THE BENEDICTINES IN THE MIDDLE AGES

Monastic Orders

ISSN 1749-4974

General Editor: Janet Burton

Monastic houses – houses of monks, regular canons, nuns, and friars – were a familiar part of the medieval landscape in both urban and rural areas, and members of the religious orders played an important role in many aspects of medieval life. The volumes in this series provide authoritative and accessible guides to the origins of each of these orders, to their expansion, and to their main characteristics.

ALREADY PUBLISHED

The Cistercians in the Middle Ages
Janet Burton and Julie Kerr

The Franciscans in the Middle Ages
Michael Robson

The Other Friars:
The Carmelite, Augustinian, Sack and Pied Friars in the Middle Ages
Frances Andrews

The Benedictines
in the Middle Ages

James G. Clark

THE BOYDELL PRESS

First published 2011
The Boydell Press, Woodbridge
Paperback edition 2014

ISBN 978-1-84383-623-0 hardback
ISBN 978-1-84383-973-6 paperback

The Boydell Press is an imprint of Boydell & Brewer Ltd
PO Box 9, Woodbridge, Suffolk IP12 3DF, UK
and of Boydell & Brewer Inc.
Mt Hope Avenue, Rochester, NY 14620-2731, USA
website: www.boydellandbrewer.com

A CIP catalogue record for this title is available
from the British Library

The publisher has no responsibility for the continued existence or accuracy of URLs
for external or third-party internet websites referred to in this book, and does not
guarantee that any content on such websites is, or will remain, accurate or appropriate.

Typeset in Garamond Premier Pro by
David Roberts, Pershore, Worcestershire

Contents

Illustrations

1 The scope of Benedictine Europe: (*above*) Þingeyrar, location of the first stable Benedictine settlement in Iceland (1133); the church now standing dates from the nineteenth century [© iStockphoto®] (*below*) Mount Tabor, Lower Galilee, Israel: the Franciscan basilica (1924) rises from the ruins of medieval buildings, among them the church and convent in the custody of Benedictines from c. 1100 until 1187. [© Shutterstock®]

2 The reading of the *Regula Benedicti*: Bishop Richard Fox's English translation of the Rule, published for the benefit of the Benedictine women of his Winchester diocese. [BL, G 10245, title page. © British Library]

3 Benedictine pioneers of polyphonic worship: Thomas Walsingham's manual of mensurable notation for the instruction of novices at St Albans Abbey. [BL, Lansdowne MS 763, fo. 98v: © British Library]

4 Benedictine supervision of the pre-Reformation parish: the new chancel of St Cuthbert's church, Oborne, Dorset, provided by the monks of Sherborne, 1533. [© Lisa Isted]

5 Benedictines and the transmission of the Latin classics: the 'class-book' connected with Dunstan, containing, *inter alia*, the first book of Ovid's *Ars amatoria*, a copy begun in a Welsh centre but apparently completed and prepared for use at Glastonbury. [Oxford, Bodleian Library, MS Auct. F. 4. 32, fo. 37v: © Bodleian Library]

6 Benedictine cultural patronage: a fifteenth-century image of the martyrdom of St Erasmus, incorporating a portrait of the monk that owned and perhaps commissioned it, John Holynborne of Christ Church, Canterbury. [© Bridgeman Art Library for the Society of Antiquaries, London]

7 The ascetic practice of late medieval Benedictines: the dry-stone *cabanes* at Breuil (Dordogne) which served as spiritual retreats for the monks of the abbey at Sarlat. [© iStockphoto®]

8 Post-Reformation Benedictines: a witness to the long life of Mary Dennys, former prioress of Kington St Michael (Wiltshire). The will of her kinsman Francis Dennys confirms she was still living, at 'St Augustine's Greene' Bristol, as late as 1593, some fifty-seven years after the surrender of her house. [© Bristol Record Office]

Maps

Acknowledgements

This book has benefitted enormously from the wide variety of colleagues, students and friends with whom I have shared, and tested, thoughts, and papers, over a number of years. Such exchanges attest to the unfailing energy of medieval monastic studies and the principal aim of this study is to stimulate them further. I would like to thank the reading-room staff of the British and Bodleian Libraries for their tireless assistance and also the community of Downside Abbey for allowing me access to their unsung but invaluable collection. I am also grateful to Janet Burton, General Editor of the series in which the book is published, and to David Roberts and to Caroline Palmer, for their advice, assistance, and patient forbearance. Above all, I thank Katherine, and the infant phenomena, Eleanor and Cecily, for their unfailing love, support and tolerance, which I will endeavour to repay.

Hadspen, August 2010

Abbreviations

AL	M. R. James, *Ancient Libraries of Canterbury and Dover. The Catalogues of the Libraries of Christ Church Priory and St Augustine's Abbey at Canterbury and St Martin's Priory at Dover, now first collected and published with an introduction and identification of the extant remains* (Cambridge, 1903)
Battle	*The Chronicle of Battle Abbey*, ed. E. Searle, Oxford Medieval Texts (Oxford, 1980)
Bede, *Historia*	Bede, *Historia gentis Anglorum ecclesiastica*, ed. R. A. B. Mynors and B. Colgrave, Oxford Medieval Texts (Oxford, 1969)
BL	London, British Library
CBMLC	Corpus of British Medieval Library Catalogues
CCM	Corpus Consuetudinem monasticarum
Chapters, ed. Pantin	*Documents Illustrating the Activities of the General and Provincial Chapters of the English Black Monks, 1215–1540*, Camden Society, 3rd Series 45, 47, 54 (1931–7)
Chatteris	*The Cartulary of Chatteris Abbey*, ed. C. Breay (Woodbridge, 1999)
Councils and Synods	*Councils and Synods with Other Documents Relating to the English Church*, 1. *871 AD–1204*, ed. D. Whitelock, M. Brett and C. N. L. Brooke, 2 vols. (Oxford, 1981)
CPL	*Calendar of Entries in the Papal Registers Relating to Great Britain and Ireland, 1198–1521*, 20 vols., ed. W. H. Bliss, C. Johnson, J. A. Twemlow, M. J. Haren, and A. P. Fuller (London, 1893–2005)
CPP	*Calendar of Entries in the Papal Registers Relating to Great Britain and Ireland. Petitions to the Pope*, I. *1342–1419*, ed. W. H. Bliss (London, 1896)
CSEL	Corpus Scriptorum Ecclesiasticorum Latinorum
DB	*Domesday Book: A Survey of the Communities of England*, ed. J. Morris, P. Morgan and C. and F. Thorn, 38 vols. (Chichester, 1983–92)
Dover	*Dover Priory*, ed. W. P. Stoneman, CBMLC 5 (1999)
Eadmer	*The Life of St Anselm, Archbishop of Canterbury by Eadmer*, ed. R. W. Southern, Oxford Medieval Texts (Oxford, 1962)
EBL	*English Benedictine Libraries: The Shorter Catalogues*, ed. R. Sharpe, J. P. Carley, A. G. Watson and K. Friis-Jensen, CBLMC 4 (1996)
EHR	*English Historical Review*
Emden, *BRUO*	A. B. Emden, *A Biographical Register of the University of Oxford to AD 1500*, 3 vols. (Oxford, 1957–9)

Gallia monastica	*Gallia monastica: Tableaux et cartes de dépendences monastiques*, 1. *Les abbayes bénédictines du diocèse de Reims*, ed. F. Poirier-Coutansais (Paris, 1974)
GASA	*Gesta abbatum monasterii sancti Albani*, 3 vols., ed. H. T. Riley, Rolls Series 28/2 (1866)
GR	*William of Malmesbury, Gesta regum Anglorum*, ed. R. A. B. Mynors, R. M. Thomson, M. Winterbottom, Oxford Medieval Texts, 2 vols. (Oxford, 1998–9)
Greatrex, *BRECP*	J. Greatrex, *A Biographical Register of the English Cathedral Priories of the Province of Canterbury, c. 1066–1540* (Oxford, 1996)
Guibert	*Memoirs of Abbot Guibert de Nogent: Self and Society in Medieval France*, ed. J. F. Benton (Toronto, 1989)
HBS	Henry Bradshaw Society
HEA	*Historia ecclesie Abbendonensis: The History of the Church of Abingdon*, ed. J. Hudson, Oxford Medieval Texts, 2 vols. (Oxford, 2002–7)
JEH	*Journal of Ecclesiastical History*
Jocelin	*The Chronicle of Jocelin of Brakelond*, ed. H. E. Butler, Nelson's Medieval Classics (London, 1949)
John of Salerno	*St Odo of Cluny. Being the Life of St Odo of Cluny by John of Salerno and the Life of St Gerard of Aurillac by St Odo*, ed. and tr. G. Sitwell (London, 1958)
John of Worcester	*The Chronicle of John of Worcester, 450–1141*, 3 vols., ed. R. R. Darlington and P. McGurk, Oxford Medieval Texts (Oxford, 1995–8)
Libellus	*Libellus de diversis ordinibus et professionibus qui sunt in aecclesia*, ed. G. Constable and B. Smith, Oxford Medieval Texts (Oxford, 1972)
LP	*Letters and Papers Foreign and Domestic of the Reign of Henry VIII, preserved in the Public Record Office, the British Museum and elsewhere in England*, ed. J. S. Brewer, J. Gairdiner, and R. H. Brodie, 22 vols. in 35 (London, 1862–1932)
MC	*The Monastic Constitutions of Lanfranc*, ed. D. Knowles and C. N. L. Brooke, Oxford Medieval Texts (rev., Oxford, 2002)
MGH	Monumenta Germanicae Historia
MO	D. Knowles, *The Monastic Order in England* (Cambridge, 1940)
MRH	*Medieval Religious Houses: England and Wales*, ed. D. Knowles and R. N. Hadcock (London, 1971)
ODNB	*Oxford Dictionary of National Biography*, ed. H. C. G. Mathew, B. Harrison and L. Goldman (Oxford, 2004)
Orderic	*The Ecclesiastical History of Orderic Vitalis*, ed. M. Chibnall, Oxford Medieval Texts, 6 vols. (Oxford, 1969–80)
Peterborough	*Peterborough Abbey*, ed. K. Friis-Jensen and J. Willoughby, CBMLC 8 (2001).

PL	*Patrologia Latina*
PP	*Past and Present*
RB	*Regula Benedicti: La règle de Saint Benôit*, ed. and tr. A. de Vogüé and J. Neufville, Source chrétienne 181, Série des textes monastiques d'Occident 49 (Paris, 1972)
RC	*Regularis Concordia: The Monastic Agreement of the Monks and Nuns of the English Nation Drawn up at the Synod of Winchester by St Dunstan, St Ethelwold and Others*, ed. and tr. T. Symons (Oxford, 1953)
Rev. Bén.	*Revue Bénédictine*
RM	*Regula magistri*
RO	D. Knowles, *The Religious Orders in England*, 3 vols. (Cambridge, 1948–59).
Selby	*Monastery and Society in the Late Middle Ages: Selected Account Rolls from Selby Abbey, Yorkshire, 1398–1537*, ed. J. H. Tillotson (Woodbridge, 1988)
STC	*A Short-Title Catalogue of Books Printed in England, Scotland and Ireland and of English Books Printed Abroad, 1475–1640*, first compiled by A. W. Pollard and G. R. Redgrave, 2nd edn revised and enlarged, begun by W. A. Jackson and F. S. Ferguson and completed by K. F. Pantzer, 3 vols. (London, 1986–91)
Stone	*Christ Church, Canterbury, I. The Chronicle of John Stone. Monk of Christ Church, 1415–71. II. List of the Deans, Priors and Monks of Christ Church*, ed. W. G. Searle, Cambridge Antiquarian Society, Octavo Series 34 (1902)
Thorne	*William Thorne's Chronicle of Saint Augustine's Abbey, Canterbury*, tr. A. H. Davis (Oxford, 1934)
TRHS	*Transactions of the Royal Historical Society*
VCH	*Victoria County History*
Walden	*The Book of the Foundation of Walden Monastery*, ed. D. Greenway and L. Watkiss, Oxford Medieval Texts (Oxford, 1999)
Warnefrid-Hildemar	M. A. Schroll, *Benedictine Monasticism as Reflected in the Warnefrid-Hildemar Commentaries on the Rule* (New York, 1941)
Wilfrid	*The Life of Bishop Wilfrid, by Eddius Stephanus*, ed. and trans. B. Colgrave (Cambridge, 1927)
Wulfstan	Wulfstan of Winchester, *The Life of St Æthelwold*, ed. M. Lapidge and M. Winterbottom, Oxford Medieval Texts (Oxford, 1991)

Introduction

The men and women that followed the sixth-century customs of Benedict of Nursia (*c.* 480–*c.* 547) formed the most enduring, influential, numerous and widespread religious order of the Latin Middle Ages. Their mode of life superseded the monastic codes of the early Christian fathers and before the close of the eleventh century it was the dominant form of monastic observance practised in the west. At this date their principal monasteries in France, Italy, Germany and the Low Countries held as many as 200 professed members, and there were the beginnings of a Benedictine presence on the eastern boundary of Christendom, in Poland-Lithuania, Bohemia and Hungary. Their Roman liturgical practice (the *opus Dei*) and their acquired taste for learning founded on the ancient liberal arts served as a model for the Church as a whole. New orders arose in the later Middle Ages, but still they took some of their customs, and something of their observant and spiritual outlook, from the *Regula Benedicti*; indeed, the reverent authority of the rule was amplified as the forms of corporate and personal religion proliferated. The plural religious culture of the later period did not extinguish the order or obviate its purpose. The opening of the sixteenth century may have seen a surge in vocations and even at the centre of the Reformation conflict (England, Germany) the Black Monks were among the last to surrender their houses.

The Benedictines may also be counted among the founders of medieval Europe. It was pioneers of the *Regula Benedicti* that created or consolidated the early Christian communities in the north and west of the Continent. These same missionary monks established many of the churches around which the social community began to cohere. Their monasteries directed the development of the new urban and extra-urban centres and the landscape on which they depended: in many regions of Europe patterns of agriculture, building and trade all bore the imprint of the Benedictines. They were also a transformative influence on cultural and social trends. To them in large part we owe the preservation of the literature of Latin antiquity. Perhaps it was the Black Monks that brought the codex itself into common use; there can be little doubt that it was their linguistic preferences and their mode of reading (at first, ruminatively, later, silently) that shaped the experience of literate Europe. Their early recovery and refinement of the decorative arts established a repertory of themes and of media which prevailed until the Renaissance. By their example, they also led early medieval Europe in the development of custom, in the care of children, in the formal conduct of social interaction – letter writing, for example, and the culti-vation of 'friendship' – and in a matter as fundamental as the marking of time.

The Benedictines reflected on their fortunes in a rich seam of historical writing which spans the seventh to the sixteenth centuries.[1] As might be expected of men and women professed to pursue the reformation of the self, their perspective was always personal; their attention and interest beyond their own precincts were patchy at best and the significance of key characters and scenes was determined by their own connection to them. They wrote of their order (*ordo*) only when it was necessary to distinguish it from other forms of monastic or clerical life; even after a system of governance by provincial or general chapter had been adopted, Benedictine annalists and chroniclers did not routinely recount their corporate affairs. Only after they had witnessed the sectarian conflict of the friars, and had reason to fear their resurgence of heresy, did they seek to record the achievements of the brethren as a whole. The narratives and inventories of the order that were compiled in the century after 1350 were modelled on the corporate histories of the friars; their focus was the origins of the *Regula Benedicti* and their readership appears to have been confined to convents, – notably in England but also in France and Germany – where the authority of chapters and congregations was most keenly felt.[2]

The Reformation transformed their historical perspective. The extinction of their life in England led exiled Benedictines to compile their first com-plete history from the Gregorian mission to the Henrician Dissolution.[3] As the confessional conflict of the Continent subsided in the second half of the seventeenth century, the reformed (Maurist) Benedictines of France began to gather records of the achievements of the order as a whole. The *Acta ordi-nis sancti Benedicti* was begun by Luc d'Achery of Saint-Germain-des-Prés

---

[1] For the tradition of historical writing among the Benedictines, see A. Gransden, *Historical Writing in England*, 2 vols. (London, 1973–82). See also D. Iogna-Prat, 'La geste des origines dans l'historiographie clunisienne des XIe–XIIe siècles', *Rev. Bén.* 102 (1992), 135–91; S. Vanderputten, 'Libri Chronicorum: A Structural Approach to the Transmission of Medieval Benedictine Historiography from the Southern Low Countries', *Rev. Bén.* 115:1 (2005), 151–86; *Dove va la storiogafia monastica in Europa?*, ed. G. Andenna (Milan, 2005); A. J. Piper, 'The Historical Interests of the Monks of Durham', in *Symeon of Durham: Historian of Durham and the North*, ed. D. Rollason, Studies in North-Eastern History 1 (Stamford, 1998), pp. 307–32.

[2] For the texts compiled in England, see W. A. Pantin, 'Some Medieval English Treatises on the Origins of Monastic Life', in *Medieval Studies Presented to Rose Graham*, ed. V. Ruffer and A. J. Taylor (Oxford, 1950), pp. 189–215. For France, see the compilation of Jean de Stavelot: D. Donadieu-Rigaut, *Penser en image les ordres religeuses: XIe–XVe siècles* (Paris, 2005), pp. 241–55. Jean's manuscript is now Chantilly, MS XIX B1. For Germany, see the compilations of Johann Trittenheim (Johannes Trithemius) abbot of Sponheim (d. 1516): *Liber penthicus seu lugubris de statu et ruina ordinis monastici* and the *De viris illustribus ordinis sancti Benedicti*, both of which date from 1492–3. See also N. L. Brann, *The Abbot Trithemius (1462–1516): The Renaissance of Monastic Humanism*, Studies in the History of Christian Thought 24 (Leiden, 1981), pp. 137–44.

[3] Clement Reyner, *Apostolatus Benedictinorum in Anglia, sive disceptatio historia de antiquitate ordinis congregationique monachorum nigrorum S. Benedicti in regno Angliae*, 3 parts (Douai, 1626).

(d. 1685) but elaborated and eventually completed by his younger contemporary, and the greater scholar, Jean Mabillon (d. 1707).[4] The *Acta* ran to nine volumes, but within a decade further *Annales ordinis sancti Benedicti* were published, the work completed at Saint-Germain by René Massuet (d. 1716) and Edmond Martène (d. 1739).[5] The Maurist monks, notably at Saint-Germain, also advanced the *Gallia Christiana*, a general history of French church, of which their order was a central feature, before the Revolution at last laid waste to their long-preserved libraries.[6] The resurgence of the order in the France of Louis Philippe (1830–48), and its successful reintroduction in England (1795–1933), against a background of papal renewal, stimulated a resumption of the historical enterprise. The leadership of the new English congregation contributed popular narratives.[7] A fresh multi-volume history emerged from the old historical heartland of France.[8] While members of the order have continued to make a distinguished contribution to historical – and specifically medieval – scholarship, and congregational histories have been renewed, there has been no history of the order from a monastic or lay scholar since the Second World War.[9]

This book offers a survey of the Benedictines from their beginnings in the sixth century to the years of reform, repression and reorganisation provoked by the European Reformation. It is not an account of convents and congregations but rather of monastic custom and its evolution over the course of eleven centuries. It traces the transmission of the *Regula Benedicti*, its rise to prominence, then pre-eminence, between the ninth and the twelfth centuries, and the regional movements that secured, and renewed its place in the clerical and lay society of Latin Europe. It charts their institutional progress, from isolated colony to corporate enterprise invested with seigniorial, fiscal and commercial capital. At the same time, it aims to uncover the currents of life in the enclosure of the monastery, between church, chapter house and cloister, dormitory and frater, not only the daily (and seasonal) obligations of the rule, but also the patterns of spiritual, intellectual and social behaviour that they fostered, or at least, they failed to suppress.

[4] *Acta sanctorum ordinis S. Benedicti*, ed. L. D'Achery and J. Mabillon, 9 vols. (Paris, 1668–1701).
[5] *Annales ordinis S. Benedicti occidentalium monachorum patriarchae*, ed. J. Mabillon, 6 vols. (Paris, 1703–7).
[6] The thirteenth volume of a projected series of sixteen appeared in 1785: *Gallia Christiana*, ed. D. Sainte-Marthe *et al.* (Paris, 1715–85).
[7] For example, F. A. Gasquet, *Henry the VIII and the English Monasteries: An Attempt to Illustrate the History of their Suppression*, 2 vols. (London, 1888); F. A. Gasquet, *English Monastic Life* (London, 1904); E. C. Butler, *Benedictine Monachism: Studies in Benedictine Life and Rule* (London, 1919). Respectively they served as prior and abbot of the new English monastery of St Lawrence at Downside, Somerset.
[8] P. Schmitz, *Histoire de l'Ordre de Saint-Benoît*, 7 vols. in 4 (Paris, 1948–56).
[9] Among recent congregational histories is E. Zaragoza i Pascual, *Història de la Congregació Benedictina Claustral Tarraconense i Cesaraugstinina (1215–1835)*, Publicacions de l'Abadia de Montserrat, Scripta et documenta 67 (Barcelona, 2004).

The result is intended neither as an apology for nor a celebration of the Benedictines, but rather as a reflection on their role, by turns directive and responsive, in the complex, mutable society of medieval Europe.

CHAPTER ONE

The Making of a European Order

In medieval Europe the Benedictines represented the archetype of a religious order, the exponents of an apparently timeless tradition from which all forms of monastic life had descended. This perception became sharply focused in the period of their political, ecclesiastical and cultural pre-eminence, but it masked the centuries in which a plural clerical and monastic culture prevailed. The *Regula Benedicti* (*RB*) was not the first monastic code of the medieval west, and, in the formative years of European Christianity, there were others, such as the Celtic customs of Columban of Bangor (*c.* 543–615), that played a greater role in the work of conversion. Yet while it lacked both the brevity and spiritual intensity of some *regulae*, it was the regime of Benedict's Montecassino that was carried furthest from the Gallo-Roman centres of the early medieval cult. In the remote, unsettled, and somewhat pagan regions to the north, east and west, the disciples of the *RB* were agents of religious change; here they were the principal architects of the institutional church – and its doctrinal and liturgical framework – that was raised from the ruins of Roman antiquity. Later, the rule informed a discourse of reform that reinvigorated clerical Europe. At the turn of the first millennium, regional networks of Benedictines had taken root; a century later they had eclipsed alternative customs and displaced the secular canons and laid claim to the ecclesiastical hierarchy.

Like so many medieval institutions, the Benedictines garnered a memory of their beginnings that was rich in legend. The life of the founder was dramatised in Gregory's *Dialogues* and never leavened with documentation. The suggestion of an apostolic succession of his disciples was encouraged by the association of regional missionaries and their churches with the advent of the monasteries: Augustine of Canterbury was remembered as an apostle of the *RB* in England; Maurus, one of the few named figures to feature in the *Dialogues*, was cast as the evangelist of France.[1] As historical writing flowered in the Benedictine precinct, the foundation narrative was enlivened not only by the great lives of these pioneers, but also by institutional histories whose successive continuations created a continuity that seemed almost tangible.[2] Visual representations reinforced the impression of a

---

[1] See below, pp. 20–2, 280.
[2] See below, pp. 224–30 at 227–8.

timeless mode of life: Benedict was bracketed with the fathers of the desert, Anthony and Pachomius, and his followers lined the route that led to the orders of the high and later Middle Ages.[3] In the century before 1517 new annals of Benedictine achievement circulated in England, claiming the origin of their customs in Moses' message to the Levites (Numbers, 8: 24–6) and commemorating the ten centuries of saints, scholars, prelates and even princes that propagated 'the vine of his holy religion ... from sea to sea to the ends of the earth' ('quomodo vinea huius sancte religionis extenderit a mare usque ad mare suos palmites propagines vero a flumine usque ad fines orbis terre').[4] The medieval view of Benedictine history persisted in the modern era. In the first half of the twentieth century the order's own historians compiled narratives that reflected the critical methods of contemporary scholarship but retained the venerable theme of an unbroken tradition.[5]

Yet the foundations of this history are hardly secure. As the text of the *RB* and its reception in early medieval Europe is better understood, the tale of a rapid and unquestioned acceptance in the clerical community appears unconvincing. At the same time, the analysis of early foundation histories has exposed a host of forgeries, inventions and spectral founders. Revisionism has even re-evaluated the achievement of the acknowledged champions of the *RB* at Aachen, Cluny, Gorze, and the England of Æthelwold, Dunstan and Oswald.[6] It has also exposed the uneasy history of Benedictine women, and their apparent regression, from the co-operative observance of the early 'double' monastery to the separation, enclosure and relative poverty of later centuries.[7] We have also been reminded of the challenge presented by the new orders of the eleventh and twelfth centuries and their early success not only in charging popular piety but

---

[3] For example, see the procession of monks from the desert to the Latin church in the nave mural of the church of the Augustinian friars of Konstanz.

[4] BL, MS Arundel 11 (Abbot John Wheathampstead of St Albans), fos. 107r–113v at 107r. For an analogous text compiled at at Bury St Edmunds (Suffolk), see *Memorials of St Edmund's Abbey at Bury*, ed. T. Arnold, 3 vols., Rolls Series 96 (1896), iii. 145–51.

[5] For example, Butler, *Benedictine Monachism*; Schmitz, *Histoire*.

[6] For example, J. Semmler, 'Réforme bénédictine et privilège impérial: les monastères autour de Saint Benoît d'Aniane', in *Naissance et fonctionnement des réseaux monastique et canoniaux*, Actes du colloque international de CERCOM (Saint-Étienne, 1991), pp. 21–32; J. Semmler, 'Benediktinische Reform und kaiserliches Privileg zur Frage des institutionellen Zusammenschlusses der Klöster um Benedikt von Aniane', in *Institutionen und Geschichte: Theoretische Aspekte und mittelalterliche Befunde*, ed. G. Melville (Cologne, 1992), pp. 259–93; J. W. Nightingale, *Monasteries and Patrons of the Gorze Reform: Lotharingia, c. 850–1000* (Oxford, 1997); N. Robertson, 'Dunstan and Monastic Reform Tenth-Century Fact or Twelfth-Century Fiction?', *Anglo-Norman Studies* 28 (2006), 153–67; I. Rosé, *Construire une société seigneuriale: Itinéraire et ecclésiologie de l'abbé Odon de Cluny* (Turnhout, 2008).

[7] For example, S. Thompson, *Women Religious: The Founding of English Nunneries after the Norman Conquest* (Oxford, 1991); R. Gilchrist, *Gender and Material Culture: The Archaeology of Religious Women* (London and New York, 1994); B. Kerr, *Religious Life for Women, c. 1100–c. 1350* (Oxford, 1999); *Female Monastic Life in Early Tudor England: with an Edition of Richard Fox's Translation of the Benedictine Rule for Women, 1517*, ed. B. Collett (Aldershot, 2002).

also in claiming a place in the ecclesiastical establishment.[8] Our greater knowledge of the later religious orders has also cast new light on the character of the Benedictines in the high and later Middle Ages. By the standards of the Carthusians, Cistercians, regular canons and, of course, the friars, the Black Monks could barely be considered an order. There was no single governmental structure, no system of fiscal subsidy, no national or international network of schools.[9] The Fourth Lateran Council (1215) promulgated general and provincial chapters for the Benedictines, instruments that were reinforced by Benedict XII in 1336, but it appears they took root only in England and Wales.[10] Regional affiliations were always potent among the Benedictines and communities were characterised by the individual customs – liturgical, pastoral and social – that prospered within the common framework of the rule. Regional congregations arose as a means of self-preservation in a volatile environment and a mechanism for reform: the largest of them endured but after their early years they lacked the centripetal force of Cîteaux, Grande Chartreuse or, indeed, the mendicant office of the Prior Provincial.[11]

Nonetheless, the men and women professed as Benedictine were conscious of a common inheritance, of a venerable, proven mode of living, an authentic witness to the pure monastic impulse of the Christian past. Their monastic and mendicant colleagues acknowledged such authority, and made a place for Benedict in their spiritual ancestry;[12] for almost a millennium it was also recognised and revered by the ecclesiastical and secular hierarchy.

Benedict of Nursia

The only feature of the Benedictine legendary left largely unscathed by post-medieval scrutiny is the figure of Benedict himself. After fifteen centuries of an intermittent but fervent following, few challenge his pre-eminence as the source and primary influence upon the monastic tradition that bears his name. His historical image remains recognisably that fashioned in the formative years of the order: indeed, the degree of continuity in the

---

[8] N. F. Cantor, 'The Crisis of Western Monasticism, 1050–1130', *American Historical Review* 66 (1960–1), 47–67; J. Van Engen, 'The Crisis of Cenobitism Reconsidered: Benedictine Monasticism, 1050–1150', *Speculum* 61:1 (1986), 269–304; P. Jestice, *Wayward Monks and the Religious Revolution of the Eleventh Century*, Brill's Studies in Intellectual History 76 (Leiden, 1997).

[9] For a revisionist account of the tensions inherent in the Cistercian system of government, see C. H. Berman, *The Cistercian Evolution: the Invention of a Religious Order in Twelfth-Century Europe* (Philadelphia, 2000). For the network of mendicant schools, see B. Roest, *A History of Franciscan Education, c. 1210–1517*, Education and Society in the Middle Ages and Renaissance 11 (Leiden, 2000).

[10] See below, p. 290.

[11] For these structures, see R. B. Brooke, *Early Franciscan Government: Ellias to Bonaventure*, Cambridge Studies in Medieval Life and Thought 7 (Cambridge, 1959), pp. 106–22.

[12] Berman, *Cistercian Evolution*, pp. 11, 20, 50; Brooke, *Early Franciscan Government*, p. 288.

representation of Benedict is perhaps unparalleled for a medieval personality. From the end of the ancient world to the Renaissance he appeared always as the venerable father of devoted disciples, presiding in person over the presentation of the rule to any supplicant inclined to 'listen to the precepts of the master' ('Obsculta filii, praecepta magistri': *RB*, prologue, 1).[13] The clarity of his reputation, of course, is not unconnected to the dearth of documentary evidence for his life and work. By contrast with the fathers of later medieval orders, whose lives made at least some imprint on institutional records, and whose *acta* and *dicta* were recorded by the early converts, the only textual trace of Benedict is the hagiography attributed to Gregory the Great, compiled as the second book of the *Dialogues*, in *c.* 590, almost fifty years after his subject's death.[14] Born in the decade Benedict died, Gregory recovered only the social memory of the man revered as Abbot Benedict: 'all the notable things and acts of his life, I could not learn' ('omnia gesta non didici': *Dialogues*, prologue). The absence of a later biography is perhaps surprising for an order renowned for its historiography, but as a testament of his life and work the *RB* itself could scarcely be bettered: from its verses Benedict continued to speak to his brethren.

To his medieval followers – and to some in subsequent centuries – Benedict was not only the father of his Black Monks but also of the order of Christian monasticism as a whole. This perception passed into the modern era: J. H. Newman declared Benedict 'found the world, physical and social, in ruins and his mission was to restore it'.[15] In fact, Benedict did not create a monastic society but was a consequence of it. Christian monasticism originated in the Middle East in the third century.[16] A wide spectrum of ascetic practices prospered among these (primarily) Coptic communities, from the extreme eremiticism of Anthony (d. 356) and his followers in Lower Egypt, to the experiments in communal living of Pachomius (d. 346) in Upper Egypt, and the followers of Julian Sabas (d. 366) in Syria.[17] The mission that advanced under the Roman hegemony during, and after, the reign of Constantine transmitted these modes into Greek and Latin society. Before the close of the fourth century, forms of monastic life flourished at

[13] Renaissance artists reinvigorated this image of Benedict. See, for example, Montagna's print of the founder instructing his order: M. J. Zucker, 'Early Italian Engravings for Religious Orders', *Zeitschrift für Kunstgeschichte* 56:3 (1993), 366–84.

[14] Gregory, *Dialogues*, ed. A. de Vögüé, 3 vols., Sources chrétiennes 251, 260, 265 (Paris, 1978). For a singular view of the *Dialogues* and a date of composition after Gregory's death, see F. Clark, *The 'Gregorian' Dialogues and the Origins of Benedictine Monasticism*, Studies in the History of Christian Thought 108 (Leiden, 2003).

[15] J. H. Newman, 'The Mission of Saint Benedict', in *Historical Sketches*, 3 vols. (London, 1888), ii. 363–430 at 410.

[16] For the beginnings of monasticism in the west, see M. Dunn, *The Emergence of Monasticism: from the Desert Fathers to the Early Middle Ages*, 2nd edn (Oxford, 2005).

[17] Dunn, *Emergence of Monasticism*, pp. 3–13, 25–30. See also P. Rousseau, *Pachomius: The Making of a Community in Fourth-Century Egypt*, 2nd edn (Berkeley, 1999), esp. pp. 87–104; J. E. Goehring, *Ascetics, Society and the Desert: Studies in Early Egyptian Monasticism* (London, 1999).

Caesarea (Cappadocia) under Bishop Basil 'the Great' (d. 379), at Aquileia (now Aglar) where the Latin historian Tyrannius Rufinus (d. 410) was professed, and at Marmoutiers, in the Loire valley, under the inspiration of Martin (d. 397), hermit bishop of Tours.[18] In the century before Benedict's birth in *c*. 480, these experiments were extended eastward at Alexandria and Antioch (under the influence of John Chrysostom (d. 407)) and westward into Roman Gaul and in the Italian peninsula itself.[19] Following his own experiences in the monasteries of the near and Middle East, John Cassian (d. 435) formed a double (male and female) convent at Marseilles, the chief port of southern Gaul.[20] Monastic colonies were settled in the same province, at Arles, the coastal island of Lérins (now Saint-Honorat), and in the Jura mountains between the Rhine and Rhone, of which Cassian himself was a patron and (in his *Conferences*) a principal witness.[21] There was nascent network in Gaul at least a generation before the cenobitic tradition had taken root beneath the Alps. Before his death Paulinus of Nola (d. 431) founded a monastery at the shrine of St Felix at Cimitile; in the decades that followed basilical monasteries – convents connected to existing churches and supporting their liturgical regime – were founded at Rome perhaps under Pope Sixtus III (d. 440) and certainly under his successors, Leo (d. 461) and Hilarius (d. 468).[22] At the turn of the fourth century, the monastic ideal was carried beyond the border of the Roman polity, to Whithorn (Scotland) and Ireland, evangelised after 431 by Palladius, and the Briton Patrick (d. 460/1–93).[23]

The close of the fifth century – the years of Benedict's youth and education – brought the extension and elaboration of the monastic movement in the same territory between Campagna (southern Italy) and Aquitania (central France). Sidonius Apollinaris offers a glimpse of an informal 'villa' monastery found in the environs of Clermont-Ferrand in *c*. 469.[24] The basilical convent was adopted in Gaul: Gregory of Tours claimed the church and convent of Saint-Denis (Île-de-France) as the achievement of St Genovefa (d. 512); the convent of Saint-Maurice at Agaune (Burgundy) was begun in 515.[25] The earliest rules for monasteries witnessed in Rome's western provinces appeared at this time: although they claimed an association with eastern monasticism, it is likely they testify to

---

[18] Dunn, *Emergence of Monasticism*, pp. 34–41, 48–50.

[19] Ibid., pp. 25–34; Rousseau, *Pachomius*, pp. 174–92 at 179.

[20] Dunn, *Emergence of Monasticism*, pp. 75–80. See also C. Stewart, *Cassian the Monk* (Oxford, 1999).

[21] Dunn, *Emergence of Monasticism*, pp. 82–4.

[22] Ibid., pp. 61, 91. See also J. T. Lienhard, *Paulinus of Nola and Early Western Monasticism* (Cologne, 1977), pp. 128–41; R. A. Markus, *The End of Ancient Christianity* (Cambridge, 1990), esp. pp. 157–80.

[23] K. Hughes, 'The Church in Irish Society: The First Phase, *c*. 400–500', in *A New History of Ireland: Pre-History and Early Ireland*, ed. T. W. Moody, D. O. Croinin, F. X. Martin, F. J. Byrne (Oxford, 2005), pp. 306–30 at 310–19.

[24] Dunn, *Emergence of Monasticism*, p. 90.

[25] Ibid., pp. 92–3. See also *The World of Gregory of Tours*, ed. K. Mitchell and I. N. Wood (Leiden, 2002).

the presence of cenobites in the western Mediterranean. Gregory's *Dialogues* (II. 1) also attest to convents of regulated religious in the region to which the young Benedict removed.[26] In the first quarter of the sixth century, probably in Campagna, an anonymous pioneer, later known as the 'Master', presided over a *cenobium*, or perhaps a network, for which he provided a disciplinary code, the *Regula magistri*.[27] In the same quarter century Bishop Caesarius of Arles (c. 470–542) founded a female monastery that served as model not only for the profession of women but also for a house that followed a daily liturgical *horarium*; Caesarius also composed his own customary, which codified the observance of the island monastery of Lérins, where he had been schooled. These communities were formed, and, from contemporary accounts, flourished, in a troubling climate of imperial and papal conflict and confessional persecution, in the closing years of the Ostrogoth Theodoric (493–526).[28] To the emergent generation of the early sixth century, the physical, social and spiritual separation of the *cenobium* was compelling. Benedict of Nursia inherited a vigorous and diverse monastic tradition, in which customary regulation, sealed in written codes and *regulae*, was increasingly common and in which a commitment to the liturgical *opus* of the institutional church already had begun to channel, and perhaps contain, the raw asceticism of the convert. His distaste (*RB*, prologue) for the irregular (the Sarabaites) and the unstable (Gyrovagues) reflected his reading of Cassian to be sure, but it was also representative of the prevailing view of his own day.

Yet it seems Benedict's first impulse was to eschew contemporary cenobitic custom. Gregory wrote of his early resolution 'to lead a life in the wilderness' (*Dialogues*, II. 1). After an interlude at the oratory of St Peter at Enfide (now, Affile), he fled 'to a desert place' (thought to have been the gorge above the River Anio, near Subiaco, only 50 miles from Rome) represented in the *Dialogues* with thee motifs of the Christian hermit, a cave, animal skins, and a rock-strewn landscape rich in natural resources. Benedict was remembered as the father of the *cenobium* but this first, solitary phase of his spiritual formation also held a powerful attraction for later generations. It was a favoured scene for visual narratives (frescoes, reliefs), and among the reformers of later centuries perhaps something of a symbol of the early purity that might be restored. The centrepiece of the Signorelli and Sodoma fresco-cycle that decorated the cloister of Monte Oliveto Maggiore – the centre of the Olivetan reform – depicted the cave-dweller Benedict receiving a loaf from Romanus (Gregory, *Dialogues*, II. 2).[29]

---

[26] Dunn, *Emergence of Monasticism*, p. 85.
[27] S. Wood, *The Proprietary Church in the Medieval West* (Oxford, 2006), pp. 185–6.
[28] Dunn, *Emergence of Monasticism*, pp. 98–107. See also W. Klingshirn, *Caesarius of Arles: The Making of a Christian Community in Late Antique Gau* (Cambridge, 1994), pp. 104–6, 117–23.
[29] The fresco cycle of thirty-six scenes in the chiostro grande was begun by Luca Signorelli in 1497 and completed by Il Sodoma (Giovanni Antonio Bazzi) in 1508.

Benedict's eremitical experiment was short lived and he surrendered to the communal imperative of the time. His hermitage became a place of pilgrimage: 'in return for the corporeal meat they brought him [many] returned with spiritual food for their souls' [*Dialogues*, ii. 2]. The *Dialogues* report his adoption by a community of monks lacking a superior only to be assaulted by them, angered at the severity of his rule. At any rate, there is no doubt disciples were drawn to the region and in time cohered into a cluster of communities which recognised Benedict's spiritual authority: the *Dialogues* present it as a colony of twelve *cenobia* each containing twelve brethren (*Dialogues*, II).

The scale of Subiaco, which if accurate would have made it surely as secure and self-sufficient as the convents at Arles and Lérins, led Benedict to remove himself to an unsettled region some 30 miles further south, at Montecassino. At the foot of the 500-metre mount, apparently on the site of a disused temple of Jupiter, he raised oratories dedicated to St Martin and St John the Baptist; at the summit, within the perimeter of an ancient fortification, he developed another monastery.

The *Dialogues* report that Benedict also assimilated into his monastic estate a nascent community at Terracina, at the invitation of an unidentified 'virtuous man of property' (*Dialogues*, II. 22). He provided a superior, prior and (presumably) monks for the foundation; in the *Dialogues* the arrangement of the buildings was also completed under his visionary direction. The church was dedicated to St Stephen, although it remains unclear if this was Benedict's original designation.[30] There was a medieval tradition that a female house was founded at nearby Plombariola (now Piumarola) for Benedict's sister, Scholastica, but there is no early documentary, or later archaeological evidence to support this; a nunnery is known there only from the reign of Pope Nicholas I (d. 867).[31]

Later regarded as the model of a Benedictine monastery, the form and size of Benedict's Montecassino remains elusive. The *Dialogues* offer contrasting impressions, of a close-knit monastic family centred on a charismatic father, and of a place of public recourse, recognised by the ecclesiastical and secular authorities of the region. There is a fleeting glimpse of its infrastructure: it appears the monks were distributed in small groups in dwellings described as *cellae*, literally 'chambers', but perhaps comprising a suite of rooms; they were stone-built, given the terrain: the *Dialogues* claim a miracle for Benedict among the masonry (*Dialogues*, II. 9). The *cellae* were sparsely furnished: the *Dialogues* describe a *psiathium* (prayer-mat); perhaps there were few further comforts. The larger part of the colony was clustered at the foot of the mount in the vicinity of the oratories and the summit

---

[30] H. Bloch, *Monte Cassino in the Middle Ages*, 3 vols. (Cambridge, MA, 1986), i. 173–4, 208–10 at 208.
[31] Ibid., II (iii–iv), p. 648.

settlement stood apart. When Willibald (d. 787) explored the site in 730, the separation between the higher and lower settlements was striking.[32]

This Montecassino was the crucible of the *RB*. The *Dialogues* (II. 36) offer it as the final act of Abbot Benedict. As discussed below, textual analysis does not support a systematic process of composition: the *RB* was a compilation and the content and structure known to its medieval disciples may have developed over time. Whether the rule captured the customs of Cassino only, or represented practice also at Subiaco, Terracina, or the shadowy convent of Scholastica cannot be known.

Benedict died at Montecassino in *c.* 547; there is no contemporary record, but the accounts of his tomb suggest it was marked with all the formality of a stable and sizeable community. The *Dialogues* recorded the names of the four superiors who followed him, among them apparently the present incumbent, Honoratus; if they are accurate, monastic life continued there at least for a generation.

The legacy of Benedict of Nursia was not a religious order, at least not in the same way as Bruno or Francis. Like Bishop Caesarius (whose own death came within a year or so of Benedict's), he bequeathed a cluster of monastic *cellae* that survived and apparently thrived on the memory of his personal charisma. In the ensuing decades disciples were drawn not only to the personal legend but also to the code that bore his name. For generations thereafter it was the figurative presence of the Benedict of the *Dialogues* and of the *RB*, not a fully realised Benedictine monastery, that shaped the spiritual impulses of medieval Europe.

The Regula Benedicti

The Benedictine tradition was founded on the *Regula Benedicti*. The *Dialogues* picture Montecassino as a community shaped by personality not precept: patrons and supplicants were drawn to the mount to experience 'a man full of heavenly doctrine' (II. 35). Yet it was the *RB* that came to be regarded as Benedict's distinctive and enduring contribution to European monasticism. Little more than a century after his death it was better known, as a code of behaviour if not always as a text, than the Gregorian *Dialogues*. Another two centuries on and the rule was synonymous with the very notion of a *regula monachalis* ('rule for monks'); from the tenth to the twelfth centuries (and even later) it served as the inspiration for innovative, monastic, clerical and secular, forms of religious living.

---

[32] Hunneberc of Heidenheim, *The Hodoeporicon of Saint Willibald*, trans. C. H. Talbot, in *Soldiers of Christ: Saints and Saints' Lives from Late Antiquity and the Early Middle Ages*, ed. T. F. X. Noble and T. F. Head (London, 1995), pp. 141–65 at 160–1.

The compilation of a rule, of course, was not a novelty. The customs of the monastic pioneers had been the subject of synthetic commentary since the turn of the fourth century: the earliest cenobitic code (extant only in Coptic) is connected to Pachomius; only a generation later Basil the Great composed a bipartite rule for his Caesarean convent, transmitted to the Latin West in the translation of Tyrannius Rufinus.[33] The next century saw a proliferation of rules, many, if not all, of which may be connected with the monastic settlements of Italia and Gaul. For the first time, ascetics were acclaimed not only as living exemplars but also as legislators. In the half-century between Benedict's birth and his arrival at Montecassino, no fewer than seven codes circulated in the Roman provinces.[34] The *RB* underlines the integration of Benedict and his colonies into the monastic culture of their time.

Indeed, the text is derivative. The inspiration of the *regulae* and *vitae* of the fourth-century fathers is acknowledged in the final chapter of the rule, for 'What are they but the monuments of the virtues of exemplary and obedient monks?' (*RB*, lxxiii). Only the rule of Basil is specified. It has been suggested Montecassino was more susceptible to Byzantine currents than other monastic settlements in middle Italy and Gaul since it was positioned on the main route south from Rome to Naples, the gateway to the eastern empire.[35] The example of 'the rule of the holy father, Basil' is recommended to brethren among other 'teachings of the holy fathers' as both inspiration and guide to 'he that hasteneth on to the perfection of the religious life' (*RB*, lxxiii. 3). Benedict's opening address 'by the toil of obedience thou may return to Him from whom ... thou have gone away' (*RB*, prologue) echoed Basil; Benedict also shared his view of obedience as the pre-eminent monastic virtue, and his fervent belief in the virtuous possibility of 'that most valiant kind of monk, the cenobite'. It was not only Basil's moral and spiritual values that shaped the *RB* but also his prescriptions for the management of a community of aspirant ascetics. The structure of Benedict's monastery itself bore the imprint of the Basilian *cenobium*. It shared the communal principle and the commitment to the possibility of social stability, moral and spiritual purity 'in common'. The conception of the abbot (*RB*, ii) as instructor of the brethren, also betrays his influence as does the importance attached to self-sufficiency through manual labour (*RB*, xlviii); the approach to children (*RB*, lix) is perhaps also inspired by Basil, although Benedict elaborates on the practicalities of their custody. Basil's influence is conspicuous, but the *RB* also carries at least a trace of

[33] Dunn, *Emergence of Monasticism*, pp. 36, 112.
[34] Ibid., pp. 111–38.
[35] A. M. Silvas, 'Edessa to Cassino: The Passage of Basil's Asketikon to the West', *Vigilia Christianae* 56:3 (2002), 247–59 at 252.

another eastern tradition: the requirement for prospective recruits to be delayed at the gate of the monastery for days is reminiscent of Pachomius.[36]

The *RB* was also shaped by the Roman Fathers. The monastic lore of Augustine is an unacknowledged presence. The humanity of the *RB*'s mode of discipline (*RB*, xliii–vi) and the paternalism of its conception of the superior (abbot's) authority (*RB*, ii) are notably Augustinian; nuances in the tools of good works (*RB*, iv) and the degrees of humility (*RB*, vii) – not novel in themselves – and especially the emphasis on *amor Dei*, also reflect the influence of Augustinian theology.[37] Benedict's unequivocal prescription for manual labour in the monastery may be informed by Augustine's contribution to the controversy it aroused in his day.[38]

The *Conferences* and *Institutes* of John Cassian were also a source of reference. Perhaps his *Institutes* are acknowledged obliquely among the examples recommended in the final chapter of the *RB*, 'the collations of the Fathers, and their institutes and lives', but there can be no doubt Cassian's witness informed the chapters on the reception of brethren, liturgy, manual labour, governance (the office of abbot, the daily 'counsel') social and spiritual discipline. Here Benedict follows the form but not the substance: the *RB* offers its disciples a degree of patience and tolerance which the fourth century would not have permitted.[39]

It might be suggested that the *RB* also bears the mark of the secular codes and customs of Rome. Within the order itself, commentators have been reluctant to confront the connections between the *RB* and contemporary communal, judicial and social structures.[40] Nonetheless, comparisons have been made between Benedict's process of counsel (*consilium*) and the consultative practice of the Roman corporation; the suggestion that an abbot may be selected by a fraction of the community of 'wise counsel' ('sive etiam pars quamvis parva congregationis saniore consilio elegerit': *RB*, lxiv. 1) perhaps recalls Justinian's *Novel*, 123. 34.[41] Such echoes were not sufficient to advance the *RB* in societies, such as that of Anglo-Saxons, where the reception of Roman law was early and marked.[42] There can be no doubt,

---

[36] Dunn, *Emergence of Monasticism*, pp. 114–17, 122–3, 128; A. de Vogüé, 'L'influence de saint Basile sur le monachisme d'occident', *Rev. Bén.* 112 (2002), 5–17 at 13–14. See also A. de Vogüé, *Community and Abbot in the Rule of St Benedict* (Kalamazoo, 1979), p. 23.

[37] Ibid., p. 24; M. de Dreuille, *The Rule of Saint Benedict and the Ascetic Traditions from Asia to the West*, trans. M. Hargreaves (London, 2000), pp. 3–32 at 29, 146–7.

[38] E. A. Clark, *Reading and Renunciation: Asceticism and Scripture in Early Christianity* (Princeton, 1999), p. 93.

[39] R. J. Goodrich, *Contexualising Cassian: Aristocrats, Asceticism and Reformation in Fifth-Century Gaul* (Oxford, 2007), pp. 253–5.

[40] For example, De Vogüé, *Community and Abbot*, p. 19.

[41] M. P. Blecker, 'Roman Law and "Consilium" in the *Regula magistri* and the Rule of St Benedict', *Speculum* 47:1 (1972), 1–28 at 2. See also De Vögüé, *Community and Abbot*, p. 24.

[42] Bede, *Historia*, ii. 5, pp. 150–1. See also F. M. Stenton, *Anglo-Saxon England*, Oxford History of England 2 (Oxford, 1947), p. 181&n.

however, that Benedict's code was formulated with reference to the frameworks of secular society: measures for the reception of the children of noble patrons and the prohibition on the exchange of letters suggest an understanding of secular custom and awareness of the threat it presented to the stability of the *cenobium*.

Yet the principal source of the *RB* came not from the ecclesiastical or social mainstream but from an obscure monastic tradition whose chronological and geographical origins remain unclear. The *Regula magistri* ('Rule of the Master', *RM*) is an elaborate, even verbose Latin rule for a monastery, arranged in ninety-five chapters, compiled before the last quarter of the sixth century, the period in which the earliest surviving copies were made.[43] The *RB* follows it closely in structure and substance, and in the prologue and first seven chapters borrows from it freely, and sometimes verbatim. The later chapters continue to follow the themes and topics of the *RM*, although *RB* diverges from them more frequently in points of detail and tone: the governance of the monastery, the abbot and other principal offices (provost or prior, infirmarer, master of novices), the balance between worship and work and the modes of communal and individual discipline remain close to the *RM* but with alterations that are original or drawn from other sources: perhaps most notable are the significant differences between the content of the day and night offices in the *opus Dei*.[44]

Long dismissed as only a late imitator of the *RB*, the role of the *RM* as a source for Benedict's rule was first recognised by the Benedictine Augustin Genestout in 1937; the indebtedness of the *RB* was reinforced by a succession of Benedictine scholars and the conviction informed the critical editions of both texts prepared by Adalbert de Vögué.[45] The premise is that the *RM* pre-dated the *RB* by as much as a generation and was perhaps compiled in the opening decades of the sixth century, possibly at, and for, a *cenobium* situated in the Campagna, or at least in southern Italy. It was appropriated by Benedict to provide a framework for his own community, and adapted in the light of his other influences and insights. It should be noted the *regula* connected with the *cenobium* of Eugippius of Castellum Lucullanum, which is dated to the second quarter of the sixth century, shares a textual

[43] Dunn, *Emergence of Monasticism*, pp. 113–18. See also *The Rule of the Master: Regula magistri*, Cistercian Studies Series 6 (1977); A. de Vögué, *Le Maître, Eugippe et Saint Benôit: Recueil d'articles* (Hildesheim, 1984).

[44] J. Dyer, 'Observations on the Divine Office in the Rule of the Master', in *The Divine Office in the Latin Middle Ages: Methodology and Source Studies, Regional Developments, Hagiography: Written in Honor of Professor Ruth Steiner*, ed. M. E. Fassler and R. A. Baltzer (Oxford, 2000), pp. 74–98. See also De Vögué, *Community and Abbot*, pp. 28–9.

[45] *La règle du maître*, ed. and trans. A. de Vögué, 3 vols., Sources chrétiennes 105–7, Serie des texts monastiques d'occident 14–16 (Paris, 1964–5); *La règle du saint Benôit*, trans. A. de Vögué and ed. J. Neufville, Sources chrétiennes 181, Serie des textes monastiques d'Occident 49 (Paris, 1972). See also De Vögué, *Community and Abbot*, pp. 25–33 at 26–8.

relation to the *RM* and may have served as a bridge to the *RB*.[46] The role of the *RM* has been questioned: Marilyn Dunn contends that the liturgical regime of the *RM* and the specific issue of the dating of the spring equinox place its composition in the period after Benedict's death when the influence of Irish monasticism passed through the former provinces north and south of the Alps, a region where Dunn would be inclined to locate the *cenobium* of the Master; the unforgiving, sometimes severe tone of the *RM* – a feature which the *RB* does not borrow – might connect it to the Irish tradition.[47] Dunn's dating would recast the *RM* not as the progenitor, but as a product of the monastic culture engendered by Benedict and his rule; her case to a degree detaches Benedict from the currents of his own day, serving to underline his originality. Dunn may be wrong to regard the dating of the equinox as a unique marker of the cultural and chronological context of the *RM* but the case for the earlier date and different context is equally insecure. Whether it preceded or followed Benedict, the identity of the *RM* was soon eclipsed by the rule of a master whose name (if nothing else) was widely known. At Corbie in the eighth century, copies of the *RM* were regarded only as an extended recension of the *RB*.[48]

In many respects, the *RB* – like its reputed author – articulated the monastic customs and values of its time, but there was a degree of originality in its treatment that arrested practitioners. It was not the first synthesis of eastern and western traditions – Augustine, Caesarius, Cassian and the *RM* drew from the same fund of authorities – but its brevity and clarity made it the most compelling. In the monastic milieus between Provence and Tuscany, the *RB* was also distinguished for its degree of humanity: the asceticism of Caesarius (and Martin before him) and the authoritarian discipline of the 'Master' were tempered by the *caritas* and communality of Augustine and Basil. There was also a novelty in the regime of the *RB* which was not found in any of the *regulae* of the early and mid-sixth century: for the night and day offices outlined in chapters 8 to 18, the *RB* adopted the new *ordo* of the secular churches of Rome.[49] Here the *RB* departs from the *RM*. The assimilation of the psalmody of the Roman church not only ensured the survival of the tradition of the *RB* in the turbulent decades after Benedict's death but also encouraged its revival when a new generation of Roman missionaries carried their brand of Christianity into northern and western Europe and into churches of their own foundation.

---

[46] A. Gometz, 'Eugippius of Lucullanum', *Monastic Research Bulletin* 11 (2005), 26–7.

[47] M. Dunn, 'Mastering Benedict: Monastic Rules and their Authors in the Early Medieval West', *EHR* 105 (1990), 567–94 at 569. See also A. de Vogüé, 'The Master and St Benedict', *EHR* 107 (1992), 95–103.

[48] Dunn, 'Mastering Benedict', 567–94; D. Ganz, *Corbie in the Carolingian Renaissance*, Beihefte der Francia 20 (Sigmaringen, 1990), pp. 38, 40.

[49] Dyer, 'Observations on the Divine Office in the Rule of the Master', p. 80.

Benedict's own connection with the *RB* is not uncomplicated. Of course, his identity as originator of the rule was axiomatic throughout the medieval and post-medieval history of the order but in modern times it has attracted critical attention. De Vögué described Benedict as the 'redactor' of the *RB*; subsequent studies have cautiously 'attributed' and 'associated' but not ascribed authorship itself.[50] The Benedict of the Gregorian *Dialogues* is a dynamic figure whose function as a legislator is referenced apparently as an afterthought in the penultimate chapter of the text. No autograph codex survives and the tradition of one was extinguished as early as the ninth century.[51] It has been observed that an attribution of the rule to the Blessed Benedict benefited Pope Zachary's promotion of the Gregorian *Dialogues*, whose translation he patronised.[52] The scope (seventy-three chapters) and structure of the text, which appears to have been stable by the eighth century, suggests a phase, perhaps as early as the mid-sixth century, of reorganisation: the office of prior, a feature not found in *RM*, is introduced in chapter 65, and the treatment of governance given earlier (for example, in the second chapter on the abbot) takes no account of it. Of course, if the *RB* did undergo a process of reorganisation, it may be further distinguished from the works on which it was founded, as one of the first codes in Western Europe to represent the customs of a living community.

Pre-Benedictine Monasticism

The advent of the *RB*, and the death of Benedict, marked the end, or the beginning of the end, of the monastic age of late antiquity. The generation of abbot ascetics and prelate patrons that extended the monastic enterprise in the years either side of 500 was receding even before Benedict arrived at Montecassino. Roman Christianity itself appeared in peril. Bishop Fulgentius of Ruspe died in *c.* 533; Eugippius of Castellum Lucullanum was dead before 540; Caesarius of Arles died in 542; nothing further is known of the 'Master' after the *RM* entered circulation, and the transmission of the anonymous rules that surfaced in the first quarter of the century, of the *Four Fathers*, of *Paul and Stephen*, also appear to have faded fast.[53] It is true that the academy-*cenobium* of Cassiodorus Senator (d. *c.* 585) flourished in the quarter century after Benedict's death, but his Vivarium was situated far to the south and apparently unconnected to the monastic networks of

---

[50] De Vögüé, *Community and Abbot*, p. 25.

[51] See below, pp. 22–6 at 25–6.

[52] *Rome and the North: The Early Reception of Gregory the Great in Germanic Europe*, ed. R. H. Bremmer, K. Dekker and D. F. Johnson (Paris, 2001), p. 208; G. Ferrari, *Early Roman Monasteries* (Vatican City, 1957), p. 249. The translation appears, in parallel with the Latin text, in *PL* 77: 149–430.

[53] Dunn, *Emergence of Monasticism*, pp. 124–8.

central and northern Italy, or, indeed, to Benedict of Nursia, as the early histories had claimed.[54]

The discontinuities in the monastic tradition were not so marked in the southern provinces of Gaul: Aurelian, Caesarius's successor at Arles, was himself the author of a conventual rule and drew the patronage of King Childebert (d. 558), whose own Gothic campaigns afforded protection to Provençal monasteries and who is credited as the founder of the basilical convent of Saint-Vincent, later Saint-Germain-des-Prés; in this region Bishop Ferreolus of Uzès (d. 581) also composed a rule for a *cenobium* of his own foundation, perhaps the last customary of the Gallo-Roman tradition.[55] In the second half of the century the Merovingian monarchs Clothar I (d. 561), Chilperic (of Neustria, d. 584) and Guntram (of Burgundy, d. 592) patronised churches at Châlons (Saint-Marcel) and Soissons (Saint-Médard) which appear to have accrued a liturgical regime reminiscent of the basilical monastery.[56]

Benedict's achievement at Montecassino also coincided with the imperial struggle for Italy which continued for almost twenty years (535–54) and saw Rome successively regained and lost by Justinian's generals. Historians are fond of the observation (surely a truism) that Benedict's appeal to the seclusion and stability of the *cenobium* – 'run thither to the tabernacle of his kingdom' (*RB*, prologue, 13, 22) – was so heartfelt because the forces of the Eastern Empire and the Ostrogoths were embattled to the north and south. Probably it would be wrong to claim the political volatility of the 530s and 40s was any greater threat to Benedict's *cenobium* than the Theodorican persecutions had been to his Cisalpine counterparts a generation before; a greater consequence of this phase of the Gothic wars was that it stifled further monastic settlement in a swathe of Subalpine Italy. Moreover, following the death of Emperor Justinian, Lombard forces swept through a region that had not recovered the evangelical spirit of forty years before, the time of Eugippius, which had shaped Benedict in his formative years. Montecassino was laid waste by the Lombards in 571.[57] The *cenobium* itself perhaps survived, since there was an early tradition that Benedict's remains, and the autograph of the *RB*, were preserved there, but the community of monks was undoubtedly dispersed. Its desolation was not an isolated incident: of ninety-seven monastic settlements documented after 500

---

[54] P. R. L. Brown, *The Rise of Western Christendom: Triumph and Diversity, 200–1000* (Cambridge, MA, 1996), pp. 196–7; J. Décarreaux, *Monks and Civilisation from the Barbarian Invasions to the Reign of Charlemagne*, trans. C. Haldane (London, 1965), pp. 237–46.

[55] A. de Vögüé, *The Rule of Saint Benedict*, trans. J. B. Hasbrouck (Kalamazoo, 1983), p. 19. For the text of his *Regula ad monachos*, see *PL* 66, 959–76.

[56] I. N. Wood, *The Merovingian Kingdoms, 540–751* (London, 1993), pp. 183–4, 186–90; P. Fouracre, *The Age of Charles Martel* (Harlow, 2000), p. 65.

[57] *Historia Langobardorum*, IV, c. 17 (MGH, p. 122). According to Warnefrid one monk escaped the assault, in fulfilment of the founder's prophecy, as recounted in the *Dialogues*, II 17.

scarcely a handful survived beyond 604.[58] Monastic observance retained a vestigial presence at Rome at intervals during this period, but in provincial Italy it all but disappeared; Vivarium again was an exception – although its celebrated library was dispersed, for a time the convent perhaps endured.[59]

The half-century following Benedict's death, when his personal cult grew enough to capture the attention of the Roman, Gregory, and the *RB* entered circulation, saw the stability of monastic life founder and its spiritual force fade. It was recovered only at the turn of the sixth century, and not from the residue of Gallo-Roman monasticism. The mission of the Irish ascetic Columban, initiated in the Vosges in 585×590 but extending west and southward as far as Lombard Italy, marks perhaps a more conspicuous watershed in early medieval monastic culture than the composition of the *RB*.[60] Columban carried with him the ascetic spirituality of Irish Christianity and the monastic customs of its early Ulster pioneers. He founded a tripartite colony at Luxeuil, Annegray and Fontaines, mixed communities of men and women whose reputation radiated in the central and southern regions of the Merovingian kingdom.[61] Although Columban himself suffered the hostility of indigenous clergy, Luxeuil itself was assimilated into the Gallican mainstream. His mission into Lombardy restored monastic life in a region where the insular tradition was threadbare: Bobbio, where Columban died in 615, became the hub of his influence south of the Alps.[62]

The demands of Columban's ascetic and liturgical regime, which contrasted with the moderation of the *RB*, appealed in regions where the earlier customs of Martin, Caesarius, and perhaps the 'Master', had flourished. In the half-century after his death, convents (male, female and 'double' houses) committed to his customs spread across a region stretching from Mediterranean to the valley of the Seine. A network of new (and renewed) foundations was formed in the patrimony of Merovingian Gaul under the patronage of Dagobert (d. 639), Clovis II (d. 657) and Queen Balthild (d. 680). Saint-Denis (630), Fleury-sur-Loire (640) and Corbie (657×661)

---

[58] M. Costambeys, 'The Transmission of Tradition: Gregorian Influence and Innovation in Eighth-Century Italian Monasticism', in *The Uses of the Past in the Early Middle Ages*, ed. Y. Hen and M. Innes (Cambridge, 2000), pp. 78–101 at 82.

[59] Brown, *Rise of Western Christendom*, pp. 196–7.

[60] For Columban, see the essays in *Columbanus and Merovingian Monasticism*, ed. H. B. Clarke and M. Brennan (Oxford, 1981). See also F. Prinz, *Frühes Mönchtum in Frankenreich: Kultur und Gesellschaft in Gallien, den Rheinlanden und Bayern am Beispiel der monastichen Entwicklung (4. bis 8. Jahrhundert)* (Munich, 1965); M. Richter, *Bobbio in the Early Middle Ages: the Abiding Legacy of Columbanus* (Dublin, 2008).

[61] His early biographer, Jonas of Bobbio (d. after 659), recounted Columban's arrival at Luxeuil and the advance of his 'fame ... in all parts of Gaul and Germany': *The Life of St Columban by the Monk Jonas*, ed. D. C. Munro (Felinfach, 1993), p. 53 (c. 31). See also P. Riché, 'Columbanus, his Followers and the Merovingian Church', in *Columbanus*, ed. Clarke and Brennan, pp. 59–72 at 62–4; Wood, *Merovingian Kingdoms*, pp. 184–9.

[62] *Life of St Columban*, ed. Munro, pp. 101–2 (c. 61); Riché, 'Columbanus, his Followers and the Merovingian Church', pp. 62–4, 66.

became the cornerstones of Frankish monasticism; satellite (male and female) convents, for example, Faremoutiers (620) and Jumièges (630), were equally well patronised.[63] The first generation of his followers carried Columban's customs eastward into the territory between the Alps and the Rhine which had not witnessed earlier monastic settlements. The communities at Saint-Gall (*c.* 613), Kreuznach (*c.* 630) and Murbach (*c.* 640) began a chain of Hibernian houses (*Schottenklöster*) which grew, and prospered, between the eighth and the twelfth centuries.[64] Columban's customs did not bear so many fruit beneath the Alps, but Bobbio prospered, and the foundation of Farfa (*c.* 680) was perhaps a late expression of Celtic enthusiasm.[65] It was also under a Columbanian banner that Amand (d. 675) led a mission into Flanders at the instigation of the Merovingian Clothar II (d. 629). He fostered monastic communities at Ghent (639) and further north at Nivelles (640).[66] Nor was the influence of Columbanian custom confined to the European mainland. There were creative exchanges between the Columbanians of Francia and the clergy of Ireland and Anglo-Saxon England. Agilbert of Jouarre held the West Saxon see of Dorchester (on Thames) before progressing to Paris in *c.* 660.[67] It was Celtic missionaries also who advanced monastic customs in the British Isles. Aidan founded a colony of cenobites at Lindisfarne in *c.* 635; the Irish mission advanced into the Borders under his disciple, Cuthbert (d. 687), who himself made an end-of-life monastic profession at Melrose.[68]

The evangelical energy of the Roman religious was not entirely spent at the turn of the seventh century and it was clerks shaped by the cenobitic customs of the Roman basilicas who led the Gregorian mission into Anglo-Saxon England in 597. Later medieval historians remembered Augustine of Canterbury as a monk of Rome, and Benedictine annalists have always

---

[63] Wood, *Merovingian Kingdoms*, pp. 192–3, 200–1; Dunn, *Emergence of Monasticism*, pp. 185–7. For Corbie, see also Ganz, *Corbie in the Carolingian Renaissance*, pp. 14–35 at 15.

[64] Riché, 'Columbanus, his Followers and the Merovingian Church', pp. 66–71. See also J. von Pflugk-Harttung, 'The Old Irish on in the Continent', *TRHS* New Series 5 (1891), 75–102. See below, pp. 48, 52.

[65] S. Boynton, *Shaping a Monastic Identity: Liturgy and History at the Imperial Abbey of Farfa, 1000–1125* (Ithaca, 2006), pp. 5–6.

[66] For Amand, see *Vita S. Amandi episcopi et confessoris*, ed. B. Krusch, MGH, SRM V (Hanover, 1910), pp. 428–49. See also Riché, 'Columbanus, his Followers and the Merovingian Church', pp. 65–6; J. M. Wallace-Hadrill, *The Frankish Church* (Oxford, 1981), pp. 72–74; Wood, *Merovingian Kingdoms*, pp. 184–9; R. McKitterick, *The Frankish Church and the Carolingian Reforms, 789–895* (London, 1977), p. 142; Décarreaux, *Monks and Civilisation*, p. 298.

[67] Bede, *Historia*, iii. 7, 28. See also P. Fouracre and R. A. Gerberding, *Late Merovingian France: History and Hagiography, 640–720* (Manchester, 1996), p. 103; P. H. Coulstock, *The Collegiate Church of Wimborne Minster* (Woodbridge, 1993), p. 89.

[68] Aidan's mission was instigated by Oswald, king of Northumbria (634–42), whose patronage conferred upon him the status of a missionary bishop ('episcopus vegans'). For a summary account, see H. M. R. E. Mayr-Harting, *The Coming of Christianity to Anglo-Saxon England*, 3rd edn (London, 1991), pp. 94–6, 161–7. See also *St Cuthbert, his Cult and his Community to AD 1200*, ed. G. Bonner, D. Rollason, and C. Stancliffe (Woodbridge, 1998). Bede of Monkwearmouth-Jarrow offered an early and influential narrative of these pioneers of Pictish and Northumbrian religion: Bede, *Historia*, iii. 3, pp. 218–20.

represented him as a pioneer of the *RB* in the British Isles.[69] Yet the earliest authorities scarcely support the tradition: Bede described the missionaries as adherents of an 'apostolic' mode of life ('coepereunt apostolicam primitiuae ecclesiae vitam imitari'); Paul Warnefrid represented them not as *monachi* but *praedicatores* (preachers).[70] Augustine did secure the patronage and practical assistance of Continental monks, some of whom visited the missionaries in England, and his royal patron, Æthelbert, did provide him with a *monasterium* of some description, dedicated to SS. Peter and Paul.[71] However, there is nothing to suggest that under Augustine or his immediate successors such connections and contexts served to cultivate cenobitic customs, still less any trace of Benedictinism. The conversion of the English was accompanied (and advanced) by the creation of devotional centres in the southern, western and northern kingdoms, but their form, infrastructure and membership were more fluid, and certainly less self-consciously clerical, than any later monastery: at most they might be described as sub-monastic, or *monasteriola* or *monasteriunculum* (terms, respectively, for small convent and cell).[72] From the middle decades of the seventh century, the form of these settlements was more sharply defined, with features, such as a designated superior, and a territorial domain, that were consistent with contemporary monastic custom. The *monasterium* established at Lyminge (Kent) under the direction of Æthelburga (?*c.* 633), daughter of Æthelbert of Kent, appears to have resembled a convent (of men and women) on the Merovingian model.[73] Sheppey (*c.* 670), Monkwearmouth (674), Malmesbury (*c.* 675), Jarrow (682), Thanet (690), Reculver (692) and Glastonbury, an erstwhile Celtic colony, formed clusters of cenobitic living approaching a century after Augustine's arrival.[74] Their foundation reflected the enterprising piety of regal authorities, not, yet, the advance of any *regula monasticae*.

It was the century after Benedict's death that marked the beginnings of cenobitic monasticism in the Iberian peninsula. Here, as in Anglo-Saxon England, there was a trace of the pre-Columbanian traditions of the Latin and Greek pioneers of the regular life. Probably Byzantine influences were predominant in the lost rule of John of Biclaro (*c.* 540–*c.* 621), bishop of

---

[69] For example, Schmitz, *Histoire*, i. 38, 42; G. Penco, 'La prima diffusione della Regola di S. Benedetto: ricerche e osservazioni', *Studia Anselmiana* 42 (1957), pp. 321–45 at p. 331.

[70] Ferrari, *Early Roman Monasteries*, pp. 387–8. It is worth noting the tenth-century narrative of Edgar's foundation of monasteries depicted Augustine as a founder of monasteries in which 'the same mode of life which the apostles maintained': *Councils and Synods*, i.142–54 at 145.

[71] Gregory's Register attests to Augustine's Continental contacts: I. Wood, 'The Mission of Augustine of Canterbury to the English', *Speculum* 69:1 (1994), 1–17 at 6. For the monastery of SS Peter and Paul at Canterbury, see *MO*, p. 22; Mayr-Harting, *Coming of Christianity*, pp. 62–3 at 63.

[72] *MO*, p. 22; J. Blair, *The Church in Anglo-Saxon Society* (Oxford, 2005), pp. 3–4, 219n.

[73] Blair, *Church in Anglo-Saxon Society*, p. 186; B. Yorke, *Nunneries and the Anglo-Saxon Royal Houses* (London, 2002), p. 23; S. J. Ridyard, *The Royal Saints of Anglo-Saxon England* (Cambridge, 1988), p. 242, n. 5.

[74] *MO*, pp. 22–4.

Girona (Catalonia), founder of a *cenobium* called *Biclarum* on a site now unidentified.[75] Fructuosus, archbishop of Braga, formed a monastic colony at Nono, for which he composed a rule distinguished for its Middle Eastern influence and its incorporation of the Mozarabic Use.[76] Perhaps the most significant force was Isidore, archbishop of Seville (d. 636), a patron and protector of the peninsula's nascent congregations, although it appears he never made his own profession.[77] He provided his own rule whose immediate reception remains unclear but which offers perhaps the earliest witness to the transmission of the *RB*. The diversity of customs in seventh-century Iberia is in contrast to the growing Columbanian consensus in the north.

The Dissemination of the Regula Benedicti

The resurgence of monastic society in Europe after the turn of the sixth century was neither the consequence of Benedict nor of the *RB*. Of the new generation of *regulae*, only that of Archbishop Isidore of Seville was deeply indebted to the Cassinese code.[78] In contrast to the customs of the living communities of Arles, Lérins and Luxeuil-Annegray-Fontaines, the *RB* appeared as a relic of a brotherhood recalled only in the Gregorian *Dialogues*. The reputation of the *RB*, and of Benedict himself, grew slowly in the century after the death of Pope Gregory (604). Before the close of the eighth century, knowledge of the *RB* may only be glimpsed or guessed at. The first phase of its transmission remains purely speculative.

Medieval accounts of Benedict and Montecassino laid claim to an early period of evangelism even before the Lombard invasion. The *Dialogues* give an impression of a lively colony of wide acclaim, witnessed by Gregory's own encounter with Abbot Honoratus. Gregory also initiated the tradition of a diaspora of Benedict's disciples elaborated by later authorities. He reported that Valentin of Montecassino carried the *RB* to the basilical monastery of the Lateran at Rome. Maurus, the noble convert to the *RB* commemorated in the *Dialogues*, was said in a ninth-century *Life* to have carried the customs of Benedict into Gaul.[79] There was an early tradition, distinct from the *Dialogues*, that Gregory introduced the *RB* in his own domestic *cenobium* of

---

[75] The Byzantine influence came from John's almost twenty-year sojourn at Constantinople. He was commemorated in Isidore's *De viris illustribus*, xxi. See also J. F. O'Callaghan, *A History of Medieval Spain* (Ithaca, 1983), p. 81.

[76] R. Collins, *Early Medieval Spain: Unity in Diversity, 400–1000*, 2nd edn (Basingstoke, 1995), pp. 84–5.

[77] Dunn, *Emergence of Monasticism*, p. 192.

[78] Ibid., pp. 185, 192.

[79] The *Vita sancti Mauri*, attributed to one 'Faustus' of Montecassino, is modelled on the second book of Gregory's *Dialogues* but also recounts the mission of 'Maurus' into Gaul, where he is represented as the founder of an abbey at Glanfeuil. Modern scholarship suggests the text is the work of the ninth-century abbot Odo of Glanfeuil, who also compiled an account of the translation of the relics of Maurus: Bloch, *Monte Cassino in the Middle Ages*, II (iii–iv), pp. 972–3.

St Andrew;[80] possible corroboration of the presence of the *RB* in Gregorian Rome is the contention that the revised version of the text, now known as the *textus interpolatus*, was formulated there before 604.[81] Paul Warnefrid reported that Placidus led a mission to Sicily: the 'Benedictine' character of the early convents at Palermo, Messina and Siracusa was reinforced by their connection to Gregory the Great.[82] Warnefrid also commemorated Marcus, another shadowy witness of early Montecassino.[83] The Cassinese chronicler Peter the Deacon (*fl.* 1130) suggested Benedict's *cenobium* attracted the patronage of the Byzantine Emperor Justinian II, although his documentary proof is doubtful.[84] If Marilyn Dunn is right to regard the *RM* as a code of *c.* 600 then it too is a marker of this first phase of transmission.[85]

Perhaps the one feature of all these narratives that has a hint of plausibility is the suggestion that the *RB* first drew attention, and perhaps a following, in ultramontane Europe. A passing reference to the observance of the *RB* in a correspondence between Venerandus of Alta Ripa and Bishop Costans of Albi (Languedoc), dateable to between 620 and 630, may constitute the very first independent testimony to the code.[86] A certain witness to its circulation is the *Regula Donati*, compiled by Bishop Donatus of Besançon for his monastery of St Paul a generation after the prelacy of Costans (655×660) and in a diocese 300 miles to the north-east.[87] This was a 'mixed rule' combining customs from Caesarius and the *Regula Columbani* together with the *RB*, knowledge of which Donatus may have born with him from Luxeuil, where he made his profession; certainly, an awareness of the code is attested in Columbanian diplomata of mid-century. It was a sign of his growing status that the 'Blessed Benedict' was specified in Donatus's prologue.[88] In the same northern and eastern region of Francia the *RB* appears to have claimed ascendancy barely a decade after Donatus's death. Bishop Drausius of the northern see of Soissons named Benedict among

---

[80] For a critical examination of Gregory's interest in the *RB*, see Costambeys, 'Transmission of Tradition', pp. 100–1.

[81] P. Meyvaert, 'Towards a History of the Textual Transmission of the *Regula sancti Benedicti*', *Scriptorium* 17 (1963), 83–110. See also M. Gretsch, *The Intellectual Foundations of the English Benedictine Reform* (Cambridge, 1991), p. 243.

[82] Such was the testimony of Gregory of Tours, *Historia Francorum*, x. 1. See also Schmitz, *Histoire*, i. 66–7.

[83] *Historia Langobardorum*, I, c. 26 (MGH, p. 68). Marcus, allegedly an early disciple of Benedict, was the attributed author of an elegy in praise of Benedict which appears in early manuscripts of the Cassinese lectionary and was reproduced in the vestibulam of the abbey church constructed by Abbot Desiderius: F. Newton, *The Scriptorium and Library at Monte Cassino, 1058–1105*, Cambridge Studies in Palaeography and Codicology 7 (Cambridge, 1999), p. 5.

[84] H. Bloch, 'Monte Cassino, Byzantium and the West in the Earlier Middle Ages', *Dumbarton Oaks Papers* 3 (1946), 163–224; Bloch, *Monte Cassino in the Middle Ages*, II (iii–iv), p. 5.

[85] Dunn, 'Mastering Benedict'. See also above, n. 42.

[86] Dunn, *Emergence of Monasticism*, p. 173.

[87] Ibid. For the *Regula Donati*, see *PL* 87: 272–98. See also J. A. McNamara and J. E. Halborg, *The Ordeal of Community: The Rule of Donatus of Besançon and the Rule of a Certain Father to the Virgins* (Toronto, 1993); G. Moyse, *Les origines du monachisme dans la diocèse de Besançon* (1973).

[88] Ibid.

the authorities to be followed by his nuns in a decree dated to 667.[89] The rule for female religious, 'regula cuiusdam patris ad virgines', derived from Donatus, repeated his debt to the *RB*.[90] A rule apparently from northern Francia and dated to the last quarter of the century, known from its incipit as 'Psallendo pro sancta devotione' (surviving as a fragment in Brussels, Royal Library, MS II 7538), is also deeply indebted to the *RB*, at least after the opening injunction culled from Caesarius.[91] A council at Autun (Burgundy), apparently convened by Bishop Leodgar (d. 679), is said to have required the religious of the region to conform either to the canonical code of a secular clerk or to the customs of Benedict.[92] There is a textual witness to knowledge of the *RB* in England also in the last quarter of the seventh century. The 'Leiden' glosses on the rule descended from an Anglo-Saxon exemplar, which must have been compiled with reference to a text of the *RB*, perhaps at Canterbury in the forty-year tenure of Abbot Hadrian of St Augustine's (d. 709).[93]

There is no trace of this early transmission in the manuscript tradition of the *RB*. The earliest extant copy, now Oxford, Bodleian Library, MS Hatton 48, has been dated to *c.* 700; made perhaps in the Anglo-Saxon kingdom of Mercia, and later in the possession of the monks of Worcester, it represents the *textus interpolatus*, the refinement of Benedict's text traditionally tied to Rome at the turn of the sixth century.[94] The text preserved in this manuscript was corrected (yielding interlinear notes) using a manuscript distinct from the exemplar; this was also a *textus interpolatus*, attesting to the presence of multiple copies in seventh-century England.[95] It has been argued that *interpolatus* was unrepresentative of the *RB* commonly read in England, which on the evidence of later copies was the *textus receptus*, a further refinement of *interpolatus* undertaken during the ninth-century reform of Benedict of Aniane; the predominance of this ninth-century

---

[89] S. F. Wemple, *Women in Frankish Society: Marriage and the Cloister, 500–900* (Philadelphia, 1985), pp. 288–9.

[90] The text is printed at *PL* 88: 1053–70. See also McNamara and Halborg, *Ordeal of Community*.

[91] A. de Vogüé, *Les règles des Saints Pères* (Paris, 1982), pp. 59–60; D. de Bruyne, 'Fragment oncial d'une règle de moniales', *Rev. Bén.* 35 (1923), 126–8.

[92] The earliest Benedictine historians held the 'Council of Autun' to be a milestone in the dissemination of the *RB*: Schmitz, *Histoire*, i. 63. The authenticity of the canon or decree, and of the record of the council itself, have been questioned by many modern scholars; a summary of the obvious problems of date, documentary evidence and context is provided in F. Clark, *The Pseudo-Gregorian Dialogues*, vol. 1, Studies in the History of Christian Thought 37 (Leiden, 1987), pp. 237–9. See also H. Mordek and R. E. Reynolds, 'Bischof Leodegar und das Konzil von Autun', *Aus Archiven und Bibliotheken: Festschrift für Raymund Kottje zum 65 Geburstag*, ed. H. Mordek (Frankfurt-am-Main, 1992), pp. 71–92.

[93] Gretsch, *Intellectual Foundations*, p. 244. The Leiden glosses were widely disseminated and survive in twenty-five manuscripts. For Abbot Hadrian and the school of Canterbury see N. P. Brooks, *The Early History of the Church at Canterbury* (Leicster, 1984), pp. 94–7.

[94] For the Hatton manuscript, see *The Rule of St Benedict: Oxford, Bodleian Library, Hatton 48*, ed. D. H. Farmer, EEMF 15 (Copenhagen, 1968). See also M. Lapidge, 'The School of Theodore and Hadrian', *Anglo-Saxon England* 15 (2007), 45–72 at 62–4.

[95] Gretsch, *Intellectual Foundations*, pp. 243–4.

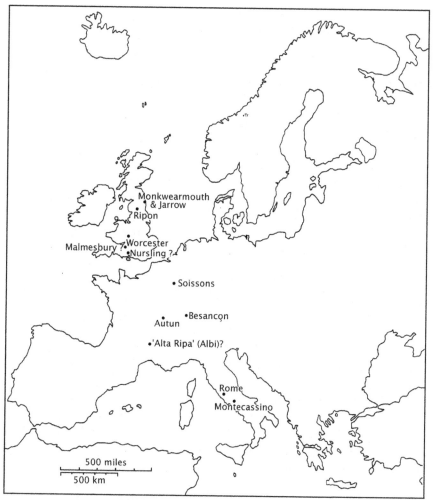

1 Presumed knowledge of the *Regula Benedicti* before *c.* 700

recension reinforces the impression that the reach of the text of the *RB* – as distinct from customs derived from it – was limited in the generations before and after 700. The codex closest in date to Hatton 48, made in *c.* 817 at the Carolingian abbey of Reichenau (now Sankt Gallen Stiftsbibliotek, MS 914) carries the recension believed to represent Benedict's text, the so-called *textus purus*: this manuscript is understood to be a copy of the lost manuscript (the Aachener Normalexemplar) copied for Charlemagne from the codex at Montecassino claimed to be the 'autograph'.[96] The descent of

---

[96] *Regula Benedicti de codice 914 in bibliotheca monasterii S. Galli servato*, ed. B. Probst (St Ottilien, 1983); *Benedicti Regula*, ed. R. Hanslik, CSEL 75 (Vienna, 1977), pp. xxiii–xxviii. See also Gretsch, *Intellectual Foundations*, p. 243.

the text from a codex of Benedict's time preserved in the 150 years between the destruction and restoration of Montecassino (571×728) cannot be proven, but certainly there is no trace of the recension in the early witnesses to the *RB*.[97] In so far as their following of Benedict had a textual base, it was probably the *interpolatus* that perhaps originated at Rome.

It is worth noting in this period that the cult of the person of Benedict was perhaps in advance of the *RB* itself. Gregory bore witness to the relic of Benedict displayed above the door of his former oratory of Enfide (*Dialogues*, II. 1. 2). The earliest manuscript fragments of the *Dialogues* may be dated to the decades either side of 700 and indicate a monastic readership.[98] The Gregorian mission perhaps brought the name of Benedict to England even if it did not bring the *RB* or religious professed under it. Here the identification of Benedict with Rome – for Anglo-Saxon prelates the model *ecclesia* – amplified his personal appeal. It was perhaps a measure of his capacity to animate a community that the monks of Fleury usurped his relics from Montecassino and not the manuscript of his rule.[99]

Regula mixta

The *RB* passed into the mainstream through the growing practice of regular observance. Mission, conversion, and the spread of church foundations in the former Roman provinces of Francia and Italia after 604, stimulated the interest of a new generation in forms of religious life. The impulse to review the record of the monastic fathers of the recent and remote past was perhaps greater in this period, not because the spiritual fervour was any stronger than in Benedict's day, but because there was a growing imperative for a monastic settlement to be integrated into the emerging ecclesiastical framework, of diocese and bishop and their royal (or magnate) patrons. The founder-abbot remained a powerful figure – Columban (Bobbio), Donatus (Besançon), Biscop (Wearmouth-Jarrow) were understood to embody the values of their communities – but their precepts were moderated by reference to a diverse and expanding corpus of codes and *regulae*. By the turn of the sixth century the *RB* was already a conspicuous presence in this repertory of monastic authorities. In the ensuing decades it emerged as one of the most popular points of reference for the formation, or re-formation, of a *regula monachalis*. Modern historians have characterised this as an age of 'mixed rules' (*regulae mixtae*) since scarcely any community of monks,

[97] Lapidge, 'School of Theodore and Hadrian', 62–4.
[98] Trier, Stadtbibliothek, Fragment, s.n.; Stuttgart, Landesbibliothek, Theologische und Philosophische Quellen, 628; Wrocław, University Library, Akc, 1955/2 + 1969/430; Barcelona, Biblioteca Capitular, s.n. Only the Wrocław fragments include sections of Book II.
[99] T. Head, *Hagiography and the Cult of Saints: The Diocese of Orléans, 800–1200* (Cambridge, 1990), pp. 23–4.

nuns or even secular clerks followed a singular code.[100] The *RB* captured the imagination of early medieval Europe not because it offered an alternative form of religious life but, on the contrary, because it could be readily assimilated into existing monastic practice.

A *regula mixta* in which the *RB* was an important ingredient appears to have been formulated first in the Columbanian heartlands of Bobbio and Luxeuil. The third superior of Luxeuil, Abbot Waldebert (d. 668), composed a customary formed from the *RB* and *RC* for the women of Faremoutiers; it was surely followed also at his own Luxeuil and perhaps other communities under his purview; the authority, if not the priority, of the *RB* was recognised at Bobbio in a diploma of 643, although no text of a *regula mixta* bearing its influence survives from this period.[101] The status of the *RB* rose slowly in the wider Columbanian network. References to the rule in foundation charters dated before 650 are scarce and generally suspect. The earliest charter of Eligius's Limousin foundation at Solignac (635) appears to prescribe the *RB*, but it survives only as a ninth-century interpolation, and the original recognised Benedict's code only on the matter of the election of the superior.[102] The communities formed under the influence of Philibert, at Jumièges and on the island of Noirmoutier, perhaps knew a fusion of *RB* and *RC* before 650; a century later the *Vita Filiberti* represented their superior as the proverbial bee prudently 'making store for the future' from the flowers of Basil, Caesarius, Columban and Benedict.[103] It is possible the customs of the old island convent of Lérins had also become mixed by mid-century: it is perhaps significant that it was here that the Englishman Biscop adopted the name-in-religion of Benedict.[104] The second half of the century saw a Benedictine *regula mixta* advance to the north and west. It was in this period that Bishop Donatus composed his own *regula* which recalled the combination of the *RB* and *RC* he had known at Waldebert's Luxeuil. Now a mixed rule also prospered in England: Biscop's community at Wearmouth (674) appears to have followed a peculiar hybrid: Bede claimed the customs came from no fewer than seventeen monasteries, although a reference in the *Life* of Coelfrid to the liturgical arrangements at Jarrow after the plague attests to *ad literam* acceptance of the *RB*.[105] Anglo-Saxon England occupied a borderland between Celtic and Roman monasticism. Celtic customs prevailed in the British Isles, and in Flanders, where Amand's

---

[100] Wallace-Hadrill, *Frankish Church*, pp. 69–70; F. Prinz, *Askese und Kultur: vor- und frühbenediktinisches Mönchtum an der Wiege Europas* (Munich, 1980), pp. 34–5.

[101] Penco, 'Prima diffusione', p. 336; Waldebert of Luxeuil, *Regula cuiusdam patris ad virgines*, PL 88: 1053–70.

[102] Dunn, *Emergence of Monasticism*, p. 166.

[103] *Vita Filiberti*, ed. W. Levison, MGH, Scriptorum Rerum Merovingicarum, V (1910), pp. 583–604 at 587; Fouracre and Gerberding, *Late Merovingian France*, p. 142.

[104] P. Wormald, 'Bede and Benedict Biscop', in *Famulus Christi: Essays in Commemoration of the Thirteenth-Centenary of the Birth of the Venerable Bede*, ed. G. Bonner (London, 1976), 141–69.

[105] Bede, *Historia*; Wormald, 'Bede and Benedict Biscop', 141, 143.

monasteries appear to have resisted the advance of *regulae mixtae* in the Pas-de-Calais, Champagne and Île-de-France.[106] Beyond Northumbria, England's emerging monastic communities were also affected by these cross-currents. The *RC* retained its appeal on the eastern seaboard, where exchanges with Flanders were frequent.[107] Canterbury's 'monasterium' of Saints Peter and Paul reflected the residual Roman influence of Augustine and Gregory, although it does not follow that the *RB* was acknowledged as an authority.[108] Perhaps it was the monastic settlements of Wessex that came closest to the mixed, but identifiably Benedictine customs of central Francia; certainly the fragmentary textual and codicological tradition of the *RB* at the turn of the eighth century tends westward.[109]

Generally a *regula mixta* constituted a composite of customs and traditions: where one rule was silent, another was substituted. There were significant differences in the scope of the source texts – in terms of its length alone, the *RB* (like its analogue the *RM*) was hardly typical – and they displayed a wide spectrum of spiritual modes, from individual asceticism to communal worship. The *RB* presented a particular contrast with the *Regula Columbani*. Columban offered his converts not an institutional code but a manual for personal spiritual transformation. Where the two texts were brought together, the *RB* was used primarily to create a framework for conventual life, adopting Benedict's preferences for the principal officers and their roles, and the election of the superior. In houses of Columbanian origin, or those where a vestige of the Caesarian tradition had been overwritten with the *Regula Columbani*, the moderate discipline and modest asceticism of the *RB* may also have been adopted as a counterbalance to the severity of their own custom. Although Benedict also offered a daily office less demanding than the Columbanian scheme, in north western regions it would appear the Celtic pattern of worship was preferred. The 'Bangor Antiphoner' offers a plausible glimpse of observance at a monastery of Columbanian origin. A conspicuous contrast with the *RB* is the priority attached to the musical performance of the monks, who in the words of one Collect were called upon to 'sing a new hymn to the god of Thunder ... create a clamour with [your] manifold spiritual melodies' ('diversis spiritalis melodiae modis');[110] indeed, the biographer of Columban, Jonas of Bobbio (d. after 659), considered the 'singing and

---

[106] Wallace-Hadrill, *Frankish Church*, pp. 73–4.

[107] S. Foot, *Monastic Life in Anglo-Saxon England* (Cambridge, 2006), pp. 52–8 at 57; B. Yorke, *Kings and Kingdoms of Early Anglo-Saxon England*, rev. edn (London, 1997), p. 65.

[108] Brooks, *Early History of the Church of Canterbury*, pp. 87–91. See also Y. Hen, 'Rome, Anglo-Saxon England and the Formation of the Frankish Liturgy', *Rev. Bén.* 112 (2002), 301–22.

[109] Foot, *Monastic Life in Anglo-Saxon England*, p. 57; B. Yorke, *Wessex in the Early Middle Ages* (London, 1995), pp. 61–2; Coulstock, *The Collegiate Church of Wimborne Minster*, p. 90.

[110] P. Jeffery, 'Eastern and Western Elements in the Irish Monastic Prayer of the Hours', in *Divine Office in the Latin Middle Age*, ed. Fassler and Baltzer, pp. 99–143 at 121.

exulting' of his brethren their distinguishing feature.[111] To the east and the extreme south it was the Mozarabic Office that prevailed.[112] Perhaps this was also true of monastic communities of a Roman orientation: the *RB* guided them through practical matters, but their liturgical regime was overlooked in favour of the customs of the basilical convents.[113] In this respect, the Northumbrian monasteries of Wilfrid and Biscop were perhaps anomalous, since it appears the Benedictine office was adopted there.[114] The earliest witnesses to the *RB* reflect the preference for the institutional Benedict: in the early seventh century it was Benedict's guidance on the election of a monastic superior that first attracted the attention of the Gaulish clergy.[115] The early currency of the institutional customs of Benedict informed the outlook of the reformers of the eighth and ninth centuries and perhaps their focus on the Benedictine *opus Dei*.

The growing status of the *RB* not only as a source of monastic custom but also as a reference work for the regulation of the whole community of clerks is reflected in its use by Bishop Chrodegang of Metz (*c.* 712–766) in his *Regula canonicorum*.[116] Chrodegang's rule, which may be dated to the second decade of his episcopate (742–66), was intended for the chapter of secular clergy that served his cathedral at Metz, yet its inspiration and principal source was the monastic customary of Benedict. Chrodegang was one of a new generation of eighth-century prelates that asserted the priority of the *RB* as a monastic code. His own foundation at Gorze, and that for which he was chief sponsor at Lorsch, were among the earliest in northern Francia to be committed to the *RB* as their sole customary.[117] Yet in his *Regula canonicorum*, Benedict's code served only as convenient framework for clerical legislation. It provided a model for the daily office, for the discipline and governance of the chapter and its administrative and domestic management, but Chrodegang did not seek to translate either the personal or communal ascetic of the *cenobium*.[118] The *Regula canonicorum* circulated widely in Francia and beyond in the century after Chrodegang's death.[119]

---

[111] Jonas, *Vitae scanctorum Columbani*, ed. B. Krusch, MGH (Hanover, 1905), pp. 275–6. See also Jeffery, 'Eastern and Western Elements', p. 121.

[112] See below, p. 50.

[113] It is notable that among his reflections on the origins of the order, Orderic Vitalis observed the preference for the Columbanian Office: 'from him they learnt the ritual and sequence of the divine offices': *Orderic*, iv. 334–5.

[114] Wormald, 'Bede and Benedict Biscop', 157&n.

[115] See above, p. 27.

[116] M. A. Claussen, *The Reform of the Frankish Church: Chrodegang of Metz and the Regula canonicorum in the eighth century* (Cambridge, MA, 2004).

[117] Ibid., pp. 20–30.

[118] Ibid., pp. 114–65.

[119] B. Langefeld, '*Regula canonicorum* or *Regula monasterialis vitae*? The rule of Chrodegang and Archbishop Wulfred's reforms at Canterbury', *Anglo-Saxon England* 25 (1997), 21–36; *The Old English Version of the Enlarged Rule of Chrodegang*, Texte und Untersuchungen zur englischen Philologie, 26 (Munich, 2003).

Certainly in the ninth, perhaps still in the tenth century, it was the rule for canons, a refinement of the *regula mixta* genre, that for many offered their first encounter with the Benedictine tradition.

The adoption of *regulae mixtae* extended, and secured, the audience of the *RB*, particularly in the northern and western regions of Europe. Yet the advent, at the turn of the eighth century, of reform movements that favoured the *RB* did not wholly displace the mixed tradition. It is likely that the foundations of Alfred of Wessex (871–99) retained a *regula mixta*: Bishop Asser represented them as communities 'of monks of all kinds'.[120] It has been suggested that even the convents reinvigorated under the Carolingian reform of Benedict of Aniane retained an attachment to the mixed customary of previous generations.[121] Before the surge in monastic professions during the spiritual revival of the eleventh century, it is possible that few convents were large enough to realise the communal observance of the *RB* in its entirety.[122]

The Beginnings of Benedictine Monasticism

There was no evolution of Benedictine monasticism in early medieval Europe – the *regulae mixtae* contained and even recast the *RB* – rather it was a movement created by a deliberate and directed process of reform. Generally it is represented as a Carolingian enterprise, the collaborative project of Charlemagne (742–814), his son and successor, Louis the Pious (778–840), and Benedict of Aniane (c. 747–821), former courtier, monastic founder and principal abbot (*abbas princeps*) of the emergent empire. Certainly, the injunctions, issued in capitularies (legislative compendia of which each entry constituted a *capitula*, i.e. chapter), from a sequence of ecclesiastical councils between 789 and 816 transformed the nature of monastic observance, and ultimately, the scale of monastic settlement, in the territory of the Franks. The capitularies, and the synoptic customary compiled by Abbot Benedict, the *Concordia regularum*, captured the imagination of their Continental neighbours not only as a charter of ecclesiastical reform but also as an *exemplum* of religious revival. Hagiographers commemorated Benedict himself as a second founder. Yet it would be wrong to regard the advance of the *RB* between the eighth and the tenth century as a unitary process powered by the ecclesiological, cultural and geo-political priorities of a single polity. The ascendancy which the *RB* had achieved by the mid-ninth century – the death of the emperor

[120] Asser, *De rebus gestis Alfredi*, in *Life of King Alfred*, ed. W. Stevenson, 2nd edn (Oxford, 1954), pp. 79–80 at 80: '... in quo monasterio diversi generis monachos undique congregavit'.
[121] A. W. Robertson, *The Service Books of the Royal Abbey of Saint-Denis: Images of Ritual and Music in the Middle Ages* (Oxford, 1991), p. 21.
[122] For example, M. C. Miller, *The Formation of a Medieval Church: Ecclesiastical Change in Verona, 950–1150* (Ithaca, 1993), p. 66.

Louis – was also the result of patterns of conversion, settlement, patronage and political hegemony that were independent of the Frankish kingdom. Moreover, if the Carolingian reform marked a watershed in the development of Europe's monasteries, for generations afterwards it remained vulnerable to a sudden reversal.

Perhaps the first instance of the imposition of the *RB* occurred not on the European mainland but in the English sub-kingdom of Deira. There was an early tradition that the West Saxon missionary and bishop Wilfrid (634–709) introduced the customs of Benedict at his monastic colony centred on Ripon (North Yorkshire). There was already a church at Ripon, and when granted to Wilfrid in *c.* 660 it may have been served by a community following the *Regula Columbani*. The account of his disciple Stephen of Ripon (Eddius Stephanus), composed in *c.* 720, attributes to him the introduction of the *RB* to the 'betterment' ('bene meliorabat') of the monastic community.[123] Stephen refers to the house as a *cenobium* and recalls a communal ethic that is reminiscent of the *RB*: when a certain Caelin aspires to the life of the hermit, Stephen contrasts his impulse with the vocation of the common life ('ad deserta loca revertere et contemplativam vitam sicut olim exercere et soli Deo servire concupsicit').[124] Wilfrid founded a dependent house at Hexham (670×680), and perhaps other satellites; certainly he was founder of minsters in Mercia and perhaps had a hand in Reculver which dates from 669: according to Stephen he drew to him 'many thousands of monks' ('multa milia monachorum') amounting to a congregation ('cum onibus subiectis nostris congregationibus'), a term which does denote a degree of conformity among the communities, although perhaps only in their recognition of Wilfrid's authority as abbot.[125] It has been suggested that he also sought the adoption of the *RB* at Lindisfarne, the monastery at which he had made his own profession as a youth; there is also a conjecture that Wilfrid's contribution to the Synod of Whitby (664) caused Hild to reform the double monastery there according to the principles of the *RB*.[126] It is possible Wilfrid also transmitted his commitment to the *RB* among the clergy of northern Francia in the course of the Continental sojourn that followed his episcopal consecration at Compiègne in 665.[127] During this period he passed through Meaux (Île-de-France), although there is no record of his involvement in

---

[123] *Wilfrid*, p. 30.
[124] Ibid., p. 138.
[125] Ibid., pp. 50, 102. See also Blair, *Church in Anglo-Saxon Society*, p. 95.
[126] For Wilfrid and Lindisfarne, see Wormald, 'Bede and Benedict Biscop', 141–69 at 158–9. For Hild of Whitby, see Schmitz, *Histoire*, i. 45. Her certain hostility to the Roman customs championed by Bishop Wilfrid at Whitby challenges this conjecture: Mayr-Harting, *Coming of Christianity*, pp. 108, 167.
[127] Fouracre and Gerberding, *Late Merovingian France*, pp. 172–8. See also Bede, *Historia*, iii. 28, pp. 314–15.

its new (*c.* 660) foundation of Sainte-Croix; Stephen claimed that Wilfrid conducted a mission among the Frisians where 'they accepted his teaching and with a few exceptions all the chiefs were baptised by him in the name of the Lord, as well as many thousands of common people', although again there is no record of any monastic enterprise of his own there, although he encouraged the later mission of his disciple, Willibrord.[128]

Stephen's representation of Ripon as a Benedictine monastery cannot easily be corroborated. The portrait provided by Wilfrid's ally Abbot Aldhelm of Malmesbury (d. 709/10) is not overtly Benedictine.[129] Bede, whose experience at Wearmouth perhaps heightened his sensitivity towards differences of custom, recalled Wilfrid as a champion not of the *RB* but of the Roman tradition: 'the first bishop of the English to introduce the catholic way of life' ('catholicum vivdeni morem': *Historia ecclesiastica*, IV, 2). Of course, it could be argued that the prevelance of *regulae mixtae*, not only in the northern kingdoms, but in the monastic colonies of the south and west (including Aldhelm's Malmesbury), would have rendered the pure *RB* more conspicuous to contemporaries. It has also been suggested that there may have been a precocious English preference for the *RB*, perhaps connected with an (unusually) wide circulation of the Gregorian *Dialogues*.[130] It remains most likely, however, that Ripon, Hexham and (perhaps) the other houses of the congregations adhered to a *regula mixta* in which the *RB* was the dominant ingredient.[131] Yet this does not diminish Wilfrid's significance. He, or at least the Bishop Wilfrid of Stephen's biography, secured the reputation of Benedict and the *RB* in a society caught in the cross-current of customs. He also represented the *RB* for the first time as a refined form of religious life, not a complement to the *Regula Columbani* but a replacement for it.

Wilfrid's episcopal career inaugurated a wave of Anglo-Saxon evangelism in Europe which may also have encouraged the wider adoption of the *RB*. Willibrord (657/8–739), who had first made his profession at Ripon under Wilfrid, was one of a cohort of Celtic and English monks inspired to conduct missions among the Frisians by Egbert, a Northumbrian divine settled at the Irish monastery of Rathmelsigi (perhaps located in Co. Connaught).[132] His mission, which began towards the end of the 680s and culminated with his consecration as Bishop of the Frisians in 695, attracted

---

[128] *Wilfrid*, pp. 52–3. Stephen represents Wilfrid as providing the foundation on which Willibrord built (*superaedificavit*). See also Wood, *Merovingian Kingdoms*, p. 315.

[129] *The Prose Works of Aldhelm*, ed. M. Lapidge and M. Herren (Cambridge, 1979), pp. 143, 150–1, 155–60, Letter IV (to Geraint), Letter XII (to the abbots of Wilfrid). See also Blair, *Church in Anglo-Saxon Society*, p. 98.

[130] Wormald, 'Bede and Benedict Biscop', 145.

[131] Ibid., 145; Blair, *Church in Anglo-Saxon Society*, p. 95.

[132] W. Levison, *England and the Continent in the Eighth Century* (Oxford, 1946), pp. 45–59. See also Y. Hen, *Culture and Religion in Merovingian Gaul, AD 481–751* (Leiden, 1995), pp. 102–7. For a sketch of Willibrord as a missionary, see R. A. Fletcher, *The Barbarian Conversion: From Paganism to Christianity* (Berkeley, 1999), pp. 199–202.

the patronage of the Frankish rulers, who presented him with ecclesiastical and secular properties from which he founded monastic communities at Echternach, Kaiserwerth and Utrecht.[133] The Benedictine character of Willibrord's foundations has always been assumed although largely on the basis of his own association with Ripon; his early biographies highlighted his debt to 'that holy and sacred monastery' (as Alcuin described it) but did not specify his ties to the *RB* itself.[134]

The Frisian mission was briefly renewed by the West Saxon monk Winfrith (who later assumed the Latin appellation Boniface, d. 754) in 716 following the resurgence of the apostate ruler Radbod (d. 719).[135] He failed, but in 719, with the patronage, and symbolic pallium, of Pope Gregory II, he embarked on a mission in the pagan territory east of the Rhine. Here he secured the first German see, and, with his followers, a network of monastic colonies.[136] His first biographer, Willibald, implied that the communities formed under his influence were Benedictine in character. He claimed that Winfrith's formation, at the West Saxon monastery of Nursling, had been under the imprint of the *RB*: 'he applied himself assiduously, according to blessed Father Benedict's prescribed form of proper arrangement to the daily manual labour and the regular performance of his duties'.[137] The most important foundation to emerge from this mission was at Fulda (744). According to the *Life* of Sturm, founder-abbot, compiled perhaps fifty years after the foundation, the first monks of Fulda had looked 'to the fathers of the monasteries of Tuscany' and 'conceived a burning desire to follow the rule of the holy father Benedict'.[138] Whatever the character of its early customs, Fulda emerged as an influential centre of Benedictinism in the wake of the Carolingian reform.

Contemporary with these monastic missions, on the northern and eastern borders of the Frankish kingdom, it appears Bishop Chrodegang of Metz advocated the adoption of the *RB* at the monasteries formed under his direction at Gorze and, at the end of his life, at Gengenbach and Lorsch. It has been suggested that the reform that spread from these houses, and the subordinate convents of Saints Evre and Maximinin, in the tenth century, was raised on the foundations of a Benedictinism that was already

[133] Fouracre and Gerberding, *Late Merovingian France*, p. 311; Hen, *Culture and Religion in Merovingian Gaul*, p. 103; Schmitz, *Histoire*, i. 70–2. See also *The Calendar of St Willibrord*, ed. H. A. Wilson, HBS 55 (1918), fo. 39v.

[134] Alcuin, *Vita Willibrordi*, ed. W. Levison, MGH (Hanover, 1920), pp. 113–41.

[135] Wood, *Merovingian Kingdoms*, pp. 309–11.

[136] Décarreaux, *Monks and Civilisation*, pp. 303–7.

[137] Willibald, *Vita Bonifatii*, ed. W. Levison, MGH (Hanover, 1905), pp. 11–57; *The Anglo-Saxon Missionaries in Germany, being the Lives of SS Wilibrord, Boniface, Sturm, Leoba and Lebium, together with the Hodoeporicon of St Willibald and a Selection from the Correspondence of St Boniface*, ed. C. H. Talbot (London and New York, 1954), p. 30.

[138] Eigil, *The Life of Sturm*, trans. C. H. Talbot in *Soldiers of Christ*, ed. Noble and Head, pp. 165–188 at 176–7.

almost two centuries old.[139] A privilege for Gorze, brought by Chrodegang to the Council of Compiègne in 757 and endorsed there by a coalition of bishops, presented the monastery as bound to observe only the customs of Benedict.[140] Of course, the impression of continuity was cultivated by the reformers and it is difficult to detach the early *acta* from their own narrative priorities. It is worth noting that in common with Willibrord and Boniface, Chrodegang's first encounter with the *RB* had probably been in the context of a Columbanian *regula mixta* at the monastery of Saint-Trond.[141]

The same period saw the restoration of monastic life at Montecassino. The site is said to have been reoccupied from 717, but the readoption of the *RB* has been connected with the return of the autograph manuscript under Pope Zachary (741–52).[142] There is no documentary evidence to underpin this tradition although if the composition of the prefatory verses attributed to Simplicius is to be dated to the mid-eighth century (as has been suggested) it might be seen as the consequence of a newly acquired Benedictine identity. This may have been part of a general resurgence of interest in the *RB* in the Italian peninsula. Gregory III (731–41) is said to have initiated a reform of the monasteries of Rome that Zachary continued. New foundations followed to the north and east, and a commitment to the *RB* appears at the outset at Volturno (731) and Nonantola (752).[143]

There was much about the constitution of these early communities that separates them from the *ad literam* regulars of later centuries. They were at once places of monastic observance and public worship, pastoral care and social welfare. They were a mix of children, clerks, laymen and priests; in England, France and northern Italy, many were conjoined with convents of women.[144] Yet increasingly, under the influence of their episcopal and monastic founders and benefactors, the Benedictine character of their customary observance was conspicuous. The traces of manuscript production and transmission in the first half of the eighth century, a contrast to the vacuum that precedes it, may be testimony to the rising status of the *RB*.[145] When Benedict of Aniane was professed at Saint-Seine (Dijon), perhaps in 774 (certainly before 780), forty years before the publication of

---

[139] Nightingale, *Monasteries and Patrons of the Gorze Reform*, pp. 69–70; Claussen, *Reform of the Frankish Church*, p. 151. See also K. Zelzer, 'Zur Stellung des Textus Receptus und des interpolierten Textes in der Textgeschichte der Regula S. Benedicti', *Rev. Bén.* 88 (1978), 205–46.

[140] Claussen, *Reform of the Frankish Church*, pp. 28–9.

[141] Ibid., p. 23.

[142] Paul Warnefrid, *Historia Langobardorum*, vi. 40 (MGH, 48 (1879), pp. 230–1 at 231). See also P. Meyvaert, 'Problems Concerning the "Autograph" Manuscript of Saint Benedict's Rule', *Rev. Bén.* 69 (1959), 3–21.

[143] G. Penco, *Storia del monachesimo in Italia dalle origini alla fine del Medio Evo* (Rome, 1961), pp. 113–14, 161, 172; *Vita Anselmi abbatis Nonantulani*, ed. G. Waitz, MGH (Hanover, 1878); Décarreaux, *Monks and Civilisation*, pp. 313–18.

[144] See below, pp. 134–5.

[145] Meyvaert, 'Towards a History', 83–110; Meyvaert, 'Problems Concerning the "Autograph" Manuscript', 3–21.

his *Concordia*, he entered a monastic environment in which the *RB* already was recognised as a valuable tool for the revival of regular observance.

The Carolingian reform, of which Benedict is regarded as the spiritual father, is commonly represented as a new departure, born not from an organic evangelical impulse but from the political imperatives of an emerging state. From the beginning of his reign, and in particular from the death of his brother and rival Carloman (768–71) in 774, Charlemagne sought to extend his control over a church whose infrastructure, personnel and spiritual charisma, duly directed, might amplify his regal, political and territorial authority. His aim was to reorganise and revitalise both secular and regular churches and their clergy, their observance and their contribution to pastoral care and to education, a new and growing priority for the monarch. These aims were not wholly novel, however: Charlemagne's father Pepin (752–89) and his uncle, Carloman, ruler of Austrasia, had also undertaken to direct the development of the Church and the evangelical initiatives of the episcopal and monastic leaders within their territory.[146] Carloman provided Boniface with an episcopal network to support and extend his mission on the borders of Austrasia; his 'Germanic' council (*concilium Germanicum*) of 742 prefigured the reforming assemblies of Charlemagne and Louis in its ambition, 'informed by the advice of the servants of God', to restore 'the laws of God and of the church corrupted'; as Charlemagne would do, both Carloman and Pepin also acknowledged, and sought to appropriate for their own advantage, the authority of the Roman papacy.[147]

Perhaps the significant difference of Charlemagne's programme was its scope. He aimed at nothing less than the transformation of ecclesiastical practice, the removal of old and anomalous customs, among them the Gallican modes shaped by Columban and other Gaulish pioneers, and the substitution of the customs of Rome. The initial injunction addressed the community of clergy as a whole 'to revive the true worship of the true God in the kingdom that God has given': the *Admonitio generalis* of 789 comprised eighty-two articles governing the observant and moral conduct of the clergy derived in large part (sixty of the articles) from the *Dionysio-Hadriana*, a digest of canon law presented to Charlemagne by Pope Adrian I in 774.[148] The principal injunctions for the reform of the monasteries were promulgated at the Synod of Aachen in 802, but in the preceding decade or so, Charlemagne had already stimulated significant developments in the governance of regular communities and their relation to magnate and royal authority. As early as 787 he had secured a manuscript of the *RB* from

---

[146] A. Barbaro, *Charlemagne: Father of a Continent*, trans. A. Cameron (Berkeley, 2004), pp. 221–3.

[147] W. Hartmann, *Die Synoden de Karolinerzeit im Frankreich und in Italien* (Paderborn, 1989), pp. 47–63; M. de Jong, 'Charlemagne's Church', in *Charlemagne: Empire and Society*, ed. J. Story (Manchester, 2005), pp. 103–35 at 109; Wood, *Proprietary Church*, pp. 223–4.

[148] Wallace-Hadrill, *Frankish Church*, pp. 259–60; McKitterick, *Frankish Church and Carolingian Reforms*, pp. 3–5.

Montecassino, from which he commissioned further copies: the surviving Saint-Gall codex is understood to be a descendant.[149] Among the synodal decrees of these years were several significant injunctions concerning the conduct of female religious: article 75 of the *Admonitio generalis* prohibited women from performing any sacerdotal function and required them to be fully enclosed; the expectation of enclosure was reiterated in 799.[150] In these years Charlemagne also encouraged initiatives undertaken independently by the prelates in his circle. He presented Alcuin of York to the abbacy of Saint-Martin at Tours in 796, where he continued the renewal of secular and scriptural learning he had initiated under the king's direction at Aachen.[151] Appointed to the metropolitan see of Lyons the following year, Leidrad reported to Charlemagne on his renewal of the region's monasteries and the restoration of regular observance.[152] Charlemagne's patronage of particular houses and their superiors in this period modelled not only a new form of monastery independent of either episcopal or papal control but bound closely to the political, social and economic priorities of its secular patron but also a novel approach to their internal administration, with abbots (underpinned by their royal patron) placed in command of a regional network of monasteries. It was as one of these privileged superiors that Benedict and the Aniane family of monasteries – granted its independence under royal protection in 787 – became bound to the royal-imperial house.[153]

Of the decrees of Charlemagne's reign, it was that of the 802 synod that was most significant for Benedictine observance since it promulgated the (sole) adoption of the *RB* not only in a given diocese but throughout the territory of the Franks. The principle was reiterated in 813 at the Council of Châlons, where it was reported that the monasteries of Burgundy had already conformed.[154] Following Charlemagne's death in 814 Emperor Louis formalised the place of Benedict of Aniane in his counsels, translating him to an abbey of his own foundation at Inde. At successive synods at Aachen in 817 and 818–19, only the second and third of Louis's reign, under Benedict's direction, two complementary capitularies were presented, the

---

[149] See above, p. 25.

[150] *Capitularia regum Francorum, I*, ed. A. Boretius, MGH (Hanover, 1883), pp. 52–62 at 60 (c. 76); *Concilia aevi Karolini, Leges III, Concilia 2/1*, ed. A. Werminghoff, MGH (Hanover and Leipzig, 1906), pp. 205–19 at 210 (c. xxvii(22)). See also H. Scheck, *Reform and Resistance: Formations of Female Subjectivity in Early Medieval Ecclesiastical Culture* (New York, 2008), pp. 29–30.

[151] For Alcuin, see S. Allott, *Alcuin of York, c. AD 732 to 804* (York, 1874). See also Wallace-Hadrill, *Frankish Church*, pp. 214–15; J. Story, *Carolingian Connections: Anglo-Saxon England and Carolingian Francia, c. 750–c. 870* (Aldershot, 2002), pp. 5–7.

[152] Jong, 'Charlemagne's Church', pp. 103–35 at 103.

[153] Wallace-Hadrill, *Frankish Church*, pp. 229–31, 290–1.

[154] Châlons was one of four regional assemblies (the others being Reims, Mainz, Tours) from which further reform might have proceeded at the Aachen assembly, convened in September, had not the emperor's death ensued: Wallace-Hadrill, *Frankish Church*, pp. 230, 261–3; McKitterick, *Frankish Church and Carolingian Reforms*, pp. 12–13.

first (817) outlining the obligations of male and female religious under the *RB* and the elaborating the detail of its different liturgical requirements and its counterpart (818–19), addressing matters of corporate governance particularly in respect of the relationship with royal and episcopal authority. At the first of these synods a commentary on the *RB* was also commissioned from Master Smaragdus of Saint-Mihiel, a work which from the evidence of its transmission may have been complete before the end of the same decade.[155] Benedict himself contributed to the legislative corpus with his *Concordia regularum*, a concordance of monastic *regulae* that served practically to contextualise the *RB* and its prescriptions and politically to underline its place in the continuum of monastic observance.[156]

In many respects the capitularies of 817–19, and the commentaries that accompanied them, constituted the framework for a monastic order. They ascribed to the *RB* a canonical status which the *Concordia regularum* and Smaragdus's commentary served to reinforce. They also bound observance of the *RB* to structural changes in the administration and governance of the monasteries: each superior was to be trained at Inde, which was offered to the religious of the empire as a model for the observance of the rule, 'Aniane is the head of all monasteries, not only those erected in the regions of Gothia but also those erected in other areas at that time or afterward', wrote Ardo, Benedict's biographer.[157] Ardo also recalled that the abbot dispatched brethren to Montecassino to learn the customs of their Nursian master *ad fontes*: 'to all a wholesome standard'.[158] There were also to be visitors, well versed in the *RB*, passing through the network of houses to monitor observance and to identify deficiencies. The adoption of the *RB*, Ardo claimed, was advanced by Father Benedict himself, who progressed from one monastery to another, 'conversing [on the rule] with them, chapter by chapter'.[159] These measures anticipated the centrifugal force of the Cluniac, and, later, the Cistercian movements, and served to create a foundation on which a congregational identity could be raised.

The canonical and critical corpus of 817–19 represented the culmination of more than three decades of royal supervision of the regular clergy. Charlemagne had fashioned himself as *rector*, responsible for their *correctio*; the young Louis was styled a *miles Christi* – the title was conferred upon him by the Benedictine Hrabanus Maurus – advancing the reformation

---

[155] Wallace-Hadrill, *Frankish Church*, p. 264. See also *Smaragdi abbatis expositio in regulam S. Benedicti*, ed. A. Spannagel and P. Engelbert, CCM 8 (Siegburg, 1974), pp. xxiv–xxix; F. Rädle, 'Studien zu Smaragd von Saint-Mihiel', *Medium Aevum* 29 (Munich, 1974).

[156] *Benedicti Ananiensis Concordia regularum*, ed. P. Bonnerue, Corpus Christianorum Continuatio Mediaevalis 168 (1999); Wallace-Hadrill, *Frankish Church*, p. 230–1.

[157] Ardo, *The Life of Benedict Abbot of Aniane and of Inde*, trans. A. Cabannis, in *Soldiers of Christ*, ed. Noble and Head, pp. 213–54 at 238.

[158] Ibid.

[159] Ibid.

begun by his father.[160] In his later decades, however, Louis's authority was undermined by external threats and internal, and dynastic instability. There was no extension of the monastic enterprise elaborated at Aachen. A council of 825 reissued the *Admonitio generalis*, but in itself this might be regarded as an acknowledgement that the codes of 817 had already lost something of their force.[161] The foundation and refoundation of houses committed to the *RB* now continued in provincial dioceses: the new community at Charlieu (Burgundy) was converted to the *RB* by Bishop Radbertus of Valence in 872; St Maximin was returned to Benedictine observance in 885 and again in 892 by Bishop Arnald of Toul.[162] Yet there are signs that the systematic conversion of customs envisaged by Benedict of Aniane had foundered, stifled by the resistance of superiors, and, in some cases, their (episcopal and secular) patrons, and by a prevailing attachment to the observant practice of a *regula mixta*. At the royal abbey of Saint-Denis, under Abbot Hilduin (814–41), the brethren wishing to follow a monastic code were driven out and the house became a community of canons; the *RB* was accepted there only in 832 and not in full: the liturgical customs remained those of the Columbanian *regula mixta*.[163] Even where the *RB* was established it is possible that only its precepts governing administration, discipline and spiritual formation were adopted and the pre-existing liturgical patterns were retained: it is telling that in the liturgical manuscripts surviving from this period there is scarcely any trace of a monastic office in the Benedictine mode. Of the spirit of Aachen, above all what was transmitted throughout the territory was an acknowledgement of the role of the ruler in the governance of the house: when a dispute erupted at Fulda in 812 the monastic community instinctively turned to the emperor to be both arbitrator and advocate.[164]

The advance of the monastic reforms, and of the ecclesiastical reorganisation of which it was an expression, was also arrested by the increasing political and social instability witnessed both within and beyond the borders of Francia. Charlemagne's *imperium* was transformed into three weak and vulnerable kingdoms under the sons of Louis the Pious, whose troubles were compounded by the advent of Norse raiders via the Garonne, Loire and Seine, 'up-river, with a favourable wind, divine judgement [made] it easy for them to launch a full-scale attack'.[165]

---

[160] E. Sears, 'Louis the Pious as *Miles Christi*', in *Charlemagne's Heir: New Perspectives on the Reign of Louis the Pious (814–40)*, ed. P. Godman (Oxford, 1990), pp. 605–28 at 625. See also *Carolingian Culture: Emulation and Innovation*, ed. R. McKitterick (Cambridge, 1994), p. 252.

[161] *Charlemagne's Heir*, ed. Godman, p. 436.

[162] Nightingale, *Monasteries and Patrons of the Gorze Reform*, pp. 13 187–90.

[163] Robertson, *Service Books of the Royal Abbey of Saint-Denis*, pp. 35–8.

[164] Jong, 'Charlemagne's Church', pp. 103–35 at 121.

[165] *The Annals of St-Bertin*, trans. J. L. Nelson (Manchester, 1991), pp. 122, 128, the latter describing the plundering of Saint-Denis.

From 787×793, the Anglo-Saxon kingdoms of England were subject to the same attrition of recurrent Norse raids.[166] The new foundations of northern Italy fell prey to Magyar incursions.[167] Secular government, settlement and trade were all interrupted, but contemporary, and near-contemporary, sources also emphasise the heavy cost paid by the church, and by the monasteries in particular. A narrative of the near extinction of the monastic tradition was initiated by the annalists and chroniclers of the eleventh and twelfth centuries and was repeated by later medieval, Renaissance and, indeed, modern historians. Asser of Sherborne's image of a wasteland has been widely used to express what many Benedictine scholars have understood to be a discontinuity comparable to the Lombard devastation of Montecassino three centuries before: 'The love of a monastic life had utterly decayed from that nation [the kingdom of England] as well as from many other nations.'[168] Since the turn of the twentieth century the evidence of monastic extinction has been re-examined: it has been observed that excavations of ninth-century monastic sites do not corroborate the annalists' claims of complete destruction; it has also been noted that houses founded or reformed under the influence of the Aachen canons underwent further renewal in the last quarter of the century, the very period when they were thought to have been laid waste. Monastic religion endured beyond the decline of the empire and the descent of the Norsemen; but there is little doubt that it did so in a form that was still far from being a Benedictine hegemony.

The Tenth-Century Reformations

The waste of the monastic order in the wake of the Norsemen and other aliens was a narrative woven by a new generation of reformers first as a call to arms and later to add lustre to the achievements of their own churches, convents and congregations. The impulse for reform which aroused them grew from the recovery of social order, royal (and magnate) authority, and the renewal of the economic, educational and legal infrastructure, as early as the turn of the ninth century in Wessex and Burgundy, a generation later in Flanders, the Rhineland and perhaps northern Italy, and a century on in the rising duchy of Normandy. It did not cohere into a single movement but was channelled into a succession of regional revivals, reflecting, and responding to, prevailing local conditions, the most energetic and enduring of which were connected with Cluny, Gorze and Winchester. Although

---

[166] *MO*, pp. 24, 32, 57–8, 69; Blair, *Church in Anglo-Saxon Society*, pp. 133, 292–323.

[167] K. Bakay, 'Hungary', in *The New Cambridge Medieval History*, iii, ed. T. Reuter and R. McKitterick (Cambridge, 2005), pp. 536–52 at 539.

[168] Asser, *De rebus gestis Alfredi*, ed. Stevenson, pp. 80–1 at 80: 'nimirum quia per multa retroacta annorum curricula monasticae vitae desiderium ab illa tota gente, nec non et a multis aliis gentibus'.

they followed their own course, they found a common source of inspiration in Benedict of Aniane's recovery of the *RB*; they also shared with the Carolingian a powerful and productive compact with secular patrons. By contrast with Abbot Benedict, these tenth-century reformers realised the full observance of the *RB*, including its liturgical programme, which, duly embellished in response to patrons with a new taste for suffrages, they represented as the *raison d'être* of monastic religion. They also refined the congregational structures pioneered by the Carolingians and achieved a degree of conformity in observance, and governance, not witnessed before. The locus of their power, their political, spiritual and cultural influence, remained at the regional centres where the reform began, but wherever they made their profession, their brethren now recognised the shared experience of a common *ordo religionis*.

Like its Carolingian precursor, the initiative for reform at Cluny originated with the lay overlord. The monastery was founded on his own lands by Duke William I (called the 'Pious') of Aquitaine (875–918) in 909. Duke William's conduct as founder was novel, however; his charter proclaimed the convent to be subject not to any lord but solely to the see of Rome, under its direction and defence (*tuitio et defensio*).[169] The formation of the community reflected the continuity; indeed, the residual strength of monastic religion in the region points to a pre-existing impulse for the pure observance of the *RB*. The founding abbot was Berno (d. 927), a monk of St Martin's, Autun, already renowned for his Benedictine reformation of the monastery at Baume, and for his own foundation, on his family estate, at Gigny.[170] Berno held Cluny together with his earlier houses and extended the family at Déols (Bourg-Dieu) and Massay. Early Cluny was characterised by a commitment to the *RB*, but further growth was stifled by the scale of Berno's *Klosterverband*. At his death the network was divided, and Cluny was placed at the head of a tripartite colony (also comprising Déols and Massay) under the direction of Odo (d. 942), former abbot of Beaume.[171] It was Abbot Odo who raised Cluny not only as a beacon of Benedictine observance but also as a powerful proprietor of the region's churches and convents. A 931 privilege of Pope John IX enabled Odo to reform monastic communities surrendered to him by their founders; a flurry of such grants followed, not only in Aquitaine but in the territories to the north and east: in the valley of the Loire, Fleury and Saint-Martin at Tours now conformed

---

[169] *Recueil des chartes de l'abbaye de Cluny*, ed. A. Bernard and A. Bruel, 6 vols. (Paris, 1876–1903), i. 124–28. See also B. H. Rosenwein, *To be the Neighbour of St Peter: The Social Meaning of Cluny's Property, 909–1049* (Ithaca, 1989), pp. 1, 14–20, 36.

[170] *John of Salerno*, pp. 6, 25&n; J. Warrilow, 'Cluny: Silentia Claustri', in *Benedict's Disciples*, ed. D. H. Farmer, pp. 118–38 at 120; Rosenwein, *To be the Neighbour of St Peter*, pp. 173–4.

[171] *John of Salerno*, p. 25. See also J. Wollasch, 'The First Wave of Reform', in *The New Cambridge Medieval History*, iii, ed. Reuter and McKitterick, pp. 63–86 at 175.

to the custom of Cluny.[172] These houses were placed under the paternal authority of Cluny as members of a family that now extended far beyond the earlier episcopal and seigniorial colonies. Odo's successors, Aymer, Maiolus and Odilo, carried the customs of Cluny further, to the northern borders of France, to Italy and the Iberian peninsula. At Pavia, Abbot Maiolus (d. 994) founded San Salvator and reformed San Pietro; it was under Odilo that Farfa accepted affiliation to Cluny, and its customs were carried so far as Salerno.[173] In the first quarter century of the foundation, there were seventeen houses bound together by Cluny; by the time of its first centenary, there were several hundred.[174]

The earliest accounts of the customs of Cluny date from its second century, reflecting the fact that in its formative years the observance of the abbey and its affiliates continued to evolve. There can be no doubt its mode of life was founded on an *ad literam* adherence to the *RB*. Berno and his successors embraced the liturgical regime of the rule, which had been eschewed by so many of the Anianian family. The special character of Cluny's *opus* strengthened the attachment of her patrons and caused her to embellish, and lengthen, the founder's offices. The regime was enforced throughout the network more effectively than the Carolingian code, since every convent was compelled to recognise the superior of Cluny as its abbot; the only exception were those well-established communities – such as Farfa – that adopted the customs of Cluny but did not formally enter the network. The abbot and convent also exercised their paternal authority over growing number of secular churches they accrued as property. By 1050 the churches of southern Burgundy bore the imprint of Cluny in their architecture, their patrons and pastors, and, presumably, their patterns of worship.

The reform, initiated in the north-eastern region of France in the second quarter of the tenth century from *c.* 933, was also raised on an existing monastic infrastructure. It began at Gorze (Lorraine), the eighth-century foundation of Bishop Chrodegang of Metz, and was passed within the Moselle to the equally venerable monastery of Saint-Evre, Toul, which claimed sixth-century origins; later it spread south to Montier-en-Der (Haute-Marne) and eastward to Vanne (Verdun), both houses of the seventh century.[175] Only at Gorze was observance wholly moribund.[176] The catalyst for change was not the collapse of conventual life but, as at

---

[172] H. E. J. Cowdrey, *The Cluniacs and the Gregorian Reform* (Oxford, 1970), p. 16.

[173] M. Stroll, *The Medieval Abbey of Farfa: Target of Papal and Imperial Ambitions* (Leiden, 1997), p. 27; Boynton, *Shaping a Monastic Identity*, p. 104.

[174] N. Hunt, *Cluny under Saint Hugh, 1049–1109* (London, 1967), pp. 124–31 at 124.

[175] Nightingale *Monasteries and Patrons of the Gorze Reform*, p. 109; *The Chronicle of Hugh of Flavigny: Reform and the Investiture Contest in the Eleventh Century*, ed. P. Healy (Aldershot, 2006), pp. 22–62.

[176] St Maximin had been the scene of successive revivals: Nightingale, *Monasteries and Patrons of the Gorze Reform*, p. 169.

Cluny, its continuing encroachment by lay magnates, one element of the mounting tensions between episcopal and seigniorial powers. A pragmatic impulse to repair the ecclesiastical infrastructure must also be recognised.[177] Bishop Adalbero of Metz reformed Gorze to free it from the interference of his secular rival, the Matfriding Count Adalbert (d. 944).[178] His seigniorial priorities were reflected in his appointment as prior of his kinsman Frederick. The work of reform was undertaken by John, 'of Gorze', a well-born ascetic, connected with the bishop's circle of *familiares*; John brought a trace of the Carolingian reformation to Gorze having made his profession and received his education at Saint-Mihiel, where Smaragdus had compiled his exposition of the *RB* in 817–19.[179] Adalbero's interventions also served to reinvigorate the Continental tradition of Celtic monasticism: he appointed the Irishman Cathróe (Cadroe) (d. 977) to the monastery at Metz, from where a reform, and a renewed Hibernian network, was extended to Wasser (945) and Cologne (953).[180] The end of secular encroachment was the primary objective of the reformers, but they regarded the *RB* as their principal tool: the rule offered a framework for the self-governance of a monastic community more complete than any other code. What the Gorzeois communicated to the chain of houses between Rhine, Moselle and Somme was strict adherence to the *RB*. To secure it for the future, Adalbero's subordinate, Bishop Gauzelin of Toul (d. 962), who introduced the reform to Saint-Evre at Toul (936) and to neighbouring monasteries under his own jurisdiction, acquired a reliable redaction of the *RB* from Fleury-sur-Loire, just as Charlemagne had done from Cassino a century and a half before.[181] Bishop Gauzelin extended the reform to new houses, such as his own foundation of Bouxières-aux-Dames.[182] In contrast to Cluny in its first century, the Gorzeois also reached religious women: in a further attempt to secure his seigniorial compact, Bishop Adelbero placed his niece Himiltrude at the head of the convent of Sainte-Glossinde.[183] The resurgence of this heartland of Gorze reform was completed in the last decade of the century by William of Volpiano, a Cluniac called into the Lorraine by the bishops of Metz and Toul. William also became a figurehead for monastic revival in the north-west. Duke Richard II of Normandy (970–1026) sponsored the restoration of convents in the burgeoning duchy, drawing William to Fécamp, 'an inconsequential little congregation

---

[177] Nightingale, *Monasteries and Patrons of the Gorze Reform*, p. 219.
[178] Ibid., p. 102. See also Wollasch, 'First Wave of Reform', p. 170.
[179] Nightingale, *Monasteries and Patrons of the Gorze Reform*, pp. 94–6; *Chronicle of Hugh of Flavigny*, ed. Healy, p. 26&n.
[180] D. Ó Riain-Raedel, 'Irish Benedictine Monasteries on the Continent', in *Irish Benedictines*, ed. Browne and O'Clabaigh, pp. 25–64 at 29&n; *Chronicle of Hugh of Flavigny*, ed. Healy, pp. 30–1&n.
[181] Nightingale, *Monasteries and Patrons of the Gorze Reform*, pp. 15–18, 141.
[182] Ibid., pp. 148–66. J. Nightingale, 'Bishop Gerard of Toul', in *Warriors and Churchmen in the High Middle Ages*, ed. K. Leyser (London, 1992), pp. 41–79 at 47.
[183] Nightingale, *Monasteries and Patrons of the Gorze Reform*, p. 76.

of clerics living in a carnal manner', where he remained until his death in 1031.[184]

Perhaps only the monastic reformation of tenth-century England represented the recovery of religious life after a period of collapse, although the clamour of contemporary charters, histories and hagiographies continues to obscure the view. The *Regularis Concordia* (*RC*), the code that carried the reform into England's religious houses, opened with the image of 'holy houses now destitute, diminished by neglect' ('sacra cenobia destitute neglegenter tabescerent').[185] The earliest *Life* of one of the movement's triumvirate of leaders, Oswald of Worcester (d. 992), a work which dates from the turn of the tenth century, claimed, 'in those days there were no monks, nor any men of the sacred rule in England' ('in diebus illis non monastici viri nec ipsius sanctae institutionis regulae erant in regione Anglorum').[186] The fragments of textual records, and the material remains from the first half of the century, challenge the claim of a complete collapse of ecclesiastical and spiritual life. It is true that Alfred's investment in monasteries had not continued under his successors, some monastic settlements had been dispersed and others secularised (or similarly rendered irregular), but churches, communities of religious, and differing degrees of regular discipline endured nonetheless. The respite from alien incursions under Egbert (809–39) appears to have allowed regular communities to prosper, albeit briefly: convents at the centre of the reform perhaps originated in these years, such as Cranborne (930) and Cerne (937).[187] The contemporary narrative, 'King Edgar's Establishment of Monasteries', an apologia for the reform, acknowledged there were indeed monks in the kingdom before the movement began but there were few 'who lived by the right rule'.[188] A public document bearing the imprint of the king, the *RC* showed greater discretion, commemorating 'the godly customs of our realm' that had prevailed hitherto.[189] Such was the clerical milieu – monastic only at the margins, scarcely Benedictine, but not moribund – that formed the leading figures of the later reform, Oswald of Worcester and Æthelwold of Winchester (909–84) and Dunstan of Canterbury (*c.* 909–988). Dunstan was said to have been converted to monastic custom by the charismatic Bishop Ælfheah of Winchester. The Dane Oswald's early formation occurred among the

---

[184] C. Potts, *Monastic Revival and Religious Identity in Early Normandy* (Woodbridge, 1995), pp. 24–6, 28–35. The description of Fécamp is by Rodulf Glaber, biographer of Abbot William: *Rodulfus Glaber Opera*, ed. and trans. J. France, N. Bulst and P. Reynolds (Oxford, 1989), pp. 272–3.

[185] *RC*, p. 1.

[186] Byrhtferth of Ramsey, *The Lives of St Oswald and St Ecgwine*, ed. M. Lapidge, Oxford Medieval Texts (Oxford, 2009), p. 38.

[187] *VCH Dorset*, ii. 53–8 at 54, 70–1 at 70; *MO*, pp. 33–6.

[188] *Councils and Synods*, i.142–54 at 145. See also Wormald, 'Æthelwold and his Continental Counterparts: Contact, Comparison, Contrast', in *Bishop Æthelwold: His Career and Influence*, ed. B. Yorke (Woodbridge, 1997), 13–42.

[189] *RC*, p. 3.

vestiges of Northumbrian religion; Æthelwold's early career also underlines that before Edgar religion had not retreated to a remote monastic fastness but flourished in the royal family.[190]

As in the age of Charlemagne, the Crown was the catalyst of the English reform. Edgar (959–75) is the principal player in contemporary narratives, as in subsequent chronicles, but it was his predecessors who were responsible for the structural changes that stimulated change. It was Eadmund (939–46) who conferred the church at Glastonbury upon Dunstan (943 or 944); it was Eadred (946–54), and his mother Eadgifu, who raised Dunstan as royal prelate and therefore a candidate for Canterbury under Edgar.[191] The contribution of the monarch was not to devise or direct a programme of reform but to engender an environment in which those of the prelates might prosper. Their regal status facilitated the transformations at the heart of the movement: the expulsion of secular clerks from Winchester (*c.* 964) and the the promulgation of a common customary, the *Regularis Concordia* (*c.* 970).[192] Their patronage secured the authority of bishops amid powerful regional magnates; and the emerging structures of their government provided the scope for a process of reform that spread countrywide. Perhaps only Edgar demonstrated a degree of engagement with the cultural dynamics of the monastic order. Contemporary accounts present him as a monarch of particular piety, who recognised the special qualities of the *RB* and, like Alfred before him, understood the importance of language and text: it was said that the king himself commissioned Æthelwold to translate the *RB* into Old English; he was also instrumental in the refoundations of Romsey (for women) and Newminster (Hyde), and perhaps Nunnaminster (St Mary's Winchester); Wherwell was founded for women by Elfrida, his queen.[193]

Yet the monastic focus, the sequence of foundations and refoundations and the spiritual tone of the movement emanated from the three principal prelates and their circle. Dunstan's commitment to Benedictinism appears to have been refined from the rich variety of monastic traditions remembered at Glastonbury, and reinforced during his exile among the observant monks of Flanders; Æthelwold and Oswald were inspired by the traces of the Carolingian reform, which the former saw in visitors from Ghent and Fleury, and which the latter witnessed at first hand.[194] In their Continental

[190] *Wulfstan*, pp. 2–14 at 10–11. See also *MO*, p. 39; N. P. Brooks, 'The Career of Dunstan', in *St Dunstan: His Life, Times and Cult*, ed. N. Ramsey, M. Sparks and T. Tatton-Brown (Woodbridge, 1992), pp. 1–24 at 5; Wormald, 'Æthelwold and his Continental Counterparts', 13–42.

[191] *MO*, pp. 37–9; Brooks, 'Career of St Dunstan', 12, 21.

[192] *Wulfstan*, pp. 32–3. For an introduction to the *Regularis concordia* see now R. W. Pfaff, *The Liturgy in Medieval England: A History* (Cambridge, 2009), pp. 78–81.

[193] Ibid., p. 43&n; *Liber Eliensis*, ed. E. O. Blake, Camden Society, 3rd Series 92 (London, 1962), p. 151; *MO*, pp. 48–52. The narrative 'King Edgar's Establishment of the Monasteries' also attested to Æthelwold's authorship of the Old English *RB*. See Gretsch, *Intellectual Foundations*, pp. 3–4, 226–30.

[194] John of Worcester recorded Dunstan's profession at Fleury, and his exile at Ghent: *John of Worcester*, pp. 396–7 (under the year 943), pp. 404–5 (under the year 956).

encounters it is likely that each of them also learned of the unusual vigour and unity of the Benedictine network centred on Cluny. His first biographers claimed Dunstan had created a Benedictine convent from the colony at Glastonbury before entered the episcopacy; his colony of monks at Westminster may have been settled while he held the custody of London (957–9), as John of Worcester claimed.[195] After his promotion to the primacy, it appears he instigated the monastic communities that returned to Bath and Malmesbury, and were newly established at Exeter, Milton (Dorset) and Muchelney. Before his death, it seems that Dunstan also presided over the foundation, or renewal, of a chain of West Country communities between the Blackmore Vale and Dartmoor, Cerne (987), Cranborne (c. 980), Horton (971) and Tavistock (961); he was surely the inspiration for the community at Sherborne, created by his disciple Wulfsige.[196]

Æthelwold had been prepared at Glastonbury under Dunstan for the vocation of a monastic evangelist. Apparently he was projected early into the role at Abingdon at the intervention of his royal patron, but from the accession of Edgar he propagated his own scheme for the renewal of the monastic network in the central, eastern and southern regions. He secured both the old and new churches at Winchester to create monastic communities (964) and in the ensuing decade he extended his network eastward, to the south to Chertsey (c. 960) and Thorney (972) and to the north to Ely (970), St Neots (974) and Peterborough (both 966); there is an early tradition that Crowland (Lincolnshire) was also connected to him.[197] Eynsham (Oxfordshire) was a western addition to the network, the foundation (1005) of a follower, Æthelmaer, and Æthelwold's former pupil, Ælfric. Likewise, Oswald initiated a cluster of monastic colonies in Worcester diocese within months of his elevation to the see (961), a western complement to the network of Æthelwold, which it intersected between the East Anglian fenland and the Thames valley. The first was in the basin of the Severn at Westbury-on-Trym (c. 962); Pershore, Winchcombe (both 972) and Worcester (after 974) followed in the upper Severn valley. Ramsey (c. 971), an eastern outpost of Oswald's influence, replaced Westbury as the training ground for Oswald's superiors.[198]

It seems that the locus of these initiatives was determined less by the diocese and its proprietorial profile than by the preference of local lordship. Indeed, as at Gorze, in certain regions the magnate interest directed the reform. Bath became one of the early refoundations only because it was granted as such by Edmund. According to the eleventh-century annalist

---

[195] *John of Worcester*, pp. 406–9; Brooks, 'Career of St Dunstan', 12–13 at 12.
[196] Ibid.; *MO*, pp. 49–50.
[197] *Bishop Æthelwold*, ed. Yorke, p. 5. Hugh Candidus claimed Æthelwold abandoned a refoundation of an earlier *monasterium* at Oundle in favour of Peterborough.
[198] Byrtferth, *Lives*, ed. Lapidge, pp. 69–71. The realisation of these foundations may have come later: John of Worcester records the dedication of Ramsey under 991: *John of Worcester*, pp. 438–9.

John of Worcester, it was Æthelweard, 'a very rich man', who facilitated the foundation at Cerne; and it may have been the same magnate that carried the influence of Dunstan into new communities at Bruton (Somerset) and Wilton (Wiltshire); the foundations made under his influence in Dorset and Devon were also facilitated by Or(d)gar, who held the earldom.[199] As John also recalled, Oswald of Worcester settled at Ramsey at the invitation of the ealdorman Æthelwine.[200] The first brethren at Ely were so bound to their patron Byrhtnoth that they retrieved his headless corpse from the field of Maldon in 991.[201] Such an association with the magnate interest was not an unequivocal benefit to a new monastic colony. A number suffered assaults, and destruction even, before the death of Dunstan. There were attacks on the foundations of East Anglia and the East Midlands; the western magnates wasted the properties and resources of the new, royal monasteries; even Dunstan's Glastonbury appears to have been vulnerable in the 970s.[202]

A synod convened in *c.* 970 sought to bring cohesion and congregational identity to the expanding network with the promulgation of a common customary. The model was conspicuously Carolingian: in its title, its tone, and to a degree, its form, the *RC* consciously recalled the code compiled by Benedict of Aniane in the wake of the Aachen *synodalia*. The *RC* is commonly attributed to Æthelwold, on the authority of his pupil, Ælfric (*c.* 955–*c.* 1010), and its prescriptions may be understood to represent the customs he pioneered at Winchester.[203] They are founded on the *RB*, but draw frequently from the interpretation of its precepts found in the customs of Cluny, Ghent, Gorze, Fleury, and, of course, the *Concordia regularum* of Benedict of Aniane: as the prologue underlined, these were the customs 'which have been constantly and everywhere observed both by the aforesaid Benedict and by his holy followers and imitators, after deep consideration and examination'.[204] The authorities were combined to create a code that contained notable novelties for Engish clerks: the liturgical regime was more elaborate and thus laborious and the emphasis on psalms a contrast with earlier Celtic, Columbanian or *regula mixta* patterns of worship. The demands of individual and institutional discipline were greater than ever before, and more rigorously enforced, perhaps the chief source of tension between the incoming monks and the incumbent secular clerks. The authority of the abbot and the independence of the monastic

[199] Ibid., p. 539. See also E. Cownie, *Religious Patronage in Anglo-Norman England, 1066–1135*, Royal Historical Society, Studies in History (London, 1998), p. 18.
[200] *John of Worcester*, p. 555 (1050).
[201] *Liber Eliensis*, ed. Blake, p. 136.
[202] D. J. V. Fisher, 'The Anti-Monastic Reaction in the Reign of Edward the Martyr', *Cambridge Historical Journal* 10 (1950–2), 254–70.
[203] *RC*, pp. li–lii, 1–2; *Ælfric's Letter to the Monks of Eynsham*, ed. C. A. Jones (Cambridge, 1995), pp. 92–7.
[204] *RC*, pp. 1–3.

domain were asserted as a challenge to the lay appropriations widespread in provincial England. The corollary, and perhaps the most significant challenge to contemporary practice in England, was the role which the *RC* proposed for the monarch (conjointly with his consort) as patron and pastor of the community of religious. Their responsibility was represented in the prologue as that of shepherd to the monastic sheep of the realm ('regali itaque functus officio veluti pastor solicitus ... oves quas Domine largiente studiosus collegerat').[205] As principal patron, the monarch was to be commemorated daily in the Office observed by all those bound to the *RC*. Only the morning office of Prime was spared of special prayers; the day's first, 'morrow' mass was to be dedicated to the royal house.[206] Moreover, the supervision of each convent was ultimately vested in the Crown: the election of the superior was subject to the approval of the king ('consenti regis').[207] The authority ascribed to the monarch in the *RC*, and at a secondary level the relationship it promulgated for the diocesan, proved a powerful legacy for later generations: it was at once a source of strength and weakness within the English network as their material and spiritual fortunes ebbed and flowed.

The earliest accounts, and the eleventh- and twelfth-century annalists and chroniclers that follow them, claimed that under Dunstan and his disciples the ecclesiastical infrastructure of England was transformed. Certainly, there was a new density of monastic foundations in the central and southern England which for the most part remained intact throughout the Middle Ages. There was also undoubtedly a new degree of conformity in their customs, of learning, liturgical practice, and, importantly, governance. Yet archival and archaeological remains suggest that neither the extent nor the stability of the monastic revival should be exaggerated. In his *Vita Oswaldi* Byrhtferth recalled that Edgar promised forty houses for the reformers, but barely half this number were founded in their lifetime.[208] Æthelwold aimed to extend his network into the East Midlands, to Barrow, Bredon and Oundle, but these were never realised. Although the community of St Cuthbert was settled at Durham, it did not adopt a monastic rule.[209] Oswald's apparent ambition to see monks returned to Ripon remained unfulfilled. Indeed, the northern region of England seems insulated from the impulses for reform that prospered further south.[210] Almost four centuries after Augustine founded his church there were still no adherents to the *RB* at Canterbury; in the mid-eleventh century this

---

[205] Ibid.
[206] See below, p. 99.
[207] *RC*, p. 6.
[208] Byrhtferth, *Lives*, ed. Lapidge, p. 77. John of Worcester claimed Dunstan 'ordered more than forty houses to be filled' with 'hosts of monks and nuns': *John of Worcester*, pp. 410–13.
[209] *MO*, p. 165. See also *St Cuthbert*, ed. Bonner *et al.*, p. xxi.
[210] *MO*, pp. 48–52.

earliest of English churches, and the cathedral church at London, remained secular.[211] Edgar's death was said to have seen 'the kingdom ... thrown into confusion'.[212] Scarcely twenty years after Dunstan's death the infrastructure of his reform was destroyed by the Danes: both Abingdon and Ramsey saw their superiors struck down, and Oswald's relics were removed from Bardney; John of Worcester recorded a raid at Tavistock and as far west as Cornwall.[213] There was a modest recovery after Scandinavian conquest was secured. Cnut patronised new monasteries in East Anglia and the Midlands although his magnates did not share the enthusiasm of their lord, or of Edgar's ealdormen.[214] The political nation of pre-Conquest England perhaps had little taste for the 'old fashioned reformed Benedictine piety of the tenth century'.[215]

The restoration of monasteries was now replicated elsewhere. Monastic life had not been extinguished within the empire but much of the energy generated by the Aachen reforms had evaporated; with it also had passed the conformity to the *RB* which the reformers had sought to secure. The spirit of renewal stirred first in the old territory of the *Schottenklöster* under the direction of a new generation of Scots evangelists. Cathróe (d. 977) restored observant monks to Metz (953), and in his lifetime the chain of Celtic convents was extended westward into Flanders, at Waulsort (Naumur). The Scots' restoration was sponsored by the lordly Archbishop Bruno of Cologne (925–65), a brother of Emperor Otto I, and the second half of the century saw a seigniorial reinvestment in monastic religion. Otto II (955–83) initiated a reform of convents under his jurisdiction.[216] Tegernsee was restored in 978 with a supply of Benedictines from Saint-Maximin, which itself had been touched by the Gorzeois.[217] Duke Henry II of Bavaria (d. 995) replaced the canons of his church at Niederaltaich with a community of monks; under Abbot Gotthard (subsequently bishop of Hildesheim, d. 1038), the customs of Cluny were adopted, and transmitted to neighbouring southern houses including Kremsmünster and Tegernsee.[218] However, it was his eleventh-century successors, Henry II (emperor,

---

[211] According to John of Worcester, when Odo was translated to Canterbury, he took the monastic habit not at his cathedral church but at Fleury. Yet John described the brethren of Christ Church as *monachi*: *John of Worcester*, pp. 390–1, 583. See also Brooks, *Early History of the Church at Canterbury*, pp. 255–66; R. A. L. Smith, 'The Early Community at Rochester, c. 604–1080', *EHR* 60 (1945), 289–99; Cownie, *Religious Patronage*, p. 12.

[212] *John of Worcester*, pp. 426–7. See also M. F. Smith, R. Fleming and P. Halpin, 'Court and Piety in Late Anglo-Saxon England', *Catholic Historical Review* 87 (2001), 569–602.

[213] *John of Worcester*, pp. 362–3, 432–3 (981), 446–7 (997), 493.

[214] Cownie, *Religious Patronage*, p. 21.

[215] Smith, Fleming and Halpin, 'Court and Piety in Late Anglo-Saxon England', 580.

[216] *Conrad II, 990–1039: Emperor of Three Kingdoms*, ed. H. Wolfram and D. A. Kaiser (University Park, PA, 2006), pp. 299–303.

[217] Ibid.

[218] I. F. von Andrian-Werburg, *Die Benediktinerabtei Wessobrun*, Germania Sacra NF 39 (Berlin, 2000), p. 88.

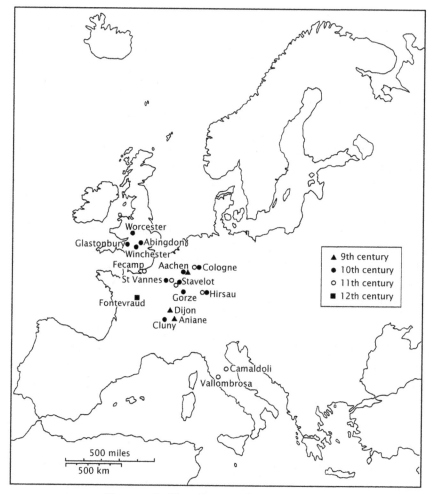

2 The spread of Benedictine reform, *c.* 817–*c.* 1073

1014–24), and the Salians Conrad II (emperor, 1024–39) and his son Henry III (emperor, 1039–56), who escalated these interventions into a programme of reform.[219] In 1020 Henry II appointed Poppo of Deinze (977–1048) as superior of the imperial double monastery of Stavelot-Malmédy. Poppo, a protégé of Richard of Saint-Vanne, carried with him the Cluniac customs of the Vanneois congregation, complemented by a commitment to the concept of the proprietary monastery (*Eigenklöster*) born of his own noble descent.[220] Saint-Maximin, whose earlier reform had failed, was also placed

[219] J. W. Bernhardt, *Itinerant Kingship and Royal Monasteries in Early Medieval Germany, c. 936–1070* (Cambridge, 1993), p. 124; Cowdrey, *Cluniacs and Gregorian Reform*, p. 33; *Conrad II*, ed. Wolfram and Kaiser, p. 298.
[220] *Chronicle of Hugh of Flavigny*, ed. Healy, pp. 42–3. See also Everhelme, *Vita sancti Popponis abbatis Stabulensis*, ed. W. Wattenbach, MGH 13 (1826), p. 301.

under his jurisdiction in 1023, and a network of communities followed, not only established convents, Echternach, Herfeld and Weissenburg-Folmar, whose regular life had stultified, but also new foundations, such as Limburg an der Haardt and Saint-Ghislain, both products of Conrad's personal patronage; in the ensuing decade the diocesans of Metz, Trier and Verdun also assigned their convents to Poppo's supervision.[221] As at Cluny, the principal houses at Stavelot and Saint-Maximinin populated these new and restored monasteries, although it appears they retained their own patronal ties. An early *Life* depicted Poppo recovering brethren 'whose way of life had separated from the observance of the rule'; the presiding influence was the Cluniac customary but coloured, it would seem, by the grandeur of the Vanneois tradition.[222] Another sequence of restorations, which stemmed from Tegernsee under Abbot Ellinger (1017–26, 1031–41), returned the *RB* to Augsburg (SS Ulrich and Afra) and Benediktbeuern; the latter convent led a revival (*c.* 1041) to the south at Santa Maria in Organo.[223] Conrad II carried the *RB* further into Italy, and under his influence Richer of Niederaltaich was elected abbot of Montecassino in 1038.[224]

Further east, the Czech missionary and martyr Adalbert Vojtěch, erstwhile primate of Prague, established Benedictine communities in his homeland at Břevnov (993) and among the neighbouring Poles at Meseritz (996–7). Early in the eleventh century, the *RB* may also have been adopted at Gniezno and Poznań, the latter perhaps constituting the chapter of the cathedral church; a Benedictine beacon at Pannonholma (Hungary) was also begun in *c.* 996.[225]

The Making of an Order

The Benedictine historians of pre-Reformation England regarded the tenth-century reform as the beginning of their order: an anonymous 'de fundacione monasteriorum nigorum monachorum in Anglia' opened at Edgar's accession (BL, Add. MS 6162, fos. 26r–31v at 26r). The reformers raised the *RB* to become the principal monastic code in Europe and projected Celtic, Gallo-Roman (and perhaps even Mozarabic) customs to the margins of ecclesiastical life. They also pioneered a new relationship between the regular religious and seigniorial authority which, once settled, would secure the monastic tradition across the Continent until the sixteenth century. Yet these regional reforms did not themselves bring to the Benedictines the clerical, cultural, economic or social pre-eminence

---

[221] *Conrad II*, ed. Wolfram and Kaiser, pp. 296–8.
[222] Wollasch, 'First Wave of Reform', p. 182; *Conrad II*, ed. Wolfram and Kaiser, p. 296.
[223] C. B. Bouchard, 'Merovingian, Carolingian, and Cluniac Monasticism', *JEH* 41 (1990), 365–88; Rosenwein, *To be the Neighbour of St Peter*, pp. 78–9.
[224] *Conrad II*, ed. Wolfram and Kaiser, p. 299.
[225] Schmitz, *Histoire*, i. 232–6, 236–8.

which they were to enjoy in the high and later Middle Ages; nor did they infuse them with a sense of corporate identity that reached beyond regional or, indeed, seigniorial affiliations. Such was the transformation that followed in the century after the last of the reformers – the septugenarian Poppo of Stavelot – had passed. In part, it was the work of a new generation of reformers, and one that achieved greater political authority and public acclaim across the Continent than its predecessors. It may also be attributed to wider political and social developments in regions destabilised by invasion and reconfigured by conquest. It might also be represented as a response to the resurgence of aesthetic spirituality on a scale not seen since the sixth century, which posed a challenge to the monastic order and which some have characterised as the 'crisis of cenobiticism'.

The spirit of reform that stimulated this change originated at Cluny. The Burgundian abbey entered the eleventh century with a seigniorial independence and a territorial influence that eclipsed Gorze and the great imperial monasteries, and without either the external threats or internal tensions that threatened Dunstan's legacy in England. Under Abbots Odilo (994–1049) and Hugues (1049–1109) the congregation continued to expand. It was Abbot Hugues who pioneered Cluniac observance for women, at Marcigny, Cluny's south Burgundy heartland, a mode of life perhaps briefly adopted in England at Delapre and Arthington.[226] Both men gave a guiding hand to the restoration of monasteries to the north-east and west: it was Odilo who first dispatched William of Volpiano to the moribund monastery of Saint-Benignus (Dijon), whence he carried reform into Normandy.[227] It was the example of Odilo's Cluny which directed the reform of Saint-Vanne and its affiliates undertaken by Richard of Verdun (d. 1046).[228] Eastward, Abbot Wilhelm (d. 1096) renewed observance at Hirsau with a customary that owed much to Cluny, at the same time appropriating its claims to fiscal and jurisdictional independence from royal, seigniorial or episcopal authorities.[229]

The audience for, and authority of, Cluny's monasticism was augmented by the prominence of its representatives in the clerical and secular establishment. Abbot Odilo drew himself and his convent into the counsels of the papacy. By the first quarter of the eleventh century, men of Cluniac origin or personal affiliation already occupied some of the most significant sees in mainland Europe; by the third quarter they also constituted a cluster in the cardinalate.[230] The century was framed by pontiffs formed under the

---

[226] Thompson, *Women Religious*, pp. 2, 89–92.
[227] Potts, *Monastic Revival and Regional Identity*, pp. 28–34.
[228] *Chronicle of Hugh of Flavigny*, ed. Healy, pp. 22–64.
[229] H. E. J. Cowdrey, *Gregory VII, 1073–85* (Oxford, 1998), pp. 253–64. See also *Hirsau St Peter und Paul, 1091–1991*, ed. K. Schreiner, Forschungen und Berichte der Archäologie des Mittelalters in Baden-Württemberg 10/2 (Stuttgart, 1991).
[230] Cowdrey, *Cluniacs and Gregorian Reform*, pp. 33–5, 78–90, 157–87. This prominence was achieved

influence of Cluny, Sylvester II (999–1003) and Urban II (1088–99); it was a reflection of the congregation's identification with the Roman see that Gregory VII was widely reputed to have made his profession at Cluny.[231] The early superiors led their brethren into the orbit of imperial hierarchy. What Jotsald wrote of Odilo was true also of his successor Abbot Hugues, '[the] Caesars ... all so magnified him in friendship, honours and imperial gifts, that he was one heart and one soul with them'.[232]

Cluny was also the catalyst for many of the new monastic settlements that carried the *RB* further into the eastern and northern territories of Europe. The new houses affiliated to the Hibernian (*Schottenklöster*) network, although fruit of the mission (*c.* 1068) of the Celts Candidus, Johannes and Marianus (Muiredach mac Robartaig), are surely to be seen as an extension of the Cluniac enterprise. *En route* for Italy, Marianus paused and propagated Benedictine colonies, first close by Ratisbon (i.e. Regensburg) as early as 1070 (Weih St Peter); thence the Scots' brand of observance expanded first within Ratisbon (1111), and thereafter to Erfurt (1136×37), Nuremberg (1140), Konstanz (1142), Vienna (1158), Kelheim (1231) and perhaps even as far as Kiev.[233] In their turn the Celtic monasteries of central Europe carried (Cluniac) Benedictinism back to Ireland, briefly, at least, at Ross Ailithir and Cashel.[234] It was said to be English monks bearing the imprint of Lanfranc's Cluniac reform who pioneered the *RB* in Denmark at Ringsted, Roskilde (before *c.* 1088), Odense (1095) and Lund (*c.* 1100); their example moulded the first monastic foundations in Norway at Selja (1080×1110), Munkeliv (1103×1110) and Nidarholm (*c.* 1100); by the second quarter of the twelfth century there was also a Benedictine presence in Iceland, at Þingeyrar and Þverá, and before the close of the century even in the eastern settlement of Greenland at Narsarsuaq.[235] Cluny itself was not responsible for these houses but its observant reputation and independent status persuaded patrons to seek affiliation. Santo Stefano (Verona) was presented to Abbot Hugues by Albert of Bonavigo; indeed, even distant Byzantium courted Cluny.[236] The Iberian rulers sought the spiritual direction of Cluny

before Gregory VII's celebrated 'commission' to Abbot Hugh to provide 'some wise men ... suitable ... as bishops': *Historiae Tornacenses*, iv.ii, ed. G. Waitz, MGH, Scriptores, 14 (1883), pp. 327–52 at 341.

[231] The story was told by Bishop Bonzio of Sutri: C. Morris, *The Papal Monarchy: The Western Church from 1050 to 1250* (Oxford, 1989), pp. 109–10.

[232] Jotsaldus, *Vita Odilonis*, I. 6 (MGH, 68 (1999), p. 156).

[233] D. A. Binchy, 'The Irish Benedictine Congregation in Medieval Germany', *Studies* 18 (1929), 194–210; A. Gwyn, 'Irish Monks and the Cluniac Reform', *Studies* 29 (1940), 409–30; D. Ó Riain-Raedel, 'Irish Benedictine Monasteries on the Continent', in *The Irish Benedictines: A History*, ed. M. Browne and C. O'Clabaigh (Dublin, 2005), pp. 25–64 at 35–9.

[234] Ó Riain-Raedel, 'Irish Benedictine Monasteries on the Continent', 25–64 at 27–8.

[235] T. Nyberg, *Monasticism in North-Western Europe, 800–1200* (Aldershot, 2000), pp. 40–3, 99–100, 103–4 (Ringsted), 40–1 (Roskilde), 55–63 (Odense), 73–4 (Munkeliv), 74–6 (Nidarholm), 71–4 (Selja); O. Vésteinsson, *The Christianization of Iceland: Priests, Power and Social Change, 1000–1300* (Oxford, 2000), p. 140. See also *Christianization and the Rise of Christian Monarchy: Scandinavia, Central Europe and Rus', c. 900–1200*, ed. N. Berend (Cambridge, 2007), p. 151. For Þingeyrar, see illustration 1.

[236] Emperor Michael VII Dukas in 1076 granted the monastery an annual pension of 23 pounds of gold and four pallia: Miller, *Formation of a Medieval Church*, p. 71.

for their monasteries and sealed the bond through the payment of tribute recovered from their Muslim neighbours. San Juan de la Peña was placed under a superior supplied from Cluny in 1028 at the request of Sancho of Navarre (d. 1035); following the presentation (in 1030) of silver sufficient to fashion a ciborium for the high altar of the mother house, further houses of Navarre were surrendered to the Burgundians. Sancho's grandson, Alfonso VI (d. 1109), ceded another four monasteries in the province of León and several dependent cells; in 1077 he compacted with Abbot Hugues to pay an annual tribute of 2,000 gold pieces.[237] There can be no doubt that the development of the abbey church in the eleventh century reflected the influx of Spanish gold; the bond between the Burgundians and the monarchs of Navarre created a Benedictine monopoly in Galicia, León and Castile.[238]

There were also further settlements independent of Cluny's influence. The chain of convents in Bohemia was extended at intervals across the eleventh century, from Břevnov to Ostrow (999), Beraum (1034), Raigern (1048), Hradisch (1077), Oppatowitz (1086) and Trebitsch (1104). These houses conformed to the *RB* in the regulation of their life and in their governance, but they continued to follow Slavic liturgical customs at least to the end of the eleventh century; nonetheless the established Slavic convent of Sázava adopted the *RB* in or after 1097.[239] The Benedictine bridgehead in Poland was extended at Lubin, Łysa Góra and Płock;[240] a monastic mission into the territory of the Rus' (Kiev) was envisaged although never achieved.[241] Here also the challenge of Slavic custom was strong: a monastic chapter at Kracøw foundered shortly after foundation, and was removed to Tyniec. Stephen of Hungary (d. 1038) is regarded as the progenitor of the monasteries at Bakonybél, Pannonhalma, Pécsvárad (Martinsberg), Zobor and Zalavár.[242] It was in this period that Benedictine monasticism also secured a foothold on the frontier between the Latin Christianity and the Islamic World. A hospice established for Christian pilgrims to Jerusalem perhaps in the second quarter of the eleventh century was initially placed in the custody of Benedictines conveyed to the city with Amalfi merchants; within a century their church evolved into the abbey of St Mary Latina; under the later Latin kingdom, Benedictine convents were also built at the site of the Holy Sepulchre and the tombs of the Virgin Mary and St Anne,

[237] J. Williams, 'Cluny and Spain', *Gesta* 27 (1988), 93–101. See also O'Callaghan, *History of Medieval Spain*, pp. 305–30 at 310.

[238] O'Callaghan, *History of Medieval Spain*, pp. 310–11.

[239] Schmitz, *Histoire*, i. 229–31 at 230.

[240] A. Buko, *The Archaeology of Early Medieval Poland* (Leiden, 2008), pp. 352–4; Schmitz, *Histoire*, i. 233–5.

[241] For the mission of Bishop Adalbert (after 959), see J. Shephard, 'Rus', in *Christianization*, ed. Berend, pp. 369–411 at 379–80; W. Duczko, *Viking Rus: Studies on the Presence of Scandinavia in Eastern Europe* (Leiden, 2004), p. 215.

[242] Schmitz, *Histoire*, i. 258–62 at 260.

and beyond Jerusalem at Bethany (for women) and Mount Tabor (for men); there was also a Benedictine foundation at Antioch.[243]

The advance of the Benedictines was accelerated by an identification of monastic and seigniorial interests which had been scarcely secure a century before. In Normandy, and after 1066, in England, Wales and even Scotland, it was the rise of a new political order that re-established, extended and secured the place of the Black Monks in the ecclesiastical hierarchy. Like the German nobility before them, the rulers of Normandy and their subordinates recognised the strategic value of religious houses in a region of continuing political, social and economic. As the conquerers of England they also understood the capacity of such foundations to stabilise the new regime. When Edward the Confessor died in 1065 there were only forty religious houses in England, for the most part confined to southern and central regions; in the half century that followed there were no fewer than a hundred new foundations and the north was renewed as a region of convents and their churches. For the first time, the Benedictines penetrated the borders of the English kingdom, planting almost twenty priories in South Wales supported by new Norman proprietors. These patrons, part of a new, close-knit but competitive cadre, also facilitated a resurgence of female communities, often providing in the first instance for their own kin.[244] William of Normandy sought to widen the Cluniac hegemony already secure in the duchy. Abbot Lanfranc of Bec, the principal school of Cluniac Normandy, was provided to Canterbury in 1070. He reinvigorated observance of the *RB* which may have become obscured, except in the crucible of reform (Winchester, perhaps Glastonbury) and he promulgated canons of his own which carried the imprint of Cluny.[245] It was a mark of their recovery that this post-Conquest generation of Black Monks renewed their missionary zeal: the monks of Winchcombe went north (1073–4) after its 'harrying' to find the ruins of Jarrow and facilitate the foundation of Durham; their confrères of Evesham mounted a mission to Denmark (Odense, *c.* 1095), the English clergy's final Continental excursion of the Middle Ages; perhaps the same men were responsible for the island community of Nidarholm and the anomalous Norman dedication to St Alban.[246] It was the pragmatic principle that also guided the monarchs

---

[243] There is a tradition that Black Monks occupied a convent on or close by the Mount of Olives as early as the turn of the eighth and ninth centuries: D. Pringle, *The Churches of the Crusader Kingdom of Jerusalem: A Corpus*, 4 vols. (Cambridge, 1993–2009), iii. 5, 118, 142, 192–3, 236–7, 254–5; J. Richard [trans. J. Birrell], *The Crusades, c. 1071–1291* (Cambridge, 1999), p. 118; D. Nicolle, *Knights of Jerusalem: The Crusading Order of Hospitallers, 1100–1565*, p. 17. For Mount Tabor, see illustration 1.

[244] *MO*, pp. 136–8; *MRH*, pp. 58–101; Thompson, *Women Religious*, pp. 220–1; F. G. Cowley, *The Monastic Order in South Wales, 1066–1349* (Cardiff, 1977), pp. 12–16; J. Burton, *The Monastic Order in Yorkshire, 1069–1215* (Cambridge, 1999), pp. 185–8.

[245] For the *Decreta Lanfranci*, see *MC*, pp. 3–195; *MO*, pp. 122–4. See also Pfaff, *The Liturgy in Medieval England*, pp. 106–9.

[246] *MO*, pp. 161–5; Nyberg, *Monasticism in North-Western Europe*, pp. 74–6.

3 Benedictine England, *c.* 1066

of Castile, León and Navarre and the magnates of northern Italy to gravitate towards Cluny.[247] Only in imperial Germany, perhaps, was it seigniorial rivalry, rather than stability, which advanced the interests of the Benedictines. Here the contest between emperor and pontiff entered the arena of monastic patronage; Cluny and its network of subordinate houses and cells were the undoubted beneficiaries.[248]

[247] O'Callaghan, *History of Medieval Spain*, pp. 201–3.
[248] The contest also exacerbated conflict within the monastic order: Jestice, *Wayward Monks*, pp. 216–17.

It was a measure of the power of the *RB* in this period of spiritual revival that it also informed experiments in ascetic religion which appear in marked contrast to the institutional culture of Cluny and its affiliate congregations. Romuald (d. 1025×1027), a Ravennese seigneur schooled at the Cluniac abbey of Sant'Apollinare in Classe, formed a chain of hermitages centred on Camaldoli (Tuscany) committed to a strict observance of the *RB*, inflected with traces of the Celtic tradition. After his conversion at Camaldoli, Giovanni Gaulberto (d. 1073), a Florentine knight, formed his own hermitage at Vallombrosa also dedicated to a form of Benedictine observance which eschewed the institutional accretions of Cluny and its affiliates. Before the close of the eleventh century the customs of Camaldoli had cohered into a code that was distinct from the *RB* (and clothed the brethren not in black but white) and the cluster of communities was designated an order in 1072. Vallombrosa developed rather as a Benedictine congregation and secured papal protection as such in 1090; its membership rose to as many as thirty monasteries by 1115. A further refinement of Benedictine observance was formulated at Fontevraud *c.* 1101 under the influence of the magnate ascetic Robert of Arbrissel: characterised by an *ad literam* adherence to the *RB* rather than any raw asceticism, Robert's movement spread rapidly, and a network recognising Fontevraud as its parent convened its first chapter in 1149.[249]

The advance of the Black Monks in the eleventh century was accompanied by the articulation of a new or newly refined Benedictine identity. The notion of a shared tradition of observance was now explicit, and the term *ordo* at least in more frequent use in both conventual and public discourse. It was in an acknowledgement of the force of this emerging idiom that Peter Damian, advocate of a new asceticism, wrote of the 'hallowed order' whose harbour draws those seeking to escape 'the shipwreck of their own soul'.[250]

The extent of Benedictine monasticism in Europe reached its peak in the years either side of 1100. Ironically, it was at this moment that the Black Monks experienced the greatest challenge to their customs since the entry of Columban into the Continent five centuries before. The dominance of Cluny, and the spiritual discourse stimulated by the reforms of Gregory VII, aroused a new aesthetic impulse among both secular and regular clergy. In 1098 men trained in the Cluniac tradition abandoned their convent for the aesthetic rigour of a remote settlement, where the spiritual principles of the *RB* might properly be realised. They established a colony at Cîteaux, only miles from Cluny, and drew to them followers from lay and clerical life and from Benedictine cloisters. Further new forms of religious life followed the

---

[249] Thompson, *Women Religious*, p. 119. See also Kerr, *Religious Life for Women*, pp. 15–63.
[250] *Letters of Saint Peter Damian: Letters 121–150*, ed. and trans. O. J. Blum and I. M. Resnick, Fathers of the Church, Medieval Continuation 6 (Washington, DC, 2004), p. 128.

Cistercians.[251] The anonymous author of the *Libellus de diversis ordinibus*, writing in the middle years of the twelfth century, reflected on the sudden diversity of regular orders developed in only fifty years: 'If they [monks and canons] all followed one observance ... there would exist a harmony more praiseworthy than all fasting, where all held a single measure of life in one order.'[252]

As their chroniclers convey, contemporary Benedictines were disturbed by the advent of these reformed religious, a new 'swarm of cowled monks spread over all the world'.[253] Some modern historians have regarded these developments as a mortal blow from which the different regional congregations were unable to recover fully before the headlong decline that followed the Black Death.[254] There is a general impression that recruitment suffered, and the defection of individuals and whole communities is well documented, the latter triggered by the preferences of the patron: at Dover, Archbishop William of Corbeil converted St Martin's Priory to a convent of Augustinian canons.[255] Yet in the first half of the twelfth century such transfers of affiliation was not accompanied by any deceleration of Benedictine foundation. It is worth noting that in the outer reaches of Europe – Ireland, Scotland, Spain and Scandinavia – where there was little or no early tradition of the *RB*, new monasteries were established as much as a century after the first Cistercian settlers arrived.[256]

Historians have concentrated on the challenge of the new monastic orders but the status of the Benedictines was also brought into question by the increasing institutional and political authority of the secular clergy. The generation of secular prelates that preceded Gregory's pontificate initiated both verbal and vocal criticism of Cluny; Gregory himself was condemned as a *pseudo-monachus*.[257] Within their dioceses they clashed with convents over their missionary involvement.[258] In England monastic commentators complained of a concerted assault during and after the difficult primacy

---

[251] For the origins of the Cistercians, see C. H. Lawrence, *Medieval Monasticism: Forms of Religious Life in Western Europe in the Middle Ages*, 3rd edn (London, 2001), pp. 172–98; Morris, *Papal Monarchy*, pp. 242–57.

[252] *Libellus*, pp. 36–7, 40–1.

[253] *Orderic*, iv. 310–11: 'in saltibus et campestribus passim construuntur cenobia, novisque ritibus variisque scematibus turbeata peragrant orbem cucullatorum examina'.

[254] Cantor, 'Crisis of Western Monasticism'; J. Leclercq, 'The Monastic Crisis of the Eleventh and Twelfth Centuries', in *Cluniac Monasticism in the Central Middle Ages*, ed. N. Hunt (London, 1971), pp. 217–37. See also Jestice, *Wayward Monks*, p. 8.

[255] J. C. Dickinson, 'Early Suppressions of English Houses of Austin Canons', in *Medieval Studies Presented to Rose Graham*, ed. V. Ruffer and A. J. Taylor (Oxford, 1950), pp. 54–77 at 56.

[256] *MRH*, pp. 57–82, 83–93, 95–101; A. Gwyn and R. N. Hadcock, *Medieval Religious Houses: Ireland, with an Appendix to Early Sites* (London, 1970), pp. 102–3; Penco, 'Prima diffusione', pp. 342–3; Schmitz, *Histoire*, i. 229–31.

[257] For example, Adalbero's satire on Odilo of Cluny: Jestice, *Wayward Monks*, p. 208&n; I. S. Robinson, *Authority and Resistance in the Investiture Contest: The Polemical Literature of the Late Eleventh Century* (Manchester, 1978), pp. 33–4.

[258] Jestice, *Wayward Monks*, p. 5.

of Archbishop Anselm. Eadmer, the archbishop's biographer, accused 'malignant' secular clerks of seeking to suppress the 'simple folk' of the monasteries, purging them from the ranks of the prelacy and threatening their independence in fundamental matters of custom and governance. Such fears were nurtured throughout the Anglo-Norman network, heightened by the impression of a profound change in the cultural and political climate, a new compact between the clerical and magnate elite.[259]

There was no sudden collapse in their material state or their ecclesiastical or spiritual status but the Benedictine foundations – new, or renewed – that endured after 1100 were profoundly affected by the continuing competition of monastic and clerical reform. It was the determination of Continental diocesans to channel the vigorous piety of their subjects that caused them to sponsor again double convents, such as those at Hirsau. Meanwhile the Cluniac preference of patrons in England created a handful of privileged newcomers, and a larger number of suspicious and perhaps increasingly introspective pre-Conquest foundations. Briefly, it is possible the papacy contemplated the reform of one party by the other.[260]

The spiritual, social and political dynamics of the Gregorian period left their mark on Benedictines but they did not project them into an existential crisis. There can be no doubt that the rapid rise of a reformed monasticism founded on *ad literam* observance of the *RB* served to sharpen Benedictine identity. Their liturgical practice, their learning, their patterns of formation, their conception of priesthood and pastoral care, now appeared in greater relief: internally, the vocation of the *professus* gained greater definition; externally their collective contribution to church, religion and society could be more clearly distinguished. It was surely no coincidence that for the first time in nearly four centuries, Benedictine scholars returned to the subject of the *RB*. Between 1100 and 1250 the most highly regarded superiors of their generation, Rupert of Deutz (d. 1129), Hildegard of Bingen (d. 1179) and Bernard of Montecassino (d. 1282), spoke out *super regulam*.[261] It was surely also a consequence of the emerging sense of corporate self that for the first, but not the last, time the dress of the Benedictines became a subject of debate: 'the men of our time reject black', reflected Orderic, 'which the earlier fathers had always adopted as a mark of humility'.[262] There can be no doubt the Black Monks and nuns professed in the half century after the death of Bernard of Clairvaux (1153) both thought of, and saw, themselves as Benedictine.

[259] D. L. Bethell, 'English Black Monks and Episcopal Elections in the 1120s', *EHR* 8 (1969), 673–98.
[260] Ibid., 689.
[261] Hildegard of Bingen, *De regula sancti Benedicti*, ed. H. Feiss, Corpus Christianorum Continuatio Mediaevalis 226 (2007), pp. 67–97; Rupert of Deutz, *Super quaedam capitula regulae divi Benedicti abbatis*: PL 170: 477–538; Bernard (Ayglier) of Monte Cassino, *Expositio in regulam S. Benedicti*, ed. A. M. Caplet (Montecassino, 1894).
[262] *Orderic*, iv. 333–5.

&

The ascendancy of the Benedictines at the turn of the eleventh century owed much to the achievements of recent generations, of the reformers, prelates and patrons that advanced the claims of the *RB* in the period of recovery and reconstruction that proceeded from the millennium. Their pre-eminence in the age of Pope Gregory could scarcely have been assured even a generation before, not only because of the still volatile political, social and economic structures but also the continuing currency of alternative models of religious life. For as many as five centuries after his death, Benedict's code did not constitute an independent order but one ingredient – increasingly, a dominant one – in a common fund of customs that informed the life of the coenobite. It was not an institutional structure that ensured it endured, and in time prevailed, but the nature of the code itself, its clarity, scope and the comparative simplicity of its liturgical, disciplinary, communal and individual demands.

CHAPTER TWO

Observance

The Benedictines were defined by the *Regula Benedicti*. Other medieval orders drew inspiration from the example of charismatic founders, from spiritual charters, and from a succession of congregational (episcopal and papal) constitutions, but none of them was bound to a single code. The *RB* gave a complete account of the monastic vocation, from the rejection of the world (*RB*, prologue) to the final reunion with God ('ad patriam caelestem': *RB*, lxxiii). Remarkably, for a text whose transmission and translation was uninterrupted for a millennium the *RB* also retained its coherence; from the time it first came together as a sequence of chapters, there were never accretions or interpolations to the text and commentators sought not to correct but to contextualise the precepts of the founder.[1] Perhaps above all the *RB* provided a simple introduction to the professed life, accessible to any condition and applicable – notwithstanding a slight Mediterranean orientation – to any clime or community. These qualities ensured a degree of continuity in Benedictine observance that eluded other orders: over the course of the Middle Ages capitular, episcopal and papal authorities sought to renew the regular life but never to reinvent it. The demands of the Benedictine day in the second quarter of the sixteenth century would have been familiar to the followers of Benedict of Aniane, and perhaps by the pioneers of the first Montecassino. Of course, the clarity of the code presented superiors, ecclesiastical supervisors, and secular patrons with a measure of pure Benedictinism with which the professed might be judged. When material conditions, and their institutional consequences, compromised communal observance in later centuries, the *RB* was sometimes read as a record of monastic decline.

The Benedictines were neither the progenitors nor the first pioneers of the regulated life. Benedict's rule was shaped by the cenobitic customs of his time, and from the traditions of Latin, Greek and Middle Eastern monasticism. These early *regulae* were reflected not only in the form of Benedict's *cenobium*, a community of brethren sharing one profession under the supervision of a single head, but also in the scope of its *horarium* (i.e. daily schedule), a balance between spiritual and bodily labours, *opus Dei* and *opus manuum*. Early eastern practice was also echoed in the ascetic regime of *RB*:

[1] For the descent of the *RB*, see above, pp. 22–6.

abstinence from meat and further restrictions on food, sleep and speech recalled the Egyptian eremites.[2] Recent reappraisals have also affirmed the influence of the early Roman church on the *RB* and its pioneers: Abbot Theodomar of the restored Montecassino maintained that his brethren followed both Benedict and the observance of Rome.[3] The continuities inherent in the *RB* were the principal theme of the *Concordia regularum*, the first synthesis of cenobitic custom that, together with the Aachen syn- odalia, advanced the Carolingian reform of Benedict of Aniane.[4] Yet the *Concordia* also sought to articulate, perhaps for the first time for the reli- gious of Western Europe, the apparent priority of Benedict's conception of regular observance.[5] This was reinforced in subsequent codes and commen- taries, as the profile of Benedict's predecessors (and sources) was steadily diminished. The partisan tone became sharply pejorative as precedence for the *RB* was claimed not only over early cenobitic custom but also over the code(s) of the secular clerks.[6] Even before the Benedictine ascendancy of the Gregorian period, Benedict's code was recognised as the best expression of the *ordo regularis*.[7] The rise of new orders did not unsettle its status, since the reformers frequently returned to the *RB* to recover the foundations of regular observance.[8] Perhaps a greater tension arose from within the order, as the growing number of congregations, national and regional networks of monasteries generated customs of their own. These particular patterns of life reflected a complex of contextual factors: the challenges of climate and topography, the demands of founders and patrons, and the dynamics of politics, society and culture within the locality. They underline, of course, that regular observance within the monastery was inseparable from its role in the world beyond.

The regime of the medieval Benedictine is not easily recovered from the sources. Like any cleric, and many layfolk, rarely did a monk regard his routine as a matter worthy of record. The *RB* and its commentaries, and the succession of codes and constitutions, are accessible to us, of course, but for the most part they offer insights into precept not practice. Customaries can

---

[2] Dunn, *Emergence of Monasticism*, pp. 59–81 at 75.

[3] D. Reilly, 'The Cluniac Giant Bible and the *Ordo librorum ad legendum*: a Reassessment of Monastic Bible Reading and Cluniac Customary Instructions', in *From Dead of Night to End of Day: The Medieval Customs of Cluny/Du cœur de la nuit à la fin du jour: Les coutumes clunisiennes en Moyen Âge*, ed. S. Boynton and I. Cochelin, Disciplina monastica 3 (Turnhout, 2005), pp. 163–89 at 167.

[4] In his prologue Benedict asks: 'At quis liber sanctorum catholicorum patrum hoc non resonat ut recto cursu perveniamus ad creatorem nostrum?', and echoes Isidore of Seville on the many precepts of reli- gious life to be recovered from the Fathers: *Benedicti Anianensis Concordia regularum*, ed. Bonnerue, pp. 15–20 at 15, 18.

[5] Ibid., prologue.

[6] The earliest reference to two orders, of regulars and (secular) canons (*ordo regularis, ordo canonicus*) was apparently at the Council of Verneuil in 755: *Capitularia regum Francorum, I*, ed. A. Boretius, MGH (Hanover, 1883), pp. 32–7 (Canon II). See also above, pp. 29–30.

[7] See above, p. 29.

[8] See above, pp. 56–8.

bring the dynamics of observance into focus and give an impression of its evolution over the generations, but they are poorly preserved: there is a concentration of them dating from the eleventh to the thirteenth centuries, but virtually nothing for the period after 1350; the rate of survival from England is especially poor.[9] There is, of course, a lively narrative of malpractice to be recovered from the documents of visitation, which are especially well preserved for the century and a half before the Reformation, but it would be misleading to reconstruct the routine of the convent from the moments when it came under strain, or collapsed. Their narratives, chronicles, *gestae abbatum* and *vitae* not only carry an echo of the regular life but also remind us that submission to the rule did not always mean the suppression of individual identity.

The Monastic Community

The core of any medieval monastery, and, after its rule, the primary influence on the character of its observance, was its professed members. Benedict provided a framework for monastic life, but it was the men and women recruited from a variety of cultural and social milieus throughout Europe, that realised, and animated, Benedictine monasticism. Medieval satirists often represented the religious orders in terms of cultural and social categories: the mendicant friar, for example, was frequently ill-educated and low-born, pressed into profession as a boy, or even infant. Their preference for the Black Monks, however, was to concentrate upon their moral condition since they seemed to defy any other form of classification.[10] The moderate regime of the *RB* was compatible with almost any condition or station of medieval life: under its governance were nurtured converts variously of status, genius, and vocation, be it personal or by the proxy of parental oblation. Benedictine profession represented the first phase of a religious life which might progress to one of the reformed orders, or even eremiticism, but for a greater number it was the ultimate expression of a personal impulse for the service of God: as the twelfth-century author of the *Libellus de diversis ordinibus* opined, the Benedictine was a monastic everyman, a servant of God but not necessarily possessed of the ascetic or pastoral ambitions of their reformed or clerical counterparts.[11]

There were many routes to the Benedictine monastery. Benedict addressed his preface to anyone with such experience of the world they might desire to leave it (*RB*, prologue). The Gregorian *Dialogues* claimed that crowds

---

[9] For the state of the evidence see Pfaff, *The Liturgy in Medieval England*, pp. 20–7, 200–42 at 242. See also S. Harper, *Medieval English Benedictine Liturgy: Studies in the Formation, Structure and Content of the Monastic Votive Office, c. 950–1540* (New York, 1993).

[10] E. Coleman, 'Nasty Habits: Satire and the Medieval Monk', *History Today* 43:6 (1993), 36–42.

[11] *Libellus*, pp. 16–26.

from the region, and from further afield, responded to Benedict's call.[12] The first followers of the *RB* did have prior experience of life, whether of the princely court, the lordly hall, the missionary church, or, in a number of notable cases, the subsistence existence of the farmstead: hagiographers held the capacity to attract mature conversions to be the hallmark of the monastic superior; end-of-life conversion was also widespread and the Aachen synodalia (817) sought to regulate it to preserve the vitality of the professed community.[13] Converts from the ruling class appear to have advanced the Benedictine revival of the tenth century: at Cluny, John of Salerno celebrated Count Fulk's knight Adhegrinus, who 'laid aside his military dress to become forthwith a soldier of Christ'; Farfa even secured the profession of the Greek governor of southern Italy.[14] The resurgence of ascetic and spiritual impulses in the eleventh century encouraged mature professions. The Norman knight Richard of Heudicourt, 'a noble knight of the Vexin', entered the abbey of Saint-Evroul following his recovery from a lance wound; the well-born Lanfranc and Anselm were also part of this movement.[15] The monastic profession was not only a penitential project but also a refuge for the world-weary. Harold Godwinson's widow, Queen Edith, retired to Wilton in 1075.[16] Count Éverard of Breteuil, count of Chartres, 'one of the foremost men of France', was professed at Marmoutiers in 1073.[17] Peter Dene, a secular clerk and supporter of the rebel Earl Thomas of Lancaster, made a rapid profession at St Augustine's Canterbury within a fortnight of the rout at Boroughbridge (1322).[18] Instances of late conversion diminished in the later Middle Ages. The leading abbeys and priories might still secure an *ad hoc* mature vocation: Ralph of Shrewsbury, a layman of Bath, entered the Benedictine priory at the beginning of the fourteenth century from where he progressed to the episcopal see.[19] Yet such recruits were scarce in England after 1350: John Kynton, secretary to Henry IV, professed at Christ Church, Canterbury, in 1400, was a rare exception.[20] Schoolmen still had recourse to the monastery as a comfortable and well-resourced alternative to a more lucrative clerical or court

---

[12] '... multi iam mundum reliquere atque ad eius magisterium festinare': Gregory, *Dialogues*, II. 2. 3, ed. De Vögué, pp. 137–40 at 138.

[13] *Wulfstan*, p. 15. *Initia consuetudinis Benedictinae consuetudinem saeculi octavi et noni*, ed. K. Hallinger, CCM 1 (1963), pp. 469–91 (473–81) at 473 [Canon 2, 817].

[14] *John of Salerno*, p. 24. There was a succession of such mature professions at Farfa: M. Costambeys, *Power and Patronage in Early Medieval Italy, Local Society, Italian Politics and the Abbey of Farfa, c. 700–900* (Cambridge, 2004), p. 137. See also Boynton, *Shaping a Monastic Identity*, pp. 1–18.

[15] *Orderic*, ii. 133.

[16] *VCH Wiltshire*, ii. 231–42 at 233.

[17] *Guibert*, p. 55.

[18] *Thorne*, pp. 436, 465–8.

[19] *Two Chartularies of the Priory of St Peter at Bath*, ed. W. Hunt, Somerset Record Society 7 (1893), ii. 159.

[20] *Stone*, pp. 7–8.

career.[21] There were instances of high-profile clerks and laymen who sought retirement in Benedictine houses but none of them were professed, even on their death-bed, although the special privilege of a monastic burial may have been conferred upon them.[22]

Benedict envisaged that a proportion of his brethren would be raised in the monastery from infancy. Patrons were invited to make an oblation of their child, both the utmost act of devotion to the abbot and his brethren and an investment in the future of their observance (*RB*, 59). As Smaragdus reminded his readers, this worthy practice was an ancient one, as witnessed by the rule of Basil, to whom Benedict himself had turned as an authority.[23] The number of oblates in the earliest *cenobia* is not recorded, although *RB* makes provision for a cohort. Gregory's account (in the *Dialogues*) of the unfortunate death of an unhappy oblate was surely intended as an *exemplum* of the moral imperative of monastic oblation.[24] The first Benedictine monasteries of northern Europe appear to have secured a ready supply of oblates; indeed, given the number of prominent monks and nuns in this period known to have been given to the monastery, it is possible the practice became the mainstay of their recruitment. The *RB* did not specify the optimum age for an oblate, and it was not unknown for adults to offer themselves.[25] However, the majority were children, generally having passed from infancy to childhood (i.e. seven years or older): in Alcuin's *Vita Willibrordi* his subject was presented to Ripon when he had 'reached the age of reason'; the oblation of nuns in Normandy refers to *puellula*, which implies girls only on the brink of childhood.[26]

Oblation was an act of benefaction to the monastery. At the *Eigenklöster* of the Frankish and German magnates it reinforced proprietorial authority – the oblate was an agent of the patron among the professed; at 'free' foundations the costs were less but the benefits were as great.[27] There was an expectation in the *RB* that parents of status would secure their oblation with a gift; since they might 'reserve to themselves the income of it, if they so desire' (*RB*, 59), temporal or spiritual property is implied; in practice the patron might offer the revenue, or a portion of it, but then retain the property itself; gifts of cash or treasure (plate, jewels, etc.) are also

---

[21] J. G. Clark, *A Monastic Renaissance: Thomas Walsingham and his Circle, 1350–1440* (Oxford, 2004), pp. 15–16.

[22] For example, the fifteenth-century record of burials at the abbey of St Albans: *Annales monasterii S. Albani, a Johanne Amundesham, monacho, ut videtur, conscripti, AD 1421–1440*, ed. H. T. Riley, RS 28, 2 vols. (London, 1870–1), i. 431–50 at 434–9.

[23] *Smaragdi abbatis expositio*, ed. Spannagel and Engelbert, pp. 299–302 at 299.

[24] Gregory, *Dialogues*, ed. De Vögué, II. xi, pp. 172–3.

[25] *Warnefrid-Hildemar*, pp. 67–8. For instances of adult oblates at Farfa, see Costambeys, *Power and Patronage*, p. 139.

[26] *Anglo-Saxon Missionaries*, ed. Talbot, p. 5; P. D. Johnson, *Equal in Monastic Profession: Religious Women in Medieval France* (Chicago, 1991), p. 15.

[27] Costambeys, *Power and Patronage*, p. 138.

attested.[28] Unpropertied parents were not prohibited from oblation but permitted 'simply [to] make the declaration, and with the oblation offer their son in the presence of witnesses' (*RB*, 59). Payments were not confined to the entry of oblates. These transactions were not unknown in connection with adult professions; between the tenth and the twelfth centuries it became commonplace for female monasteries to demand a 'dowry' from each recruit; condemned by the Fourth Lateran Council in 1215 (Canon 10), the practice endured although in many parts of Europe the dowry was reduced to a fixed cash sum in the later Middle Ages.[29]

At its peak, in the eleventh century, oblation served to extend and secure the endowment of the new foundations made in England, Lombardy and Normandy. Battle Abbey grew from the 'great many that offered their children there ... for the service of God'.[30] Orderic Vitalis observed the benefit brought to Saint-Evroul from the donation of the church of St Nicholas by Fulk of Bonneval when he promised his son Thierry to the abbey.[31] Oblation also created a cadre of able and committed Benedictines. It is surely no coincidence that the most prolific and influential writers of the Gregorian period, authorities on the history of Benedictine observance, were oblates: Abbess Hildegard of Bingen, oblated at eight under the supervison of the anchoress Jutta of Sponheim; Orderic Vitalis, monk of Saint-Evroul, offered at Shrewsbury, before 1085, also Rupert of Deutz and Suger of Saint-Denis.[32]

Yet in the decades either side of 1200, the impulse faded, at least among the northern monastic networks of France and England. Few of the houses here were wholly subject to their secular lord (*Eigenklöster*), the context that encouraged oblation. Also, there appears to have been a growing anxiety over the place of children in the monastery, their involvement in the solemn observances to which it was bound, and the danger they posed to the moral integrity of the adults. A fourteenth-century chronicler of Canterbury, William Thorne, claimed his forebears had rejected oblation because 'certain abbots [were] induced by carnal affection' and 'coerced by the importunity of the rich and powerful' to the 'scandal of religion and the loss of the church'.[33] The practice had disappeared entirely from England's male monasteries by 1200 but it remained a feature of admissions to nunneries perhaps to the end of the medieval period; there

---

[28] For example, Johnson, *Equal in Monastic Profession*, p. 23; Costambeys, *Power and Patronage*, p. 140.

[29] E. Power, *Medieval English Nunneries, c. 1275–1535* (Cambridge, 1922), pp. 16–24; M. Oliva, *The Convent and the Community in Late Medieval England: Female Monasteries in the Diocese of Norwich, 1350–1540* (Woodbridge, 1998), pp. 148–50. See below, p. 68&n.

[30] *Battle*, pp. 70–1.

[31] *Orderic*, ii. 85.

[32] *The Letters of Hildegard of Bingen*, ed. J. L. Baird and R. K. Ehrman, 3 vols. (Oxford, 1994–2004), i. 5; M. Chibnall, *The World of Orderic Vitalis* (Oxford, 1984), p. 3; J. H. Van Engen, *Rupert of Deutz* (Berkeley, 1983), p. 53.

[33] *Thorne*, p. 94.

is little doubt it also continued in central, eastern and southern regions of Europe.[34]

The different routes to profession created a monastery of multiple generations. This appears to have been a feature of Benedictine houses throughout their medieval history. Æthelwold's community at Winchester Old Minster was remembered as one of 'old men who had been professed, novices, and child oblates'.[35] The generational divide did generate tension, conspicuous at moments of inevitable division, such as an election or visitation. Yet it also served to stimulate cohesion, assuring brethren of the continuity and, so it appeared, the enduring value of their enterprise. At a practical level, generational exchanges cemented patterns of liturgical practice, and study, as books, and the unique texts and glosses they contained, were passed from elder to younger.[36] These interactions also cultivated a collective identity. The history of the house was transmitted orally (at least at first) from one generation to another and even at the end of the Middle Ages, when the textual inheritance of the greater abbeys and priories was formidable, the lives of brethren past still afforded a framework for the construction of conventual chronicles: John Stone of Christ Church, Canterbury, created a continuous narrative of his house from the obituaries of his confrères.[37]

Benedict did not conceive of his *cenobium* as socially exclusive: 'we all bear an equal burden of servitude under one Lord, "for there is no respect of persons with God"' [Romans 2:11] (*RB*, 2). Yet the *RB* did not seek entirely to efface distinctions of status: oblation was undertaken differently for the offspring of nobles and paupers (*RB*, lix). The *RB* also recognised the special qualities that converts of status might convey to the community and its early followers actively sought professions from the social and political elite. The ties of the early monastery to its patron served only to intensify the preference for well-born recruits. Patrons commonly asserted the right to nominate candidates and could even dictate the progression of the candidate after profession: Guibert de Nogent owed his schooling as a monk to the intervention of a patron.[38] The emergence of Cluny, and its pursuit of an independence founded on territorial power, amplified the interest in professions from the seigniorial families. According to Orderic, the masters

---

[34] Jacques de Vitry (d. 1240) preached on the persistent parental impulse for oblation: Johnson, *Equal in Monastic Profession*, p. 23. The mystic Gertrude 'the great' was oblated at Helfta, near Eisleben (Saxony) in 1260: C. Larrington, *Women and Writing in Medieval Europe: A Source Book* (London, 1995), p. 143.

[35] *Wulfstan*, pp. 34–5.

[36] See, for example, the transmission of books through successive generations of Durham monks: A. J. Piper, 'The Libraries of the Monks of Durham', in *Medieval Scribes, Manuscripts and Libraries: Essays Presented to N. R. Ker*, ed. M. B. Parkes and A. G. Watson (London, 1978), pp. 213–49.

[37] *Stone*, pp. 5–118. The final portion from 1460–71 (81–118) becomes as much an annal of regional and national occurrences, although the sporadic record of obituaries continues. See also M. Connor, 'Brotherhood and Confraternity at Canterbury Cathedral Priory in the Fifteenth Century: the Evidence of John Stone's Chronicle', *Archaeologia Cantiana* 128 (2008), 143–64.

[38] *Guibert*, p. 77.

of the Norman clergy chose Herluin as abbot of Bec 'recognising his high birth'.[39] Orderic reflected the prevailing view that nobility reinforced the monastic order: 'he came of noble stock, and drew at will on the resources of his relatives, with their friendly consent, for the needs of his monks'.[40] In this period of expansion, perhaps naturally it was brethren of noble stock that were charged with colonisation: Roger, a priest monk of Saint-Evroul, led the new community at the revived Saint-Martin of Séez.[41] Generally men and women of good birth gravitated towards houses of proven prestige: Guibert claimed a 'great swarm of men of knightly rank' gravitated to the abbeys of the Seine valley.[42] New settlements struggled to secure high-status conversions, and the political and territorial influence they carried with them. The anonymous annalist of the foundation of Walden noted ruefully the modest origins of the first professions.[43] The affiliations of the seigniorial class shifted in the course of the twelfth century as first the crusade and subsequently ascetic forms of monasticism offered an alternative focus for their spiritual investment. In England men of noble birth no longer led the Benedictines, but, given their pre-eminence in the prelacy – an Arundel, Courtenay and Bourchier as primate between 1397 and 1459 – now they governed them. The fall in numbers of noble or magnate monks both reflected and compounded their growing separation from royal and seigniorial patronage: in pre-Reformation England monks were now the clients, not the kinsmen, of the political nation.

By contrast, nobility was a feature of female houses to the end of the Middle Ages. The impulse for the foundation of a nunnery was not infrequently the vocation (natural or contrived) of a noblewoman. The female foundations that followed the Dunstanian reform depended upon the patronage of such women; the expansion of female houses after the Conquest was also accelerated by noble interest: Stephen of Blois provided Lillechurch for his daughter, Mary, who was subsequently elected abbess of Romsey.[44] In the high and later Middle Ages, the magnate class continued to provide the mainstay of these houses: Eileen Power's characterisation of them as 'aristocratic institutions' cannot be discarded as mere caricature.[45] Abbess Anne de Prye of La Trinité, Poitiers, was perhaps not untypical of the female superiors of her time: the daughter of a distinguished family of minor nobility (her father was a seigneur and Grand Queux de France) whose male and female members monopolised secular and ecclesiastical

[39] *Orderic*, i. 13.

[40] Ibid., i. 87.

[41] Ibid., i. 49. For magnate monks leading new foundations in England, see Burton, *Monastic Order in Yorkshire*, pp. 156–7, 159, 163.

[42] *Guibert*, p. 58.

[43] *Walden*, pp. 26–7.

[44] S. K. Elkins, *Holy Women of Twelfth-Century England* (Notre Dame, NC, 1988), p. 189&n.

[45] Power, *Medieval English Nunneries*, p. 4. See also *Chatteris*, p. 102.

offices in their own region.[46] It was not only that nunneries continued to appeal to royal, noble and gentry families as a secure and socially acceptable refuge for their unmarried maids, but that, against a background of a lively domestic piety, the vocation of nun still held a powerful appeal for many girls of good birth; of course, the persistence of the 'dowry' also constrained the social catchment.[47] In England, France and Italy the social composition of female houses did stratify somewhat in the generations after 1300 and professions from mercantile and urban families were more common, but given the commercial and political power of such groups, the character of these convents was no less exclusive.[48]

At the core of any Benedictine convent were entrants of less exalted origin. The regional prominence of the monastery as landowner and employer made it an obvious objective for those born into the tenantry and perhaps even the prosperous peasantry. There can be no doubt that many monasteries drew recruits directly from the settlements, manors, villages, towns, under their jurisdiction, although where sufficient data survives (notably from England) it appears demesne or tenanted estates were rarely the principal source of recruitment.[49] Dependent cells – priories, chapelries – also appear to have filtered regional recruits through to the mother house. Granges may have served the same purpose. These patterns appear predominant in the records of English houses, athough an easy correlation between a personal toponym and place of origin cannot be assumed.[50] The origin of such monks is sometimes reflected in conventual records where the tribulations (climate, market) of the farmer are mentioned in passing; it might also be observed how skillfully successive generations of Benedictines undertook the responsibilities of estate management.[51] In the high Middle Ages men of such status formed the mainstay of monastic professions. After the Black Death there was a rise in the number recruited from mercantile and reinvigorated urban contexts. In England the leading monasteries now

---

[46] V. P. Day, 'Recycling Radegund: Identity and Ambition in the Breviary of Anne de Prye', in *Excavating the Medieval Image: Manuscripts, Artists, Audiences: Essays in Honor of Sandra Hindman*, ed. D. Areford, N. Row and S. Hindman (Aldershot, 2004), pp. 151–78 at 151–2.

[47] Power, *Medieval English Nunneries*, pp. 16–24 (dowries), 25–9 (vocations); S. T. Strocchia, *Nuns and Nunneries in Renaissance Florence* (Baltimore, MD, 2009), pp. 25–31; M. E. Mate, *Women in Medieval English Society*, New Studies in Economic and Social History 39 (Cambridge, 1999), p. 73. As an example of the financial arrangements precipitated for a female profession in the later Middle Ages, see the case of Eleanor Fairfax (1429–30) at Nun Monkton: *VCH County of York*, iii. 122–3.

[48] Oliva, *Convent and Community*, pp. 57, 60–1. The shift was perhaps as much as a century earlier in some regions. The nunneries of Normandy attracted women of urban (and indeed mercantile) origins from early in the thirteenth century: Johnson, *Equal in Monastic Profession*, p. 17.

[49] E. H. Pearce, *The Monks of Westminster*, Notes and Documents Relating to Westminster Abbey 5 (Oxford, 1909), p. 38; Clark, *Monastic Renaissance*, pp. 15–17; B. Harvey, *Living and Dying in England: The Monastic Experience, c. 1100–1540* (Oxford, 1993), pp. 75–6; Oliva, *Convent and Community*, pp. 58–9; Selby, p. 24. Durham did not recruit in this way: R. B. Dobson, *Durham Priory, 1400–1450* (Cambridge, 1973), pp. 57–8.

[50] Dobson, *Durham Priory*, pp. 56–8.

[51] *Walden*, pp. 33, 63, 109; *Battle*, p. 65.

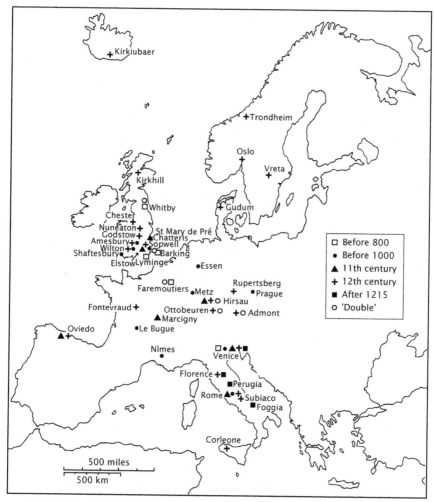

4 Benedictine foundations for women, *c.* 700–*c.* 1349

recruited from the merchant elite of London, York, Norwich, Bristol, and subordinate trading centres.[52]

Profession as a Benedictine was rarely possible for those of the lowest status. Benedict had prescribed 'let not a free-born be preferred to a freedman' yet implicitly his code was presented to the Latinate patriciate from whose society he himself had withdrawn. The early codes of northern Europe were clear in their exclusion of the *plebs*.[53] There was perhaps

---

[52] Dobson, *Durham Priory*, pp. 57–8; *Selby*, p. 24: monks came to Selby from middle ranks of rural and urban society; Harvey, *Living and Dying*, pp. 76–7.

[53] The presumption of the early commentators was that the adult or oblate entrant would be from families of property. Hildemar represented the monastic state as one intended for the chosen few: *Warnefrid-Hildemar*, pp. 66–9 at 68, 76–81 at 77–8, 189.

greater scope for the meanest sort to pursue a Benedictine vocation in the later Middle Ages, particularly as superiors and other senior monks now sponsored the schooling of worthy, and notably able, plebians under their authority. Abbot Richard of Wallingford of St Albans (d. 1334) was one such, owing his early schooling and university studies to the support of Prior William de Kirkeby of Wallingford (Oxfordshire).[54]

The social mix of the Benedictine monastery was matched by a blend of national and regional identities. Certainly Benedict's model colonies at Cassino and Subiaco drew converts from beyond the region. The first northern colonies were equally cosmopolitan. Their reputation as exponents of the pure *RB* attracted a migrant population: Wilfrid sojourned at Fleury, as Benedict Biscop had done a generation before.[55] Frankish monks were tempted into English monasteries as teachers. The scholarly authority Abbo of Fleury came to Ramsey in 997, where he taught and compiled his compendious *Quaestiones grammaticales*.[56] As the pace of recruitment slowed, the catchment of Benedictines became more confined. Before the Reformation, English monasteries recruited from within their own liberty, or the regions that bordered it, and for the most part from families whose ties to the house were of long standing.[57]

Among the Benedictines of the early and high Middle Ages a greater importance was attached to social status than either learning or literacy. By implication, Benedict expected his brethren to be Latinate, whether from their prior experience in the world, or their preparation, from infancy, in the claustral *schola*. The classical culture of the *cenobium* faded as the *RB* advanced northwards to locations where schooling on the Roman model had disappeared, if, in fact, it had ever been present. In the first Frankish and English monasteries perhaps only the missionaries who had passed through Rome and its remaining satellites (such as Marseilles) could claim an education equal to Benedict's own. The synodalia of 817 required at least one member of the community learned enough to converse with visitors in the *hospitium*.[58] The Aachen reforms encouraged a general recovery of learning already apparent in the greatest Frankish abbeys; yet a century later the English reformers were conscious of their dependence on committed but 'unlearned laymen' ('ungelaeredum woroldmonnum').[59] The reformed observance required a Latin culture, and literacy advanced as far as the new customs and congregations. Learned culture competed with liturgy as a priority, an *opus speciale*, for Otloh of Saint-Emmeram, a prerequisite of

[54] *GASA*, ii. 200. See also J. D. North, *Richard of Wallingford and the Invention of Time* (London, 2005).
[55] See above, pp. 27, 31.
[56] Byrhtferth, *Lives*, ed. Lapidge, pp. xxiv, 90.
[57] Clark, *Monastic Renaissance*, pp. 15–17.
[58] *Initia consuetudinis Benedictinae*, ed. Hallinger, pp. 472–81 at 479 (Canon 29).
[59] Such was the address of Æthelwold's translation of the *RB* (973): *Councils and Synods*, i.1151–2. See also *Wulfstan*, pp. liv–v; 38–41.

monastic profession for Rupert of Deutz.[60] Before the close of the eleventh century the illiterate entrant was already a rarity. At Orderic's Saint-Evroul they were disparaged as *rustici*, although new colonies were unlikely to turn such converts away: at Walden (*c.* 1148) 'To tell the truth [the first monks were] few in number and barely literate.'[61] The unlettered Benedictine was now confined to the *claustrales* (cloister monks), although character could sometimes compensate for education: Abbot Ording of Bury St Edmunds 'was an illiterate man' but 'a good abbot'.[62] The parallel demands of communal observance and domestic administration left no place for a fervent but incapable *professus*. Fifty years after its foundation, only two unlettered monks remained at Walden; at Bury St Edmunds, Jocelin of Brakelond exposed them to open mockery.[63] Rarely was a Benedictine profession open to the ill-educated in the later Middle Ages. The fall in the rate of admissions in later centuries was accelerated by an increasing selectivity at least among prestige convents: the formula for a letter of rejection preserved in a fourteenth-century abbatial register bears witness to an exacting process of application, requiring sponsors' references.[64] It may be their exacting standards that explain the small number of almonry boys that progressed to profession.[65]

Co-existent with the members of the monastery was a variety of men and women living under the regular discipline of the house but without the formality of profession. The early medieval convent contained a sizeable and transient community of clerks closely bound to the observant and domestic life of the monastic enclosure although unprofessed.[66] Their status did not preclude them from positions of seniority: the deacon Waldo, of Saint-Gall (d. 813), held the abbacy itself.[67] The integration of the professed and unprofessed did not persist in the later Middle Ages, although clerks retained a place in the liturgical and pastoral work of the monastery and in its precinct.[68]

The Benedictines also harboured lay brethren. The opportunity of a cenobitic life for the unprofessed (and uneducated) layman is often presented as a unique feature of the reformed monasteries of the Cistercians, but *conversi* were equally common in the precincts of Black Monks and Nuns. They are not seen in the *RB* but are well attested in the early convents that

---

[60] I. M. Resnik, 'Litterati, Spirituales and Lay Christians according to Otloh of Saint Emmeram, *Church History* 55 (1986), 165–78; Van Engen, *Rupert of Deutz*, p. 321.

[61] *Orderic*, ii. 296; *Walden*, pp. 26–7.

[62] *Jocelin*, p. 11.

[63] *Walden*, pp. 30–1; *Jocelin*, p. 130.

[64] Cambridge University Library, MS Ee.4.20, fo. 68v.

[65] J. G. Clark, 'Monasteries and Secular Education', in *Monasteries and Society in Medieval Britain*, ed. J. Burton and K. Stoeber, Studies in the History of Medieval Religion 35 (Turnhout, 2008), pp. 145–67.

[66] For example, *MO*, p. 39.

[67] M. Hildebrandt, *The External School in Carolingian Society* (Leiden, 1992), p. 112.

[68] See below, pp. 165–7.

followed it: the thirty *laici* accommodated in three chambers at Corbie in the ninth century were presumably lay brethren.[69] The duties of the *conversi* are not described in early codes but it appears they experienced the life of the enclosure to a greater extent than their Cistercian counterparts. In Lanfranc's *Decreta* the *conversi* were called upon to assist in the celebration of the principal liturgical feasts. Lanfranc distinguished two tiers of the unprofessed – the *conversi* and the *fratres laici*.[70] The admission of lay brethren declined after 1250, just as it did across the Cistercian network. Perhaps they were subject to the same pressure on income that constrained monastic professions, although the greater abbeys and priories, of men and women, continued to admit them *ad hoc*, sometimes only under episcopal licence.[71] The 1277 statutes of the general chapter of English Benedictines incorporated special measures (notably punishments) for *conversi*.[72]

Benedict set no limit on the scale of his *cenobium*. There is no record of the numbers at Montecassino, Subiaco or 'Alta ripa', but excavations at the first two suggest a cluster of inter-dependent communities served by as many as twelve oratories. The scale of the individual communities is difficult to judge but the extent of the sites and the number of oratories are consistent with an overall population not in tens but in hundreds. The scale of the first colonies that followed the *RB* can also only be estimated. Hagiographers claimed crowds came to the pioneering communities at Fleury, Ripon and Whitby.[73] The churches on these sites were not small and the precinct, and its infrastructure, were often extensive. The later monasteries of the Carolingian reform were large, recruiting 200 or more.[74] In a climate of reform and religious revival, the most renowned of these houses became oversubscribed: at Corbie Abbot Adalard allowed for 350 in 822, although, perhaps deliberately, only 130 had been admitted in *c.* 830.[75] By contrast, the English houses of the Anglo-Saxon reform were modest: the dispersal of irregular canons from Winchester and elsewhere at first confined these convents to a handful of committed professions.[76]

---

[69] Hildebrandt, *External School in Carolingian Society*, p. 89&n.

[70] *MC*, pp. 36–7, 74–5, 156–7, 168–9. See also *The Letters of Lanfranc, Archbishop of Canterbury*, ed. H. Clover and M. Gibson (Oxford, 1979), pp. 86–7 (Letter 14).

[71] BL, Cotton MS Nero D VII, fos. 81v–82v at 82v; Power, *Medieval English Nunneries*, pp. 213, 288; D. Logan, *Runaway Religious in Medieval England, c. 1240–1540* (Cambridge, 1996), p. 127.

[72] *Chapters*, ed. Pantin, i. 64–92 at 72.

[73] *Wilfrid*, pp. 18–19.

[74] For a survey of scales, see H. Fichtenau, *Living in the Tenth Century: Mentalities and Social Orders* (Chicago, 1991), pp. 269–70. See also G. Constable, *The Reformation of the Twelfth Century* (Cambridge, 1996), pp. 28, 89.

[75] Ganz, *Corbie in the Carolingian Renaissance*, p. 26&n.

[76] Æthelwold's model *monasterium* at Abingdon supplied monks for his subsequent (re)foundations, responding no doubt to a dearth of brethren able or willing to commit to a regular life: A. Thacker, 'Æthelwold and Abingdon', in *Bishop Æthelwold*, ed. Yorke, pp. 43–64 at 43&n; D. H. Farmer, 'The Progress of the Monastic Revival', in *Tenth-Century Studies*, ed. D. Parsons (London, 1975), pp. 10–19 at 16–17.

The liturgical complexity of the Clunic customary demanded communities on a grand scale, and the mother house and its main affiliates expanded exponentially between the tenth and the twelfth centuries. During the abbacy of Peter the Venerable there were at least 220 professed brethren at Cluny and numbers exceeding 100 at the best-known abbeys in its network, such as Bec.[77] The English monasteries grew in the wake of their post-Conquest reorganisation, the beneficiaries not only of Norman patronage but also a general surge in popular piety. The Conqueror envisaged a community of 140 to serve his commemorative foundation at Battle.[78] If any number of English houses did reach these heights, they had fallen again by the beginning of the fourteenth century. The communities of the greater abbeys and priories in England – Christ Church, Canterbury, Durham, Glastonbury, Westminster – settled between fifty and eighty in the years either side of 1300.[79] The Black Death devastated monastic Europe and in a number of locations monastic life was entirely extinguished. Those that survived never again sustained the numbers seen before 1250. Their depressed (if not diminished) resources at any rate for decades militated against disproportionate expansion. In England the capitular authorities now monitored admissions, anxious that for the purposes of observance they achieved the 'plenum numerum monachorum'.[80] Lacking capitular supervision, Continental houses declined to levels that could scarcely sustain regular observance.[81] Quite apart from unfavourable economic and social conditions, it has been suggested the monasteries of this period also suffered from a growing problem of apostasy. Donald Logan has estimated that prestige monasteries such as Christ Church, Canterbury, and Durham lost as many as one-third of their professed brethren in each generation.[82] This instability was characteristic also of mendicant convents and secular colleges in the later Middle Ages and at least in part reflected the growing complexity of clerical career paths.[83]

It has often been suggested that the monastic community of the Middle Ages constituted a microcosm of society. It is true that the principal orders of society, and many of its occupations, from higher clergy to lowly, unskilled labourer, were contained within the precincts of the greater

[77] G. Constable, *Cluny from the Tenth to the Twelfth Centuries: Further Studies* (Aldershot, 2000), p. 407.
[78] *Battle*, pp. 68–9. See also V. H. Galbraith, 'Monastic Foundation Charters of the Eleventh and Twelfth Centuries', *Cambridge Historical Journal* 4 (1932–4), 214–22.
[79] *MRH*, pp. 61, 64, 66, 80; Harvey, *Living and Dying*, p. 122.
[80] *Chapters*, ed. Pantin, ii. 43.
[81] See below, p. 263.
[82] Logan, *Runaway Religious*, p. 67. See also Dobson, *Durham Priory*, p. 77.
[83] For examples of the career patterns of regular and secular clergy in the later period, see D. Lepine, 'The Origins and Careers of the Canons of Exeter', in *Religious Belief and Ecclesiastical Careers in Late Medieval England*, ed. C. Harper-Bill (Woodbridge, 1991), pp. 87–120; R. B. Dobson, 'The Monks of Durham', and 'The Residentiary Canons of York in the Fifteenth Century', in *Church and Society in the Medieval North of England* (London, 1996), pp. 47–82, 195–224.

abbeys and priories. The parallels between the community of the monastic enclosure and the community beyond the walls, however, should not be overdrawn. The longevity of the monastic community set it apart from lay society: this was an environment where it was not unknown for an entire generation to achieve old age. The interaction between the generations, in which the four ages of man lived and laboured together, was not replicated beyond the precinct walls, not, perhaps, because of a lower life-expectancy, but due to the expanding opportunities of a diversifying – and in some regions, urbanising – economy.[84] The social blend of the Benedictine monastery was also a feature for which there was no exact parallel in wider society. There can be little doubt the lives of layfolk were strictly stratified, even in the vibrant urban centres of the later Middle Ages. Nor was there another community of regular or secular clerks which saw such variation in its social profile, at least until the sons of nobility, gentry and tradesmen began to share benches in the Renaissance schoolroom.

Noviciate

Whatever the impulse behind their arrival at the monastery, the making of a Benedictine was the subject of a strict and, over time, an increasingly elaborate programme of work. The *RB* cautioned the prospective convert, 'the way of salvation cannot be but narrow' (*RB*, prologue). Admission was deliberately difficult to secure (*RB*, 58): the supplicant was to be detained at the gate 'for four or five days' to demonstrate their capacity 'patiently [to] bear the harsh treatment'; when finally they gained entry, it was only to the guesthouse and a further period of observation. Although these formalities may have faded away, there can be no doubt a degree of selectivity endured. The customary of Eynsham Abbey (Oxfordshire) required candidates for admission to be examined by the abbot, prior 'et alii fratres spirituales' and to be impressed by the 'poverty of the house, the barrenness of the place and the severity of its discipline' ('paupertas domus, asperitas loci, severitas disciplinae').[85] Later, the capacity of the (male or female) postulant to pay the customary entry fee was perhaps the principal criterion.[86] Benedict's code was for 'beginners' in the Lord's service, but it demanded nothing less than the transformation of the self: 'Let [them] be shown', the founder ordered 'all the hard and rugged things through which we pass to God' (*RB*, 58). In common with his predecessors, Benedict prescribed a formal period of preparation for such a mode of life. His noviciate reflected a

[84] Harvey, *Living and Dying*, pp. 127–9.
[85] *The Customary of the Benedictine Abbey of Eynsham in Oxfordshire*, ed. A. Gransden, CCM 2 (Siegburg, 1963), p. 27. The scrutiny of candidates can be found even in the fifteenth century: *Visitations of the Diocese of Norwich, AD 1492–1532*, ed. A. Jessopp, Camden Society, New Series 43 (London, 1884), p. 33 (Thetford, 1492).
[86] Power, *Medieval English Nunneries*, pp. 16–24; Oliva, *Convent and Community*, p. 50.

Roman instinct for codification. Its term was to be twelve months, a period punctuated by three examinations on the *RB* after two, eight and twelve months (*RB*, 58); the novice was to be placed in the custody of a senior who was to be both guide and governor; the culmination was a ceremony of profession in which the novice pledged, in his own words (committed where possible to parchment), his adherence to the monastic code, the precondition for citizenship in the *patria monachorum*.

The noviciate retained the shape and the spirit of Benedict's code throughout the Middle Ages. In the period of the Benedictines' greatest expansion, between the tenth and twelfth centuries, the term contracted and it was not uncommon for a novice to pass from clothing to profession in a matter of weeks: Lanfranc's *Decreta* (*c.* 1070) envisaged profession only after 'many days have passed'.[87] The breadth of their liturgical, pastoral and administrative obligations exposed the inadequacy of such arrangements, and in the later Middle Ages, for the men the noviciate of a year was reaffirmed; for women the shorter term may have persisted.[88] The term during which the entrant was understood to be under the tutelage and supervision of their seniors did expand.

In the early monasteries a promising recruit might be schooled for several years, as Æthelwold was at Glastonbury, 'eventually' (*tandem*) receiving the habit of the order.[89] Orderic Vitalis recalled that Ralph 'the badly tonsured' trained at Marmoutiers for seven years.[90] Later customaries lengthened the period of custody beyond the point of solemn profession: in the century before the Reformation in England it was between eight and perhaps as many as twelve years.[91] Given the pattern of academic and clerical careers, these arrangements meant English Benedictines might be ordained priest or complete a university degree before they had been released from the supervision of an elder.

The novices formed a discrete cohort within the monastery, subject to a distinct regime of their own. The *RB* placed them in the charge of a master invested with absolute authority, the superior of the unprofessed. Orderic remembered his master, Osbern, 'drove the novices hard and did not hesitate to use the whip as well as words'.[92] The office appears unchanged at pre-Reformation Durham, where the master was responsible 'for the

---

[87] *MC*, p. 159. 'A year made my professioun' recalled John Lydgate (*c.* 1370–*c.* 1451) of Bury in his *Testament* (l. 671): *The Minor Poems of John Lydgate*, ed. H. N. MacCracken, EETS, Extra Series 107 (1911), pp. 329–62 at 354.

[88] For the male noviciate, see *Chapters*, ed. Pantin, i. For the female noviciate, see Oliva, *Convent and Community*, p. 52.

[89] *Wulfstan*, pp. 14–15.

[90] *Orderic*, ii. 74–7: 'monachili regulae septem annis militavit'.

[91] 'iuvenes qui sunt in custodia': *MC*, p. 138; Harvey, 'A Novice's Life at Westminster in the Century before the Dissolution', in *The Religious Orders in Pre-Reformation England*, ed. J. G. Clark (Woodbridge, 2002), pp. 51–74 at 56–7.

[92] *Orderic*, ii. 107.

contynewallie instructing of ther youth in vertew and lerning'.[93] The *RB* placed the novices in a *domus* of their own. They were to sleep in their own chamber ('in cella noviciorum') and there also they were to take their meal(s) ('ubi et manducent et dormient': *RB*, lviii), a pattern repeated in the earliest commentaries.[94] Benedict of Aniane's *Concordia* reinforced their alterity, requiring the habit to be withheld until their profession.[95] The separation was relaxed somewhat in later centuries. At Eynsham, the novices were accommodated in the monks' dormitory.[96] Later they also took meals in the frater with the professed. They were assigned their own table and apparently were served from the kitchen – at the 'dresser window' at Durham – perhaps to expedite the meal since many customaries required them to wait upon the brethren; they were not to receive meat on flesh days and one of their number was deputed to read as the brethren dined.[97] They also attended the conventual chapter, although they were forbidden to speak.[98] Yet their subordinate status was also underlined: the English capitular canons of 1277 and 1343 denied novices the mobility beyond the enclosure permitted to the professed and prohibited their access to keys, a prohibition enforced by episcopal visitors.[99]

Entrants of clerical status, or otherwise educated, were dispensed from the full rigour of these preparations. The thirteenth-century customary of Eynsham designated such converts *provecciores*, and they were to pass briskly to profession and participation in the Office.[100] In England the concession was codified in the capitular statutes of 1343, under which clerks (*clerici*) were wholly exempt from the requirements of the noviciate.[101] Nor did the oblates follow a formal noviciate.[102] They were bound by domestic regulations of their own and as they passed out of infancy (as they turned seven, according to classical custom) they embarked on an education which encompassed the verbal and vocal demands of the Office as well as grammar and the computus. The *Liber Eliensis* offers an image of its children *in schola* (among them Edward Atheling) at the far end of the cloister walk

[93] *Rites of Durham: A Description of all the Ancient Monuments, Rites and Customes with the Monastical Church of Durham before the Suppression*, ed. J. Raine, Surtees Society 15 (1842), p. 69.
[94] *Warnefrid-Hildemar*, p. 66.
[95] *Benedicti Anianensis Concordia regularum*, ed. Bonnerue, pp. 549–90 at, for example, 555 (extract from Pachomius), 590 (extract from Aurelianus).
[96] *Customary of Eynsham*, ed. Gransden, p. 35. For the arrangement of female dormitories, see L. V. Hicks, *Religious Life in Normandy, 1050–1300: Space, Gender and Social Pressure* (Woodbridge, 2007), pp. 108–11; M. C. Erler, 'Private Reading in the Fifteenth- and Sixteenth-Century English Nunnery', in *The Culture of Medieval English Monasticism*, ed. J. G. Clark (Woodbridge, 2007), pp. 147–67.
[97] *Rites of Durham*, ed. Raine, pp. 69–70.
[98] *MC*, pp. 163, 167, 213.
[99] *Chapters*, ed. Pantin, i. 64–92 at 74, ii. 50; *The Register of Thomas Bekynton, Bishop of Bath and Wells, 1443–1465*, 2 vols., ed. H. C. Maxwell-Lyte and M. C. B. Dawes, Somerset Record Society, 49–50 (1934), ii. 555–6.
[100] *Customary of Eynsham*, ed. Gransden, p. 33.
[101] *Chapters*, ed. Pantin, ii. 28–62 at 50.
[102] For example, *Warnefrid-Hildemar*, p. 80.

within sight of the professed brethren 'and there learnt ... the psalms ... and the Sunday office hymn'.[103] The earliest customaries expected the children (although not the infants)[104] to contribute to both hebdomadal and festive observance[105] and there was a compulsion for them to practise at every opportunity, even as they washed their faces.[106]

The purpose of the noviciate was to initiate a spiritual transformation yet the guiding principle of its syllabus was pragmatic, to prepare the novice for a life under the rule. The first lesson was the most practical of all: as Lanfranc's *Decreta* described how, on the second day of their term, the novice was to be led to the frater to be shown how to don and doff the habit, 'in a seemly (*honeste*) manner'.[107] As a mode of teaching, the Benedictine noviciate differed from the pedagogy of the schoolroom. Novices were expected to learn as much from their active participation in the *horarium* as from the study of the codes in which it was enshrined. Early witnesses represent the noviciate as the experience of walking closely with an *exemplum* of monastic discipline, whether it was Benedict of Aniane, Dunstan, Odilo or Anselm. Bernard of Cluny advised novices that liturgical customs were learned best through what he termed 'demonstrated experience' ('*probatae experientiae didicit*').[108]

The first objective of the noviciate was, of course, to master the *RB*. For Benedict it was its only object: the novice was to read and demonstrate their understanding to their brethren. The earliest commentaries confirm their reading conformed to the pattern of the Roman schools, where the master read, glossed and expounded the text and their pupils repeated it. The reading of the *RB* remained central to the experience of the novice. The Eynsham customary commanded: 'Hear the rule, read it and reread it' ('*regulam audiat, legat et relegat*').[109] Such was John Lydgate's recollection of his fourteenth-century noviciate; a century on and there were still examiners to test the entrants on their rule.[110]

Reading elaborated the literal sense of the *RB*. For the first Black Monks, the oral exposition of the master, and the interlinear glosses carried in some manuscripts, constituted the sole critical apparatus. Before 1100 a single authority served as the novices' guide to the *RB*. The exposition of Smaragdus of Saint-Mihiel (d. *c.* 840) provided an authoritative but concise elaboration of Benedict's precepts together with meditations on their

[103] *Liber Eliensis*, ii. 91: trans. J. Fairweather (Woodbridge, 2005), p. 191.
[104] The eighth-century commentators prescribed only the eldest children: 'for the sake of learning ... and ... propriety': *Warnefrid-Hildemar*, p. 163.
[105] *RC*, p. 35; *MC*, pp. 6–7, 28–9, 32–3, 40–1, 44–7, 52–3, 86–7.
[106] *RC*, p. 16.
[107] *MC*, p. 201.
[108] Boynton, *Shaping a Monastic Identity*, p. 125.
[109] *Customary of Eynsham*, ed. Gransden, p. 31.
[110] *Testament*, l. 684, in *Minor Poems*, ed. MacCracken, p. 354. The fifteenth-century example is from St Albans: *GASA*, ii. 484.

spiritual *sensus*.[111] The monastic reform and rivalry of the twelfth century generated a new repertory of commentaries, of Rupert of Deutz, Hildegard of Bingen and Bernard Ayglier, abbot of Monte Cassino (1263–82), which added a further source of reference for the advanced novice.[112] This period also saw a surge of para-regular literature, works which mediated on the primary themes of the *RB*: humility, obedience, the renunciation of the world. These works, such as Hugh of Fouilloy's *De claustro animae* and Hugh of Saint-Victor's *De institutione noviciorum*, also transmitted the spirit of neo-Augustinian spirituality into Benedictine cloisters.[113] As the preparation of novices assumed something of the character of conventual clerical instruction, textual authorities played a greater role in the teaching of the rule. Books and library catalogues surviving from the later Middle Ages suggest novices came to rely on a wide range of cribs and simple commentaries, perhaps not only as a supplement to claustral teaching but as a substitute for it.[114]

The *RB* provided an introduction to the principles, and (some of the) seasonal patterns, of the *opus Dei*, but it did not prepare the novice for full participation in the daily office. In any period of the Middle Ages, an observant Benedictine was required to know the complete canon of the liturgy, the antiphons, psalms, prayers, readings and responses which, in different combinations, formed the offices of day and night. The early codes and *consuetudines* assumed a working knowledge of all these texts; in the capitular canons of the later Middle Ages, the minimum expectations of a Benedictine novice were codified: the 1277 canons of the English chapter expected nothing less than the antiphons, canticles and hymns and the responses and sentences (presumably incorporating readings). John de Cella of St Albans (abbot, 1195–1214) claimed to know his psalter back to front.[115]

Practice was perhaps the only means to ensure the novice was ready to take their place in the oratory. From the tenth century, if not before, customaries expected the novices to contribute both to festal and routine observance. At the same time, the novice master directed their practice of (at least) portions of the Office, perhaps in the same corner of the cloister where they listened to the rule.[116] In the early Middle Ages this work was

---

[111] *Smaragdi abbatis expositio*, ed. Spannagel and Engelbert, pp. 1–337.

[112] See Hildegard of Bingen, *De regula sancti Benedicti*, ed. Feiss, pp. 67–97; Rupert of Deutz, *Super quaedam capitula regulae divi Benedicti abbatis: PL* 170: 477–538; Bernard (Ayglier) of Monte Cassino, *Expositio*, ed. Caplet. For a novice-manual incorporating the latter commentary, see Cambridge, Corpus Christi College, MS 137 (Christ Church, Canterbury), fos. 33v–92v.

[113] For these texts, see *PL*. For their presence in Benedictine collections, see, for example, *EBL*, B68. 75, 468a, pp. 359, 400 (Ramsey); B120. 369–72, pp. 720–1 (St Mary's, York); *Dover*, BM1. 104g, 105m,p, 107a, 126d,e, 207b,f, 210c, 212g, pp. 74–6, 84, 108–10, 124; *Peterborough*, BP21. 237m, 241e, 276e, 321a, 330c, pp. 140–3, 155, 168, 171.

[114] See, for example, Cambridge University Library, MS Dd.9.38 (Reading Abbey), the *RB* incomplete at fos. 64r–75r. *AL*, pp. 127 (Christ Church, Canterbury), 405 (St Augustine's, Canterbury).

[115] *Chapters*, ed. Pantin, i. 64–92 at 73–4; *GASA*, ii. 232.

[116] *MC*, p. 157; *RC*, p. 8.

undertaken without reference to any textual authority; the monastic office was still in genesis and even well established abbeys had yet to form the liturgical compendia – antiphoner, breviary, diurnal, gradual, responsory – that later filled the book cupboard of the sacrist. To improve the uniformity and quality of liturgical performance, the Carolingian reformers compiled summaries of the Mass for the instruction of novices (and the refreshment of the professed) known from their incipits as *Dominus vobiscum* and *Primum in ordine*.[117] The novice of this period may also have been directed to the anonymous *expositio missae* and to Isidore of Seville's *De ecclesiasticis officiis*.[118] Yet even the elaborate liturgical programme of Cluny at first did not yield any critical apparatus for the assistance of novices: it is a reflection of the remarkable appeal of the Cluniac reform that it was adopted across northern Europe without the assistance of a single customary. The rapid rise of the Benedictine population after 1050 transformed these patterns of liturgical training. Customaries were now commonplace, as were, at least from the mid-twelfth century, compendia containing key elements of the Office. An early example from Farfa (Farfa Abazia MS A 209) brought together glossed copies of the Athanasian Creed, a Confiteor, the Nunc dimittis and the psalter.[119] A codex from Canterbury (now Cambridge, Corpus Christi College, MS 441) contains the texts of prayers, psalms, and responses, presented to the novice reader as the 'traditional teaching' ('traditionis huius doctrina') of the monastery.[120]

The *opus Dei* required both verbal and vocal skill. There is little doubt that the Benedictine noviciate involved at least a modicum of musical training. The early anecdotes of Anglo-Saxon, Carolingian and Norman novices refer to their practice in chant or song.[121] As these witnesses imply, and as contemporary illustrations would suggest, the novices learned their liturgical music directly from the lectern of the precentor (or cantor) in the monastic church, perhaps supplemented with sessions with the novicemaster in their corner of the cloister.[122] The plainchant of the early and high Middle Ages was perhaps more compatible with, or presented fewer obstacles to, oral transmission. The polyphony which became more widely practised in Benedictine houses from the turn of the fourteenth century presented a formidable challenge to the novice. Visitors perceived

---

[117] *Dominus vobiscum*: PL 147: 1891–200; *Primum in ordine*: PL 138: 1173–86.

[118] *Expositio missae Romanae*: PL 96: 1481–1502; Isidore of Seville, *De ecclesiasticis officiis*, ed. C. Lawson, Corpus Christianorum Serie Latina (Turnhout, 1989).

[119] Boynton, *Shaping a Monastic Identity*, pp. 233–4.

[120] *MC*, p. liii.

[121] See below, p. 104.

[122] In the later Middle Ages, it appears it was almost always the work of the cantor: *Customary of the Benedictine Monasteries of Saint Augustine, Canterbury, and Saint Peter, Westminster*, ed. E. M. Thompson, HBS 23, 28, 2 vols. (London, 1902–4), i. 90–1, ii. 28–9. Historiated initials commonly represent the performance of the office as a handful of brethren gathered at the lectern: e.g. Zwettl, Zisterzienserstift, Codex Zwettlensis, 400, fo. iv.

a decline in the standard of the musical performance.[123] Monastic pioneers of the *ars nova* now sought to train novices to negotiate pricksong: Thomas Walsingham's *Regulae de figures formisque musicae* introduced novices to the mensurable note forms that were its standard feature.[124] At Glastonbury a student monk was compelled to turn from academic study to address his deficiency 'in cantu ad monachandum'.[125] In the pre-Reformation period the greater abbeys and priories resorted to professional cantors and organists to prepare their brethren, alongside the unprofessed boys who now also performed in the offices.[126]

The novice's observation and practice of liturgical performance were underpinned by readings in Holy Scripture. The Eynsham customary expected the novices 'frequenter in divinarum litterarum se exerceat'.[127] Particular emphasis was placed upon those biblical readings prominent in the daily office: it was these 'histories' that John Lydgate of Bury St Edmunds recalled when reflecting on his own noviciate.[128] It is likely this reading began, like the exposition of the *RB*, as a communal lesson led by the novice master. A late glimpse of the noviciate in England, from visitation injunctions issued at St Benet Hulme, Norfolk, in 1494, indicates that the mode of instruction, exposition and repetition, was unchanged on the eve of the Reformation: here the novice-master was reprimanded for failing to rehearse his charges to repeat their 'histories' ('recitationem historiae').[129] Novices might also absorb passages of scripture from their daily reading in the frater, which in England continued to the end of the Middle Ages.[130] The intention, however, was to instil a habit of scriptural study which would become the mainstay of the monk's personal regime. Book cupboards in the cloister walk set aside for novices were supplied with glossed copies of the scriptures and a selection of reference works.[131] There was a practical dimension to these preparations: since scripture was the predominant idiom of the monastic community, not only in the choir but also in the conduct of daily conventual business, mastery of its narratives,

---

[123] *Visitations of Religious Houses in the Diocese of Lincoln*, ed. A. H. Thompson, Lincoln Record Society 7, 14, 21, 27, 4 vols. (Lincoln, 1914–47), i. 54 (Eynsham, 1432), 106 (Ramsey, 1432).

[124] BL, MS Lansdowne 763, fos. 97v–104r; see also illustration 3.

[125] *Chapters*, ed. Pantin, iii. 27.

[126] For example, Glastonbury Abbey's indenture for the employment of a cantor and organist: NA, E135/2/31. Such appointments are also documented at Gloucester and Muchelney. See also R. Bowers, 'An Early Tudor Monastic Enterprise: Choral Polyphony for the Liturgical Service', in *The Culture of Medieval English Monasticism*, ed. Clark, pp. 21–54 at 40.

[127] *Customary of Eynsham*, ed. Gransden, p. 53.

[128] John Lydgate, *Testament*, l. 729, in *Minor Poems*, ed. MacCracken, p. 356.

[129] *Visitations*, ed. Jessopp, p. 61.

[130] *EBL*, B14 (Bury), B74 (Reading), pp. 87–9, 451–3 at 451; *Catalogi veteres ecclesiae cathedralis Dunelmensis*, ed. Raine (Durham, 1838), pp. 81–4.

[131] For example, at Durham *Catalogi veteres*, ed. Raine, pp. 46–79. See also A. J. Piper, 'The Monks of Durham and the Study of Scripture', in *The Culture of Medieval English Monasticism*, ed. Clark, pp. 86–103.

exemplae and imagery was a precondition for profession. Yet, after the *RB*, scripture was also the principal tool of the Benedictine's spiritual development, their aid and guide on their progress into God. The reading of it was not a studious exercise but a meditative experience. Benedict termed it *opus* (*RB*, xlviii. 1); later commentators and codes elaborated it: the *Statuta Murbacensia* described it as 'in meditatione lectionis diuinae'.[132] The novice was encouraged to reflect and to ruminate on the text, and in the early medieval era of reading aloud (if not in later centuries) this was expected to lead to the physical mastication of particular phrases. The measure of a monk of promise was his commitment to such *lectiones* and early monastic letters and *vitae* always celebrated the young monk eager for his hours of *opus*: 'strive with unflagging zest to pursue your study of the scriptures', Boniface counselled Nithard (*c.* 716–17) 'and thus acquire the nobility of mind which is divine wisdom'.[133] Orderic Vitalis remembered Richard of Fourneaux as a monk who 'made a particular study of Holy Scripture and from the time of his adolescence (i.e. from his noviciate) had travelled swiftly along the way of God in the footsteps of the fathers of old, singing psalms'.[134] The diversity of the novice cohort led to variations in the level of these scriptural *lectiones*. There may have been some that progressed to patristic and contemporary exegesis, but many others were limited to extracts from the familiar 'histories' and *exemplae*. Orderic wrote of the 'country priests', 'simple converts' and Durand 'the gardener' at Saint-Evroul, unable to understand the 'more profound books of scripture', whom the novice master 'sustained with colloquies within their grasp'.[135]

The able novice was encouraged to engage with sources of spiritual nourishment beyond the Bible. The works Benedict recommended for the refectory reader – patristic glosses and homilies – may have been followed independently during the hours assigned to reading in the cloister. The hagiographers of early Benedictine leaders such as Æthelwold, Dunstan, Lanfranc and Anselm laid claim to a sophisticated adolescent diet for religious works which is not wholly implausible.[136] Certainly it seems there was no obstacle to an eclectic programme of reading for the ambitious young monk. Wulfstan employed the image of the bee, beloved of Anglo-Saxon masters, to recall the novice Æthelwold at his books: '[He was] a provident bee that habitually flits around looking for scented trees and settling on

---

[132] *Statuta Murbancensia*, in *Initia consuetudinis Benedictinae*, ed. Hallinger, pp. 439–50 at 449.
[133] *Anglo-Saxon Missionaries*, ed. Talbot, p. 66.
[134] *Orderic*, iv. 306–7 at 307.
[135] Ibid., ii. 21.
[136] For example, *Memorials of St Dunstan, Archbishop of Canterbury*, ed. W. Stubbs (London, 1874), p. 11: 'ita vero vitae suae stadium coherebat ut quoties cuique divinae scripturae libros scruteretur Deus cum eo parite loqueretur'; *Wulfstan*, pp. 8–11: 'quod studiose et diligenter in ipsa pueritia sacris litterarum studiis animum dederit'.

greenery of pleasant taste, he laid toll on the flowers of religious books. He was eager to read the best-known Christian writers.'[137]

The *RB* and their instruction in liturgy and music turned novices into Benedictines but in isolation they did not integrate them fully into the life of their own monastery. From early centuries it was widely recognised that a novice must at the same time absorb the culture of the community in which they were to make their profession. The chain of glosses on the *RB* itself, whether they were delivered orally by the novice master, at the parchment face, or in one or other local commentary, offered valuable insights into local practice. The idiom of the house was perhaps ideally suited to oral transmission: Orderic describes how the customs of Thierry and his predecessors, the pioneers of Norman monasticism, were passed with great care to each new generation of novices ('et noviciis ad religionis conversationem conuersis sollerter insinuant').[138] From the twelfth century, and perhaps earlier, this source was supplemented with longer narratives of the house, its foundation, furnishings, and celebrated forefathers. In the later Middle Ages these narratives were collected together in compendia that were at least equal in scale to the liturgical codices that also occupied the novices. At Bury St Edmunds, in the decades following the Black Death, the novice master(s) compiled more than 400 folio leaves of narratives and notes (now Oxford, Bodleian Library, MS Bodley 240) on the history, sanctity and traditions of the the English church, the order of Black Monks, and of their own house.[139] The gathering of local knowledge reinforced the identity of the community and its transmission from one generation to another. As the author of the foundation history of Walden Abbey expressed it, 'amid the fluctuations of fortune in this passing world, the memory of past events is apt very easily to suffer loss through forgetfulness'.[140] Memory was the primary reflex to be refined by the young monk. The early monastic hagiographers saw feats of memory as an unequivocal sign of future greatness in a novice. Wulfstan of Winchester related how the boy Æthelwold had impressed his elders with his 'retentive memory'.[141] Orderic Vitalis appraised his peers in the same way, observing the 'tenacious memory' of William of Bonneval, which mastered the Pauline epistles, Proverbs 'and other books of Holy Writ'.[142] The exercise of memory was enshrined in the *RB*; Old Testament readings were to be recited at Matins (in the summer) and at Lauds by heart 'memoriter'

---

[137] *Wulfstan*, pp. 14–15.
[138] *Orderic*, ii. 74.
[139] For an analysis of this manuscript, see Pantin, 'Some Medieval English Treatises', pp. 194–6. Historical passages relating to the abbey were printed in *Memorials of St Edmund's Abbey*, ed. Arnold, ii. 362–8. See also N. Heale, 'Religious and Intellectual Interests at St Edmund's Abbey at Bury and the nature of English Benedictinism, c. 1350–1450: MS Bodley 240 in Context' (DPhil diss., Oxford, 1994).
[140] *Walden*, p. 3.
[141] *Wulfstan*, pp. 10–11.
[142] *Orderic*, i. 87.

(*RB*, x, xiii, xix); in its disciplinary chapters, the rule also commanded its readers repeatedly to recall the *dicta* of the apostles, or the *verbum Dei* itself. As a mode of behaviour, mindfulness (*memor* in the Latin of the *RB*) was to be a key attribute not only of the abbot (*RB*, ii) but also of his brethren (*RB*, iv. 61).

Education

Benedict addressed his rule to the educated Roman. The passage of the *RB* beyond the locus of Latinate culture presented the Benedictine life to men and women of little, if any, formal schooling. From the time of the first fully observant Benedictine monasteries, the learning of Latin and other elementary disciplines was widely acknowledged to be a necessity for the novice. Given the different age and status of entrants, certainly in the early centuries, and later also, perhaps there was never a common experience of elementary education in the monastery. There was always a minority educated before their profession. The Carolingian and Anglo-Saxon abbeys attracted *alumni* of royal and episcopal curia (courts) which were already acknowledged centres of teaching and learning.[143] Later, novices also came from the cathedral schools now burgeoning in the European mainland.[144] Women recruited from royal and noble contexts also carried learning with them; in the early and high Middle Ages, a large proportion may have possessed both vernacular and Latin literacy.[145] In the later Middle Ages the greater abbeys and priories also attracted recruits from merchant or gentry families which now dispatched their sons to grammar school as a matter of course.[146] There was a handful in the later period professed after undergraduate studies. These graduate novices were surely exempt from elementary education although they may have continued their study in the liberal arts.[147] Women in the later period might still enter with literacy although it was likely to have been the vernacular culture that now thrived in households of high and middling status.[148] Abbot Thomas de la Mare of St Albans prohibited the entry of unlettered novices to St Mary de Pré but few supervisors were so proscriptive.[149] When Bishop Richard Fox sought to restore female observance in his diocese of Winchester, he provided a translation of the *RB* in the idiomatic English of the early Tudor gentry.[150]

[143] For example, Æthelwold, whose youth was spent at the court of King Æthelstan: *Wulfstan*, p. 11.
[144] For the recruitment of monks trained in these schools, see Hildebrandt, *External School in Carolingian Society*, pp. 108–29, 180.
[145] Power, *Medieval English Nunneries*, pp. 245–52 at 246–8.
[146] Clark, *Monastic Renaissance*, p. 44; Dobson, *Durham Priory*, pp. 61–2.
[147] Clark, *Monastic Renaissance*, pp. 57–60 at 59–60.
[148] Power, *Medieval English Nunneries*, p. 242.
[149] *GASA*, ii. 401.
[150] For Fox's translation, see Collett, *Female Monastic Life in Early Tudor England*, and illustration 2. See also Power, *Medieval English Nunneries*, pp. 248–54.

There can be little doubt there were always a number, at times a majority, that received their elementary education on entry. The children presented for profession were surely illiterate; a proportion of the mature recruits, especially those seignieurs converted from a martial life, are also likely to have lacked the polish of the schoolroom: a (presumably well-born) youth entering Cluny was urged at once to apply himself to his letters 'since he was illiterate'.[151] In the later period in the women's houses it seems there was an expectation that the novice cohort as a whole would be placed under an 'eruditricem'.[152]

There are only hints and suggestions of the nature of this education in the earliest communities. Where a quantity of books was available, pupils probably followed some approximation of the syllabus of late antiquity, beginning with the precepts of Donatus and Priscian and progressing to selection of both pagan and Christian poetry. Odo of Cluny was said to have been schooled in Priscian and tempted by Virgil.[153] Michael Lapidge's analysis of the reading of Anglo-Saxon writers from Aldhelm to Wulfstan suggests a wider range of authorities than we might readily associate with an early monastery. The parity between monastic and secular pedagogy is reflected in the attraction of clerks and courtiers to the Benedictine cloister.[154] There were no purpose-made primers in the early period, and where no other works were available the psalter and the simple prayers of the liturgy were the most likely substitute. The reform movements of the ninth and tenth centuries ushered in texts for teaching prepared by monastic masters themselves. At Fulda, Master Hrabanus prepared a grammar which garnered classical principles for the use of a new generation of monastic students.[155] At the same period in England monastic culture was bilingual, and the structure of language was unfolded to pupils in manuals such as Ælfric's Latin–English grammar; according to Wulfstan, Æthelwold expected his Winchester novices to work from Latin to English and back again.[156] The Cluniac and Norman reform of the Benedictines, which coincided with the resurgence of secular schools in northern Europe, saw the return of a classicised curriculum of grammar teaching. At the abbey of Bec, Anselm encountered an array of ancient *auctores*, although he admitted later in a letter to Maurice there were many he had not mastered ('et aliis auctoribus quos a me non legisti').[157] Book lists give a good impression of the changing

[151] *John of Salerno*, p. 63.

[152] *Visitations*, ed. Jessopp, p. 243.

[153] The Augustan he judged 'a ... vessel, most beautiful indeed outside, but full of serpents within': *John of Salerno*, p. 14.

[154] M. Lapidge, *The Anglo-Saxon Library* (Oxford, 2006), p. 66; A. A. Grotans, *Reading in Medieval St Gall* (Cambridge, 2006), pp. 27–8.

[155] Hrabanus Maurus, *De institutione clericorum libris tres*, ed. D. Zimpel (Frankfurt, 1996). See also V. Law, *Grammar and Grammarians in the Early Middle Ages* (London, 1997), pp. 129–53 at 137.

[156] *Wulfstan*, pp. 46–8.

[157] *Eadmer*, p. 8&n.

character of the syllabus in the Gregorian period: at Reading Abbey, for example, a selection of Augustan poets appears, apparently by means of donation; at Christ Church, Canterbury, there were multiple copies, suggestive of the independent study of these authors; the collections of the female houses are poorly documented, but the testimony of Latin literacy suggests the schoolroom *auctores* were also known there.[158]

The range of these resources affirms that a Benedictine education embraced not only grammar, but also the remaining arts of the *trivium* (logic and rhetoric), and the *quadrivium* (arithmetic, astronomy, geometry, and music). The principal centres of the Carolingian reform (Fulda, Reichenau, Saint-Gall) had pioneered a monastic syllabus that recovered the ancient *artes liberales* as early as the eighth century. In the manuscripts of Saint-Gall it is possible to identify a programme of reading from which an able entrant might proceed from elementary grammar to early experiments in astronomical calculations.[159] It was this Carolingian model of monastic instruction which provided the foundation for teaching in the revived monasteries of the Low Countries, Normandy and England.[160]

Here there was an intersection between the novices and the unprofessed that were attracted into Benedictine precincts to learn from their masters. These secular pupils were intent on a syllabus of study which embraced the full complement of liberal arts, and it would appear that a proportion of the novices, the abler and elder among them, studied alongside them. This syllabus could not have been suited to every novice, nor could it have been accommodated in the twelve months or less that was the typical term. Those that pursued this programme therefore may have continued *in studendo* after their formal profession, or postponed their profession to prove their mastery in arts. This, apparently, was the experience of Æthelwold, who studied 'the liberal art of grammar and the honey-sweet system of metrics' for no fewer than seven years.[161]

Not every novice pursued such advanced studies. Generally it was only those that taught in the monastery school that wrote at length on the arts of *trivium* and original works in the *quadrivium* were rare indeed before the Benedictines arrived at the universities. If there was a tradition of monastic studies in grammar it was brief, beginning with Hrabanus and fading after Anselm's *De grammatico*, itself apparently little used in subsequent decades. Even when Anselm's fame was at its apogee, there was no expectation that everyone living under the *RB* should excel in arts. Jocelin of Brakelond believed there was much to be said for a monk who knew 'much concerning

[158] *AL*, pp. 8–10 (catalogue dating from *c.* 1170); *EBL*, B71. 172, 202–4, pp. 420–47; D. N. Bell, *What Nuns Read: Books and Libraries in Medieval English Nunneries*, Cistercian Studies Series 188 (1995), p. 118 (1a, b, Virgil, Cicero, *De officiis*, Barking).

[159] Grotans, *Reading in Medieval St Gall*, p. 77.

[160] Lapidge, *Anglo-Saxon Library*, p. 275&n. See also Law, *Grammar and Grammarians*, pp. 129–53 at 137.

[161] *Wulfstan*, pp. 14–15.

the rule and the customs of the Church though he be not so perfect a philosopher'.[162]

With the rise of the cathedral schools, and peripatetic masters, the monasteries lost their secular students, and perhaps also something of the vigour (and rigour) of their claustral schools. It is generally assumed their style of their schooling in the thirteenth century and later was introspective, in its scope limited to the requirements of customary observance. In fact the century after 1200 is too sparsely documented, in terms of book lists, surviving examples of primers, textbooks, or original compositions, to make any definitive deductions. Nonetheless, it would appear that Benedictine novice-masters were sensitive to wider trends in the teaching of grammar, and other elementary arts. Classical authorities fell out of favour, and in their place came the speculative grammars of contemporary scholastics, such as the *Summa* of Peter Elias.[163] The advent of academic study after 1250 compelled the monks to revise their provision for the teaching of arts. The capitular authorities envisaged the introduction of a curriculum that closely paralleled the arts course of the universities, 'primitive sciences' of grammar, logic and philosophy. To what extent this was ever realised in any house remains difficult to judge from the handful of books and documents now surviving. If library catalogues can offer any clue to patterns of teaching, it would appear, at least in England, the teaching of grammar did conform to contemporary clerical trends. In the century after 1350 the manuals of contemporary grammar masters were widely used by the monks, and classical *auctores* (and the medieval imitators) returned to the cloister cupboards. In England there was some effort to support the study of logic but texts of moral and natural philosophy appear only rarely.[164] There is some evidence of student monks pursuing Aristotle and his commentators in their university *studia*, an indication perhaps that opportunities were limited at home.[165] Of greater appeal in England were studies in applied rhetoric and the *ars dictaminis*: Thomas de la Mare, monk of St Albans, was dispatched to a dependent cell for a year after his profession to learn to compose letters 'as they do in the papal chancery'.[166] In the reformed congregations of Bursfeld, Melk and Padua, the teaching of arts in the cloister adhered self-consciously to humanist precepts. Here novices were introduced to the translations of Bruni and Guarino and the hitherto inaccessible learning of Greek antiquity. Nikolaus Ellenbog of Ottobeuren recalled a noviciate

---

[162] *Jocelin*, p. 10.
[163] For example, *EBL*, B68. 134, 369, B79. 198, pp. 365, 390, 520.
[164] Academic logic is represented in the fourteenth-century catalogue from Ramsey, but not among other extant inventories of the period: *EBL*, B68 (pp. 350–415).
[165] For example, the patterns of reading among the student monks of Worcester Priory: R. M. Thomson, 'Worcester Monks and Education, *c.* 1300', in *The Culture of Medieval English Monasticism*, ed. Clark, pp. 104–10.
[166] *GASA*, ii. 374.

passed compiling excerpts from the Plato of Marsilio Ficino.[167] Before the Reformation a taste of these trends could be found in English convents: at Reading the schoolmaster composed his own primer on classical rhetoric.[168]

As a counterpoint to language work, a Benedictine novice may have been taught the craft of writing. Scribal skills were prized by the Carolingian and Anglo-Saxon reformers, and although their scriptoria attracted secular craftsmen in the convents of men and women, there were also scribes and illuminators to be found among the professed. The training of the novice with stylus and parchment can be glimpsed in Orderic's account of Saint-Evroul, where the novice-master Osbern 'with his own hands ... made the metal stylus and wax covered tablets for the boys and beginners, and exacted the daily tasks from each individually'.[169] It is possible such training was paralleled throughout Benedictine networks in a period notable for book production. Female scribes flourished in the convents of Germany and northern France (although not England, it appears) before the close of the twelfth century.[170] Orderic understood 'to excel ... in writing' was a precondition of profession although not every house could claim a master craftsman.[171] The training of entrants in the craft of the scriptorium, and perhaps also the chancery, may have persisted in houses with a tradition of book production, or a volume of diplomatic business; among the women it appears to have been abandoned, and superiors of the later Middle Ages were obliged to employ a clerk for copying.[172] With a humanist sensibility towards the quality of script, the reformed congregation of Melk promulgated a programme of scribal training for their recruits in the mid-fifteenth century, although it does not appear to have spread to their affiliate congregations or further afield.[173]

At the same time as they were instructed in monastic observance, the (male) Benedictine also prepared for ordination to the priesthood. Benedict had not envisaged a community of monastic priests; his *opus Dei* was to be undertaken by *lay* brethren; priests were to be admitted into the community as a discrete body (*RB*, lx) but he displayed doubts as to the compatibility of priesthood with the monastic vocation: 'in consequence of the priesthood let him not forget the obedience and discipline of the rule'. He permitted brethren 'worthy to discharge the priestly office' to pursue ordination but only if the superior perceived the need (*RB*, lxii):

---

[167] F. Posset, *Renaissance Monks: Monastic Humanism in Six Biographical Sketches* (Leiden, 2005), p. 163.

[168] Leonard Coxe, *The Arte and Crafte of Rhetorycke* (London, 1532), STC5947. See also Clark, 'Monasteries and Secular Education', pp. 145–67.

[169] *Orderic*, ii. 107.

[170] A. I. Beach, *Women as Scribes: Book Production and Monastic Reform in Twelfth-Century Bavaria* (Cambridge, 2004), pp. 36–9 at 36 (Wessobrun), 68–72 (Admont).

[171] Ibid.

[172] *Visitations*, ed. Thompson, ii. 91; Power, *Medieval English Nunneries*, p. 250.

[173] S. H. Steinberg, 'Instructions in Writing by Members of the Congregation of Melk', *Speculum* 16:2 (1941), 210–15.

Abbot Berno of Cluny ordained the young Odo 'foreseeing what this most virtuous man was going to become'.[174] In these early centuries a monk might assume a position of some authority without priesthood: Paul Warnefrid, commentator on the *RB*, was styled 'deacon'; the diaconate does not appear to have been a bar to the office of superior.[175] Yet the elaboration of the Office between the ninth and eleventh centuries, and the growing interest in monastic intercession, stimulated a demand for priests in the professed community unforeseen by the founder. As the English Benedictines embraced common customs in the *Regularis Concordia*, Cluny began to extend its influence over the houses of France and northern Italy and reformed congregations arose elsewhere, there was an expectation that at least a fraction of the monastic community should be priested. Lanfranc's *Decreta* of *c.* 1070 referred to the presence of priests singular and plural, reflecting the diverse resources of the houses for which legislated; he also recognised the reliance on secular priests. While it was not yet a universal pathway, twelfth-century witnesses would suggest those that did not take orders were now a diminishing number. Orderic Vitalis, writing in 1100, referred to the progression 'by the usual stages' to the priesthood (in respect of his contemporary, Thierry of Bonneval) as a predictable, customary process ('per singulos gradus usque ad sacerdotium legitime ascendens').[176] By the end of the thirteenth century scarcely any Benedictine failed to ascend at least to the diaconate and only the demonstrably incapable were not presented for the priesthood.[177] In the pre-Reformation period the unpriested were classified by both regular and secular authorities as brethren of lower status. At the Tudor suppressions they were assigned only a meagre pension.[178]

For the male Benedictine, the ascent towards the priesthood was aligned closely, perhaps wholly, with the term of the noviciate itself. The rate of the novice's progress varied: there can be little doubt the ablest candidates were accelerated towards ordination, passing from acolyte to subdeacon in successive months, subject only to the sequence of the diocesan (or suffragan); by the same token candidates of doubtful competence or dubious conduct saw their progress stalled, or arrested, and sometimes were never

---

[174] *John of Salerno*, p. 39.

[175] For Paul the Deacon, see R. McKitterick, 'Paul the Deacon's *Historia langobardorum* and the Franks', in her *History and Memory in the Carolingian World* (Cambridge, 2004), pp. 60–83 at 68–9; H. Taviani-Carozzi, 'Le souvenir et la légende de Paule Diacre', in *Haut Moyen Âge: Culture, éducation et société: Études offertes à Pierre Riché*, ed. M. Sot (Paris, 1990), pp. 555–73. See also D. A. Bullough, '"Baiuli" in the Carolingian "regnum Langobardorum" and the Career of Abbot Walso (d. 813)', *EHR* 77 (1962), 625–37.

[176] *Orderic*, ii. 85.

[177] The trend towards a universal priesthood was perhaps more pronounced in England. It it worth noting that even in the fourteenth century (1320) scarcely half the professed brethren of Cluny were priests: D. Riche, *L'ordre de Cluny à la fin du moyen âge: le vieux pays clunisien, XIIe–XVe siècles* (Saint-Étienne, 2000), p. 378.

[178] *RO*, ii. 287.

permitted to progress further than their minor orders.[179] The pedagogic link between the noviciate and ordination was underpinned by the efforts of convents wherever possible to progress their candidates together as a cohort. At Westminster Abbey, for example, in the pre-Reformation period the brethren were presented for ordination in generational groups, approaching this sacramental rite alongside the colleagues with whom they had also shared their admission and clothing.[180] Of course, progression to the priesthood did not always coincide strictly with the completion of the noviciate. Where, for reasons of practicality, prior learning, or other privileges, the noviciate itself had been truncated, brethren were priested months, even a year or more, after their profession. In the later Middle Ages, candidates were presented for ordination from the monastic *studia* at Cambridge and Oxford, an indication that recruits had been hurried to the university ahead of their completion of the customary period of preparation.[181]

Customaries offer few insights into the instruction of ordinands. Above all, they were led to an understanding of the diaconate or priesthood by the example of their elders, as they did, to a degree, the *RB* and the Office. As priesting became more commonplace, there appears to have been greater recourse to preceptive manuals and other works of reference. Primers providing guidance on the mass, on confession and the pastoral code to be imparted to the penitent – comprising the commandments, mortal sins and cardinal virtues – were compiled for the particular use of monastic candidates. A compilation from Farfa (Perugia, Bibliotheca Communale Augusta, MS I. 17) contains the *Ordo penitentis*, perhaps for the purpose of preparing monk priests for the office of confessor.[182] In the later Middle Ages ordinands were also provided with examples of the expanding secular literature of priestcraft and pastoral theology. In pre-Reformation England Benedictine priests digested the same clerical manuals as their secular counterparts.[183] It should be noted that although Benedictine women did not receive holy orders, the record of their book collections suggests that in the high, and later Middle Ages, they were exposed to examples of the same pastoral literature as the men.[184]

The climax of the noviciate was the ceremony of profession. In the presence of the professed, and for the female novice, the supervisor of the house, the novice made a three-fold promise of stability, obedience and the conversion of morals.[185] The form of their profession was to be written, if possible, in their

---

[179] Clark, *Monastic Renaissance*, pp. 50–1.

[180] Harvey, 'A Novice's Life at Westminster', pp. 51–74.

[181] Clark, *Monastic Renaissance*, pp. 62–72 at 65.

[182] Boynton *Shaping a Monastic Identity*, pp. 235–6.

[183] *EBL*, B30. 12, B30. 98, B30. 107, B43. 40, 41a, 42, B100. 3, 66, 74, pp. 140, 149, 225–6, 599, 602.

[184] Bell, *What Nuns Read*, pp. 108–9 (4c: Beleth, Barking), 118 (2a: *De modo confitendi*, Barking), 120 (17b: Voragine, Barking).

[185] The supervisor of the nunnery sought to enforce the terms of the profession since it was feared that

own hand, and if not at least to bear their mark, and to be expressed in 'the name of the saints whose relics are there preserved' (*RB*, lviii).[186] The written profession was to be placed upon the altar as the novice intoned 'Uphold me O lord, according to Thy Word and I shall live, and let me not be confounded in my expectations' (Psalm 118 [119]:116). Profession was a moment of personal re-formation: the Eynsham customary reminded its brethren that in profession they became *new* men.[187] At their profession, the novice also released any remaining ties to the secular world, not least any properties to which they might lay title. The surrender of the self was underlined in the 817 injunction that the monk should remain hooded for three days following their profession.[188]

It was perhaps also at their profession that medieval Benedictines adopted their name in religion. The substitution of a baptismal name for one of devotional resonance was not a universal custom, and waned and waxed with successive currents of reform. It would seem such names were conferred upon the monk as often as they were chosen. At times they were a mark of distinction. The Norman novice William Bollein 'grew to be of such sound character and application in his studies that he earned the name of Gregory'.[189] Here, in a period before family names and with a common fund of popular forenames, the impulse was as much pragmatic as it was spiritual: personal suffixes were popular. In England it would seem names in religion were outmoded from the end of the twelfth century; the pre-Reformation generation of English Benedictines was notable for its choice of names connected with the early history of the monastic order in England: Augustine, Dunstan, Oswald.[190] In the later Middle Ages, profession was also the moment that the brethren shed their family name for what was usually a toponym. The rationale for the selection of toponyms and their precise connection with place of birth or family remain obscure. However, their diversity might suggest they did reflect individual identity.

Profession was also a point of departure. The Benedictines' formal entry into the community of the professed was not infrequently followed by dispatch to a house distant from the one where they had passed the noviciate. The proliferation of foundations, and the formation of affiliate networks, demanded this diaspora not only to secure observant life in remote

women would find themselves 'unable to bear the burden of the quire': *Visitations*, ed. Thompson, i. 53; Oliva, *Convent and Community*, p. 52.

[186] See also *Smaragdi abbatis expositio*, ed. Spannagel and Engelbert, pp. 291–9. Lanfranc recognised that the *professus* might not have been able to write: *MC*, pp. 158–9.

[187] *Customary of Eynsham*, ed. Gransden pp. 30–1.

[188] MGH Capitula I: xvi, p. 476 (469–81).

[189] *Orderic*, ii. 87.

[190] Such names are recorded among the religious of suppressed houses: D. S. Chambers, *Faculty Office Registers, 1534–49* (Oxford, 1966), pp. 123, 158, 202. J. G. Clark, 'Humanism and Reform in Pre-Reformation English Monasteries', *Transactions of the Royal Historical Society*, 6th series, 19 (2009), 57–94.

settlements but also to sustain the spirit of reform. In Cluniac Normandy, novices may have been trained in the principal monasteries but they were subsequently dispersed among their smaller satellites.[191] Throughout the medieval period there were houses that served as seminaries for the regional congregation as a whole. In the earliest period of English Benedictinism, Glastonbury appears to have played such a role; after the Dunstanian reform, Winchester was also prominent as a seed-bed of monastic leaders; later the Canterbury convents, Westminster and St Albans each saw their *professi* pursue careers elsewhere.[192] In the later Middle Ages the new congregation of Padua practised the 'migration of brethren' ('mutationes fratrum') as a tool of reform. Independent abbeys that retained dependent cells also deployed their ablest in this way. St Albans Abbey, the parent of no fewer than ten cells, drew novices to the mother-house for their profession and then returned them to the provinces.[193] A *professus* might also make a personal request to transfer to another monastery. Later medieval generations, in particular, were conscious of the variations in discipline and observant character among houses of the same congregation and sometimes sought greater (and lesser) rigour, or even a better quality of liturgical music, elsewhere.[194]

Opus Dei

The *opus Dei* was the *raison d'être* of the professed Benedictine. The physical and mental strictures of the *RB*, and the intellectual and spiritual training devised by its disciples, were conceived purely to support the sequence of offices, masses and other observances that punctuated the conventual day: 'giving up their own will' to follow 'the master's command and the disciple's finished work' (*RB*, v). The sequence of day and night offices was not new to Benedict: it had been an evolving element of monastic practice since at least the second century and appeared in a form comparable to the *RB* in fourth-century monasteries witnessed by Cassian and in the pioneering colonies of southern France, such as those supervised by Caesarius of Arles.[195] It is often claimed that Benedict's achievement was to codify diffuse forms of observance, but the foundation of a common *horarium* was already apparent at the beginning of the sixth century, and to his

[191] Chibnall, *World of Orderic Vitalis*, pp. 65–8.
[192] Clark, *Monastic Renaissance*, pp. 50–1; Thomas Elmham, of St Augustine's Canterbury, was promoted to the priorate at the Cluniac house of Lenton.
[193] Clark, *Monastic Renaissance*, p. 50.
[194] For example, William Powns, monk of St Albans, who may be identified as one of the two monks of that house who requested a transfer on the grounds of the poor quality of the music: Amundesham, *Annales monasterii S. Albani*, ed. Riley, i. 89–91; *Stone*, pp. 186–7. Christ Church, Canterbury, certainly valued its music. Stone commends the contributions of a long-serving precentor and organist: ibid., pp. 11–12.
[195] Dunn, *Emergence of Monasticism*, pp. 93–6.

contemporaries the *RB* appeared to be only one of a number of regional and stylistic variants. Benedict's primary contribution was to synthesise the practice of the churches of Rome with emerging monastic custom. Over time his recension also proved to possess a clarity and simplicity – a certain sparseness of description – that rendered it more adaptable to different cultural, ecclesiastical and institutional circumstances.

The development of Benedictine life over the Middle Ages was driven in large measure by the demands of the *opus Dei*. The primary impulse in the first phases of reform in the ninth (Benedict of Aniane) and tenth (Berno of Cluny) centuries was for a return to *ad literam* observance of the Office. The pioneers at Cluny privileged the *opus* at the expense of other occupations: Anselm of Canterbury later confessed to a fear of their regime: 'If at Cluny ... all the time I have spent in study will be lost.'[196] Later codes, Æthelwold's *Regularis Concordia* and Lanfranc's *Decreta*, aimed to embellish the *opus* so as to enhance its spiritual power but not to alter its essential structure. In the Gregorian period, as the clerical orders multiplied, the *opus Dei* was upheld by the governors of the order, and by its secular observers, as the monks' distinctive contribution to Mother Church and their most valuable currency in the material world. After 1215 papal reformers sought to stem what they saw to be an incipient decline. Yet the chapters of the Benedictines were concerned to lighten the liturgical burden, not only the supernumerary commemorations required by benefactors, but also the incremental elaboration of the Office itself. The 1277 canons of the English chapters trimmed psalms and responses from the daytime offices and sought to standardise and simplify the seasonal variations; further revisions were promulgated in 1343 and again in 1444.[197] The pressure for pure observance of the Benedictine Office remained constant at least in England, where the intervention of the Lancastrian regime – at the Council of Westminster in 1421 – added weight to the views of episcopal visitors. These tensions should not be interpreted as a sign of the terminal decline of the *opus Dei* or the abandonment of the Office. The capitular canons had removed accretions and anomalous variations, but the rhythm of the liturgical round remained intact. There were perhaps greater interruptions to traditional observance in the reformed congregations of Bursfeld, Melk and Padua, where the observant hours were eclipsed by a programme of claustral lectures. Certainly, in England the patterns of liturgy familiar to Black Monks of the early and high Middle Ages were still performed on the eve of the Dissolution. At Evesham Abbey the completion of the office was the final act of the brethren before passing out of the precinct forever.[198]

---

[196] *Eadmer*, p. 9.
[197] *Chapters*, ed. Pantin, i. 64–92; ii. 28–62; iii. 187–220.
[198] M. D. Knowles and T. Dart, 'Notes on a Bible of Evesham Abbey', *EHR* 79 (1964), 775–8.

The *opus* was laborious indeed. The Office occupied the Benedictines for fourteen of their nineteen daytime hours. Benedict prescribed seven day offices – Lauds, Prime, Terce, Sext, Nones, Vespers, Compline – since thus the 'sacred sevenfold number [Psalm 118] will be fulfilled' (*RB*, xvi), to be preceded by a night office commonly known as Matins or Nocturns, from the phases of which it is comprised. The sevenfold sequence was not Benedict's invention but the offices of Lauds, Prime and Compline were only in their infancy and his, and other monastic rules of the period, did represent a refinement of the leaner, five-office sequence of the patristic pioneers. To these eight offices a conventual mass (High Mass or Principal Mass) was added after Sext. Although not prescribed by Benedict, its place in the *horarium* appears to have been fixed before the close of the seventh century. From the tenth century another, subsidiary, mass was adopted to be celebrated after Terce. In England this 'morrow' mass was codified in the *Regularis Concordia*, although perhaps it reflected earlier customs.[199] Such additions in the day hours perhaps contributed to the eclipse of Compline as a communal office. Certainly by the close of the eleventh century it appears to have become a semi-private observance, at least in England. Lanfranc expected it to be 'recited in a low voice by groups of two or three' ('dicant completorium bini aut terni sub silentio') although followed by the *Trina oratio*. Although the length and timing of these offices did vary somewhat over time and region, there was no further development in the sequence before the Reformation.

The Benedictine Office was built on the psalms. Early cenobitic observance had incorporated the psalms, but Benedict made them the core of his *horarium*. The night office, and each of the daytime offices, comprised a sequence of psalms, seven principals at night and three for each of the daytime hours, interwoven with hymns, prayers and readings, verses and responses. The centrality of the psalms was reflected in the *RB*'s concern for the manner of its performance: 'sing wisely [Psalm 46[47]:8]' the brethren were warned, as it 'becometh us to behave in the sight of God and His angels, and let us so stand to sing, that our mind may be in harmony with our voice' (*RB*, xix). Benedict adopted the pattern of *psalterium per hebdomadum*, common in the churches of Rome, by which the psalms were recited over the course of one week, in preference to the older custom of *psalterium currens* which required the psalter to be performed in fixed order, and then repeated. Moreover, he assigned particular psalms, and sequences of psalms, to each of the offices, the selection made to match the theme of the psalm with the mood or purpose of the hour. Although the principals were always different, a common thread of sequential verses from Psalm 118 connected the four daytime hours of Prime, Terce, Sext and Nones. Benedict did not

---

[199] *RC*, p. 34.

93

reject the contemporary ideal of completing the psalter in a single cycle of the Office but prescribed that 'the rest of the psalms which remain over be divided equally into [the] seven night offices' (*RB*, xviii). The psalmody of the *RB* set it apart not only from contemporary monastic customs, of Caesarian and Cassinian origin, but also from the later rules of Columban, Fructuosus and Isidore of Seville.[200]

The Carolingian, Anglo-Saxon and Cluniac reform movements each elaborated on the sequence of psalms prescribed by the *RB*. Benedict of Aniane required the recitation of the fifteen gradual psalms (and their respective collects (prayers) before Matins. The *Regularis Concordia* introduced three substantial cycles: the seven penitential psalms (6, 32, 38, 51, 102, 130, 143) to be performed at Matins and Prime; the *Trina oratio*, a three-fold subdivision of all, or some of the same seven, performed daily at Matins, Terce and Compline, together with prayers (*oratio*), an appropriate collect and *Pater noster*; and, of the three, the most significant innovation, a sequence of between two and four *psalmi familares*, chosen to commemorate the monarch and any other patron, benefactor or kinsfolk known to the monastery. Æthelwold also prescribed the reading of the sequence as 'apt for driving away the temptations of the devil' ('ad tentationem diabolicam devincendam psallendo').[201] Lanfranc's *Decreta* added no fewer than thirty psalms to the winter observance of Matins, the first ten (*decedae*) for the dead, the second for the monastic community, and the last for benefactors and kinsfolk.[202] As the obligation for extra-liturgical observance grew, the burden of these extended offices became intolerable. At least from the thirteenth century it was common for the strict requirements to be relaxed. In England the capitular authorities codified this in their canons of 1277 and 1343, under which several psalms were trimmed from the Office; the reformed congregations of mainland Europe also made reductions to make space for an expanded programme of study.[203]

Psalmody was the dominant language of the cloister. Even as they processed every hour to and from the choir, the early codes required the monastic community, man and boy, to recite the psalms. Between the offices, and seasonally, when a given office was cut short, the unoccupied brethren were to take up their psalter. Whatever duty they undertook, whether spiritual or temporal, the brethren were to preface it with the blessing 'Deus in adiutorium meum intende', derived from Psalm 69.[204] Psalter discipline ('de disciplina psallendi': *RB*, xv) also served as a punishment for egregious errors.

---

[200] Dunn, *Emergence of Monasticism*, pp. 87–95, 105–7; J. Dyer, 'The Monastic Psalmody of the Middle Ages', *Rev. Bén.* 99 (1989), 241–74; 100 (1990), 41–84; Dreuille, *The Rule of St Benedict and the Ascetic Traditions*, pp. 189–204.

[201] *RC*, p. 16.

[202] *MC*, p. 11.

[203] *Chapters*, ed. Pantin, i. 64–92; ii. 28–62.

[204] *RC*, pp. 20–1.

The negligent monk might be sentenced to the recitation of the psalter in its entirety.[205]

The psalm sequences were connected by a repertory of antiphons, prayers, readings, responsories and hymns. For the most part, the *RB* imported these features from contemporary monastic and secular practice. Antiphons were sung scriptural phrases and sentences that were paired with the psalms. Latin antiphony was still evolving in the sixth century, and it was to Benedict's disciple and hagiographer, Gregory, that the popular medieval cycle is attributed.[206] The purpose of the antiphon was to attenuate the psalm and at first they were particularly focusd on Matins for which the psalmody was most elaborate. The *RB* required antiphons to follow all but one of the eight psalms (*RB*, ix) but there was to be only one antiphon at Lauds and none at Prime; they were only to be performed at Terce, Sext and Nones 'if the brotherhood is large' (*RB*, xvii). Later, antiphons were added to the day offices for particular feasts.[207]

The collects and prayers of the *RB* were also derived from those in common use, although Benedict prescribed their performance, with 'humility and reverence', observing also, 'prayer ought to be short and pure, unless, perhaps it is lengthened by the inspiration of divine grace' (*RB*, xx). Prayers for special purposes were added in subsequent centuries. Lanfranc's *Decreta* promulgated prayers 'for every degree of the church' and required the *preces*, one of the earliest prayer cycles of the Roman church, to be performed after each of the four principal day offices.[208]

The Office was attenuated by readings. The *RB* required three readings at Matins, together with the lesson of the Apostle, but none at Lauds, Vespers or Compline and one only in the four principal day hours (*RB*, xvii). The adoption of the Roman *ordo librorum ad legendum* in the ninth century imported a larger schedule of readings: its scale is embodied (literally) in the 'giant' bibles of Cluny, whose format was to facilitate their reading at night.[209] Within a century of the Anianian reform it appears the *ordines librorum* had passed into general use. The readings were not only from scripture; the *RB* also prescribed 'the most eminent orthodox and Catholic Fathers' (*RB*, ix). By the tenth century, patristic authorities were prominent among the daily *lectiones*: for the feast of the Holy Trinity at the Cluniac convent of Farfa there were no fewer than eleven readings from the

---

[205] For example, *Statuta Casinensia*, ii. 115–41, ed. K. Hallinger *et al.*, CCM 7 (Sieburg, 1975), pp. 224–6.

[206] J. Harper, *The Forms and Orders of Western Liturgy from the Tenth to the Eighteenth Century* (Oxford, 1991), pp. 78–97.

[207] For the integration of antiphons in the Office, see Harper, *Forms and Orders of Western Liturgy*, pp. 73–107; A. W. Robertson, 'From Office to Mass: The Antiphons of Vespers and Lauds and the Antiphons before the Gospel in Northern France', in *Divine Office in the Latin Middle Ages*, ed. Fassler and Baltzer, pp. 300–23. For the elaboration of antiphons at Cluny under Odo, see *John of Salerno*, pp. 11–12.

[208] *MC*, pp. 14–15, 30–1, also 10–11, 26–7, 44–5, 52–3.

[209] Reilly, 'Cluniac Giant Bible', pp. 164–5.

pseudo-Ambrose and nine from Bede's Homily on John.[210] The sequence of readings for Matins constituted a self-contained scriptural commentary and it is indicative that one early codex containing the liturgy was annotated in the same manner as a book of biblical glosses. To these scriptures in time were added historical narratives of devotional significance. For the feast of Benedict, readings were extracted from the *acta* recounted in Gregory's *Dialogues*. As the number of new foundations and the scale of their networks steadily grew, the *lectiones* of the Office also served as an arena for formulating, and reinforcing, conventual identity. At Farfa, passages from the foundation history of the house were employed in the readings for Matins.[211]

Of these features of the Office, it was Benedict's use of hymns that represented the greatest novelty. Hymns had been performed in the secular church at least since the fourth century; Ambrose of Milan (d. 397) was widely known as the father of the tradition. Yet before the *RB* they were not a routine feature of monastic worship. Benedict required a hymn in each of the offices, night and day; those for the night and the principal day offices were to be selected according to the hour, those for Lauds and Vespers were taken from the Ambrosian hymnary (*RB*, xii, xvii). The hymn offered an opportunity for innovation within the framework of the Office; the number of new compositions rose steadily from the eighth to the twelfth century. Lanfranc of Bec commissioned the monk Osbern to compose a passion of St Alphege as a hymn which might be performed at Matins on the saint's feast day ('auctorizatam in ecclesia Dei legi cantarique instituit').[212] Orderic remembered a fellow monk of Saint-Evroul, Roger of Le Sap, for his composition of hymns.[213] Even at the height of the monastic schools, the hymn remained a popular genre among monastic writers. Abbot Peter the Venerable of Cluny was the author of two celebrated hymns in honour of St Benedict.[214]

Throughout the Middle Ages the exact form of the Benedictine Office was varied by season, festival, and even by virtue of regional affiliation. The *RB* varied the content of night and daytime offices according to the seasonal and hebdomadal cycle. There was a general distinction between the summer and winter months. The heat of the Beneventan day, and the need for the self-sufficient *cenobium* to secure its harvest, necessitated the trimming of day and night offices: at Matins there was only one (Old Testament) reading and responsory (*RB*, x). The short hours of daylight and the harsh climate of the winter months required their own remissions: in *RB* Matins

---

[210] Boynton, *Shaping of a Monastic Identity*, p. 70.
[211] Ibid., pp. 39–41.
[212] *Eadmer*, p. 54.
[213] *Orderic*, ii. 109.
[214] Boynton, *Shaping a Monastic Identity*, p. 187.

was to be earlier, to enable a rest-period before Lauds; the tenth-century *Regularis Concordia* required shorter hymns on these shorter days. There were also particular customs for Sunday. The first day of the week, in the *RB* it marked the resumption of the psalter cycle, since the brethren should 'always start again from the beginning' (*RB*, xviii). Sunday matins was a longer observance, involving two clusters of four lessons and responsories as well as a gospel reading from the abbot (*RB*, xi); Sunday Lauds was therefore shorter (*RB*, xii). The four principal day offices were to be lengthened on a Sunday with portions of Psalm 118 (*RB*, xviii). These variant forms were followed by later Benedictines, although northern houses did not always recognise the need for summer remissions: in his open letter to the brethren of Eynsham, Ælfric reminded them that the *RB* was written for a *cenobium* in the climate of the Benevento.[215] The diversity of liturgical forms here cannot be underestimated. Before the close of the twelfth century Benedictine Europe, even its Italian and French heartland, still harboured at least trace of eastern liturgies; in Iberia the Mozarabic tradition was formally rejected in 1085 but remained pervasive at least until the fifteenth-century *reconquista*.[216]

The greatest number of additions and elaborations were made for the feasts of saints and other seasonal festivals. In the *RB* itself the festive variations were few: Matins was to be observed in its Sunday form (*RB*, xiv), and there were to be seasonal changes to the Alleluia, from Easter to Pentecost and from the latter to Lent (*RB*, xv). Later codes were more complex. The *Regularis Concordia* specified additional ceremonies for the celebration of Christmas and Epiphany and also acknowledged that local cults would require special observance.[217] Lanfranc's *Decreta* added further to the tally of festal observances for English Benedictines: Holy Innocents, John the Apostle, Stephen and Sylvester were all to be marked with special observances.[218] While Æthelwold had placed particular emphasis on Christmas observances, Lanfranc elaborated the ceremonies for Easter, which included the presentation of boughs, flowers and palms on a carpet before the High Altar (for Palm Sunday), the performance of antiphony between the offices of the day and the Cluniac custom of lighting the High Altar with candles

---

[215] '... but we who live in Britain': *Ælfric's Letter to the Monks of Eynsham*, ed. Jones, pp. 138–9.
[216] Harper, *Forms and Orders of Western Liturgy*, p. 17. See also P. Jeffrey, 'Eastern and Western Elements in the Irish Monastic Prayers of the Hour', in *Divine Office in the Latin Middle Ages*, ed. Fassler and Baltzer, pp. 99–143 at 101. For a useful summary of the Mozarabic tradition, see L. M. F. Bosch, *Art Liturgy and Legend in Renaissance Toledo: The Mendoza and Iglesia Primada* (University Park, PA, 2000), pp. 57–60. See also L. Vones, 'The Substitution of the Hispanic Liturgy by the Roman Rite in the Kingdoms of the Iberian Peninsula', in *Hispania Vetus: Musical-Liturgical Manuscripts from Visigothic Origins to the Franco-Roman Transition (9th–12th Centuries)*, ed. S. Zapke (Bilbao, 2007), pp. 43–59; J. F. O'Callaghan, 'The Integration of Christian Spain into Europe: the Role of Alfonso VI of Léon-Castile', in *Santiago, Saint-Denis and Saint Peter: The Reception of the Roman Liturgy in Léon-Castile in 1080*, ed. B. F. Reilly (New York, 1985), pp. 101–30.
[217] *RC*, pp. 28–31.
[218] *MC*, pp. 22–3.

on the eve of Good Friday. The Aachen synod had favoured no fewer than eleven feast days in the calendar, but later customaries were more selective.[219] Bernard of Cluny identified five to be observed as major feasts: Christmas, Easter, Pentecost, Peter and Paul and the Assumption of the Blessed Virgin Mary.[220] The English codes, *Regularis Concordia* and the *Decreta Lanfranci*, incorporated All Saints among the major feasts. Lanfranc also identified feasts of second rank: the Ascension, the Annunciation and Purification of the Virgin, SS Gregory, Michael and Andrew, and the saints of English affinity, Alphege and Augustine of Canterbury.[221] Second only to the principal feasts of the calendar was that of the monastery's patronal saint. Orderic Vitalis described how the feast of his patronal saint, Evroul, was elaborated with 'nine antiphons and three repsonsories'.[222] From the twelfth century, such was the number and variety of feasts, it became common for customaries to distinguish between major and minor festivals; in calendars the status of the feast was identified in terms of the different vestments required, albs, caps, copes, etc.[223] Festive variations were a means for the monastic community to formulate their local identity, to foster internal cohesion, external patronage, and to respond to corporate colleagues and rivals. The nuns of Swaffham Bulbeck (Cambridgeshire) were said (1373) to have adapted their offices for the commemoration of their own saints to the extent that the customary of Ely, their supervisor, was scarcely recognisable.[224]

In the secular church, the mass represented the summit of observance, but for the Benedictines it was an adjunct to the Office. The mass entered the monastic *horarium* before the close of the eighth century. Its advance coincided with, and perhaps accelerated, the decline of manual labour. In his commentary on the *RB* Hildemar reflected 'now the mass is sung, the brethren do no work until the end of the tenth hour'.[225] The mass was positioned at the mid-point of the day's observance, after Sext. It was formed of four phases: the introit, incorporating a psalm, antiphon, epistle and gospel readings and the *Gloria in excelsis* and Alleluia; the preparation, comprising prayers and responsories, the *Credo, Sanctus, Benedictus*, Lord's Prayer and *Agnus Dei*; the communion, and closing prayers. The mass differed sharply from the Office since it was not, strictly speaking, a communal performance: the celebrant priest and (where present) his assistants conducted the liturgy of the mass in the sanctuary of the oratory, set apart from their

[219] *Initia consuetudinis Benedictinae*, ed. Hallinger, pp. 469–81 at 475–5.
[220] Boynton, *Shaping a Monastic Identity*, pp. 39, 156&n, 159.
[221] *RC*, pp. xxxii, 15, 22, 26, 29, 55, 58; *MC*, pp. 89, 95.
[222] *Orderic*, ii. 109.
[223] Harper, *Forms and Orders of Western Liturgy*, p. 54.
[224] *VCH Cambridgeshire*, ii. 226–9 at 227. Interestingly, the women were advised to reserve these commemorations for their private devotions.
[225] *Warnefrid-Hildemar*, p. 116.

brethren assembled in the choir. The choir monks or nuns contributed to the chanted portions of the Office – the antiphons, verses and responses. The result was a liturgical and musical dialogue, the aural effect of which was comparable to a motet.

At least from the tenth century a second mass entered the *horarium*, positioned after Terce. In England it was known as the 'morrow' mass; under the *Regularis Concordia* it was to be performed as a commemoration of the monarch, or 'for any other pressing need' ('uel quacumque imminente necessitate').[226] Before the end of the eleventh century the 'morrow' mass became enshrined in English customaries. Lanfranc's *Decreta* suggested brethren might be absent from this secondary mass, but over time it appears that English Benedictines were accustomed to attend the first mass of the day but not the later service, by which time they were occupied with their administrative or pastoral offices.[227]

For much of the medieval period, the Office was accompanied by discrete offices dedicated to a special purpose. The most common was the Office of the Dead, which comprised the three offices by which the brethren marked the turn of the day: Vespers, routinely the final office before they retired to the dormitory, Matins, the night office, and Lauds, the office with which they greeted the dawn. For the Dead, these offices were recast, to incorporate psalms, antiphons, readings and responsories appropriate to the theme; hymns were also omitted. The Office of the Dead was formulated during the reform of Benedict of Aniane; by the tenth century it was a common feature of customaries, and it remained among the principal obligations of observant Benedictines to the end of the Middle Ages. Conceived as a commemoration for deceased brethren, it was soon appropriated as a suffrage for patrons and benefactors. In the later Middle Ages capitular and episcopal visitors complained of its decline as a monastic observance: in England the capitular president, Abbot Thomas de la Mare of St Albans (1349–96), attempted to revive it at his own house, and within the congregation as a whole.[228]

The Little Office of the Blessed Virgin Mary also emerged in the eighth century, perhaps first in a Benedictine context, at Montecassino, where Warnefrid described it simply as an office 'which it is customary to perform in honour of the Holy Mother of God'.[229] The Little Office was integrated within the day's cycle of offices, offering a concurrent sequence of antiphons, prayers, psalms, readings and responsories with a Marian theme.

---

[226] *RC*, p. 16.
[227] *MC*, pp. 7–9.
[228] *GASA*, ii. 418–44 at 428–9.
[229] Harper, *Forms and Orders of Western Liturgy*, pp. 46, 133–4; R. A. Baltzer, 'The Little Office of the Virgin, and Mary's Role at Paris', in *Divine Office in the Latin Middle Ages*, ed. Fassler and Baltzer, pp. 463–84. See also *The Monastic Breviary of Hyde Abbey, Winchester*, ed. J. B. L. Tolhurst, HBS (1932), p. 148.

It was known in northern monasteries before AD 1000, but was not a universal feature of the *horarium* until the end of the eleventh century.[230]

The Office was cemented in the *horarium* by a cycle of quasi-liturgical ceremonies and processions. There was a foretaste in the *RB*: the reception of guests incorporated communal prayer and reading ('Legatur coram hospite lex divina ut aedificetur': *RB*, liii) and the ceremony of the Maundy also. Later codes increased their frequency and elaborated their form. The *Regularis Concordia* required formal processions of professed brethren and children to precede each of the daily offices; these were retained in the *Decreta Lanfranci*, which for certain festivals required the brethren to be vested in albs.[231] For Sunday observances, the processions, like the offices, were lengthened. At Durham Priory not only did it pass every one of the subordinate altars on its progress to the choir, but also each chamber of the monastic enclosure, even the dormitory.[232]

For their patronal festival, and perhaps for other major feasts, the monastic community carried their processions beyond the monastic precinct. On the feast of St Alban the abbot led his brethren through the gatehouse bearing precious plate and relics; they crossed the marketplace and gathered at the door of the principal parish church to preach a sermon.[233] These processions could also be mobilised *in extremis* to provide succour to the unprofessed: in the summer of 1437 the monks of Worcester priory processed to meadows outside the city to call upon their patron to end the 'continuall reine'.[234] The continued elaboration of these ceremonies tended to eclipse the Office itself: Jocelin of Brakelond described, with frustration implied, how 'thrice every week [we] prostrate[e] ourselves in the choir after leaving the chapter house and singing the seven penitential psalms'.[235] At least at the principal monastic churches, the commitment to ceremonial remained undiminished. A memoir of Durham Priory described the daily procession preceding the high (principal) mass, in which three monks and a verger 'with a tipt staffe in his hand as it was his office so to doe' proceeded to the lectern for the reading of the epistle and gospel.[236]

It should be noted there was a liturgical dimension to other duties of the daily *horarium*. The profession of the novice incorporated a phrase from Psalm 118, also performed in the four principal offices of the day. The Maundy ceremony culminated with a phrase from Psalm 47:10 repeated by the superior, 'We have received Thy mercy, O God, in the midst of Thy

[230] Harper, *Forms and Orders of Western Liturgy*, pp. 133–6; *Divine Office in the Latin Middle Ages*, ed. Fassler and Baltzer, pp. 463–84. See also *Monastic Breviary of Hyde Abbey*, ed. Tolhurst, pp. 120–9.

[231] *RC*, pp. 13, 16, 21, 23; *MC*, pp. 4–5, 24–5, 34–5, 66–7, 72–3, 94–5.

[232] *Rites of Durham*, ed. Raine, p. 7.

[233] Clark, *Monastic Renaissance*, pp. 33–4 at 33.

[234] *VCH Worcestershire*, ii. 94–112 at 107.

[235] *Jocelin*, p. 11.

[236] *Rites of Durham*, ed. Raine, p. 7.

temple'. The daily chapter – embedded from the end of the ninth century – carried its own liturgical routine. The *Regularis Concordia* required the reading of the conventual martyrology, the verses, *Pretiosa in conspecti Domini, Deus in adiutorium meum intende*, repeated three times, together with the collect, to be followed by the Gloria, the verse *Et ne nos inducas* (recited by the prior) and conventual response, *Respice in servos*, closing with the Gloria and two further collects. After the business was concluded, the chapter was to close with the recitation of five psalms for the dead. Cluniac customaries also developed observances for certain moments of community action: the *Adventus* was a liturgical greeting for a visiting prelate; the *Clamor* was a liturgical malediction conveyed to the enemies of the community.[237]

In parallel with the *opus Dei*, the Benedictine was expected to follow a pattern of private devotion. Benedict conceived of prayer (*RB*, xx) as both a communal exercise ('in conventu') and a personal experience ('in puritate cordis et compunctione lacrimarum'); thus following the Office the community were encouraged (if not obliged) to remain in the oratory for private prayer (*RB*, lii). The earliest evidenced customs of Cluny referred to these solitary suffrages in the oratory as *particular* (*peculium*; a phrase later given for the monk's stipend).[238] Some later customaries assigned the period between Matins and Lauds as the (only) time for such prayer but at the Cluniac abbey of Vallombrosa in the eleventh century the particular had been reinvented as a communal observance of individual devotion, directed by the superior.[239]

The liturgical regime of the Benedictine monastery placed a formidable burden on its members. The early canons and commentaries on the *RB* admitted no dispensations from the daily round. The rapid growth of administrative, educational and pastoral responsibilities, however, required superiors and their deputies to be freed from the demands of the full *horarium*. Lanfranc's *Decreta* accounted for the absence of the superior from the offices and the masses of the day.[240] The division of conventual administration among a succession of obediences created a further challenge to full observance: neither local nor capitular canons formally dispensed the obedientiaries from the *horarium* but their frequent injunction for officers to attend a minimum of the hours indicates that non-attendance was widespread; Lanfranc expected the professed to recite the offices as best they could when absent on business, even on horseback.[241] The advent of formal academic study at the end of the thirteenth century detached

---

[237] Boynton, *Shaping of a Monastic Identity*, pp. 127, 131–5.
[238] Ibid., p. 90.
[239] Ibid, p. 90.
[240] *MC*, p. 57.
[241] *Visitations*, ed. Thompson, iii. 273, 277, 279 (Peterborough, 1437), 290, 292 (Peterborough, 1446–7); *Chapters*, ed. Pantin, iii. 280 (visitation of Whitby, 1366); *MC*, pp. 96–8.

another section of the community from their liturgical duties. Ostensibly monks at the university *studia* were to observe the hours in their chapel, but capitular correspondence suggests the requirement was often ignored.[242] At any rate, at home the students were released from the morning offices to allow time at their books.[243] Beyond these elites, the cloister monks and nuns were prone to resist the daily duties of the *horarium*.[244]

Music

The *opus Dei* was always a musical performance. Benedict appointed a cantor to chant the verses and responses (*RB*, ix), but he impressed upon all his brethren their individual responsibility as singers: 'let us consider how it becometh us to behave in the sight of God and His angels and let us so stand to sing, that our mind may be in harmony with our voice' (*RB*, xix). The brethren were expected to be adequate singers, but Benedict recognised that not every one would be able; for the solo performance in the frater he advised 'the brethren will not read or sing in order, but only those who edify their hearers' (*RB*, xxxviii). The priority that Benedict attached to aural, as much mental and spiritual experience of their worship challenged the conservatism of earlier rules and the precepts of the fathers: for Jerome, 'sweetness of voice is not required, but a proper mental disposition'.[245] Benedict reflected the values of the church(es) of Rome, which were already renowned for their refinement of customary patterns of liturgical performance. It was an approach that was not always affirmed by the early adherents of the *RB*: the commentators Warnefrid and Hildemar felt it necessary to remind the cantor of their obligation to please 'not with their voices but with the words they sing, for thus they will seek the advancement and salvation of the people'.[246] Yet as foundations proliferated following the Carolingian reform, it was articulated with increasing force.[247] For the patrons of this period the style of liturgical performance appealed as much as its substance. Patronal charters sometimes specified the musical mode of the proposed commemoration: Pope John VII (705–7) granted Farfa Abbey a privilege on condition the brethren 'persist day and night in the singing of hymns, psalms and spiritual songs'.[248] Cluny represented the high-water mark of this trend. Before 1100 and the emergence of cathedral and collegiate chapters the Burgundian mother-house and its significant satellites served as the creative heartland of Latin music. The monastic commitment to music came under strain, however, as the demand for suffrages drew brethren away

[242] *Chapters*, ed. Pantin, ii. 55–8 at 57; iii. 54–5 at 55.
[243] Clark, *Monastic Renaissance*, pp. 66, 128–32; Dobson, *Durham Priory*, pp. 68–9.
[244] *Visitations*, ed. Thompson, i. 51 (Elstow, 1421–2), 66 (Godstow, 1432–4), 102, 104 (Ramsey, 1432).
[245] Ep. 125, *Ad Rusticum monachum*, 15: CSEL 56: 134.
[246] *Warnefrid-Hildemar*, pp. 163–4.
[247] Boynton, *Shaping a Monastic Identity*, p. 4.
[248] Ibid., p. 4.

from the daily Office. From 1300 visitors frequently complained of the poor quality of monastic voices, an indication perhaps that regular and sustained performance was no longer a matter of course. Nonetheless, monastic music appears to have held its appeal among lay benefactors, if only by force of the number of potential performers (in a monastery of fifty or more). In the century before the Reformation their innovations in polyphony and their investment in secular cantors, organists, and singers (both men and boys) brought the greater Benedictine abbeys and priories again into the vanguard of contemporary music.

The *RB* prescribed the manner of the musical performance. The choir was led by the cantor: when he began 'all [were to] rise at once from their seats in honor and reverence' (*RB*, ix). The conventual chant was to be carefully structured, with contributions from the brethren determined apparently by both seniority and capability: 'Let those who have been ordered, intone the psalms or the antiphons in their turn after the Abbot. No one, however, should presume to sing or read unless he is able so to perform this office that the hearers may be edified' (*RB*, xlvii).

Later customaries add detail to these arrangements. The brethren were positioned on both sides of the choir and they performed the verses of the psalms alternately. The cantor stood on the right-hand side of the choir and served both as leader and conductor, 'to decide when the chant is to be begun, and the note raised or lowered'; he was also to be both prompt and understudy for his brethren and to provide the correct note and phrase when others faltered. It was common for the role of cantor to be rotated, underlining the necessity for each of the brethren to be competent in chant.

The presence of oblates in later centuries provided further scope for variation. The children contributed phrases from the verses and responsories; during festivals the *Decreta Lanfranci* assigned them solos in each of the day and night offices.[249]

Benedict made only passing reference to the style of music appropriate for his *cenobium*: (at the day offices at least) it was to be 'as the Roman church singeth it' (*RB*, xiii). During the early Benedictine diaspora three forms of chant were prevalent: the 'Roman' familiar to Benedict and popularised through its association with his disciple Gregory the Great; the Ambrosian, associated with Ambrose of Milan and followed in northern Italy; and the Beneventan, a form more fluid but with fewer tonal variations practised at Montecassino and other monasteries to the south.[250] The advance of Roman Benedictinism reinforced the status of Gregorian custom, and in 1058 Beneventan chant was formally proscribed.[251] Yet variant forms persisted

---

[249] *MC*, pp. 28–9, 32–3, 44–7, 52–3, 74–5, 80–1.

[250] W. P. Apel, *Gregorian Chant* (New York, 1958), pp. 51–83, 465–83 [R. Jesson]; T. F. Kelly, *The Beneventan Chant* (Cambridge, 1989), esp. pp. 181–8. See also K. Levy, *Gregorian Chant and the Carolingians* (Princeton, 1998), pp. 3–18.

[251] Kelly, *Beneventan Chant*, p. 39.

in the north and west to the close of the twelfth century. Abbot Thurstan of Glastonbury was said to have rejected Gregorian chant in favour of the form pioneered by William of Fécamp.[252]

Liturgical music offered medieval Benedictines opportunities for individual creativity as much as the *studium* and scriptorium. From the early times it seems cantors, and other brethren, were encouraged to compose new settings for psalms, verses, responses and hymns. As early as the ninth century a number of abbeys had secured a reputation for innovation in music. Paul the Deacon at Montecassino was said to have set to music his own verses in honour of St Benedict.[253] The Carolingian and Anglo-Saxon reforms, and the reintroduction of the full Benedictine Office, fostered a further phase of original composition: it seems the names of the musicians of Frankish and Saxon abbeys were celebrated throughout the network.[254] Within the family of Cluny, a musical ability attracted as much, perhaps more, acclaim than scholarship since it contributed to the collective *opus* of the choir. Among the Cluniac abbeys of Normandy, Orderic Vitalis recalled three celebrated composers of his time, Gerbert of Saint-Wandrille (1062–89), Ainard of Dive (1046–c. 1078) and Durand of Troarn (1059–88), each of whom 'had music in their souls'.[255] Benedictine women found a degree of independence in the music of the Office denied them in its sacerdotal dimensions. Their local embellishments appear to have been a frequent frustration for their episcopal visitors.[256]

The Benedictines renewed their reputation for music in the century before the Reformation. It is often overlooked that polyphony, the mode of expression that introduced a new colour, depth and (of course) harmony to sacred music, was pioneered, and popularised, in Benedictine monasteries.[257] Polyphony, the so-called *ars nova* (new art), originated in the secular churches of fourteenth-century France but it attracted the early attention of monastic cantors on either side of the English Channel. Before the end of the century, polyphonic performance had been introduced into the extra-liturgical offices – such as the Lady Mass – of a handful of English abbeys; before 1500 it had passed over into the liturgical hours. Fragments may be found in the manuscripts of a number of houses.[258]

The practice of polyphony transformed Benedictine music. The integrity of the monastic choir was compromised as secular professionals (men) and

[252] *The Chronicle of John of Glastonbury*, ed. J. P. Carley (Woodbridge, 1985), pp. 156–7.
[253] Boynton, *Shaping a Monastic Identity*, p. 42.
[254] Wallace-Hadrill, *Frankish Church*, pp. 175–6; Claussen, *Reform of the Frankish Church*, pp. 274–6. See also S. Rankin, 'Carolingian Music', in *Carolingian Culture*, ed. McKitterick, pp. 274–316.
[255] *Orderic*, ii. 299.
[256] Power, *Medieval English Nunneries*, p. 662; *VCH Oxfordshire*, ii. 71–5 (Godstow, 1520).
[257] Bowers, 'Early Tudor Monastic Enterprise', 21–54.
[258] For example, BL, MS Harley 4664, fos. 181r–197r (perhaps from Durham); Oxford, Bodleian Library, MS e.Mus.7 (Bury).

boys were recruited to provide the necessary vocal range and skill.[259] The aural experience was also changed: the richness of polyphony presented a stark contrast to the sonic simplicity of plainchant, and it was underpinned by the use of the organ in which many monasteries now invested; for the first time since the twelfth century, the musical repertory of the quire was refreshed. Their practice of polyphony attracted composers: the abbeys and priories of England commissioned and were offered new works from influential figures including John Dunstable, Lionel Power, Robert Fairfax and Thomas Tallis.[260] Reformers mocked their modish ways: Erasmus (citing Jerome) ridiculed their cultivation of 'almost as many ways of chanting the psalter as there are different nationalities'.[261]

Manual Labour

The labour of the choir was complemented by the *opus manuum*, a daily period of physical labour applied to the material needs – food, infrastructure, furnishings – of the monastery. Benedict's precursors had commended these labours but had not prescribed their form and frequency.[262] Benedict focused on the spiritual benefits of manual labour, as a means of discipline, to direct the physical energies of the brethren, and mental preparation for their performance in the choir. The hours passed outside the choir were those of greatest peril for the professed monk for 'idleness is the enemy of the soul' ('Otiositas inimica est animae': *RB*, xlviii. 1). Yet there was also a practical dimension: the monastery was meant to be free from worldly interference, self-sufficient in all its needs: so situated 'that there may be no need for the monks to go about outside, because it is not good for their souls' ('ut non sit necessitas monachis vagandi foris, quia omnino non expedit animabus eorum': *RB*, lxvi). The oratories for which the *RB* was first compiled lay at the centre of colonies supported by a network of fields and farms. The labour of their members was essential for their survival, perhaps especially under the threat of continuing Lombard incursions. Gregory's *Dialogues* evoke the art and craft of these colonies, where walls were raised (and razed) by the brethren's own hands (II. 11). Benedict's *cenobium* was not to be a commune, however, an alternative *urbs*: building was to be undertaken only as 'the needs of the place, or poverty should require'.

---

[259] For example, Amundesham, *Annales monasterii S. Albani*, ed. Riley, i. 106.
[260] Bowers, 'Early Tudor Monastic Enterprise', 23, 32; M. Bent, 'John Dunstaple (*d.* 1453)', *ODNB*, 8286; N. Sandon, 'Robert Fayrfax (1464–1521)', *ODNB*, 9089; J. Milsom, 'Thomas Tallis (*c.* 1505–1585)', *ODNB*, 26594.
[261] *The Correspondence of Erasmus*, ed. R. A. B. Mynors, D. F. S. Thomson and P. G. Beitenholz, 12 vols. (Toronto, 1974–2003), vi. 72–91 at 89, citing Jerome, *Epistulae*, 46.10.
[262] Dunn, *Emergence of Monasticism*, pp. 79, 84, 87, 125. Among Benedict's precursors, Martin of Tours was notable for not prescribing the *opus manuum*. See also Décarreaux, *Monks and Civilisation*, p. 228.

Reading was to be an annexe to these physical labours. Benedict did not regard book work as an intellectual exercise but as another mode of discipline, the analogue of the other 'necessary work' and the antidote to carelessness, sloth, idleness and 'vain talk' (*RB*, xlviii). If reading was to be undertaken for a purpose other than personal and communal discipline, it was as a further source of spiritual succour, as a foundation for private meditation, since it was an obligation of their profession to engage 'willingly with Holy Reading' (*RB*, iv. 56: 'Lectiones sanctas libenter audire orationi frequenter incumbere').

The *RB* prescribed two periods of manual labour in the summer months, between Prime and Terce and Nones and Vespers (approximately five hours in total) and for the winter one period (which could amount to four hours but was interrupted by Sext) between Terce and Nones. Reading was to be taken up between these periods of other work: after Terce and before Sext and after mealtime a period of rest or reading, 'if anyone desires it' (summer); this post-prandial period was retained (and perhaps extended) in the winter months and paired with a daybreak hour of reading after Prime; on Sundays the time between each of the hours was to be occupied in reading unless the brethren were required for other duties. There was also to be a period of reading before the day closed at Compline, so timed to allow those occupied in outdoor work to re-enter the enclosure. During Lent the early hour of reading was to continue until Terce; at this time there was to be a distribution of books from the conventual collection to each of the brethren which were 'to be read in order' ('quos per ordinem ex integro legant': *RB*, xlviii. 15), an indication perhaps of a programme of reading prescribed for the season.

In later customaries the opportunities for the pure *opus manuum* were curtailed. The growth of their temporal possessions in successive phases of expansion in the ninth, tenth and eleventh centuries released many Benedictine monasteries from the necessity to provide for their own of their own. Even before this expansion, at Montecassino Hildemar noted the reduction of morning work to make way for Mass.[263] A century later, Smaragdus recommended a division of labours – the morning for manual duties, the afternoon for devotion to books.[264] In the *Regularis Concordia* the morning worktime had contracted, confined to the period between chapter and the High Mass although the (two) hours between None and Vespers remained in place and work was permitted on particular feast days.[265] By the end of the eleventh century the work hours had been eroded almost entirely. The *Decreta Lanfranci* refers to manual labour once only,

---

[263] *Warnefrid-Hildemar*, p. 116.
[264] *Smaragdi abbatis expositio*, ed. Spannagel and Engelbert, pp. 271–5 at 272.
[265] *RC*, pp. 20–1 (work, where necessary, to be undertaken between Chapter and Sext). See also *MO*, p. 454.

requiring an oblate to read when the brethren engage in some unspecified, perhaps domestic, occupation.[266] In subsequent centuries it seems manual duties were undertaken by a resident population of retainers, domestic servants, husbandmen, tradesmen and labourers.[267] It is possible that in small or remote and rural settlements professed brethren still took a share of these practical tasks. In the greater number of urban, or suburban, Benedictine houses, however, like many of the Benedictines' gentry and mercantile kinsfolk, work was no longer a shared experience but the object of their daily, but detached supervision. A nostalgic sense of its observant significance remained.[268]

The abandonment of manual labour enabled the extension of the reading hours. Already in the tenth century, to the morning and afternoon *lectiones* the *Regularis Concordia* allowed another moment for the brethren to give themselves to reading ('vacant fratres lectioni') after daybreak, and the observance of Prime, and before the sounding of the second hour.[269] Lanfranc's *Decreta* replaced these readings with psalmody but offered further opportunities for *lectio* (or conversation) after chapter and after Sext.[270] The continued attenuation of the morning hours, with both commemorative and festive sequences of psalms, encroached further on preprandial reading and in customaries compiled after 1200 the period is often scarcely noticeable.[271] The adoption of an academic programme at the turn of the thirteenth century encouraged a new approach to reading in the enclosure, in a *studium* built for the purpose, under the eye of a magister.[272] Yet in some centres there appears to have been a resurgence of claustral *lectiones*, and in a number of later consuetudines the length of the morning hours, and the moment of the meal itself, were adapted to allow for reading time.[273]

From earliest times there was an expectation that brethren might engage in less formal *lectiones* during the hours of rest between Compline and Matins. The fragmentary customs of Corbie contain a reference to brethren reading 'in lectulo suo' ('in their bed').[274] Wulfstan witnessed Æthelwold's taste for nocturnal reading 'with a candlestick in his hand ... keeping his eyelids hard at work', though not always with success.[275] The subdivided

---

[266] *MC*, p. 120&n.

[267] For example, the number and variety of occupations represented in a 1398–9 record of *stipendia famulorum* (staff salaries) from Selby Abbey: *Selby*, pp. 56–7.

[268] *Chronicle of John of Glastonbury*, ed Carley, pp. 116–17.

[269] *RC*, p. 15.

[270] *MC*, p. 61.

[271] *Customary of Eynsham*, ed. Gransden, p. 181; *Customary of St Augustine and St Peter*, ed. Thomson, i. 190 (St Augustine's); ii. 144 (Westminster). Only the St Augustine's customary specifies reading ('occupant se in leccionibs de servicio reddendis vel de divinis scripturis'), although it also permits brethren with responsibility for private masses to absent themselves.

[272] *GASA*, ii. 300.

[273] Amundesham, *Annales monasterii S. Albani*, ed. Riley, i. 101–16.

[274] *Consuetudines Corbeienses*, CCM, i. 369–422 at 421.

[275] *Wulfstan*, pp. 52–3.

dormitories of the later Middle Ages incorporated cupboards and shelves for the books which the brethren were now permitted to keep in their possession.[276] The representation of the bookish monk in his sleeping quarters that appears in a number of post-1300 Benedictine manuscripts might suggest that nocturnal reading now served as a metaphor for independence not only in reading but also in patterns of thought.[277]

The individual *opus* of the Benedictine *horarium* was complemented by communal reading – exercises which grew in number over the medieval centuries. Benedict prescribed a formal reading at mealtime since the spiritual nourishment it offered 'must not be wanting at the table of the brethren when they are eating'. The duty of reader was to rotate on a weekly cycle, although it was only to be undertaken by 'those who edify their hearers' (*RB*, xxxviii); the reader was to take 'a little bread and wine before he begins' but otherwise take his meal with the servers after the meal was over. The reading was always to begin with the verse *Domine, labia mea aperies, et os meum annuntiabit laudem tuam* (Psalm 50[51]: 17), recited by the brethren following the reader's lead; the reading continued without further interruption, although Benedict permitted the superior to provide 'a few words for edification' on the theme. The latter was elaborated into an exegetical lesson in later centuries: Eadmer recalled that Anselm of Canterbury could rarely hold back from leading a discussion; one correspondent recalled an entire sermon expounded 'ad prandium'.[278] The *RB* also required the observant day to close with a brief period – four or five pages' worth – of communal reading (*RB*, xlii). The purpose was to allow time for the brethren to gather themselves, and those occupied with work elsewhere, before 'having assembled in one place' they could perform the final office of Compline as one. The reception of guests was also to incorporate the reading of the divine law 'so that [they] may be edified', although at the end of the twelfth century Adam of Eynsham found it 'almost forgotten everywhere by all monks'.[279] The advent of the chapter added another daily reading and exposition: in the *Regularis Concordia* 'the prior shall explain what has been read ... as the Lord shall inspire him'; in the *Decreta Lanfranci* the reading of the *RB* was followed by a sermon.[280] The sermon may have been abandoned in the later Middle Ages but it was substituted by further readings, not least from the canons of the capitular authorities of the order; at Chester Abbey, and at Ebersberg (Bavaria), the injunctions or sermons of visitations past were transcribed for (perhaps communal)

---

[276] A. Coates, *English Medieval Books: The Reading Abbey Collections from Foundation to Dispersal* (New York, 1998), p. 85; Erler, 'Private Reading', 147–67; Strocchia, *Nuns and Nunneries*, p. 24.

[277] See, for example, Oxford, The Queen's College, MS 304.

[278] *Eadmer*, pp. 73–8.

[279] *Magna vita sancti Hugonis: The Life of St Hugh of Lincoln*, ed. D. L. Douie and D. H. Farmer (Oxford, 1985), p. 176.

[280] *RC*, p. 17; *MC*, 105, 159.

reading.[281] Under the influence of the Fourth Lateran Council (1215), the injunctions (in England at least) of the general and provincial chapters, and the canons *Summi magistri* (1336) of Benedict XII, many houses also introduced a daily lecture in theology delivered by a qualified doctor of theology.[282] It appears the practice faded in the fifteenth century, but in the reformed congregations of Bursfeld, Melk and Padua they were replaced with humanist inspired lectures in polyglot exegesis, Latin, Greek and Hebrew.[283]

There are few contemporary descriptions of the Benedictines at work. There can be little doubt their outdoor labours were largely agricultural. Ardo of Aniane depicted his brethren in the fields 'with plowmen ... diggers ... reapers' although it appears there were also duties in the (kitchen) gardens of the precinct.[284] The customs of Corbie incorporated an *ordinatio hortorum* ('garden ordinance'); the humility of Æthelwold of Winchester was such that at his own hand he 'cultivated the garden and gathered fruit and vegetables ready for the monks' meal'.[285] Early Benedictine hagiographers hailed their subjects as accomplished builders and craftsmen. Wulfstan represented Æthelwold as the builder of Abingdon and the Old Minster at Winchester, leading his brethren by example to the extent that he broke his ribs in a fall.[286] These were self-consciously rhetorical representations intended to complement the contemplative with *exemplae* of active devotion: it would be wrong to regard them as objective proof of the craft of the Benedictines. There is no doubt the monks of many periods displayed an informed interest in architecture. Where resources were meagre, and in a period when adult profession brought men with artisanal skills into the community, it is possible a minority of brethren did make a contribution to the work of building: at Battle, while construction 'progressed poorly', the brethren 'built themselves plain little huts where they could live'.[287] Yet it was surely more common for them to act in a supervisory role. It is telling perhaps that the popular miracle story of Dunstan, who is said to have suspended a beam fallen from the scaffold of the church at Glastonbury, presented the saint as a bystander.[288] Some early accounts specify the use of secular labourers: Oswald's church at Westbury (Gloucestershire) was the work of the lowest sort ('contemptibiles personae'); at Æthelwold's

---

[281] BL, Royal MS 8 F IX, fos. 73r–93r; P. B. Pixton, *The German Episcopacy and the Implementation of the Decrees of the Fourth Lateran Council, 1216–1245: Watchmen on the Tower*, Studies in the History of Christian Thought 64 (Leiden, 1995), p. 227. See also C. R. Cheney, *Episcopal Visitation of Monasteries in the Thirteenth Century*, 2nd edn (Philadelphia and Manchester, 1982), pp. 15–16.

[282] *Chapters*, ed. Pantin, i. 28, 75, 181–5.

[283] Posset, *Renaissance Monks*, p. 158&n.

[284] Ardo, *Life of St Benedict of Aniane*, ed. Head and Noble, p. 233.

[285] *Consuetudines Corbienses*, CCM, i. 369–422; *Wulfstan*, pp. 16–17.

[286] *Wulfstan*, pp. 28–9.

[287] *Battle*, pp. 44–5.

[288] The Life of Eadmer of Canterbury: *Memorials of St Dunstan*, ed. Stubbs, p. 188.

Abingdon it was the responsibility of the monk Ælfstan to provide meals for the workmen, 'cooking meat every day and serving it painstakingly to the workmen, lighting the fire, fetching the water and keeping the pans clean'.[289] In fact, kitchen duties were a familiar substitute for outdoor labour. The *RB* prescribed that 'no one be excused from the work in the kitchen' (*RB*, xxxv) and presented it as the most common locus of daily labour, 'if one is engaged in any work' ('Si quis dum in labore quovis': *RB*, xlvi. 1). These indoor and outdoor obligations diminished in the Gregorian period: not only did greater endowments enable monasteries to maintain a permanent staff but also there was a growing perception that the principal *opus* of the order was in the service of the institutional church, in pastoral care, and scholarship: Rupert of Deutz opined 'the whole world could be starving ... yet the teachers of the Word ave a right to see their needs provided for'.[290] It was suggestive of a shift in attitudes that the council of Rouen (1072) ruled that apostate monks and nuns, if refused the opportunity to return by their superior, were to labour by their own hands and to receive alms until it could be judged whether they had mended their ways.[291]

Benedict defined the book time of the brethren as *lectio divina* (*RB*, xlviii. 1), literally sacred reading. He did not specify a text but the canon of scripture was surely the focus; indeed, it has been suggested that his direction for the Lenten distribution of books from the library may have been interpreted in the sixth century as the collected (*de bibliotheca*) booklets (*codicis*) of the Old and New Testaments (*RB*, xlviii. 15). The final chapter of the *RB* also points to a programme of reading beyond scripture, the books of 'our holy catholic fathers' which 'proclaim how we may proceed to our Creator' together with the 'the collations of the Fathers, and their institutes and lives, and the rule of our holy Father, Basil' which are 'the monuments of the virtues of exemplary and obedient monks' (*RB*, lxxiii). Benedict distinguished between *lectio divina* and its diet of scripture and patristics, and the (liturgical) reading of the psalms: after mealtime the brethren were permitted to engage in *lectio divina* or to take up the psalms ('vacent lectionibus suis aut psalmis': *RB*, xlviii. 15). This distinction was respected in later generations: psalters and other service books were rarely deposited in the cloister book cupboards. Later Benedictines continued to identify a repertory of texts deemed appropriate for *lectio divina* but in practice the works which occupied them in the reading hours were more diverse. The record of a Lenten distribution at eleventh-century Farfa reveals the variety of authors and texts even at an early date: one monk received the Pauline epistles, one the *Historia ecclesiastica* of Bede and one the Roman History

[289] *Wulfstan*, pp. 28–9.
[290] Van Engen, *Rupert of Deutz*, p. 322.
[291] *Orderic*, ii. 284–92. See also R. Foreville, 'The Synod of the Province of Rouen in the Eleventh and Twelfth Centuries', in *Church and Government in the Middle Ages: Essays Presented to C. R. Cheney*, ed. C. N. L. Brooke *et al.* (Cambridge, 1976), pp. 19–40 at 30.

of Livy.[292] Later medieval records reveal a wider variety of genres but also a core group of traditional *lectiones* assigned to almost every borrower.[293] The reformers of the fifteenth and early sixteenth centuries encouraged a return to the original staples of monastic *lectio* – Basil, Cassian and the *Vitas patrum* – which from number of new manuscript anthologies, and the popularity of pioneer names-in-religion, appears to have born fruit in some regions.[294] It appears communal reading served as an arena for the exposition of a wide variety of works throughout the Middle Ages. Scripture was the first focus: Ælfric commanded his brethren to complete in the frater that part of the *ordo librorum* which 'we do not cover in church'.[295] Yet early accounts of books assigned to the refectory record exegesis and ecclesiastical history alongside scripture; in the later Middle Ages, standard authorities of academic and pastoral theology were also be found on the frater lectern.[296] In the later period the *lectiones* in chapter were legislative. In England the capitular authorities required the exposition of the sequence of statutes: Benedict XII's *Summi magistri* was also to be reasserted and expounded in this context.[297]

The *RB* does not refer to the making of books; indeed, the brethren were enjoined to possess 'neither a book, nor a writing-tablet, nor a pen' (*RB*, xxxiii. 1), but from early times there was an expectation in Benedictine communities that their book time might also incorporate bookcraft. At the pioneering houses of the eighth and ninth centuries – Corbie, Fleury, Fulda, Glastonbury, St Gall – there was a culture of writing as much as reading.[298] As attitudes to the *opus* of the monastic order sharpened in the course of the eleventh century, there was an emerging consensus that bookcraft represented an appropriate channel – perhaps the most appropriate – for their practical impulses. Orderic captured the prevailing view in his portrait of Abbot Thierry of Jumièges (d. 1067), a distinguished scribe ('scriptor erat egregius') who 'performed the manual work that was proper for him', producing a sequence of service books with his own hand.[299] It was an act of devotion required of everyone from the superior downward: Eadmer witnessed the nocturnal Anselm 'busy in the cloister correcting books' ('in claustro emendandis libris').[300] Undoubtedly autograph production

[292] Lawrence, *Medieval Monasticism*, p. 112.
[293] For example, *EBL*, B87 (St Albans); B100 (Thorney), pp. 555–64, 599–604.
[294] B. Collett, *Italian Benedictine Scholars and the Reformation: The Congregation of Santa Giustina of Padua* (Oxford, 1985), pp. 86–7; Posset, *Renaissance Monks*, pp. 148.
[295] Reilly, 'Cluniac Giant Bible', p. 177.
[296] For example, *EBL*, B14, pp. 87–9 (Bury).
[297] *Chapters*, ed. Pantin, ii. 40.
[298] R. McKitterick, 'Script and Book Production', in *Carolingian Culture: Emulators and Innovators* (Cambridge, 1994), pp. 221–47; Ganz, *Corbie in the Carolingian Renaissance*, pp. 36–67, 121–3. See also *The Culture of the Abbey of St Gall: An Overview*, ed. J. C. King and W. Vogler (Stuttgart and Zurich, 1990), pp. 69–118.
[299] *Orderic*, iv. 49.
[300] *Eadmer*, p. 24.

declined in the later Middle Ages as the Black Monks, like their regular and secular counterparts, acquired a greater number of books from professional workshops. There remained a nostalgic commitment to *ars scribendi* as a devotional act, a commitment renewed in the fifteenth century by rising humanist sensibilities. In the reformed congregation of Melk, the art of writing was enshrined in the new curriculum of the cloister.[301]

Bookcraft was also a communal labour. The fragmentary customs of Corbie refer to a custodian of the books (*bibliothecarius*) responsible for reading and writing ('omnium librorum cura habeat, lectionum atque scriptorium'); Adelhard's capitulary refers to Corbie's chamber or solar (*solarium*) for the scribes.[302] As these early customaries demonstrate, the work of the scriptorium was always regarded as specialised, and only brethren with the appropriate skills were assigned to apply their labour there. As their material resources grew, monasteries turned to unprofessed professionals to complete commissions within their precincts under their direction.[303] For Benedictines of the high and later Middle Ages, there was a distinction to be drawn between bookcraft as a claustral act of devotion and the professional labour required to provide the monastery with its learned and liturgical needs.

Discipline

The Benedictine regime of the *opus Dei* and the *opus manuum* was reinforced by a simple, hierarchical system of governance and instruments for daily, collective and individual supervision. These structures were not original. Both the *ordo* of Caesarius and the *RM* had conceived of a *cenobium* under central authority and had prescribed divers disciplinary mechanisms.[304] Benedict refined their framework, drawing on the legislative idiom of the Roman *urbs*. His measures for the management of the monastery remained enshrined in Benedictine practice to the end of the Middle Ages. The successive phases of expansion and revival between the ninth and the twelfth centuries added further dimensions to this system of governance, although for the most part external to the monastic community itself. The reform of Benedict of Aniane first asserted the authority of regional councils and synods to legislate for monasteries independently founded.[305] Benedict also pioneered a congregational structure founded on filial ties between houses, a structure recreated in later centuries at Cluny, Bursfeld and elsewhere, as a key instrument of reform. Historians have made much of the novelty of the capitular structure of the Cistercians, but the origins

[301] Steinberg, 'Instructions in Writing'.
[302] *Consuetudines Corbeienses*, CCM, i. 369–422; Ganz, *Corbie in the Carolingian Renaissance*, p. 28.
[303] A great bible made at Cluny in the early twelfth century appears to have been the work of secular craftsmen, a scribe, Albert, and Opizo: Reilly, 'Cluniac Giant Bible', p. 179.
[304] Dunn, *Emergence of Monasticism*, pp. 117–21.
[305] See also Wallace-Hadrill, *Frankish Church*, pp. 258–303 at 263–9.

of their centrifugal network are to be found in the Benedictine foundations of the tenth and eleventh centuries.[306] The Gregorian years ushered in a new era of papal, legatine and episcopal intervention and imposed upon the order an arrangement of national congregations.[307] Ironically, it was also these disciplinary instruments that enabled the reformers of the sixteenth century to suppress them.

The superior, abbot or abbess for an independent house, prior or prioress for a dependency, presided over the monastery, the head (*paterfamilias*) and master (*praesul*) of the professed community (*RB*, ii. 1, 7). The office was the ultimate administrative and disciplinary authority for the house and its members; it was also invested with the grave duty of the pastoral care and spiritual direction of the brethren: 'Let he [who undertakes the office of abbot] understand what a difficult and arduous task it is to govern souls' ('regere animas': *RB*, ii. 31). The commentator, Smaragdus, elaborated: the good superior was the ghostly (i.e. spiritual) parent of the professed, as Christ to His disciples, a Good Shepherd to the sheep in his fold; and as a parent to their offspring, the superior should inspire fear and love in equal measure.[308] The parental motif was perennial in Benedictine culture: Eadmer represented Abbot Anselm as a mother for his gentleness.[309] Such texts also represent the superior as a source of affective love: John of Salerno recalled how Odo's brethren caressed and his kissed his garments.[310] The *RB* describes the range of the superior's responsibilities, to admit novices (*RB*, lviii), to determine their dress (*RB*, lv), daily duties and degree of mobility (*RB*, xxxiii, l–li), to identify, and punish, individual misdemeanours (*RB*, ii. 26–30), to receive guests, and perform the Maundy (*RB*, liii), and to supervise the artisans and craftsmen of the precincts (*RB*, lvii). The scope of their authority altered little in later centuries at least in the houses of men, although often the direction of daily observance was delegated to subordinate officers. The superiors of female monasteries saw their authority frequently challenged in the later Middle Ages; the principle that informed the decretal *Periculoso* (1298) appears to have encouraged episcopal and monastic supervisors to curb both the physical and the constitutional horizons of the women within their jurisdiction.[311] The *RB* did not address the goods of the monastery, their custody and use, but even in the *regula mixta* communities of the seventh century – Luxeuil, Ripon, Wearmouth

---

[306] For the capitular principle, its early adoption and its Cistercian application, see Lawrence, *Medieval Monasticism*, pp. 168, 189, 284–5. For the Cistercian model, see also Berman, *Cistercian Evolution*, pp. 153–4.
[307] For these later developments, see below, pp. 289–304.
[308] *Smaragdi abbatis expositio*, ed. Spanngel and Engelbert, pp. 61–80 at 79.
[309] *Eadmer*, p. 23.
[310] *John of Salerno*, p. 46.
[311] For the decretal *Periculoso*, see J. A. Brundage and E. M. Makowski, 'Enclosure of Nuns: The Decretal *Periculoso* and its Commentators', *Journal of Medieval History* 20 (1994), 143–55.

– the administrative duties of the superior were well defined.[312] The burden of such business grew rapidly between the tenth and the twelfth centuries, to the extent that the secular stewardship of the superior eclipsed their role as conventual pater-(or mater-)familias. Jocelin of Brakelond captured this tension in his account of the administration of Bury, which opens with the wretched spectacle of Abbot Hugh, a 'godly and pious monk', diminished in his office by matters 'outside'.[313] The dignity of the office also increased in direct proportion to the material resources and temporal responsibilities with which it was invested. The superior of the great, endowed (and predominantly, male) monastery of the Gregorian period, and after, was not merely a steward but a magnate, and perhaps, in his own conception, prelate and even prince: '[Abbot Samson of Bury] said that a new seal must be made and that he should be represented with a mitre, though his predecessors had none such', reported Jocelin, 'and he made arrangements for his own house[hold] ... saying that he had already determined to keep twenty-six horses in his court, and further declaring that "a child must crawl before he can stand and walk securely".'[314]

Generally the superior was elected by 'the whole community with one consent' (*RB*, lxiv. 1), the selection informed by the 'merit of life and wisdom of doctrine' regardless of rank or seniority since any *professus* might be a candidate 'though [s]he be the last in the community'. The right to elect their superior remained a shibboleth for the Benedictines throughout the Middle Ages, but in many periods and regions they accepted, or conceded to, a degree of interference not envisaged by the founder. The *RB* recognised the right, and value, of intervention of 'the Bishop to whose diocese the place belongs' (*RB*, lxiv) if the abbot should prove unsuitable but the authority to act was unequivocally vested in the consensus of the monastic community. The episcopal or monastic supervisors always presided at the election of a female superior. The growing taste for ecclesiastical endowment carried with it a new cast of patron that expected an interest in the governance of the church in which they had invested. The status of *Eigenklöster* was secured at the cost of electoral independence; in England where, generally, proprietors were more restrained, there was a general recognition of the secular interest. It was natural, given its patronage of Benedictines, that under the *Regularis Concordia* the Crown itself was cast as the arbiter of all appointments.[315] Nor did reform restore their independence: the Cluniac customary of Farfa expected the election to occur in the presence of 'the one to whom the abbey belongs'.[316]

---

[312] *Wilfrid*, p. 31.
[313] *Jocelin*, p. 1.
[314] Ibid., p. 26.
[315] *RC*, p. 6.
[316] Boynton, *Shaping a Monastic Identity*, p. 120.

The Cluniac restorations in Normandy echoed English practice, placing elections under the authority of the duke.[317] It would be wrong to assume the consequences of such intervention were always detrimental to the convent. Elections stirred internal tensions, which could be settled by the assertion of patronal authority: the monks of St Augustine's, Canterbury encouraged their patron, Earl William of Huntingdon, to umpire the contest.[318] Moreover, in the early and high Middle Ages, the presence of the patron appears to have secured not only placemen but also a succession of scholars and skilled administrators.[319] Equally, it would be wrong to exaggerate the positive effects of 'free' elections; as Lanfranc's *Decreta* recognised unanimous outcomes were unlikely, the internal divisions could become intractable, or a minority candidate could take office with disastrous consequences.[320] The constitution, status and growing wealth of the greater abbeys and priories also encouraged the interference of episcopal and papal authorities. In England, conflict with the diocesan was most common at the cathedral priories, where the superior was under-mighty by comparison with their bishop.[321] In mainland Europe papal provision was widespread and in the later Middle Ages might also incorporate a presentation *in commendam*.[322] In general, the English Benedictines experienced a new independence in the century before the Reformation, and their commentators were conscious of canonical election 'under the *Regula Benedicti*'; although royal presentation occurred, repeatedly in the fifteenth century for the priory of Blyth.[323] Only after 1515, and the cardinalate of Thomas Wolsey, did interference again become frequent.[324]

[317] Chibnall, *World of Orderic Vitalis*, p. 298&n; *Orderic*, ii. 29.

[318] *Thorne*, p. 557. This was the election of 1332.

[319] H. E. J. Cowdrey, *The Age of Abbot Desiderius: Montecassino, the Papacy and the Normans in the Eleventh and Early Twelfth Century* (Oxford, 1983), pp. 123–44; J. Howe, *Church Reform and Social Change in Eleventh-Century Italy: Dominic of Sora and his Patrons* (Philadelphia, 1997), pp. 123–48 at 133–4.

[320] For example, see the case of the disputed election at Bury (1371), which was carried to the papal curia: *The Heads of Religious Houses, England and Wales, 940–1540*, ed. D. Knowles, C. N. L. Brooke, V. C. M. London and D. M. Smith, 3 vols. (Cambridge, 1972–2008), iii. 23–4. See also the minority candidate at Wilton (1317), whose weakness caused the house to be transferred to a lay administrator: *VCH Wiltshire*, ii. 231–42.

[321] For a survey of the cathedral priories, see R. B. Dobson, 'English Monastic Cathedrals in the Fifteenth Century', *TRHS* 6th Series 1 (1991), 151–72. For a case-study reporting a relatively peaceable relationship, see B. Dodwell, 'The Monastic Community', in *Norwich Cathedral: Church, City and Diocese, 1096–1996*, ed. I. Atherton, E. Fernie and C. Harper-Bill (London, 1996), pp. 231–54. The monks of Tewkesbury tailed their diocesan to the English encampment at Calais to legitimate their election: R. Haines, *Ecclesia Anglicana: Studies in the English Church of the Later Middle Ages* (Toronto, 1989), p. 16.

[322] For example in Caroline Bohemia: J. Eršil, 'Les rapports administratifs et financiers de la papauté avignonaise avec les pays de la couronne de Bohème entre 1352 et 1378', *Rozprávy československá akademie věd* 69 (1959), p. 131; P. H. Stump, *The Reforms of the Council of Constance, 1414–1418* (Leiden, 1994), p. 67.

[323] *Chronicle of John of Glastonbury*, ed. Carley, pp. 174–7; *VCH Nottinghamshire*, ii. 83–8 at 88.

[324] For example, T. Thornton, 'Cardinal Wolsey and the Abbot of Chester', *History Today* 45:8 (1995), 12–17. See also G. W. Bernard, *The King's Reformation* (New Haven, 2005), pp. 228–30; *RO*, iii. 157–63.

Benedict recognised the authority of the superior required delegation but in the *RB* the precise nature and scope of such a role remained unresolved. The rule provides for an office of provost (*praepositus*) charged with the 'government of the monastery' under the abbot, although with the caveat that 'still it is best [it] ... should depend on the will of the Abbot' (*RB*, lxv). It also advises that any colony of size should be subdivided into deaneries, each dean of which exercises the delegated authority of the single abbot. There was much variation in the description and deployment of these roles in early Benedictine communities. The commentaries of Hildemar and Warnefrid reinforced the importance of counsel and collaboration but did not elaborate on the office, or role, of the deputy.[325] The fragmentary constitutions of Corbie describe the dean as the custodian of regular observance in the cloister, 'de conversatione fratrum et cottidianus cum fratribus in obedientia sit'.[326] At Fleury, under Abbot Wulfald (943–62), the dean was recognised as the deputy of the abbot.[327] At Dunstan's Glastonbury it appears the terms, and roles, of dean and provost were interchangeable.[328] The *Regularis Concordia* clarified the arrangement, at least for English brethren: here the provost was the abbot's deputy and in turn their deputy was the dean.[329] The *Decreta Lanfranci* confirmed this a century later, placing the *praepositus* as 'after the abbot the first among all the brethren'.[330]

The provost (prior)'s custody of the cloister was achieved with the assistance of deputies. The *RB* advised the appointment of 'one or two seniors ... to go about the monastery ... lest perhaps a slothful brother be found who gives himself up to idleness or vain talk ... and is unprofitable, not only to himself, but also disturbs others'. In the eighth-century commentary of Paul Warnefrid these were known as the *circas* (i.e. *circumatores*), since they circulated the monastery for the enforcement of regular discipline ('duo seniores qui circumeant monasterium': *RB*, xlviii. 17).[331] The term and the role were retained in the canons of Benedict of Aniane, Æthelwold's *Regularis Concordia*, and the *Decreta Lanfranci*; only at Cluny, and its affiliates, was it unknown, although the *diaconi* (deans) of the cloister served the same purpose.[332] After 1100 the several *circas* were substituted with a single 'claustral' or second provost (prior) although in England there were still *scrutatores* – literally, watchmen – who assisted provost and deputy in their scrutiny of claustral discipline and in some cases assisted in the preparation of novices.[333]

[325] *Warnefrid-Hildemar*, pp. 60–2.
[326] *Consuetudines Corbienses*, CCM, i. 355–422 at 421.
[327] *RC*, p. xxx&n.
[328] Ibid.
[329] *RC*, pp. 39, 56.
[330] *MC*, p. 113. Abbot Eldred of Abingdon was provost (*prepositure officium*) before his election: *Historia ecclesie Abbendonensis*, ed. J. Hudson, 2 vols. (Oxford, 2002–7), p. 221.
[331] *Warnefrid-Hildemar*, pp. 61, 83, 146.
[332] *RC*, p. 56&n.
[333] *GASA*, iii. 424–6 at 425.

Other conventual officers, the cantor (precentor) and novicemaster, also acted as delegates of the principal and second provost (prior). The cantor (precentor) was responsible not only for the technicalities of the liturgical performance but also for general quire discipline. In greater abbeys and priories of the high Middle Ages, the offices of cantor and precentor were often separated.[334] Here the precentor was responsible for the preparation of the brethren for the *opus Dei* and also for the supervision of their bookwork. The novicemaster also acted under the authority of the provost (prior) to maintain the disciplined observance of the novice cohort.[335]

In Benedict's *cenobium* governance depended upon the personal authority and charisma of the abbot. The dissemination of the *RB*, and the expansion of its form of *cenobium* in scale and scope, stimulated the creation of a formal framework for conventual discipline, the daily chapter. The commentators Warnefrid and Hildemar were familiar with the concept in the mid-eighth century; it appears in the code for Frankish convents formulated at the second synod (Canon 36) of 816 although Ardo, the biographer of Benedict of Aniane, knew it not as a chapter but as an assembly.[336] Another century and the form and function of the meeting had been finalised: the *Regularis Concordia* describes the daily chapter in terms recognisable to Benedictines at the end of the Middle Ages.[337] Chapter was a forum for the instruction of the brethren in monastic discipline, the focus of which was the reading of a chapter of the *RB*; but it was also intended to be a forum for discussion for the community of brethren – to this extent the term echoed early secular usage of *capitula* as a congregation of clergy.[338] Chapter was also a microcosm of the monks' daily routine: in a period of perhaps 45 minutes were concentrated a cycle of psalms, prayers, readings and responsories, together with a collation, confessions, due penance and punishment, and even conversation. The *RB* was a constant – on feast days it was substituted for a Gospel – although in the later Middle Ages in England it was supplemented with readings from the canons *Summi magistri* (1336) and the Benedictine general and provincial chapters (1277, 1343, 1444).[339] The disciplinary centrepiece was the confession and performance of penance. Bearing the imprint of early penitential thought, by the tenth century the moment had been suffused with elaborate ritual. The *Regularis Concordia* presented it as a process of spiritual purgation ('spiritualis purgaminis'); the *Decreta*

---

[334] *Customary of St Augustine and St Peter*, ed. Thompson, i. 90–101 at 90–1 (cantor), 91–7 (precentor), ii. 28–36 at 28–9 (cantor), 29–36 (precentor). Generally in the later period the precentor was supported by a deputy, called the succentor: ibid., i. 97–101, ii. 37–42.

[335] Ibid., i. 73; ii. 35.

[336] Ardo, *Life of St Benedict of Aniane*, ed. Head and Noble, p. 247; *Warnefrid-Hildemar*, pp. 64, 115–16.

[337] *RC*, pp. 17–18, 28.

[338] Chrodegang of Metz's *Regula canonicorum*, c. 8, conceived of a chapter for his secular canons as a meeting in which 'the bishop, archdeacon, or whoever is in charge may give whatever commands he has to command': *The Chrodegang Rules*, ed. J. Bertram (Aldershot, 2005), p. 60.

[339] *Chapters*, ed. Pantin, ii. 40.

Lanfranci required the penitent to remove his clothes in readiness for corporal punishment ('corporale iudicium').[340] The drama of the moment should not be underestimated: Wulfstan recalled the 'extreme terror' of a monk disciplined before Abbot Æthelwold; at Farfa the fearful formality of chapter caused a brother to confess to a vision of a murder.[341] Even so, chapter was known to foster learned and lively discourse: Eadmer remembered Father Anselm 'discoursing freely' about matters which concerned their rule ('et ex more de huius modi liberius agens dicendi fine complete').[342] It was at chapter that news was digested and decisions debated. It was a reflection of the function of chapter that certain English convents conceded to surrender following their daily meeting.

The governance of the monastery was secured not only through the community of the convent but through the person of the *professus* themselves. The prescriptions on diet, sleep, recreation, and dress ensured the subjection of the self to the authority of the abbot under the rule. Benedict's emphasis upon bodily discipline was consistent with early monastic codes, although he allowed a degree of discretion not found in all of his models; as knowledge of pre-Benedictine custom faded, his precepts were widely regarded as the paradigm of mortification for the individual *devotus*.[343]

The dietary regulations were perhaps the most challenging of all; their precise terms, and their prohibitive force, generated a debate greater than any other prescription in the *RB*. The rule permitted a principal daily meal, 'dinner', to be taken after Sext, that is to say, around midday, and a supplementary meal, 'supper', to be taken after Nones; on Wednesdays and Fridays in the summer months dinner was forgone and the brethren were to fast until the ninth hour (*RB*, xxxix; xli), although this discipline was to be relaxed if the summer was especially hot, or there was much work to be done in the fields. For each mealtime no more than two dishes of cooked food ('cocta duo pulmentaria') were to be provided (*RB*, xxxix). Their content was not specified, but red meat (literally, the meat of quadrupeds) was prohibited (*RB*, xxxix. 11: 'Carnium vero quadrupedum omnimodo ab omnibus abstineatur comestio'); fruit and vegetables could constitute an additional dish and up to a pound of bread might accompany the meals (*RB*, xxxix. 3–4). The restrictions on quantity and variety were raised 'making allowance for infirmities', notably in the case of infants, children, the elderly and infirm (*RB*, xxxix, 1); the professed adult received a larger portion only when the labours were great, presumably at harvest time (*RB*, xxxix. 6:

---

[340] *RC*, p. 18; *MC*, p. 150.

[341] Boynton, *Shaping a Monastic Identity*, p. 26.

[342] *Wulfstan*, pp. 50–1; *Eadmer*, p. 70.

[343] A. Seebohm, 'The Crucified Monk', *Journal of the Warburg and Courtauld Institutes* 59 (1996), 61–102. See also D. M. Bazell, 'Strife among the Table-Fellows: Conflicting Attitudes of Early and Medieval Christians towards the Eating of Meat', *Journal of the America Academy of Religion* 65:1 (1997), 73–99.

'si labor forte factus fuerit maior ...'). Wine was also permitted – a *hemina* (half a sextary, i.e. 10 fl. oz.) per day: Benedict presented this clause (*RB*, xl. 6) as a relaxation of the ascetic practice of the recent past, a pragmatic concession since 'monks in our times cannot be persuaded' that 'wine is not at all proper [for them]' ('Licet legamus vinum omnino monachorum non esse, sed quia nostris temporibus id monachis persuaderi non potest'). The frequency of meals required under the *RB* was generally observed, even at the end of the Middle Ages. Their communal character, implicit in the *RB*, xxxix, was challenged by Benedict's own requirement that the weekly reader and those designated as servers dine separately; the elaboration of liturgical duties, and, later, of administration, undermined this further.

The early adherents of the *RB* applied the dietary restrictions *ad literam*. Hildemar and Warnefrid argued that the prohibition on meat extended to fowls.[344] The Carolingian reformers reinforced these strictures. The Aachen synod of 817 (canon 21) forbade the feeding of (red) meat to oblate children, except in case of sickness; in his commentary Smaragdus reported six months of penance for the offence of meat eating.[345] Dietary reform was said to be among the principal objectives of Odo of Cluny.[346] The *Decreta Lanfranci* required brethren returning from the infirmary (where they had been restored to health with 'flesh meat and ordinary fare') to request formal absolution from the abbot in the quire.[347] Yet it also came to be widely accepted that (bipedic) poultry and waterfowl were exempt from Benedict's prohibition; the routine of the daily meals was also relieved by the *mixtum*, a portion of bread and wine (ale, in England, at least in the later Middle Ages), served after Prime as a form of breakfast, except in Lent and during principal liturgical feasts, and provided to the aged, infirm and to children as a supplement. Twelfth-century commentators were bolder in their reading of the dietary strictures, perhaps reflecting the human sensitivity of the new generation of schoolmen and undoubtedly responding to the renewed debate over ascetic practice aroused by the new religious orders. Abbot Rupert of Deutz did not regard the regulation on meat to be proscriptive.[348] Since the dishes (other than fruit and vegetables) were unspecified in the *RB*, in her exposition, Abbess Hildegard of Bingen suggested that cheese, eggs and fish might be permitted; moreover Benedict's prescriptions reflected the particular context of his *cenobium* ('rudis et adhuc fere insolita fuit').[349] The divergence between dietary precept and practice appears to have grown

---

[344] *Warnefrid-Hildemar*, pp. 173–75.
[345] *Initia consuetudinis Benedictinae*, ed. Hallinger, pp. 473–81 at 477. See also *Smaragdi abbatis expositio*, ed. Spannagel and Engelbert, pp. 255–7 at 257.
[346] *John of Salerno*, p. 76; Bazell, 'Strife among the Table-Fellows', 73–99.
[347] *MC*, p. 177.
[348] Rupert of Deutz: *PL* 170: 480A–481A.
[349] Hildegard of Bingen, *De regula sancti Benedicti*, ed. Feiss, pp. 67–97 at 80; Bazell, 'Strife among the Table-Fellows', 73–99.

in later centuries. From the earliest, thirteenth-century examples onward, dietary indiscipline was a recurrent theme of visitation injunctions; indeed, the advent of a cycle of visitations perhaps distorts the picture of a pattern of behaviour that began far earlier. The Black Monks of Bacqueville, Normandy, entirely abandoned abstinence from meat during the episcopate of Odo Rigaud (1248–75).[350] The English injunctions include repeated complaints of dietary lapses in the later Middle Ages, but domestic accounts also bear witness to a continuing structural commitment to the observance of the *RB*.[351] Diverse vegetables were cultivated; the pattern of purchasing at the greater abbeys and priories, which has been examined in detail for Durham and Westminster, suggests that fish, poultry and (wild) waterfowl (including the unusual – crane, whooper swan) were the mainstay; the most conspicuous contravention of the rule was in the (rising) consumption of veal. It has been suggested that the fare of the female monasteries was modest by comparison. It may be that the more modest foundations depended upon the home farm rather than commercial (urban) food markets, and it seems some women were expected to purchase food from their personal stipends, although deposit evidence demonstrates the diet of the wealthiest was as indulgent as the men.[352] It is worth noting that visitors also found houses unable or unwilling to provision adequately: Bishop Wakefield of Worcester reprimanded Abbot Thomas Parker of Tewkesbury in 1378 for failing to ensure his brethren enjoyed the capon which once they had known.[353]

The mobility of the Benedictine was strictly circumscribed. Outside the places of conventual work – choir, chapter house, cloister – the *RB* regulated when, where and by what route the brethren might move in the domestic space. At Cluny, these movements took on a quasi-liturgical character, one which also passed into English custom through the *Decreta Lanfranci*.[354] The *RB* did not specify the hours of rest or sleep, although it did require brethren to remain clothed 'that they may be always ready' and 'hasten to outstrip one another in the work of God' (*RB*, xxii. 6: 'et ut parati sint monachi semper et, facto signo absque mora surgentes, festinent invicem

[350] Cheney, *Episcopal Visitations*, p. 155.
[351] *Visitations*, ed. Thompson, iii. 338–9 (Spalding, 1438–9), attesting to the dominance of fish in diet and an alimentary regime perhaps too spartan for the infirm; Haines, 'Stratford's injunctions', 154–80 at 159. See also Harvey, *Living and Dying*, pp. 34–71 at 43–57; *Selby*, pp. 11–12, 150–93 at 161–3 (1416–17 account of the kitchener, noting the scale of purchases of fish); M. Threlfall-Holmes, *Monks and Markets: Durham Cathedral Priory, 1460–1520* (Oxford, 2005), pp. 220–2.
[352] *Visitations*, ed. Jessopp (Carrow); Gilchrist, *Gender and Material Culture*, pp. 76, 86, 88–9; J. H. Harvey, 'Vegetables in the Middle Ages', *Garden History* 12:2 (1984), 89–99 at 94–5; A. Evans, 'Battle Abbey at the Dissolution: Expenses', *Huntington Library Quarterly* 6 (1942), 53–101 at 65–6. For provisioning at a male establishment, see Threlfall-Holmes, *Monks and Markets*, which argues that produce from their own estates remained essential for basic foodstuffs, pp. 136–61 at 137.
[353] R. M. Haines, 'Some Visitation Injunctions for Worcester Cathedral Priory Appended to the Register of Bishop Simon de Montacute', *Rev. Bén.* 106 (1996), 332–55.
[354] Boynton, *Shaping a Monastic Identity*, pp. 119 134, 137.

se praevenire ad opus Dei'). Visitation injunctions from the later period give an impression of unregulated mobility but nocturnal enclosure at least continued to be enforced.[355] A post-Reformation memoir of Durham Priory claimed the conventual buildings had been locked 'evin at vi of the clocke ... untyk vii of the clock the next morninge'.[356] In principle, Benedictine women of the later period were bound by *Periculoso*; they complained of the constraints it placed on domestic administration although their supervisors and visitors maintained that its strictures were widely ignored.[357]

The rule's governing principles on dress were simplicity and utility. Brethren were clothed in tunic and cowl, with a scapular (i.e. tabard) added for work time; only one change of clothes was permitted but the demands of different climates were recognised (*RB*, lv. 2: 'in frigidis regionibus'). The habit was the exclusive possession of the *professus* conferred only after their solemn profession; its significance as a symbol of their *officium* was underlined in the later Middle Ages by the sentence of excommunication *latae sententiae*.[358] It was an indication of the increased formality of the noviciate that in a number of regions before the Reformation the unprofessed were also required to wear a uniform habit. Of course, dress was susceptible to secular influence as much as any of the personal dynamics of the monastic community. The preference of Black Monks for fine garments of high status was proverbial generations before the popular, vernacular satires of the fourteenth century.[359] In his contempt for Cistercian novelty, Orderic betrayed an irregular preference for breeches and sheepskin ('formalibus pelliciisque').[360] Sartorial indiscipline drew criticism both from capitular and episcopal visitors in England. The chapter visitor condemned the taste for soft garments among the Malmesbury monks in 1527.[361] Like many of their secular kinsfolk, modish footware seems to have been a special interest. On the brink of the Henrician suppressions, Bishop John Longland reminded the brethren at Westminster, 'let your shabby attire be the sign of a spotless mind'.[362] Complaints of self-conscious and secular patterns of dress were widespread at houses of women both in Britain and Europe.[363]

---

[355] For example, *Visitations*, ed. Thompson, i. 48–54 (Elstow, 1421–2), 66–8 at 67 (Godstow, 1432–4).

[356] *Rites of Durham*, ed. Raine, p. 73.

[357] Power, *Medieval English Nunneries*, pp. 343–91 at 343–54; *Visitations*, ed. Thompson, i. 67 (Godstow, 1432–4).

[358] B. F. Harvey, *Monastic Dress in the Middle Ages: Precept and Practice* (Canterbury, 1988), p. 12; L. F. Hodges, *Chaucer and Clothing: Clerical and Academic Costume in the General Prologue to the Canterbury Tales* (Cambridge, 2005), p. 115.

[359] In the age of Gregorian reform, a commitment to the habit was also represented as an index of monastic sincerity: Jestice, *Wayward Monks*, p. 64.

[360] *Orderic*, iv. 324–5.

[361] *Chapters*, ed. Pantin, iii. 124–36.

[362] M. Bowker, *The Henrician Reformation: The Diocese of Lincoln under John Longland, 1521–47* (Cambridge, 1981), p. 23.

[363] For example, *Visitations*, ed. Jessopp, p. 200 (Norwich); Power, *Medieval English Nunneries*, p. 674 (St Cyriac's, Erfurt).

The physical infirmity of the brethren was also to be managed in disciplinary mode. The sick were to be treated with care (*RB*, xxxvi), the aged, like children, with 'compassion' and 'tender regard' (*RB*, xxxxvii), yet in their impotence they were not to make 'unnecessary demands' or 'grieve their brethren' both of which, by implication, would endanger regular observance. The sick were to be 'set apart' in their own cell (*RB*, xxxvi) in the charge of a custodian (later, infirmarian) where they would be subject to disciplined care (a modicum of meat, baths), graduated according to the gravity of their condition. It seems the disciplined care of the infirmary was steadily eroded. At the wealthiest abbeys and priories the infirm were perhaps provided with a higher concentration of luxury than was accessible to their healthy colleagues: a sixteenth-century memoir of Durham recalled a decrepit monk 'conveyed with his appurtinans or furniture, from his own chamber ... to the Fermery ... wher he might have both fyre and more convenient kepynge'.[364] Yet where there was no surfeit of luxury, it seems the infirmary brethren were the first to be neglected. A Norwich visitor found them obliged to take their meals in the refectory regardless of their condition.[365]

Throughout the medieval centuries, monastic discipline was also determined and enforced by external authorities. Benedict himself recognised the possibility of external supervision, from the diocesan, or a senior monastic superior from within the region, in respect of the conduct of superiors and their provost (prior) (*RB*, lxv). The earliest networks of monasteries in Burgundy, Normandy and Northumbria were subject at least to the informal surveillance of the diocesan; in these regions the monasteries also attracted the interest of the magnate or monarch and their clerical advisors.[366] The formation of a network of houses under the Carolingian and Anglo-Saxon reforms fostered a new approach to congregational supervision and visitation. The synod of Aachen inaugurated instruments for the enforcement of regular discipline throughout the kingdom of the Franks.[367] Both Ælfric and Wulstan remembered Æthelwold's personal visitation of monasteries founded, or refounded, under his influence.[368] The reform of the monasteries advanced in parallel with episcopal authority and the spirit of monastic renewal proved a poor defence against the ambition of the diocesan. The heads of Frankish houses were compelled to offer fealty to the see: Abbo of Fleury (*c.* 945–1003) famously refused, and sought the protection of papacy.[369] In England it seems the earliest systematic diocesan visitations

---

[364] *Rites of Durham*, ed. Raine, p. 44.
[365] *Visitations*, ed. Jessopp, pp. 19, 24–6.
[366] Wallace-Hadrill, *Frankish Church*, pp. 55–109; Riché, 'Columbanus, his Followers and the Merovingian Church', pp. 66–71; *MO*, pp. 22–30.
[367] See above, pp. 36–7.
[368] *Bishop Æthelwold*, ed. Yorke, p. 58.
[369] M. Mostert, *The Political Theory of Abbo of Fleury* (Hilversum, 1987), p. 36.

occurred under the primates Richard of Dover (1184–84), Baldwin (1184–90) and Hubert Walter (1193–1205).[370] The regular scrunity of religious houses was acknowledged as the duty of the diocesan by 1215: canon 33 of the Fourth Lateran Council placed restrictions on the *procurationes* demanded by visitors; the Councils of Rouen (1214) and Oxford (1222) also asserted scrutiny of monasteries as an episcopal responsibility.[371] Yet in many regions a cycle of visitations was not seen before the second quarter of the thirteenth century: the monks of Peterborough recorded their earliest visit in 1231; visitation reached Wales only with Archbishop Peckham in 1284.[372] The rights of the visitor, whether diocesan or metropolitan, were repeatedly challenged, and the venerable, well patronised and obdurate still would concede only to the authority of a papal commission. Discipline – and ultimately, dispersal – at Lorsch succeeded only after the intervention of Gregory IX in 1231.[373] The formation of a capitular structure under the authority of Lateran IV added a further tool for the enforcement of conventual discipline. The chapters of the Black Monks were empowered to visit the monasteries of the province; Benedict XII's canons *Summi magistri* (1336) required the capitular visitation on a triennial cycle.[374] The record of the Continental chapters is too slight to assess the frequency or efficacy of these visitations, but in England, where the cycle was unbroken to the brink of the Reformation (1527), they were perhaps the most productive consequence of the capitular organisation.[375] It was perhaps their similarity to the machinery of visitation that caused English monks to co-operate with the injunctions of Cromwell's commissioners in 1535–6.

The discipline of the conventual hierarchy, and their external supervisors, was enforced with an elaborate scheme of punishments. The *RB* promulgated a scale of correction (affecting a symmetry with the scale of humility: *RB*, iv): the brother in error for the first time was admonished by his superior; a second offence was addressed 'in secret' (*secrete*), a third publicly; further disobedience was to be met with excommunication or corporal (i.e. physical) penalities (*RB*, xxiii). It was for the superior to determine the degree of excommunication: for minor misdemeanours it might amount only to exclusion from the frater, but grave offences were met with banishment from the oratory. Whatever their error, the excommunicate was expected to perform public penance before returning

---

[370] Cheney, *Episcopal Visitations*, p. 37.

[371] Ibid., p. 20. See also *Councils and Synods*; Pixton, *German Episcopacy*, p. 280.

[372] E. King, *Peterborough Abbey, 1086–1310: A Study in the Land Market* (Cambridge, 1973), p. 94; Cowley, *Monastic Order in South Wales*, p. 101.

[373] Pixton, *German Episcopacy*, pp. 388–9.

[374] *Concilia magnae Britanniae et Hiberniae, 446–1717*, ed. D. Wilkins, 4 vols. (London, 1737; repr. Brussels, 1964), iii. 589–91. The chapter was to convene on such a cycle, *de triennio in triennium*, and the (provincial) chapter was to co-ordinate the visitation: '… in huiusmodi provincialibus capitulis deputati, sint idonei, soliciti, et discreti circa visitationis officium eorum exequendum' (591).

[375] *Chapters*, ed. Pantin, iii. 124–36.

to the community (*RB*, xxiv). The same scheme was applied to the children (*RB*, xxx), although coerced fasting was offered as an alternative to corporal interventions. Oblates could not be expelled; indeed, if they attempted to abscond they could be forcibly returned. For the truly incorrigible the *RB* recommended finally the force of prayer before the superior was compelled to expel them. These measures were reiterated by the early commentators; in their time chapter was established as the forum for public admonition and custody was also a common sanction for the persistent offender; the capitulary of 817 required the conventual prison to be heated in winter.

The maintenance of monastic discipline was a fierce, often futile, struggle with human nature and wider social forces; whether in pioneering seclusion or at the centre of urban conglomeration it was not uncommon for Benedictine monasteries to suffer bouts of individual and collective disorder. Minor infringements of the *RB* were frequent. The earliest commentaries and customaries recognised that errors, omissions and outright non-observance were inevitable.[376] The response to them changed little over centuries of customary revision, a measure of their acceptance as a structural feature of regular life. Instances of gross indiscipline were not uncommon. Throughout the Middle Ages, communities were destabilised by the persistent disobedience of individual brethren who absented themselves from the Office and other daily obligations; those that attended but refused to conform – chatting in choir, at mealtime and the dormitory absence were also commonplace.[377] Moral misdemeanours were widely reported by both capitular and episcopal visitors, although since the surviving *comperta* are concentrated in the century before the Reformation it would be wrong to infer the general prevalence of drunkenness and sexual impropriety. Also notable is the level of physical violence attested. Brawling, both armed and unarmed, was widespread and grievous injury and death not unknown.[378] These episodes focus on a recurrent threat to conventual order, a certain predisposition to factionalism that may be found throughout the Middle Ages.

The Culture of Observance

The experience of the Benedictine was shaped not only by the precepts of the *RB* but also by the patterns of behaviour that were woven around them. Historians have often represented the monastery as a microcosm of medieval society, seeing in the administrative, domestic and personal records a concentration of the cultural dynamics of the communities beyond their walls. The common conception of the monk, however, was of a cultural

---

[376] *Warnefrid-Hildemar*, pp. 83–106.
[377] For example, *Visitations*, ed. Thompson, i. 22–3.
[378] *Visitations*, ed. Jessopp, p. 97.

community that was the antithesis of the unprofessed, one shaped by a self-conscious rejection of secular norms, a veritable *Gegenkultur* (counter-culture). Life according to the *RB* was informed by this perception and it became a guiding principle of movements for Benedictine reform, a purification of the enclosure, a reinforcement of the cultural boundary between the cloister and world. Secular commentators were sensitive to this self-image and played upon the perpetual struggle of the monasteries to preserve it: the worldly monk uneasy in the unworldly enclosure was a familiar figure of estates satire.[379] Yet as popular interest in monastic spirituality was renewed in the later Middle Ages, their claim to a cultural separation from the world (re-)captured public imagination: 'for if hevene be on this erthe,' reflected Clergie in *Piers Plowman* (B Text, Passus X, 297–9) 'and ese to any soule / it is in cloistre or in scole, by manye skiles I fynde / For in cloistre cometh no man to chide ne to fighte / But al is buxomnesse there and bokes, to rede and to lerne'; in the decades before the Reformation the lay divine cultivated a domestic devotional culture that drew on the monastic model.[380] There were aspects of life, and attitudes of the mind, that proved resistant to influences from beyond the precinct, but no Benedictine monastery maintained complete cultural isolation and traces of secular trends in domestic, social and personal behaviour are perceptible in every period: at any rate, there was no sudden descent into secularism at the end of the Middle Ages.

The Black Monks propagated their own approach to the division and regulation of time, one which also informed patterns of life among the later religious orders. While for the secular world the working day was set between daybreak and nightfall, for observants of the *RB* its beginning (Matins) and end (Compline) fell in the night hours, for much of the year (particularly in northern Europe) the hours of darkness. The transition from night- to daytime was also distinctive: for the brethren there was a formal change of clothes and shoes unknown to any secular and a daybreak meal (the *mixtum*) which for much of the Middle Ages had no exact equivalent in wider society. The division of the hours was determined by the demands of the liturgy, at least until the development of the mechanical clock and, perhaps, for some time after: as customaries required, and contemporaries attest, Matins continued until the readings were completed which could mean until daybreak.[381] Perhaps only the marking of the hour by the sound of a bell would have been familiar to those that laboured outside the monastery; at any rate in many customaries it was not the bell

---

[379] The most conspicuous examples in English literature are Clergie's representation of Religoun in Passus X of *Piers Plowman* and Chaucer's portrait of the monk among the pilgrims in his *Canterbury Tales*.

[380] M. Kaartinen, *Religious Culture and English Life in the Reformation* (Basingstoke, 2002), esp. pp. 126–41.

[381] For example, Boynton, *Shaping a Monastic Identity*, pp. 65–80.

that summoned the brethren to their work but the beating of the board. The passage of greater portions of time, week, month, and year was also self-consciously separated from the chronological framework increasingly familiar in the secular world. The monastic framework was the liturgical calendar, the regnal year of the superior and the personal term of profession providing a parallel point of reference.[382]

The monastery might also claim a linguistic culture of its own. Benedict conceived of a Latinate community, which later followers sought to recreate and secure, but regional vernaculars were never entirely removed from the discourse of the convent and in some periods – under the Anglo-Saxon reformers of the tenth century, for example – there was a formal bilingualism in education and worship. No other social community, clerical or lay, maintained a multilingual compact over such a period: vernaculars flowered among secular clerks and regular canons in the later Middle Ages but at the expense of their Latin tradition. The Black Monks also pioneered non-verbal communication for which there was no parallel beyond their precincts. The *RB* placed a premium on silence, but it was the Benedictine reformers of Cluny who sought to preserve it through the practice of a sign language. Apparently under the direction of Abbot Odo, Cluny raised silence from a matter of discipline to a mark of ascetic rigour, a further means by which the *professus* might be released from the corporeal world.[383] The proscriptions of the *RB* were extended: there was to be no speech on the days of an office of twelve lessons and during the octaves of Christmas and Easter; silence was to be kept even in the kitchens; the infirmarer could converse with the sick only in order to treat them. Cluny's signs were fully formed, 'grammarians', wrote John of Salerno, 'would call it a language of the fingers and eyes'.[384] Signs were also adopted in Anglo-Saxon houses before the middle of the eleventh century: a manuscript written at Christ Church Priory, Canterbury (BL, Cotton MS Tiberius A III) contains a directory of 127 manual signs 'to observe diligently God's service', that is to say to ensure conformity with the rule of silence.[385] The directory did not originate at Canterbury but was derived from the customs of Cluny. It may represent a general initiative to inculcate reformed customs in England, although no other copy of this text is known: signing appears to have been current in Æthelwold's reformed community.[386] Signs seem to have

---

[382] For example, the obituaries compiled by the Canterbury monk, John Stone, generally beginning with the liturgical calendar and closing with the years since profession 'vixit in habitu monachali': *Stone*, p. 54.

[383] S. G. Bruce, *Silence and Sign Language in Medieval Monasticism: The Cluniac Tradition, c. 900–1200* (Cambridge, 2007), pp. 20–1, 25.

[384] *John of Salerno*, p. 33.

[385] *Monasteriales Indicia: The Anglo-Saxon Monastic Sign Language*, ed. D. Banham, 2nd edn (Hockwold cum Wilton, 1996).

[386] Wulfstan records the story of Theodoric coming to Æthelwold and 'wanting to tell him by signs (*indiciis*) about some important matter': *Wulfstan*, pp. 52–3.

faded with the force of the Cluniac spirit of reform; although an *instructio signorum monasticorum* appears in the Canterbury library in the early fourteenth century, there can be little doubt (as visitors complained) that daily discourse was freer in the later Middle Ages.[387]

In their shared observance of the *RB*, Benedictine monasteries also developed distinctive social dynamics. Above all, the brethren were bound together by a powerful sense of (con-)fraternity. The *RB* configured the *cenobium* as a community of kinsmen under the authority of an abbot father bearing an obligation of mutual obedience one to another, the younger subordinate to the elder as among well managed siblings (*RB*, lxxi): the monastic brotherhood effaced the earthly family and not only provided a peer group but also an alternative genealogy. Perhaps John of Salerno was not untypical in his impression of separation from forebears of one 'living under the rule and nurtured in the cradle of the church'.[388] The elaboration of the process of admission, profession and the noviciate (with its *schola*) reinforced the notion of brotherhood: biographies and letter books bear witness to the enduring appeal of affective bonds often formed in early adolescence. These texts also attest to the emotional depth possible in the personal ties between brethren: the homo-eroticism of the discourse is sometimes unmistakable.[389] Literary expressions of monastic fraternity also proved susceptible to secular trends. From the turn of the eleventh century the Benedictines engaged with the Ciceronian concept of *amicitia* and cultivated formal networks of political, social and spiritual correspondents. Monastic friendship acquired something of the political character of secular *amicitia* but the priority of spiritual fraternity was never challenged.[390] The corollary of the intense attachment that arose between individuals was a brand of collegial sociability articulated in humorous, often highly comic banter. Nicknames were commonplace: the Notkers of Saint-Gall were recognised by their physical traits; Odo of Cluny was called 'digger' because he kept his head bowed and his eyes fixed to the ground; Orderic commemorated a contemporary known as 'the badly tonsured'; at pre-Reformation Evesham one of the brothers was affectionately known as 'Luther'.[391] The bond between professed brothers experienced greater strain from the shift in patterns of recruitment in the later Middle Ages, and the growing dominance of kinship groups in the monastery; it is worth noting

---

[387] Signing appears to have been current when the customary of Eynsham was compiled in the thirteenth century: *Customary of Eynsham*, ed. Gransden, pp. 145–6; *AL*, no. 1352g, p. 115 (St Augustine's, Canterbury).

[388] *John of Salerno*, p. 5.

[389] J. Haseldine, 'The Monastic Culture of Friendship', in *The Culture of Medieval English Monasticism*, ed. Clark, pp. 177–202.

[390] Ibid., pp. 177–201.

[391] *John of Salerno*, p. 52; *Orderic*, ii. 64; *The Letter Book of Robert Joseph, Monk-Scholar of Evesham and Gloucester College, Oxford, 1530–3*, ed. H. Aveling and W. A. Pantin (Oxford, 1967), p. 106 (Letter 74).

that among the well-born nuns of the later period the weakening of sorority was less marked.

The fraternal bonds of the Benedictines were fostered by the shared experience of observance, but their social culture was also coloured by the occupations of the monks outside the hours of work and worship. Here the traces of the secular life they had left behind (and which continued to flourish beyond the precinct walls) were most conspicuous. The *RB* recognised the need for rest periods, but only under strict regulation: throughout the year the brethren could retire between Sext and Nones, or else occupy themselves in reading; in winter a brief respite was allowed before Matins (*RB*, viii); after Compline and supper (where it was taken) the brethren were released from the day's duties, but the *RB* prescribed a programme of reading – Cassian's *Conferences*, the *Vitas patrum*, 'or or something else that will edify the hearers' (*RB*, xlii) – to occupy the time before bed. In practice, the rest period was always more permissive. A wide variety of diversions are documented: lively discourse, drink, entertainments – players, and, at least in England, a performance from a fool employed for the purpose – and gaming.[392] At Durham Priory the monks were said to drift into the garden and other places after Compline 'and there, impudently sport and idle' ('et ibidem ludunt et vacant insolenciis'); before the Reformation the garden was apparently equipped with a 'bowlinge allie'.[393] Legitimate recreations were permitted, indeed promoted by superiors and congregational authorities, to divert or disengage the brethren from rival attractions. Leave of absence from the *horarium* was offered, a 'holiday' which might be enjoyed beyond the precincts: a monk of fifteenth-century Canterbury chronicled the names of those granted leave in successive years.[394] Medicinal bleeding might also be granted as a privilege, sometimes to be undertaken at a dependency, grange or manor and thus to coincide with a period of 'holiday'. Known among English Benedictines as the *seyney*, it remained general practice to the Reformation.[395] Throughout the Middle Ages there were monks that sought to erode, or ignore, the distinction between recreation and work. The evidence of their personal pastimes is preserved in inventories and visitation *comperta*: archery, falconry, and the paraphernalia of the page-squire – buckler, dagger and sword – are frequently found.[396] Historians have associated these abuses of regular discipline with later monasticism, but they are to be found in every era of the Middle Ages. It has been argued

[392] A. Evans, 'Actors in the Accounts of Battle Abbey', *Huntington Library Quarterly* 6 (1942), 103–5; *RO*, iii. 67. It was reported that the monks of Ramsey played at dice when they should have been at Mass: Bowker, *Henrician Reformation*, p. 25. For backgammon at Norwich in 1532, see *Visitations*, ed. Jessopp, p. 265.

[393] Dobson, *Durham Priory*, p. 70; *Rites of Durham*, ed. Raine, p. 75.

[394] Smith, *Canterbury Cathedal Priory*, p. 199.

[395] *MC*, pp. 138–40; Harvey, *Living and Dying*, pp. 96–9.

[396] *Visitations*, ed. Jessopp, p. 97.

that the atmosphere of the Anglo-Saxon monastery recalled the beer hall of an ealdorman.[397] The boys of Anselm's household kept dogs to course for hares.[398] The women of later medieval houses retained the attachment to domestic animals which they had known in their gentry and noble households.[399] The greater privacy afforded the brethren in the later Middle Ages, arising from the partition of the dormitory and the provision of personal camera (chambers, offices) for senior obedientiaries, allowed these personal pleasures to become a permanent feature of their conventual life.

There was a growing anxiety about the irregular nature of monastic life at the end of the Middle Ages. It was not only a matter of disapproval at the secular pleasures – alimentary, sartorial and recreational – apparently widespread across the network but also of suspicion that those observances that survived diverged significantly from the precepts of the founder and no longer displayed the distinct qualities of the Benedictine: in particular there was a perception that the *opus Dei* had been stripped of the sequence of psalms, antiphons, readings and hymns which once set it apart from secular use and at any rate was now eclipsed by the extra-liturgical suffrages of secular patrons, the formation of monks had been overwritten with the pedagogic programme of the secular clerk, and the mental and physical labour of quire, cloister and field had been replaced with the social and sometimes secular intercourse of the pulpit and the schoolroom. These were not the sectional tensions of the community of clergy but were of wider currency, and perhaps as much as a generation before 1517. The issue at the heart of this discourse, of course, was hardly new: the narrow way of the Benedictine had widened over the course of the Middle Ages and their lives had become interwoven with the ways of the world.

---

[397] J. Campbell, 'Elements in the Background to the Life of St Cuthbert and his Early Cult', in *St Cuthbert, his Cult and his Community*, ed. Bonner *et al.*, pp. 3–21 at 12–13.
[398] *Eadmer*, p. 89.
[399] For pets discovered at visitations, see Power, *Medieval English Nunneries*, pp. 662–3.

CHAPTER THREE

Society

Benedict called upon his followers to forsake society, but those that adopted his rule fashioned a life that acknowledged and assimilated the economic, social and cultural ways of the world. In the medieval mind the monastery was conceived of as a city, certainly a centre of worship, but also a focus of material, social and political commerce. The Benedictines were the monks of society ('qui iuxta homines habitant'), a counterpoint to the monks outside society, 'away from all disturbance' ('a turbis omnino segregati'), the archetype of early monasticism to which the reformed orders aspired.[1] The social integration of the Black Monks was a consequence of their early years. The pioneers of the *RB* were public figures, prelates and princes, and the customs of Benedict became an instrument of their confessional and territorial ambitions; the endowment of property secured the first colonies in unsettled regions and unstable polities but also bound them forever to the emerging infrastructure. Yet the social dynamics of the Benedictines were also inherent in the *RB* itself: Benedict's *cenobium* was sustained by social ties: the paternal care of the superior for his brethren, the fraternal bond of the professed, the blend of age, status and skill in the liturgical and manual *opera* of the *horarium*, the *caritas* of the community for wayfarers and pilgrims; of course, its premise was that a life of spiritual fulfilment, of perfection even, was not only the possession of the solitary but might also be the reward of a life in common.

Their social ties were the chief source of tension in their medieval history. A recurrent theme among reformers, the instinctive worldliness of the Benedictines should not be exaggerated. As individuals they were not immune to eremitical impulses; collectively they repeatedly challenged the encroachment of secular interests, particularly in successive phases of reform. Yet they also accepted their place in the material world, and in the later Middle Ages sought to defend it in the face of growing opposition; when compulsory enclosure was required by sixteenth-century reformers, they rejected it; they also cultivated the interest of society in their observance and adapted their liturgical, pastoral and charitable customs accordingly. The laity shaped the social identity of the Benedictines, yet they harboured doubts over their worldly involvement which only heightened in

[1] *Libellus*, pp. 16–17.

the later Middle Ages as their own hierarchy was threatened. The secular clergy were early critics of monastic endowment and as their own social role and self-image were refined they were projected into open conflict: canonists (and the preachers that parroted them) condemned the Black Monk beyond the enclosure as the proverbial fish-out-of-water, while clerical readers responded warmly to the satirist's portrait of a 'lord ful fat', an 'outridere' and a 'prikasour'.[2]

There can be no doubt the social integration of the Benedictines cast them into a role that differed significantly from the intentions of their founder. With the lay elite they shared seigniorial authority and the income and territorial influence that sustained it; it presented them with administrative responsibilities that undermined the *horarium* and removed many of them from the observant life, but as a corporate body it also invested them with fiscal, judicial and social rights over individuals and communities, their labour, resources and personal conduct, which made their houses almost impregnable. For Benedictine women, the social position of their house sharply exposed the tensions inherent in their status. It turned the precinct of both male and female monasteries into a marketplace where material and spiritual commodities were traded. Their social and economic status also encouraged interventions, in pastoral care and social welfare, which, while not prescribed by the rule, appeared to give expression to its precepts.

At the same time the Benedictines left their imprint on the world beyond their walls. In many regions of Europe it was the early monasteries that shaped the very patterns of settlement, land use and trade which determined the distribution of cities and towns, markets and places of worship. The populace of these places surrendered labour and livelihood to their monastery, and in the boroughs of the later Middle Ages, also their hope of economic and political independence, but also they looked to it for material succour, and for spiritual and perhaps cultural inspiration. Even at the Reformation, at regional level there was rarely a simple polarity between monastery and society; rather, a recognition that their fates were intertwined.

The Benedictine Environment

Benedict inspired his brethren with the image of a tabernacle retreat (tabernaculum) on 'Thy holy hill' [Psalm 14:4: *RB*, Prologue, 23]. It remained at the heart of later representations, and in decorated capitals the founder (and his followers) might be found beneath the tracery of a temple canopy.[3]

---

[2] In his popular *Summa summarum*, a popular source of reference in the later Middle Ages, the English canonist William of Paull (de Pagula) repeated the charge that the monk out of his cloister was as a fish out of water: Book III, c. 38: De statu monachorum: Oxford, Bodleian Library, MS Bodley 293, fos. 103v[d]–132r[b] at 131v. See also Geoffrey Chaucer, *Canterbury Tales*, General Prologue, ll. 166, 189, 200.

[3] For example, Zettel, Zisterzienserstift, Codex Zwettlensis 84, fo. 128v; Michaelbeuern Stiftsbibliothek, Codex Michaelburanus perg. 2, fo. 115r.

Yet Benedict's colonies arose at moment when the form, and infrastructure, of the monastic oratory had evolved far beyond a biblical archetype. The *cenobia* which Benedict discovered in Cassian's *Institutes* constituted whole villages of the devout, which developed the environs and exploited its resources to sustain their common spiritual enterprise.[4] The convents of the Gallo-Roman pioneers recreated these colonies (and much of their energy), albeit on a smaller canvas: according to Cassian, the monastery at Lérins claimed the whole surface area of the island.[5] The Celtic communities first established in the half-century before Benedict's birth were distinguished by the scale of the enclosure that surrounded the *clymiterium* (i.e. place of worship).[6] Benedict would have also known the urban, or suburban, basilical monastery whose precinct was constrained but whose buildings were more advanced (stone and permanent) than any isolated colony.[7] His own settlements have left little trace, but early anecdote and later history suggest a form reflecting these models: while the oratory occupied a conspicuous, central position, the colony as a whole incorporated, populated, and perhaps controlled and defended, a wider area. Here there remained a distinction between the monastic colony and the society of the villa or the *urbs*.[8] Yet as the infrastructure of the ancient world crumbled and the *RB* was carried north, the *cenobium* became a template for the development of territories with either little, or long forgotten social organisation. Indeed, in regions of France, Germany and the British Isles, it could be said the social community was formed in a Benedictine environment. The monastic influence endured in the later stages of mercantile and urban development. Of course, its role as source of and stimulus for social organisation shaped the Benedictine monastery itself. The professed monk entered an enclosure that always bore the imprint of the world beyond, just as the unprofessed were always conscious of their community beginnings within the sanctuary.

The first Benedictine monasteries were raised from the foundations, however vestigial, of an existing ecclesiastical and social infrastructure. The convents that were called upon to adopt the *RB* in the dioceses of Albi, Besançon and Soissons were connected to established churches.[9] Some of the earliest Anglo-Saxon monasteries to prioritise the customs of Benedict also emerged from a pre-existing network of churches. Certainly, Wilfrid's monastic colony at Ripon appropriated a church which had been served

---

[4] See above, p. 10.
[5] Cassian, *Conlationes*, xi, pref. 1. See also Klingshirn, *Caesarius of Arles*, pp. 23–4 at 23.
[6] Blair, *Church in Anglo-Saxon Society*, p. 218.
[7] Dunn, *Emergence of Monasticism*, pp. 92–3; Blair, *Church in Anglo-Saxon Society*, p. 204 (on ecclesiastical building 'in the manner of the Romans').
[8] Dunn, *Emergence of Monasticism*, pp. 90, 98.
[9] See above, pp. 23–4.

probably by Celtic monks.[10] A number of the English convents formed in the 'boom' years either side of 700 were also connected with earlier, and in some cases, Celtic churches: Aldhelm's Sherborne (*c.* 705) was a new minster in what may have been a much older place of observant worship.[11] Whether or not there was already a church, the early Anglo-Saxon converts to monastic religion conceived their convents within existing settlements, 'engrossing for themselves small estates and villages' ('agellulis sive vicis'), as Bede described it.[12] Pioneering communities were also propagated amid the residue of Roman social and sacral occupation. Famously, Columban's Luxeuil (*c.* 600) was once Luxovium, a Roman settlement which apparently retained its 'baths constructed with unusual skill [and] a great number of stone, idols, which in the old heathen times had been worshipped with horrible rites'.[13] The site of Fleury, first colonised from *c.* 640, was believed to have been a villa complex called Floriacum.[14] The *locus* of the first monastery at Abingdon (*c.* 675) appears to have been determined by its connection with a former centre of Roman administration; the minster at Reculver (Kent) was raised on the remains of a Roman fort.[15] Willibrord's model community at Echternach, established in the years after 698, originated both as villa and non-monastic basilica before being granted to the missionary.[16] Even in regions which had not witnessed earlier occupation, the Benedictine pioneers showed a preference for natural points of contact, *foci* of communication, trade and travel: Farfa was planted above a tributary of the Tiber; the first monastic foundations of upper Normandy (Jumièges, Saint-Ouen, Saint-Wandrille) modelled later patterns of settlement in the valley of the Seine; Reichenau (724) may have been an island monastery but it was strategically significant, presiding over the isthmus between the upper and lower lakes of Constance.[17]

[10] Ripon had first been placed in the custody of brethren from Lindisfarne: Mayr-Harting, *Coming of Christianity*, p. 107; Blair, *Church in Anglo-Saxon Society*, p. 95.

[11] Blair, *Church in Anglo-Saxon Society*, pp. 29–30; Glastonbury also may claim Celtic origins: *MO*, p. 2; L. Abrams, *Anglo-Saxon Glastonbury: Church and Endowment* (Woodbridge, 1996), pp. 1–9.

[12] Blair, *Church in Anglo-Saxon Society*, p. 101. The phrase is found in the twelfth chapter of Bede's letter to Egbert, archbishop of York: *Historiam Ecclesiasticam Gentis Anglorum*, ed. C. Plummer (Oxford, 1896), pp. 405–23 at 415.

[13] Jonas, *Life of St Columban*, c. 17 [ed. Munro, p. 32]. See also I. Wood, 'Prelude to Columbanus: The Monastic Achievement in the Burgundian territories', in *Columbanus*, ed. Clarke and Brennan, pp. 3–32.

[14] For Fleury, see T. Head, *Hagiography and the Cult of Saints: The Diocese of Orléans, 800–1200* (Cambridge, 1990), pp. 23–5; J. Laporte, 'Fleury', *Dictionnaire d'histoire et de géographie écclesiastique* 17 (Paris, 1969), col. 441–76.

[15] Mayr-Harting, *Coming of Christianity*, p. 245; Blair, *Church in Anglo-Saxon Society*, p. 249.

[16] Brown, *Rise of Western Christendom*, p. 417.

[17] Costambeys, *Power and Patronage*, p. 9. For the first phase of monastic foundation in Normandy, see J. Laporte, 'Les origines du monachisme dans la province de Rouen', *Revue Mabillon* 31 (1941); Fouracre and Gerberding, *Late Merovingian France*, p. 148; Potts, *Monastic Revival and Regional Identity*, pp. 1–13 at 11. For Reichenau, see H. J. Hummer, *Politics and Power in Early Medieval Europe: Alsace and the Frankish Realm*, Cambridge Studies in Medieval Life and Thought, 4th Series 65 (Cambridge, 2005), pp. 10, 57–9.

It has been suggested there were deliberate differences in the location and form of the female monastery. A study of nunneries in England has drawn attention to the marginal sites offered by founders, peripheral to settlement and remote from natural resources. These houses did not match the scale and scope of the greater abbeys and priories of the men, but we should be wary of generalisation: there were convents of women which were bound closely to settlement centres; moreover, their material and documentary records continue to challenge critical assumptions.[18]

The form of these first (semi-)Benedictine settlements was variable. There may have been a broad spectrum of *monasteria* in seventh-century France: the shadowy convents known only from episcopal decrees, which perhaps followed the basilical model, the communities which recognised Bishop Donatus as their master which in their scale and infrastructure may have constituted colonies, and between the two constituencies, the novel villa monasteries of the Loire, Seine and Somme.[19] England in the same period seems comparable, the diversity of form perhaps amplified by the peripheral presence of Celtic monks; the early prevalence of the double monastery is perhaps a measure of their influence.[20] These early, experimental Benedictines may even have lacked a common experience of worship in their respective oratories. The character of the earliest churches remains unclear: stone was not universal but perhaps also not as scarce as is often assumed, at least for the church building; although not necessarily indicative of the first churches on the site, excavations in England have revealed churches of great scale (200 ft at Abingdon) and grandeur (fragments of bronze decoration at Glastonbury); Wilfrid's church at Ripon was 'adorned ... with gold, silver and various purples'; Hexham was said to have no parallel north of the Alps.[21] There were also significant differences in the structure and scale of the monastic enclosure and its immediate environs. Benedict's vision of the common life of dormitory, refectory and chapter house was perhaps realised at Fleury, and other Continental convents, but in England traces of the eremitical alternative endured: from Wessex to Northumbria, the earliest *monasteria* incorporated individual cells at least for senior and sick brethren.[22] The largest of these houses may have incorporated a complex of domestic buildings conspicuous for its contrast to secular settlements. Certainly the discrete but complementary accommodation for men and

---

[18] Gilchrist, *Gender and Material Culture*, pp. 63–90. Thompson, *Women Religious*, pp. 16–79, noting both the eremitic and social sources of female communities; Vernarde, *Women's Monasticism*, pp. 141–2.

[19] For these foundations, see above, pp. 19–24.

[20] Blair, *Church in Anglo-Saxon Society*, p. 72.

[21] *The Archaeology of Anglo-Saxon England*, ed. D. M. Wilson (London, 1976), pp. 217, 244; Gilchrist, *Gender and Material Culture*, pp. 92–3; *Wilfrid*, pp. 34–7.

[22] Mayr-Harting, *Coming of Christianity*, pp. 139–44 (the traces of asceticism in Wilfrid), 149–59 at 150 (evidence of cells at Whitby), 163–4 (the diversity of modes that persisted); Blair, *Church in Anglo-Saxon Society*, pp. 212–20 at 219&n.

women of mixed communities was a configuration of space that had no obvious parallel in the wider world.[23] Yet lesser (and less populated) houses, and those remote from ecclesiastical centres, may have been remarkable for their resemblance to the halls and huts of the still nucleated clusters of layfolk; perhaps there was a trace in their fabric of the royal origin of their foundation; the cave dwelling Benedictines of Brantôme (Dordogne) adopted a domestic mode that pre-dated Christianity itself.[24] Nor was there yet any common pattern in the shape or extent of their immediate environs. It has been suggested that the first Roman monasteries in England maintained modest precincts by comparison with their Celtic counterparts. The *Lives* of the early Continental missionaries convey an impression of concourses crowded with converts and pilgrims, although also where space was severely constrained, 'the walls ... could with difficulty hold so great a throng of converts'. An anonymous eighth-century verse from England, *De abbatibus*, suggests the precinct did not provide (permanent) space for the unprofessed.[25] Bede described minsters with well defined (and perhaps stone-built) boundaries, which suggest fortification, although archaeological evidence reveals that precinct boundaries could also be of sufficient size and distance from the enclosure to employ hedgerow or earthworks; such works also distinguished them from secular settlements.[26]

The reform movements of the tenth century promoted common patterns for both the church and enclosure. The liturgical regime of the reformers, and in particular the customs of Cluny, required a church with an enlarged choir that was integral to the monastic enclosure.[27] The renewal of regular discipline *ad literam* also demanded a common living space and the removal of any trace of eremitic individualism. The tripartite structure of church, chapter house and cloister was now widely disseminated. It was under Archbishop Dunstan that the cloister was developed in England; the prototype was perhaps developed at Glastonbury during his brief tenure of the abbacy (c. 957–63).[28]

Indirectly, the reform also led to the further elaboration of the precinct. The cause of reform was advanced in France, Germany and Anglo-Saxon England through collaboration with seigniorial authorities, and the houses they founded, or refounded, were bound to their own centres of administrative and political power. Now the environs of the monastery were invested with strategic, social or economic significance not because of past associations but by present need. The pioneers' monasteries had prefigured

[23] Blair, *Church in Anglo-Saxon Society*, pp. 81–2.
[24] Ibid., pp. 202–3, 205.
[25] Jonas, *Life of St Columban*, ed. Munro, p. 32; Blair, *Church in Anglo-Saxon Society*, p. 222; see also pp. 189, 196&n, 203–4.
[26] Ibid.; Gilchrist, *Gender and Material Culture*, pp. 92–3, 194.
[27] See above, pp. 92, 94, 102–3.
[28] *The Archaeology of Anglo-Saxon England*, ed. Wilson, p. 242; *MO*, pp. 38–9.

such a transformation: Stephen had written of the 'dignitaries of every kind gathered together' at Wilfrid's Ripon, 'reeves and the subkings' among them.[29] The precinct became the *locus* of political transactions, of negotiations, treaties and seigniorial *acta* recorded in diplomata (i.e. charters) now issued from the monastery's own chancery, inscribed by its own copyists and witnessed by its leadership.[30] As a consequence it also became the common recourse not only of magnates and their household but also their militia, their tenants and at times their enemies. The precinct was adapted to their needs with accommodation, workshops, armaments and fortifications which were not always rudimentary. The abbey at Corbie was fortified under the terms of a charter issued by Charles the Simple in 867.[31] The infrastructure developed further as the number of seigniorial foundations steadily rose, at the turn of the eleventh century in Normandy, England, Lombardy, Aragon and Castile. The female monastery of Castle Hedingham was co-located at the castle of its founder, Aubrey de Vere, earl of Oxford.[32] Guibert de Nogent, whose house was a product of this later phase of foundation, neatly reflected the conjunction of worship and lordship in the monastic landscape, 'a new residence for monks [whose] use for worship by worldly society is very old ... standing below the stronghold of Coucy ... and closely surrounded by very rich manors'.[33] Excavation has brought the broad scope of these precincts into focus, yielding traces of diverse husbandry (e.g. fishponds), manufacture (e.g. metals) and weaponry.[34]

Such was the seigniorial significance of these new monastic foundations that not only did they transform their immediate environs but also they carried an imprint of their mode of life, authority and business to outlying settlements. This was (and is) palpable in the pastoral landscape of southern Burgundy where so many market centres, farm networks and fortified *bastides* were redeveloped at the direction of Cluny and its cadre of secular clients.[35] It was also apparent among the great abbeys of northern France whose early endowment enabled in many cases the *ab initio* development of farms, mills, villages and markets.[36] Within a narrower radius, it was also true of the independent houses founded in England in the years

---

[29] *Wilfrid*, pp. 36–7.

[30] For example, St Gall in the ninth century: R. McKitterick, *The Carolingians and the Written Word* (Cambridge, 1989), p. 80; Winchester in the tenth century: M. T. Clanchy, *From Memory to Written Record. England, 1066–1307* (Oxford, 1993), pp. 156, 163.

[31] *Recueil des actes de Charles II le Chauve*, ed. G. Tessier, 2 vols. (Paris, 1952), ii. 170–6.

[32] Gilchrist, *Gender and Material Culture*, p. 63.

[33] *Guibert*, p. 119.

[34] For example, Verhulst, *Carolingian Economy*, p. 78 (Bobbio, St Gall); Gilchrist, *Gender and Material Culture*, pp. 77–8, 83.

[35] For Cluniac Burgundy, see R. H. Leech, 'Cluny et le développement urbain en Bourgogne du sud', in *La ville de Cluny et ses maisons, XIe–XVe siècles*, ed. P. Garrigou Grandchamp (Paris, 1997), pp. 76–87; M. Angheben, *Les chapiteaux romans de Bourgogne: thèmes et programmes* (Turnhout, 2003). See also J. Evans, *The Romanesque Architecture of the Order of Cluny* (Cambridge, 1938), rev. K. J. Conant and N. Stratford (Farnborough, 1972).

[36] For Normandy, see Chibnall, *World of Orderic Vitalis*, pp. 58–85.

before and after the Norman Conquest. The estates of Glastonbury Abbey were on a scale comparable to its Norman counterparts and the built and husbanded environment that surrounded it owed its shape, use and yield to the monastery and its subordinates.[37] Yet smaller monasteries also shaped satellite communities: the vill of Barnhorn (Sussex) owed its very existence to Battle Abbey as a manorial retreat for its weary brethren.[38]

The creative force of the Benedictine monastery was most conspicuous in the formation of urban centres. Throughout Europe there were towns whose early development was directed by an adjoining abbey.[39] The *vicus monasterii* (literally, monastic city) was evident in mainland regions even in the mid-ninth century; in England it was a century later, in the wake of the Benedictine reform, that new and renewed foundations were chartered with the right to develop the burgh beyond the precinct boundary.[40] Some of the principal towns of provincial England were the product of monastic foundations: Bury (Suffolk), known in the Middle Ages as St Edmund's Bury, was a planned grid-pattern town, whose settlement, trade and spatial orientation were wholly determined (from the end of the eleventh century) by the monastery, itself a tenth-century foundation; St Albans arose from the ruins of Roman Verulamium, but its Benedictine abbey not only controlled its redevelopment but also changed the location of its principal marketplace which had naturally gravitated towards the London road. Here the monastery not only regulated patterns of residence and trade but also that of time itself: in the fifteenth century the abbot and convent erected a clock in their marketplace which matched the claustral clock inside the enclosure.[41] The force of these male houses in the urban environment was rarely matched by their female counterparts: the site and limited scope of their endowments left the women subordinate to the development of the town: the convent of St Radegund, Cambridge, was contained within a bend of the River Cam.[42]

[37] *MO*, pp. 100–2. See also M. M. Postan, 'Glastonbury Estates in the Twelfth Century', *Economic History Review* 2nd Series, 5 (1953), 358–67, (1956), 106–18. See also Abrams, *Anglo-Saxon Glastonbury*, pp. 42–257; P. Clery, *The Wealth and Estates of Glastonbury Abbey at the Dissolution* (Sutton Bridge, 2003).

[38] A. Evans, 'Actors in the Accounts of Battle Abbey', *Huntington Library Quarterly* 6 (1942), 103–5 at 103. See also E. Searle, *Lordship and Community: Battle Abbey and its Banlieu, 1066–1538* (Toronto, 1974), pp. 40–2. Janet Burton has highlighted Benedictine foundations (Selby, Whitby, St Mary's, York) shaping satellite economic and social centres in post-Conquest Yorkshire: Burton, *Monastic Order in Yorkshire*, pp. 42–3, 245–9.

[39] A. E. Verhulst, *Carolingian Economy* (Cambridge, 2002), p. 22.

[40] Blair, *Church in Anglo-Saxon Society*, p. 333; M. de Jong, 'Carolingian Monasticism: The Power of Prayer', in *The New Cambridge Medieval History*, ii, ed. R. McKitterick (Cambridge, 1995) pp. 622–53; A. E. Verhulst, *The Rise of Cities in North-West Europe*, Themes in International Urban History 4 (Cambridge, 1999), p. 53; Searle, *Lordship and Community*, pp. 69–88; *Gallia monastica*, i. 13.

[41] For Bury St Edmunds, see A. Gransden, *A History of the Abbey of Bury St Edmunds, 1182–1256: Samson of Tottington to Edmund of Walpole*, Studies in the History of Medieval Religion 31 (Woodbridge, 2007), pp. 44–50. For St Albans, see T. R. Slater, 'Benedictine Town Planning in Medieval England: Evidence from St Albans', in *The Church in the Medieval Town*, ed. T. R. Slater and G. Rosser (Aldershot, 1998), pp. 155–76.

[42] Gilchrist, *Gender and Material Culture*, p. 64.

The Benedictines fostered urban communities but it is often suggested that in the later Middle Ages their supervision curtailed their development.[43] Certainly, in trade they were as restrictive to external investment or involvement as any guild or mistery, and in governance as inherently unrepresentative as any seigniorial authority. They also determined the focus and form of spiritual life and the provision of education, charity and other forms of social welfare. Their hold over the horizons of their inhabitants incited recurrent rebellion. Yet many of these towns endured, expanded and prospered even in the difficult decades after the Black Death. The pre-Reformation buildings of Bury or Charlieu (and Reading or Saint-Omer, had they survived) bear witness to the enterprise and investment that could be propagated under Benedictine patronage. The scale of these communities suggests the continuity and security connected with a monastic environment attracted migrants at a time when urban depopulation was widespread. The formation of a rudimentary corporate structure, recognised by the monastic superior, in England, for example, at Reading and Shrewsbury, is perhaps a sign of a new collaboration in the shadow of the Henrician suppressions.[44] It is worth noting that the corporate structures, and in many cases the patterns of residence, trade and spirituality, of the monastic *urbs* persisted in the post-Reformation period.[45]

The conurbation of the Benedictines marked them indelibly in the medieval imagination. Their presence in the commercial and residential concourses of secular society was rationalised by clerical commentators: the author of the *Libellus de diversis ordinibus* drew attention to an Old Testament precedent for their role (1 Samuel 10:5), 'the company of prophets' which came down to the people 'from the high place', that is, the 'hill of God' which adjoined the garrison of the Philistines ('collem Domini iuxta stationem Phylistinorum').[46] Still satirists sharply rebuked them: 'religion is a rider, a runner-by-streets'.[47] The sociability of the Black Monks served to shape the physical environment and the identity of the reformed orders. The Cistercians sought simple settlements in rural seclusion as a conscious rejection of the monastic 'cities' of contemporary Cluny. The Carthusians recast the monastic enclosure itself, to secure isolation in individual cells

---

[43] For example, at Bury St Edmunds: R. S. Gottfried, *Bury St Edmunds and the Urban Crisis, 1290–1539* (Princeton, 1982), pp. 215–36 at 215.

[44] For example: J. Martin, 'Leadership and Priorities in Reading during the Reformation', in *The Reformation in English Towns, 1500–1640*, ed. P. Collinson and J. Craig (Basingstoke, 1998), pp. 113–29; B. Coulton, 'The Establishment of Protestantism in a Provincial Town: a Study of Shrewsbury in the Sixteenth Century', *Sixteenth Century Journal* 27 (1996), 307–35.

[45] For example: C. J. Litzenberger, 'The Coming of Protestantism to Elizabethan Tewkesbury', in *The Reformation in English Towns*, ed. Collinson and Craig, pp. 79–93; *VCH Hertfordshire*, ii. 477–83 at 480–1.

[46] *Libellus*, pp. 18–20.

[47] *Piers Plowman*, B text, Passus X, l. 311.

configured around a common oratory, a re-creation of the presumed setting of the pre-Benedictine pioneers.[48]

The Monastic Economy

The Benedictines' presence in society was, above all, a product of their material status. Of course, every medieval religious, even the mendicants who aspired to the poverty of Christ, entered into the economic nexus, but only the Black Monks were so closely identified with their resources and transactions: they were 'possessioners', defined and, in polemic, damned by their desire for temporal goods.[49] Benedict had conceived of a subsistence community ('monachi sunt si manuum suarum vivunt': *RB*, xlviii) but his own *cenobium* was not wholly detached from the wider economy, collaborating with neighbouring farmers in times of dearth (*Dialogues*, 2. 19). The earliest Benedictine foundations required significant resources – territory, raw materials, infrastructure, personnel – to secure them in unstable regions; a growing recognition of the strategic and spiritual rewards of such foundations encouraged further endowment; the liturgical and scholarly programmes of the tenth- and eleventh-century reformers undermined the daily *opus manuum* and intensified the demand for resource. Before the turn of the millennium Benedictine monasteries had already emerged as valuable and vigorous economic enterprises; by the twelfth century the largest of them – Christ Church, Canterbury, Durham, Cluny, Cassino – contributed as much to the regional economy, and in a number of cases on a national scale, as any city entrepôt. The political and spiritual climate of the fourteenth and fifteenth centuries curtailed further growth but the scale and relative strength of the monastic economy remained formidable in the long shadow cast by the Black Death.

Like any magnate of the Middle Ages, the material resources of the Black Monks were founded on land, and the labour to exploit it. There is no precise measure of the site occupied by Benedict's *cenobia* at Montecassino, Subiaco and Terracina, although when it was restored after 718 Cassino was said to have been presented with a patrimony 'cuncta in circuitu montana et planiora'.[50] The pioneers of Benedictinism in England and Gaul held significant territory. Sigebert III (d. 656×600) provided Stavelot-Malmédy with the entirety of 'terra nostra silva Ardenense'.[51] Bishop Wilfrid's grant

---

[48] For the physical and spatial organisation of the reformed orders, see, for example, G. Coppack and J. Hall, 'The Church of Mount Grace Priory: its Development and Origins', in *Studies in Carthusian Monasticism in the Late Middle Ages*, ed. J. Luxford, Medieval Church Studies 14 (Turnhout, 2008), pp. 299–322; J. Hogg, 'The Architecture of Hinton Charterhouse', *Analecta Cartusiana* 25 (1975), 1–96.

[49] John Wyclif, *Responsiones ad XLIV conclusiones sive ad argucia monachales*, in *Opera minora Iohannis Wycliffe*, ed. J. Loserth, Wyclif Society (1913), pp. 201–57 at 235–6.

[50] Bloch, *Monte Cassino in the Middle Ages*, i. 264–72.

[51] J. M. Wallace-Hadrill, *The Long-Haired Kings* (Toronto, 1982), p. 234.

of Ripon (660) included 30 hides (3,600 acres) of land, to which was added 'one quarter of the Isle of Wight' in 686.[52] The eighth-century foundation of Saint-Hubert-en-Ardennes was endowed with no fewer than forty villages which came to be known as 'la terre de saint-Hubert'.[53] These first, formidable domains were diminished over time. The incursions of Norsemen interrupted monastic interests in the valley of the Seine, and in the north, east and extreme west of England, but in these regions and elsewhere it may have been seigniorial interference (of both bishops and lay magnates) – the 'robbery of evil men', as a contemporary commentator termed it – that resulted in the permanent loss of lands.[54] Such illicit seizures meant the new or renewed monasteries of the tenth and eleventh centuries were generally raised on reduced and geographically concentrated gifts of lands, although the very fact of their recovery perhaps bears witness to the coherence of their original holdings.[55] Ramsey (Cambridgeshire) was endowed with 30 hides, a compact of estates from the ealdorman Æthelwine and Bishop Oswald's own patrimony; likewise, the 'terra' of Wherwell (Hampshire) lay within 6 miles of the abbey.[56] The restored Saint-Evroult (Normandy) received only a modest portion which was grown gradually through 'the gifts of a few ploughlands'.[57] Glastonbury Abbey, which appears by 1066 to have held as many as 100 hides (12,000 acres), was apparently an exception.[58] In this period the nature of the monastery's property emerges from a greater profusion of written records. The territory of these reformed convents comprised farmsteads, hamlets and villages which increasingly were clustered in a form that was recognisably manorial.[59] The wealth of a monastery was measured not only by the extent of its lands but also by the number and significance of its manors, supplemented, of course, by the presence of natural resources such as woodland; there was a disparity in the tally of manors between male and female houses.[60] The Gregorian period witnessed extraordinary growth in the territorial wealth of the Benedictines. The advance of Cluny, and the Norman hegemony, yielded

---

[52] *MO*, pp. 21–2; Blair, *Church in Anglo-Saxon Society*, p. 87&n. See also *Wilfrid*, pp. 16–17.

[53] Wood, *Proprietary Church*, p. 110&n.

[54] 'King Edgar's Establishment of the Monasteries', in *Councils and Synods*, i.142–54 at 153.

[55] *The Monks of Redon: Gesta sanctorum rotonensium and Vita conuuoinionis*, ed. and trans. C. Brett, Studies in Celtic History 10 (Woodbridge, 1989), p. 4. T. Pestell, *Landscapes of Monastic Foundation: The Establishment of Religious Houses in East Anglia, c. 650–1200* (Woodbridge, 2004), pp. 118–19; Foot, *Monastic Life*, pp. 341–3.

[56] *MO*, pp. 51, 55, 59; Gilchrist, *Gender and Material Culture*, p. 71. See also A. R. DeWindt and E. B. DeWindt, *Ramsey: The Lives of an English Fenland Town, 1200–1600* (Washington, DC, 2006), p. 12; C. J. R. Hart, 'The Foundation of Ramsey Abbey', *Rev. Bén.* 104 (1994), 295–327 at 308–9.

[57] Chibnall, *World of Orderic Vitalis*, p. 63. For patterns of growth in this period see also *Gallia monastica*, i. 11–13, 29 (Saint-Remi de Reims) 152 (Saint-Thierry) 224–6 (Saint-Nicaise); Searle, *Lordship and Community*, pp. 21–35.

[58] *DB*, viii. 90a–d; *Chronicle of John of Glastonbury*, ed. Carley, pp. 154–5.

[59] Foot, *Monastic Life in Anglo-Saxon England*, pp. 251–82; Blair, *Church in Anglo-Saxon Society*, pp. 253–4.

[60] Barking held 13, Peterborough 27: Gilchrist, *Gender and Material Culture*, p. 72.

a harvest of foreign estates for the abbeys of northern and western France.[61] It was also the final period of medieval expansion. Cultural, economic and political change curbed monastic endowment in England even before the 1279 Statute of Mortmain prohibited it, except under licence.[62] Although the pressure on land was perhaps less pronounced, the prevalence of grants *in commendam* – the transfer of revenue from the foundation to another beneficiary – in mainland Europe also acted as a constraint on benefaction. There was a cultural change of which the monks were conscious: 'kings, princes ... and nobles' [were] devoted servants of Christ' but 'now the charity of many grows cold'.[63] The later medieval monastery was sustained by an extensive and rich portfolio of property but one whose proportions had been set two, three or four centuries before.

It should be noted that in the early and high Middle Ages it was not wholly unknown for individual brethren to retain their interest in temporal property after their profession. The well-born recruits of the eighth and ninth centuries carried their inheritance into the precinct; indeed, the model communities of Bishop Chrodegang and Abbot Benedict of Aniane were founded on such family properties. The practice continued into the Gregorian period, when it became a conspicuous cause of reform: looking back, the Abingdon annalist observed ruefully, 'it was then the custom among the English that those monks who wished might receive goods and patrimonies [and] enjoy them'.[64]

The main source of revenue from monastic property was the mixed agriculture practised throughout the Middle Ages, notwithstanding the different forms of manorial setting. The division of pasture and plough land, the number of livestock and the labour resources of these properties are poorly documented before the twelfth century. Certainly, there was regional (and, of course, topographical) variation: the early Benedictines of southern and western England, Flanders and Normandy were for the most part arable farmers, while their counterparts in the north, Germany and northern Italy were stockmen.[65] The Black Monks of Normandy maintained, indeed extended, their arable enterprise in subsequent centuries. Even

[61] For example, J. Potter, 'The Benefactors of Bec and the Politics of Priories', *Anglo-Norman Studies* 21 (1998), 175–92; Cownie, *Religious Patronage*.
[62] For the effect of Mortmain on monastic England, see S. Raban, *Mortmain Legislation and the English Church, 1279–1500* (Cambridge, 1982); P. Brand, 'The Mortmain Licensing System, 1280–1307', in *English Government in the Thirteenth Century*, ed. A. Jobson (Woodbridge, 2004), pp. 87–96; E. D. Jones, 'The Crown, Three Benedictine Houses and the Statute of Mortmain, 1279–1348', *Journal of British Studies* 14:2 (1975), 1–28. See also M. Mate, 'Property Investment by Canterbury Cathedral Priory, 1250–1400', *Journal of British Studies* 23:2 (1984), 1–21 at 12; B. J. Thompson, 'The Church and the Aristocracy: Lay and Ecclesiastical Landowning Society in Fourteenth-Century Norfolk' (PhD diss., Cambridge, 1990), p. 197.
[63] *Chronicle of John of Glastonbury*, ed. Carley, pp. 38–9.
[64] McKitterick, *Frankish Kingdoms*, p. 45; Lawrence, *Medieval Monasticism*, p. 74; *HEA*, i. 212–13.
[65] Verhulst, *Carolingian Economy*, pp. 76–8; Blair, *Church in Anglo-Saxon Society*, pp. 252–4; Gilchrist, *Gender and Material Culture*, p. 72.

before 1100 the houses of the upper and lower Seine – Saint-Germain-des-Prés, Saint-Wandrille – held scores of mills; the monks of Saint-Omer changed the course of the River Aa for the construction of further mills at Arques.[66] Here, and in regions of France to the south and west, and in the Rhineland, the Black Monks also turned their lands over to vines: Prüm Abbey had produced 120,000 litres of wine *per annum* even before the turn of the millennium.[67] The English Black Monks also advanced their arable activity, not least as a result of fenland and wetland reclamation.[68] There are indications of an interest in the science of yields not seen among other landlords of the period: the compotus rolls record early purchases of lime for marling.[69] Later records also show rising levels of livestock: the monks of Peterborough ran 1,500 head of sheep on their thirteen manors in *c.* 1125; the cathedral priory of St Swithun, Winchester, had amassed 20,000 head by the fourteenth century.[70] The agriculture of the women's houses was predominantly pastoral.[71] From this period, the Black Monks in England and Normandy also profited from warrening: Bury St Edmunds received 15 shillings from a single warren at Mildenhall by 1247–8.[72] Benedictine herds in England did not reach the scale of those run by the Cistercians, routinely numbered in the thousands, but they remained a conspicuous presence on their properties even at the Reformation; a resurgence of pastoral farming was also apparent in France at the end of the Middle Ages.[73]

Revenue was also raised from the natural resources of their lands. Indeed, the presence and material potential of these resources were guiding principles of the early foundations. It was with an awareness of its material value that Sigebert III assigned the 'new forest' ('silva nova') to his twin house of Stavelot-Malmédy.[74] The lands of the early monasteries of north, eastern and central France were notably rich in woodland and in the raw materials, and fish, to be recovered from their rivers and wetlands: the

---

[66] Verhulst, *Carolingian Economy*, p. 69.

[67] Ibid., p. 71.

[68] For example, S. Raban, *The Estates of Thorney and Crowland*, University of Cambridge Department of Land Economy Occasional Paper 7 (Cambridge, 1977), pp. 47–9. See also Searle, *Lordship and Community*, pp. 269–323; Gilchrist, *Gender and Material Culture*, p. 68. For reclamation projects of the religious in south west France, see E. Ladurie, *Peasants of Languedoc* (Urbana, IL, 1974), pp. 36–7.

[69] Gransden, *History of the Abbey of Bury St Edmunds*, p. 258.

[70] King, *Peterborough Abbey*, pp. 154–5; 'The Southern Counties', in *The Agrarian History of England and Wales*, iii. *1348–1500*, ed. E. Miller (Cambridge, 1991), pp. 285–303 at 292.

[71] Gilchrist, *Gender and Material Culture*, pp. 72–3; A. Savine, 'English Monasteries on the Eve of the Suppression', in *Oxford Studies in Legal and Social History*, ed. P. Vinogradoff, vol. 1 (Oxford, 1909), pp. 140–217 at 186–8, 193–7.

[72] M. Bailey, *A Marginal Economy: East Anglian Breckland in the Later Middle Ages* (Cambridge, 1989), p. 132.

[73] For France in this period, see Ladurie, *Peasants of Languedoc*, pp. 43–4.

[74] C. Wickham, *Land and Power: Studies in Italian and European Social History, 400–1200* (London, 1994), p. 177; Wood, *Proprietory Church*, pp. 117, 221.

income of Fécamp was dependent upon its fisheries.[75] The harvest of the rivers and water meadows was equally important to the Benedictine pioneers in England. Aldhelm of Malmesbury pursued a particular estate for his house because it was 'especially suitable for the catching of fish'.[76] The early foundations of Germany were able to exploit salt deposits (for example, at Mondsee, Tegernsee, Niederaltaich) and iron ore (at Fulda, Lorsch and Saint-Gall).[77] The direct farming of estates may have diminished during the later Middle Ages, but the religious continued to exploit their natural environment. The Cistercian women of Esholt and Marrick (Yorkshire) profited from quarries; Benedictine Tavistock owed a large proportion of its £900 per annum (1535) to the extraction of tin from its estates.[78]

The monasteries also raised revenue from the rights associated with their lands. Those with authority over wide areas of woodland exercised a monopoly on the production and sale of timber, reinforced by fines for its illicit removal. Those situated by navigable rivers, and associated freshwater fishing grounds, such as the Seine abbeys, Stavelot–Malmédy, and those of the English East Midlands, levied lucrative tolls.[79] Their agricultural infrastructure was also a source of income: within their territory they held exclusive rights to the construction and use of mills, with punitive sanctions for any farmer (land-holding peasant, tenant, or, indeed, magnate) who sought to circumvent it.[80] Founders and patrons elaborated these rights to underpin the material and seigniorial independence of their favoured houses. They empowered them not only to levy fees and fines but also to be exempt from those levied by higher authorities. Domesday Book (1086) demonstrates that a number of Anglo-Saxon foundations had been dispensed from the royal geld on all of their demesnes.[81] As regional economies, and towns and markets, developed, to these fundamental rights were added particular privileges to place tariffs on the transport and sale of goods within the territory of the monastery; a local monopoly on seasonal markets was secured by many monasteries in post-Conquest England.[82]

---

[75] Fécamp benefited from rights to the English ports of Hastings, Rye, Winchelsea and Steyning: Potts, *Monastic Revival and Regional Identity*, p. 129; *VCH Sussex*, ii. 3–4, 264–71 at 265. See also M. Aston, *Medieval Fish, Fisheries and Fishponds in England*, 2 vols. (Oxford, 1988).

[76] *Charters of Malmesbury Abbey*, ed. S. E. Kelly, Anglo-Saxon Charters 11 (Oxford, 2005), p. 148: 'precipue pro captura piscium apto et competenti loco'.

[77] Verhulst, *Carolingian Economy*, pp. 76, 80–2 at 82.

[78] Gilchrist, *Gender and Material Culture*, p. 71; H. P. R. Finberg, *Tavistock Abbey: A Study in Social and Economic History of Devon*, Studies in Medieval Life and Thought, New Series 2 (Cambridge, 1951), pp. 167–91.

[79] Verhulst, *Carolingian Economy*, p. 95; Aston, *Medieval Fish, Fisheries and Fishponds*, p. 81.

[80] For example, at Bury St Edmunds Abbot Samson's fury at the construction of a mill by Herbert the Dean: *Jocelin*, p. 94. See also J. S. Loengard, 'Lords' Rights and Neighbours' Nuisances: Mills and Medieval English Law', in *Wind and Water in the Middle Ages*, ed. S. A. Walton, Penn State Medieval Studies 2 (Tempe, AZ, 2006), pp. 129–52.

[81] For example, Ramsey: *DB*, I. 203b. Domesday remained an authority on monastic property on the eve of the Dissolution: Evans, 'Battle Abbey at the Dissolution: Expenses', 66.

[82] For example, Bury St Edmunds: Bailey, *A Marginal Economy*, p. 144.

The income raised from these resources was in cash and in kind. Before 1100 the bulk of their estates were farmed directly, which brought their yields to the monastery itself, or at least to one of its outlying manors, for use, re-deployment or sale. Raw materials were also presented to the monastery in whole or in part: Saint-Germain-des-Prés received consignments of fresh iron ore; at Fulda iron was worked on the manors and dispatched to the abbey as a finished article.[83] From the twelfth century, in England in particular but also in regions of mainland Europe, a greater proportion of monastic land was tenanted and the lion's share of the income was rental, although renders in kind continued, commonly paid to particular obedientiaries, at least until the thirteenth century.[84] Their reliance on the produce of their own lands appears to have declined sharply in the later Middle Ages. Certainly compotus rolls from England show that many monasteries were at least partially provisioned from commercial, urban food markets.[85] From the fourteenth century the greater abbeys and priories also supplemented their income with rents raised from urban properties, some secured from benefactors perhaps conscious of the curb on landed endowments but many others converted, developed or purchased especially for the purpose. As early as 1292 the treasurers of Christ Church Priory, Canterbury, expended £58 17s 2d, on building in the city.[86] Westminster Abbey bought residential, commercial and industrial property regularly, and on some scale, between the mid-thirteenth and the sixteenth centuries: as many as nine manors were purchased during the abbacy of John Islip (1510–32).[87] The monks of this period also became increasingly dependent on purchases for their resources in kind. Barbara Harvey has suggested the larger monasteries of England, such as Westminster, could not have maintained their standard of living without buying much of their produce.[88]

Throughout the Middle Ages the Benedictines also benefited from the income of 'spiritual' properties – that is, churches and other foundations invested with intercessory and pastoral functions, and served by a body of clergy, such as chapels, chantries and hospitals. The ties that bound churches to monasteries originated in the missionary objectives of the early pioneers. It was not an impulse confined to those that favoured the *RB*, but was common to all monastic movements of the seventh and eighth centuries: Columban's communities incorporated clusters of

---

[83] Verhulst, *Carolingian Economy*, pp. 77–8.
[84] B. F. Harvey, *The Obedientiaries of Westminster Abbey and their Financial Records, c. 1275–1540*, Westminster Abbey Record Series 3 (Woodbridge, 2002), pp. xxiv-xxv.
[85] Threlfall-Holmes, *Monks and Markets*, pp. 35–6.
[86] R. A. L. Smith, *Canterbury Cathedral Priory: A Study in Monastic Administration* (Cambridge, 1943), pp. 9–11, 195; Mate, 'Property Investment by Canterbury Cathedral Priory', 5.
[87] B. F. Harvey, *Westminster Abbey and its Estates in the Middle Ages* (Oxford, 1977), pp. 425–7 at 425–6. For comparable instances: Smith, *Canterbury Cathedral Priory*, pp. 9–11&n; *VCH Salop*, ii. 30–7 at 32 (Shrewsbury Abbey).
[88] Harvey, *Living and Dying*, pp. 34–72.

churches.[89] In Merovingian Gaul, Northumbria and Frisia, the primary role of the monastic colony was to sustain and extend the community of Christian believers, while the superior commonly served as their bishop. Their relationship to the nascent network of churches and chapels was represented in terms of pastoral leadership, but from its first beginnings it was also regarded, as much by the monks as by their royal and episcopal patrons, as collateral, another dimension of the material foundation of the monastery. The royal grant made to Wilfrid in *c.* 660 gave the churches of Ripon and Hexham as property (*proprietas*).[90] Although the documents are sparse, there is little doubt that many monasteries of the early period accrued churches, or at least pecuniary or tributary rights to them, as an adjunct to their territorial holdings.[91] The scale and significance of such spiritual property grew in the tenth century as the reformers aimed not only to consolidate the material status of their houses but also to challenge the seigniorial authority of regional magnates and prelates.[92] There was scarcely a church in the whole of the Charolais and Mâconnais that was not subject to Cluny: the abbey held 110 churches across the dioceses of Autun and Mâcon.[93] England's reformed convents also commanded a wide circle of churches: before the Conquest Abingdon apparently claimed authority over twenty-one Berkshire churches and another six in neighbouring counties.[94] In the final phase of Benedictine foundation and refoundation in the century after *c.* 1050, the currency of churches was widely employed as a means to enhance new and existing endowments. In the century after its revival in 1025, Orderic's Saint-Evroult received no fewer than thirty churches.[95] The new royal abbey of Reading, founded by Henry I in 1121, was granted three principal churches in its initial foundation charter; the abbey of Whitby secured as many as twenty-seven from its foundation to *c.* 1215.[96] The currency retained its use and value for the Benedictines and their benefactors for several generations after temporal endowments had declined: the greater nunneries extended or defended their income by grants of churches and chapels at least until the middle years of the thirteenth century.[97]

Churches were invested with a variety of resources, agricultural

[89] E. James, 'Archaeology and the Merovingian Monastery', in *Columbanus*, ed. Clarke and Brennan, pp. 33–55 at 41–4.

[90] *Wilfrid*, pp. 16–17. See also Blair, *Church in Anglo-Saxon Society*, pp. 87, 92–7.

[91] Blair, *Church in Anglo-Saxon Society*, pp. 155–60, 212–20.

[92] Wood, *Proprietary Church*, pp. 681–2.

[93] Ibid., p. 682. See also Rosenwein, *To be a neighbour of St Peter*, pp. 9–10, 196–7.

[94] Blair, *Church in Anglo-Saxon Society*, p. 300.

[95] Chibnall, *World of Orderic Vitalis*, p. 63; Wood, *Proprietary Church*, pp. 681–2.

[96] Chibnall, *World of Orderic Vitalis*, p. 63; *VCH Berkshire*, ii. 62–73 at 62–3.; Burton, *Monastic Order in Yorkshire*, p. 235. See also the fifteen churches on which Walden was founded: *Walden*, p. 7.

[97] For example, the Fontevraud priory (from 1177) of Amesbury: *VCH Wiltshire*, ii. 231–42 at 236; *MRH*, p. 94.

estates and, in time, tenements, and their associated revenues and rights, comparable to any temporal property. The nature and level of income which monasteries raised from 'their' churches in early centuries are not entirely clear; it is likely that tributes in kind were taken at least from nearby churches, although from the tenth century, and perhaps earlier, an annual tribute or pension in coin was also commonplace, at least in England.[98] The emergence of a parochial system served to establish a common tariff, of which the tithe was the principal element, although, of course, as proprietor the monastery might alienate the revenue of the church and its incumbent at will.[99] The parish system also propagated an array of customary charges connected with the rites required by all parishioners. Perhaps the most burdensome were funerary fees: charges obtained to burial whether within or beyond the parish or precinct cemetery; a mortuary payment was also due for tithes forgotten: both were frequently alienated by the monastic proprietor.[100] Of course, there was much variation in the value of monastic churches, and the tiny timber oratories of isolated settlements presented fabric and pastoral demands for only a meagre return. Yet the church that was well endowed was a source of revenue arguably more secure than tenanted temporal properties. In England they served to anchor the Black Monks through the turbulent waters of the post-Black Death depression.[101]

The permanent income raised from the (temporal and spiritual) property of the monastery was complemented by the *ad hoc* income accrued from fees, the most important of which were perhaps the entry fees charged on the *professus*, since they might convey a combination of cash, moveable goods and property. Certainly in the early Middle Ages it was commonplace for the entrant (male or female) to carry with them the prospect of a payment of some kind; in the age of expansion from the tenth to the twelfth centuries these transactions cemented the bond between the Benedictines and their seigniorial patrons. For women religious the process was formalised in the requirement for a dowry, generally a cash sum, for every profession. Dowries were prohibited under the Lateran canons of 1215, which subsequent supervisors and visitors sought to enforce, but they endured in England and mainland Europe into the sixteenth century.[102] In

[98] For example, the pensions paid at Walden: *Walden*, pp. 20–1.
[99] For a survey, see R. H. Snape, *English Monastic Finances in the Later Middle Ages* (Cambridge, 1926), pp. 74–91. For case-studies, see Harvey, *Westminster Abbey and its Estates*, pp. 45–55; Smith, *Canterbury Cathedral Priory*, p. 11; E. Stone, 'Profit-and-Loss Accountancy at Norwich Cathedral Priory', *TRHS* 5th Series 12 (1962), 25–48.
[100] Snape, *English Monastic Finances*, pp. 84–7. For case-studies, see M. Harvey, *Lay Religious Life in Late Medieval Durham* (Woodbridge, 2006), p. 90; Riche, *L'ordre de Cluny*, pp. 341–2 at 341.
[101] Snape, *English Monastic Finances*, pp. 76–9. For examples of recourse to spiritual resources, see Harvey, *Westminster Abbey and its Estates*, pp. 48–51, 402–9; *Canterbury College, Oxford*, ed. W. A. Pantin, 3 vols. (1947–85), iv. 14–16.
[102] For payment on entry see J. H. Lynch, *Simoniacal Entry into Religious Life from 1000–1260: A Social, Economic and Legal History* (Columbus, OH, 1976), pp. 61–81. For women see also Oliva, *Convent and Community*, pp. 148–50. The women religious of sixteenth-century Venice were dependent on dowry

the later Middle Ages no such transactions were required of male *professus*, although in England, and probably in Europe, each entrant was expected to purchase (or otherwise provide for) the clothing requirements (habit, undergarments, shoes, etc.) for their noviciate; in England no less a fee than £5 was paid, equivalent to the annual income of a skilled labourer at the beginning of the sixteenth century and not far from the total income of the poorer chantry foundation.[103]

It should not be forgotten that the financial well-being of the Benedictines was underwritten by the rich treasure they had accrued through patronage, persuasion, or penalty, over many generations. The earliest communities attracted gifts of precious plate and were also called upon to be the custodians of coinage and other valuable treasures. Whatever had been lost in the years of instability between the eighth and the tenth centuries was recovered or renewed in the age of reform, at least by the larger foundations. Battle Abbey acquired 300 amulets 'well made of gold and silver' from its founder; Wilton received a jewel in 1297 at the profession (at Amesbury) of Mary, daughter of Edward I.[104] The treasures of Cluny and its principal satellites stirred the dissatisfaction which powered the Cistercian and Carthusian movements. Impecunious monarchs and magnates made recourse to their treasuries: Geoffrey de Mandeville seized from Ramsey the 'gold and silver vessels ... [and] copes ... interwoven with precious stones' in 1144; Edward III borrowed plate to the value of £277 4s from Reading Abbey in 1338.[105] Their reserves of gold, and their role as guarantors of loans, also made a number of convents the locus for a public mint.[106]

Assessment of either the individual or collective wealth of Europe's Benedictines is still perilous. The surviving account rolls continue to present anomalies in the calculation of acreage and yield and in the record of irregular and regular payments which constrain an accurate estimate of *per corpora* income; the number of houses documented by decade after decade of accounts is too few to develop very detailed comparative data. Certainly, the Benedictine monasteries of England appear to have been of modest income before the Norman Conquest; indeed, during the difficult decades after the reformers' death some may have struggled, with low numbers, only a little above the level of subsistence. The patronage of the post-Conquest generation transformed their position; a network of independent abbeys emerged,

---

income: J. G. Sperling, *Convents and the Body Politic in Late Renaissance Venice* (Chicago, 1999), p. 187. See also Strocchia, *Nuns and Nunneries*, pp. 23–30.

[103] *RO*, i. 285; Oliva, *Convent and Community*, pp. 148–50.

[104] *Battle*, pp. 90–1; *VCH Wiltshire*, ii. 231–42 at 234 (1297).

[105] *Walden*, pp. 16–19; *VCH Berkshire*, ii. 62–73 at 66.

[106] For example, St Augustine's Abbey, Canterbury, profited from a mint franchise until the mid-twelfth century: T. C. R. Crafter, 'Henry II, the St Augustine's Dispute and the Loss of the Abbey's Mint Franchise', in *Coinage and History in the North Sea World, c. AD 500–1250*, ed. B. Cook and G. Williams (Leiden, 2006), pp. 601–16.

Christ Church, Canterbury, Glastonbury, Bury St Edmunds, St Albans, Westminster, as among the kingdom's richest churches.[107] The appeal to patrons of the principal houses (and shrines) and the general reduction in the scale of religious endowment stratified the English congregation: after 1300 at the head there was only a handful of abbeys and cathedral priories, a rump of roughly 'middle income' and a tail whose resources, while above subsistence, were small enough to threaten their survival.[108] The *Valor ecclesiasticus* of 1535 offers an indicative if not definitive measure of Benedictine means before the Reformation: here Shaftesbury was valued at £1,000, St Albans at £2,000, Westminster at £3,000 and Glastonbury at £4,000, Tavistock at £900, Selby at £600, Ramsey at £400, and a number of dependent houses and nunneries at between £100 and £200. Even here it is necessary to distinguish between wealth in cash and kind: while in 1535 the nunnery at Wilton claimed an income of a little over £650, it also held stocks of raw wool valued at 600 marks (a little under £400).[109] Such figures suggest the Black Monks experienced incomes higher than many of their monastic and mendicant colleagues; only the Yorkshire Cistercians could rival the revenue of the independent abbeys and cathedral priories.[110] Moreover, the nunneries and poorer priories of the Benedictines were often better resourced than their counterparts in other orders, or than many hospitals, schools or university colleges.[111] The largest of the Continental convents were wealthier than their English colleagues. The Black Monks of Normandy experienced a comparable fall and incremental expansion in their endowments between the early eleventh and the late twelfth centuries, but in Burgundy, the Rhineland, the Alps and northern Italy, there was no such interruption in the advance of their interests and income.[112]

There was scarcely a generation in which the greater and smaller monasteries enjoyed these resources undisturbed. Their tenure of temporal estates was repeatedly challenged. This was not only a feature of later medieval life, when the political and social pressure to preserve monastic property undoubtedly weakened. In the wake of the tenth-century revival of the *RB*, and a century later at the time of the Gregorian reform, the Black Monks

---

[107] Glastonbury's income was recorded as over £800 as early as Domesday Book (1086): *DB*, viii. 90a–d. See also *MRH*, pp. 66, 80.

[108] *MRH*, pp. 58–93; Savine, 'English Monasteries on the Eve of the Dissolution', pp. 269–88.

[109] Savine, 'English Monasteries on the Eve of the Dissolution', pp. 272, 274, 282, 287–8; *VCH Wiltshire*, ii. 231–42. See also *Valor ecclesiasticus tempore Henrico octavo auctoritate regia institutus*, ed. J. Caley, 6 vols. (London, 1810–34).

[110] Burton, *Monastic Order in Yorkshire*, pp. 230–1; C. V. Graves, 'The Economic Activities of the Cistercians in Medieval England', *Analecta sacri ordinis Cisterciensis* 13 (1957), 3–60.

[111] Power, *Medieval English Nunneries*, pp. 96–130; Thompson, *Women Religious*, pp. 161, 165, 167–8 (Elstow, Godstow, Nuneaton, although Thompson emphasises that from the outset many female foundations 'lacked a wealthy patron': ibid., 161); Kerr, *Religious Life for Women*, pp. 129–79; *MRH*, pp. 209–22. The *Valor ecclesiasticus* (1535) assessed the wealth of Amesbury above £400 p.a., Barking above £800 p.a., and Shaftesbury above £1,000 p.a.

[112] Potts, *Monastic Revival and Regional Identity*, pp. 36–80 at 63.

suffered significant losses. Reflecting on the consequences of conquest, William of Malmesbury underlined the number of estates wrested from Anglo-Saxon abbeys that were never restored.[113] Further losses were suffered by the English monks in the years of civil (1135–54) and baronial (1215–17) war;[114] their Norman brethren suffered in their turn during the English conquest (1417–20): Fécamp was compelled to cede its territories to the conquering English captain.[115] Revenues were also threatened by the ineluctable forces of disease and demographic crisis: between 1348 and 1360 Durham Priory lost more than half its tenants from twenty-eight towns under its jurisdiction; persistent depression compelled the convent to commute its rents by the turn of the fifteenth century.[116] The inflationary periods of the early thirteenth, mid-fourteenth and late fifteenth centuries also constrained their incomes.[117] Of course, the Black Monks also undermined conventual income by their own hands, whether through wanton grants (which Jocelin attributed to Abbot Hugh), wasteful expenditure, or the quasi-criminal alienation of conventual resources for personal use.[118] Certainly, throughout the high and later Middle Ages, many middling and larger monasteries were laden with debts. Such insolvency strengthened their ties to the social community beyond the gatehouse since it was to their own burghal neighbours that they turned for loans.[119]

Administration

The administration and management of these diverse resources engaged the monastic community as a whole. There was no place for such business in Benedict's *cenobium*: the brethren were to labour together for self-discipline and to sustain the community but only the cellarer under the supervision of the superior was to be charged with the mundanities of domestic management (*RB*, xxxi: 'Cellararius monasterii ... curam gerat de omnibus'). Even the earliest monasteries to adopt the *RB* may have placed greater demands

---

[113] *GR*, iii. 278, pp. 506–7: 'it would have been better to preserve the old foundations ... than to rob them to build new ones' ('melius fuisse ut antique in suo statu conservarentur quam illius semimutilatis de rapina nova construerentur'). See also R. Fleming, *Kings and Lords in Conquest England*, Cambridge Studies in Medieval Life and Thought 4th Series 15 (Cambridge, 1991), pp. 84–6.

[114] For example, *Walden*, pp. 16–19.

[115] *L'abbaye bénédictine de Fécamp*, Ouvrages scientifiques du XIIIe centenaire, 4 vols. (Fécamp, 1959–63), i. 148.

[116] R. H. Britnell, 'Feudal Reaction after the Black Death in the Palatinate of Durham', *PP* 128 (1990), 28–47 at 31; M. Bonney, *Lordship and the Urban Community: Durham and its Overlords, 1250–1540* (Cambridge, 2005), p. 144.

[117] The experience of inflation in England was part and parcel of the expansion of trade at the turn of the twelfth century in which the monasteries, particularly the wool producers, were prominent. See P. D. A. Harvey, 'The English Inflation of 1180–1220', *PP* 61 (1973), 3–30; P. Spufford, *Money and its Use in Medieval Europe* (Cambridge, 1987), pp. 243–5.

[118] *Jocelin*, pp. 1–5.

[119] Gottfried, *Bury St Edmunds and the Urban Crisis*, pp. 240–1 at 240; Riche, *L'ordre de Cluny*, pp. 266, 273, 390.

upon the principal officers and their brethren than the founder had envisaged. As the number and variety of their properties grew, administration challenged other occupations as a priority for the professed community; indeed, it may be observed that as the opportunity and need for manual labour receded, the hours required for administration rose; ironically, at the moment of the order's greatest influence in the years of the Gregorian reform, a growing number of Benedictines found themselves diverted from observance, *pastoralia*, or study, by the manors, townships and hundreds without the walls.[120] These demands intensified in the inclement economic environment of the later Middle Ages. A life of devoted administration was the experience of many Black Monks between their noviciate and their dotage in the infirmary, one that separated them from their reformed colleagues (Cistercians, Carthusians), from all but a minority of Regular Canons, and from the mendicant friars, a distinction that did not pass unnoticed by critical voices among clergy and laity.[121]

It appears the prescriptions of the *RB* prevailed in early centuries, although the management of the monastery's resources is rarely glimpsed in narrative sources. The cellarer assumed general responsibility for expenditure and receipts pertaining to the monastery itself: the cellarer's office at Saint-Gall lay at the centre of the monastic enclosure; Wifrid's administration of Ripon was assisted by a treasurer.[122] Chrodegang of Metz also adopted the office and its obligations for his *regula canonicorum*, where the role is elaborated in greater detail, perhaps reflecting prevailing custom in regular communities.[123] Matters of principle, of seigniorial or tenurial right, seem to have been the preserve of the superior; they represented the monastic community in negotiation as it may be with monarch, magnate, tenant or labourer: anecdotal evidence suggests they might even descend to the detail of determining labour service among their lowliest subjects.[124] There was a growing identification of the abbacy with administration: at Saint-Denis the date clause of charters even cited the *annus administrationis*.[125] The expansion of the monastery's properties and proprietorial interests, and its growing population, from at least the tenth century (and perhaps some time before) urged a greater distribution of responsibilities: the cellarer's management of internal resources was now supplemented by a sacrist, to whom responsibility for the furnishings of the oratory, altars and chapels now passed, and a chamberlain (*camerarius*) responsible for the domestic

---

[120] *Jocelin*, p. 1.
[121] *Piers Plowman*, B text, passus X, l. 313, represented (monastic) religion as 'a prikere on a palfrey from place to manere'.
[122] R. A. Stalley, *Early Medieval Architecture* (Oxford, 1999), p. 185; *Wilfrid*, p. 19.
[123] Claussen, *Reform of the Frankish Church*, pp. 84, 97–8.
[124] Gransden, *History of the Abbey of Bury St Edmunds*, p. 48.
[125] R. Berkhofer, *Day of Reckoning: Power and Accountability in Medieval France* (Philadelphia, 2004), p. 126.

needs of the monastic community, from the soap and towels for their bathing and shaving to the tallow to light the chapter house, dormitory and refectory.[126] External administration was now assisted by a bailiff assigned to each burgh, manor or vill in the possession of the monastery.[127] The monastic bailiff resided on the estate for which they held their office and exercised authority over land, labour and livestock equivalent to their lay counterpart, although in purchase or sale they deferred to the superior or their delegated representative; in the early and high Middle Ages the bailiff was a professed member of the monastic community; only when estates were put out to farm did monasteries come to rely on seculars.[128] The administrative duties of the superior at the same time were distributed among assistants, stewards of the household, and for the greatest of them, perhaps their own chamberlain. Such were the offices and responsibilities recognised by the *Decreta Lanfranci* of 1070, presented to some of the principal Benedictine houses in England.[129] Yet there was further proliferation. By the beginning of the twelfth century it was becoming increasingly common for conventual resources to be distributed to a chain of administrative officers alongside the cellarer, chamberlain and sacrist: in the custody of each, as it may be, the almoner, the hostillar, the refectorer, etc., was placed a portion of the temporal and spiritual resources, an 'obedience', to be administered discretely, and from which the officers were known collectively as 'obedientiaries'.[130] There were regional variations in the title and scope of the obediences, at Saint-Denis, for example, after the cellarer there were capicer (i.e. sacrist), chancellor, infirmarer and treasurer, but a common structure is recognisable throughout Benedictine Europe.[131]

There were additional administrative duties associated with the spiritual property of the monastery. Churches, and other clerical foundations, held demesnes and often further estates of their own, which required supervision. They also bore obligations toward their institutional life, to appoint clergy, and other officers, to promulgate codes or customs for their observance, and to undertake formal visitation at appropriate intervals. Their conduct in early centuries remains obscure, but in the high and later Middle Ages, spiritual properties were distributed among the obedientiaries to be managed together with their temporal

---

[126] *MO*, 431–9. For the rise of the chamberlain at Abingdon, see *HEA*, ii. 88, 224, 226.

[127] *MO*, 434–9; Smith, *Canterbury Cathedral Priory*, pp. 100–12 at 111–12. See also R. A. L. Smith, 'The *Regimen Scaccarii* in English Monasteries: The Alexander Prize Essay', *RHS* 4th Series 24 (1942), 73–94.

[128] For example, the arrangements at Westminster: *Documents Illustrating the Rule of Abbot Walter de Wenlok, 1283–1307*, ed. B. F. Harvey, Camden Society, 4th Series 2 (1965), p. 10.

[129] *MC*, pp. 112&n, 122, 126.

[130] For the development of obedientiary offices, see *MO*, pp. 431–9; Smith, *Canterbury Cathedral Priory*, pp. 36–49; Harvey, *Obedientiaries of Westminster*, pp. xix–xxii.

[131] Berkhofer, *Day of Reckoning*, p. 127.

estates.[132] An exception was churches exempt from episcopal jurisdiction, a privilege perhaps originating from the grant to the monastery but often secured after lengthy litigation. These monastic 'peculiars' were administered by an archdeacon, generally recruited from among the brethren, a role which first appears in Benedictine records at the turn of the eleventh century.[133] It has been suggested the archdeaconry was assigned to the sacrist *ex officio* but in later medieval England the office often passed to one of the university monks, particularly where there was a graduate of canon law.[134]

The obedientiary system distributed (although not always evenly) the burden of temporal administration placed upon the brethren, but it also diluted the authority of the conventual hierarchy (abbot, prior, cellarer) and exposed precious resources to the exigencies of a variety of individuals whose capability was generally untrained and untried. The dangers were underlined in the opening lines of Jocelin's life of Abbot Hugh of Bury, 'in temporal matters ... unskilful and improvident' whose 'infirmity spread from the head to the members', his officials (notably the sacrist) binding themselves tighter in debt with every passing year.[135] A common treasury (*thesaurum*) acted as a check on the obedientiaries: there was such supervision at Saint-Denis as early as 1137 although it is unclear whether it was common to Continental convents.[136] In the course of his metropolitan visitations of 1281–4 Archbishop John Peckham of Canterbury promulgated systematic reform for the English system: the income of the monastery was to be received from the obedientiaries by a triumvirate of treasurers, recruited from the monastic community, who were to render a complete account to their brethren *in capitulo* three times a year; a monastic and a secular supervisor were to be appointed to act as auditors.[137] As might be expected, Peckham's system appears to have been adopted at Canterbury (Christ Church) and Rochester, where a common treasury appears from the turn of the thirteenth century; at Rochester the arrangements were retained to the end, a burgess of the town being named as auditor on the brink of the Reformation.[138] A common treasury also appears in the records of Glastonbury and St Albans; at Abingdon there was an office of treasurer, supported by 'pensions' from each obedientiary.[139] Since Archbishop Robert Winchelsea sought to renew the reform in 1299 the impulse does not

---

[132] For examples: Smith, *Canterbury Cathedral Priory*, pp. 14–28 at 24; Harvey, *Lay Religious Life in Late Medieval Durham*, p. 41.

[133] J. Sayers, 'Monastic Archdeacons', in *Church and Government in the Middle Ages*, ed. Brooke *et al.*, pp. 177–204 at p. 179.

[134] *RO*, i. 192; ii. 281–4; Clark, *Monastic Renaissance*, p. 71; Harvey, *Lay Religious Life in Late Medieval Durham*, pp. 19, 69.

[135] *Jocelin*, p. 2.

[136] Berkhofer, *Days of Reckoning*, p. 125.

[137] M. D. Knowles, 'Aspects of the Career of Archbishop Pecham', *EHR* 57 (1942), 178–201 at 191–201.

[138] R. A. L. Smith, 'The Central Financial System of Christ Church, Canterbury, 1186–1512', *EHR* 55 (1940), 353–69.

[139] Ibid.

appear to have penetrated the entire congregation.[140] Compotus rolls from the fourteenth and fifteenth centuries attest to a variety of arrangements, although the independence of the obedientiaries was generally preserved. In the century before the Reformation and in the face of falling recruitment it was not uncommon for one officer to hold multiple obediences; whether or not they were pluralist, maladministration was widespread and often discovered only after the damage (costs, debts) was irrecoverable.[141] It appears Peckham's principle was acknowledged at Durham and Norwich since their obedientiaries were each accustomed to audit their own treasuries.[142] Elsewhere the earlier arrangements persisted: at Evesham the cellarer was charged with 'the whole care of the abbey except incomes assigned to the [obedientiaries]'; at Barking Abbey the cellarer retained the authority envisaged in the *RB*.[143]

As obedientiary administration was subject to reform, a separation between the resources of the superior and the convent was also widely adopted. Benedict's superior was the head of a subsistence community (*RB*, ii), but by the twelfth century, in many instances, (s)he commanded a monastery invested with resources that vastly exceeded its own needs, integrated in a network of affiliate and dependent convents and subordinate institutions (chapels, hospitals); and it was not uncommon for them to preside over a personal household of officials and clerks comparable to any secular prelate. Their administrative separation from their monastic community was a practical measure, and also responded to the potential threat that a superior possessed of such resources presented to their brethren. In England the subdivision of resources between abbot and convent at Westminster was proposed as early as the abbacy of Gilbert Crispin (1085–1117), although the arrangements were not cemented for another century.[144] The thirteenth century saw the separation adopted in the European mainland, where it perhaps accelerated the advance of grants *in commendam* – under which the income of the monastery was alienated to an unprofessed appointee – after 1250.[145] The separation did not settle conflict between the superior and their subordinates: the prodigious consumption of the superior was a

---

[140] R. Graham, 'The Metropolitan Visitation of the Diocese of Worcester by Archbishop Winchelsey in 1301', *TRHS* 4th Series 2 (1919), 59–93.

[141] For example, *Registrum abbatiae Johannis Whethamstede*, ed. H. T. Riley, RS 28, 2 vols. (London, 1870–1), ii. 230–2 at 231.

[142] Snape, *English Monastic Finances*, pp. 43–4; *RO*, ii. 328–30; Dobson, *Durham Priory*, pp. 250–96 at 290; Stone, 'Profit-and-Loss Accountancy at Norwich Cathedral Priory', 25–48.

[143] *Chronicon abbatiae de Evesham ad annum 1418*, ed. W. D. Macray, Rolls Series 29 (1863), p. 207; *MO*, 439. The administrative authority of the 'high' cellarer at Barking is described in the fifteenth-century memorandum, *Charthe longynge to the Office of the Celeresse of the Monastery of Barkinge*, now BL, Cotton MS Julius D VIII.

[144] Abbot Richard de Berking granted the convent the administration of its own lands in 1225: *Walter de Wenlok*, ed. Harvey, pp. 19, 217–22 (text of agreement). See also A. Gransden, 'The Separation of Portions between Abbot and Convent at Buy St Edmunds: The Decisive Years, 1278–121', *EHR* 119 (2004), 373–406.

[145] See below, pp. 294–5.

persistent theme in the discourse of the convent and stirred frequent disputes and sometimes deep divisions, such as between Abbot Walter de Wenlok of Westminster and his brethren in 1307; at Romsey it led the abbess to alienate administrative responsibility *in toto*.[146]

It should be remembered that the management of the monastery's resources was never an exclusively monastic enterprise. From early times it is likely that an array of secular clerical and lay advisors and assistants supported the brethren in their tasks. Temporal properties may have been served by lay representatives even before the office of bailiff (alter, warden) tied them to monastic supervisors. In post-Conquest England, at a time when the role of the bailiff was already well established, each manor was served *in situ* by a reeve; Jocelin attests to the 'laymen [who] make ... prudent provision for ourselves and our lands'.[147] In the later Middle Ages monasteries also appointed stewards to represent their temporal interests at regional level.[148] The superior of the monastery maintained administrators of their own. Even the pioneering abbots benefited from *familiares*: many were bishops, and a curia or household was already the common apparatus of the prelate. Later, the superior was served by a substantial staff of professed and unprofessed officers, and at the greater abbeys and priories a permanent council of advisors, which may have included representatives of the lay elite, perhaps burgesses, merchants or, indeed, neighbouring landlords.[149]

The development of administrative offices in the high and later Middle Ages was accompanied by shifting approaches to the custody of the monastery's resources. It has always been assumed that over time the monasteries abdicated from the direct management of their properties, and that long before the Reformation all but a token remnant of their ancient demesnes was scattered among a wide variety of grantees. It is true that the Benedictines ceased to exploit (i.e. to farm for themselves) every one of their estates at an early point in their medieval history. Moreover, the later Middle Ages were marked by the alienation of many properties, and the progressive subdivision of rents and rights (tithes, fees, fines, etc.), the 'putting out to farm' of which pre-Reformation critics frequently complained: as David Knowles characterised it, 'the monks [of the later Middle Ages] became high farmers'.[150] Yet it would be wrong to suggest there was a systematic and irreversible shift. As a growing number of charters, cartularies and compotus (i.e. account) rolls are analysed, it is becoming clear that patterns of estate management were regional – indeed, highly individual approaches prevailed within the same region, reflecting the particular nature of their

---

[146] *Walter de Wenlok*, ed. Harvey, p. 17; Power, *Medieval English Nunneries*, pp. 64–6.

[147] *MO*, p. 446; *Jocelin*, pp. 28–9.

[148] For example, Savine, 'English Monasteries on the Eve of the Dissolution', pp. 245–60.

[149] For examples, see Smith, *Canterbury Cathedral Priory*, pp. 68–82; *Walter de Wenlok*, ed. Harvey, pp. 6–7.

[150] *RO*, ii. 310.

endowments and natural resources – and responsive to the dynamics of the wider economy. In England, Bury St Edmunds had dispersed almost all of its eight hundreds as early as 1182, when Jocelin lamented, 'all the hundreds and townships [are] given out'.[151] The trend was followed in Yorkshire, but not in central, eastern and southern counties, where direct exploitation continued down to the Black Death.[152] At Christ Church, Canterbury, it did not end until the close of the fourteenth century; in the extreme west at Tavistock (Devon) it endured into the sixteenth century.[153] The abbot and convent of Westminster appear extraordinarily sensitive to the exigencies of the economy, recovering their tenanted estates in the inflationary instability of the early thirteenth century and dispersing them again in the last quarter of the fourteenth century when the worst effects of the post-Black Death were over.[154] Westminster's management was not perhaps unique: the rare survival of an obedientiary's register from pre-Reformation Peterborough reveals that portions of the same estate were managed differently – arable land, for example, being farmed at a fixed rent, and pastures exploited directly.[155] At the women's houses there was an enduring commitment to the 'home' farm although a drift towards tenancies has been detected.[156] Reviewing monastic estates at the Reformation, the agents of the crown and the Court of Augmentations did not always distinguish reliably between demesne and dispersed land.[157] The later medieval patterns in mainland Europe remain fully to be recovered from (more fragmentary) sources, but it would appear that at least in south-west France 'direct management triumphed' as ecclesiastical landlords 'recruited their harvest hands themselves and directed the haymaking, reaping, binding and the threshing'.[158]

The later Middle Ages saw a significant, and unequivocal, shift in the monastery's management of its spiritual property. Churches and their appurtenances were as likely to be farmed as any temporal property; they were also subdivided for sale.[159] The constraints on conventual income

---

[151] *Jocelin*, p. 1.
[152] Burton, *Monastic Order in Yorkshire*, pp. 248–52.
[153] Smith, *Christ Church, Canterbury*, p. 192; Finberg, *Tavistock Abbey*, pp. 258–9 at 258. By contrast, Battle Abbey: Searle, *Lordship and Community*, pp. 324–37.
[154] Harvey, *Westminster Abbey and its Estates*, pp. 148–51.
[155] *The Book of William Morton, Almoner of Peterborough Monastery, 1448–67*, ed. W. T. Mellows, intr. C. N. L. Brooke, Northamptonshire Record Society 16 (1954), pp. xxxii–xxxvii at xxxv–vi (direct exploitation of pasture, including arrangements for the loaning of cattle and cows).
[156] Gilchrist, *Gender and Material Culture*, p. 76.
[157] J. Youings, *The Dissolution of the Monasteries* (London, 1971), pp. 36–7, 57, 61. For the intersection of demesne and tenanted property in the pre-Reformation period, see also Power, *Medieval English Nunneries*, p.101&n; R. A. Lomas, 'The Priory of Durham and its Demesnes in the Fourteenth and Fifteenth Centuries', *EHR* 31 (1978), 339–53.
[158] Ladurie, *Peasants of Languedoc*, pp. 37–40 at 38.
[159] For example, the Prior of Thetford sold prebends for cash: Thompson, 'The Church and the Aristocracy', p. 240&n.

experienced in the decades after the Black Death led many of them to appropriate the revenue of their churches in its entirety, that is, to suspend the living and to transfer the annual income, and all contiguous benefits such as customary fees, to the monastery. The mechanism appears in monastic administration as early as the twelfth century.[160] It was widely employed in the post-Black Death period by a variety of foundations, not only monasteries, but also secular colleges and even individual magnates, as a means of raising revenue without recourse to either sale or loan.[161] Since generally it contradicted the terms of the original grant which had conveyed the church, appropriation could only be secured by episcopal or papal dispensation. Here the Benedictines profited from their prominence among the higher clergy, particularly at Avignon (1305–78). In England, appropriations were sought to fund specific schemes: at Abingdon, they were to repay losses incurred during the civil disturbance of 1327; at Canterbury and St Albans they were channelled into the creation of a *domus studiorum* at Oxford; at Clifford Priory the appropriated parish paid for hospitality for 'a great multitude of Welshmen' who 'cannot be denied without great risk'.[162] Appropriation aroused condemnation from pre-Reformation critics of the monasteries, but such discourse should not obscure the continued investment which churches received from their monastic proprietors. The renewal of provincial parish churches in early Tudor England owed much to their monastic patrons: the abbot and convent of Sherborne provided the parishioners of their satellite village of Oborne with a new chancel as late as 1533.[163] In the Benedictine heartlands of Burgundy, Rhineland and Tuscany, town and village churches, chantries and chapels carried the imprint of their monastic proprietors far beyond 1517.

Lordship

The evolution of the Benedictine monastery from the subsistence colony of the sixth century to the burgeoning corporations of the tenth century (and after) bound it into Europe's emerging structures of lordship. In later centuries the status of the Black Monks as the source and subject of seigniorial authority shaped not only their relations with the world

---

[160] Smith, *Canterbury Cathedral Priory*, p. 11; Smith, 'Central Financial System of Christ Church, Canterbury', 353–69.

[161] Snape, *English Monastic Finances*, pp. 79–91; *RO*, ii. 290–2; K. L. Wood-Leigh, 'Appropriation of Parish Churches during the Reign of Edward III', *Cambridge Historical Journal* 3 (1929), 15–22.

[162] G. Lambrick, 'The Impeachment of the Abbot of Abingdon in 1368', *EHR* 82 (1967), 250–76; Clark, *Monastic Renaissance*, pp. 26–31 at 27; *Canterbury College, Oxford*, ed. Pantin, iv. 1–50; Cowley, *Monastic Order in South Wales*, p. 204. For an abortive appropriation attempted by Ramsey Abbey to support scholar monks at Oxford, see Thompson, 'The Church and the Aristocracy', p. 243.

[163] For example, M. Heale, 'Monastic Parochial Churches in Late Medieval England', in *The Parish in Late Medieval England*, ed. C. Burgess and E. Duffy (Donnington, 2006), pp. 54–77. For Oborne, see illustration 4.

beyond their walls but also the rhythms of conventual life – indeed, the very identity, corporate and individual, of the convent itself. Benedict was born to the Roman patriciate, and his *Regula* reflects a familiarity with classical and biblical concepts of lordship. His *cenobium* represented a counterpoint to the contemporary social hierarchy, since the brethren bore 'an equal burden of servitude under one Lord' (*RB*, ii. 20: 'et sub uno Domino aequalem servitutis militiam baiulamus'), spiritually, Christ, and practically, the superior, who was 'to hold the place of Christ in the monastery' (*RB*, ii. 2: 'Christi enim agere vices in monasterio creditur'). There was a trace of an external ecclesiastical authority, the 'spiritual superiors' (*RB*, xlvi. 3: 'ante abbatem vel congregationem') to whom the abbot might be required to defer but in large measure the monastery was conceived as autonomous and discrete. Yet the earliest communities to follow the *RB* were often initiated and frequently sustained by sources of authority beyond the professed community, a diocesan, magnate or monarch. Their scale and scope were generally determined by the grant of sites, incorporating sometimes churches and, certainly, outlying lands, which invariably were invested already with the social, political and perhaps fiscal obligations. The strength of the seigniorial bond varied, but the vast majority of the monastic foundations that endured in the early centuries, in the European mainland and in England, were *Eigenklöster*, wholly the possession of their episcopal, magnate or royal patron.[164] At the same time, the properties (spiritual and temporal) they accrued empowered them to exercise lordship over subjects (clerical and lay) of their own. These seigniorial exchanges intensified during the phases of expansion initiated by the reform movements of the tenth century. Within the networks of Gorze and Vannes it was the very subjection of the monks to their patrons that advanced the cause of reform; in England, the seigniorial authority of patrons shaped the scale and geographical spread of the reform.[165] Cluny, by contrast, challenged the concept of *Eigenklöster*, creating a foundation favoured by the very *libertas Romana* that was the preserve of the papacy and 'freed from every kind of earthly lordship'.[166] The reinvigoration of Benedictinism that followed during the years of the Gregorian reform saw the extension of the monks' own seigniorial powers and obligations, as properties and populace were presented to them. The economic, social and political turbulence of the later Middle Ages weakened the old bonds of lordship in much of Europe. In the generations before the Reformation, the Black Monks were released from many features of their former subjection,

---

[164] Wood, *Proprietary Church*, pp. 115–17; *MO*, pp. 569–70, 589–90; Levison, *England and the Continent*, pp. 27–33.

[165] For Gorze and Vannes, see Nightingale, *Monasteries and Patrons of the Gorze Reform*, pp. 30–9, 132–47. For England see *MO*, pp. 48–52, 128–38; Burton, *Monastic Order in Yorkshire*, pp. 23–44 at 39.

[166] Cowdrey, *Cluniacs and Gregorian Reform*, p. 3.

but as seigniors themselves also struggled to retain their authority and the resources it offered them.

As a seigniorial possession, an *Eigenklöster*, the Benedictine monastery was the instrument of their proprietor's financial, political and strategic priorities. The revenue of the monks represented an additional resource. The early communities were often bound by demands for tribute; later, their lord might levy customary fines, for example at the election of a superior, and in England might insist on the escheat of conventual income during a vacancy, that is, to be the sole financial beneficiary until the new superior entered his office.[167] The seigniorial authority might also take advantage to seize, or insist on the surrender of, property at will, whether for their own benefit or for that of a client.[168] Interference in the monastery's own transactions was frequent; an interest was also commonly declared in the presentation of livings, and other offices.[169] Like an individual vassal, in the early and high Middle Ages, and in a number of instances as late as the fourteenth century, the monastery was also bound to pay service to its lord. Given the geographical extent of their estates, even in the early period, it was possible for a monastery to owe different obligations to different lords: the convent of Saint-Florent-de-Saumur was exempt from knights' service for the king but bound to provide it for a magnate of the region.[170] In England there was early pressure to commute (render in cash) martial obligations: in an addendum to the *Regularis Concordia*, Edgar exempted the monasteries from the customary *heriot*; scutage (cash sums in lieu of martial service) was widespread among ecclesiastical vassals after the reign of Henry I (1100–35), although the scale of such payments had risen significantly as a result of renewed endowment and a higher rating of service per fief.[171] Here the final summons of a feudal host was seen in 1385, but in other regions of Europe the expectation of (commuted) payments endured into the pre-Reformation period.[172] There were also demands for labour service, which in early centuries diverted labourers from the monastery's demesne. Such demands had been commuted in England by the turn of the twelfth century, but they endured in regions of Europe where there was a greater degree of direct exploitation of monastic estates.[173] The monastery was also required to act in any cause of their seignior, to advise and assist in any territorial or political dispute and *in extremis* to bear the burden of any

---

[167] N. E. Stacy, 'Henry of Blois and the Lordship of Glastonbury', *EHR* 114 (1999), 1–33; Jones, 'The Crown, Three Benedictine Houses and the Statute of Mortmain'.

[168] For example, Bernhardt, *Itinerant Kingship*, pp. 55, 173, 245.

[169] S. M. Wood, *English Monasteries and their Patrons in the Thirteenth Century* (London, 1955), p. 113.

[170] W. Ziezulewicz, 'The Fate of Carolingian Military Exactions in a Monastic Fisc: The Case of Saint-Florent-de-Saumur (*c*. 950–1118)', *Military Affairs* 51:3 (1987), 124–7.

[171] *RC*, p. 69; *MO*, pp. 607–12.

[172] N. B. Lewis and J. J. N. Palmer, 'The Feudal Summons of 1385', *EHR* 100 (1985), 729–46.

[173] T. Scott, *The Peasantries of Europe from the Fourteenth to the Eighteenth Centuries* (London, 1997), p. 247; H. Kamen, *Early Modern European Society* (New York, 1999), p. 134.

conflict in which they were involved: monasteries were the focus of magnate violence even in the midst of the tenth-century reform in the regions of England; later, in the eleventh and twelfth centuries, they were projected into the persistent struggle between imperial and papal authority; those under the authority of an episcopal magnate did not escape the violent consequences of such conflict and also suffered the repeated pressure of the ecclesiastical hierarchy.[174] Their subjection was cemented by ceremonial. It was commonplace for the superior to perform homage to the proprietor of the monastery, although from the twelfth century, superiors sought to evade the obligation by means of proxies, or arrant non-attendance.[175]

Submission not only surrendered rights and resources to the proprietor but also secured their protection. The proprietor was their common advocate in the courts of both secular and clerical authority.[176] Throughout the Middle Ages, and in all regions of Europe, such protection came only on the terms of the proprietor themselves: in Anglo-Saxon England defence against Norse incursion was bought only at the cost of endowments; in thirteenth-century Germany assistance in the face of the diocesan came at the cost of reform; at the Reformation the advocacy of the patron was conditional upon the payment of fines, the grant of a stewardship, or the surrender of the monastery to their own seigniorial advantage.[177]

Their own seigniorial authority placed comparable obligations on subordinates of variable status, from tenants of the gentry or 'knightly' class, to urban burgesses and peasantry both propertied and not. Like its own ecclesiastical or secular proprietor, the monastery laid claim to a portion of their income and also levied fees and fines for such formalities as entry into and termination of tenancies and the marriage of a tenant, and, certainly, the election of a new superior of the monastery and certain practicalities, such as the use of (hand, wind or water) mills within the liberty, and the passage of road and waterways.[178] There was some variation in the scope of these levies. The burgesses of Battle were obliged to pay a fine of 100 shillings for their liberties whenever an abbot took office; the town's guilds were bound to make offerings to the abbey church.[179] The prior and convent

---

[174] For example: Cowdrey, *Age of Abbot Desiderius*, pp. 56–71: 'the papacy's need for the help of the institutions was great' (p. 56); Potts, *Monastic Revival and Regional Identity*, pp. 13–35, 105–32; Burton, *Monastic Order in Yorkshire*, p. 201.

[175] The anonymous *De professionibus abbatum* condemned the superior that submitted to demands for homage: *Three Treatises from Bec on the Nature of Monastic Life*, ed. G. Constable and B. S. Smith (Toronto, 2008), p. 21. See also the requirements of the Constitutions of Clarendon (1164): *Councils and Synods*, pp. 852–93 at 877–83; Gransden, 'Separation of Portions', 373–406.

[176] For example, Burton, *Monastic Order in Yorkshire*, p. 196.

[177] Searle, *Lordship and Community*, pp. 12–22, 89–105; E. Mitchell, 'Patrons and Politics at Twelfth-Century Barking Abbey', *Rev. Bén.* 113 (2003), 347–64; Savine, 'English Monasteries on the Eve of the Dissolution', pp. 245–60.

[178] Snape, *English Monastic Finances*, pp. 71–94 at 92; L. Mellinger, 'Politics in the Convent; the Election of a Fifteenth-Century Abbess', *Church History* 63 (1994), 529–40.

[179] *Battle*, pp. 58–9, 64–5.

of Durham did not scruple at the confiscation of estates from tenants who were elderly or infirm.[180] In the Champagne, monasteries charged *mainmorte*, a fee levied for the death of every incumbent tenant regardless of the value of the property: the abbot and convent of Saint-Loup denied the heirs of Thierry de Thuisy the right to his market stall for their default of the fee of 15 *livres*.[181] In the early and high Middle Ages, as a vassal of the overlord, or 'tenant-in-chief', the monastery also passed part of the burden of martial service to its own tenants. Before the thirteenth century these obligations were often paid in kind: the knightly tenants of Bury St Edmunds offered themselves in service to Henry II, and when they saw action against Earl Robert of Leicester in 1173 they bore the banner of the abbey's patronal saint.[182] Of course, the tenants were also obliged to offer labour to the monastery. In England the monasteries had ceased to enforce their customary rights to labour by the end of the fourteenth century, and may have purchased it instead, although in the depressed economic climate a century later they accepted labour in lieu of cash rents and also retained service for their leased demesnes.[183] The principal tenants of the monastery were obliged to perform homage for their estates, an obligation observed more frequently than it was by the superior for their own proprietor. For certain fiefs they could command the fealty of comital lords: Thibaut IV of Champagne performed homage to the abbot of Saint-Denis for Nogent in 1226.[184] Homage brought the tenant and his train into the heart of the convent (not only the chapter house but also the high altar) serving to the unworldly brethren of their worldly bonds. Jocelin's discomfort was clear when Thomas Hasting paid homage to Abbot Samson 'cum magna multitudine militum ...'.[185]

The seigniorial status of the monastery also conferred upon the superior the responsibility to administer secular justice. In England the possession of a hundred or its constituent manor empowered the superior to convene a court; within this jurisdiction the superior (or his delegated representative) was also responsible for the supervision of such mechanisms as wardship and gaol delivery.[186] Where they survive, the formal record of these courts, the court books, provide perhaps the most vivid illustration of the monastery's intervention in the lives of the laity.[187] As the arbiter of justice within the

[180] Britnell, 'Feudal Reaction', 34.
[181] T. Evergates, *Feudal Society in Medieval France: Documents from the County of Champagne* (Philadelphia, 1993), p. 21.
[182] *Jocelin*, p. 57.
[183] For the purchase of labour by the nuns of Minster-in-Sheppey, see Gilchrist, *Gender and Material Culture*, p. 69. See also Harvey, *Westminster Abbey and its Estates*, pp. 233–4.
[184] Evergates, *Feudal Society in Medieval France*, p. 106.
[185] *Jocelin*, p. 27.
[186] R. B. Pugh, 'The King's Prisons before 1250', *TRHS* 5th Series 5 (1955), 1–22. For the exercise of such rights, see, for example, *Jocelin*, pp. 123–4.
[187] For example, the evidence of the extant court books of St Albans Abbey examined in A. E. Levett, 'Courts and Court Rolls of St Albans Abbey', *TRHS* 4th Series 7 (1924), 52–76; A. E. Levett, *Studies in Manorial History*, ed. H. Cam and L. Sutherland (Oxford, 1938), pp. 103–77.

locality, the superior also collaborated with representatives of royal justice in the intermittent commissions of *oyer et terminer* and other extraordinary enquiries.[188] In fifteenth-century England, as presiding justice, the monastic superior participated in the arraignment of alleged heretics under novel statutes which had recast heresy as a felony.[189]

Just as for the monastery and its proprietor, in principle the ties between abbot, convent and tenant were reciprocal. The reform-minded monks of the tenth and eleventh centuries reflected at length on the moral superiority of ecclesiastical lordship and condemned their magnate colleagues for their customary abuses.[190] Yet the Benedictines' relations with their tenants were almost always turbulent: fiscal and social obligations were frequently disputed, and acts of violence were common from both sides.[191] The recurrent conflict between the independent abbeys of England and their tenants, notably Bury St Edmunds and St Albans, are well documented; the records of regional and royal justice give a glimpse of many others, on a smaller scale, but equally irreconcilable.[192] Nonetheless, there are a number of instances in the century before the Reformation of English Benedictines coming to the aid of their tenants, to assist in the repulsion of French pirates, and to stir direct action against a neighbouring magnate determined on enclosure.[193] It is also worth noting that the spiritual ties of their subjects to the monastery and the cult (s) of which it was (generally) custodian remained strong throughout the later centuries.[194]

The Black Monks' exercise of secular lordship did much to shape the dynamics of regional and even national politics between the twelfth and the fifteenth centuries. In the still unstable regions of twelfth-century England (especially the north and Wales), eastern Germany and the frontier of Christian Spain, the monasteries, or their superiors, served as invaluable deputies for a succession of oppressed and under-mighty princes.[195] Later the stasis of the monastic liberty did much to secure regional communities

---

[188] R. W. Kaeuper, 'Law and Order in Fourteenth-Century England: the Evidence of Special Commissions of Oyer et Terminer', *Speculum* 54 (1979), 734–84.

[189] For example, N. P. Tanner, *Heresy Trials in the Diocese of Norwich, 1428–31*, Camden Society, 4th Series 20 (1977).

[190] For example, the principles examined in the *Collectio de ecclesiis et capellis* of Hincmar of Reims (806–82): Wood, *Proprietary Church*, pp. 806–15.

[191] Wood, *Proprietary Church*, pp. 830–50.

[192] Bury's and St Alban's troubles were narrated by their brethren: *Memorials of St Edmund's Abbey*, ed. Arnold, ii. 327–5 (*Depredatio*), iii. 125–31. For unrest elsewhere, see M. Müller, 'The Aims and Organisation of a Peasants' Revolt in Early Fourteenth-Century Wiltshire', *Rural History* 14:1 (2003), 1–20; A. Jones, 'A Dispute between the Abbey of Ramsey and its Tenants', *EHR* 91 (1976), 341–3.

[193] For the repulsion of pirates, see the exploits of Prior Haimo of Lewes in 1373: *The St Albans Chronicle: The Chronica maiora of Thomas Walsingham*, ed. J. Taylor and W. R. Childs (Oxford, 2003), pp. 164–5. For direct action against enclosure, see R. B. Manning, *Village Revolts: Social Protest and Popular Disturbances in England, 1509–1640* (Oxford, 1988), pp. 45–6.

[194] Harvey, *Lay Religious Life in Late Medieval Durham*, pp. 34–5, 67. It is worth noting that at Durham devotion to Cuthbert could be eclipsed by recent popular figures.

[195] Bernhardt, *Itinerant Kingship*, pp. 85–105.

during periods of economic and social disturbance; the defeat of the peasant rebels at Bury and St Albans in 1327 and 1381 stifled what might have become a nationwide uprising.[196] As modern historians have underlined, the corollary was that their fiscal and juridical monopoly also curbed the development of provincial and urban politics, in England, northern Italy and the commercial cities of the Rhine valley. Here, the seigniorial presence of the monastery also arrested cultural and religious innovation and perhaps also the spread of Reformation.[197]

Lordship also left a powerful imprint on the monastery itself. The verbal and visual identity of the monastery was infused with its seigniorial obligations: the charters of the abbot and convent couched their transactions in terms identical to monarch or magnate and were authenticated by seals which depicted the superior as seignior; the conventual buildings carried many of the symbolic and some of the practical badges of lordship, including a corporate and personal blazon of arms, and, at least from the fourteenth century, the crenellation now featured on almost any fortification. Elements of this identity were appropriated by the brethren themselves. From at least the eleventh century, and perhaps earlier, the superiors of the greater monasteries readily adopted the trappings of lordship, in deportment, dress and personal appearances and, as they developed among their secular counterparts, in accommodation, recreation and display. Jocelin of Brakelond recalled Samson as Caesar *alter* ('Caesar omnia erat').[198] Henry of Blois, abbot of Glastonbury, was remembered for his luxuriant beard, an unmistakable mark of his enthusiasm for the style of a secular lordship.[199]

The Precinct Community

The Benedictines' interaction with the unprofessed, both clergy and lay-folk, was not confined to their administrative and feudal obligations. They also came to rely on their assistance in the routine tasks – domestic, clerical and manual – of their internal life. It seems there was always some such (i.e. unprofessed) presence in the precincts of the monastery. They pass by in the shadows of the *RB* although there is sufficient detail to distinguish their roles: a porter (*portarius*: *RB*, lxvi), tradesmen (*artifices*: *RB*, lvii), and priests 'who may choose to live [there]' ('Si quis de ordine sacerdotum in monasterio se suscipi rogaverit': *RB*, lx. 1). As the earliest Benedictine monasteries became established, and expanded in size and the scale of their

---

[196] R. B. Dobson, *The Peasants' Revolt of 1381*, 2nd edn (London, 1983), pp. 233–7, 269–77.

[197] For a study of the problem: R. Tittler, *The Reformation and the Towns in England: Politics and Political Culture, c. 1540–1640* (Oxford, 1998), pp. 3–57. For a case-study, which suggests radical religion could prosper in a monastic environment, see L. M. Higgs, *Godliness and Governance in Tudor Colchester* (Ann Arbor, MI, 1998), pp. 57–9, 87–9.

[198] Jocelin's description was derived from Lucan: *Jocelin*, p. 33.

[199] Stacy, 'Henry of Blois and the Lordship of Glastonbury'.

endowments, the precinct populace also grew. They are often seen only as bystanders in the narrative sources, but the material remains of the monastery bear witness to their numbers and the range of their activities: the greater abbeys and priories of the high and later Middle Ages provided workshops, offices, stable, kitchen, chambers and even self-contained cottages to meet their needs and those of their families.[200] In the early Middle Ages the precinct community not only served the professed brethren but also acted as a commercial and social focus, and a place of refuge, for the wider community. Later, as markets and urban communities expanded, the largest of them came to represent the town in microcosm: a lively and competitive hub for employment, residential settlement and a host of commercial, social and cultural transactions. The seigniorial and spiritual supervisors of the monasteries at times were uneasy at the energy of the precincts, but there is little doubt that when they were abandoned at the Reformation the regional economy, and its commercial and labour opportunities, were diminished.

Servants

The largest constituent of the precinct population were the servants of the professed community. Given the social status of the men and women that entered the order in the early and high Middle Ages, the priority attached to domestic service was perhaps inevitable. Although Benedict had recommended the employment of staff outside the monastic enclosure, inside he required the brethren to fend for themselves: they were to 'serve one another in charity' ('ceteri sibi sub caritate invicem serviant': *RB*, xxxv), taking a turn at the tasks of the kitchen (*RB*, xxxv) and to have the custody of clothing and other necessaries (*RB*, lv). His ideal of self-sufficiency was respected in early centuries: Warnefrid's eighth-century commentary acknowledges the presence of kitchen staff only in the guest house. Later codes, the customs of Cluny, the *Regularis Concorda* and *Decreta Lanfranci*, were inclined to treat the descriptions of fraternal service as preceptive.[201] Certainly, from the eleventh century, the number and variety of domestic servants employed in the enclosure rose steadily, staff not only for the kitchen but for other departments of the monastery. Before the beginning of the thirteenth century, servants may have already outnumbered monks by a ratio of 2:1; in the later Middle Ages the imbalance was greater, in England perhaps 4:1 or 5:1.[202] When rising debts forced Abbot Nicholas

---

[200] Dobson, *Durham Priory*, pp. 168, 264; J. Kerr, *Monastic Hospitality: The Benedictines in England, c. 1050–1250* (Woodbridge, 2007), pp. 67–9 at fig. 5.

[201] *RC*, p. 63; *MC*, p. 51; *Warnefrid-Hildemar*, p. 51.

[202] For examples, see Smith, *Canterbury Cathedral Priory*, pp. 49–50; *The Account Rolls of the Obedientiaries of Peterborough*, ed. J. Greatrex, Northamptonshire Record Society 33 (1984), pp. 12–13; Savine, 'English Monasteries on the Eve of the Dissolution', pp. 225–7.

Quappelade of Reading (1305–27) to reduce the number of permanent staff to thirty-seven, there was still one servant for every two of the monks.[203] The superior retained their own cohort of servants, and in the case of abbots and cathedral priors of great dignity, it may have been a greater than the conventual staff. The household of Abbot Wenlok of Westminster comprised eight discrete departments, buttery, kitchen, larder, pantry, private chamber and public hall, together with the chapel and marshalsea; the presiding officer of each department rendered a daily account to the household steward.[204] In the century before the Reformation the household of the abbot of Peterborough doubled, rising from thirty-eight to 109.[205]

The departments of the monastery that served the community beyond the precinct walls, the almonry and hostelry, and those officers charged with the custody of relics, shrines and pilgrims, also employed domestic servants. Both the almonry and hostelry required staff for the preparation and presentation of food and for the maintenance of both remedial and recreational accommodation; a hostelry might also employ a household steward (maniple); these departments and officers are also likely to have turned to the ostlers that were surely present in the precincts.[206]

The household servants should be distinguished from the tradesmen also retained in the precincts. The greater abbeys and priories of the high and later Middle Ages are likely to have supported their own smithy, perhaps their own saddler, tanner and wheelwright.[207] It would be wrong to assume that the early monastery was less well equipped; albeit from a handful of centres, archaeological evidence has pointed to the working of precious metals and stone in the precincts; anecdotal evidence, such as Warnefrid's commentary connected with Montecassino, attests to the presence of a cobbler and tailor.[208] At almost any period there was also likely to be a transitory population of labourers. Joiners, masons, metalworkers, and painters were employed for a fixed term to undertake a specific task, although the greatest monasteries perhaps retained them.[209] At regular intervals there were also book craftsmen, scribes, limners and illuminators active in the precinct; palaeographical analysis suggests they were engaged for both books and chancery documents. Of course, it was not only tradesmen that entered the precinct for periodic work: like any medieval householders of high status, the Black Monks also sought the services of entertainers,

---

[203] *VCH Berkshire*, ii. 62–73 at 65.
[204] *Walter de Wenlok*, ed. Harvey, p. 6.
[205] *Account Rolls of Peterborough*, ed. Greatex, p. 12 (from 1434/5 to 1504/5).
[206] For example: *Selby*, pp. 236–40, 243 (almoner's office and sample account).
[207] At Selby, the service of the saddler appears to have been bought in *ad hoc*, but the recurrent employment of the smith(s) suggests they were close at hand: *Selby*, pp. 75, 77, 167.
[208] *Warnefrid-Hildemar*, pp. 41–7 at 47.
[209] See below, pp. 247–9.

musicians and players to mark the major festivals of the liturgical calendar: between Martinmas and Pentecost 1520–1, the brethren of Battle Abbey paid no less than 16d for a troupe of players 'with puppets' ('cum popetys').[210]

The cohorts of servants and tradesmen that were based permanently in the precincts, or passed through, became closely integrated with their professed employers. Servants of the household wore the livery of the convent, or its superior, just as they did if they served a secular house: at Carrow Priory the colours were varied (red, black) by department.[211] The criticism of capitular and episcopal visitors suggests there was often a degree of collegiality, even conspiracy, between masters and servants. There is evidence from the later Middle Ages of cultural exchange also: the chamberlain of the abbot of St Albans maintained an impressive library of English and Latin poetry and prose which is likely to have attracted readers within the enclosure.[212]

Secular Clerks

The precinct population also incorporated clergy. Benedict had conceived of a monastery of professed laymen served by both priests (*sacerdoti*) and clerks (*clerici*, the designation for those in minor orders): they were to be encouraged to enter the community and were expected to adhere to its rule; they were not to be given seniority by virtue of their ordination alone, and those in minor orders were to be granted middling status ('loco mediocri collocentur': *RB*, lx); at the same time the brethren were to consider ordination for themselves. The early monasteries seem to have respected these arrangements and distinctions in the conventual hierarchy of the community; for female Benedictines it was a structural necessity. The clergy of the monastery, priested and unpriested, were prominent in its internal and external affairs, as charters, liturgical and learned texts attest.[213] The elaboration of liturgical obligations in later centuries, both in and beyond the *horarium*, led a greater proportion of the monks to be ordained. Secular clergy continued to assist at their services, however, and it was surely in recognition of a trend that was already widespread that general and provincial chapters of England permitted the employment of clerks for specific offices in 1343.[214] Now the monasteries also employed secular clerks to extend their liturgical and pastoral provisions for the laity: the parochial chapels

[210] For references to players, see also *Extracts from the Account Rolls of the Abbey of Durham from the Original MSS*, ed. J. T. Fowler, Surtees Society, 99–100, 103, 3 vols. (1898–1901), ii. 522, 526–7 (1334, 1335–6); Evans, 'Actors in the Accounts of Battle Abbey', 103–5 at 104.

[211] *Walter de Wenlok*, ed. Harvey, p. 247&n; Oliva, *Convent and Community*, p. 139.

[212] Hertford Record Office, ASA, AR1, fo. 70v.

[213] For example, Clark, *Monastic Renaissance*, p. 18; Oliva, *Convent and Community*, pp. 112–15, 125–9 (relative number of male clergy).

[214] *Chapters*, ed. Pantin, ii. 33.

and churches located in their precincts were served by secular priests; the Lady Chapels which many created in the later Middle Ages also saw secular as well as monastic officiants.[215] The greater abbeys and priories were also presented with a growing number of patronal chantries (whether a discrete chapel or associated with a nave altar), some, though not all, of which were endowed with secular priests.[216] Nor were such chantries the sole preserve of prestige convents.[217] In the pre-Reformation period the spiritual labour of the Benedictine monastery, intercession, hebdomadal and festal observance, and pastoral care were a collaboration between regular and secular clergy.

Secular priests were always a significant presence in the female monastery. In the mixed monastery of early times, as a source of spiritual authority they may have been subordinate to the coterminous brethren, but in the self-contained nunneries of later centuries they were at once the officiants, pastors and preachers. Only the most meagre foundation was served by a single priest; it was not uncommon for women to be supported by several priests and assistant chaplains; in addition to resident, stipendiary clergy, the women also secured *ad hoc* the (paid) service of passing secular and regular (particularly mendicant) clerics.[218] Within the enclosure their workspace was the sacristy, although the convents of the Fontevraud reform provided their priests with conventual buildings, and a church, of their own.[219]

Secular clerks also entered the precincts, among the professional administrators, advisors and lawyers that served the convent and the household of the superior. This was a transitory population, and the most prominent among them served more than one institution. Nonetheless, favoured advisors might serve the monastery for the lifetime of their career, and might also seek the succour of the community at the end. Indeed, it seems the ties between the monks and the seculars that shared in their work were close throughout the medieval centuries. Although accommodated beyond the enclosure, the clerks were engaged in its intellectual and social dynamics. Monastic books bear witness to the passage of clerical borrowers and readers.[220] Pre-Reformation reports show clerks and monks taking meals together and conversing on matters of conventual and general political

---

[215] R. Bowers, 'The Musicians and Liturgy of the Lady Chapels of the Monastery Church, *c.* 1235–1540', in *Westminster Abbey: The Lady Chapel of Henry VII*, ed. T. Tatton-Brown and R. Mortimer (Woodbridge, 2003), pp. 3–57.

[216] Harvey, *Lay Religious Life in Late Medieval Durham*, pp. 132–56 at 134–8, 145–6. The Mautravers chantry (1392) at Abbotsbury (Dorset) provided for a monk to celebrate a commemorative mass: *VCH Dorset*, ii. 48–53 at 50.

[217] For example, the endowment (1403) of the Stafford mass at Cerne to be said at the altar of the Holy Cross or at the nearby parish church of St Michael: *VCH Dorset*, ii. 53–8 at 56.

[218] *Chatteris*, pp. 104–5; Oliva, *Convent and Community*, pp. 112–13.

[219] Gilchrist, *Gender and Material Culture*, pp. 103, 111; Kerr, *Religious Life for Women*, pp. 55–6: the statutory strictures placed on the priests were significant.

[220] For example, *AL*, pp. 146–9 (1337 inventory from Christ Church, Canterbury).

interest.[221] Such company was not always conducive to monastic discipline: at Worcester Bishop Cobham sought the removal of one 'Master J' who occupied a chamber and was 'odious and burdensome to the community'.[222] Records of benefaction from this period attest to the powerful devotional attachment of clerks to the monastery to which they owed their livelihood.

The Benedictine environment also proved a powerful draw for clerks whose careers had not drawn them into the precincts. Curialists chose a Benedictine retirement: Becket's ally, Herbert of Bosham, did so to complete his commentary on the psalter.[223] Schoolmen also: Master Simon Bredon, an Oxford astronomer and mathematician, ended his days at Battle and bequeathed some of his scholarly books to the brethren.[224]

Guests, Corrodians and Pensioners

The majority of the precinct population contributed to the material and spiritual life of the monastery but there was a conspicuous minority that was itself sustained by it. The Benedictine monastery was as secure and well resourced an environment as any in medieval society. Even in the sixteenth century there was scarcely any secular cathedral, church or college and only a handful of noble households that could rival either the commons (i.e. food and drink) or the domestic comforts offered to its residents. The sustenance of the monastery was sought, and provided, throughout the Middle Ages. The earliest settlements sheltered passers-by as well as prestigious guests. Later, there was provision for an array of passing traffic, pilgrims, travellers, troops on campaign and the monarch in progress, and a permanent body of beneficiaries of the foundation.[225] There was, of course, a significant difference in the scale of this population, and the provision for them, between the greater and smaller abbeys and priories. Yet it was rare for a Benedictine monastery to be without these dependents: the reports of the Henrician commissioners show that on the eve of reformation, when observant life had all but collapsed, there were still sojourners to be found in the outer courts.[226] From early times the monasteries and their patrons shared a common understanding of the political, social and commercial value of these benefits, but also conflicted over the nature and number of the beneficiaries.

Hospitality was a duty of the Benedictine. The second commandment

---

[221] For example, *Account Rolls of Peterborough*, ed. Greatrex, pp. 12–13. There was perhaps greater opportunity for such exchanges after the imposition of the injunctions of the Royal visitors in 1535, given their requirement for a *lector* in divinity: for example, at Reading: *LP*, xiii/1, 147, 264, 571.
[222] Haines, 'Visitation Injunctions', 349.
[223] B. Smalley, *The Study of the Bible in the Middle Ages*, 3rd edn (Oxford, 1983), p. 186.
[224] Emden, *BRUO*, i. 257–8; F. M. Powicke, *The Medieval Books of Merton College* (Oxford, 1931), pp. 5–6, 25, 28, 82–6 (will), 138.
[225] Kerr, *Monastic Hospitality*, pp. 94–120.
[226] *Account Rolls of Peterborough*, ed. Greatrex, pp. 12–13.

(i.e. Love thy neighbour) was the second instrument of good works (*RB*, iii. 2), which scheme also reminded the *professus* 'not to forsake charity' (*RB*, iii. 26). The *RB* required specific provision for pilgrim and pauper ('pauperum et peregrinorum maxime susceptioni cura sollicite exhibeatur': *RB*, liii). They were to be given food, drink and shelter, set apart from the monastic enclosure in kitchens and a guesthouse or hostelry prepared for the purpose, but served by the brethren themselves. It appears the guest house was a priority even in the earliest precincts: the church of San Vincenzo al Volturno was demolished to create a space for the guests' palatium.[227] The entry of the guest was to be a spiritual experience for both recipient and host: they were to be greeted with communal prayers and the kiss of peace conferred by the superior, after which there was to be a brief collation ('legatur coram hospite lex divina ut aedificetur') and the ceremonial washing of hands and feet (*RB*, liii). According to Hildemar, these obligations were recognised in the eighth century but so also was the burden they represented, advising their fulfilment not *ad literam* but in spirit.[228] Later codes and customaries retained the commitment to hospitality; the principle was reiterated in the capitular and papal canons of the thirteenth and fourteenth centuries although other ceremonial duties were abandoned. The high Middle Ages had seen many houses invest in lavish accommodation for the guests; in spite of the inclement conditions of the fourteenth and fifteenth centuries, these ranges were generally retained and even renewed; their maintenance was not infrequently given a higher priority than the conventual buildings.[229] In this period the paupers and pilgrims of the *RB* were often eclipsed by guests of greater status. The monks consciously courted distinguished guests: the abbot of St Albans went so far as to divert a royal progress to ensure a visit to his costly 'King's Hall'.[230] Royal and noble guests exploited their monastic hosts, requiring hospitality for their household, their knights, esquires and other hangers-on, remaining in the precincts for weeks at a time: in January 1296 Edward I required the abbot and convent of Abingdon to accommodate his servant, two horses and two grooms until Michaelmas.[231] Guests also compromised the discipline of the convent: at the turn of the thirteenth century the brethren of Brecon Priory complained to their visitor of the compulsion to 'feign drunkenness' when receiving the Welsh.[232]

For much of the Middle Ages the monasteries also provided a permanent

---

[227] R. Hodges, *Light in the Dark Ages: The Rise and Fall of San Vincenzo al Volturno* (Ithaca, 1997), p. 101.
[228] *Warnefrid-Hildemar*, pp. 147–9 at 148–9.
[229] For example, Dobson, *Durham Priory*, p. 102; Savine, 'English Monasteries on the Eve of the Dissolution', 241–5. The trend was matched among the Cistercians of this period: Kerr, *Monastic Hospitality*, pp. 89–90.
[230] Clark, *Monastic Renaissance*, p. 40. See also *GASA*, iii. 274–5, 277, 387.
[231] *VCH Berkshire*, ii. 51–62 at 54 (1296).
[232] Cowley, *Monastic Order in South Wales*, p. 204.

residence for guests. The early communities occasionally may have accepted sojourners into their custody, often under the duress of the patron. Later these arrangements became both formal and financial: a commercial value was ascribed to the daily bed and board of the monastery, which might be purchased or provided by a patron for themselves or a dependent, or conferred as a privilege by the abbot and convent. In England the provision was called a 'corrody', and from the thirteenth century corrodies were sought and traded as commodities by patrons and their clients. They became the currency with which royal patrons rewarded their pensioners. In the straitened circumstances of the post-Black Death decades, the monks also treated them in these terms: the compotus rolls of Selby Abbey record sales of corrodies to local investors and their use as a convenient alternative to cash compensation in the settlement of disputes.[233] Female communities also accepted paying boarders, called 'prebendaries' in the accounts of English convents.[234] Not every boarder was a patron or purchaser; visitors reported a concentration of kinsfolk, particularly at poor or poorly patronised houses, where the family network was perhaps more powerful than the commercial attractions of the corrody.[235]

The permanent presence of the unprofessed not only encroached on the social culture of the precinct but also on its infrastructure. In the later Middle Ages it was common for the conventual church to be furnished with a 'viewing gallery' to accommodate the resident worshippers; at Cistercian Marrick Priory (Yorkshire) they reached closer to the centre of the enclosure, occupying chambers aligned on three sides of the cloister.[236]

Men, Women and Children

The *RB* was an inclusive code. Brethren were required not only to 'love thy neighbour' but also to 'honour the aged' and 'love youth' (*RB*, iii. 2, 69–70) and to 'let ... natural weakness be always taken into account' (*RB*, xxxvi. 1). Even those members of society apparently incompatible with the spiritual purity of the oratory were to be tolerated within the precinct wall. There is no mention of women in the *RB*, but, as Gregory bears witness in his *Dialogues*, there was a contemporary perception that Benedict's code could also offer them spiritual nourishment. Some of the first communities to follow the *RB* in England and France were 'double' monasteries of men and women. None of the English houses survived the Norman Conquest but closely connected, if not intersected, convents endured on the European

---

[233] Smith, *Canterbury Cathedral Priory*, pp. 50–2; Selby, pp. 52–4; Harvey, *Lay Religious Life in Late Medieval Durham*, pp. 171–2.
[234] Oliva, *Convent and Community*, p. 117.
[235] *Visitations*, ed. Thompson, iii. 274–5 (Peterborough, 1437); Haines, 'Visitation Injunctions', 346.
[236] Gilchrist, *Gender and Material Culture*, pp. 74, 107–8.

mainland. In Anglo-Norman England a number of Benedictines cultivated connections with communities of (male and female) anchorites.[237]

From early times women were also to be found among the workers of the precinct. The labour of the laundry was exclusively female, and its demands required that washerwomen passed in and out of the monastic enclosure.[238] There may have been women engaged in the characteristically female crafts of baking and brewing. The recurrent complaint of episcopal visitors in the later Middle Ages that women had been found in the cloister may reflect the variety of domestic tasks undertaken by women even in monasteries of modest size. There were also women among the guests, corrodians and pensioners accommodated, if they were not merely annuitants, in the chambers or cotts often built into the precinct walls.[239] The collateral presence of the sexes was also an inherent feature of female houses. Not only was the observant life supported by men but also the administration of the household.[240] The recourse of unauthorised unprofessed males was a recurrent complaint of visitors; errant clerks from Oxford found good cheer ('omnimodas solaciones') at Godstow in 1432.[241] Much of the skilled and unskilled labour on which the nunnery depended was also surely male; labourers engaged for seasonal work might still be accommodated within the precinct.[242]

Children were a licit presence in the precinct although not unproblematic. Benedict placed children at the centre of the professed community. The oblation of their parents, their lifetime commitment to the *cenobium*, was recognised in their exemption from the formalities of the noviciate. They were to 'take their place in oratory' (*RB*, lxiii) although it was only in later customaries that their own contribution to the Office was codified.[243] There were oblates in the pioneering male, female and double houses, and between the ninth and eleventh centuries oblation was perhaps the principal means of recruitment. The disciplinary and moral difficulties arising from a cohort of (respectively) boys and girls in the enclosure caused its decline in later centuries but children remained on the edge of the enclosure. The foundation of open schools from the turn of the thirteenth century, as discussed below, placed boys of variable status aged seven to thirteen in the custody of the monastery; houses of men and women also accepted boys and girls into the custody of the superior before their entry into the world, for some by means of marriage.[244] Certainly in later centuries there were also

---

[237] The celebrated instance is the patronage of the hermit, Roger, and his protégée, Christina, by Abbot Geoffrey Gorham of St Albans (1119–46), for which see *GASA*, i. 97–105.

[238] *Selby*, p. 254 (1413–14).

[239] For example: *Selby*, pp. 52–3 (1398–9).

[240] Oliva, *Convent and Community*, pp. 112–14.

[241] *Visitations*, ed. Thompson, ii. 66–68 at 67; *VCH Oxfordshire*, ii. 71–5.

[242] Oliva, *Convent and Community*, p. 115&n.

[243] For example, *RC*, iii. 31; iv. 36–7.

[244] Oliva, *Convent and Community*, p. 119.

children employed as servants in the domestic departments. The guesthouse or hostel, kitchen and infirmary might retain pages; they were also attached to the kitchen, hall and perhaps private apartments of the superior.[245]

Service

The Benedictines' engagement with the world was not only the effect of their endowments; it was also the expression of a vocation of service which evolved in their early centuries. Service was articulated in the *RB* as a principle of personal morality and not primarily a corporate responsibility: the *professus* was challenged neither 'to do no evil to his neighbour, nor to take up reproach against him' (Psalms, 14[15]: 2–3) to reinforce their re-formation as 'heir of the kingdom of heaven (*RB*, prologue); there were six modes of service advanced in the tools of good works, to sustain the poor and naked, visit the sick, bury the dead, to help in trouble and to console the sorrowing (*RB*, iv. 14–19) to deepen personal spirituality, an 'art [which] applied without ceasing day and night ... will merit for us that reward which He hath promised' (*RB*, iv). The reception of guests was the only outward act of service with which Benedict charged his *cenobium* and it was presented as an observance, incorporating prayer and procession; practical provisions, the kitchen and dormitory of the guests and the number of beds, were addressed only in the closing lines of the chapter (*RB*, liii). The environment in which the *RB* was propagated in the generations after Benedict, and the place of the church within it, invested the first communities of monks with a wider social significance. They were raised with regional settlements and the emerging polities that governed them and responded to their needs. Already the eighth-century commentaries on the *RB* elaborated the services of the *cenobium* in response to the crowds that came there.[246] They were further elaborated between the tenth and the twelfth centuries as, under the influence of a novel, penitential theology, founders and benefactors adopted the Benedictine monastery as the principal agent of their necessary good works. The Black Monks accepted a role which owed less to the principles of the founder than the personal, social and political imperatives of the laity: it offered them the security of continued endowment and the status of social leadership. Yet the rise of the mendicant friars and reformed orders of monks, and the proliferation of penitential foundations, in the later Middle Ages challenged their monopoly on social and spiritual welfare. Now the monasteries faced criticism for their performance of functions which society had projected upon them.

[245] For example, *Selby*, pp. 165, 254 (1413–14; 1416–17).
[246] *Warnefrid-Hildemar*, pp. 147–51.

Prayer

The greatest service offered to the outside world was the very *opus* undertaken within the monastery, the perpetual enterprise of prayer and praise in the oratory. Prayer was the *raison d'être* of Benedict's *cenobium*, but his intended beneficiaries were the brethren themselves. To the world beyond the precinct wall, the *RB* offered only an admonition: 'Hear what the spirit says' and 'Run while you have the light of life, that the darkness of death does not overtake you' (John 12:35); the rewards of the *opus Dei* were for those that laboured at it. Yet even among the pioneering colonies of the seventh century, there was general interest in the properties of Benedictine observance. It was not only that it brought Christian worship to a community of believers that was small and insecure – the *RB* was pioneered in the heartland of the Celtic and Gallo-Roman Church – but rather that it carried the imprint of Rome, and the authority, continuity, and prosperity conjured by its legend. Stephen of Ripon represented the thegn Alhfrith's grant to Bishop Wilfrid as 'for the good of his own soul'.[247] This was his interpretation of the impulses of the recent past but already at the turn of the seventh century charters gave credence to the efficacy of monastic observance outside the enclosure and beyond the precinct wall. The unequivocal expectation of a charter of 762, presented to Prüm by Pepin the Short, is of personal (and indeed social) participation in the spiritual profit of the professed community, 'for the good of our soul and [for those of] our kinsfolk, and for the continuance of our kingdom' ('pro remedio anime nostre et coniugis prolisque nostre et pro longevitate regni nostri').[248] The public utility of the monastic *opus* was elaborated by Benedict of Aniane: the capitulary of 817 added daily prayers to the Office in honour of the royal house; the *Notitia de servitio monasteriorum* of 819 codified the three-fold service the monastery owed to the founder: gifts (*dona*), martial aid (*militia*) and prayer 'for the salvation of the emperor, his sons and the stability of the empire' ('pro salute imperatoris vel filiorum eius et stabilitate imperii').[249] The reformers of the tenth century rediscovered Benedict's prescriptions and reinforced them: Æthelwold's *Regularis Concordia* placed prayers for the royal house after Prime and High Mass and pairs of psalms and collects (i.e. prayers) in honour of the monarch and other benefactors were required after Matins, Terce, Sext and Vespers;[250] Cluny initiated the custom of prefacing Matins with fifteen gradual psalms, five for departed brethren, five for the living community, and five for the prince and principal benefactors; in the eleventh century, when Cluny's customary was first codified, the congregation also added to its calendar a distinctive observance

[247] *Wilfrid*, pp. 16–17.
[248] MGH *Diplomata Karolinum I*, no. 16, pp. 22–3 at 22.
[249] Bernhardt, *Itinerant Kingship*, p. 77.
[250] *RC*, pp. 12–14, 16, 20–3.

for the feast of All Souls dedicated to the souls of all the faithful departed.[251] The patrons of these reformed monasteries sharpened their perception of their share in the Office: in his charter for Winchester, Edgar was explicit that the 'intercessions' ('eorum intercessionibus') of the Black Monks were intended 'for us and for ours' ('pro nostris nostrorumque').[252] Cnut's charter for Fécamp, restored under the influence of Cluny by William of Volpiano, held the expectation of 'perpetual service' with his grant ('ut nostrum beneficium inviolabile permaneret regali gravitate roboravi, quatinus ispis mee meritis ad celestia indesinenter studeant elevare').[253]

In the generations between the Carolingian and the Gregorian reforms, monastic and secular authorities established a theological foundation for this emerging spiritual economy. The refinement of the penitential imperative provided a powerful rationale for the transaction between patron and monastery. It was work in which the monastic order participated through the preparation and transmission of penitentials, and through preaching and teaching.[254] The making of purgatory as place and process, although not complete until after the taste for monastic patronage had passed its peak, was also advanced, not least in the popular homilies of the Benedictine Hrabanus Maurus; in parallel the liturgical commemorations for the souls of the faithful departed took shape.[255] Such theology informed the justification of Cluny offered by its early chronicler Jotsaldus: 'due to the prayers of religious men often the souls of the damned were freed from their punishment through God's mercy'.[256] Renewed reflection on the celestial hierarchy and its terrestrial counterpart clarified the spiritual capacity of clergy as well as their moral authority and social status: those that follow 'the rule of religion', wrote the eremitical prelate Peter Damian, are 'set above warriors' as 'the army of spiritual service'.[257]

Before the beginning of Gregory's pontificate (1073), a conceptual framework for the service of the monasteries had been formed. Famously, in his *carmen* dedicated to Robert II of France, Bishop Adalbero of Laon

---

[251] Boynton, *Shaping a Monastic Identity*, pp. 108–9.

[252] *Councils and Synods*, i.12.

[253] C. H. Haskins, 'A Charter of Canute for Fécamp', *EHR* 33 (1918), 342–4 at 343; Potts, *Monastic Revival and Regional Identity*, p. 39&n.

[254] M. F. Giandrea, *Episcopal Culture in Late Anglo-Saxon England*, Anglo-Saxon Studies 7 (Woodbridge, 2007), p. 110.

[255] For the rise and refinement of these liturgical provisions, see G. Constable, 'The Commemoration of the Dead in the Early Middle Ages', in *Early Medieval Rome and the Christian West: Essays in Honour of Donald A. Bullough*, ed. J. M. H. Smith (Leiden, 2000), pp. 169–95; Dunn, *Emergence of Monasticism*, p. 208; V. Schier, 'Memorials Sung and Unsung: Liturgical Remembrance and its History', in *Care for the Here and the Hereafter: Memoria, Art and Ritual in the Middle Ages*, ed. T. van Bueren and A. van Leerdam (Turnhout, 2005), pp. 125–35; R. Horrox, 'Purgatory, Prayer and Plague: 1150–1380', in *Death in England: An Illustrated History*, ed. P. C. Jupp and C. Gittings (Manchester, 1999), pp. 90–118. See also Harper, *Forms and Orders of Western Liturgy*, pp. 126–31.

[256] Jotsaldus, *Vita sancti Odilonis*: PL 142. 897–940 at 927A, reworked by Peter Damian, PL 144. 925–44 at 936B.

[257] Peter Damian, *Letter to the Cardinal-Bishop Boniface of Albano*: PL 145, 463–6.

represented contemporary society as three orders – *bellatores, laboratores, oratores* (warriors, workers and those who pray) – although his characterisation was hardly an *apologia*, since his verses were also sharply critical of Cluny.[258] The Benedictine Otloh of Saint-Emmeram elaborated on the bond between the orders: the professed depend for their sustenance on 'the labour of secular men' while in turn secular men owe their salvation to their prayers.[259]

It should be acknowledged there was a divergent trend in the devotional literature of the Benedictines. Just as Cluny's spiritual commerce prospered, in the middle years of the eleventh century, John of Fécamp called upon his brethren to reawaken the affective contemplation of the monastic pioneers in which 'the weight and misery of our mortal condition no longer deaden[s] the faculties ... the spirit is filled with joy ... the mind is clear, and the whole soul, burning with a desire for the vision of thy beauty, is ravished by a love of things invisible'; Odo of Cluny himself celebrated the 'coelestis disciplina' that was the practice of the perfect monk.[260] A belief that an experience of the divine was the exclusive reward of the professed persisted in the later Middle Ages even as the monasteries became burdened by the schedule of suffrages for their benefactors. The decorative scheme of the Sherborne Missal (*c.* 1400) was directed towards the depiction of the personal vision of the Trinity that was the privilege of the observant Abbot Robert Brunyng.[261]

Yet the penitential conviction and practice of patrons recast the public role of monastic religion. In its second century, under the rule of Abbot Odilo, as many as two-thirds of the charters presented to Cluny conveyed particular requests for prayers;[262] the endowments of the new foundations of conquered England and those revived in regions of Italy and Normandy were raised for the most part from these transactions. Guibert maintained the old church at Nogent was passed to the monastic order 'to have there a full offering of the divine offices'.[263] The service of prayer promised to strengthen the authority of the proprietorial *Eigenklöster*, but patrons invested widely and the typical Benedictine monastery became bound by obligations of diverse origins. The scale of the spiritual economy stirred sectional tensions in the clergy and certainly stimulated a resurgence of the ascetic impulse, but it also served to fix the identity of the Benedictines in

---

[258] Adalbero of Laon, *Carmen ad Rotbertum regem*, ll. 295–6, ed. C. Crozzi, *Poème au roi Robert*, Classiques de l'histoire de France au moyen âge, 32 (Paris, 1979), p. 22.

[259] G. Constable, *Three Studies in Medieval Religious and Social Thought* (Cambridge, 1995), p. 313.

[260] John of Fécamp, *Confessio theologica*, in *Un maître de la vie spirituelle au XIe siècle: Jean de Fécamp*, ed. J. P. Bonnes and J. Leclercq (Paris, 1946), p. 182. Odo's characterisation comes in his *Life of Gerald of Aurillac*, ed. G. Sitwell (London, 1958), pp. 139–40; see Bruce, *Silence and Sign Language*, p. 20.

[261] J. Backhouse, *The Sherborne Missal* (Toronto, 1999), p. 24; J. M. Luxford, *The Art and Architecture of English Benedictine Monasteries, 1300–1540: A Patronage History* (Woodbridge, 2006), p. 70.

[262] Van Engen, 'Crisis of Cenobiticism Reconsidered', 293.

[263] *Guibert*, p. 125.

Church and State. The clerical compiler of the *Libellus de diversis ordinibus* distinguished between the two species of monk in the contemporary church but acknowledged that both merited the term 'in the proper sense' ('qui monachi nomen proprie');[264] in England their status was even enshrined in statute: the Statute of Carlisle (1307) promulgated the principle that the purpose of such foundations was 'to perform prayers and alms in places where the churches were founded for the souls of the founders, their heirs and all Christians'.[265]

As the spiritual economy grew, it also diversified. The demand for prayers was too great to be met by the daily office, since prayers or psalms were added to the *ordo* of the Office to acknowledge a patron, as well as the now customary commemorations of the prince or the principal founder. The response was to offer observances in parallel. The likelihood of private masses was recognised in the *Regularis Concordia* but it was from the turn of the eleventh century that it became common for patronal requests to be met by diverse observances, 'suffrages', outside the *horarium* and in spaces beyond the monastic quire.[266] If not the origin of the shift itself, patrons did much to shape the schedule of extra-liturgical services; indeed, the record of services might be read as a summary history of lay piety in the high and later Middle Ages. Before 1250 a mass was the most common observance offered to a patron outside the *horarium*. While they remained the principal currency in the centuries before the Reformation, particularly for prominent patrons, other offices (of the Dead, of the Virgin) or parts of offices (the gradual psalms) might also be performed; in this period patrons were also served by chantries of variable scale, some little more than a stipend for a priest (monk or secular) to perform commemorative prayer in perpetuity, but some comprising a fully furnished chapel within the conventual church; there were fewer in the houses of women although they were not unknown.[267]

These extra-liturgical suffrages transformed the observant life of the monastery. Their demands drained personnel and, in the constrained circumstances of the later Middle Ages, even resources (vestments, incense, wax) away from the daily Office.[268] They also ended the seclusion of the monastic quire: as early as the twelfth century the change was visible at Cluny as the 'closed' church of Cluny II was replaced by the open Cluny III.[269]

[264] *Libellus*, p. 16.
[265] *Councils and Synods*, ii.1235.
[266] *RC*, p. 66.
[267] For example, Bishop Walter Skirlaw of Durham's chantry (1398) at Selby, which paid for a daily mass and an annual obit as well as a commemorative dole to the monastic community: *Selby*, pp. 236–9; Gilchrist, *Gender and Material Culture*, p. 105.
[268] Constable, *Reformation of the Twelfth Century*, p. 200.
[269] C. E. Armi and E. B. Smith, 'The Choir Screen of Cluny III', *The Art Bulletin* 66 (1984), 556–73; O. K. Werckmeister, 'Cluny III and the Pilgrimage to Santiago de Compostela', *Gesta* 27 (1988), 103–12.

There was pressure from seigniorial and episcopal supervisors, and visitors, to prioritise patronal obligations and counter initiatives in the thirteenth century and later, from the chapters of the order, to curb, or simplify these performances: at Worcester in 1301 Archbishop Robert Winchelsea commanded the brethren to assist one another in the completion of their private masses.[270] Although they might be served by monks, the creation of chantries made secular clerks a permanent presence in the conventual church; they also carried with them further changes to its fabric. In England suffrages also bound the monastery to obligations beyond the precinct: Earl Edmund of Cornwall placed his parochial chapel dedicated to St Edmund of Canterbury in the care of the abbot and convent of Abingdon.[271] Given the new constraints on their endowment, such as Mortmain legislation in England, the Black Monks were generally unable to resist the continuing requests for suffrage. The purchase of property could be sealed by the promise of spiritual service.[272] The rewards remained significant even in a clerical marketplace now crowded with ecclesiastical foundations: for daily prayers performed by chaplains in their conventual church, in 1331 Reading Abbey received no fewer than 240 acres of land.[273]

The rich variety of suffrages sought by patrons reflected the character of their spiritual ties to the Benedictines. The cult of saints was a constant source of and stimulus for their interest. There were many early monasteries that owed their foundation or formative development to figures later venerated as saints: Wulfstan of Worcester was a focus of popular devotion in his lifetime, and at his death his disciples remained at the monastery for three days of observance; others secured significant relics at an early stage in their history: Fleury secured its pre-eminence among Loire monasteries by the seizure of Benedict's relics; perhaps uniquely, Glastonbury created contemporary shrines to concentrate the devotion to its ancient associates, Arthur and Joseph of Arimathea; later convents were given the custody of relics, or competed for them by their own enterprise, as a conscious strategy to secure and extend their endowments.[274]

The shrine of the saint became the focus of forms of spiritual service that

---

[270] *Chapters*, ed. Pantin, ii. 32; Haines, 'Visitation Injunctions', 337.

[271] *VCH Berkshire*, ii. 51–62 at 54.

[272] For example, Bury St Edmunds purchased a messuage at Dereham when suffrages were offered to the vendor: Thompson, 'The Church and the Aristocracy', p. 241.

[273] *VCH Berkshire*, ii. 62–73 at 64.

[274] For Worcester see E. Mason, *Wulfstan of Worcester, c. 1008–1095* (Oxford, 1990), pp. 254–85. For Fleury see Head, *Hagiography and the Cult of the Saints*, pp. 23–5; J. Nightingale, 'Oswald, Fleury and the Continental Reform', in *St Oswald of Worcester: Life and Influence*, Studies in the Early History of Britain, The Makers of England 2 (London, 1996), pp. 23–45; for Glastonbury's shrines, see A. Gransden, 'The Growth of Glastonbury Traditions and Legends in the Twelfth Century', *JEH* 27 (1976), 37–58; V. M. Lagorio, 'The Evolving Legend of St Joseph of Glastonbury', in *Glastonbury Abbey and the Arthurian Tradition*, ed. J. P. Carley (Cambridge, 2001), pp. 55–82. See also J. P. Carley, *Glastonbury Abbey: The Holy House at the Head of the Moors Adventurous* (Glastonbury, 1995), pp. 87–94, 122–4, 147–50. See also Luxford, *Art and Architecture*, pp. 134–6.

were distinct from suffrages or a collateral share in the daily Office. From the turn of the eleventh century, in a climate of reform, renewed asceticism and the ambition for crusade, pilgrimage emerged as a powerful and popular expression of the penitential impulse. The Black Monks encouraged pilgrims into their precincts for periods of personal prayer at the shrine; they also harnessed the inherent power of the relics for their individual and collective benefit: the shrine was constructed with arches or niches to allow the pilgrim the utmost proximity; the reliquary was also processed at regular intervals even out of the precincts: the Ely monks carried the relics of St Wendred onto the battlefield of Ashington in 1016 to assist the fallen; in their turn, the regional community treated the shrine as a locus of public penance.[275] In later medieval England a number of monasteries also offered benefactors the perpetual benefits of the shrine through membership of the fraternity of the saint. Membership was conferred on prominent patrons but might also be purchased by willing benefactors.

In the later Middle Ages, to cultivate the interest of lay benefactors, the monasteries also adopted the extra-liturgical celebration of the Marian Office. The greater abbeys and priories constructed (or converted) Lady Chapels; although committed to a formidable liturgical schedule, invariably they observed a daily Lady Mass; from the turn of the fourteenth century the larger houses also employed clerks and boys to perform polyphony that was to the taste of their patrons.[276]

Lay piety in the later Middle Ages was 'vigorous, adaptable and popular' and the later Benedictines proved responsive to evolving tastes.[277] The dedication of their subordinate altars reflected not only domestic traditions but also popular and regional trends. Here the service of the monastery was to provide an environment for personal prayer, although there was still a transaction with the penitent: as the sacrist's account from Selby attests, at each of the nave altars there was a box for alms and oblations.[278]

The Parish

The Benedictines not only offered the laity a share in their observances but also they became involved in their own worship. There was no place in the *RB* for pastoral responsibility beyond the professed community, still less for common or collaborative worship. Yet the early foundations that followed

---

[275] *Liber Eliensis*, ed. Blake, p. 148.
[276] Bowers, 'Early Tudor Monastic Enterprise', 21–54 at 35–8; B. Harvey, 'The Monks of Westminster and the Old Lady Chapel', in *Westminster Abbey: The Lady Chapel of Henry VII*, ed. Tatton-Brown and Mortimer, pp. 5–31.
[277] E. Duffy, *The Stripping of the Altars: Traditional Religion in England, c. 1400–c. 1580* (New Haven, 1992), p. 5.
[278] *Selby*, pp. 217–18.

the rule eroded the boundary between monastic and lay religion: they took possession of churches which already served a social community; they were led by missionary prelates charged with pastoral, if not, yet, strictly diocesan obligations; they flourished in regions with few, if any secular churches and fewer secular priests to serve them. The evolution of the provincial church, of settled dioceses and, eventually, parishes did not disengage them since so much of this ecclesiastical infrastructure was now placed under their supervision.[279] The spiritual properties of the Benedictines formalised their early ties to the secular church with material, juridical and pastoral duties. At the same time, the rise of the precinct community established lay worshippers on the edge of the enclosure itself. As the authority of the secular clergy advanced in the high and later Middle Ages, their discomfort over the clerical interests of their monastic colleagues only deepened. Even before the resurgence of heresy aroused fears of a pastoral crisis at the turn of the fourteenth century, canonists had condemned the monk of the parish and pulpit.[280] The commitment of the monks only hardened in the face of such criticism. The experience of academic study had led them to appropriate the identity and interests of the masters of theology that were now widespread in the secular church. The spread of heresy among the laity and sectarian discord among their mendicant colleagues served to strengthen their conviction that in their hands alone lay the hope and salvation of the people: as a Benedictine preacher pronounced at a meeting of the English general chapter, 'we are the masters of the priesthood and the princes of the people'.[281]

Throughout the Middle Ages, the churches of the Benedictines witnessed lay worship. In Gaul, Lombardy, Flanders and Anglo-Saxon England the monastic churches were the principal churches of their respective regions, sometimes raised from the residue of earlier clerical centres, often the locus of what passed for episcopal administration.[282] The Columbanian monasteries which later adopted the *RB* were, at least in origin, the cult centre for the whole region; the minsters of Anglo-Saxon England also served as a devotional focus for a diverse community of monks, priests, layfolk and pilgrims.[283] Observant reform forced the removal or at least separation of these lay worshippers, but not uniformly. The abbey at Gembloux acted as a parish church until the mid-eleventh century; a number of English abbeys and priories, both male and female, retained the role long after the Norman

---

[279] Guibert de Nogent was notably engaged with the prevalence of heresy in his province: *Guibert*, p. 210.

[280] William of Paull [de Pagula], *Summa summarum*, III. 38: Oxford, Bodleian Library, MS Bodley 293, fos. 130v*-132r* at 131v. See also B. Smalley, *Studies in Medieval Thought and Learning from Abelard to Wyclif* (London, 1981), pp. 297–8.

[281] W. A. Pantin, 'A Sermon for a General Chapter', *Downside Review* 51 (1933), 291–308 at 295.

[282] Worcester Cathedral Library, MS F10, fos. 81r*; Blair, *Church in Anglo-Saxon Society*, pp. 212–20; 384–5, 393–5.

[283] Ibid., pp. 153–60.

Conquest.[284] Here an often uncomfortable cohabitation continued into the fifteenth century: the shared monastic and parochial space at Rochester and Sherborne was the subject of violent discord which at the latter led to the destruction of the church.[285] In the pre-Reformation period the Black Monks proved hostile to cohabitation, although the arrangement in communities of women apparently remained collaborative.[286]

It was not uncommon for the parish church rather to be positioned on the edge of the precinct. Such churches were either the survival of an earlier ecclesiastical infrastructure or the foundation of the monastery, to serve a laity that might otherwise share its space. Separated by the courts and outbuildings of the precinct, these churches still placed parish worship more or less cheek-by-jowl with the professed community. In the high and later Middle Ages the greater abbeys and priories also made spiritual provision for the residents of the precinct with a parochial chapel (sometimes in the gatehouse) or church, served by secular clergy but under the jurisdiction and, surely, the devotional regime of the monastery; certainly their clergy were as closely bound to the religious as any serving the monastic community.[287]

The bond between the monastery and parish was strengthened by the brethren's performance of the pastoral office. The earliest recruits to the *RB* were not routinely ordained but it was not uncommon for their superiors to occupy sees and the obligations they carried: Stephen of Ripon recalled Wilfrid's demanding pastoral circuit, undertaken on horseback.[288] The terms of later foundations, formed from pre-existing secular churches, or to implant them in regions lacking such infrastructure, could invest the convent as a whole with a corporate cure of souls: the prior of Leominster (Herefordshire) was known as the deacon and held the cure not only of the professed brethren but of the entire parish.[289] Where secular churches were the possession of the monastery, constituting a jurisdictional peculiar, the cure of souls passed to the monastic archdeacon.[290] In early times this

---

[284] Oliva, *Convent and Community*, p. 148; A. E. Verhulst, *The Rise of Cities in North West Europe* (Cambridge, 1999), pp. 111, 114.

[285] A. Oakley, 'Rochester Cathedral Priory, 1185–1540', in *Faith and Fabric: A History of Rochester Cathedral, 604–1994*, ed. N. Yates and P. A. Welsby (Woodbridge, 1994), pp. 29–56 at 35–6; *VCH Dorset*, ii. 62–70 at 67.

[286] G. Coppack, 'The Planning of Cistercian Monasteries in the Later Middle Ages: the Evidence from Fountains, Rievaulx, Sawley and Rushen', in *The Religious Orders in Pre-Reformation England*, ed. J. G. Clark (Woodbridge, 2002), pp. 197–209; Oliva, *Convent and Community*, p. 147.

[287] A. Brown, *Popular Piety in Late Medieval England: The Diocese of Salisbury, 1250–1550* (Oxford, 1995), pp. 37–9; Gilchrist, *Gender and Material Culture*, pp. 72–3; Wood, *Proprietary Church*, pp. 681–2; T. Cooper, *The Last Generation of English Catholic Clergy: Parish Priests in the Diocese of Coventry and Lichfield in the Early Sixteenth Century* (Woodbridge, 1999), pp. 42–3.

[288] 'equitanti et pergenti ad varia official episcopatus sui, baptizandi utique et cum manus impositione confirmandi populos': *Wilfrid*, pp. 38–9.

[289] B. R. Kemp, 'The Monastic Dean of Leominster', *EHR* 83 (1968), 505–13.

[290] For monastic peculiars, see *MO*, p. 605.

responsibility was a matter of principle, not practice.[291] Rarely did the archdeacon act as the officiant in such instances, but certainly they exercised their canonical jurisdiction over the parishes in their custody: at Durham the monastic archdeacon convened his court in the cathedral, determining cases not only of routine indiscipline but also heresy. The pastoral authority of the monastic community was channelled for the correction of lay heretics.[292] Their spiritual leadership was also visible in the seasonal festivals of the parish. The convent took precedence in processions; it appears they also presided over the liturgical dramas which were widespread in England and mainland Europe: at twelfth-century St Albans Abbot Geoffrey lent vestments for a play of St Katherine; at Chester and Bury St Edmunds the dramatist himself may have been among the brethren.[293]

It was not uncommon for Black Monks to be charged with such responsibilities in their own right. Throughout the Middle Ages there were monks promoted to the episcopacy; they were prominent in the Gregorian period at the peak of the order's expansion and Cluny's political influence; in England the Benedictines entered episcopal service again in the decades after the Black Death when the mendicants were diminished by discord.[294] While it would be wrong to generalise over their contribution as bishops, the documentary traces of their diocesan service present them as committed pastors and, perhaps especially, popular preachers. The *Libellus de diversis ordinibus* observed the fervour for Benedictine sermons; Guibert de Nogent regarded his store of narratives as 'examples useful for sermons'.[295] The public sermons of the monastic prelates of fourteenth-century England appear to have attracted a clerical if not a lay audience beyond their own houses.[296]

There were few monks elevated to the episcopacy but there were many that fulfilled the duties of the secular priesthood. As the sacerdotal office gained greater definition during the period of the Gregorian reform, there was a growing contest as to its place in the monastic life: although the First Lateran Council of 1123 proscribed regulars from performing the cure of

---

[291] Blair, *Church in Anglo-Saxon Society*, pp. 163–4.

[292] For example: evidence of the Durham monks' critical engagement with Wyclifism and Lollardy in their supervision of observance and their preaching: Harvey, *Lay Religious Life in Late Medieval Durham*, p. 29; the abbot and convent of St Augustine's, Canterbury, acting as custodians of a convicted Lollard in 1511: *Kent Heresy Proceedings, 1511–12*, ed. N. P. Tanner, Kent Archaeological Society (Maidstone, 1997), pp. 110–11.

[293] *GASA*, i. 73; G. M. Gibson, *Theater of Devotion: East Anglian Drama and Society in the late Middle Ages* (Chicago, 1989), pp. 108–14 at 108.

[294] *RO*, iii. 369–75. Even when not elevated to the see monks at the English cathedral priories frequently undertook their responsibilities as suffragans or vicar generals: for example, Dobson, *Durham Priory*, pp. 203–49 at 223–4, 230; R. M. Haines, 'Bishop John Stratford's injunctions to his Cathedral Chapter and other Benedictine houses in Winchester', *Rev. Bén.* 117 (2007), 154–80 at 165–6.

[295] *Guibert*, p. 195; *Libellus*, p. 25.

[296] Wenzel, *Latin Sermon Collections*, pp. 278–87 at 286. See also *A Macaronic Sermon Collection from Late Medieval England: Oxford, MS Bodley 649*, ed. and trans. P. J. Horner (Toronto, 2006), pp. 6–7.

souls and the reformist Vallombrosians self-consciously rejected it, the spokesman of mainstream Benedictinism, Rupert of Deutz, embraced it as the highest expression of monastic spirituality.[297] There is no doubt that Black Monks occupied benefices, although the circumstances, and the degree of their incumbency, are not always clear: perhaps many instances shared the fiscal impulse of Chester Abbey to secure licences for the brethren to serve cures as a means of recovering the resources of their churches.[298] In later medieval England a benefice was a refuge for a monk unable to remain in the common life, and a reward for a superior, obedientiary or distinguished graduate seeking retirement; it appears a monk might also be presented to a benefice by a personal patron.[299] Clerical status and its canonical advantages acted to efface monastic identity.[300] Contemporary commentators complained of the monasteries' encroachment into the parish and pastoral care, but the extent to which monks served as pastors in provincial centres remains unresolved.[301] At any rate, in this period it appears the greater part of the monastery practised their priestcraft. The superior, prior, obedientiaries and prominent graduates might be engaged as personal chaplain, confessor or spiritual counsellor to a patron; they would also execute their wills.[302] It was the prior of Dover who performed the hasty exequies for the drowned duke of Suffolk (William de la Pole) at the port's parish church.[303] Only half a century before the Dissolution Abbot Thomas Ramridge of St Albans ministered to the household of King Henry VII.[304] Even without such affiliations, they might be called upon to minister to the permanent or temporary residents of the precinct and certainly to preach. It was an experience common to Black Monks at the beginning and end of the Middle Ages: Hrabanus's eighth-century homilies were written 'for the people' ('confeci ad praedicandum populo').[305]

---

[297] Van Engen, *Rupert of Deutz*, pp. 326–8.

[298] *VCH Cheshire*, iii. 132–46 at 141.

[299] For example, John Nyghtyngale, rector of Sneaton, buried in 1474 bearing the habit in which he had made his profession at Whitby: *VCH Yorkshire*, iii. 101–5 at 104.

[300] For example, an apostate accused of concealing the monastic habit with the garb of a secular clerk: Logan, *Runaway Religious*, p. 197.

[301] For example, Thomas Gascoigne's complaints of the damage done by monastic appropriation of churches and their sacramental functions (such as baptism): *Loci e libro veritatum: Passages selected from Gascoigne's Theological Dictionary*, ed. J. E. Thorold Rogers (Oxford, 1881), pp. 147–8, 197: 'et abbatiae diversae haent licenciam et usum quod omnes de certis parochiis baptizent in eorum monasteriis, et tamen non possunt in nocte, mec in aliis temporibus, commoe ad fontem ibidem accedere'.

[302] Oliva, *Convent and Community*, pp. 150–1.

[303] *Stone*, p. 49. See also C. R. Haines, *Dover Priory: A History of the Priory of St Mary the Virgin and St Martin of the New Work* (Cambridge, 1930), p. 286.

[304] *LP*, i/1, 308.

[305] McKitterick, *Frankish Church and Carolingian Reforms*, p. 97.

Charity

The Benedictines not only offered spiritual service to their neighbours; they also provided for their bodily needs. Benedict's *cenobium* was animated by the notion of *caritas*, an affective bond, an analogue of kinship, which Christ bore to his apostles and now bears to the whole family of the faithful. *Caritas* was to be the guiding principle of personal and communal conduct in the convent; it was also to be conspicuous to those beyond the enclosure by the common use of six instruments of good work, respectively care for the poor, naked, sick, dead, the troubled and sorrowing. In the *RB* these informed a number of routine acts of charity: the cellarer was to set aside the surplus commons of the monastery for the poor and the sick (*RB*, xxxi); worn clothes were to be 'put away in the vestry cupboard for the poor [*pauperes*]' (*RB*, lv). The cleansing of the hands and feet of guests (*RB*, liii) was articulated as a service for all visitors, but the founder required special solicitude to be shown to pilgrims and to the poor ('pauperum et peregrinorum maxime suceptioni cura sollicite exhibeatur': *RB*, liii. 6). The early Benedictines elaborated these prescriptions. The commentaries of Warnefrid and Hildemar attest to the presence of paupers and a hostel (*hospitale*) for their care; Hildemar, the later of the two, describes the arrangements governing their admission: two monks were to watch for alms seekers, to refer to the superior who would determine the worthy, and to assign those approved a place in the precinct.[306] Such provisions were common enough at the last quarter of the eighth century for Pepin I to require them of the Black Monks of Prüm, 'to feed and foster the helpless and the poor for the love of Christ' ('inopibus et pauperibus pro amore Christi gubernare atque educare'); here the currency of the phrase 'caritate in refectorio' suggests paupers were supported directly from the common table.[307] Their place in the Benedictine programme was codified by the Carolingian and Anglo-Saxon reformers. Æthelwold's *Regularis Concordia* recast the cleansing of hands and feet – called here *mandatum*, remoulded in English as *Maundy* – as a service for the poor alone; the code also required the brethren to build a surplus, 'laid up as a treasure in heaven', for the sustenance of the poor.[308]

In the Gregorian period of expansion, the relief of the poor was institutionalised as a discrete dimension of the monastery's administration, managed by an obedientiary, the almoner, and occupying dedicated accommodation often positioned adjoining the gatehouse through which outsiders passed. Like any of the 'obediences', the almonry was sustained by a portion of the monastery's income. The portfolio was diverse, perhaps as a means to guarantee its income: as early as 1174×1184 at Christ Church,

306 *Warnefrid-Hildemar*, p. 151; O. G. Oexle, 'Les moines d'Occident et la vie politique et sociale dans le Haut Moyen Âge', *Rev. Bén.* 103 (1993), 255–72 at 263.
307 MGH *Diplomata Karolinum I*, no. 16, pp. 22–3 at 22.
308 *RC*, pp. 39–40, 61–2,

Canterbury, churches, shops and tenements were all diverted to the almonry.[309] Generally the building offered facilities comparable to the guesthouse, kitchen, chamber and perhaps a dormitory; at greater abbeys and priories the almonry also offered a chapel: the relief of the monastery was as much spiritual as physical. The almonry range attracted the same investment in the high Middle Ages as the guesthouse or hostel: Jocelin of Brakelond noted the 'new stone' almonry at Bury St Edmunds, successor to an unstable wooden structure ('elemosinaria nostra lapidea que prius erat debilis et lignea').[310] The scale and vigour of the office should not be underestimated, although it is rarely visible in the physical remains of the monastery: it was perhaps a common perception of the twelfth-century public that these were 'cities of refuge in the possession of saints' [Numbers, 35:6].

From this period, if not before, Benedictine monasteries also offered 'out-relief' to the poor either at the gate of the monastery, or before the almonry building. The distribution was sometimes seasonal, to mark the patronal festival or a principal date in the liturgical calendar, although in the later Middle Ages at the greater abbeys and priories it appears to have been a weekly routine. The earliest recorded general chapter of the order in England reminded delegates of their duty to offer 'out-relief'.[311] The accounts of obedientiaries from the post-Black Death period show that officers also made distributions from their departmental income: Margery Palmer, the fifteenth-century cellarer of Carrow, gave clothes as well as cash.[312] It was not uncommon for it to be a condition of benefactions to be undertaken on the day of, or days following, the benefactor's funeral or on the anniversary of their death. As benefactor of Westminster Abbey, Edward I requested a distribution as a commemoration for Queen Eleanor of Castile.[313]

It has long been assumed the monastic commitment to charity diminished in the later Middle Ages as the pressure on institutional income intensified and the preservation of patronage became the main priority. Pre-Reformation critics claimed the genuine poor were now eclipsed by prestigious guests and privileged corrodians and pensioners.[314] Certainly in England the monasteries made provision for their most exclusive visitors and fostered a dining culture familiar only to Crown and nobility. In the complex parallel accounts of an income subdivided between obedientiaries,

---

[309] Smith, *Canterbury Cathedral Priory*, pp. 14, 15, 23.

[310] *Jocelin*, pp. 95–6.

[311] *Chapters*, ed. Pantin, i. 8–14 at 10.

[312] These distributions should be distinguished from gifts, commonly bestowed by the obedientiary upon those whose services they employed, such as the Christmas gift presented to the clerk of the refectory at Selby: *Selby*, pp. 143, 196, (Granger's account); Haines, 'Visitation Injunctions', 343–4; Oliva, *Convent and Community*, p. 141.

[313] N. S. Rushton, 'Spatial Aspects of the Almonry Site and the Changing Priorities of Poor Relief at Westminster Abbey, *c.* 1290–1540', *Architectural History* 45 (2002), 66–91.

[314] *Visitations*, ed. Thompson, iii. 290 (Peterborough, 1446–7); Haines, 'Visitation Injunctions', 346. See also Harvey, *Living and Dying*, pp. 179–209.

the full extent of their expenditure in alms and commons in this period is not always conspicuous.[315] Yet recent studies of English abbeys have revealed no significant reduction either in the value of their charitable provisions. Where *Valor ecclesiasticus* returns had recorded barely 2 per cent of conventual income devoted to charity, modern analysis has argued a more reliable figure may be as high as 10 per cent.[316] In the century before the Reformation, the expenditure of the best-endowed houses may have risen to between 15 and 20 per cent, although an analysis of provision of the female houses of East Anglia has shown little connection between conventual income and the provision of alms.[317] The scale of their charity remained stable but there can be no doubt it narrowed in scope. The conurbation and partition of the precinct curbed the daily passage of the itinerant poor.

The Black Monks also followed the founder's call to care for the sick. There is no trace of medical aid for outsiders in the early Middle Ages. Later, those admitted into the almonry might receive treatment alongside bed and board: perhaps it was his medical skill that secured Walter the Physician the office of almoner at Bury St Edmunds.[318] At a visitation in the first quarter of the fourteenth century, Worcester Priory was called upon to resume the care of the sick in the almonry, offering a loaf and wine to all that were known to be infirm, as well as access to an appropriate physic.[319]

In a handful of cases, the Black Monks directed, or served, a dedicated hospice. At the turn of the twelfth century a hospice under the *RB* was raised alongside the church of the Holy Sepulchre at Jerusalem, although it was later refounded for the Knights Hospitaller.[320] Abbot William of Whitby founded a hospice in 1109; it was intended for lepers, but later it was open to all.[321] There was a hospice in the precinct of Bermondsey, adjoining the cellarer's range, and at Ramsey, the church of St Thomas which stood at the gatehouse served variously a guesthouse, hospital and infirmary.[322] The turn-of-the twelfth-century vision of the monk of Eynsham represented a nun of Godstow (Oxfordshire) cleansing the limbs of a leper.[323]

When endowments and extra-mural interests were extended between 1050 and 1250 a number of abbeys initiated the foundation of secular

[315] As early as 1306 for this reason Bishop Cobham of Worcester commanded the brethren of the priory to resume the central administration of alms: Haines, 'Visitation Injunctions', 344.

[316] Savine, 'English Monasteries on the Eve of the Dissolution', pp. 235–40.

[317] N. S. Rushton and W. Sigle-Rushton, 'Monastic Poor Relief in Sixteenth-Century England', *Journal of International History* 32:2 (2001), 193–216; Oliva, *Convent and Community*, pp. 144–5.

[318] *Jocelin*, pp. 96, 113.

[319] Haines, 'Visitation Injunctions', 343–4.

[320] Pringle, *Churches of the Crusader Kingdom of Jerusalem*, p. 5.

[321] *Cartularium abbatiae de Whiteby: The Chartulary of Whitby Abbey*, 2 vols., ed. J. C. Atkinson, Surtees Society, 69–72 (1879–81), i. 329.

[322] *VCH Surrey*, ii. 64–77 at 66; *VCH Huntingdonshire*, i. 377–85; *MRH*, pp. 254, 301.

[323] *Eynsham Cartulary*, ed. H. E. Salter, 2 vols., Oxford Historical Society 49, 51 (1907–8), ii. 285–371 at 355–6.

hospitals, beyond the precinct but within their jurisdiction. The monks of St
Mary's, York, were co-patrons of the hospital of St Nicholas which received
its first charters between 1108 and 1118.[324] St Albans was sole founder of
a leper hospice sited on Watling Street in the period 1119×1146: Abbot
Geoffrey promulgated constitutions for its members, which bore some
resemblance to the *RB*.[325] A hospice was provided by the prior and convent
of Bath in *c*. 1180 for the care of the sick that resorted to the renowned hot
spring.[326] Bury St Edmunds secured the patronage of six secular hospitals
before 1215; the largest, St Saviour's, was staffed by twelve and supported the
same number of male and female inpatients.[327] These provisions were not
always uncontested, of course: at Castle Hedingham the women objected
to the co-location of their hospital.[328] The Black Monks did not serve their
secular hospitals – the monastic master of the leper hospice at Peterborough
is surely an exception – but under their patronage the greater part of them
endured to the end of the Middle Ages.[329] Certainly they were as susceptible
to appropriation as any monastic property: the women of St Bartholomew,
Newcastle, had appropriated their hospital at Gateshead before 1400.[330] Yet
it seems wealthy houses were also moved to remodel them to respond to
changing economic and social conditions: it was perhaps a measure of their
understanding of the provincial laity in the early sixteenth century that one
Benedictine hospital (Glastonbury) became an almshouse for women and
another (Reading) became a grammar school.[331]

It was not unknown for the Black Monks to offer *ad hominem* medical
care to the unprofessed. The skill of particular brethren attracted unsolicited
enquiries for aid. Generally these came from persons of status, or at least
property: Abbot Faricius of Abingdon received the gift of a hospice and
lands at Colnbrook (Buckinghamshire) in return for treatment provided
to one Miles Crispin in 1106.[332] Master Walter the Physician of Bury St
Edmunds had amassed 'a large sum of money which he had acquired by his
practice of the art of medicine' ('multum apposuit, quod arte medicinali
adquisiuit').[333] Edward II sent one of his servants to Reading Abbey to
recover from an injury to his hand.[334] In the later Middle Ages the monastic
infirmary, or at least its staff, were made accessible to select layfolk, notably
the monks' own kin: in 1533 there were seven kinsmen in the Durham

[324] *MRH*, p. 323.
[325] *GASA*, i. 77–8.
[326] *VCH Somerset*, ii. 69–81.
[327] *MRH*, p. 260; *VCH Suffolk*, ii. 134–6.
[328] *VCH Essex*, ii. 184.
[329] *MRH*, p. 299.
[330] *MRH*, p. 272.
[331] *MRH*, pp. 273, 301.
[332] *HEA*, ii. 143.
[333] *Jocelin*, pp. 95–6.
[334] *VCH Berkshire*, ii. 62–73 at 65.

infirmary.³³⁵ The care of the infirmary was also offered as a privilege to favoured patrons: at Bury St Edmunds the widows of the town's burgesses benefitted from the care of the infirmary.³³⁶

As an extension of their charitable enterprise, the Benedictines also offered elementary schooling to children from beyond the precinct. The *schola* of the *RB* was strictly for the children of the enclosure, the oblates, but even in the earliest communities the boundary appears to have been porous. The flowering of intellectual life that followed in the eighth and ninth centuries generated a general interest in the cloister school. Now it was neither the preserve of the oblate or the poor scholar but a training ground for courtiers and churchmen.³³⁷ Benedict of Aniane condemned the open school and called for a resumption of a school exclusively 'of the Lord's service': children or youths were not to be admitted unless they were to make their profession.³³⁸ Yet the open school survived, and between 950 and 1150 the Black Monks served as settled Europe's principal schoolmasters. The expansion of secular schools and the establishment of *studia generale* (i.e. universities) stemmed the flow of established scholars to the monasteries although it may be there was no interruption to their provision of elementary schooling for the poor. From the turn of the thirteenth century the Black Monks of England formalised these *ad hoc* provisions in a school foundation attached to and administered by the monastic almoner.³³⁹ The almonry school provided for poor scholars but also permitted paying pupils, creating a degree of social diversity on the schoolroom benches. There can be little doubt there was an expectation that poor scholars might repay the convent with their own profession, but the paying pupils were of gentry or even noble stock and their studies were only the first stage in their preparation for propertied or public life. The school endured at least at the greater monasteries, to the Henrician suppressions; indeed, in some instances, there was a cohort of children there at the end.³⁴⁰

Both male and female monasteries also admitted unprofessed (i.e. non-oblated) children into the enclosure for teaching and training. At any point in their medieval history the household of the superior was likely to see a number of boys accepted on behalf of the patron or benefactor to be raised by the brethren, generally for a fixed period. In the later Middle Ages, as personal households and staff were maintained by prior and principal

---

³³⁵ Harvey, *Lay Religious Life in Late Medieval Durham*, p. 174.
³³⁶ Gottfried, *Bury St Edmunds and the Urban Crisis*, p. 204.
³³⁷ Grotans, *Reading in Medieval St Gall*, p. 50.
³³⁸ *Initia consuetudinis Benedictinae*, ed. Hallinger, p. 473 (Canon II, 817).
³³⁹ N. Orme, *Medieval Schools: From Roman Britain to Renaissance England* (New Haven, 2006), pp. 255–88; R. Bowers, 'The Almonry Schools of the English Monasteries, c. 1265–1540', in *Monasteries and Society in Medieval Britain: Proceedings of the 1994 Harlaxton Symposium*, ed. B. J. Thompson (Stamford, 1999), pp. 177–222.
³⁴⁰ J. Bettey, 'The Dissolution and After at Cerne Abbas', in *The Cerne Abbey Millennium Lectures*, ed. K. Barker (Cerne Abbas, 1988), pp. 43–53 at 50.

obedientiaries, such children might be seen in a number of households: there were seven or eight boys and girls in the household of the prioress of Stamford (Lincolnshire).[341]

Public Service

The Benedictines were always members of the social hierarchy. Benedict appealed to the literate (and urban) layman of his own day, and as his rule was carried beyond the Campagna it was men and women of authority and status that were among the first to answer its call. In the turbulent centuries that followed, the monastic community was a natural and necessary source of social and political leadership, and its early intellectual energy also generated highly skilled servants of government. Their material wealth and territorial influence and their continuing recruitment of men and women of royal, noble and mercantile origin ensured their affinity with secular authority endured in spite of a strengthening secular church and the spread of reformed religious orders. In the century before the Reformation there were colonies of Black Monks, such as those in commercial cities, that were marginal to the social and political dynamics of the region, but in many European states they still retained their role in the governing class.

There was scarcely a period of the Middle Ages when the monks did not serve as the agents of royal authority. The pioneers of the *RB* purchased their patronage by collaboration with regional monarchs; the success of the reformers of the ninth and tenth centuries was secured by their political service; indeed, the monastic programme of Benedict of Aniane or Dunstan might be construed as an extension of their service to (respectively) Louis the Pious and Edgar. In the Gregorian period the ambitions and achievements of Benedictine leaders and their royal benefactors were mutually dependent: England's post-Conquest abbots acted to settle the new regime in the provinces, just as the new regime advanced the cause of the *RB* in the clerical establishment. In the high and later Middle Ages, Benedictines continued to secure a place among the principal counsellors of the king. In England even Henry VII and his son sought the advice of Benedictine superiors.[342] Their royal favour faltered less on the European mainland: Vicente de Ribas, prior of Santa Maria de Montserrat, served as chancellor of Martin el Viejo of Aragon (1396–1410).[343] Like any secular seignior, the Benedictines also undertook royal service in their own region, not least in

---

[341] *Chatteris*, p. 98.
[342] See below, p. 307.
[343] 'Vicente de Ribas', *Diccionario de historia eclesiástica de España*, 4 vols., and Supplement, ed. Q. A. Vaquero, T. M. Martínez and J. V. Gatell (Madrid, 1972–5, 1987), suppl., 645–6. See also P. N. Morris, 'Patronage and Piety: Montserrat and the Royal House of Medieval Catalonia-Aragon', *Mirator* (October 2000), 1–14 at 7–8.

the administration of justice and taxation.[344] They also demonstrated an enduring taste for martial service: Lupus, abbot of Ferrières (d. 862) served in the armies of Charles the Bald and adopted the name 'Servatus' after his miraculous recovery from a battlefield wound; famously, the Cluniac Odo of Bayeux rode with his cousin's horsemen on the field of Hastings, where William Faber of Marmoutier also 'joined the army with the rest'; Abbot Samson of Bury St Edmunds was present at the siege of Windsor 'where, with certain other abbots of England, he carried arms having his own standard and leading a number of knights at great expense, though shining rather in counsel than in prowess'.[345] The taste for feats of arms endured; no fewer than forty Black Monks answered Henry Despenser's call for the Flanders crusade in 1384.[346] Of course, royal service compromised their professed status and also presented personal costs: Thomas Merke of Westminster Abbey suffered imprisonment for his involvement in deposed Richard II; Prior Edmund Bocking of Christ Church, Canterbury was executed for his clumsy conspiracy against Henry VIII.[347]

The Benedictines were a key constituent of the social hierarchy. They were a source of spiritual authority in principle and (pastoral) practice; as the members of a community they also exerted the seigniorial rights, ceremonial, fiscal, judicial, and personal of any lay lord. Their presence was a legacy of the formative years of Christian Europe, in which they had played a leading, at times decisive role. It also reflected the strategic priorities of successive governing elites in the ninth, tenth and eleventh centuries. Yet it would be wrong to regard their pre-eminence as pragmatic: it was the *opus* of the Benedictines that bound them to the world. The social utility of their observance was recognised, and promoted, from earliest times; the vocation of service articulated in the *RB* was elaborated in later centuries. Nonetheless, the extent of their exchanges carried ineluctable change into the cloister, not only in its social dynamics but also in its culture.

---

[344] For example, *Chapters*, ed. Pantin, iii. 18 (1338).

[345] T. F. X. Noble, 'Lupus of Ferrières in His Carolingian Context', in *After Rome's Fall: Narrators and Sources of Early Medieval History. Essays presented to Walter Goffart*, ed. A. Callender Murray (Toronto, 1998), pp. 232–50 at 237. *Battle*, pp. 36–7; *Jocelin*, p. 55.

[346] Thomas Walsingham, *Historia Anglicana*, ed. H. T. Riley, RS 28, 2 vols. (London, 1862–4), ii. 416. John Canterbury of Westminster retained his armour from the Flanders adventure: Harvey, *Monastic Dress*, p. 26.

[347] *RO*, iii. 182, 184–90 at 186.

CHAPTER FOUR

Culture

The profile of the Benedictines in economic and social life was matched by their cultural power. From early times the Black Monks cultivated a commitment to learning not only in the clerical fields of scripture and theology but also in the secular arts which they, together with the courts of Charlemagne and Otto, were responsible for recovering from the ruins of antiquity. In the formative centuries of medieval Christendom it was principally Benedictine scholars that set the pattern not only for the exposition and transmission of Christian doctrine but also for the use of language, the practice of reading (ruminatively, silently) and writing (miniscule, cursive) itself. Their writings on history, literature and the physical sciences determined the development of these disciplines and genres at least until the spread of secular schools and universities in the twelfth century. The culture of the Benedictines, moreover, was not narrowly an intellectual culture. In their precincts the applied arts also flourished; in the absence of a settled urban existence the secure infrastructure of the Black Monks offered to craftsmen both the prospect of patronage and a constantly expanding creative canvas. These practical occupations passed into the monastery itself, and at times, perhaps especially in the early Middle Ages, the Benedictines were widely acclaimed for their skill as miniaturists and metalworkers. The later Middle Ages saw the economic and social position of the monasteries subject to increasing challenges, but there was no corresponding shift in their cultural significance. The size, wealth and accumulated resources of the Black Monks assured their continued presence alongside an increasingly complex cluster of intersecting cultural communities; the largest of them proved not only resilient but also receptive in the face of current trends and remained vigorous enough to play a role in the transmission of the artistic and scholarly Renaissance.

The flowering of Benedictine culture in these diverse forms had not been envisaged in the *RB*. Benedict's *cenobium* represented a cultural community in so far as it enshrined the principal mores and values of Roman patrician society. It was also, at least by implication, an educated environment since it was presented as an opportunity for the literate layman who, like the founder himself, had been schooled in the traditions of Latin antiquity. Yet the cultivation of a cultural life, of learning, or, indeed, of art or craftwork, was not the objective of Benedict's brethren. The sole purpose of study was to provide the monks with a means of mental and physical discipline that might better prepare them for the performance of the liturgy (*RB*, xlviii); craftwork was a practical necessity, supplying the monastic colony with all its material needs (*RB*, lvii). The rapid decline of the late Roman society represented in the *RB*, however, and the transmission of the text into the outer reaches of settled Europe, required subsequent disciples to re-examine these principles. On the northern frontier of Christendom there was no alternative but to make the monastery a school not only for the Lord's service but also for the secular arts; and schools stimulated teaching, learning and the copying and transmission of texts. The reformers of the ninth century recognised the potential of the learned monk not only for the advance of monasticism but also for the furtherance of the Christian mission itself. Before the death of Charlemagne (814) the traditional values of the Benedictine had been transformed and a space created for the *studia litterarum*. Later phases of reform and revival reinforced the Benedictine commitment to literate culture. The Gregorian period witnessed the final passing of the *opus manuum*, to be replaced by the labour of reading, and for some the reproduction of, the monastery's books. A greater challenge to the letter of the *RB* came in the wake of the Fourth Lateran Council (1215), when the Black Monks embraced the universities and began to train their most able members using the same syllabus as their secular colleagues. Conservative canonists cited the celebrated dictum, 'monachus non doctoris habet sed plangentis officium', but members of the order accepted a further departure from their observant traditions. The congregational reforms of the fifteenth and early sixteenth centuries widened the breach, cementing ties to the academic community and cultivating a contemporary, humanist curriculum in the cloister.

The advent of a vigorous artistic and intellectual culture transformed the nature of Benedictine monasticism. The emergence of a programme of teaching and scholarship in the monastery not only displaced manual work in early times but also encroached upon the observance of the liturgy itself. The promotion of intellectual pursuits also profoundly affected the character of the monastic community: barely a century after Benedict's death the *cenobium* had changed from a lay to a clerical community, and in the later Middle Ages it turned again from a community of clergy to one largely of graduates. The cultural life of the Benedictines also compromised the isolation of the monastic enclosure. Whether they were scholars, teachers, copyists or craftsmen, the creative activities of the Black Monks were both stimulated and sustained by continuous interactions with the world beyond the convent walls. Yet it would be wrong to infer that it was the cultural achievement of the Benedictines which weakened the order at the end of the Middle Ages. It was their presence at the universities, the public profile of their theologians, and some other scholars, and their continuing involvement in the production and publication of (even printed) books that reaffirmed much of their remaining status in pre-Reformation Europe. Perhaps it was these factors that also assured them an easier passage than their regular colleagues into post-Reformation society.

The Beginnings of Benedictine Culture: Language, Liturgy and Lectio

The *RB* was the primary influence on the culture of the Black Monks. While often distinguished for its universality, the document was indelibly marked with the mores of first-millennium Italy. The rhythm of life it proposed was unmistakably Roman: the very act of codifying the customs of the *cenobium* recalled the Justinian regulation of the *urbs*. The daily *horarium* reflected the blessed climate of Benevento, as followers of the rule in northern Europe were wont to bewail in later centuries.[1] At the same time, Benedict sought consciously to create a community whose customs and values clearly separated it not only from secular, patrician society but also from the established religious groupings, the Girovagues, Sarabites and Stylites (*RB*, prologue).

A key element in this scheme was the emphasis on Latinity, which was only implied in the *RB* but made explicit in many later codes and commentaries. Latin distinguished Benedict's brethren from their counterparts in the east, and in the centuries that followed the cultural and political weight it carried with it enabled the *RB* to survive and ultimately to rise above the abundant vernacular monastic traditions of the north. It also bound Benedict's monks umbilically to a textual tradition – of Latin antiquity – that was to become the source and stimulus of their intellectual endeavours ever after. It also placed a premium on education, a high order of learning, which for many medieval commentators on both sides of the enclosure came to be regarded as the hallmark of the Benedictine monastery. In the view of one twelfth-century chronicler, it was their Latinity that set the Black Monks apart from other orders; before his own house adopted the *RB* the brethren had been illiterate.[2] It was the same outlook which led many chroniclers also to appraise abbatial candidates according to their linguistic ability: at St Albans Abbey, their facility with Latin was always the first quality to attract comment.[3] Latinity was also a standard applied to Benedictine women, although in the later Middle Ages supervisors, and visitors, qualified their demands.[4] It would be wrong to suggest that the Benedictines were immune to the European vernacular tradition. In the

[1] *Ælfric's Letter to the Monks of Eynsham*, ed. Jones, pp. 138–9.
[2] *Walden*, pp. 26–7.
[3] *GASA*, ii. 113 (comment on the election of Abbot Hugh Eversden).
[4] Power, *Medieval English Nunneries*, pp. 244–55 at 246–7; *Chatteris*, pp. 98–9.

Anglo-Saxon and Frankish monasteries of the eighth and ninth centuries the vernacular was valued as a means of education, both monastic and secular, and evangelisation, by way of glosses, homilies and sermons.[5] It resurfaced in the fifteenth century among the Benedictines of Bursfeld and, to an extent, among their English colleagues, as both groups again became involved in teaching, preaching and pastoral care.[6] In the female houses, from the turn of the fourteenth century to the Reformation, vernacular reading probably pushed Latin to the margins, or at least separated a literate leadership from their sisters.[7] The culture of the monastic enclosure, however, was always avowedly monolingual. This may not be explicit in the *RB*, but the *cenobium* is presented as community of laymen, in the Late Antique sense of adults already schooled in the Liberal Arts, and beyond the oblate children no provision is made for elementary education (*RB*, lix). It was defended by a strict admissions policy that on occasion excluded men of rank or real promise, such as Nicholas Brakespear (Pope Hadrian IV), allegedly turned away from St Albans Abbey in *c*. 1135.[8] In the interests of reform, from the fourteenth century episcopal and conventual authorities were inclined to relax the restrictions on language in monasteries of women, but no such concessions were ever extended, formally at least, to the men.[9] There are signs in this later period that vernacular languages did edge their way into the teaching of grammar in the monastery, a response perhaps in part to a fall in the age of profession but also a reflection of new trends in the teaching of Latin which brought the widespread use of bilingual dictionaries and glossaries. Yet it appears that in spite (or perhaps because) of this trend there was a determined effort to confine the texts of monastic formation – the rule, the canons and related commentaries – to their original Latin. Novices at the greater English abbeys and priories were provided with multiple copies of these texts, presumably to facilitate independent study, but translations or glossaries were not widely available.[10] It is possible that there was greater latitude elsewhere, perhaps especially in small monasteries that struggled to recruit: a rare bilingual copy (fourteenth-century) of the *RB* in Latin and Swabian German survives from the abbey of Ottobeuren,

---

[5] McKitterick, *Frankish Church and Carolingian Reforms*, pp. 184–205; Wallace-Hadrill, *Frankish Church*, pp. 377–87; Lapidge, *Anglo-Saxon Library* (Oxford, 2006), pp. 31–52 at 33, 47.

[6] Brann, *Abbot Trithemius*, pp. 105–204.

[7] Power, *Medieval English Nunneries*, pp. 247–55.

[8] *GASA*, i. 112; J. E. Sayers, 'Adrian IV, d. 1159', *ODNB*, 173.

[9] For example, the injunctions presented to the women of Romsey in 1311 were translated into French for their better understanding: Power, *Medieval English Nunneries*, pp. 248–9. See also *Chatteris*, pp. 98–9; Oliva, *Convent and Community*, pp. 64–5 & n. 135, where it is observed that injunctions for women religious in Norwich diocese were never translated.

[10] For the variety of copies of the *RB*, related *regulae*, and commentaries present in English houses, see *EBL*, pp. 910–11. The inventories edited there record an Old English *RB* and a copy of Richard Fox's 1519 English translation, both at Worcester (B114. 7 B117. 76: pp. 653, 672) and two copies of the text in Anglo-Norman at Ramsey (B68, 467, 474: pp. 400–1); *AL*, pp. 130–1 (Christ Church, Canterbury), 405 (St Augustine's, Canterbury).

near Memmingen, Bavaria, although in this region the presence of unlettered or semi-lettered boys in the monastic *schola* cannot be discounted.[11] In the greater Benedictine houses the transmission of humanist trends served only to reinforce this already powerful impulse to preserve the tradition of monastic Latinity. Certainly in the fifteenth century there were masters, both in the cloister and in the Benedictine *studia generales*, who aimed to deepen not dilute the linguistic skill of their students, offering them a sophisticated syllabus of classical *auctores*.[12]

The culture of Benedict's *cenobium* was also determined by its diet of liturgy. It was not only the scale and regularity of the regime – the 'sacred' seven daylight hours of observance – that set the *RB* apart from its predecessors, but also its communal character. The brethren were bound together by their patterns of worship, the pursuit of spiritual perfection was not be a solitary prize, but their common purpose, and every hour passed outside the oratory – asleep, at table, at their books or at work – was only to serve and strengthen this observance. It is perhaps difficult for anyone unprofessed to understand fully how far the liturgy pervaded monastic life. The *RB* filled the few unoccupied minutes of the *horarium* with liturgical reading; if the brethren returned to their beds after Lauds, or retired early after Vespers, they were to take their psalter with them; for anyone who strayed from the rule the preferred punishment was the recitation of all of the psalter, or, for minor offences, just part. To be possessed by liturgy was more than merely a metaphor. Ardo, biographer of Benedict of Aniane, recalled how his brethren would rehearse the liturgical hours even when labouring in the fields.[13] This image of Carolingian monasticism was perhaps one of the few that would have been recognisable to the Benedictines of the later Middle Ages. The monks of this period may have been allowed greater independence and individual status, as academic masters, as prelates, and stewards of substantial properties, but for the majority the liturgical hours had lost little, if any, of their significance. The formation of reformed orders of Benedictines, the Cistercians, Carthusians and Celestines, which consciously favoured private devotion over common observance, appears to have redoubled the Black Monks' determination to retain their liturgical regime for the most part. The trimming of offices sanctioned by the two English chapters in 1277 should be seen in terms of rationalisation rather than reduction: the length of the offices as outlined in these canons was not significantly different from the *Decreta Lanfranci* two centuries before.[14] Moreover, in the decades that followed the same capitular authority formulated new prescriptions for

[11] University College London, MS GERM 12.
[12] Brann, *Abbot Trithemius*, pp. 25, 55; Clark, *Monastic Renaissance*, p. 57; Posset, *Renaissance Monks*, pp. 63–92, 204–21.
[13] Ardo, *Life of St Benedict of Aniane*, ed. Head and Noble, p. 233.
[14] For the *Decreta Lanfranci* see *MC*, pp. 3–195; for the canons of 1277 see *Chapters*, ed. Pantin, i. 64–92 at 67–71.

the observance of the offices by monks travelling, or living for periods away from the monastery. Student monks at Gloucester College, Oxford, were to observe the daylight *horarium* in the same way as their brethren at home.[15] It is sometimes suggested that the monasteries' obligations to lay patrons in the later Middle Ages undermined the purity of their own observances. In fact their greater exposure to the devotional inclinations of the laity appears to have persuaded them to elaborate further their own forms of worship. In the fifteenth century polyphonic music passed from the Lady Chapel into the monks' quire; indeed, the complexity of the liturgical music in contemporary monasteries was one of the contemporary 'abuses' condemned by reformers in 1521.[16] It is surely a measure of the place of liturgy in the life of the pre-Reformation Benedictine that in the last chronicles of conventual life, such as that compiled by John Stone, of Christ Church, Canterbury, the centrality of the conventual church, and the offices, festivals, funerals and other ceremonies it witnessed, is more conspicuous than in many narratives of earlier centuries.[17]

The only *culture* that Benedict recognised and sought for his *cenobium* was the *cultus* of continuous, common worship. There was no place in his programme for the purely intellectual pursuits that became associated with the Black Monks in subsequent centuries. Yet the intellect of the monk in itself was not unimportant. The proper performance of the liturgy required periods of mental and physical preparation and while manual labour might to an extent channel their physical energies, the cerebral exercise could only be achieved through regular *lectio*. The *RB* represents *lectio* only as an adjunct to the offices, but over time it became an equally distinctive element of the Benedictine experience. Benedict's conception of reading in part reflected contemporary practice – his brethren read aloud (and continued to do so until custom changed across Europe at the end of the first millennium) – but its communal character and its regularity did represent a new departure. The community as a whole was to enter the cloister twice daily for *lectio*, in the morning before Prime and in the afternoon between mealtime and Vespers, a period of time amounting to approximately two hours. The active *lectio* of the cloister hours was also complemented in *RB* by a daily reading in the refectory, to which the brethren were to listen but on which they might also be permitted to comment, if only by way of correction, a concession retained by subsequent commentators (Warnfrid, Smaragdus), but later elaborated into something akin to a collation.[18] By contrast with contemporary currents (which reached fruition in Cassiodorus's Vivarium)

---

[15] *Chapters*, ed. Pantin, ii. 55–8 at 57.

[16] Bowers, 'Early Tudor Monastic Enterprise', pp. 21–54.

[17] Stone's chronicle took its structure from the liturgical calendar; he recorded the expenditure of Prior Chillenden on church plate, vestments and images (*Stone*, p. 18), ceremonies such as the consecration of oil at the shrine of St Thomas (pp. 29, 30), and notable processions (pp. 49, 51) and sermons (p. 78).

[18] *Warnefrid-Hildemar*, pp. 119–20; *Smaragdi abbatis expositio*, ed. Spannagel and Engelbert, pp. 252–4 at 254. See also p. 108 above.

Benedict also confined his *cenobium* to a syllabus of sacred texts (*opus*), scripture, scriptural exegesis (the principal patristic authorities as he knew them) and monastic homiletics. Such a syllabus underlined for the professed that *lectio* was not primarily a pedagogic or scholarly exercise but one of profound spiritual enlightenment; for women it was one observant mode in which they participated wholly and which offered scope for independent thought.[19] The early reformers (Benedict of Aniane, Dunstan of Glastonbury) placed particular emphasis on the *opus*, and their codes defended and even expanded its place in the *horarium*; before the turn of the eleventh century it had become truly the engine room of Benedictine spirituality. The expansion and diversification of both liturgical and administrative obligations undoubtedly undermined communal observance, including the daily *lectiones*, in the later Middle Ages. At the same time, a growing number of Black Monks found alternative approaches to reading in the academic community, and many also carried into the cloister the private reading practices learned in literate lay households. It would be wrong to assume that the traditional *opus* was abandoned. Indeed, its symbolic importance intensified as, increasingly, it came to be identified as a means of monastic, and specifically, Benedictine, renewal. Reforming superiors presented manuscripts to their monks pointedly as for the *opus claustralium*.[20] This was coupled with a strong nostalgic impulse, particularly among those monks with academic studies behind them. John Uthred of Boldon (d. *c.* 1397), perhaps the greatest of the English Benedictine graduates, wrote with great affection of the virtues of such an *opus*; a Glastonbury monk compiling a personal anthology at Oxford *c.* 1400 commissioned a sequence of miniatures each representing different attitudes of traditional *lectio*.[21]

Scripture

The *RB* did not in itself create the learned culture that later became so characteristic of the medieval Benedictines, but the customs of language, liturgy and *lectio* that it codified created a climate in which it could flourish. Firstly, it wove both the language and sense of scripture into the fabric of conventual life. The text of the *RB* itself impressed on brethren not only the literal meaning of scripture in its narrative outline, but also much of its spiritual significance. Moreover, the readings recommended for cloister and refectory, the Old and New Testaments, the Collations, Institutes and Lives of the Catholic Fathers (*RB*, lxxiii), exposed them to the possibilities

---

[19] At Admont, the daily *lectio divina* was the foundation for female scholarship: Beach, *Women as Scribes*, pp. 69, 115.

[20] For example, the gifts of Abbot Walter de Monington of Glastonbury: *EBL*, B43, pp. 220–32.

[21] For Uthred of Boldon, see R. Sharpe, *A Handlist of the Latin Writers of Great Britain and Ireland before 1540* (Turnhout, 1997), pp. 699–702 at 700–1. The Glastonbury manuscript is Oxford, The Queen's College, MS 304. For the development and dynamics of the *lectio divina* see also pp. 91–102.

of exegesis. The practical process of providing these texts, securing exemplars and reproducing them accurately, may also have served as a stimulus to study, although there are few codicological fragments that can firmly be connected with the first Benedictines. It is, of course, impossible to know how often and how far the earliest monks strayed from meditative *opus* into the *study* of scripture, but the presence of even a handful of patristic writings must surely have inclined them to intellectual enquiry. At any rate, there was an expectation that the refectory reading might arouse discussion that might be channelled by the superior into an impromptu collation, *magister ad discipulum*. Whether there was also scope for such collations from the outset for the children of the cloister or the novices is not specified in *RB*, although the lay status of early recruits is likely to have necessitated some degree of scriptural instruction.

Certainly the precepts of the *RB* were enough to establish a place for the study of scripture from early, if not quite the earliest, times. Little more than a century after Benedict's death, it seems there were active studies in scripture at various levels in monasteries where the *RB* was present, if not predominant. Not only were the prescribed periods of *lectio* providing opportunities for such study individually and in common but the provisions in the rule for the training of children, youths and prospective novices were elaborated to the extent that monastic schools, whether formally or informally, were now established. Bede commemorated the 'crowd of students' attracted to Canterbury in the time of Archbishop Theodore (668–90) for 'instruction in scripture'; of English houses Nursling (Hampshire) was similarly renowned at the end of the seventh century for its 'love of spiritual learning' ('spiritali litterarum diligentia provocatus') although Ripon after Wilfrid (d. 709) appears remarkably barren.[22] The refounded Montecassino also saw a flowering of both sacred and secular studies in the second quarter of the eighth century.[23] Bede's autobiographical notes also underline that barely a century and a half after Benedict, independent studies were now countenanced in these quasi-Benedictine convents:

> I have spent all my life ... applying myself entirely to the study of scriptures ... I have made it my business for my own benefit and that of my brethren to make brief extracts from the works of the venerable fathers on the holy scriptures, or to add notes of my own to clarify their sense and interpretation.[24]

The expansion and renewal of Benedictinism between the eighth and the ninth centuries transformed these somewhat uneven patterns of learning and teaching into a programme for the 'order' as a whole. Although the

[22] Bede, *Historia*, iv. 2, pp. 332–3; Willibald, *Vita Bonifatii*, ed. Levinson, p. 435. See also Lapidge, *Anglo-Saxon Library*, pp. 42–3.
[23] Bloch, *Monte Cassino in the Middle Ages*, i. 648; Kelly, *Beneventan Chant*, p. 238&n.
[24] Bede, *Historia*, v. 24, pp. 566–7.

aim of the Aachen reform was to achieve *ad literam* observance of the
RB, education was also recognised as an essential tool, and in the wake
of the synods a network of new monastic schools was established in the
Frankish kingdom. The schools offered an introduction to the liberal arts
(as discussed below) as well as training in the sacred texts, but it was for
their scriptural exegesis, and their skill in training both secular and regular
clergy, that they became widely known. Perhaps the greatest school of
this period was at Fulda, where the principal master (and subsequently
abbot) was Hrabanus Maurus (*c.* 776–856), who produced no fewer than
twelve influential commentaries on historical and prophetic books of the
Old Testament and on the gospels of Matthew and John.[25] Exegesis also
blossomed among the French Benedictines at Corbie in the east, where
Radbertus Paschasius (d. 865) was the best-known master, and Auxerre in
the west, which nurtured a cadre of commentators in the second half of
the ninth century, Haimo (d. 875), Heiric (d. 876) and Remigius (d. 908);
Haimo became a staple authority for Benedictine readers in subsequent
centuries.[26] The renewal of monastic life in England in the following century
did not yield any school of equal stature, although codicological fragments
suggest that scriptural studies were well established at the principal centres,
such as Abingdon, Glastonbury, Winchester and Worcester.[27]

These pioneers of Benedictine exegesis drew primarily on patristic
tradition. Their reading of the sacred page still sought out the literal and
historical senses privileged by Augustine and Gregory, but they were more
persuaded to probe further into the linguistic foundations of the text,
and also to regard this textual and contextual analysis as preliminary to a
possible exploration of allegorical and moral meanings.[28] There was also a
distinctly pastoral dimension to their exegesis, perhaps especially among the
masters and students of busy Benedictine entrepôts such as Auxerre, Fulda
and, a generation later, Luxeuil. Here exegesis was channelled not only into
commentaries but also into homiliaries and sermons, some of which were
even rendered into regional vernaculars.[29] A similar pastoral impulse seems
to have passed through the English monasteries between the mid-ninth and
mid-tenth centuries, generating Old English glosses but no more substantial
works.[30] The scale and scope of these studies reflect the rich manuscript
resources accessible to some early Benedictines. The Continental convents

[25] Wallace-Hadrill, *Frankish Church*, pp. 281–2; Smalley, *Study of the Bible*, pp. 37–46 at 37, 43.
[26] Smalley, *Study of the Bible*, pp. 37–46 at 39–40; Ganz, *Corbie in the Carolingian Renaissance*, pp. 82–7, 103–20.
[27] Lapidge, *Anglo-Saxon Library*, pp. 63–70.
[28] Smalley, *Study of the Bible*, pp. 26–36; Lapidge, *Anglo-Saxon Library*, p. 177.
[29] Hummer, *Politics and Power in Early Medieval Europe*, pp. 137–9; McKitterick, *Carolingians and the Written Word*, pp. 255–65.
[30] M. Cayton, 'Homiliaries and Preaching in Anglo-Saxon England', in *Old English Prose: Basic Readings*, ed. P. Szarmach and D. A. Oosterhouse (London, 2000), pp. 151–236. See also R. Morris, ed., *Old English Homilies*, EETS, Original Series (1873); Lapidge, *Anglo-Saxon Library*, pp. 128, 135.

were especially well equipped with patristic authorities in Latin and Greek and a ready supply of systematic glossed scriptures. Their counterparts in Anglo-Saxon England appear to have been poorer, at least in terms of patristics and scriptures (the Latin Vulgate did not circulate before the last quarter of the tenth century), but glossaries in general circulation gave access to a remarkable array of authorities, some of which were distinctly scarce in subsequent centuries.[31] The Leiden glossary, copied at Saint-Gall in *c.* 800 from an English exemplar, gave the reader forty-eight chapters of *glossae collecta*, that is to say source texts and glosses from nineteen books of the Bible and another twenty patristic authorities.[32]

The Norman revival of the tenth and eleventh centuries saw a succession of new schools eclipse the houses of the Frankish heartland. Under the influence of Cluny, Bec became the pre-eminent Benedictine *studium* in northern Europe and as a focus for exegesis perhaps eclipsed even Montecassino under Abbot Desiderius (1058–87).[33] The Norman conquest of England brought new, or renewed, monasteries into the orbit of Bec which in turn stimulated a surge in scriptural studies, notably at Canterbury, Durham, St Albans and Worcester. Beyond the Anglo-Norman sphere there were scattered centres of scriptural study, at Deutz (at least under Abbot Rupert), Liège (where Rupert was professed) and perhaps also Burgundy, where Honorius Augustoniensis has been associated with Autun, although none of these achieved the stature of the Frankish houses of two centuries before.[34] Perhaps at the turn of the twelfth century Benedictine exegesis achieved its peak.

Of course, not every one of these monasteries developed the same intellectual dynamics. At Bec the atmosphere was magisterial and students, secular and regular, cohered around a charismatic master (Lanfranc, Anselm). In England, by contrast, the climate was claustral and the work of exegesis was undertaken at individual initiative: Lawrence of Durham (*fl.* 1150) compiler of the *Hypognosticon*, a collection of scriptural precis, described his work as the 'occupation of his leisure hours'.[35] It should also be observed that in both contexts original scholarship was produced by only a small circle of monks. At Bec, Canterbury, Durham and elsewhere elementary studies continued in parallel with the pursuits of the masters. A Canterbury

[31] Lapidge, *Anglo-Saxon Library*, pp. 63–70 at 69.
[32] M. Lapidge, *Anglo-Latin Literature, 600–899* (London, 1996), pp. 150–5. See also S. Lake, 'Knowledge of the Writings of John Cassian in Early Anglo-Saxon England', *Anglo-Saxon England* 32 (2003), 27–41.
[33] M. T. Gibson, *Lanfranc of Bec* (Oxford, 1978), pp. 23–97; H. E. J. Cowdrey, *Lanfranc: Scholar, Monk and Archbishop* (Oxford, 2003), pp. 46–74; Cowdrey, *Age of Abbot Desiderius*.
[34] Van Engen, *Rupert of Deutz*, p. 53; R. W. Southern, *Saint Anselm: A Portrait in a Landscape* (Cambridge, 1991), pp. 376–80. See also M. Parisse, 'Lotharingia', in *The New Cambridge Medieval History*, iii, ed. Reuter and McKitterick, pp. 299–328.
[35] Sharpe, *Latin Writers*, pp. 359–61; A. G. Rigg, *A History of Anglo-Latin Literature, 1066–1422* (Cambridge, 1992), pp. 54–7 at 55. See also Piper, 'The Monks of Durham and the Study of Scripture'.

manuscript of *c.* 1100 contains a copy of Jerome's essay on the difficult words of the Bible, apparently prepared for the most inexperienced reader, since it carries a decorated capital depicting Jerome bearing the 'ABC'.[36] The coterie of original commentators nonetheless captured an audience for their works that stretched far beyond Benedictine circles. Even in the second quarter of the twelfth century, as secular schools expanded to rival, and ultimately to reject, the contribution of the monasteries, the monastic masters and their work remained the focus of many scholastic discussions. Abbot Rupert of Deutz, author of no fewer than seven scriptural commentaries, was drawn into a public disputation with Master Anselm of Laon (d. 1117), an event abandoned at the eleventh hour after the master's sudden demise.[37]

The public stature of Benedictine exegetes in this period was a product of the methodological flux that existed among scholars in both monastic and secular contexts. The response of the monastic masters to this climate, and to the challenge of their secular counterparts, was to refine their own methodology. They continued to proceed initially by means of thorough linguistic analysis but now they also incorporated the scholastic tools of the *distinctio* and *quaestio*. As Hrabanus and Paschasius had pioneered two centuries before, from here they pursued the senses of scripture – allegorical, spiritual – which now they confidently claimed were the special calling of the monastic commentator. Unafraid of controversy, Abbot Rupert of Deutz went so far as to claim that only the professed religious could perform such a task: 'those who study sacred letters in Christ's school ... give everything to buy that single pearl [i.e. the truth of scripture]'.[38] The parallel development of a distinctive exegetical method among the Augustinian canons of Saint-Victor, which drew on the knowledge of secular masters to offer a study of the literal sense of scripture more systematic than that of any monastic scholar, diminished the force of such claims.[39] Yet before the end of the twelfth century, while the Benedictines still held the lion's share of scholarly books, this was a judgement some secular masters were inclined to accept. Alexander Nequam (1157–1217) abandoned the schools and sought admission (unsuccessfully) at St Albans; Herbert of Bosham (d. *c.* 1194) merely acknowledged that so long as he was unprofessed he might never master the sacred page.[40]

The energy of scriptural exegesis in the Carolingian schools also stimulated claustral studies in theology. At Corbie in the second half of the ninth century the monks Radbertus Paschasius (d. *c.* 860) and Ratramnus (d. *c.* 868) composed complementary tracts on transubstantiation. As the

---

[36] Cambridge, Trinity College, MS O.4.7, fo. 75r.
[37] Van Engen, *Rupert of Deutz*, pp. 97–9 at 98.
[38] Rupert of Deutz, *Commentary on John*, CCM 9, p. 6.
[39] Smalley, *Study of the Bible*, pp. 83–111.
[40] R. W. Hunt, *The Schools and the Cloister: The Life and Writings of Alexander Nequam, 1157–1217* (Oxford, 1984); Smalley, *Study of the Bible*, p. 188.

network of Benedictine schools expanded over the next two centuries, the theological interests of monastic masters intensified. It was the advanced students and teachers of the schools of northern and western France that were most active in the tenth and eleventh centuries, although after 1100 theological studies also thrived in several southern English (Canterbury, St Albans) and German houses. Their theological enquiries were founded on, and framed by, their exegetical training and tended to focus on a repertory of fundamental themes such as the Incarnation and the Trinity. The rapid expansion of secular schools at the turn of the twelfth century, and the radical methodology of at least some of their masters, persuaded some monastic scholars to engage more directly with the themes current in their halls. Abbot Rupert of Deutz attacked the secular masters Anselm of Laon and William of Champeaux and agreed to a public disputation with Master Anselm, entering Laon on a donkey accompanied by a small band of disciples.[41]

The theological impulses emerging in these early schools were also expressed in meditations on insular themes, not least the nature of the monastic vocation itself. In his *Diadema monachorum* Smaragdus of Saint-Mihiel (*fl.* 805) drew from scripture, patristics and the *RB* itself to offer reflections on such topics as prayer and the performance of the liturgy. In the greater schools of the eleventh and twelfth centuries further reflections on the theology of the cloister were composed, generally within the framework of a commentary on the *RB*, although at times the reflections amounted almost to self-contained tracts. Although focused on the *materia* of the *RB*, the commentary of Abbot Rupert of Deutz reflected his familiarity with the theological currents of the secular schools. Perhaps the most popular of this period were Abbot Bernard of Montecassino's commentary and companion piece, the *Speculum monachorum*, itself modelled on Smaragdus's *Diadema*.[42] There was a brief, regional revival of this brand of monastic theology in fourteenth-century England. The *Philosophia monachorum*, which owed much to Bernard of Monte Cassino, may have originated at Christ Church, Canterbury, and was also known at Evesham; the rule commentaries of Richard of Wallingford (d. 1334: St Albans) and Edmund Stourton (*fl.* 1375: Glastonbury) no longer survive but since one, and perhaps both, were university graduates it is possible these texts also used the *RB* as a framework for further theological reflection.[43] Certainly this was the case with the companion tracts of Uthred of Boldon, *De perfeccione vivendi* and *De substantialibus regulae*, which employed both monastic (Smaragdus, Bernard) and

---

[41] Van Engen, *Rupert of Deutz*, pp. 97–9 at 98, 200–15.

[42] Bernard (Ayglier) of Montecassino, *Expositio*, ed. Caplet; *Speculum monachorum*, ed. H. Walter (Freiburg, 1901). For extant copies of English Benedictine provenance see Cambridge, Corpus Christi College, MS 252 (Norwich) and BL, MS Harley 1206 (Bury); for copies in English collections, see *EBL*, B30. 42 (Evesham), B58.12, pp. 143.

[43] *AL*, no. 1829f; *EBL*, B30. 45 (Evesham), 58.16 p. 143; Sharpe, *Latin Writers*, p. 108. See also Cambridge, Corpus Christi College, MS 137, fos. 1r–33r.

academic authorities to elaborate the spiritual strengths of the monastic vocation.[44]

Benedictine exegesis blossomed in these early exchanges with the emergent groups of secular masters, but in the second half of the twelfth century, as the schools expanded, and the masters and students became settled within them, the open schools of the monasteries fell into sharp decline and the vigour of scriptural studies seen there was greatly diminished. After 1200 there were few if any Benedictine exegetes whose work attracted the attention of regular and secular scholars Europe-wide. The evidence of surviving book lists suggests that even before Oxford and Paris elected their first chancellors, the greater abbeys and priories were exposed to the teaching of the secular schools, and the textbooks of their masters – Peter Comestor and Peter Lombard, Alexander of Hales and Hugh of Saint-Cher – eclipsed Bede and Hrabanus in the cupboards of the cloister.[45] The insular tradition of scriptural study was not wholly stifled, however. The canons of the Lateran Council of 1215 placed a renewed emphasis on the public exposition of scripture in clerical communities, requiring monastic and secular cathedrals to make provision for a claustral *lector*.[46] The canons also reminded the regulars of their pastoral responsibilities and stimulated a return to public preaching, certainly in some monasteries. The English Benedictine chapters repeated the call for a permanent lector in a canon of 1247; the imperative for conventual instruction underpinned the papal canons *Summi magistri* of 1336.[47] The better survival of books and book lists, library catalogues and other documents from the post-1250 period allows us to assess the currents in the cloister in some detail. Certainly the larger Benedictine monasteries continued to maintain major collections of scriptural scholarship. The largest entries in the *Registrum Anglie*, a union catalogue of, principally, patristic and later exegesis, compiled by Franciscans in England between 1314 and 1317, represented the holdings of a handful of Benedictine houses.[48] These resources supported the studies of a steadily expanding cohort of Benedictine students in the theological faculties of Oxford, Cambridge and Paris, although it is only from the last that a lively group of active commentators can be glimpsed. The English scholar monks may have been underproductive in this field but they did stimulate some vigorous preaching activity, and several original sermon sequences emerged in the second half of the fourteenth century. While these texts were generally the work of graduate monks, exposed to the full range of scholastic commentators,

---

[44] Pantin, 'Some Medieval English Treatises'.

[45] *EBL*, B71. 25, p. 423 (Reading, *c*. 1192); B79. 64, 68, pp. 505–6 (Rochester, *c*. 1202).

[46] *Disciplinary Decrees of the General Council*, ed. H. J. Schroeder (St Louis, 1937).

[47] *Chapters*, ed. Pantin, i. 28 (1247), 75 (1277); ii. v. For *Summi magistri*, see also *Concilia magnae*, ed. Wilkins, ii. 585–613 at 588–613 (594–6).

[48] *Registrum Anglie*, ed. R. A. B. Mynors, R. H. Rouse and M. A. Rouse, CBMLC 2 (London, 1991), pp. 246–322. Thirty houses are recorded, but there are few full entries.

there is an unmistakable affection for earlier monastic authorities, Bede, Hrabanus and Anselm.

Perhaps the greatest energy in this period was to be found at the level of elementary instruction. The only 'original' exegetical work to emerge from the English Benedictines after 1250 was a companion to the ordinary gloss compiled by Roger, a monk and (it must be presumed) a novice-master of Bury St Edmunds (*fl.* 1320). The compilation and (albeit limited) circulation of the text in the age of the Black Death does tend to confirm that junior monks were still likely to be schooled in the basics of exegesis, an experience that John Lydgate (d. 1449) (also a monk of Bury) later recalled as 'learning my histories'.[49] The editorial efforts of Henry Kirkstead (*fl.* 1370), again of Bury, were intended to prepare a repertory of texts, a number of them exegetical, for a cohort of novice readers.[50]

In many Benedictine monasteries the study of scripture may have never again advanced far beyond these basics, but the re-emergence of heresy, and the parallel progress of a powerful impulse for reform, challenged a handful of Black Monks, among other regulars, to extend their horizons beyond the routines of teaching and preaching. Among the earliest academic opponents of John Wyclif, Nicholas Radcliff of St Albans (d. 1400) displayed formidable exegetical expertise in his *Dialogues*.[51] Benedictine books from the next generation suggest scholar monks were inspired by the work of William Woodford and Thomas Netter to seek their own defence of orthodoxy in the pages of scripture and patristic commentaries.[52] Nicholas Faux, a Glastonbury monk, commissioned at Oxford a remarkable compendium combining orthodox commentaries with Wyclif's *Trialogus* for critical scrutiny.[53]

The monastic reformers that emerged against the background of the alarm over both heresy and schism also encouraged a renewal of Benedictine Biblicism. Indeed, the restoration of traditional patterns of scriptural *lectiones*, both publicly, in chapter and frater, and privately, in cloister and dormitory, was fundamental to the parallel reform programmes pursued at Bursfeld, Melk, Padua and, ultimately, Valladolid in the course of the fifteenth century. Peter von Rosenheim mounted the reform of Melk from his position as *Cursor Biblicus* from 1423.[54] The chapter general of the Paduan

---

[49] For Roger 'Computista' of Bury, see Oxford, Bodleian Library, MS Bodley 238, fos. 213v–262r; Sharpe, *Latin Writers*, p. 585. John Lydgate, *Testament*, l. 729, in *Minor Poems*, ed. MacCracken, p. 356.

[50] For these efforts see especially R. H. Rouse, 'Boston Buriensis and the Author of the *Catalogus scriptorum ecclesiae*', *Speculum* 41 (1966), 471–99. See also Henry of Kirkestede's *Catalogus de libris autenticis et apocrifis*, ed. R. H. Rouse and M. A. Rouse, CBMLC (2004). See also Sharpe, *Latin Writers*, p. 172.

[51] J. I. Catto, 'Wyclif and Wycliffism at Oxford, 1356–1420', in *The History of the University of Oxford*, ii. *Late Medieval Oxford*, ed. J. I. Catto and T. A. R. Evans (Oxford, 1992). See also Sharpe, *Latin Writers*, pp. 391–2 at 392.

[52] *EBL*, B88. 20, 26, B90. 7a, pp. 567–8, 583 (St Albans).

[53] Oxford, Oriel College, MS 15.

[54] Posset, *Renaissance Monks*, p. 20.

congregation codified their commitment to exegesis in 1465, commanding brethren 'to spend more time in the reading of holy Scripture than of Cicero and of the Greek poets and literature' ('Hortamur etiam et admonemus ut patres et fratres plus operam dent lectioni sacre scripturae quam Ciceronis, poetarum et litterarum graecarum').[55] The reformed congregations also became early enthusiasts for humanist exegesis. Greek gospels were employed at Padua as early as the mid-fifteenth century.[56] The brethren of Ottobeuren, a house of the Melk congregation, went so far as appointing their own instructor in Hebrew in 1510, a decade before such a position existed even at Wittenberg. Leonhard Widenmann and Nikolaus Ellenbog of Ottobeuren corresponded with Johann Reuchlin on the original languages of the scripture.[57] These impulses were conspicuous in the reformed congregations but not perhaps confined to them. Certainly in England there were individual Black Monks with an interest in Christian humanism, and at Evesham and Winchcombe at the turn of the fifteenth century it may be the brethren were treated to biblical lectures on the model of Melk.[58] The presence of polyglot bibles and other hallmarks of contemporary scriptural scholarship did not, however, serve to radicalise the majority of these pre-Reformation Benedictines. The best-known Black Monks of the period, Nikolaus Ellenbog of Ottobeuren, and Richard Kidderminster of Winchcombe, publicly denounced the reformers, and in the most advanced convents it appears the atmosphere was Erasmian at most, and never Lutheran.[59]

The Liberal Arts

It was the central paradox of Benedictine culture that the study of the sacred page was powered by a mastery of the secular arts. The liturgical and lectionary requirements of the *RB* were predicated on the presence of brethren immersed in the liberal arts tradition of late Roman antiquity. There was no suggestion that such elementary training be provided to the professed members of the community. Yet as the *RB* was carried out of Italy, and the classical tradition of the arts faltered and finally collapsed, converts to the Benedictine customs had no choice but to make a space for *litterae saeculares* inside the *cenobium*. An approximation of the ancient *trivium* and *quadrivium* appears to have been in place at the semi-Benedictine monasteries of the later seventh century.[60] At Wearmouth and Jarrow, Bede compiled preceptive treatises on orthography and metre presumably for

[55] Collett, *Italian Benedictine Scholars*, p. 29n.
[56] Ibid.
[57] Posset, *Renaissance Monks*, pp. 155–72 at 171.
[58] W. A. Pantin, 'Abbot Kidderminster and Monastic Studies', *Downside Review* 47 (1929), 198–211 at 200; *RO*, iii. 91–3 at 92, 100–7.
[59] Posset, *Renaissance Monks*, pp. 170–1; *RO*, iii. 91–5. See also pp. 317–23 at 319, 321.
[60] Lapidge, *Anglo-Saxon Library*, pp. 31–40 at 38–9 (Monkwearmouth-Jarrow and Nursling).

the immediate benefit of his own brethren.[61] The Benedictine expansion of the eighth and ninth centuries codified this emergent curriculum. A capitulary of 789, called the *Admonitio generalis*, required all Frankish monasteries to establish an elementary school, an injunction reinforced in subsequent synodalia.[62] The cloister schools that flourished in the wake of the Carolingian reforms and, subsequently, the Anglo-Saxon reorganisation realised a more complete arts curriculum, which extended the Black Monks beyond grammar and rhetoric to logic and even elementary philosophy.[63] The commitment to the *artes* continued into the twelfth century until the expansion of the secular schools drained much of the energy, and many of the students and masters, from the monastic enclosure. The monastic and papal reformers of the thirteenth and fourteenth centuries aimed to revive these early traditions and the creation of Benedictine academic *studia* attached a new imperative to primary work in the 'primitive sciences'.[64] Wherever there were university monks in large numbers in the later Middle Ages, it seems there were studies not only in grammar but also logic, philosophy and the physical sciences; in the reformed congregations of the Rhineland and northern Italy the vigorous schools of *litterae saeculares* returned.[65]

Grammar was the first and the foremost of the monastic arts. As *RB* impressed upon its readers, a proper understanding of language was not only of practical utility but also of profound spiritual importance in the performance of the *opus Dei*: the brethren were required to 'sing His praises with understanding' ('psallite sapienter': *RB*, ix [Psalm 44: 8]) 'that mind and voice may accord together' ('ut mens nostra concordat voci nostrae': *RB*, ix). Grammar was the necessary discipline of the novice and also the enduring duty of the professed, to be repeatedly refreshed. The Benedictine expansion of the ninth and tenth centuries saw grammar established both as the cornerstone of the novices' curriculum and the legitimate study of the senior monk, whether or not he held magisterial responsibility. The primary focus in this and later periods was on learning and teaching, and to the end of the thirteenth century the only original Benedictine compositions were textbooks. Yet the self-conscious rejection of *litterae saeculares* made by the *seniores* is so common a trope, especially before the end of the twelfth century, as to be suggestive of the opposite. The decline of the mixed monastic school after 1200 may have diminished for a time the place of grammar in many Benedictine monasteries. The advent of the order's academic *studia* appears to have stimulated a revival however, at least in the greater abbeys and priories, which now sought to prepare their ablest

---

[61] For Bede's work see Sharpe, *Latin Writers*, pp. 70–6; M. Irvine, 'Bede the Grammarian and the Scope of Grammatical Studies in Eighth-Century Northumbria', *Anglo-Saxon England* 15 (1986), 15–44.

[62] MGH Capit. I, no. 22; *Charlemagne: Translated Sources*, ed. P. D. King (Kendal, 1987).

[63] Lapidge, *Anglo-Saxon Library*, pp. 140–3 at 143, 243, respectively Worcester (perhaps) and Ramley; Grotans, *Reading in Medieval St Gall*, pp. 49–110 at 81–91.

[64] *Chapters*, ed. Pantin, ii. 91.

[65] Collett, *Italian Benedictine Scholars*, pp. 28–54 at 29–31; Posset, *Renaissance Monks*, pp. 1–28, 133–54.

1 The scope of Benedictine Europe: (*above*) Þingeyrar, location of the first stable Benedictine settlement in Iceland (1133); the church now standing dates from the nineteenth century (*below*) Mount Tabor, Lower Galilee, Israel: the Franciscan basilica (1924) rises from the ruins of medieval buildings, among them the church and convent in the custody of Benedictines from c. 1100 until 1187.

2 The reading of the *Regula Benedicti*: Bishop Richard Fox's English translation of the Rule, published for the benefit of the Benedictine women of his Winchester diocese.

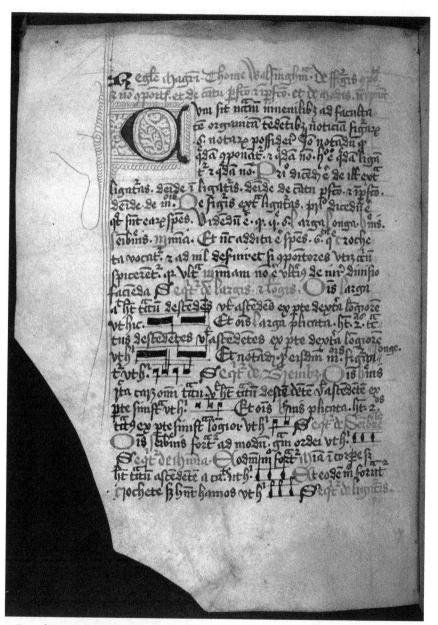

3 Benedictine pioneers of polyphonic worship: Thomas Walsingham's manual of mensurable notation for the instruction of novices at St Albans Abbey.

4 Benedictine supervision of the pre-Reformation parish: the new chancel of St Cuthbert's church, Oborne, Dorset, provided by the monks of Sherborne, 1533.

5 Benedictines and the transmission of the Latin classics: the 'class-book' connected with Dunstan, containing, *inter alia*, the first book of Ovid's *Ars amatoria*, a copy begun in a Welsh centre but apparently completed and prepared for use at Glastonbury.

6 Benedictine cultural patronage: a fifteenth-century image of the martyrdom of St Erasmus, incorporating a portrait of the monk that owned and perhaps commissioned it, John Holynborne of Christ Church, Canterbury.

7 The ascetic practice of late medieval Benedictines: the dry-stone *cabanes* at Breuil (Dordogne) which served as spiritual retreats for the monks of the abbey at Sarlat.

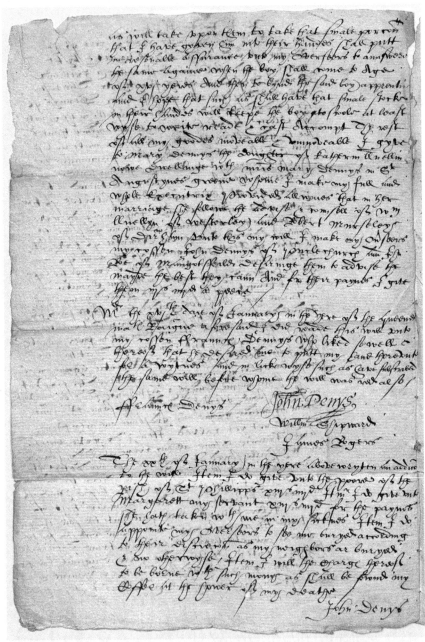

8 Post-Reformation Benedictines: a witness to the long life of Mary Dennys, former prioress of Kington St Michael (Wiltshire). The will of her kinsman Francis Dennys confirms she was still living, at 'St Augustine's Greene' Bristol, as late as 1593, some fifty-seven years after the surrender of her house.

men for admission into the higher faculties of the university. The greater frequency of capitular and episcopal visitation from the fourteenth century also exposed the deficiencies of elementary education tolerated in many houses and forced them to appoint (perhaps for the first time in more than a century) a dedicated grammar master. These contingencies were short lived in many, perhaps the majority of, late medieval convents, and in the century before the Reformation the study of grammar may most commonly have been reduced to the ragged tuition of a tiny cohort of novices.[66] Certainly there was a gulf between the generality of Benedictines and the handful of reformed houses which saw the introduction of a wholly humanist syllabus, which in isolated cases incorporated tuition in Greek and Hebrew.[67]

Monastic grammar was founded on the authorities and approaches of the late antique schoolroom. At least until the later Middle Ages, the preferred reference works remained those of the principal Roman masters, primarily Priscian's *Institutiones grammaticae* and Donatus's *Ars minor*. These two were staples of the medieval schoolroom, but some early monasteries also held on to authorities already forgotten elsewhere. Aldhelm of Malmesbury (d. 709) was apparently familiar with the works of Phocas and Sergius on the parts of speech.[68] Classical grammars were written for native Latin speakers, and in the growing monastic colonies of the north they were supplemented with indigenous guides which digested Roman lore for a Germanic audience. Alcuin's *Dialogus Franconis et Saxonis de octo partibus orationis*, drawn from Latin and Greek authorities, was offered to brethren at ninth- and tenth-century Saint-Gall in preference to Priscian.[69] Hrabanus Maurus prepared his own digest of the *Institutiones* for his pupils at Fulda. The Winchester master, Ælfric (d. *c.* 1010), went further with his *Excerptiones de arte grammatica anglice,* transmitting the principles of Priscian into an English vernacular vigorous in the reformed convents of the tenth century.[70] The monks of this period not only produced new expositions of these old principles but also pioneered novel teaching practices. The Saint-Gall Tractate, a ninth-century compendium of grammar attributed to the novice master Notker Balbulus (d. 912), encouraged readers to proceed from parsing words and phrases for themselves, into testing exchanges with their masters, and finally to vocal performance before their peers.[71] Abbo of Fleury's (d. 1004) *Questiones grammaticales*, dedicated to his former pupils at Ramsey Abbey, which tackle the problems of pronunciation, among others, perhaps recall the patterns of teaching he

---

[66] For example, *Visitations*, ed. Jessopp, pp. 19, 77 (Norwich Cathedral Priory).
[67] Brann, *Abbot Trithemius*, pp. 52, 56, 59. Posset, *Renaissance Monks*, pp. 28, 138, 171.
[68] Lapidge, *Anglo-Saxon Library*, pp. 178–89 at 184, 186.
[69] Grotans, *Reading in Medieval St Gall*, p. 309&n.
[70] D. W. Porter, *Excerptiones de Prisciano: the Source for Ælfric's Latin-Old English Grammar*, Anglo-Saxon Texts 4 (Cambridge, 2002), pp. 9–12, 23–31.
[71] Grotans, *Reading in Medieval St Gall*, pp. 155–98.

adopted.[72] Later generations hardly matched the originality of these early grammar masters, although Osbern of Gloucester's mid-twelfth-century *Panormia*, an elaborate glossary, served as a model for the later word-lists of Uguccio of Pisa and Giovanni Balbus.[73] Generally original grammar work faded from Benedictine houses from the end of the twelfth century, and patterns of teaching and independent study appear to have been increasingly dominated by the textual traditions of the secular schools. The early monastic textbooks were replaced first by a new brand of scholastic commentary, such as Peter Elias on Priscian, and, from the fourteenth century, by the expanding corpus of bilingual grammars generated by the growing number of secular schools.[74] In England the Benedictines were among the earliest readers of the new vernacular grammars, a product perhaps of their association with the independent schools of grammar and *dictamen* now found on the fringes of the universities. It is possible they played a direct role in the transmission of these texts.[75]

Grammar was the gateway to the two remaining arts of the *trivium* – rhetoric and dialectic (i.e. logic). Neither discipline could claim the special status of grammar in the monastery, but over the course of time both captured the attention of Benedictine students. The teaching of grammar in the greater Carolingian and Anglo-Saxon schools incorporated an introduction to the basic principles of rhetoric and dialectic. Notker Labeo summarised rhetorical rules for the Saint-Gall *schola* in his own *De arte rhetorica*. His *Distributio* offered them a corresponding conspectus of logical categories and concepts, definition, predicate, proposition and syllogism.[76] As the schools reached the peak of their activity in the eleventh and twelfth centuries, these subjects were not confined to the schoolroom but also became the occupation of many more senior monks. Early book lists suggest Benedictine convents were comparatively well equipped with the key classical and late antique authorities on dialetic – Aristotle, Boethius, Porphyry – but rather less so on rhetoric.[77] An unprovenanced eleventh-century manuscript of Cicero's *De inventione* (Dublin, Trinity College, MS 927) that migrated from France to England must surely have monastic connections but this essential work appears only rarely in catalogues before the thirteenth century. The growing popularity of epistolography among the Black Monks of the Gregorian generation provides a better witness to

[72] Lapidge, *Anglo-Saxon Library*, pp. 51, 242; Sharpe, *Latin Writers*, pp. 1–4 at 3.
[73] Rigg, *Anglo-Latin Literature*, p. 92; Sharpe, *Latin Writers*, pp. 407–9.
[74] *EBL*, B79. 198 (Rochester, *c.* 1202), p. 520. For the rich variety of grammar primers, see B30 (Evesham, fourteenth-century) and p. 902 (index entry); *Dover*, BM1. 439, pp. 168–9; *Peterborough*, BP21 149, 333b, pp. 110–11, 172; *AL*, pp. 76, 85.
[75] Clark, *Monastic Renaissance*, pp. 57–9 at 59. See also D. Thomson, *A Descriptive Catalogue of Middle English Grammatical Texts* (London, 1979), e.g. pp. 147–56 at 157, 316–22.
[76] Grotans, *Reading in Medieval St Gall*, pp. 86, 95, 155–6.
[77] Lapidge, *Anglo-Saxon Library*, pp. 142–3; Grotans, *Reading in Medieval St Gall*, pp. 77, 81–2; *AL*, pp. 7–12.

Culture

the extent of their rhetorical expertise.[78] Logic was equally well established as a subject worthy of study in its own terms but also as the basis for philosophical reflection. Eadmer of Canterbury recalled the time devoted by Anselm to 'solving many dialectical questions' in his *De grammatico* before he proceeded to his ontological proof in *Monologion* and *Proslogion*; the language of his anecdote suggests Eadmer himself was well versed in Aristotle's *Categoriae*.[79] A major stimulus to these studies was the continued interaction of monks and seculars in the context of the claustral school and as the status of these *schola* diminished and the seculars departed, the monastic commitment to the arts of the *trivium* steadily declined. There are few signs of original scholarship from the later twelfth and thirteenth centuries. It was only as the academic studies of the Benedictines advanced after 1300 that rhetoric, dialectic (and philosophy) returned to the majority of monasteries. The canons capitular and *Summi magistri* compelled the monks of England and France to make provision in 'the primitive sciences' and book lists of the Black Death period show the principal abbeys and priories restocking their libraries with the standard academic authorities, most notably the commentaries on the Aristotelian logical corpus.[80] The primary aim was to prepare student monks for their entry into the theology faculties of the university, but in some houses these logical and philosophical studies gathered a momentum of their own. The work of a cohort of Worcester monks between *c.* 1290 and *c.* 1320 went far beyond the basic requirements of the theology baccalaureate.[81] It was perhaps the strength of the primitive sciences among the English Benedictines that persuaded secular masters such as Roger Swineshead (d. *c.* 1366) to enter the monastery themselves.[82]

In parallel with the preparation of monk students, rhetoric attracted renewed interest in this period in its practical application as the basis of prose composition. The growing burden of secular business in the larger Benedictine abbeys and priories placed a greater premium on administrative skills than in previous centuries and those men marked out for high office were offered dedicated training in the applied rhetorics of the *ars dictaminis*. The dictaminal manuals of the French, Italian and English masters now entered Benedictine book collections in significant numbers;

[78] For epistolography, see also J. Leclercq, *The Love of Learning and the Desire for God: A Study of Monastic Culture*, trans. C. Misrahi (New York, 1961), pp. 179–82; Southern, *Saint Anselm*, pp. 138–65; B. P. McGuire, *Friendship and Community: The Monastic Experience, 350–1250* (Kalamazoo, MI, 1988), pp. 184–5 (letter-writing), 222–3 (Lanfranc, Anselm), 233–4 (rhetoric), 255 (Peter the Venerable). See also J. P. Haseldine, 'Epistolography', in *Medieval Latin: an Introduction and Bibliographical Guide*, ed. F. A. C. Mantello and A. G. Rigg (Washington, DC, 1996), pp. 650–58.
[79] *Eadmer*, p. 28.
[80] *EBL*, B43 (Glastonbury), B68 (Ramsey), pp. 220–32, 350–415, 824–5, 830; *AL*, nos. 1465–6, 1473, 1475–6, 1787, pp. 126, 140 (Christ Church, Canterbury), nos. 1024–1104, pp. 307–18 (St Augustine's, Canterbury); *Catalogi veteres*, ed. Raine, pp. 46–79 at 77–8. See also *Chapters*, ed. Pantin, ii. 91.
[81] Thomson, 'Worcester Monks and Education'.
[82] For Swineshead, see Emden, *BRUO*, iii. 1837; G. Molland, 'Roger Swineshead, d. 1365?', *ODNB*, 52682; Sharpe, *Latin Writers*, p. 597.

some monks may have attended the schools of such masters in person.[83] In England, where the training in *dictamen* was undoubtedly vigorous, Benedictines of the post-Black Death generation became preoccupied with *dictamen*. In their own precincts, and possibly also at the Oxford *studia*, several served as masters of the art: Thomas Merke (d. 1404), a Westminster monk, compiled his own manual *Formula*.[84] These preoccupations were not the sole preserve of the advanced scholar monk. The commonplace book of a Canterbury cloister monk, compiled in the second quarter of the fifteenth century, contains a list of twenty-nine colourful (in the rhetorical sense) epistolary salutations to be put to practical use.[85] Some progressed from the practicalities of *dictamen* to the pure principles of classical rhetoric. John Bamburgh, a mid-fifteenth-century monk of Tynemouth Priory (Northumbria), compiled an anthology for the study of rhetoric in theory and literary practice which contained an *accessus* to Horace's *Ars poetica* together with a copy of Alain de Lille's *De planctu naturae*, which he himself had annotated noting the application of different rhetorical colours.[86] From the rhetorics of poetry and prose a number of English monks of this same period pursued an interest in metre. Anonymous compilations of metrical paradigms are preserved in several monastic anthologies from the period 1375–1450, and a manual on metre that attracted the attention of secular masters has been attributed (without corroboration) to a Benedictine of St Benet Hulme (Norfolk).[87]

The higher arts of the *quadrivium* – arithmetic, astronomy, geometry and music – were never fundamental to the monastic vocation, but nonetheless they became embedded in the culture of the Black Monks from early times. There were traces of the *quadrivium* in the quasi-Benedictine monasteries of the seventh and eighth centuries – contributions on computation and music can be counted among Bede's lesser-known compositions – but it would be unsafe to assume on this basis alone that a complete curriculum was in place at all these pioneering communities.[88] The cloister schools of the Carolingian revival, however, did recreate the ancient syllabus of studies, and entrants were now expected to gain a grounding in the mathematical and musical arts. The experience of learning and teaching stimulated

---

[83] *EBL*, B10. 107 (Bermondsey), B30. 52 (Evesham) B76. 13b (Reading – Leominster), pp. 32, 143, 463; *AL*, nos. 542v, p. 66 (Christ Church, Canterbury), nos. 954d, 956–60, 966, pp. 299–300 (St Augustine's, Canterbury); *Dover*, BM1. 134j, 262c, 439j, q, pp. 88, 120, 168–9.

[84] For Merke, see Emden, *BRUO*, ii. 1263–4; R. G. Davies, 'Thomas Merke, d. 1409/10', *ODNB*, 18596; Sharpe, *Latin Writers*, pp. 668–9.

[85] Oxford, Corpus Christi College, MS 256, fos. 171v–176v. The monk was William Glastynbury. See also J. Greatrex, 'Culture at Canterbury in the Fifteenth Century: Some Indications of the Cultural Environment of a Monk of Christ Church', in *The Culture of Medieval English Monasticism*, ed. Clark, pp. 169–75 at 174–5.

[86] Oxford, Corpus Christi College, MS 144, fo. 18v.

[87] See, for example, Oxford, Bodleian Library, MS Digby 100, fos. 178r–189r. For the attribution of a metrical manual to Thomas Langley, monk of St Benet Hulme, see Sharpe, *Latin Writers*, p. 663.

[88] Sharpe, *Latin Writers*, pp. 71–6 at 75; Lapidge, *Anglo-Saxon Library*, pp. 31–8 (Canterbury, Malmesbury, Monkwearmouth, Nursling).

original scholarship, at least in the largest of the schools. At Saint-Gall the monastic leader in the *artes liberales*, Notker Labeo, composed his own *Computus* as a substitute for contemporary computational manuals; his contemporary, Byrhtferth of Ramsey (d. 970), compiled a comparable text, *Enchiridion*, although probably for an audience of secular priests rather than professed religious.[89] A Winchester anthology (Cambridge, Trinity College, MS R.15.21 (945)) of *c.* 1025 offers a conspectus of the mathematics and science studied in the reformed English convents. The extent of an insular English tradition should not be exaggerated here: Byrhtferth's work was remembered at Peterborough and Thorney after 1100 but not thereafter, and although a residual interest in Bede remained it did not spark original English scholarship.[90] New manuals of music theory, building on the Boethian-Bedan tradition, were compiled in the same context. The anonymous *Musica enchiriadis*, which offers the earliest description of the primitive polyphonic form, *organum*, may be of monastic origin.[91] The *De musica* of Hucbald of Saint-Amand (d. 930) was undoubtedly a monastic text and perhaps indicative of the approach – as much grammatical and rhetorical as it was musical – that thrived in the monastic and secular schools of northern France.[92] Astronomy, however, appears to have been less well established in these northern houses. Hermann of Reichenau (d. 1054), called 'Contractus', was known for his experiments in horology but appears isolated among the German houses.[93] It may have been the relatively poor resources for scientific study that persuaded Gerbert, monk of Aurillac (subsequently Pope Sylvester II; d. 1010), to pursue his studies in Catalonia where the cathedral schools had already benefited from Arabic contacts.[94]

The decline of the major Benedictine schools in the twelfth century drained much of the energy from the monastic *quadrivium*, but what might be termed *routine* work in mathematics and music continued in subsequent centuries, at least in the major centres. The provision of books in the post-1200 period would suggest entrants were still expected to have a passing familiarity with the principles of computation, musical notation and astronomical prediction (with particular regard to Easter tables). Some book lists show a selection of the staple authorities on the shelves holding other standard fare for the newly professed, such as copies of the *RB* and its commentaries and collections of the canons concerning monks.

---

[89] Grotans, *Reading in Medieval St Gall*, p. 144; Lapidge, *Anglo-Saxon Library*, pp. 121–2.
[90] Lapidge, *Anglo-Saxon Library*, p. 51.
[91] D. E. Cohen, 'Notes, Scales and Modes in the Early Middle Ages', in *The Cambridge History of Western Music Theory*, ed. T. S. Christiansen (Cambridge, 2002), pp. 307–63 at 323–4.
[92] Rankin, 'Carolingian Music', 298. See also Cohen, 'Notes, Scales and Modes', p. 318.
[93] *Science in the Middle Ages*, ed. D. C. Lindberg (Chicago, 1978), pp. 37, 64; S. C. McCluskey, *Astronomies and Cultures in Early Medieval Europe* (Cambridge, 2000), p. 179.
[94] For a sketch of his career, see also D. C. Lindberg, *The Beginnings of European Science: the European Scientific Tradition in Philosophical, Religious, and Institutional Context, Prehistory to AD 1450*, 3rd edn (Chicago, 2007), pp. 199–203.

The evidence of books, both attested and extant, would also suggest that seasoned cloisterers were encouraged to renew their knowledge of these disciplines. The *sors* (allocation) of Lenten borrowers invariably included an antiphoner.[95] The personal libraries of the later Benedictines commonly contained at least one collection of *Canones*, if only for the customary Easter calculations.[96] Music was markedly less common, but snatches of notation were sometimes scribbled into the manuscript margins, often of wholly unrelated works.[97] While many monks of this period were preoccupied with grammar, and the perfection of verbal pronunciation, it seems a minority were still moved to practise their vocal performance.

Generally the arts of the *quadrivium* drifted to the margins of monastic reading after 1350 but there remained a handful of houses where advanced studies in mathematics, the physical sciences, and even, to some extent, music survived into the pre-Reformation period. There was a surge of interest in applied mathematics and astronomy among a closely knit network of English Benedictine monasteries during the decades either side of the Black Death. These currents might be connected with the recruitment of a succession of secular masters who carried with them the preoccupations, and probably the text exemplars, of the Oxford schools, although it is also possible they were themselves attracted to the pre-existing resources and scholarly reputation of these monasteries. This appears to have been the impulse for John of London (d. *c.* 1325), who may have been active as an arts master from the turn of the fourteenth century, to gravitate towards St Augustine's Abbey, Canterbury, and perhaps to be professed there. John bequeathed his books to the brethren and his presence seems to have reinforced a trend in astronomy that continued in the convent at least to the last quarter of the fourteenth century.[98] Likewise, Reginald Lambourne (d. 1377), a fellow of Merton College, Oxford, until at least 1357, entered the order in 1363 and was professed at Eynsham Abbey (Oxfordshire). As a monk he continued the astrological studies for which he was known in academic circles, completing an account of the lunar eclipse in the same year as his profession.[99] Roger Swineshead, an Oxford logician, entered Glastonbury Abbey in the second quarter of the fourteenth century where he appears to have continued his work both on logic and on mathematics, completing *De motis naturalibus*, an analysis of motion, not only of locomotion but also alteration, augmentation and diminution. In a contemporary couplet he was celebrated as 'subtle Swineshead, son of Glastonbury' ('subtilis Swynyshed, proles Glastoniae').[100] The most important of these masters was Richard of

---

[95] For example, at St Albans: *EBL*, B87. 1, 7–8, 28, 3, 57, 62–3, pp. 555–63.
[96] For example, *EBL*, B23. 27–8, p. 112 (Coventry).
[97] For example, Dublin, Trinity College, MS 444, fos. 9v–10r.
[98] *AL*, esp. pp. 23–6, 329, and 540; W. R. Knorr, 'John of London (*fl.* 1260)', *ODNB*, 14853.
[99] Sharpe, *Latin Writers*, p. 457; K. Snedgar, 'Reginald Lambourne, fl. 1351–1377', *ODNB*, 15945.
[100] Ibid.

Wallingford, a charity boy of Wallingford Priory but a secular master of some stature at Oxford before his profession at St Albans Abbey in *c.* 1320. Richard rose to the abbacy but also remained prolific in experimentation and writing. His enduring achievement was to design and build a ground-breaking mechanical clock, the most sophisticated timepiece of its day.[101] A similar scientific impulse surfaced a century later among the reformed Benedictines of Melk and the Bursfeld. Vitus Bild of the abbey of SS Ulrich and Afra attracted the interest of secular masters for his experimental work with a variety of scientific instruments. He entered into exchanges with Ellenbog, who pursued similar studies at Ottobeuren on the eve of the Reformation.[102]

The development and dissemination of polyphonic music in the fourteenth century, and its adoption by the monastic orders, first for the Lady Mass only but later for the offices of the monks' quire, was accompanied by a revival of music training in several of the greater Benedictine abbeys.[103] A new generation of theorists eschewed early, and monastic, authorities and engaged closely with contemporary academic work emerging from France (where the *ars nova* first appeared) and the English 'Mertonian' School. Their approach perhaps acknowledged the new complexities of polyphonic music and its mensurable notation but can more probably be attributed to their growing affinity with the culture of the academic community. Walter of Oddington (*fl.* 1330), a monk of Evesham Abbey, was one of several secular masters who entered the English congregation before the Black Death. His excursus on the nature of music, *De species musicae*, neatly summarised discussions in the contemporary schools, but surely separated him from the musical knowledge and practice of the majority of his monastic peers.[104] Thomas Walsingham, precentor at St Albans Abbey before 1394, also with an academic background, did seek to dilute the complexities of contemporary notation for monastic consumption, directing his *De modis* specifically to 'the youngsters' of the monastery. Walsingham's work was transmitted through monastic networks, at least in England, but by the beginning of the fifteenth century a growing number of monasteries employed professional cantors, organists and singers, and while they continued to witness original compositions, musical as much as technical, it was the work of their employees and not of the monks themselves.[105]

It should be noted of course that like other clerks, secular and regular, the scientific interests of the Black Monks extended beyond the disciplines of the *quadrivium*. Probably there was a degree of interest in the practice

---

[101] North, *Richard of Wallingford and the Invention of Time.*
[102] Posset, *Renaissance Monks*, pp. 139, 145.
[103] Bowers, 'Early Tudor Monastic Enterprise'.
[104] Sharpe, *Latin Writers*, p. 738.
[105] Ibid., p. 690. See also Clark, *Monastic Renaissance*, pp. 54–5.

and, perhaps, the theory, of medicine since earliest times. Certainly, early manuscripts connected with the convents of the Carolingian and Anglo-Saxon reforms contain traces of medical lore.[106] There was no place for such material in the syllabus of the monastery school, but independent study, and apparently even the practice of medicine, was permitted among the senior monks. The reputation of Notker Physicus (d. 975) as a learned physician was recognised by the emperor, who offered him patronage.[107] The practice and study of medicine survived at least in a small way in subsequent centuries. It would be wrong to assume that every monastery always maintained an accomplished physician – there are many instances of convents sending their sick brethren away for treatment – but their residue of medical texts was not wholly neglected.[108] The development of medical studies at the universities, and the tendency, which was marked at least by the mid-fifteenth century, for practitioners to seek training there, probably served to eclipse any early reputation the monasteries may have had for medical studies.

There were also traces among the medieval Benedictines of studies on the margins of science – in alchemy, astrology and the occult. The Eadwine psalter, copied at Christ Church Priory, Canterbury, in *c.* 1160, contains a series of chiromantic figures.[109] Like their secular counterparts (Ficino *et al.*) the humanist monks of the late fifteenth century made their own forays into the occult. Abbot Johann Trittenheim of Sponheim (d. 1516) speculated on the possibilities of steganography, the communication of angelic messengers. Trittenheim wrote a number of works on the dangers of the diabolic presence, and intervention in human society, *Antipalus maleficiorum, De daemonibus* and *De septem secundeis*, which examined the occult influences on human behaviour. He believed himself to be pursuing a 'theologica magica', to recover the religious roots of certain magical beliefs and rites.[110]

Classical Literature

The study of the liberal arts also served to embed the literature of classical antiquity as one of the cornerstones of Benedictine culture. In institutional terms, of course, Benedict's *cenobium* was inextricably linked with the

---

[106] Grotans, *Reading in Medieval St Gall*, p. 145&n; Lapidge, *Anglo-Saxon Library*, pp. 135, 390, 392–3, 395.

[107] For Notker Physicus, see J. Duft, *Notker der Arzt: Klostermedizin und Mönchsarzt im frühmittelalterlichen St. Gallen* (St Gallen, 1972).

[108] Of extant catalogues and inventories, only the fourteenth-century list from Ramsey shows a concentration of medical texts: *EBL*, B68. 90, 125, 258, 261, 307, 522, 525–6, pp. 360, 364, 378, 384, 405; *Catalogi veteres*, ed. Raine, pp. 78–9; Coates, *English Medieval Books*, pp. 37, 77, 89; Greatrex, 'Culture at Canterbury in the Fifteenth Century', pp. 169–75; C. O'Boyle, *The Art of Medicine: Medical Teaching at the University of Paris, 1250–1400* (Leiden, 1998), p. 171&n.

[109] *The Eadwine Psalter: Text, Image and Monastic Culture in Twelfth-Century Canterbury*, ed. M. T. Gibson, T. A. Heslop, and R. W. Pfaff (Philadelphia, 1992).

[110] Brann, *Abbot Trithemius*, pp. 16–19, 44–5; N. L. Brann, *Trithemius and Magical Theology: A Chapter on the Controversy over Occult Studies in Early Modern Europe* (New York, 1999), pp. 2–3.

linguistic, legal and social dynamics of the late Roman world. Yet Benedict did not share the desire of his contemporary Cassiodorus (*c.* 490–*c.* 585) to combine the discipline of Christian living with a cerebral diet devoted to pagan authorities. He sought to separate his 'beginners' in *RB* from the secular literature of their background, for 'What page, or what passage is there in the divinely inspired books of the Old and New Testament, that is not a most perfect rule of man's life?' (*RB*, lxxiii: 'Quae enim pagina aut qui sermo divinae auctoritatis veteris ac novi testmenti non est rectissima norma vitae humanae'). There is no manuscript trace of these first Benedictine colonies but it must be assumed that patterns of reading there differed markedly from Vivarium and other southern colonies that arose, albeit briefly, under its influence. Notwithstanding Benedict's scruples, however, as it travelled out of Italy, the *RB* came increasingly to be regarded as a shibboleth of Roman society, and its strongest appeal was among those – such as Biscop and his brethren at Wearmouth and Jarrow – already inclined to adopt the trappings of Latin culture. Before the end of the seventh century the *RB* was followed most faithfully in those monasteries which had already done much to restore the syllabus of the ancient schoolroom. As the presence of pagan learning was accepted as a positive virtue in the monastery school at the turn of the seventh and eighth centuries, although senior monks demurred, the classics soon passed over into the reading patterns of the professed.

The Benedictine bond with the classics began in the monastic schoolroom. As the early masters (re-)established a regime of Latin grammar teaching, so they also formulated a repertory of 'readers', poetry and prose texts that might reinforce, and test, the principles of speech, syntax, and style. The key criterion for selection was always the display of literary devices, and to a degree poetry was preferred to prose. An early form of the repertory may be glimpsed from the quotations scattered in seventh- and eighth-century monastic writing, reinforced by the few manuscript fragments from this period. The satirists Juvenal and Persius, no strangers to the schoolrooms of late antiquity, were read widely: a monk of Verona recalled how 'their joking and witty words / made us burst out laughing' ('sepe suia verbis iocundis ateqe facetis nos quae fecerunt risum depromere magnum').[111] There are also signs of Ovid (the amatory poetry and the *Metamorphoses*), Statius, Valerius Maximus, Virgil and the late antique *auctores*, Boethius, Macrobius and Martianus Capella.[112] Scattered references suggest there were also some remarkable rarities among these readers such as Ausonius, Avianus, Probus

---

[111] Miller, *Formation of a Medieval Church*, p. 68.
[112] B. Bischoff, 'Benedictine Monasteries and the Survival of Classical Literature', in *Manuscript and Libraries in the Age of Charlemagne* (Cambridge, 1994), 134–60; Lapidge, *Anglo-Saxon Library*, pp. 66–7, 98–9.

and Quintus Serenus.[113] These rarities did not resurface in subsequent centuries, but the masters of the Carolingian and Anglo-Saxon schools did extend the syllabus to incorporate such *auctores* of pagan and Christian antiquity as Aristotle, Boethius, Prosper, Prudentius and Sedulius.[114] The systematic stocking of Benedictine libraries in the century after 1100 saw these authors and texts enshrined as a core element of the book collection in every major monastery. The earliest extant catalogue from Christ Church Priory, Canterbury (*c.* 1170) records multiple copies of the principal Roman authors, Horace, Juvenal, Lucan, Ovid, Persius, Statius, Terence and Virgil, provisions which suggest not only perhaps patterns of group teaching *viva voce* but also that a prescribed syllabus was now in place.[115] This might explain the specificity of Anselm's story of being put to the reading of Virgil 'et aliis auctoribus quos a me non legisti' on his arrival at Bec.[116] In this period the burgeoning corpus of pseudo-classical literature also began to find a place alongside the *bona fide auctores*. Already the monks of Anselm's generation may have been presented with the anonymous *comediae Babio*, *Geta* and *Pamphilus* and by the turn of the twelfth century their successors would have entered the pseudo-classical world of the *Alexandreis* (Walter of Châtillon), *Architrenius* (Jean de Hauteville) and *Dissuasio Rufini* (Walter Map).[117] The blurring of the boundary between authentic and contemporary *auctores* was indicative of the Benedictine, and more generally the clerical, conception of the classics, as, primarily, vehicles for the exposition and perfection of Latin style.

Monastic readers were encouraged to engage with the classical *auctores ad literam* unencumbered by any apparatus of authorities (liturgical, patristic, exegetical) comparable to that which always accompanied their reading of scripture. As the masters presented it to their pupils in the cloister school, the reading of the classics was in itself an exegetical exercise in which any or every feature of grammar, orthography, syntax, metrical structure or rhetorical style might be elaborated for profit. There appears to have been limited use of late antique commentaries in the earliest schools, and although the Carolingian masters were conscious of Donatus (on Terence), Macrobius (on Cicero) and Servius (on Virgil), their preference was for schemes of interlinear glosses, scholia and other para-textual apparatus. Their manuscripts bear witness to some of the earliest scholia, some of which may have entered the networks surrounding Corbie, Fulda and Saint-Gall in a

---

[113] Lapidge, *Anglo-Saxon Library*, pp. 66–7, 292, 332, 404.

[114] Ibid., pp. 50, 54; Grotans, *Reading in Medieval St Gall*, pp. 73, 197. See also V. Law, 'The Study of Grammar', in *Carolingian Culture*, ed. McKitterick, pp. 88–110.

[115] *AL*, pp. 7–12 at 9–10.

[116] Letter to Maurice (letter 64), i. 55.

[117] For these attested in Benedictine book-collections, see *AL*, nos. 1445, 1482, 1594, pp. 365, 369, 384 (St Augustine's, Canterbury). For the works themselves, see Rigg, *Anglo-Latin Literature*, pp. 88–91, 152, 156; Rigg also reviews literary anthologies of this period, pp. 148–53.

more or less unbroken line of transmission from the schools of late antiquity.[118] The masters of this period were also among the first monks of any tradition to contribute interlinear glosses of their own. A marginal commentary on Martianus's *De nuptiis* attributed to Remigius of Auxerre is preserved in several manuscripts.[119] Several anonymous hands were responsible for the apparatus that accompanies Ovid's *Heroides* in the tenth-century codex known as the Dunstan classbook which belonged to, but did not originate at, the Anglo-Saxon monastery at Glastonbury.[120] Some of these glosses are in the vernacular, underlining the importance of translation (in general if not at Glastonbury) in this early period. The Carolingian masters themselves translated selected works of key *auctores*. Notker Labeo is known to have rendered both Boethius (*Consolatio*) and Martianus Capella (*De nuptiis*) into German; translations of Virgil's *Bucolica* and Terence's *Andria* were also completed but no longer survive.[121] This interest in translation did not survive into the high Middle Ages. The commentaries of late antiquity and later were more widely available, and widely used, in the monasteries after 1100, but readers of this period also broadened the range of textual apparatus which they applied to classical *auctores*. They borrowed the analytical *accessus* developed by the masters of the burgeoning secular schools, and – although authorship of any such text is surely questionable – probably originated versions of their own. There were no Benedictine successors to the handful of Carolingian commentators, however, before the open schools faded at the close of the twelfth century. A resurgence of interest in the curriculum *auctores* at the greater English abbeys and priories in the second half of the fourteenth century led to the reproduction of early works and the composition, or compilation, of several new commentaries. Several St Albans monks of the same generation produced fresh *accessus* collections and semi-original commentaries on such works as Boethius's *Consolatio*, Lucan's *De bello civili* and the mock-classical *Architrenius* of Jean de Hauteville.[122]

The patterns of reading and study instilled in the claustral schoolroom in large part determined the ways in which the Latin classics became integrated into Benedictine culture as a whole. The priorities of the schoolmaster and his pupils appear to have passed into the cloister carrels and, later, the

---

[118] Bischoff, 'Benedictine Monasteries', 134–60; Grotans, *Reading in Medieval St Gall*, pp. 38, 165–7; *Texts and Transmission: A Survey of Latin Classics*, ed. L. D. Reynolds (Oxford, 1983), pp. 224–31 (Macrobius, noting Corbie's witness), 385–8 (Servius, noting Fulda's witness to the DS tradition of the text), 419–20 (Terence, noting Corbie's witness to scholia Bembinus).

[119] C. E. Lutz, 'The Commentary of Remigius of Auxerre on Martianus Capella', *Mediaeval Studies* 19 (1957), 137–56. See also *Texts and Transmission*, ed. Reynolds, pp. 245–6.

[120] R. J. Hexter, *Ovid and Medieval Schooling: Studies in Medieval School Commentaries on Ovid's Ars amatoria, Epistulae ex Ponto and Epistulae Heroidum*, Münchener Beiträge zur Mediävistik und Renaissance-Forschung 38 (Munich, 1986), p. 28–9. See illustration 5.

[121] Grotans, *Reading in Medieval St Gall*, pp. 41, 367.

[122] Clark, *Monastic Renaissance*, pp. 217–34.

cells and *studia*, for the most part unchanged. This was reflected clearly in the balance of authors and texts in Benedictine book collections. Almost without exception, the classics that entered the cloister were Latin. The quasi-Benedictines of the seventh and eighth centuries laid the foundation for this syllabus but there are scarcely any substantive traces of this in surviving manuscript fragments. The poetry and prose providing the richest source of literary paradigms – Lucan, Ovid, Terence, Virgil – were perhaps most common, and most commonly provided in multiple copies.[123] Works of history, secular manuals and reportage – Caesar, Suetonius, Vegetius – were also popular, a natural extension, for readers of greater experience, of the schoolroom glosses and scholia that elaborated the literal and historical sense of each text.[124] The strongest attachment among monastic readers appears to have been to the authors and texts that were their closest companions in the schoolroom. As a veteran of the cloister, Guibert de Nogent (1053–1124) confessed to a certain guilty pleasure in returning to the Ovid of his schooldays.[125] Later, in the fourteenth and fifteenth centuries, when classical works were commonly collected by Benedictines building personal libraries, such preferences were still apparent. A circle of collectors at St Augustine's Abbey Canterbury gathered an impressive corpus of texts, almost all of them the traditional curriculum *auctores*.[126] Manuscript anthologies were compiled according to the same principle as the curriculum *auctores* were glossed, the *materia* of poetry was unravelled with reference to history, or at least to parallel poetics treating the same theme, thus the *Aeneid* or the *Metamorphoses* were bound together with, for example, Dares' *De excidio Troiae*.[127] Even advanced monastic readers remained a little aloof from the expanding corpus of critical literature, and it was only in the later Middle Ages, and in the specific field of mythography, that there is evidence of a close engagement with the work of contemporary commentators.[128] When they turned to their manuscripts, the schoolroom skills of textual analysis resurfaced. William of Malmesbury (d. 1125) marked the margins of his celebrated anthology of Cicero with notes of the literary devices (*declamacio*, etc.) displayed, almost as a reflex action.[129]

Only rarely did the Benedictine readers translate these patterns of study into original scholarship. In the wake of the open cloister schools, there was no consistent or co-ordinated impulse to comment on, translate or

[123] Bischoff, 'Benedictine Monasteries', 134–60; Lapidge, *Anglo-Saxon Library*, pp. 66–8, 99, 110, 112, 122&n.

[124] Ibid.

[125] *Guibert*, p. 87.

[126] *AL*, nos. 1408, 1471, 1478–80, pp. 360, 367–8 (St Augustine's, Canterbury).

[127] For example: *AL*, no. 937, p. 297 (St Augustine's, Canterbury).

[128] Perhaps most notable in the reception of Pierre Bersuire's *Ovidius moralizatus*: J. G. Clark, 'Ovid in the Monasteries: the Evidence from Late Medieval England', in *Ovid in the Middle Ages*, ed. J. G. Clark, F. Coulson and K. L. McKinley (Cambridge, 2010), pp. 177–96.

[129] R. M. Thomson, *William of Malmesbury*, rev. edn (Woodbridge, 2003), pp. 51–6.

otherwise transmit the classical tradition within or beyond the order. This might be connected to a growing unease towards the presence of pagan and secular literature in the cloister towards the end of the twelfth century, and later. Certainly the last generation of Benedictine writers to have been trained when the schools of Bec, Canterbury, etc., were at their apogee articulated a greater anxiety over their classical and literary enthusiasm than many of their predecessors. There was a defensive edge to the claim of Ralph of Dunstable (*fl.* 1190) that 'the trifles of the Muses are not incompatible with the discipline of the cloister'.[130] Even a cautious approach to the pagan classics may have carried little weight with superiors, and episcopal visitors, in the years after the Lateran reform of 1215. Occasionally conventual sermons of the later Middle Ages expressly condemn the fading of pure contemplation in the *opus claustalium*.[131] It was perhaps in response to such concerns that original scholarship, where it occurred, was now more conspicuously hermeneutic in character. Naturally, perhaps, Boethius's *Consolatio* was a favoured subject of the few commentaries known to have been composed by Benedictine scholars.[132]

The historical *materia* of the classical *auctores*, of course, was always less controversial and a modest, but in many ways influential, tradition of studies in ancient history continued to thrive in a number of Benedictine houses, most notably in England. William of Malmesbury's *Polyhistor* reached Benedictine readers in Britain and Continental Europe and perhaps provided late medieval monks with a valuable link to the literary vigour of the eleventh and twelfth centuries.[133] Monastic interest in the narratives of the ancient world was reinvigorated by the encyclopaedic genre which proliferated in the period after 1150. It was the work of Vincent de Beauvais and his analogues, as much any prevailing monastic tradition, which shaped the Chester Benedictine Ranulf Higden's synthesis of Greek and Roman histories in his *Polychronicon*.[134] Higden transformed monastic historiography, and *Polychronicon* was a principal source for Thomas Walsingham's *Historia Alexandri magni principis*. Like Higden, Walsingham attached weight equally to poetry and prose history, and in the companion piece to Alexander, *Dites ditatus*, literally 'Dictys expanded', he interwove the empirical details of the destruction of Troy (from Dares) with fabulous tales of the deities and their descent into the world (from Dictys).[135]

[130] Ralph of Dunstable, *Vita Albani*, prologue: 'pieridum ludis claustri laxare rigorem non est emeritae religionis opus'. See also W. McLeod, 'Alban and Amphibal: Some Extant Lives and a Lost life', *Mediaeval Studies* 42 (1980), 407–30 at 412.

[131] For example, Oxford, Bodleian Library, MS Laud 706, fos. 153r–56r at 156r.

[132] For example, Simon Southerey, on whose lost commentary, see Sharpe, *Latin Writers*, p. 617; Emden, *BRUO*, iii. 1734.

[133] Thomson, *William of Malmesbury*, pp. 189–203; *Texts and Transmission*, ed. Reynolds, p. 49.

[134] See also J. Taylor, *The Universal Chronicle of Ranulf Higden* (Oxford, 1966), pp. 33–50 at 38–45.

[135] Clark, *Monastic Renaissance*, pp. 163–208 at 192–5.

Perhaps a comparable chronicle of Troy was composed by the Glastonbury monk John Seen (*fl.* 1350); the work was commended by his Oxford contemporaries but no longer survives.[136]

A resurgence of interest in classical mythography among clerical readers in the decades either side of the Black Death stimulated a further, albeit brief, period of critical creativity in the Benedictine convents of northern Europe. Pierre Bersuire (d. 1362), superior of the Parisian priory of Saint-Éloi, and a Franciscan convert to the *RB*, composed a systematic exposition of Ovid's *Metamorphoses*, called *Ovidius moralizatus*, which emerged as one of the most widely read classical commentaries in pre-Reformation Europe. Bersuire's work was the product of the extra-mural intellectual exchanges made possible for many regulars by the papal exile at Avignon: for Bersuire it brought an encounter with the *Africa* of Francesco Petrarca.[137] The English Benedictines were early readers of Bersuire's *Ovidius* – it is possible exemplars were carried into the country by colleagues returning from the Avignon curia – and it was his work which inspired imitations by Thomas Walsingham (d. *c.* 1422) and John Wheathampstead (d. 1465), both monks of St Albans.[138] Bersuire's moralised fables from Ovid also became the stock-in-trade of English Benedictine preachers. It was perhaps the influence of the *Ovidius* which led English monks to rediscover the rudimentary mythographic analysis of earlier centuries. Certainly, elementary genealogical trees showing the descent of the pagan deities, which probably originated in earlier centuries, were recopied in fifteenth-century codices.[139]

Their immersion, in their formative years, in the structure and style of the classical *auctores* also inclined many Benedictines to appropriate the idiom for themselves. From early times, much of their original prose became embroidered with the vocabulary and verbal effects borrowed from the Roman masters. No doubt these borrowings encouraged the compilation of *florilegia*, often regarded as the archetypal monastic codex, although lemmata could also be culled from *accessus*, scholia and other sources, and surely also reflected their close reading – and perhaps ability to reminisce from – the original texts themselves. This tendency to classicise ebbed and flowed from the tenth and the fifteenth centuries. It peaked perhaps in the first half of the twelfth century, although in this renaissance climate the most cultured monastic writers – Anselm of Canterbury, Peter the Venerable –

---

[136] Seen's work was recalled by the Franciscan Richard Trivetlam. See also Rigg, *Anglo-Latin Literature*, p. 273&n; Sharpe, *Latin Writers*, pp. 312–13, 516.

[137] There is still no systematic study of Bersuire; see J. Engels, 'L'édition critique de l'*Ovidius moralizatus* de Bersuire', *Vivarium* 9 (1971), 19–24; W. D. Reynolds, 'Sources, Nature and Influence of the *Ovidius moralizatus* of Pierre Bersuire', in *The Mythographic Art: Classical Fable and the Rise of the Vernacular in Early France and England*, ed. J. Chance (Gainesville, FL, 1990), pp. 83–99. K. Rivers, 'Another Look at the Career of Pierre Bersuire, OSB', *Rev. Bén.* 116 (2006), 92–100.

[138] Clark, *Monastic Renaissance*, pp. 200–5, 234–8.

[139] For example, Dublin, Trinity College, MS 632, 89v–109v at 90v–96v, 99r–104v. See also Clark, 'Ovid in the Monasteries'.

remained more conservative than many secular masters.[140] The years either side of 1400 saw a return to this self-conscious classicism, particularly in the prose writing of the English Benedictines. This generation of monks wrote under the influence of the elaborate euphuism of late medieval masters of *dictamen*, but they also approached even the most routine writing – conventual letters, domestic chronicles, sermons – as vehicles for their knowledge of ancient authors.[141]

The first full experiments in classical form were found in the Carolingian and Anglo-Saxon schoolrooms. Clever versification became the currency of their masters. The tenth-century trilogy of verses titled *Altercatio magistri et discipuli* was the work of the Winchester schoolmaster, perhaps Lantfred of Old Minster.[142] Abbo of Fleury's acrostic *carmina* extended the genre to encompass secular and even political subjects.[143] Later masters, especially those of the eleventh and twelfth centuries, were persuaded to apply the structure and style of secular, classical poetry also to the treatment of monastic and theological themes. Marbod of Rennes (d. 1123) ended his life a Benedictine of Anjou and applied his skills as an arts master to the composition of hexametrical verse in honour of the Virgin which ends with the invocation that she will 'grant to the blessed an eternal dwelling in the Elysian fields' ('supplicum post iudicium removeto gehennae Elisios concede pios habitare').[144] The exegetical digest of Lawrence of Durham, *Hypognosticon*, was likewise written in verse; Ralph of Dunstable departed from convention with Latin pentameters for his *Passio Albani*.[145] There was only ever a handful of monks in any generation with the requisite skills to compose original poetry in the classical style, but throughout the high and later Middle Ages many ordinary *claustrales* expressed their passion for versification in less polished ways. Anonymous memorial verses, quatrains, couplets and other fragments are frequently found in the margins of manuscripts. A pen-try on a front or rear pastedown might also reproduce a passage of poetry.[146] They may have been unable to compose verse themselves, but they were more than capable of measuring the quality of others. Orderic

---

[140] J. Martin, 'Classicism and Style in Latin Literature', in *Renaissance and Renewal in the Twelfth Century*, ed. R. L. Benson, G. Constable and C. D. Lanham (Cambridge, MA, 1982), pp. 537–68.

[141] Clark, *Monastic Renaissance*, pp. 211–17; Coates, *English Medieval Books*, p. 104; E. F. Jacob, '*Florida verborum venustas*: Some Early Examples of Euphuism in England', *Bulletin of the John Rylands Library, Manchester* 17 (1933), 264–90. For the masters of *dictamen* in late medieval England, see M. Camargo, *Ars dictaminis, Ars dictandi* (Turnhout, 1991), pp. 37–41; M. Camargo, *Medieval Rhetoric of Prose Composition: Five English Artes dictandi and their Tradition* (Binghamton, NY, 1995), pp. 20–32.

[142] Lapidge, *Anglo-Latin Literature*, pp. 122, 235–41.

[143] M. Lapidge, 'Appendix II: The Acrostic verses of Abbo of Fleury', in Byrhtferth, *Lives*, ed. Lapidge, pp. 318–40.

[144] Martin, 'Classicism and Style in Latin Literature', p. 552.

[145] For both versifiers, see Rigg, *Anglo-Latin Literature*, pp. 54–61, 124. For Ralph's verse, see also McLeod, 'Alban and Amphibel'.

[146] For example, Worcester Cathedral Library, MS Q61, backsleeve of the over-cover: Thomson, *Descriptive Catalogue*, p. 158.

Vitalis reveals an unvarying eye for the niceties of metre, noting an epitaph 'composed in the adonic metre, which consists of a dactyl followed by a spondee' ('adonico metro quod dactilo spondeoque constat').[147] Verse, often of an indifferent quality, became a favourite idiom of the Benedictine cloisterer. It was perhaps a direct evocation of the banter of the cloister which Jocelin of Brakelond evoked in the claim of the Bury brethren that 'they have declined Musa, Musae so that they count themselves bemused'.[148]

Other forms also inspired Benedictine imitation. Of course, to any monastic reader epistolography was as much a patristic as it was a pagan genre, but from the tenth century onward the letter writing of the Benedictines was modelled closely on classical originals, Cicero in particular.[149] The Black Monks were bound up in the general interest in epistolary *amicitia* which emerged in the Gregorian period.[150] The exchange, collection and critical examination became for a generation or more a conspicuous occupation of the monks of the leading Benedictine houses. Their letter collections circulated within their own fraternal networks and as such served to reinforce the programme of spiritual and intellectual renewal propounded in such centres as Bec and Canterbury. A minority, such as those of Anselm of Canterbury, were also known in secular milieus.[151] Less literary forms of letter writing lived on in later medieval monasteries. At the turn of the fourteenth and fifteenth centuries, as humanism revived the classicism of earlier centuries, a handful of high-profile houses – the Canterbury convents, Evesham, Sponheim, Würzburg – saw a return to the perfect epistles of the past.[152]

The prominence of Juvenal and Persius among the curriculum *auctores* also tempted some Benedictines into the controversial territory of the satirist. The twelfth century saw a flowering of satirical poetry, and some of the most popular works were those poured from monastic pens. The *Speculum stultorum* was the work of a Canterbury monk, Nigel Witeker [Whiteacre] (*fl.* 1190), which celebrated the misadventures of the ass Brunellus.[153] Like Latin verse, satire thrived also among those of lesser learning in the cloister and a taste for texts of this kind survived at this level long after the twelfth century. Late medieval monks were voracious consumers if not composers of contemporary satire, and such verses were among the few vernacular texts to find a place in the margins, or pastedowns, of their manuscripts.

[147] *Orderic*, iii. 19.
[148] *Jocelin*, p. 130.
[149] For background, see J. Haseldine, 'Epistolography', in *Medieval Latin*, ed. Mantello and Rigg, pp. 650–8; Martin, 'Classicism and Style in Latin Literature', p. 550.
[150] McGuire, *Friendship and Community*, pp. 184–5, 187, 233–4; Haseldine, 'Monastic Culture of Friendship'.
[151] Southern, *Saint Anselm*, pp. 394–403, 458–81.
[152] *RO*, iii. 94–5, 100–7; Brann, *Abbot Trithemius*, pp. 281–9. For example, the Canterbury letter-book, BL, Royal MS 10 B IX; R. Weiss, *Humanism in England during the Fifteenth Century*, 2nd edn (Oxford, 1957), pp. 130–1&n.
[153] Rigg, *Anglo-Latin Literature*, pp. 102–5; Sharpe, *Latin Writers*, pp. 400–1 at 401.

Pseudo-classical satires resurfaced among the scholar monks of the Oxford *studia* at the turn of the fourteenth and fifteenth centuries and seem sufficiently well regarded to have reached the commonplace books of secular scholars: the early Tudor antiquarian William Worcester owned a collection of this late flowering of monastic satire.[154]

The commitment to the classical heritage which coloured Benedictine culture in the high and later Middle Ages has been characterised as a *monastic* humanism (*Klosterhumanismus*), comparable to, but distinct from, the *scholastic* humanism connected with the cathedral and secular schools of the twelfth century and subsequently with the arts masters of the new universities.[155] Where the methodology of the secular masters was speculative, and what they derived from the ancients above all was the potential of dialectic, their monastic counterparts' *modus operandi* was primarily literary and their purpose was to appropriate the grammatical, metrical and rhetorical power of the pagan masters. They were humanists, Jean Leclercq contended, to the extent that they drew on the classics 'to develop and refine their own human faculties', particularly in terms of an appreciation of the aesthetic value of language, but they shared neither the sensibilities of the high medieval scholastics nor of the humanists of the *quattrocento*: 'They were neither antiquarians nor bibliophiles, theirs was in no sense a collector's mentality.'[156] There is no doubt it was their literary tastes and techniques that bound the Benedictines to the Latin classics, but it would be wrong to deny the signs of a deeper attachment to the traces of antiquity. Leclercq overlooked the extent to which, from early times, the Black Monks became actively involved in the recovery, reproduction and transmission of the textual traditions of pre-Christian authors. It is now clear that it was among the cenobites of the seventh and eighth centuries – at Bobbio, Malmesbury, Montecassino – that the last classical codices were broken, turned over to the palimpsest, and then recast in the forms they were known throughout the Middle Ages: Bishop Aldhelm (d. 709) was the only witness to the *Tragediae* of Seneca between antiquity and 1100.[157] The Benedictines of the Carolingian and Anglo-Saxon reforms were proactive in the reproduction and transmission of the burgeoning canons of *auctores*. By the mid-ninth century Fulda was recognised as a repository of classical *originalia*, preserving the work of authors – Dictys Cretensis, Nonius

---

[154] *Canterbury College, Oxford,* ed. Pantin, i. 68–72; Clark, *Monastic Renaissance,* pp. 209–38. See also BL, Cotton MS Julius F VII, fos. 129r–135r.

[155] For this interpretation, see R. W. Southern, *Scholastic Humanism and the Unification of Europe,* vol. 1 (Oxford, 1997), p. 20; R. W. Southern, *Medieval Humanism and Other Studies* (Oxford, 1970).

[156] Leclercq, *Love of Learning,* p. 140.

[157] Bischoff, 'Benedictine Monasteries', 134–60; *Texts and Transmission,* ed. Reynolds, pp. 378–81 at 378; Lapidge, *Anglo-Saxon Library,* pp. 68, 94–5, 332.

Marcellus, Pliny – which remained rare throughout the Middle Ages.[158] The stocking of Benedictine libraries between 1050 and 1250, and the systematic book production it brought to many precincts, served to transmit key texts to both regular and secular readers. Both in Britain and Europe it is possible to show that several popular works were descended from a single monastic exemplar. It is possible the Benedictines continued to play an important role in the preservation and publication of texts in the period after the Black Death when monastic scriptoria were thought to have entered a terminal decline. The accounts of the Italian humanists, of rare discoveries in remote convents, have fostered a false impression of the moribund character of monastic libraries in the later fourteenth and fifteenth centuries.[159] Book lists from this period show a surge in the number and range of classical authors and texts available at least in the greater Benedictine abbeys and priories. There are signs that some returned to co-ordinated book production and that there were both individual and collective efforts to acquire earlier, better exemplars of existing works, and to secure known rarities for the first time.

Whatever the character, or depth, of their classical enthusiasm in earlier centuries, there can now be no doubt the Benedictines were receptive to the currents of humanism that emerged in Italy, and elsewhere, over the course of the fourteenth century. The personal connections between Benedictines and the pioneering humanists would probably repay further study, especially in connection with monastic representatives present at the papal court at Avignon. The Italian Benedictines cultivated, and secured, the interest of leading humanists from an early stage; indeed, there were a number of high-profile conversions at the turn of the fifteenth century. The Benedictines of Badia (Florence) secured the library of Antonio Corbinelli, containing no fewer than 105 classical *auctores*, donated in spite of opposition from Poggio Bracciolini.[160] Even English Black Monks may have had fleeting exchanges with fourteenth-century Florentines: Poggio Bracciolini came to England in 1419 believing he would find like-minded *littérateurs*.[161] The evidence of both surviving and attested books suggests the translations and treatises of early humanists – Leonardo Bruni's Aristotle, Petrarch's *De remediis* – had entered even into the remoter northern monasteries by 1425: Abbot John Wheathampstead of St Albans wrote admiringly in one of his notebooks of 'Arretinus' [i.e. Leonardo Bruni] and his 'most cultured pen' ('calamo

[158] Lapidge, *Anglo-Saxon Library*, p. 84; Bischoff, 'Benedictine Monasteries', 134–60; *Texts and Transmission*, ed. Reynolds, pp. 248–52 at pp. 251, 321.

[159] *Two Renaissance Book Hunters: The Letters of Poggius Bracciolini to Nicolaus de Niccolis*, ed. P. W. G. Gordon, Records of Civilisation, Sources and Studies 91 (New York, 1974), pp. 31–77 at 34, 36, 42, 46, 48, 55. See also *Texts and Transmission*, ed. Reynolds, p. xli.

[160] Collett, *Italian Benedictine Scholars*, p. 30.

[161] Weiss, *Humanism in England*, pp. 13–21 at 14–15.

cultissimo').[162] In the majority of Benedictine houses such inclinations were confined to the independent studies of a handful of advanced scholars but in a number of cases they affected the community as a whole. The congregations of Padua, Melk and Bursfeld made a co-ordinated effort to re-form the cloister curriculum according to humanist principles. The introduction of a new syllabus of humane letters proved so successful at Santa Giustina and its dependents that the chapter general was compelled (in 1465) to remind the convents of their obligations with regard to scriptural study.[163] The Benedictines of Melk attracted a succession of humanist masters whose work transformed both in 'letters' and in scripture. The new learning became established in the Bursfeld congregation only in the last quarter of the fifteenth century but a number of its houses – Nuremberg, Sponheim – soon eclipsed more established centres of northern humanism.[164] Their scholarship not only brought them to prominence in their order, but also secured them the recognition and patronage of secular humanists. Benedikt Schwalbe (*c.* 1460–1521), called Chelidonius (i.e. the swallow), of St Giles's Abbey, Nuremberg was commissioned to contribute memorial verses for the triumphal arch of Emperor Maximilian, a project on which he collaborated with Albrecht Dürer.[165] Recent work would suggest these Rhenish houses represented the heartland of monastic humanism but the parallels in other parts of Europe should not be overlooked. The *commendam* Abbot Guillaume de Briçonnet recast the abbey of Saint-Germain-des-Prés as a humanist seminary sufficient in its bibliographic resources for the pioneering exegete Jacques Lefèvre d'Étaples to settle there.[166] Prior William Sellyng, of Christ Church Canterbury, encouraged his able brethren to pursue the *studia humanitatis* in the secular schools of northern Italy; they returned with some examples of contemporary humanist scholarship although whether the cloister curriculum itself was wholly transformed remains somewhat doubtful.[167] There are glimpses of renewed interest in the classical inheritance – if not in Italian humanism *per se* – in the greater Benedictine monasteries of the Iberian peninsula. The monks of Montserrat possessed an early copy of the Catalan translation, by Pere Plana OP (d. 1365), of Boethius's *Consolatio*.[168] More than a century later the Spanish Benedictines

---

[162] BL, MS Arundel 11, fo. 92r.

[163] Collett, *Italian Benedictine Scholars*, p. 29.

[164] Brann, *Abbot Trithemius*, esp. pp. 355–77; Posset, *Renaissance Monks*, pp. 63–92.

[165] Posset, *Renaissance Monks*, p. 66.

[166] P. Imbart, *Les origines de la réforme*, 2nd edn, 2 vols. (Paris, 1944), ii. 488–523; G. Bedouelle, *Lefèvre d'Étaples et l'intelligence des écritures* (Geneva, 1976).

[167] Weiss, *Humanism in England*, pp. 153–9.

[168] D. Briesemeister, 'Die Überlieferung der *Consolatio Philosophiae* des Boethius im mitteralterlichen Spanien', in *Sinn und Sinnverständnis: Festschrift für Ludwig Schrader zum 65. Geburtstag*, ed. K. Holz et al. (Berlin, 1997), pp. 15–25 at 17.

contributed to a conference at Valladolid that examined the orthodoxy of
Erasmus.[169]

Where it was promoted, humanism transformed monastic studies. It
removed the old, and in many cases, muddled 'arts' curriculum of earlier
centuries, and substituted the systematic study of grammar, rhetoric, history and moral philosophy. It also served to revive scriptural studies and in
some cases promoted pioneering work in polyglotism. The traces of traditional monastic classicism, however, were not entirely effaced. The culture
of these humanist cloisters remained for the most part Latinate. Certainly,
there was a new recognition of the importance of Greek *auctores*, and Greek
codices were collected in some numbers, especially in the Bursfeld and
Melk congregations. Yet the teaching of Greek made little headway. Abbot
Trittenheim hailed his own Sponheim as a Hellenist academy where even
the hounds barked in Greek, but even here, in the heartland of Benedictine
reform, the learning of Greek remained a remote fantasy in the half century
before the Reformation.[170]

History

The intellectual horizons of the Benedictines were not confined to the
canonical authorities of the quire and the schoolroom. From earliest
times, in their reading and their original writing, they also reflected upon,
and responded to, the dynamics of the social, political and public spheres
beyond the monastery. These impulses were channelled, perhaps above
all, into the consumption and composition of a wide variety of histories,
not only annals and chronicles but also biographies and hagiographical
vitae. Indeed, over the course of the medieval centuries, the Black Monks
came to be regarded by many, and to consider themselves, as human society's appointed historians. Royal governments deposited documents in
abbey archives, even after their own chanceries developed record keeping.[171]
Princes and prelates deferred to Benedictine chroniclers not only, or indeed
principally, for their knowledge of past history, but rather for their research
skills in the recovery and (re-)interpretation of early documents.[172] It was his
mastery of early records, and his skill in determining their reliability, that
recommended the St Albans chronicler Matthew Paris to King Henry III,
who in 1247 requested him 'to write an accurate and full account of [all]

[169] Abbot Alonso Enriquez (d. 1577) of Valladolid was a key member of the Erasmian party: *Contemporaries of Erasmus: A Biographical Register of the Renaissance and Reformation*, ed. P. G. Bietenholz (Toronto, 1985), p. 432. See also *The Correspondence of Erasmus: Letters 1658 to 1801: January 1526–March 1527*, ed. C. G. Nauert and A. Dalzell (Toronto, 2003), p. 476 (Letter 1791, from Pedro Juan Olivar).

[170] Brann, *Abbot Trithemius*, p. 243.

[171] Gransden, *Historical Writing in England*, ii. 457; M. T. Clanchy, *From Memory to Written Record: England, 1066–1307* (Oxford, 1993), pp. 152–3, 156–8, 165–8.

[172] For example, the summons of the Chester chronicler Ranulf Higden in 1352: J. G. Edwards, 'Ranulf, monk of Chester', *EHR* 47 (132), 94.

events'.[173] The historical legacy of the order even determined to a degree the treatment of their houses, and their treasures, during the sixteenth-century dissolutions. In England especially, the recovery of chronicles, cartularies and other collections of records was almost complete in some regions and, apparently, co-ordinated centrally.[174]

The Benedictines' conception of history was formed by their experience of cenobitic life. To be professed a monk was to join a community of past as well as present, and it was incumbent on any novice to seek to understand, and to share in, this inheritance, this social memory. In the later Middle Ages such a process became a formal part of the preparation of novices, and anthologies of texts were compiled to inculcate newcomers into the history of the house.[175] This process was perhaps particularly imperative for Benedictines, since they lacked, for much of the Middle Ages, not only a corporate superstructure but also a clear, coherent chronological framework of their own. The *RB* and Gregory's *Dialogues* spoke not of temporal but of spiritual origins: there was nothing within the order to be compared to the Cistercians' *Carta* or the Franciscans' *Adventus ordinis in Anglia*.[176] The historical sensibilities of the Black Monks were sharpened by the daily regime of reading and study. The liturgical lectionary, of course, laid bare the outline of human history, and the principal patristic authorities – Augustine, Orosius – introduced them to the chronology of the Christian community, past, present and future. These readings also impressed upon them the moral value of such reflections on the past: 'the thoughtful listener is inspired to imitate the good' ('ad imitandum bonum auditor sollicitus instigator'). Historical *exemplae* were not only prominent in their public and private reading of scripture but were also central to the schoolroom analysis of classical *auctores*. These reflections were vividly reinforced by their visual environment and the frequent representation of historical figures and scenes in murals, statuary and, in the later period, stained-glass windows. There was a taste for historical themes in the glazing of the cloister walks and other conventual spaces at the greater English abbeys and priories, such as Bury, Christ Church, Canterbury, and Durham.[177] It should be noted, of course, that through their exposure to patristic and pagan authorities, the Benedictines also learned to love the literary quality of historical writing, an appreciation which became an important part of their own contributions to the genre.

[173] Matthew Paris, *Chronica majora*, ed. H. R. Luard, RS 57, 7 vols. (London, 1872–83), iv. 644–5; R. Vaughan, *Matthew Paris* (Cambridge, 1958), p. 3.

[174] J. P. Carley, *The Libraries of King Henry VIII*, CBLMC 7 (London, 2000), pp. xxxiii–xxxix, xliii–xlvi.

[175] For example, Oxford, Bodleian Library, MS Bodley 240, pp. 765b–852b; BL, Cotton MS Claudius E IV, where following a copy of the *Gesta abbatum* comes apologetics on monasticism: fos. 322v^d–331r^b.

[176] For these texts, see A. Kehnel, 'The Narrative Tradition of the Medieval Franciscan Friars on the British Isles: Introduction to the Sources', *Franciscan Studies* 63 (2005), 461–530.

[177] Oxford, Corpus Christi College, MS 256, fos. 185v–188r; M. R. James, *On the Abbey of St Edmund at Bury, I: The Library; II: The Church*, Cambridge Antiquarian Society 28 (1895), 186–203 at 186, 190–3, 199. *Rites of Durham*, ed. Raine, pp. 91–102.

Original historical writing flourished from the earliest times. The unsteady fortunes of the first foundations, and their (often) frontier position within the community of the faithful, encouraged a focus on the struggles of their people as a whole. The quasi-Benedictine Bede compiled his *Historia ecclesiastica gentis Anglorum* so 'the multitude of the isles [might] be glad and give thanks at the remembrance of His holiness'.[178] The *Historia* celebrated the achievements of conversion and kingship. In the same way, a generation after Bede's death Paul Warnefrid at Montecassino marked the making of the Lombard hegemony with his *Historia gentis Langobardorum* (787×795/6), which traced the triumph of those men from 'the region of the north ... so ... fitted for the propagations of nations'.[179] The expansion of the Benedictinism in northern Europe of the ninth and tenth centuries brought a new intensity to this historical enterprise. The affiliation between Crown and convent now apparent in the kingdoms of the Franks and the Anglo-Saxons extended the range of monastic writers from *res gestae* to biography and even political polemic. At the same time, the triumph of secular letters in their schools only served to strengthen their attachment to classical models. It was at the foremost of these schools – Fulda, Winchester – that there emerged the greatest energy for historical writing. Annals of the recent past were initiated at Fulda before 800 and were maintained to the end of the ninth century.[180] Einhard (d. 830), an early product of the school and subsequently founder abbot of Muhlsheim, composed the most significant history (monastic or secular) of this period, a *Vita Caroli magni* which owed much to Suetonius's *De vita Caesarum* in structure and style.[181] The historical impulses in Anglo-Saxon houses were expressed in the same high style but generally in the hagiographical genre. When Wulfstan of Winchester (*fl. 996*) produced a valuable account of his mentor, Bishop Æthelwold, it was presented in the form of a devotional *vita*.[182] The annalistic tradition originated outside the monasteries of the English reform but Abingdon and Canterbury (Christ Church, St Augustine's) certainly contributed to its later development and dissemination.[183]

It was not the process of monastic reform but the political transformations of the eleventh and twelfth centuries that saw the peak of this activity in the northern monasteries. The triumph of ducal Normandy, in which Benedictines had a material share, stimulated a return to the grander narratives of the distant past. The *Gesta Normannorum ducum*, begun by William, monk of Jumièges (d. *c.* 1090), and continued by brethren both of Bec and Saint-Evroul, recalled the scope and contemporary political

---

[178] Bede, *Historia*, v. 23, pp. 560–1.
[179] Paul, *Historia langobardorum*, I. 1: ed. Bethmann and Waitz, pp. 47–8.
[180] *Annales Fuldenses sive annales regni Francorum orientalis*, ed. G. H. Pertzii and F. Kurze, MGH (1891). See also T. Reuter, *The Annals of Fulda* (Manchester, 1992).
[181] Einhard, *Vita Karoli Magni*, ed. C. P. González (Hildesheim, 1998).
[182] Æthelwold is one of the 'many apostolic teachers' to have followed Christ: *Wulfstan*, pp. 2–3.
[183] Lapidge, *Anglo-Latin Literature*, p. 53; Gransden, *Historical Writing in England*, i. 39–41.

commentary of the early classics.[184] Their English counterparts responded to the experience of conquest and colonisation with equally ambitious narratives which aimed to conserve their independent past and bind it to their present predicament. This was fully realised in the *Gesta regum Anglorum* of William of Malmesbury, in style and documentary substance perhaps the greatest of all medieval monastic histories, but there was also now a flow of narratives from other Benedictine houses, Peterborough, Winchester, Worcester, where the juxtaposition between English and Norman custom was felt most acutely.[185] The gathering storm over empire and the Gregorian papacy equally engaged the Black Monks of mainland Europe. The epic character of these conflicts encouraged them to explore a larger canvas and a new 'universal' history was pioneered at a number of houses. A universal chronicle which culminated in the confrontation between Gregory VII and Henry IV was begun at Reichenau by Hermann 'Contractus' (d. 1054) and continued by Berthold (d. 1088).[186] The Irishman Marianus Scotus (d. 1083) completed his own universal history at Fulda.[187] Another narrative, the *Chronographia*, incorporating biographies of the first Frankish kings, was compiled at Gembloux by Sigebert (d. 1112); comparable chronicles were also completed at Bamberg (by Frutolf) and Flavigny (by the monk Hugh).[188] The voluminous *Historia* of Orderic Vitalis (d. *c.* 1142), monk of Saint-Evroul, was likewise a universal history, which began with the biblical narrative.[189]

The (re-)foundations that followed these political transformations also fuelled a new trend in insular history. The reformed and restored houses of England and Normandy necessarily sought to unite the documentary traces of the distant past with the now rich portfolio of privileges and properties that underpinned their present status. The rapid expansion of churches and convents also encouraged them to reassert the dignity and priority of their patronal saints and shrines. These imperatives were neatly reflected in the title of the treatise on the new Benedictine monastery of Durham ascribed to the monk, Symeon (d. 1128), *Libellus de exordio atque procursu istius hoc est Dunhelmensis ecclesie*, an essay in its *origin* and

---

[184] William of Jumièges, *Gesta Normannorum ducum of William of Jumièges, Orderic Vitalis and Robert of Torigini*, ed. and trans. E. M. C. van Houts, Oxford Medieval Texts, 2 vols. (Oxford, 1992–5); Gransden, *Historical Writing in England*, i. 94–7 at 95–6.

[185] *GR*. See also Gransden, *Historical Writing in England*, i. 142–6, 252–3, 272–83, 301, 307, 333, 405; Thomson, *William of Malmesbury*, pp. 159–60.

[186] *Eleventh-Century Germany: The Swabian Chronicles*, ed. I. S. Robinson, Manchester Medieval Sources (Manchester, 2008).

[187] Gransden, *Historical Writing in England*, i. 145.

[188] P. Classen, 'Res gestae, Universal History, Apocalypse: Visions of Past and Future', in *Renaissance and Renewal in the Twelfth Century*, ed. Benson *et al.*, pp. 387–420 at 399–400; *Chronicle of Hugh of Flavigny*, ed. Healy, pp. 63–88; P. Magdalino, *The Perception of the Past in Twelfth-Century Europe* (London, 1992), p. 33.

[189] Chibnall, *World of Orderic Vitalis*, pp. 170–7.

progress.[190] Durham could claim a complex prehistory, but histories were also composed to commemorate *ab initio* foundations. The author of the *Liber de fundacione* of Walden Abbey, compiled *c.* 1203, offered not only an account of the foundation itself but more especially a working record of the monastery's first endowment, in effect a narrative cartulary.[191] The origins of saints' cults and shrines were elaborated in the same way. The monks of the refounded St Albans Abbey embarked on a systematic re-examination of their patronal saint which extended to the discovery of a co-martyr, Amphibel.[192] As a work of contemporary history, the *Libellus alter de consecratione ecclesiae sancti Dionysii* of Abbot Suger of Saint-Denis served not only to document his own devotion to his church but also to defend the claims of its cult.[193]

After this period of rapid expansion, however, the active historical impulse was confined increasingly to a hierarchy of houses, particularly those that retained a pre-eminence in political or public life. Among the English Benedictines, it was the monks of St Albans Abbey that were most prolific. Matthew Paris (d. 1259) compiled not only a national narrative, the *Chronica maiora*, but also a complete history of his house, the *Gesta abbatum*; both works were continued by a succession of contributors to the beginning of the fifteenth century.[194] The monks of Saint-Denis, like St Albans the custodians of a national shrine, also continued to compile national narratives in Latin and, from the 1270s, the French vernacular, under the general heading of *Grandes chroniques de France*.[195] It was once believed these histories were in some way officially sanctioned, if not by the Crown, then certainly by the order or convent themselves. There was some degree of co-ordination at Saint-Denis where the office of historiographer appears to have been held in more than one generation and where the Latin chronicles were systematically translated for the *Grandes chroniques*. In England the circumstances were considerably more *ad hoc*. Here the chroniclers appear to have acted on their own initiative, although they were regarded, and treated to some extent, as the representatives of their house and order by ecclesiastical and secular authorities. The chroniclers of St Albans, and also Chester and Glastonbury, were called upon sporadically

[190] Symeon of Durham, *Libellus de exordio atque procursu istius, hoc est Dunhelmensis ecclesiae*, ed. D. W. Rollason, Oxford Medieval Texts (Oxford, 2000).
[191] *Walden*, pp. 5–10.
[192] McLeod, 'Alban and Amphibel', 408.
[193] *Abbot Suger on the Abbey Church of St Denis and its Arts Treasures*, ed. and trans. E. Panofsky, 2nd edn (Princeton, 1979), pp. 82–121.
[194] For Matthew, see Vaughan, *Matthew Paris*; Gransden, *Historical Writing in England*, i. 356–79; Sharpe, *Latin Writers*, p. 373.
[195] *Les Grandes Chroniques de France*, Société de l'histoire de France, 10 vols. (Paris, 1920–53); *Les Grandes Chroniques de France: Chroniques de règnes de Jean II et de Charles V*, Société de l'histoire de France, 4 vols. (Paris, 1910–20); G. Spiegel, *The Chronicle Tradition of Saint-Denis: A Survey* (Brookline, MA, 1978).

in the thirteenth and fourteenth centuries for their wise counsel by bishops, and the Crown itself.[196]

It has long been assumed that historical writing, like many other literary traditions of the monasteries, fell into abeyance in the later Middle Ages. However, in England the compilation of chronicles revived in a handful of houses in the wake of the *Polychronicon* of the Chester Benedictine Ranulf Higden. Higden's text not only replaced earlier universal chronicles in the reading patterns of many monasteries but also provided them with a framework for compositions of their own. The St Albans author Thomas Walsingham presented his contemporary history as a *Polychronicon* continuation.[197] Anonymous continuations have also been connected with Glastonbury, Westminster and Worcester.[198] The interest in classical and literary scholarship in these same English convents also initiated a new era of experimentation in historical writing. Walsingham infused his *Chronica maiora* with the vocabulary, and imagery, of Ovid and Virgil. Thomas Elmham (d. after 1427), initially of St Augustine's Abbey, Canterbury, employed Horatian metres for his metrical *Vitae Henrici Quinti*.[199] The classicising tendency of these monastic historians was not dissimilar from – and perhaps to some extent anticipated – the techniques of second-generation humanists, such as Leonardo Bruni and Tito Livio Frulovisi, himself the author of a florid, fulsome life of Henry V.[200] Elmham himself was not only a self-conscious stylist, but, like the humanists, displayed a strong antiquarian sensibility. His *Speculum Augustinianum*, a study of his abbey's early history, showed a sharp awareness of chronology, and an almost philological precision in the transcription of sources, which he was at pains to reproduce in script appropriate to their age and origin.[201] A comparable antiquarianism was evinced by John Washington (Wessington), prior of Durham, who composed a sequence of forty-seven tracts on the early history of his house.[202]

The sectarian struggles of this post-Black Death period also brought a new partisan tone to Benedictine history, at least among the English congregation. The polemics of Archbishop Richard Fitzralph of Armagh (d. 1360) had provoked the mendicants to record their past achievements. John Wyclif renewed this critique and condemned the monastic orders as well as their mendicant colleagues. The response of the Black Monks, which

---

[196] Gransden, *Historical Writing in England*, i. 356–79.

[197] For the development and descent of Walsingham's chronicle, see ibid., ii. 124.

[198] J. Taylor, 'The Development of the *Polychronicon* Continuation', *EHR* 76 (1961), 20–36; Gransden, *Historical Writing in England*, ii. 43–57, 124, 157.

[199] Clark, *Monastic Renaissance*, pp. 163–208; Rigg, *Anglo-Latin Literature*, pp. 299–201; Sharpe, *Latin Writers*, pp. 653–4.

[200] Weiss, *Humanism in England*, pp. 41–8 at 45&n. For Frulovisi, see Grandsen, *Historical Writing in England*, ii. 210–13; Sharpe, *Latin Writers*, p. 698.

[201] Gransden, *Historical Writing in England*, ii. 353–4.

[202] For Washington see Sharpe, *Latin Writers*, pp. 342–3; Dobson, *Durham Priory*, pp. 378–86.

has remained largely unregarded by modern historians, was to compile a succession of short tracts, some of them little more than time-lines, which served, cumulatively, to underline the intellectual, social and spiritual significance of the order.[203] These short works were not simply an extension of the insular historical tradition since they carried with them a sense of corporate identity, of the *ordinis nigrorum monachorum*, not seen in earlier domestic chronicles, and also offered an explicit challenge to their critics, as one tract expressed it, 'the detractors and defilers of the present time'.[204] These works are significant not only because they reflect the engagement of at least some Benedictines with contemporary ecclesiological debates, but also because they reveal something of a new approach to the history of the order and of their own houses in England. A number of the tracts begin with an exploration of the biblical origins of Benedictine monasticism, one which tends to nominate both Old Testament prophets and New Testament evangelists as proto-Benedictines; interestingly, the reflection on biblical history has at least one parallel among Continental Benedictines: in about 1432 Jean Stavelot of Liège compiled an account surviving in his own autograph codex, which he illustrated with a genealogical tree tracing the growth of Benedictine monasticism from its Old Testament roots.[205] They also contain a common narrative of the coming of monasticism to England, which names century King Lucius as the legendary father, and founder of the first English abbeys. In the pre-Reformation period these tracts attracted the attention of secular antiquarians, such as William Worcester, who cited them freely in his commonplace book. Ironically, they were also consulted by the compilers of the *Collectanea satis copisoa* to support King Henry's claim to the headship of the church.[206]

Academia

For much of the medieval period the culture of the Benedictines was fashioned by the patterns of reading and writing established in their earliest centuries. Yet in the later Middle Ages it has often been suggested the Black Monks fell under the spell of academia. Jean Leclercq characterised this period, pessimistically, as the age of the *'moine universitaire'* and he stopped

---

[203] Pantin, 'Some Medieval English Treatises'; Gransden, *Historical Writing in England*, ii. 343, 397–401.
[204] BL, Cotton MS Claudius E IV, fo. 333r.
[205] For English examples that explore the Biblical foundations of the Benedictine profession, see Pantin, 'Some Medieval English Treatises'; BL, MS Arundel 11, fos. 107r–113v at 107r (St Albans); BL, Cotton MS Claudius A XII, fos. 142r–45r, printed in *Memorials of St Edmund's Abbey*, ed. Arnold, iii. 145–51 (Bury). For Jean de Stavelot, see Chantilly, MS XIX B1, the genealogical tree at fo. 126r. See also Donadieu-Rigaut, *Penser en image les ordres religeuses*, pp. 241–55. See jacket illustration.
[206] For Worcester's commonplace book see *Itineraries, by William Worcestre, Edited from the Unique MS Corpus Christi College, 210, and Translated*, J. H. Harvey, Oxford Medieval Texts (Oxford, 1969), e.g. pp. 42–7; Gransden, *Historical Writing*, ii. 327–41 at 334. The *Collectanea* is now BL, Cotton MS Cleopatra E VI, fos. 16–139.

his own survey of pure, monastic culture, significantly short of 1300.[207] Of course, the intellectual currents of the secular schools had found their way into the cloister long before the thirteenth century and in the Gregorian period the masters and students of the greater monastic schools observed closely the controversies, and novel methodologies, of their secular counterparts. But it was the advent of the Benedictine *studia* at Paris, Oxford, and other northern universities in the century after 1215 that first exposed the order to the full range of academic studies. The number of student monks was small initially but their engagement with academic trends appears to have been extensive from the outset. Scarcely fifteen years after the foundation of Gloucester College, Oxford, a circle of students at Worcester Priory were copying and circulating the work of contemporary arts masters.[208] Moreover, as participation increased, many superiors were persuaded to recast the cloister curriculum to prepare their students for university and also to make proper provision for academic texts in the monastic library. Library catalogues from the fourteenth century point to a stocking-policy which privileged academic works above many more traditional genres.[209] Even so, it would be wrong to exaggerate the effects of these academic currents in European cloisters. In the majority of Benedictine monasteries university textbooks served only as a source of reference, although the occasions on which readers made recourse to them grew markedly, not only in the preparation of sermons, for example, but also in the tackling of administrative problems. It was only ever a handful of Black Monks that made an active contribution to academic culture, principally at Paris and Oxford. Their work is poorly preserved and often known only from the *reportationes* of other scholars. Nonetheless, at certain peaks of academic activity, such as the initial alarm over Wyclif, the final stages of the papal schism, and the first appearance of Lutheran apologists, their influence, both within and beyond the universities, far exceeded their modest numbers.

As with regulars, the Benedictines were barred from the university arts course and were obliged to make their own preparations for the higher faculties in their home communities. While the manuscript evidence suggests such preparations represented something of a rag-bag of approaches, it seems they presented monastic readers with a wide range of works in logic, and philosophy, both natural and metaphysical. The Worcester monks were perhaps the first in England to form a working collection of Aristotelian texts and commentaries but these works had become widely available to

---

[207] Leclercq, *Love of Learning*, p. 252.
[208] Thomson, 'Worcester Monks and Education'.
[209] *EBL*, B43, B68, pp. 220–32, 350–415; *AL*, pp. 211–15, 253–63, 307–17 (St Augustine's, Canterbury); *Catalogi veteres*, ed. Raine, pp. 46–79 at 68, 72–5, where staples of the academic syllabus, Aquinas, Henry of Ghent, Nicholaus de Gorron, Peter of Tarentaise appear as subheadings in the library catalogue.

Benedictines by the end of the fourteenth century.[210] The purpose of these texts was to provide student monks with the analytical tools for their projected studies in theology and canon law, and thus very few are known to have produced original scholarship of their own. A number of the anonymous cribs and guides to logic and elementary philosophy surviving in anthologies of this period may have originated in cloister schools.[211] The arts masters drawn into the order in fourteenth-century England – Richard of Wallingford, Roger Swineshead – continued to contribute to the disciplines which had formed them, but their work found little following among their brethren.[212]

Among the higher faculties, the university monks were encouraged to study not only in their natural territory of theology, but also in canon law. This reflected the importance increasingly attached to the canons in community life. The early reformers had called for their reading and exposition not only in the novices' *schola* but also in the daily chapter. The growing portfolio of spiritual properties held by the greater abbeys and priories made the mastery of the canons also a practical imperative. There is very little evidence of the texts that were read or the approaches adopted in this early period, although it seems studies were sufficiently advanced for some monks to make significant contributions to what was still a nascent discipline. At the opening of the eleventh century Abbot Olbert of Gembloux contributed to the *Collectarium canonum* of Burchard of Worms; two generations later Anselm of Lucca (d. 1086), a monk of Polirone Abbey (Mantua), completed a collection of canons which subsequently served as the basis of Gratian's celebrated *Decretum*.[213] In the monastic *studia* of Oxford, Paris and the other northern schools, however, only a minority of monks appear to have studied the canons, at least to the level appropriate for a degree. The largest number of law students is recorded in England, at Oxford, although even here there were houses that refused to allow their monks to divert their attention from theology. These English Benedictine canonists attracted some attention in academic circles in the decades either side of the Black Death, attested by an anthology of their doctoral exercises.[214] A handful of French monks were also known for their legal expertise in

---

[210] Thomson, 'Worcester Monks and Education'.

[211] For example, the anonymous commentary to Petrus de Isolella's *Summa grammaticae* which includes such observation as 'Philosophia genus est ceterarum disciplinarum': Worcester Cathedral Chapter Library, MS F 123, fo. 1r. See also Thomson, *Descriptive Catalogue*, p. 84.

[212] Clark, *Monastic Renaissance*, pp. 148–9 at 149.

[213] For these early canonists, see A. Boutemy, 'Un grand abbé du XIe siècle: Olbert de Gembloux', *Annales de la Société archéologique de Namur*, 41 (1934), 43–85; K. G. Cushing, *Papacy and Law in the Gregorian Revolution: the Canonistic Work of Anselm of Lucca* (Oxford, 1998), pp. 47–8 & n. 27. See also C. Rolker, *Canon Law and the Letters of Ivo of Chartres* (Cambridge, 2010), pp. 50–88.

[214] For example, BL, Royal MS 9 E VIII, which references monks of Battle, St Augustine's, Canterbury, and, perhaps, St Albans at fos. 71, 95, 109. See also BL, Royal MS 6 E VI–VII, English codices compiled by a monk, Jacobus, and containing, among other extracts, a copy of the Benedictine constitutions *Summi magistri* (1336).

the first half of the fourteenth century. Guillaume de Grimoard (d. 1370), monk of Marseilles, held the chair of canon law at Montpellier before his election as Pope Urban V.[215] The academic curriculum concentrated on the key collections of canons, the decretals of Gregory IX, the Sext, and the Clementine Constitutions, and their commentators, and to this the monastic canonists made no original contribution. Yet it appears they did develop new approaches in the narrower study of canons that addressed the monastic orders directly. An anthology of these canons, known by its *incipit* as *Abbas vel prior*, appears to have originated among the English Benedictines at the beginning of the fourteenth century, possibly at Durham Priory.[216] Notwithstanding their modest numbers, these monastic canonists transformed the legal book collections of many Benedictine monasteries. At St Albans Abbey, there emerged an exceptional group of fourteenth-century *decretalia*, some of which were copied and illustrated in Italy.[217] These collections were prized by the monks but they do not seem to have stimulated legal studies in the community at large. The only *legalia* that passed under the eyes of cloister monks in the later period were reminders of the canons – the legatine constitutions of Ottobuono, the papal canons *Summi magistri* – which directly determined their own pattern of life.[218]

It was in the field of theology that academic authorities, and methodologies, appeared to flood Benedictine cloisters in the later Middle Ages. The greater abbeys and priories, which maintained, and sometimes exceeded, the prescribed ratio (1:20) of monk students amassed comprehensive collections of academic theology. The glossed scriptures that had filled their book cupboards since early times were substituted with the postils that were the staple of the schools. It appears that the English Benedictines pioneered contemporary postillators before they were staples of the academic community. The earliest manuscript editions of Nicholas of Lyra's postils are recorded not at Oxford or Cambridge, as might be expected, but at Durham Priory.[219] In the same way, the principal works of Aquinas, Scotus and other *doctores perspicuus*, displaced the old diversity of monastic, patristic and pre-scholastic theologians. The reorganisation of books at Durham Priory (again) at the end of fourteenth century might be taken as typical; works of patristic and early medieval theology were transferred to the novices' collection, and academic textbooks

[215] L. Vones, *Urban V: 1362–1370: Kirchenreform zwischen Kardinalkollegium, Kurie und Klientel* (Stuttgart, 1998).
[216] For a Durham copy of the text see Cambridge, Jesus College, MA 61, fos. 48r–69v. See also Dobson, *Durham Priory*, p. 381. See also L. E. Boyle, 'The *Oculus sacerdotis* and some other works of William of Pagula', *TRHS* 5th Series 5 (1955), 81–110.
[217] Clark, *Monastic Renaissance*, p. 87.
[218] *EBL*, B43 (Glastonbury), B68 (Ramsey), pp. 220–32, 350–415.
[219] Durham Cathedral Chapter Library, MSS A.I. 3–5. See also Piper, 'The Monks of Durham and the Study of Scripture', 86–103.

replaced them in the cloister cupboards accessed by the seniors in study periods.[220] Superiors also now seized on these authorities as symbols of their commitment to learning. After his election to a second term, Abbot John Wheathampstead of St Albans presented his brethren with a *de luxe* four-volume manuscript of Lyra.[221]

There is no doubt of the traffic in texts but it remains difficult to document in any detail the work of the monks who passed through the theology faculties. The university registers show that the majority did meet the requirements of their degrees, but there is scarcely any trace of their academic exercises in any surviving manuscripts. A collection of *lecturae* and *reportationes* compiled at Paris and Oxford by John of St Germans, a monk of Worcester between *c.* 1290 and *c.* 1310 may include the work not only of John but of a number of other Black Monks present alongside him in both theology faculties.[222] Another anthology dating from the third quarter of the fourteenth century contains *reportationes* of disputations at Oxford to which several Benedictine scholar monks contributed, among them men of Bury St Edmunds, St Albans and Worcester.[223] An isolated manuscript from the mid-fifteenth century offers a different impression of the scholar monk's position: a collection of notes and summary studies of lectures in the theology faculty compiled *c.* 1432–50 by John Lawerne of Worcester Priory (again) is interspersed with drafts of letters on mundane matters of business with his home community.[224] Many scholar monks were denied a period of regency due to their conventual responsibilities, which may account for the absence of Benedictine commentaries on the Sentences of Peter Lombard. The fourteenth-century commentators Adam Wodeham and Gregory of Rimini were aware of the Sentence commentaries of a Joannes Normannus, perhaps a monk of the Norman abbey of Marmoutiers, and two Englishmen, one identified only as 'Monachus', the other named as (John) Uthred of Boldon; none of these works is known to survive. A third Englishman, 'Wicerius', may be the Glastonbury monk Swineshead, at Oxford in the second quarter of the century.[225]

The scant traces of their studies in the schools obscure to some extent the significant contributions of Benedictine theologians to the theological controversies of the period. There are some signs of their interest in

---

[220] *Catalogi veteres*, ed. Raine, pp. 85–116 at 94–7, 100–1; Piper, 'Monks of Durham and the Study of Scripture'.

[221] Cambridge University Library, MS Dd.7.7–10.

[222] Worcester Cathedral Chapter Library, MS Q99; Thomson, *Descriptive Catalogue*, pp. 183–4.

[223] Worcester Cathedral Chapter Library MS F 65. See S. L. Forte, 'Some Oxford Schoolmen of the Middle of the Fourteenth Century' (BLitt diss., Oxford, 1947).

[224] Oxford, Bodleian Library, MS Bodley 692, fos. 30v–31r, 65r, 116r.

[225] W. J. Courtenay, *Adam Wodeham: An Introduction to his Life and Writings* (Leiden, 1978), pp. 92–4. For Joannes Normannus, see also T. Sullivan, *Benedictine Monks at the University of Paris, AD 1229–1500: A Biographical Register*, Education and Society in the Middle Ages and Renaissance 4 (Leiden, 1995), p. 256.

the closing stages of the mendicant controversies aroused in the mid-thirteenth century but reawakened in the 1350s by Archbishop Fitzralph of Armagh. When John Wyclif emerged as controversialist in the mid-1370s the Black Monks were the first, or among the first, to raise the alarm and to respond to him in the schools. It would appear that the danger of Wyclif's doctrine was a topic for discussion between Oxford Benedictines before his name was well known in wider clerical circles. At the Curia, the Benedictine Cardinal Adam Easton had heard enough from his English correspondents to request copies of his offending works.[226] The record of Oxford disputations is muddled, but Wyclif himself spoke of his assault at the hands of a 'black dog' ('canis niger'); John Wellys and Nicholas Radcliff, masters of the theology, respectively from Ramsey and St Albans, are known to have disputed with him and a number of their colleagues also claimed the distinction. Radcliff was the author of several *quaestiones* which elaborated the orthodox view of topics – devotion to images, religious vows – tackled by Wyclif, and these lively tracts perhaps carry more than a hint of his original *disputatio*.[227] In the aftermath of the papal condemnation (1378), the scholarship of these Benedictine theologians was acknowledged by the authorities and a selection was invited to serve at the councils of Blackfriars (1382) and Stamford (1392). Radcliff's home community, St Albans, was also assigned for the re-education of Oxford masters that abjured Wyclif's heresies.[228] Like many in the theology faculties, at the turn of the fourteenth century the Benedictines also applied their academic training to the problem of the papal schism. Nicholas Radcliff examined the various routes to a resolution in perhaps the last of his *quaestiones*.[229] Another summary of the *viae solutionis, De modis uniendi ac reformandi ecclesiam* (sometimes attributed to Dietrich of Niem), was offered by the Iberian Benedictine Andreas of Randuf at Bologna.[230] Theologians at Paris were more openly partisan and added their academic authority to the Avignon cause although it would appear no monastic scholar was particularly prominent.[231] The order's theologians not only fuelled the debate over the schism but also actively participated in the deliberations, at Pisa (1409), Constance (1414–17) and Basel (1430/1–1438),

[226] *Chapters*, ed. Pantin, iii. 76–7.
[227] *Fasciculi zizaniorum magistri Johannis Wyclif cum tritico Ascribed to Thomas Netter of Walden provincial of the Carmelite order in England and confessor to King Henry the Fifth*, ed. W. W. Shirley, RS 5 (London, 1858), p. 239; A. Hudson, *The Premature Reformation: Wycliffite Texts and Lollard History* (Oxford, 1988), pp. 58, 93, 95, 98. For Radcliff and Wellys, see also Emden, *BRUO*, iii. 1539, 2008; Sharpe, *Latin Writers*, pp. 343, 391–2.
[228] John Aston: *Fasciculi zizaniorum*, ed. Shirley, p. 332; Walsingham, *Historia Anglicana*, ed. Riley, ii. 65.
[229] BL, Royal MS 6 D X, fos. 277v–283r.
[230] Andreas of Randuf, *De modo uniendi*: Johannes Gerson, *Opera*, 5 vols., ed. L. Du Pin (Antwerp, 1706), ii. 161(163)–200.
[231] R. N. Swanson, *Universities, Academics and the Great Schism*, Cambridge Studies in Medieval Life and Thought 12 (Cambridge, 1979), pp. 45–7, 64–6, 162–8. See also the 'personalities' listed at 209–15.

where even English Benedictines appear to have been in attendance for a time.[232]

Although the Benedictines remained a major presence in the theology faculties in the century after 1450, they were markedly less prominent in later controversies. This should not be interpreted as a sign of any qualitative decline in the scholars passing through their *studia* in the shadow of the Reformation but rather of a shift in the focus of current clerical (and extra-clerical) debates. Perhaps there was no English Benedictine master to challenge Bishop Reginald Pecock in 1457 because his principal target was the ministry of the secular clergy.[233] Only after Luther – for many Benedictines, a Wyclif *alter* – began his assault on the entire edifice of Holy Church were they again persuaded to engage in public debates. The English Black Monks acted early and energetically; Luther's works were under scrutiny by Ely monk-scholars by 1519, and by 1521 the order had selected one of its number to join a university commission charged with the refutation of his false doctrines.[234] As late as 1528 King Henry himself turned to the veteran theologian Abbot Richard Kidderminster of Winchcombe, for his own assessment of Lutheran error (the work is not known to survive).[235]

The theology faculties of the universities were communities not only of scholars but also of serving members of the secular church. The entry of the monks into this environment heightened their awareness of pastoral theology. There had been a growing emphasis on these texts and themes in monastic education and formation following the Fourth Lateran Council, but it was the increased interaction between the cloister and the schools that exposed the later medieval Benedictines to the full range of recent work in the field. The interests, indeed, in the face of heresy and schism, and the plight of the parochial clergy, were impressed upon university monks and it appears they returned to their home communities armed with many of their most popular manuals – William of Paull's *Oculus sacerdotis*, John of Frieburg's *Summa confessorum* – and the values that underpinned them.[236] Their awareness of these authorities is reflected in the small number of graduate sermons that survive from the century after 1350, but it seems it was only in mainland Europe that Benedictine scholars made significant contributions to the genre. Here, particularly in the imperial territories, determined diocesans pursued programmes of reform and the principal

[232] For the Benedictine contribution to the councils, see Stump, *Reforms of the Council of Constance*; A. Breck, 'The Leadership of the English Delegation at Constance', *University of Colorado Studies* 1 (1941), 289–99.

[233] For Pecock see D. B. Foss, '"Overmuch blaming of the clergy's wealth": Peacock's Exculpation of Ecclesiastical Endowment', in *The Church and Wealth*, ed. W. J. Sheils and D. Wood, Studies in Church History 24 (1987), pp. 155–60.

[234] Greatrex, *BRECP*, pp. 438–9.

[235] *RO*, iii. 91–5 at 94. See also pp. 322.

[236] For example, *EBL*, B30. 12, 99, 107 (Evesham), B87. 12, 51, 61(St Albans), pp. 140, 149, 557, 562–3.

monasteries, and their scholars, played a prominent role. Abbot Martin von Senging of the Vienna Schottenkloster, a Black Monk of Hungarian extraction (d. 1464×1470), compiled a reflective account (*Senatorium*) of the visitations he had undertaken at the instigation of Cardinal Archbishop Nicholas of Cusa (d. 1450×1451).[237]

Whether the theologies of the schools were actively studied in the cloister by a cross-section of monks remains difficult to assess across all regions of Benedictine Europe. The English evidence, most recently, and thoroughly, analysed, would suggest original scholarship resided, almost exclusively, with the coteries of university monks themselves. Moreover, it would appear their most significant compilations and compositions were made while still in academia. The exceptional collection of contemporary Sentence commentaries compiled by Nicholas Faux of Glastonbury in the second quarter of the fifteenth century may be typical: the book was made and used at Oxford by Faux and his brethren and appears never to have seen Glastonbury.[238] Among the books that were already at home we tend to see only provisional notes and studies, such as the tabula to Aquinas' *Summa* constructed by the Westminster student William Sudbury, apparently in about 1375.[239] Cloister monks continued to choose theology in their seasonal *sors*, but these were almost always the works of the traditional monastic doctors.[240]

Material Culture

The learned culture of the Benedictine monastery was complemented by a variety of practical arts and crafts that flourished both within the monastic enclosure and in the precincts beyond. As Benedict knew it, the *cenobium* was not a community but a colony that attracted a host of followers, of whom a number were artisans (*artifices*) occupied with craftwork 'practise[d] with all humility ... to confer benefit upon the monastery' ('cum omni humilitate faciant ipsas artes. Quod si aliquis ex eis extollitur pro scientia artis suae, eo quod videatur aliquid conferre monasterio': *RB*, lvii), and also 'to be sold', although not for profit ('si quid vero ex operibus artificum venumdandum est, videant ipsi per quorum manus transigenda sint ne aliquam fraudem praesumant': *RB*, lvii). As the order expanded in subsequent centuries, craftwork came to be seen not only as a means of sustaining the monastic community in its material needs but also of enhancing

---

[237] G. G. Coulton, *Five Centuries of Religion*, IV. *The Last Days of Medieval Monachism* (Cambridge, 1950), pp. 210–12.

[238] Oxford, Oriel College, MS 15; J. Catto, 'Some English Manuscripts of Wyclif's Latin Works', in *From Ockham to Wyclif*, Studies in Church History, Subsidia 5 (Oxford, 1987), pp. 353–9.

[239] BL, Royal MS 9 F XIV, fos. 1r–399r. See also Sharpe, *Latin Writers*, p. 811.

[240] For example, *EBL*, B87. 41, 59b, pp. 560, 563 (St Albans), B100.18, 51, pp. 600, 602 (Thorney); R. Sharpe, 'Monastic Reading at Thorney Abbey, 1323–47', *Traditio* 60 (2005), 243–78.

its spiritual status. Benedictine superiors of the eleventh and twelfth centuries presided as proudly over their artisanal workshops as they did over their claustral schools and their masters. In this period, female houses (or the female portion of double foundations) attracted equal renown for their art and craft.[241] Their interest in material culture intensified in the later Middle Ages as it attracted a new currency among leading clerical and lay magnates.

For much of the medieval period there were aspects of this craftwork practised by the monks themselves. The *opus manuum* outlined in the *RB* focused primarily on the physical labour of farm and field but over time, and certainly before the Benedictine expansion of AD 800–1000, a broader interpretation was admitted that allowed for the cultivation of certain craft skills. The change in attitude could be regarded as pragmatic – many early monasteries were remote from major settlements – but it might also be connected to contemporary exegetical trends and the growing emphasis on the artistry of the creator-God. Certainly, from the Carolingian period onwards, monastic writers openly acknowledged that Lord's service might be fulfilled in the workshop just as it was in the quire or the schoolroom.[242] The sanction was never made explicit in codes and customaries until the later Middle Ages, when the statutes of the English Benedictine chapters (1277, 1343) prescribed the scribal arts as a suitable occupation for any ordinary cloister monk.[243] Nonetheless, it appears to have been common for men to be professed and promoted on account of their artistry; the office of sacrist, for example, was frequently held by a monk possessing practical skills. The resurgence of learning in the fourteenth century, following the advent of the university *studia*, appears also to have revived the tradition of the monastic workshop. The influence of Italian humanism heightened the artistic sensibilities of both southern and northern Benedictines in the post-Black Death period and broadened their horizons to embrace domestic architecture, portraiture and in time the new technology of printing. The role of the Black Monks in the emergence of Renaissance culture should not be underestimated.

Books

The earliest and most enduring craftwork of the Benedictine cloister was the making of books. Benedict expected each monastery to maintain a book collection, called *bibliotheca* in the *RB*, glossed by Smaragdus (d. 868) as 'cellula ubi libri reconduntur'.[244] The first books originated outside the monastery: the quasi-Benedictine houses of seventh-century

---

[241] Beach, *Women as Scribes*, pp. 45–104. See also Power, *Medieval English Nunneries*, pp. 255–8.
[242] See above, pp. 111–12.
[243] *Chapters*, ed. Pantin, i. 74; ii. 50–1 at 51.
[244] *Smaragdi abbatis expositio*, ed. Spanngel and Engelbert, p. 273.

Northumbria were equipped with codices that came from Rome, primarily, although perhaps also from clerical centres in France.[245] Yet within a generation, there was a writing room (scriptorium) established in many of the greater monasteries. The primary impulse was a practical one, since the *opus Dei* depended on the provision of books, of liturgy, scripture and patristics. As attitudes to the *opus manuum* shifted and sharpened, the making of books also came to be regarded as one practical art – perhaps the only one – in which the Lord would always be served. It was a view readily articulated, and illustrated, by early Benedictine writers: the first full leaf (fo. 1r) of the so-called Dunstan classbook (Oxford, Bodleian Library, MS Auct. F.4.32) features a portrait of the saint kneeling at the feet of Christ; this conception of monastic *ars scribendi* was constantly reiterated in subsequent centuries and became the focus of much nostalgia among humanist monks of the fifteenth century. The schools of the Carolingian and Anglo-Saxon reform stimulated a surge in Benedictine book production and a handful of houses – Corbie, Saint-Gall, Winchester – hosted the most influential scriptoria in northern Europe.[246] The artistry of these scriptoria attracted secular patrons. Archbishop Egbert of Trier commissioned a richly illuminated gospel book from the brethren of Reichenau. The growth of the Gregorian period engendered another prolific phase of production as libraries were systematically stocked, in some cases for the very first time. The scriptoria of Benedictine Spain at the beginning of the twelfth century were among the most accomplished in the peninsula.[247] The demise of the cloister schools diminished the demand for texts and at many, perhaps the majority, of Benedictine houses, the production of books dwindled to the level of routine repairs and occasional one-off productions. The advent of academic studies necessarily revived more extensive schemes of copying in some of the greater houses committed to the university experiment.[248] The promotion of humanist values in houses of the reformed congregations likewise led to renewed programmes of book production at Bursfeld, where the 'Ceremonial' of 1463 called for a resumption of manufacture, and Padua.[249] Johann Gutenberg's concentration on the monasteries of the Mainz hinterland

[245] Lapidge, *Anglo-Saxon Library*, pp. 25–7, 33, 35.
[246] Ganz, *Corbie in the Carolingian Renaissance*, esp. pp. 121–58; B. von Scarpatetti, 'Das St Galler Scriptorium', in *Das Kloster St. Gallen im Mittelalter: Die kulturelle Blüte vom 8. bis zum 12. Jahrhundert*, ed. P. Ochsenbein (Stuttgart, 1999), pp. 31–67; D. H. Turner, *The Missal of the New Minster, Winchester*, HBS 93 (1962); S. Rankin, 'Making the Liturgy: Winchester Scribes and their Books', in *The Liturgy of the Late Anglo-Saxon Church*, ed. H. Gittos and M. Bradford Bedingfield, HBS Subsidia 5 (2005), pp. 29–52.
[247] Notably, at the abbey of Santo Domingo at Silos: M. C. Vivancos, 'El monasterio de Silos y su scriptorium', in *El scriptorium silence y los orígenes de la lengua castellana* (Burgos, 1995).
[248] For example, the English priories of Durham and Worcester: Thomson, 'Worcester Monks and Education'.
[249] C. J. Cyrus, *The Scribes for Women's Convents in Late Medieval Germany* (Toronto, 2009), p. 176&n; Collett, *Italian Benedictine Scholars*, pp. 28–9.

was not, as it has often been represented, a measure of his conservatism, but rather of his recognition of the dynamic heart of the regional market.[250]

The early codes are opaque on the organisation of book production in the monastery. Historians have always fondly imagined a scriptorium set at the heart of the conventual buildings, a scene of calm but committed manufacture, the serried scribes carefully contributing to a page, or phase, of the same codex. There is scarcely any early documentary evidence either to confirm or confound this impression. The first accounts of quasi- or fully Benedictine convents do not refer directly to the scriptorium, although their authors, such as Eddius Stephanus, were nonetheless conscious of the scribal activity that surrounded them.[251] It would appear a properly organised approach to book production was in place by *c.* 1100. The first, full customaries of the English Benedictines assign the repair or renewal of books to the precentor (also designated 'cantor'), also custodian of the conventual seal and master of the monks' choir and the choir books, the codices most likely to require his attention.[252] It is probable that the arrangement prevailed right across Europe. The customaries do not always name the scriptorium, but archaeological evidence confirms the creation of central chamber, located, like the warming room, chapter house and other communal spaces, adjacent to the cloister walk.[253] There are no detailed descriptions of such a writing room, but late inventories indicate that it was likely to be furnished with desks, presses and possibly chests and quantities of raw materials (parchment, and from *c.* 1350, paper) and tools. Customaries are unclear as to the rhythm of the writing room, whether its work (and workers) ran wholly in parallel to the monastic *horarium* or only in occasional periods outside it. The number and the quality of the books produced at the height of the Carolingian and Gregorian periods are indicative of highly professional, intense periods of copying. By contrast, the clumsy, crowded script and muddled *mise en page* of many later medieval monastic manuscripts suggests that writing was begun (and rarely completed) in moments snatched from other burdens. Nonetheless, in a number of late customaries, the scriptorium was transformed into a fully funded obedience of the monastery supported by conventual income.[254]

It is equally difficult to establish the precise contribution of the professed religious to the practical work of the writing room. The supervision of the scribes it seems was always a monastic responsibility; in many cases

---

[250] Davies, *Gutenberg Bible*, pp. 42–53. See, for example, R. Nolden, 'Reste einer verschollenen Klosterbibliothek: Zwei Inkunabeln aus dem Benedikterinnenkloster Walsdorf, *Gutenberg-Jahrbuch* 65 (1990), 75–8.

[251] *Wilfrid*, p. 37.

[252] For example, *Customary of Eynsham*, ed. Gransden, pp. 164–8.

[253] R. J. Cramp, 'Monastic Sites', in *The Archaeology of Anglo-Saxon England*, ed. Wilson, pp. 201–372 at 211.

[254] *GASA*, ii. 306.

it remained among the principal charges of the precentor, although in the years after 1350 some abbeys appear to have appointed a dedicated *scriptorarius.*[255] Whether supervision amounted to routine interventions at the parchment face, of course, is more difficult to establish; compositors' notes appear frequently in the margins of monastic manuscripts but there is nothing in the character of these scribbles to connect them unequivocally with the work of a monastic officer. Moreover, it is is far from clear how often the scribes themselves were recruited from the monastery. There has always been a tacit assumption that many of the earliest manuscripts were the work of monastic scribes. Early *vitae* encourage the impression that the monks of the eighth, ninth and tenth centuries were frequently accomplished and prolific copyists. Two of the three English reformers, Æthelwold and Dunstan, were remembered as accomplished scribes, and while it may be that every virtue, artistic as well as spiritual, was attributed to acknowledged monastic fathers, it was a skill also ascribed to many lesser brethren of the period.[256] There are a number of extant manuscripts that explicitly credit a monastic scribe in the colophon.[257] Yet there are almost as many whose colophons are ambivalent, naming a scribe without confirmation of their clerical status.[258] A re-examination of manuscripts connected Corbie revealed that some of the abbey's most significant codices were the work of professional, secular scribes; indeed, the correspondence between Corbie and other convents would indicate this great 'monastic' scriptorium served as a hub for hired hands.[259] It is possible that smaller monasteries engaged in only sporadic production were able to rely on their own professed scribes, but the larger scriptoria, whose artistry attracted the attention of royal and episcopal patrons, probably sought the assistance of professional copyists from an early stage.[260] The expansion and renewal of monastic book collections in the Gregorian period brought the work of the writing room to a wider range of Benedictine monasteries. The *ars scribendi* was now represented not only as an appropriate *opus* for the devout *professus* but also as a tool of conventual reform; nonetheless it is likely that scriptoria continued to be served by both monastic and professional copyists.[261] Contemporary accounts suggest the scribal arts were still the preserve of a minority in the

---

[255] Ibid.

[256] For Æthelwold, see *Wulfstan*, pp. 18–18, 54–5; *Bishop Æthelwold*, ed. Yorke, p. 10&n.

[257] For example, BL, MS Arundel 57, a Canterbury manuscript, which at the opening bears the inscription: 'Þis boc is dan Micheles of Northgate ywrite an Englis of his oÿene hand'.

[258] For example, at Mont Saint-Michel, the scribe Antonius: J. J. G. Alexander, *Norman Illumination at Mont St Michel, 966–1100* (Oxford, 1970), pp. 234–5.

[259] Ganz, *Corbie in the Carolingian Renaissance*, pp. 48–56 at 56.

[260] Ibid., pp. 48–56 at 56; Beach, *Women as Scribes*, pp. 32–64 (Wessobrun), 65–103 (Admont).

[261] R. M. Thomson, *Manuscripts from St Albans Abbey, 1066–1235*, 2 vols. (Cambridge, 1982), i. 2–43, where the acceleration of scribal activity between the first and third quarters of the twelfth century can be clearly evidenced; Beach, *Women as Scribes*, pp. 32–103; T. A. Heslop, 'The Production and Artistry of the Bury Bible', in *Bury St Edmunds: Medieval Art, Architecture, Archaeology and Economy*, ed. A. Gransden, BAA Conference Transactions 20 (Leeds, 1998), pp. 172–85.

convent; superiors who cultivated an elegant script were duly celebrated.[262] The candid colophon comment of the monk scribe of the Silos Apocalypse (*c.* 1100) would suggest the work of writing was not shared with many of his brethren:

> The work of writing makes one lose his sight, it hunches his back, it breaks ribs and bothers the stomach, it pains the kidneys and causes aches throughout the body. Therefore, you, the reader, turn the pages carefully and keep your fingers from the letters, because just as hail destroys the fields, the useless reader erases the text and destroys the book.[263]

The status of this cadre of monk scribes is not clearly defined. Like other craftsmen that practised in the precincts, there may have been professionals that later sought profession. It is also possible there were some schooled in the monastery itself, a task to which a semi-professional scriptorium would have been well suited. The distinctive scripts displayed in the manuscripts of major Benedictine monasteries – Corbie, Mont Saint-Michel, Canterbury, Durham, St Albans – between the tenth and the twelfth centuries are indicative at the very least of stability in the scriptorium, but might also suggest the scribes shared a common origin and training.[264] Customaries say nothing of the arrangements for scribes, but, like other specialists in the monastic community, their position perhaps attracted privileges, even exemption from a portion of the daily offices: the scribe Dietmut was accorded the status of *inclusus* within her convent at Wessobrun.[265]

The monasteries may have lost something of their status as sponsors of book production in the later Middle Ages, but probably a greater proportion of monks were now capable of producing a competent book hand. The parallel experiences of administrative office and academic study in the schools placed a new premium on writing skills. As early as 1277 there was an expectation, expressed in the canons of the English general chapter, that any monk might be able to occupy himself, during the prescribed reading time in the cloister, in writing and in other forms of

---

[262] Abbot Simon of St Albans (1167–83) was commemorated as a patron of scribes, who he maintained 'at his own expense', though evidence of his own scribal practice is lacking: Thomson, *Manuscripts from St Albans*, i. 52.

[263] C. R. Dodwell, *Painting in Europe, 800–1200* (Harmondsworth, 1971), p. 261; A. Boylan, *Manuscript Illumination a Santo Domingo de Silos, Tenth to Twelfth Centuries* (Pittsburgh, 1990); BL, Add. MS 11695.

[264] Ganz, *Corbie in the Carolingian Renaissance*, pp. 36–67; J. Châtillon, 'Notes sur quelques manuscrits dionysiens, érigéniens et victorins de l'abbaye du Mont Saint-Michel', in *Millenaire monastique du Mont-Saint-Michel*, 2: *Vie montoise et rayonnement intellectual*, ed. R. Foreville (Paris, 1967), pp. 313–20; Alexander, *Norman Illumination at Mont St Michel*, pp. 23–43. Alexander observes (p. 24) that 'scribal practice [at Mont Saint-Michel] progressed to great uniformity'; Thomson, *Manuscripts from St Albans*, i. 23–6. See also *Durham Cathedral Manuscripts to the End of the Twelfth Century*, ed. R. A. B. Mynors (Oxford, 1939).

[265] Beach, *Women as Scribes*, p. 35.

bookcraft.[266] As the pastedowns of later manuscripts attest, it seems there was scarcely a senior monk in the post-Black Death period unable to scribble at least a couplet in a legible, if highly cursive script; the hagiographers now remembered only superiors whose penwork was hopeless.[267] The scriptoria that survived, or revived, in the fourteenth and fifteenth centuries seem to have been served by a higher proportion of monastic scribes than in the more intense phases of production three centuries before. The monks of St Albans Abbey, whose twelfth-century books were, for the most part, the work of secular professionals, now turned out a series of densely copied codices at their own hands; there was also a return to copying at another early centre, the abbey of Corbie, led by Étienne de Conty.[268] It would appear the *ars scribendi* was still widely practised among Benedictine women of the period: Cyrus has identified fifty-one female scribes active in twenty-one houses of the order.[269] With more personal freedom than their predecessors, many monks of this period also wrote manuscripts for their own use outside the context of the conventual writing-room. These personal compilations provided for their scholarly and recreational reading, but also proved a popular devotional outlet. The writing of a psalter, or some other liturgical text, was an exercise undertaken by many senior, often office-holding Benedictines, conscious, presumably, of their own distance from traditional monastic occupations.[270] Abbot Johann Trittenheim's celebrated paean for the scribal art, *De laude scriptorium* (1492), was not, as it is often presented, a reiteration of the original Benedictine conception of bookcraft, but rather a reflection of the fond nostalgia for an imagined past self-consciously cultivated by some of the most educated monks of the pre-Reformation period.[271]

Throughout the medieval period there were as many, indeed perhaps rather more, monks that were adept in manuscript painting. It would appear many of the most accomplished painters of the Anglo-Saxon and Carolingian scriptoria were professed monks. In England Dunstan himself was remembered as an accomplished painter: 'Hic etiam ... artem scribendi ... pariterque pingendi diligenter excoluit.'[272] His co-reformer Æthelwold was said to have been the artist of the Winchester Psalter (BL, MS Harley 2904), although acclaim in the manual as well as the contemplative arts also conformed to a monastic ideal.[273] The artwork of the Benedictional of

---

[266] *Chapters*, ed. Pantin, i. 74.

[267] For example, the reputation of Abbot Thomas de la Mare of St Albans: *GASA*, iii. 410.

[268] Thomson, *Manuscripts from St Albans*, i. 20–43; R. H. and M. A. Rouse, *Manuscripts and their Makers: Commercial Book Producers in Medieval Paris, 1200–1500*, 2 vols. (London, 2000), pp. 61–2.

[269] Cyrus, *Scribes for Women's Convents*, pp. 217–20 at 216.

[270] *EBL*, B88. 37–42, pp. 570–1 (St Albans).

[271] Brann, *Abbot Trithemius*, pp. 149–74.

[272] *Vita Dunstani*, B, c. 12: *Memorials of St Dunstan*, ed. Stubbs, p. 20.

[273] For modern scepticism, see Smith, Fleming and Halpin, 'Court and Piety in Late Anglo-Saxon England', 573.

Æthelwold (*c.* 1000) has been attributed to the Winchester monk Godeman, who became Abbot of Thorney.[274] The artistry of the manuscripts copied at Corbie, Fulda and Reichenau in the same period may be attributable to accomplished monastic painters; indeed, there are stronger grounds for suspecting a monastic identity for the painters of these codices than (necessarily) for their scribes.[275] In the later Middle Ages the greater abbeys and priories looked to professional painters for their manuscripts, but professed members of the community continued to cultivate their artistic ability. Matthew Paris of St Albans Abbey (d. 1259) was perhaps the pre-eminent monastic artist of the post-Conquest period, a polymath who composed, copied and illustrated a series of hagiographies and histories.[276] Surviving manuscripts of the fourteenth and fifteenth centuries show there were some Benedictines still capable of such fine art: reformed under Abbot Henri Ade (1403–34), the abbey of Saint-Laurent de Liège fostered the art and scribal craft of Jean de Stavelot; the decorative scheme of a manuscript made at the Bavarian nunnery of Sankt Walburg is assumed to be the work of one of the sisters.[277]

The Black Monks came to book production when the codex was still in its infancy and their contribution, both as copyists, and as patrons of copyists, did much to shape its subsequent development. Their earliest extant manuscripts replicate Roman styles in *mise en page*, script, and decoration, and the transmission of these books throughout Europe served to preserve such Late Antique forms.[278] The monastic scriptoria of southern and central Europe also transmitted into the mainstream elements of the Byzantine aesthetic – higher and lower registers of script, elaborate borders to the writing space: the Codex Egberti (Trier, Staadtsbibliothek, 24), made at Benedictine Reichenau but commissioned by Archbishop Egbert reflects this fusion of eastern and western styles.[279] With the emergence of the monastic schools in the eighth and ninth centuries, their scriptoria turned from imitation to innovation. It is to the ninth-century copyists of Corbie that the minuscule script is commonly attributed.[280] The scriptoria of this period also settled on a pattern of *mise en page*, script and decorative style that became the standard for monastic books – indeed, for all scholarly and service books at least until the advent of the universities at the end of the

[274] An alternative suggestion is that Godeman was a monk of Ely: Lapidge, *Anglo-Latin Literature*, p. 124&n.

[275] Ganz, *Corbie in the Carolingian Renaissance*, pp. 36–67.

[276] Vaughan, *Matthew Paris*, pp. 205–34.

[277] For Jean de Stavelot see above, n. 205; K. L. Scott, *Later Gothic Manuscripts, 1390–1490*, 2 vols. (London, 1996), i. 26, 45; ii. 23, 57, 64; J. F. Hamburger, *Nuns as Artists: The Visual Culture of a Medieval Convent* (Berkeley, 1997), pp. 9–19.

[278] R. McKitterick, 'Script and Book Production', in *Carolingian Culture*, ed. McKitterick, pp. 221–42. See also Lapidge, *Anglo-Saxon Library*, pp. 33, 35.

[279] H. M. R. E. Mayr-Harting, *Ottonian Book Illumination: An Historical Study*, 2 vols., rev. edn (London, 1999), ii. 60–2, 70–81.

[280] Ganz, *Corbie in the Carolingan Renaissance*, pp. 48–56.

twelfth century.[281] The creative force was concentrated in the monasteries of northern and western France and the Rhineland, but English scriptoria also made a significant contribution to the development of vernacular scripts and to some decorative schemes – acanthus border decoration, the so-called 'Winchester style', the distinctive line drawing exemplified in the Utrecht Psalter – later adopted in France and the Low Countries.[282] The artistic ferment found in the monastic scriptoria of this period is another testament to the vitality of the order's regional networks, which nurtured a vigorous traffic in books. It should be noted that the influence of Benedictine bookcraft was not confined to books of high status. Their methods of maintaining administrative records, and the cartulary in particular, provided a model which many clerical institutions were persuaded to follow.[283]

It is generally assumed that the expansion of secular workshops at the universities, and, generally, in urban centres, and the growing influence of academic studies on the arrangement of texts robbed monastic books of much of their distinctive character in the later Middle Ages. Although latecomers to the academic community in institutional terms, it does appear that monastic compilers and copyists were quick to adopt many of the main *mise en page* innovations of the schoolbook.[284] The thematic index or tabula that became a standard feature of an academic reference work was widely adopted in monastic books of this period. Much of the other textual apparatus of the school textbook was imported into monastic books, such as running-heads, titles, annotated tables of contents and the schematic *accessus*.[285] The new formats of textbooks were emulated in many monastic scriptoria; in England at least, the soft-bound parchment wrapped single text *quaterni* which was the staple of the stationers' shops was widely emulated.[286] It would appear that *quaterni* were employed to provide multiple copies perhaps in the novices' *schola*, and perhaps also for the preparation of monks, and monastic singers, in the quire. Yet there were aspects of their book production where the Benedictines, like other regulars, still diverged from contemporary clerical practice. Their use of

---

[281] A. Derolez, *Palaeography of Gothic Manuscript Books: From the Twelfth to the Early Sixteenth Century* (Cambridge, 2003), pp. 49–55.

[282] *The Utrecht Psalter in Medieval Art: Picturing the Psalms of David*, ed. K. van der Horst, W. Noel and W. C. M. Wüstefeld (Utrecht, 1996). See also C. R. Dodwell, 'The Final Copy of the Utrecht Psalter and its relationship with the Utrecht and Eadwine Palters (Paris, BN lat. 8846, c. 1170–1190)', *Scriptorium* 44:1 (1990), 21–53.

[283] Clanchy, *From Memory to Written Record*, pp. 101–2, where Hemming, monk of Worcester, is presented as the progenitor of the genre.

[284] Piper, 'Libraries of the Monks of Durham'.

[285] See, for example, the books of Durham Priory, such as Durham Cathedral Chapter Library, MS B.IV.32, fos. 50r–114r, and MA B.IV.49, fos. 18v–24r. See also the books of Worcester Priory, many of which can be connected to named scholar monks, such as Worcester Cathedral Library, Q 13, probably made by the monk John Aston: Thomson, *Descriptive Catalogue*, pp. 127–8.

[286] *EBL*, B68. 593, p. 414, B87. 49, p. 561; *Dover*, BM1. 308, p. 131; *AL*, nos. 1470, 1473, 1475, pp. 367–8 (St Augustine's, Canterbury).

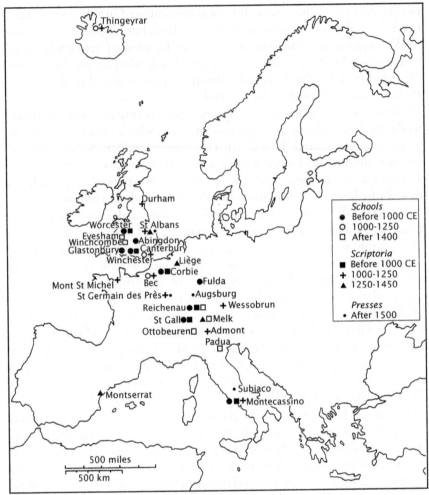

5 Benedictine schools, *scriptoria*, and presses

cursive scripts which by the end of the thirteenth century had become almost synonymous with the university textbook remained highly selective. Even in the fifteenth century, there remained a marked preference for the formal *textura* scripts of earlier centuries, especially for certain classes of book, such as a work of liturgy, a chronicle, etc.[287]

By contrast with the universities, notably in northern Europe, the Benedictines also demonstrated an early and enduring enthusiasm for the technology of printing. While much of Gutenberg's project remains conjectural, it would appear the Benedictine monasteries of the Mainz hinterland provided the bulk of the market, and perhaps the exemplar, for the

[287] Clark, *Monastic Renaissance*, pp. 97–120.

forty-two-line Bible of 1455.[288] Within a decade, the brethren of Benedict's Subiaco welcomed the German pioneer printers Arnold Pannartz and Conrad Sweynheim into their precincts, where they produced the first full text to be printed south of the Alps.[289] Probably these were acts of patronage, not partnership, but in the same decade a more direct involvement in the production process appears to have begun at the Melk affiliated abbey of SS Ulrich and Afra.[290] It is possible there was a degree of monastic involvement also in the near-contemporary press established at St Albans in 1479.[291] In the shadow of the Dissolution several English Benedictine abbeys showed an active interest in the press. At Tavistock, South Devon, printing equipment was acquired in the early 1520s and a translation of Boethius's *Consolatio* was produced, together the text of the statutes of the stannaries under the jurisdiction of the abbot and convent.[292] At Abingdon it appears a press was briefly established in the precincts to produce a print of the abbey breviary; at St Albans and St Augustine's, Canterbury, a precinct press also appeared after 1530, on which were produced not only conventional devotional and literary texts but also a controversial tract.[293]

Architecture

The monks also expressed their artistic sensibilities and craft skills in many other fields. It seems likely that there were some in every medieval generation that were architecturally adept, whether or not this was a natural aesthetic, or whether it was acquired through a working relationship with a professional architect or stonemason. Among the *miracula* attributed to Dunstan was the tale of his timely intervention at the building of the church at Glastonbury when a beam suspended by a rope snapped suddenly.[294] Such hands-on supervision of construction work was commonly claimed in chronicle narratives, and also represented in the illustrations that accompanied them.[295] There is very little evidence of Black Monks of any period who were competent in the finer points of building

[288] M. Davies, *The Gutenberg Bible* (London, 1996), pp. 42–53; A. Kapr, *Johann Gutenberg: The Man and his Invention*, trans. D. Martin (Aldershot, 1996), pp. 61–4, 182–3.

[289] For their work see E. Hall, *Sweynheym and Pannartz and the Origins of Printing in Italy: German Technology and Italian Humanism in Renaissance Rome* (McMinnville, OR, 1991).

[290] The press was established under Abbot Melchior von Stamhaim (d. 1474): 'The Ulrich and Afra Vincent of Beauvais', *The Library* 4th series 2 (1921), 115–16. For background, see Posset, *Renaissance Monks*, p. 135.

[291] J. G. Clark, 'Print and Pre-Reformation Religion: The Benedictines and Press, c. 1470–c. 1540', in *The Uses of Script and Print, 1300–1700*, ed. J. Crick and A. Walsham (Cambridge, 2004), pp. 77–92.

[292] Finberg, *Tavistock Abbey*, pp. 290–3.

[293] Clark, 'Print and Pre-Reformation Religion', 77–92.

[294] BL, Royal MS 10 E IV, fo. 246v.

[295] For example, a twelfth-century image of Cuthbert building his Farne hermitage, BL, Yates Thompson MS 26, fo. 39, and a fifteenth-century copy of Lydgate's Lives of Edmund and Fremund showing labourers and monks constructing the church of Bury St Edmunds: BL, MS Harley 2278, fo. 115v.

work, although it is possible that the brethren provided unskilled labour, particularly in the formative, foundation period. Nonetheless, it was not uncommon, in any period of the Middle Ages, for a monk to take a key role in the planning and supervision of a building project. Abbot Suger's vision for the church and shrine of Saint Denis was undoubtedly genuine, and certainly there were Benedictines before and after his day who shared his eye, if not his resources, or the number and quality of his craftsmen.[296] This sympathy for the structure and style of a building seems to have continued to have thrived in the later Middle Ages; indeed, even in the shadow of the sixteenth-century surrenders. There was perhaps more to this than merely a well-informed, well-connected patron. The work of Abbot William Middleton at Milton Abbey, Dorset (*c.* 1520), would surely suggest the presence of at least one member of the community, if not the abbot himself, who understood the principles of the perpendicular style they pioneered.[297]

Decorative Arts

It would appear a number of those who were painters were capable in a variety of media. There is no reason to assume that Dunstan's accomplishments in paint were confined to the scriptorium, nor those of other monks of his generation.[298] Three centuries later Matthew Paris may have applied his art to an (altar?) panel (at Faaberg) during his Scandinavian embassy.[299] There is no doubt that the illumination of a manuscript became a more specialised enterprise in the later Middle Ages, and even if they could count the requisite skill among the brethren, the majority of monasteries might prefer to commission itinerant professionals.[300] The painting of murals and other interior furnishings, however, may have accommodated an amateur spirit for rather longer, perhaps especially in the northern Europe unaffected by currents of the Renaissance. Perhaps there were Benedictines capable of producing panel, and perhaps wall, paintings at the beginning of the fifteenth century.[301]

[296] *Abbot Suger*, ed. Panofsky, pp. 1–37 at 26–9, 35–7.
[297] Luxford, *Art and Architecture*, p. 281. See also J. P. Traskey, *Milton Abbey: A Dorset Monastery in the Middle Ages* (Tisbury, 1978), pp. 149–59 at 150–5.
[298] For wall-paintings of this early period which may be the work of the monastic community, see *RO*, i. 296.
[299] Vaughan, *Matthew Paris*, pp. 205–7.
[300] J. J. G. Alexander, *Medieval Illuminators and their Methods of Work* (New Haven, 1992), pp. 26–34, 122–5.
[301] The fifteenth-century work of the Liègeois Jean de Stavelot and of the female artists of Bavaria examined by Jeffrey Hamburger would support this: Stavelot's colophon claim was as 'scriptor' and 'pictor' (Chantilly, MS XIX B1, fo. 2r: 'iste liber fuit scriptus et ac depictus per manus ...'). See also Hamburger, *Nuns as Artists*, pp. 9–19. The variety of raw, sometimes crude murals of the later period extant in church and conventual interiors may represent the activity of painters among the professed.

The specialist skills of the metalworker and jeweller were also not wholly uncommon in the Benedictine convents, especially in the early Middle Ages. The Anglo-Saxon prelates of the tenth century appear to have been sufficiently adept in these arts for their skills to be celebrated by near-contemporary biographers. Dunstan was remembered as a metalworker as much as a painter; the monks of Abingdon claimed he cast two of their church bells.[302] His co-reformer, Æthelwold of Winchester, was believed to have cast not only bells but also a golden coronal (from which were suspended bells and lamps) and a retable in gold and silver.[303] Nothing is known of their training in these arts; Spearhavoc of Bury, abbot of Abingdon (d. *c.* 1050), however, may have practised as a craftsmen before his profession. According to his biographer his renown resulted in a personal commission from Emperor Henry IV in 1053.[304]

Benedictine women, at least those of the high and later Middle Ages, were also practised in needlecraft. They worked the richly embroidered vestments for their own churches and also accepted external commissions, although visitors sought to curb such commerce. The tenor of these prohibitions suggests they also accepted domestic tasks: *Ancrene riwle* demanded '[They] make no purses to gain friends ... but shape and sew and mend church vestments and poor people's clothes.'[305]

Patronage

The range of art and craft skills current in Benedictine cloisters was remarkable but they remained confined to only a minority of monks. The magnificence of their monasteries, their fabric and their furnishings, was, for the most part, a measure of their energy not as producers but as patrons. For the successful settlement of even a modest monastic community such acts of artistic patronage were almost a practical necessity; indeed, such was the struggle to secure skilled labour that some superiors were compelled to offer spiritual services – indulgences, special suffrages – to persuade masons, metalworkers, glaziers to work within their precincts. The expansion of monasteries and the growing importance of lay patrons overlaid these imperatives with additional corporate and political pressures. It was now essential even for established churches to underpin their special claim to sanctity with conspicuous schemes of building and beautification. Such schemes were as significant in the struggle for spiritual, social and political status as any temporal endowment: Abbot Suger of Saint-Denis (d. 1151) described the

---

[302] His role in crafting them has been doubted: C. R. Dodwell, *Anglo-Saxon Art: A New Perspective* (Manchester, 1982), p. 49.
[303] *Bishop Æthelwold*, ed. Yorke, p. 57&n.
[304] *MO*, p. 536.
[305] Power, *Medieval English Nunneries*, pp. 257–8.

decoration of his abbey church as further 'increments' (*incrementa*) for the monastery.[306] Secular patrons expected an investment in the physical fabric of their foundations, and monastic superiors recognised the potential in such schemes to reinforce, and perhaps extend their patronal relationships. At the completion of his church Abbot Suger anticipated 'kings, princes, and many outstanding men following our example' (*De administratione*, XXXI).[307] It would be wrong, however, to represent the artistic and cultural enterprise of the Black Monks exclusively as pragmatic or narrowly political. The spiritual impulses that persuaded individual monks to cultivate the practical arts were equally powerful at an institutional level. Abbot Suger's *apologia* for his own artistic patronage reflected attitudes widespread in the order as a whole: the 'beauty of the house of God' was an aid to monastic contemplation and 'The loveliness of the many coloured gems [transfers] that which is material to that which is immaterial ... and by the grace of God I can be transported from this inferior to that higher world.'[308]

In the later Middle Ages the patronage of the monks was infused with a number of new impulses. The growing interest of the nobility, gentry and merchant class in the personal, social and political advantages of such artistic and cultural projects passed over to monastic superiors, many of whom were recruited from these strata.[309] The values shared by superiors and their secular kinsfolk and supporters even encouraged collaborative projects.[310] The aesthetic values of the humanists also appealed to many superiors and caused them to champion certain crafts – notably, the making of manuscripts – with an almost antiquarian sense of their intrinsic worth. The increased independence of conventual life in this period allowed individual monks themselves to act as patrons. It was not uncommon now for obedientiaries to commemorate their service to the community with a gesture of artistic patronage – perhaps a reliquary, richly embroidered altar-hanging or a painted tablet: John Holynborne of Christ Church, Canterbury, perhaps commissioned the image of St Erasmus that bears his apparent *ex dono* (illustration 6).[311] Successful scholar monks, in receipt of fees and other rewards from their time in the schools, commissioned *de luxe* codices. John Moorlinch of Glastonbury commissioned from an Oxford workshop companion volumes with an exquisite sequence of miniatures depicting different attitudes of traditional monastic *lectio*.[312]

[306] Suger, *De administratione*, I: *Abbot Suger*, ed. Panofsky, pp. 40–1.
[307] Ibid.
[308] Ibid.
[309] See above, pp. 66–9.
[310] For example, the Sherborne missal, the fruit of affinities between Benedictines, Dominicans, secular prelates and, via the Lovel Lectionary, lay patrons: Backhouse, *Sherborne Missal*, pp. 48–55.
[311] For example, BL, Cotton MS Nero D VII (St Albans Abbey Liber Benefactorum), fos. 83v–85r. See also Luxford, *Art and Architecture*, pp. 83–114 at 83.
[312] Oxford, The Queen's College, MS 304; Oxford, Bodleian Library, MS Laud Lat. 4; BL, Add. MS 74236.

To medieval contemporaries the Benedictines' most conspicuous achievements were as patrons of architecture. In northern Europe they were the pioneers of building in stone, and perhaps in some regions solely responsible for the adoption of the Roman style of basilica.[313] The Romanesque style was spread by means of the Benedictine expansion after 1050, not only, as might be expected, in western France and the British Isles, but also to the east (Lubin, Poland) and south (San Juan de la Peña, Aragon).[314] The octagonal bell-tower of Cluny was echoed in churches throughout central and southern Burgundy, and although lacking the same congregational ties, in Lanfrancian England the robust arches, columns and towers of the Romanesque became the brand image of the new Benedictinism. Early and elaborate experiments in Gothic form were also witnessed at Benedictine abbeys and priories, not only Suger's Saint-Denis but also Ely and Peterborough.[315] It is sometimes overlooked that the Black Monks remained a significant source of architectural innovation even in the post-Black Death period. Certainly in England Benedictine superiors were early enthusiasts for the perpendicular style and willingly experimented with developments that represented both a decorative and a technical triumph, such as chimney-pieces, oriel windows and fan-vaulted ceilings.[316] In the shadow of the Reformation they also contributed to the transmission of Renaissance styles in England: for example, at the last stages of the reconstruction of Milton Abbey (Dorset).[317]

Yet it was in the production of books that the influence of Benedictine patrons was perhaps most profound. In the unstable centuries of conversion and colonisation the semi-Benedictine communities of middle Italy, France and England were virtually the sole stimulus to the transmission of texts.[318] The Anglo-Saxon and Carolingian recovery saw royal and episcopal courts emerge as alternative focus for scribes and illuminators but the larger Benedictine monasteries still matched them both in productivity and quality.[319] Moreover, in the century after 1050 the scriptoria of the re-formed Benedictine foundations of England, Normandy and the Île-de-France attracted the services of some of northern Europe's most

[313] See above, pp. 9, 20.
[314] R. Cassanelli, 'Romanische Kunst und benediktinisches Mönchtum', in *Benediktinische Kunst*, ed. R. Cassanelli and E. Lopez-Tello Garcia (Regensburg, 1997), pp. 139–55; J. Mann, *Romanesque Architecture and its Sculptural Decoration in Christian Spain* (Toronto, 2009), p. 56.
[315] *A History of Ely Cathedral*, ed. P. Meadows and N. Ramsay (Woodbridge, 2003), pp. 95–111; L. Reilly, *An Architectural History of Peterborough Cathedral* (Oxford, 1997).
[316] For example, the abbot's solar at Muchelney (Somerset).
[317] Traskey, *Milton Abbey*, pp. 150–5.
[318] Bischoff, 'Benedictine Monasteries', 134–60; McKitterick, 'Script and Book Production', pp. 226–7. For the books, citations and verbal echoes which bear witness to their pivotal role, see Lapidge, *Anglo-Saxon Library*, pp. 34, 37–40, 53–60, 65–9, 84–5, 93–126.
[319] McKitterick, 'Script and Book Production', pp. 221–47; M. Garrison, 'The Emergence of Carolingian Latin Literature and the Court of Charlemagne (780–814)', in *Carolingian Culture*, ed. McKitterick, pp. 111–40; G. Henderson, 'Carolingian Art', in *Carolingian Culture*, ed. McKitterick, pp. 248–73.

accomplished scribes and illuminators.[320] Few patrons in the Gregorian period presided over a book of the quality of Master Hugo's Bury Bible.[321] It has often been assumed that the advent of the universities, and the stationers that supported them, diminished the creative and commercial role of the monasteries in the production of books. The *studia generales* may now have provided the primary stimulus for the production scholarly books, but the Black Monks remained prominent in other genres, and the laity, acquiring books in any quantity for the first time after 1200, received many, if not most, from the hands of monastic patrons. The abbot and convent of Evesham appear to have presented a remarkable psalter (BL, Add. MS 44874) to Richard earl of Cornwall to commemorate the Battle of Evesham in 1265.[322] There were regions of Europe where the Benedictines remained a powerful force in the marketplace. The little that is known of commercial book production in provincial England would suggest that workshops were most active within the orbit of one or other of the greater monasteries.[323] It would be equally wrong to assume the conservatism of these communities acted as a check on artistic or scriptorial innovation. The artistry of the East Anglian school of manuscript painters, whose pioneering work emerged in the middle years of the fourteenth century, appears to have been sustained largely by the Benedictine abbeys of the region.[324] The émigré scribes who pioneered humanist and Greek text in fifteenth-century England were also supported by Benedictine patrons.[325]

These projects were as prominent in the cultural life of the Benedictine monastery as any pedagogic or pastoral activity. The building and beautification of the house was a protracted process and generally passed from one generation to another; at the greater abbeys and priories there can scarcely have been a period when there were no artisans or craftsmen at work within the precincts. Although the majority of these specialists entered the service of the monastery for a specific commission, they were thoroughly integrated into the community, living, working and worshipping alongside

[320] R. Gameson, 'La Normandie et l'Angleterre au XIe siècle: le temoignage des manuscrits', in *La Normandie et l'Angleterre au Moyen Âge: Colloque de Cerisy-la-Salle (4–7 Octobre 2001), Actes*, ed. P. Bouet and V. Gazeau (Caen, 2003), pp. 129–72; R. Gameson, 'Hugo Pictor, enlumineur normand', *Cahiers* 44:2 (2001), 121–38. M. Bourgeois-Lechartier and F. Avril, *Le scriptorium du Mont Saint-Michel* (Paris, 1967).
[321] Heslop, 'Production and Artistry of the Bury Bible'. See also *The Bury Bible*, ed. R. M. Thomson (Woodbridge, 2003).
[322] D. H. Turner, 'The Evesham Psalter', *Journal of the Warburg and Courtauld Institutes* 27 (1964), 23–41.
[323] For example, L. Dennison and N. Rogers, 'A Medieval Best-Seller: Some Examples of Decorated Copies of Higden's *Polychronicon*', in *The Church and Learning in Late Medieval Society*, ed. C. M. Barron and J. Stratford, Harlaxton Medieval Studies 11 (Donnington, 2002), pp. 80–99.
[324] L. F. Sandler, *The Peterborough Psalter in Brussels and other Fenland Manuscripts* (London, 1974); L. F. Sandler, *Gothic Manuscripts, 1285–1385*, 2 vols. (London, 1986), i. 25, 27, 54.
[325] R. A. B. Mynors, 'A Fifteenth-Century Scribe: T. Werken', *Transactions of the Cambridge Bibliographical Society* 1:2 (1950), 97–104; M. B. Parkes, 'A Fifteenth-Century Scribe: Henry Mere', *Bodleian Library Record* 6 (1961), 654–9; Coates, *English Medieval Books*, pp. 10–12.

the other unprofessed and, not infrequently, wearing the same livery.[326] In some cases the interest of the abbot and convent was enough to convince them to trade from inside the monastery: in the fifteenth century binders and other book artisans appear to have based themselves at English Benedictine abbeys; in the second quarter of the sixteenth century several pioneers of provincial printing did the same.[327] The interest and involvement of the abbot and convent in a permanent workshop were not confined to their own precinct. There is evidence, some of which requires further examination, that suggests that scriptoria, in particular, within the orbit of some major monasteries were in effect client branches of the conventual workshops.[328] Occasionally, artisans attracted to the monastery by the prospect of patronage were persuaded to be professed. The twelfth-century reconstruction of the shrine of St Albans was the achievement of the mason Anketil, who entered as an employee but completed the work (in 1129) as a professed monk.[329] The professional painter Walter also sought profession at St Albans and continued his work after his solemn vows, rising to the rank of sacristan.[330]

In the Middle Ages, as in later periods, artistic patronage was a collaborative enterprise. It is likely that whenever the Black Monks commissioned a piece or a project they were also closely involved in its planning, preparation and execution. In early centuries the extent of their interaction is, of course, difficult to document, although anecdotal accounts, both illustrative and narrative, consistently assert an ideal of constant monastic supervision.[331] The previously mentioned account, among the miracles of Dunstan, of the archbishop's timely intervention to stop a scaffold beam from falling on a stonemason vividly captures the monks' self-perception as committed, conscientious builders.[332] In the later Middle Ages the full extent of their creative control was elaborated in formal contracts agreed with their craftsmen. The terms under which the mason John de Middleton was engaged to construct the dormitory at Durham Priory in 1398 specified not only the size and capacity of the new building, but also the materials to be used and even the shape and size of the window apertures.[333]

---

[326] Harvey, *Living and Dying*, pp. 168–9.

[327] M. J. Foot, 'Bookbinding', in *The Cambridge History of the Book in Britain*, iii. *1400–1557*, ed. J. B. Trapp and L. Hellinga (Cambridge, 1999), pp. 109–27 at 116.

[328] Dennison and Rogers, 'A Medieval Best-Seller'.

[329] *GASA*, i. 83–7, 108; *MO*, pp. 537–8.

[330] *GASA*, i. 37, 242; *MO*, p. 538.

[331] For example, *Wulfstan*, pp. 38–41, 54–5.

[332] *Memorials of Saint Dunstan*, ed. Stubbs, p. 189. For supervision of building work, see ibid., 7, 25, 182, 271–2.

[333] L. R. Shelby, 'Monastic Patrons and their Architects: A Case-Study of the Contract for the Monks' Dormitory at Durham Priory', *Gesta* 15:1–2 (1976), 91–6.

The creative oversight of the monks was matched in other craft activities. The contract agreed with the text-writer Thomas Preston at Westminster Abbey for the completion of Abbot Litlyngton's missal specified the character of the text and the stints at which it was to be copied.[334] The monks' concern for the aesthetic character of the manuscript also caused them to employ, simultaneously, a workshop remote from the abbey, to undertake the work of finishing.[335] Their pursuit of artistic perfection now caused them not only to call upon a network of craftsmen and workshops but also upon co-patrons whom previously they may have regarded as corporate or seigniorial rivals. Abbot Robert Bruyning of Sherborne sought the services not only of a Dominican artist but also his diocesan, Bishop Richard Mitford of Salisbury, to complete his lavish missal, now known as the Sherborne Missal.[336] These collaborations are indicative of the fact that the regular and secular clergy of the pre-Reformation period shared a common set of cultural values, aesthetic and intellectual, just as, increasingly, they shared common patterns of education and formation, observance and pastoral mission. On the eve of the sixteenth-century surrenders, the boundary between the cultural world of the Benedictines, and wider society, was being steadily eroded.

---

[334] See L. F. Sandler, *Gothic Manuscripts, 1285–1385*, 2. vols. (Oxford, 1986), i. 36–7; ii. 172–5. P. Tudor-Craig, 'The Large Letters of the Litlington Missal and Westminster Abbey, in 1383–4', in *Illuminating the Book*, ed. M. P. Brown and S. McKendrick (London, 1998), pp. 102–19.
[335] Ibid.
[336] Now, BL, Add. MS 74236. See also Backhouse, *Sherborne Missal*, pp. 49, 53.

CHAPTER FIVE

The Later Middle Ages

Benedictine monasticism flowered when European society was in its infancy. The order, self-sufficiency and stability of the *cenobium* captured the imagination of peoples for whom a settled existence, and even subsistence, remained elusive. The early Benedictine monastery was not only a refuge but also an essential building block of the medieval community, a surrogate economic and social unit and, in the absence of an institutional church or state authority, a source of spiritual and temporal governance. Yet as the order neared the apex of its influence, and a pope (Gregory VII, 1073–85) widely credited as Benedictine announced a new Christian age, Europe was already in the process of rapid change. Between the twelfth and the fifteenth centuries the economic, social and political structures of the Continent were transformed. As the incidence of invasion and internal warfare fell sharply and population levels rose, a new urban environment, economy and identity emerged. The institutional church retained, indeed reinforced, its influence in this demographic, economic and social flux, but it was the new ascetic orders and the secular clergy to which many now turned first for spiritual direction. The authority of kings, princes and republics (in later centuries at least) also grew steadily, strengthened not only by a buoyant economy but also by a battery of permanent institutions, an exchequer, judiciary and representative assembly. These were forms of authority with which lordship, whether exercised by a great magnate or a great monastery, could scarcely fail to collide. In the centuries before the Reformation the Benedictines confronted a world beyond the convent in which the place and purpose of their observant life was no longer certain.

Historians have always associated the later Middle Ages with the downfall of the monastic order. This view originated with the very first narratives of the European Reformation which necessarily regarded the failure of the monastic tradition as a principal prerequisite for religious change.[1]

---

[1] The 'corruption of religion' which ensued after Constantine's emancipation of the 'Church of Christ' was offered as the overture to John Foxe's *Acts and Monuments: Acts and Monuments of these latter and perillous days touching matters of the Church* (London, 1563) STC 11222, bi–ii (Preface to the Queen). More particularly, John Bale argued the 'practyse of hypocratsyhe monkery' had provided for the 'further mayntenaunce of that myghtye monarchy of Antichriste'; moreover, 'why [the King's Grace] plucked he downe their monasteryes ... yf that kinde of chastite had bene indispensable': *The Apology of Iohan Bale agaynste a ranke papyst answering both hym and hys doctours* (London, 1550) STC 1275,

It was reinforced by the first generation of modern researchers, many of whom shared the sensitivities and prejudices of their Protestant predecessors. The arch-Anglican G. G. Coulton considered 'the pioneers of one generation became the laggards of a later age', guilty of 'a lamentable gulf between monastic theory and practice'.[2] Even respected monastic authorities of this era – Jean Leclercq, David Knowles – proved reluctant to challenge the prevailing view.[3] For Knowles the lustre of early and high medieval monasticism was irrevocably muddied after the mid-thirteenth century, and in England at least the later Middle Ages represented 'one long slow decline'.[4] Reformation revisionism has restored the reputation of the later medieval Church but has preferred not to recover the monasteries from their accustomed position on the cultural, social and spiritual margins.[5]

Recent case studies of communities, and congregations, have offered an alternative view, however.[6] Here it has become possible to see not only the changing nature of Benedictine life after 1215, or even 1349, but also their continuing success in the reform of observance, in learning, and their wider participation in the causes of Church and State. There can be no doubt that the Black Monks suffered under the prevailing economic and social trends, from a fundamental shift in cultural attitudes, and from the escalation of ecclesiastical, secular and seigniorial authority. Yet these difficulties did not stifle the Benedictine spirit completely but served to stimulate a process of institutional reorganisation and intellectual and spiritual revival which enabled them to reclaim something of their old ascendency in national and even international affairs. By comparison with their monastic and mendicant colleagues, the Benedictines entered the sixteenth century with some confidence for the future of their order.

---

pp. xviii, xxv. Bishop John Jewel reminded readers that '*Of late yeeres' sundry cardinals and other 'frendes' of Rome, among them Wolsey and Fisher,* had acknowledged the *'abuse there is to be reformed in the* Orders of Monkes, and Freers, *for many of them are so vile, that they are a shame vnto the seculares, and with their example doo mutche il'*: *A Defence of the Apologie of the Churche of Englande* (London, 1567), STC 14600.5, p. 510. Likewise, Robert Parson's Counter-Reformation perspective: 'as when the rivers of any country, or veins or arteries do wax dry, or are corrupted ... all the rest must needs perish and putrifie; so when religious people themselves be corrupted, and do infect, or scandalize others, by their evil example ... all the rest must needs come to desolation': *Letters and Memorials of Father Robert Persons*, ed. L. Hicks, Catholic Record Society (London, 1942), p. 185.

[2] G. G. Coulton, 'The Last Generations of Medieval Monachism', *Speculum* 18:4 (1943), 437–57 at 437; Coulton, *Five Centuries of Religion*, iv. 1

[3] Leclercq defined the later Middle Ages as 'non-monastic centuries': *Love of Learning*, p. 252. For Knowles 'the age was undoubtedly marked by a lack of distinction': *RO*, ii. 364.

[4] D. Knowles, 'Some Developments in English Monastic Life, 1216–1336', *TRHS* 4th Series 26 (1944), 37–52 at 37.

[5] Duffy, *Stripping of the Altars*; C. Haigh, *English Reformations: Religion, Politics and Society under the Tudors* (Oxford, 1993); B. A. Kümin, *The Shaping of a Community: The Rise and Reformation of the English Parish, c. 1400–1560* (Aldershot, 1996).

[6] For example, Clark, *A Monastic Renaissance*; Luxford, *Art and Architecture*; Collett, *Italian Benedictine Scholars*; Posset, *Renaissance Monks*.

The Benedictines after 1215

The council that convened in the Lateran basilica on 11 November 1215 represented a church transformed. It was not only the presiding figure of Pope Innocent III (1198–1216), himself a product of the new schools of theology and law, that bore witness to a century of change, but also the presence of as many as 800 abbots and priors, the delegates of almost a dozen different religious orders founded since the end of the eleventh century.[7] The Fourth Lateran Council is often considered a turning point in the fortunes of the Benedictines.[8] If the profile of the council underlined the rapid advance of the new orders, so too did its pronouncements, which, for the first time, included an intervention into the governance of the old monastic order, requiring it to replicate the capitular structure of the Cistercian *avant-garde*. This measure of reform may have marked a shift in the relationship between the monks and the masters of the church, initiating a programme of monastic reform continued by Innocent's successors until the middle years of the fourteenth century. Yet, in the wake of 1215 and for decades after, the Black Monks maintained much of their original dominance, both in the ecclesiastical hierarchy, and among the community of the faithful. The surge of new religious orders and houses had been rapid but also relatively short-lived. By the beginning of the thirteenth century only the Black Canons continued steadily to secure new foundations.[9] The general chapter of Cîteaux now sought to limit the number of new affiliations to its network.[10] The reformers had seen significant successes in the sparsely populated north and west but remained a minor presence in the monastic heartlands of south-east England, northern France, and northern Italy. Their search for a simple life had stimulated a general interest in the monastic vocation, from which all orders appear to have benefited, and its focus on the *RB* as an authentic evocation of early monasticism served only to reinforce the primacy of the Black Monks.

[7] For Innocent III's pontificate, see J. E. Sayers, *Innocent III: Leader of Europe, 1198–1216* (London, 1994); B. Bolton, *Innocent III: Studies in Papal Authority and Pastoral Care* (London, 1994). For the Fourth Lateran Council in particular, see N. P. Tanner, 'Pastoral Care: The Fourth Lateran Council of 1215', in *A History of Pastoral Care*, ed. G. R. Evans (London, 2000), pp. 112–25; R. Foreville, *Les conciles de Latran I, II, II et de Latran IV: 1123, 1139, 1179, et 1215*, vol. 1 (Paris, 2007); *Councils and Synods*, ii.1, 48&n. See also J. Avril, 'Moines et chanoines réguliers dans les conciles et synodes des XIIe et XIVe siècles', in *Moines et monastères dans les sociétés de rite grec et latin*, ed. J.-L. Lemaître, M. Dmitriev and P. Gonneau (Geneva, 1996), pp. 313–34.

[8] Knowles, 'Some Developments in English Monastic Life', 37–8.

[9] For the dispersal of Cistercian, Augustinian and the other orders of canons, see J. Burton, 'Past Models and Contemporary Concerns: the Foundation and Growth of the Cistercian Order', *Studies in Church History* 44 (2008), 27–45; P. Burton, 'The Beginnings of Cistercian Expansion in England: The Socio-Historical Context of the Foundation of Rievaulx (1132)', *Cistercian Studies Quarterly* 42:2 (2007), 151–82; L. J. R. Milis, 'Hermits and Regular Canons in the Twelfth Century', in L. J. R. Milis, *Religion, Culture and Mentalities in the Medieval Low Countries: Selected Essays*, ed. J. Deploige *et al.* (Turnhout, 2005), 181–246.

[10] From the 1160s new foundations nearby religious houses were discouraged: Berman, *Cistercian Evolution*, p. 86.

The presence and profile of the Benedictines after 1215 rested for the most part on the network of houses founded in their formative years. The expansion of the order was over long before the Lateran Council. Never exactly a missionary movement even in early centuries, the monks now ceded the Continent's remaining uncolonised territories and unconverted souls to the reformed orders and thereafter to the mendicants; on the periphery of the Continent – Ireland, Scandinavia – where the institutional church remained in its infancy, the Benedictines were all but eclipsed.[11] The twelfth and thirteenth centuries saw the formation of many new towns and even sees, but it was the new orders, for the most part, that were chosen to serve their churches. Even venerable foundations were vulnerable in the devotional vigour of the urban environment. San Cosimato in Rome, a Benedictine convent from the tenth century, was surrendered to the nuns of St Clare in 1230.[12] Moreover, convents deemed to be in material or moral decline were now required to accept the modish rules of the reformers: the venerable female community of Frauenwörth was transformed into a community of canonesses in 1209.[13]

Yet it would be wrong to present the Benedictines of this period as on the point of retreat. When Orderic Vitalis wondered at the crowds attracted to the 'lonely wooded places' of the Cistercians, it was the prospects for this novel mode of life, and its 'unaccustomed rigour', that worried him, not his own.[14] The early fortunes of some of the new foundations seemed to bear out his concerns: the experience of Grimbergen, which passed from regular canons to (Black) monks before returning to canons again, was not untypical of this volatile period.[15] Orderic's generation knew their order to be resurgent, not only in his own Anglo-Norman homeland but also to the west and south of Europe, below the Alps and the Pyrenees.[16] Their incremental growth, in numbers, of brethren as well as houses, and in regional influence, continued to the close of the thirteenth century.

After 1200 there were few new Benedictine foundations on a grand scale. The establishment in 1333 of Ettal Abbey, near Oberammergau, by Duke Ludwig IV of Bavaria (d. 1347), was exceptional not only for its status and

---

[11] C. Ó Clabaigh, 'The Benedictines in Medieval and Early Modern Ireland', in *Irish Benedictines*, ed. Browne and Ó Clabaigh, pp. 79–121 at 80: 'the foundations shared in the general fate of the Anglo-Norman colony, experiencing decline, uncertainty and hardship'; B. and P. H. Sawyer, *Medieval Scandinavia: From Conversion to Reformation, c. 800–1500* (Minneapolis, 1993), pp. 112–16, 126–7.

[12] J. H. Moorman, *Medieval Franciscan Houses* (New York, 1983), p. 655.

[13] Pixton, *German Episcopacy*, p. 226.

[14] *Orderic*, iv. 326.

[15] B. L. Venarde, *Women's Monasticism and Medieval Society: Nunneries in France, 890–1215* (Ithaca, 1997), p. 69. A transfer of order was not unknown at the end of the Middle Ages: the Cistercian convent of St Giles, Münster, adopted a Benedictine identity as late as 1468: R. P. Hsia, *Society and Religion in Münster, 1535–1618*, Yale Historical Publications Miscellany 113 (New Haven, 1984), p. 34.

[16] *Orderic*, iv. 326.

seigniorial patronage but also for its date.[17] A handful of new houses were founded in Iberia, where Cluniac Benedictines retained their ascendancy at least until the mid-thirteenth century, and Italy (Tuscany, Romagna), although not all of them survived, or retained the *RB*, for more than a century; the most significant and sustained success was seen in female foundations.[18] The convent for women established by Santuccia Carabotti (*c.* 1250–1305) near Gubbio (Umbria) had carried its brand of *ad literam* observance to a further six convents before her death.[19] A Benedictine nunnery was born from the spiritual resurgence of Florence at the turn of the fourteenth century, although Le Murate, which became affiliated to Paduan congregation, was hardly typical of the city's reform.[20] The spiritual awakening of the Venetian convent of Corpus Domini momentarily augured the renewal of Benedictine life in the city, but under the direction of the Dominican Giovanni Dominici, the prioress Lucia Tiepolo rejected the *RB* for mendicant custom.[21] Only in central and Eastern Europe, regions which earlier phases of colonisation had failed to penetrate, were there new endowments of any size. The late twelfth and thirteenth centuries saw intense monastic settlement in Bohemia and Moravia. Although the Cistercians and Premonstratensians were prominent in the region, the Benedictines also attracted benefactors and secured some key sites.[22] Želiv was founded for Premonstratensians in 1145 but had turned to the *RB* by 1148; Podlažice followed perhaps a decade later. Přemysl Otakar I (d. 1230) presented a site at Broumov to the Benedictines of Břevnov in 1213, although it was another century before the monastery there was properly established.[23] Ann, widow of Duke Henry I of Silesia (d. 1238), founded a monastery at Krzeszów in 1242; in the precinct of Pražský hrad (Prague Castle) a convent was colonised in 1347 by Croatian Benedictines (thus klášter Na Slovanech) at the

[17] S. Deutinger, 'Klosterreform und historisches interesse: Ettaler Geschichtspflege am Ausgang des Mittelalters', *Zeitschrift für bayerische Landesgeschichte* 68:1 (2005), 75–92.
[18] O'Callaghan, *History of Medieval Spain*, pp. 310–11; L. Provero, 'Monasteri, chiese e poteri nel Saluzzese (secoli XI–XIII)', *Bollettino storico-bibliografico subalpino* 92:2 (1994), 385–476; K. Jansen, *The Making of the Magdalen: Preaching and Popular Devotion in the Later Middle Ages* (Princeton, 1999), pp. 120–1.
[19] K. Gill, '*Scandala*: Controversies Concerning *Clausura* and Women's Religious Communities in Late Medieval Italy', in *Christendom and its Discontents: Exclusion, Persecution and Rebellion, 1000–1500*, ed. S. Waugh and P. D. Diehl (Cambridge, 1996), pp. 177–203; Jansen, *Making of the Magdalen*, p. 121&n; J. C. Ward, *Women in Medieval Europe, 1200–1500* (Harlow, 2002), p. 171.
[20] K. J. P. Lowe, *Nuns' Chronicles and Convent Culture in Renaissance and Counter-Reformation Italy* (Cambridge, 2003), pp. 108–12.
[21] *Life and Death in a Venetian Convent: The Chronicle and Necrology of Corpus Domini, 1395–1436*, ed. and trans. D. E. Bornstein (Chicago, 2000), pp. 4–5.
[22] For Brevnov, see P. Sommer, 'Das Kloster Brevnov', in *Europas Mitte um 1000*, ed. A. Wieczorek and H.-M. Hinz, Beitrage zur Geschichte, Kunst under Archaologie I (Prague, 2000), 418–19.
[23] L. Wolverton, *Hastening Towards Prague: Power and Society in the Medieval Czech Lands* (Philadelphia, 2001), pp. 136–331. See also J. W. Thompson, 'Medieval German Expansion in Bohemia', *Slavonic Review* 4 (1926), 605–28 at 615–16.

invitation of Charles IV.[24] At Nicosia a Benedictine convent dedicated to Our Lady of Tyre was founded in the early fourteenth century.[25]

The network of smaller Benedictine houses also expanded, at least until the middle years of the thirteenth century. In the Benedictine heartland – the British Isles, France, and the Rhineland – the most profitable monasteries continued to colonise dependent priories, particularly on those estates furthest from the home community. Between 1100 and 1450 the abbot and convent of St Albans acquired a tally of ten dependencies from west Wales to the border with Scotland.[26] No other English houses could lay claim to such a congregation, but several in this period – Durham, Reading, St Mary's York – populated at least one priory community.[27] Economic (if not also evangelical) impulses projected some into the Celtic periphery. Durham and Reading could claim Scottish outposts (Coldingham, Isle of May) by the mid-twelfth century.[28] The years either side of 1200 also brought Benedictine forays into Ireland. The monks of Chester established a priory at Downpatrick to serve the cathedral church there in 1183; Glastonbury founded a priory (Ocunild) near Killarney (Co. Kerry) after 1171, Bath, a priory, from the remains of a hospital, at Waterford after 1204, which in turn created a tiny colony at Youghal (Co. Cork) in about 1350.[29] The early Benedictine bond between Germany and Ireland was renewed in the same period in the foundation of an outpost of St James's Abbey, Würtzburg, at Rosscarbery (Co. Cork).[30]

In England, the multiplication of cell colonies continued even in the century after the Black Death. Nunneries were placed under the closer control of their male superiors. Several alien priories suppressed between 1360 and 1415 were annexed by wealthy English abbeys; in their weakness some of these houses (Lenton, Montacute) were compelled to accept superiors provided by their powerful Benedictine neighbours.[31] It is worth noting the counterforce witnessed on the European mainland where the regional congregations that flourished in the Gregorian period – Camaldoli, Vallombrosa – now fragmented into febrile clusters.

[24] For the foundation of this community, later occupied by Iberian Benedictines, and rededicated to Emmaeus, see A. Thomas, *Anne's Bohemia: Czech Literature and Society, 1310–1420* (Minneapolis, 1998), p. 77.

[25] J. R. Riley-Smith, *The Crusades: A History*, 2nd edn (London, 2005), p. 172.

[26] *MRH*, pp. 58–93 at 59, 67, 73–4, 79–81.

[27] Durham maintained dependencies at Farne, Finchale and Stamford, Reading at Leominster and St Mary's York at, Boston, Lincoln, Richmond (North Yorkshire), Rumburgh (Suffolk), St Bees (Cumbria) and Wetheral (Cumbria): *MRH*, pp. 60, 69, 74–5, 80.

[28] Ibid., pp. 64, 74. See also G. W. S. Barrow, 'The Scottish Rulers and the Religious Orders, 1070–1153', *TRHS* 5th Series 3 (1953), 77–100.

[29] Ó Clabaigh, 'Benedictines in Medieval and Early Modern Ireland', 113–14.

[30] Ibid., 45.

[31] Headley Priory (West Yorkshire) was granted to the Cluniac Priory of Holy Trinity, York, the (probable) grange at Panfield (Essex) to Christ Church, Canterbury, and Steventon (Berkshire) to Westminster: *MRH*, pp. 83–93, 97–8 (Lenton, Montacute).

In the half-century after 1215, a new form of dependency developed, the *domus studiorum* (house of studies), a monastic community but also a school, set within sight of the university, to support the scholastic studies now expected of the Benedictines. Cluny established such a house at Paris (known as the Collège de Cluny) in 1269; the general chapter of the English Benedictines founded a *studium* at Oxford for brethren of the southern province in 1277.[32] The cathedral priories in England made provisions of their own. Christ Church, Canterbury, built a *domus* at Oxford on a privileged site adjoining the ancient priory of St Frideswide; Durham established two *domus*, at Oxford and Stamford (Lincolnshire), an Oxford *alter*, for much of the fourteenth century.[33] The abbot and convent of Crowland (Lincolnshire) established a *domus* at Cambridge in 1428, known as Buckingham College, apparently after an early benefactor.[34] Cluny founded further provincial (i.e. extra-Parisian) *studia* at Avignon (1378) and Dole (1491); the Vallombrosans also sought a *studium* of their own in this period.[35] Although lacking the full range of conventual buildings, and providing private chambers for the brethren, these *domus* were intended to be fully observant monastic foundations. As a refinement of the traditional Benedictine model, blending observance and higher forms of learning, the monastic house of studies held some attraction for secular humanists. Bishop Richard Fox of Winchester (1501–28) founded a short-lived college at Oxford for the Black Monks of St Swithun's Priory in 1511, the penultimate Benedictine foundation in pre-Reformation England.[36]

The order also reinforced its influence in this period through the change of status, or conversion, of existing convents. Prosperity, both before and after the Black Death, persuaded a number of modest foundations to secure denization (i.e. the status of an independent abbey). Paisley (Renfrewshire) was declared denizen as early as 1245.[37] Several English and Welsh houses secured denization in the fifteenth century following the severance of their French ties: the independence of Abergavenny (Monmouth), Bermondsey and Boxgrove (Sussex) raised their profile in regions where the order was not well represented.[38] The anti-Pope Felix V raised Peterlingen (Swiss Confederation) to the status of abbey (1440–9), although his intervention

---

[32] The effort to establish Cluny's college commenced in 1259: Riche, *L'ordre de Cluny*, pp. 212–13. *Chapters*, ed. Pantin, i. 64–92 at 75.

[33] *Canterbury College, Oxford*, ed. Pantin, iv. 1–50 at 9–38; Dobson, *Durham Priory*, pp. 343–60.

[34] *MRH*, p. 61.

[35] J.-M. Le Gall, 'Les moines et la ville: l'exemple de Paris au début du XVIe siècle', in *Moines et monastères dans les sociétés de rite grec et latin*, ed. Lemaître *et al.*, pp. 255–70 at 268; Riche, *L'ordre de Cluny*, pp. 664–5.

[36] *VCH Oxfordshire*, iii. 219–28 at 219.

[37] *Medieval Religious Houses, Scotland, with an Appendix on Houses in the Isle of Man*, ed. I. B. Cowan and D. Easson, 2nd edn (1976), p. 64.

[38] Respectively in 1339, 1318×1399, 1415: *MRH*, pp. 58, 60, 95.

failed to prevent its rapid decline.[39] While there is no doubt that a number of their own monasteries abandoned the *RB* in the twelfth or thirteenth centuries and adopted the customs of the Cistercians or the Regular Canons, it is worth noting that the Benedictines themselves benefited from the misfortunes of reformed communities. Pluscarden Abbey (Elgin), presented to the Valliscaulians in 1230 by the Scots king Alexander II (1214–49), reverted to the *RB* in 1454, perhaps in formal recognition of a far earlier change.[40] The Augustinian priory of Spinney (Cambridgeshire) adopted the *RB* in 1449 and became a dependency of Ely Cathedral Priory.[41] Only eighteen months before the final suppressions in England and Wales, Bisham became Benedictine after two centuries under Augustinian rule.[42] A number of affiliate foundations intended initially to follow alternative customs (i.e. the *Regula Augustini*) also reverted to the *RB* in the later Middle Ages.[43]

The extension of their institutional and regional influence was accompanied by perhaps the greatest expansion in their population since the Anglo-Saxon and Carolingian revivals. Between 1150 and 1250 the monasteries of the Benedictine heartland saw a surge in recruitment. Their growth owed much to the general level of interest in the religious life in this period, but it must also be a measure of the (still) growing prosperity and public profile of the older monastic order. There are few, if any, precise statistics for this period, but anecdotal and circumstantial evidence suggests that houses of hitherto modest size – forty to fifty monks – had risen by more than 50 per cent to between seventy and a hundred by the beginning of the thirteenth century.[44] In England, where some effort has been made to trace the ebb and flow of numbers, even monasteries of recent foundation – Gloucester, Reading – numbered close to a hundred monks in the years either side of 1200. In the time of Matthew Paris (d. after 1259), the quorum for an abbatial election at St Albans Abbey was considered to be 100; at Christ Church, Canterbury, numbers were said to have risen as high as 150 and rarely fell far below 100. The extension of monastic churches in this period – for example at Jumièges in 1256 – provides some impression of

---

[39] J. W. Thompson, 'Church and State in Mediaeval Germany', *American Journal of Theology* 22 (1916), 513–40 at 516.

[40] *Medieval Religious Houses: Scotland*, ed. Cowan and Easson, p. 72. See also P. F. Anson, *A Monastery in Moray: The Story of Pluscarden Priory, 1230–1948* (London, 1959).

[41] *MRH*, p. 78; *VCH Cambridgeshire*, ii. 249–54 at 252.

[42] *MRH*, p. 59; *VCH Bedfordshire*, ii. 82–5 at 85.

[43] For example, the hospital of St Mark, Bristol, known as the Gaunt's hospital: M. C. Skeeters, *Community and Clergy: Bristol and the Reformation, c. 1530–c. 1570* (Oxford, 1993), p. 12.

[44] For example, Bury (80), Durham (70), Reading (100), St Albans (100), Winchester (70): *MRH*, pp. 61, 66, 74–5, 81; *Gallia monastica*, i. 14.

the scale of these thirteenth-century communities, and the spectacle of a hundred monks (or more) *in choro*.[45]

It would be misleading, of course, to suggest the Black Monks were wholly immune to the forces, material and political, which arrested the progress of other religious orders in this period. The Benedictines suffered as much as their younger counterparts from the proliferation of poorly endowed monasteries. The Irish outposts of the English abbeys had faded almost to the point of extinction before the end of the fourteenth century: Ardaneer Priory (Co. Limerick) survived for only three years (1202–5).[46] The small convents of central and southern Italy could not survive the combined effects of economic stagnation, schism and war. The 'few monks' of San Fermo (Verona) surrendered their convent to the Franciscans as early as 1261; Varatella was ceded to the Carthusians as early as 1315; San Martino di Gallinaria was abandoned in 1473; Santa Maria di Canneto ceded to the Dominicans in 1516.[47] These losses were generally of peripheral and poor houses whose viability had long been problematic, but the contemporary perception was of a greater crisis: one fifteenth-century observer opined that 'the monastic order in Italy has collapsed utterly' ('ordo monachorum nigrorum in tota Italia pene collapsus est').[48] Northern Europe saw fewer such losses, at least before 1450, but a small number of its earliest and most successful foundations struggled after the twelfth century to sustain numbers sufficient even for the most minimal observance. Fulda, Reichenau and Saint-Gall failed to recover from the fading reputation of their schools, and numbers dwindled to single figures after 1300; by the beginning of the fifteenth century Saint-Gall had been abandoned.[49]

These foundations, too meagre, or too neglected, to function, amounted only to a minority of Benedictine monasteries, even in the later Middle Ages. Perhaps a greater challenge to the order was the expansion of their rivals into territories, and communities, in which they had not, previously, established a commanding presence. On the fringes of Christian Europe – Ireland, Scandinavia and Spain – the Black Monks were soon eclipsed by the reformed orders, not only as the custodians of principal churches and shrines but also as the presiding influence in popular religion. The dominance, and then indifference, of a handful of English houses in Anglo-Ireland prevented further colonisation, while the new orders expanded and

[45] *MRH*, pp. 61, 66, 74–5, 81; R. Vaughan, 'The election of Abbots of St Albans in the 13th and 14th Centuries', *Proceedings of the Cambridge Antiquarian Society* 47 (1954), 1–12; C.-A. Deshayes, *Histoire de l'abbaye royale de Jumièges* (Montfort, 1980).

[46] Ó Clabaigh, 'Benedictines in Medieval and Early Modern Ireland', 98; E. St J. Brooks, 'Irish Daughter Houses of Glastonbury', *Proceedings of the Royal Irish Academy*, section C, 56:4 (1954), 287–95.

[47] Coulton, *Five Centuries of Religion*, iv. 59.

[48] Luigi Barbo, abbot of Santa Giustina di Padua, *De initiis congregationis sanctae Justinae de Padua*, ed. G. Campeis (Padua, 1908), pp. 8ff.: Collett, *Italian Benedictine Scholars*, p. 1.

[49] R. W. Southern, *Western Society and the Church in the Middle Ages* (Harmondsworth, 1970), p. 234.

widely within and (especially) beyond the Pale. In Scandinavia, the customs of Cîteaux and the *Regula Augustini* proved more attractive to patrons, and prospective recruits, than the observance of the early Benedictine colonists. The Danish abbeys of Esrum (*c.* 1151) and Sorø (*c.* 1162) adopted Cistercian customs; the cathedral chapter at Odense also abandoned the *RB* finally in 1484.[50] In Norway the White Monks, Regular Canons, and in the next century the mendicant orders, advanced far beyond the two Benedictine foundations. By the fifteenth century there were no fewer than forty-eight mendicant convents in the province of Dacia (combining Denmark and Sweden) and the Benedictine Munkeliv became Brigittine in 1426. In Sweden the Cistercians secured the patronage successively of Sverkar I (1130–56) and Knut Eriksson (1167–95).[51] The White Monks also succeeded in Spain, where the Benedictines had struggled, and celebrated the conversion of one of their early (*c.* 1085) settlements, San Salvador de Leyre (Navarre), in 1236.[52] In central Europe the early dominance of the Black Monks was also challenged. Venerable convents were eclipsed in a burgeoning urban environment of new churches, and a vigorous religious culture under the influence of the Fourth Lateran Council: at Erfurt the foundations of the friars, and in particular the church of the Augustinians (1277×1291), replaced the Benedictine abbey as the city's principal pastoral and spiritual focus.[53] The Benedictines of the later Middle Ages were an order of the old Europe – of the Angevin and Hohenstaufen hegemonies – and if not wholly rural, found themselves in many cases to be extra-urban.

Their reach across Christendom may have been challenged after 1215 – and in some regions perhaps as much as half a century before – but at the same time their status as a monastic movement was enhanced by the emergence, for the first time, of a properly corporate structure. It was the council of 1215 itself which called upon the Black Monks to create a capitular system of governance for each province, modelled on the chapters of the reformed monastic orders.[54] The canon was accepted and adopted in England where the first provincial chapters of the Benedictines were convened as early as 1218×1219.[55] Over the course of the thirteenth century the chapters transformed the character of the congregation in England. What had been an informal confederation of convents bound together at regional level by a whole complex of historical, jurisdictional and seigniorial ties now became a

---

[50] Nyberg, *Monasticism in North-Western Europe*, p. 176. See also B. P. McGuire, *The Cistercians in Denmark*, Cistercian Studies 35 (Kalamazoo, 1982), p. 45.

[51] For these developments see Nyberg, *Monasticism in North-Western Europe*, pp. 141–6. J. France, *The Cistercians in Sweden*, Cistercian Studies 131 (Kalamazoo, 1992), p. 344.

[52] *Leire, un señorio monástico en Navarra*, ed. L. J. F. Pérez de Ciriza (Pamplona, 1993), p. 167.

[53] A. Zumkeller, 'Geschichte des Erfurter Augustinerklosters vom Ausgang des Mittelalters bis zur Säkularisation im Jahre 1828', *Augustiniana* 55 (2005), 321–55.

[54] Tanner, *Decrees*, i. 227–71 at 240–1.

[55] *Chapters*, ed. Pantin, i. 3, 7–8.

congregation, which, in its two provinces of Canterbury and York, possessed a single centre of gravity. Regional affiliations remained, of course, and were overt in early initiatives such as the foundation of the order's Oxford *studium* in 1277.[56] The creation of a single chapter after 1336, under the terms of the papal canons *Summi magistri*, brought greater cohesion, and as the presidency of the chapter was rotated frequently from the end of the fourteenth century, it was the chapter and its officers, rather than any one regional monastery, that were regarded truly as the governors of the order. The chapters not only established a new tier of governance which enforced common patterns of observance, its own cycle of conventual visitations, and a schedule of annual levies; they also fostered exchanges between houses, of books, reform initiatives and even of monastic personnel themselves. To an extent this made the English Benedictines of the later Middle Ages more homogenised. Certainly in early centuries, a monk was commonly identified by his home affiliation – *monachus Dunelmensis, et al.* Later he was as likely to be noted as *monachus niger*. It also sharpened confrontations with the secular clergy.[57] Their Continental counterparts were slow to respond to the canon of 1215. The pre-existence of Cluny perhaps prevented the development of another capitular framework in France. Benedictine chapters were convened in the imperial territories after 1400, where they served as the crucible of the reformed congregations, but there is little evidence of such a structure in the preceding centuries. Gregory IX commissioned the superiors of Břevnov and Kladrau to summon a chapter in 1234, but since Innocent IV renewed the commission a dozen years later it seems the intervention was ignored.[58]

The experience of capitular governance in England contributed to a growing sense of corporate identity that was evident among Benedictines in the century after 1215. The canons and correspondence of the English chapters were imbued with the image of a national congregation ('ordo monachorum nigrorum in Anglia') and an international order ('ordo noster'). In the fourteenth century the general chapter also sought to raise the status of the feast of St Benedict in English convents, conscious perhaps that national and regional cults, and the observance of benefactors' obits, had eclipsed the commemoration of the founder.[59] The English chapter was perhaps also responsible for the circulation, if not composition, of a series of historical narratives recounting the origins and achievements of the order, which first appear in the second half of the fourteenth century.[60]

---

[56] V. H. Galbraith, 'New Documents about Gloucester College', in *Snappe's Formulary*, ed. H. E. Salter, pp. 338–386b at 342–51.
[57] For example, in 1280 clergy of the province of Canterbury protested at the Benedictine Chapter's changes to the Office and levies for their Oxford *studium*: *Councils and Synods*, ii.2. 866.
[58] Pixton, *German Episcopacy*, p. 407.
[59] *Chapters*, ed. Pantin, i. 68, 98; ii. 30, 65, 83.
[60] Pantin, 'Some Medieval English Treatises'.

The narratives reflect a new interest in the origins of monasticism and the early expansion of the Black Monks in the pre-Conquest period. The catalogues of Benedictine saints and scholars they contain represent the first attempt to create a systematic record of the intellectual and spiritual contribution of the order.[61] The form of these texts is analogous to the mendicant apologia which appeared a generation earlier, and it is possible they were intended not only as an expression of identity but also as response to the assault on the monastic order made by Wyclif and his followers in the 1370s and after.[62] The new expressions of monastic identity in mainland Europe were perhaps less politically charged. The prevalence of portraits of Benedict and his early followers in the aesthetic schemes of fourteenth- and early fifteenth-century churches and cloisters was indicative rather of the antiquarian impulses now passing through the convents of Italy and France, powered, at least in part, by the pervasive influence of early humanism.[63]

The status of the Benedictines in this period was also reinforced by their return, in some regions of Europe at least, to the ecclesiastical and secular hierarchies. The rise of reformed monasticism had displaced them from pontifical and episcopal counsels; the protracted conflict between Crown and Church in England, France and the Empire had also distanced them, to a great extent, from heads of government. The external criticisms and internal divisions that beset the mendicants in the century after 1250, however, undermined their public authority, and the Benedictines were the main beneficiaries of their faltering fortunes. Before 1349 the Black Monks were again well established in the cardinalate and in the higher ranks of the episcopacy in England, France and the imperial territories.[64] The Black Monks retained their position during the Great Schism, on all sides, and also in the restored and resurgent papacy after 1417. In England the Benedictines were the backbone of the smaller dioceses, not only serving as diocesan but also his vicar-general and several suffragan under honorary titles *in partibus*.[65] Towards the end of the century, as Edward III (1327–77) and his grandson (Richard II, 1377–99) both encountered mendicants tainted by treason, the Black Monks also returned to their former place in the counsels of the king. Abbot Thomas de la Mare of St Albans was said to have become a trusted councillor of King Edward and his son, the Black Prince.[66] Ironically, at any early stage in their regime, the Tudor dynasty appears

---

[61] Ibid., 189–215.
[62] Ibid.
[63] For example, the frescoes depicting the life of Benedict at Monte Oliveto (Tuscany).
[64] *RO*, ii. 370–5.
[65] *RO*, ii. 374–5, 494.
[66] *GASA*, ii. 409, iii. 382.

to have held some affection for the abbots of their greater Benedictine abbeys.[67]

As well as their public presence, it is important to recognise the continued conceptual pre-eminence of their own code, the *RB*. The early expansion of the new orders may have encouraged criticism of unreformed monasticism for a time but its more enduring consequence was to remind pious Europe of the many possibilities of Benedict's rule. A rich tapestry of traditions and trends shaped the religious culture of Europe after 1215, but it remains difficult to support the claim of R. W. Southern that 'no-one [now] looked to [the Benedictines] for new ideas or new forms of spiritual life'.[68] The century after 1150 witnessed devotional and intellectual interest in the precepts of the *RB*. In England Robert Grosseteste and Edmund Rich (of Abingdon) made the rule the basis of their own novel reflections on the religious life.[69] Bernard Ayglier (d. 1282), abbot of both Lérins and Montecassino, composed two meditations on the *RB* whose profile within the order eclipsed earlier authorities.[70] Benedict's rule also played a part in the regulation of the Poor Clares.[71] In the Abruzzi mountains of the mid-thirteenth century, Pietro di Murrone (d. 1296) and his followers attempted a new *ad literam* observance of the *RB* which attracted the formal recognition of Urban IV in 1264, taking their name from that chosen by their founder when he took the papal throne as Celestine V.[72] The same period saw the first colleges endowed at the universities and at Cambridge the founder of Peterhouse, Bishop Hugh of Balsham, turned 'freely, allusively and appositely' to the *RB* for the framework for his learned society.[73]

---

[67] For example, the abbot of St Albans was present at the funeral of Henry VII, *LP*, i/1, 20 (p. 15), and he and the abbots of Abingdon, Battle, Chester, Crowland, Reading and Sherborne were named among his legatees, ibid., 308; the abbot of Abingdon was also the recipient of a gift of plate from Henry VIII, ibid., 1549.

[68] Southern, *Western Society and the Church*, p. 237.

[69] In a letter to the abbot and convent of Peterborough, Grosseteste wrote: 'in the rule of St Benedict you have been able to contemplate, as in the plane surface of a mirror, the beauty of the life you lead': F. S. Stevenson, *Robert Grosseteste: A Contribution to the Religious, Political and Intellectual History of the Thirteenth Century* (Oxford, 1899), pp. 147–167 at 166. It is worth noting that contemporary Benedictines suspected him of hostility to their order. Matthew Paris described him as 'hammer of the monks': *Historia Anglorum*, ed. F. Madden, Rolls Series, 3 vols. (1800), iii. 149. For Edmund of Abingdon: *Speculum religiosorum*, ed. H. Forshaw (London, 1973); Sharpe, *Latin Writers*, p. 106.

[70] For Bernard's Commentary on the *RB* and *Speculum monachorum*: Bernard (Ayglier) of Monte Cassino, *Expositio in regulam sancti Benedicti*, ed. A. M. Caplet (Montecassino, 1894); *Bernardi I abbatis Cassinensis Speculum monachorum*, ed. P. H. Walther (Freiburg, 1901).

[71] Ward, *Women in Medieval Europe*, p. 156.

[72] 'Célestins', *Dictionnaires d'histoire et géographie ecclésiastiques*, vol. 12 (Paris, 1953), pp. 79–104; B. Guenée, *Between Church and State: The Lives of Four French Prelates in the Late Middle Ages*, trans. A. Goldhammer (Chicago, 1991), p. 52; P. Herde, *Cölestin V (1294) (Peter vom Morrone) der Engelpapst*, Papste und Papsrtum 16 (Stuttgart, 1981).

[73] H. Mayr-Harting, 'The Foundation of Peterhouse, Cambridge (1284) and the Rule of Saint Benedict', *EHR* 103 (1988), 318–38.

Europe in the Later Middle Ages: Economy and Society

For the readers that returned to it after 1215, the *RB* was redolent of a different age, a pre-urban world of pioneers who, although no strangers to sufferings, natural and man-made, or to a variety of personal trials, were apparently unaffected by the interplay of political, ecclesiastical and economic structures that governed their own lives. The condition of society in Europe, and the changes, crises, and conflicts, which marked it between the thirteenth and the fifteenth centuries, left an indelible imprint upon the Benedictines. The order had seen, and survived, years of turbulence in early centuries, from the conquest of the Lombards to the coming of the Norsemen, but their record was now confined to early, legendary narratives, and the immediate inheritance of late medieval monks was an institutional memory of the peaceable period of prosperity and public pre-eminence between *c.* 1050 and *c.* 1200. It is generally understood that the economic, political and social upheavals of the post-1215 period undermined the monastic order in Europe and perhaps even projected it into a permanent decline. Certainly the climate proved far less favourable to the flourishing of perpetual foundations than preceding centuries, and some convents suffered a collapse from which they never recovered. Yet it should be remembered there were also instances, both in and beyond the monastic heartland, of houses which responded robustly to the pressures of the period and which benefited, whether directly or indirectly, from the failure of poorer (and poorly protected) communities in their midst. The triple spectre of famine, plague and war did not spell doom for every European Benedictine.

The Black Death

The pandemic which between 1347 and 1352 passed across the Continent from its easternmost fringes affected monastic Europe more profoundly perhaps than any of its earlier trials. Although contemporary accounts concentrate on the effects of the first pestilence, it is now evident that equal, if not greater, destruction was wrought by further outbreaks in subsequent decades: England was devastated by the *pestis secunda* in 1361–2 and further infections in 1369, 1374 and 1437–9; in northern and middle Italy (i.e. Tuscany) second and subsequent waves were recorded in 1366–7, 1399–1400 and 1405.[74] The plagues of this period have been examined at length but the coverage of case studies is uneven. In terms of institutional and individual impact, the English experience is especially well documented. Here the sufferings of the monastic order in general, and the Black Monks in particular, were as great as in any part of mainland Europe. A swathe

---

[74] J. Hatcher, 'Plague, Population and the English Economy, 1348–1550', in *British Population History: From the Black Death to the Present Day*, ed. M. Anderson (Cambridge, 1996), pp. 15–25.

of monastic England, stretching from the south east to the Humber in the north and the Bristol Channel in the west, appears to have met the full force of the infection. Contemporaries commented that the plague was indiscriminate in its passage through society but there is no doubt that the institutionalised were particularly vulnerable. At St Albans Abbey it was reported that half the monastic community, the abbot among them, fell prey to the plague in 1348–9.[75] The suffering was similar at Bury St Edmunds, where the monastic community fell from over eighty to fewer than fifty after three successive bouts of infection.[76]

While much of the most vivid testimony is from monasteries in the south and west, their brethren throughout Britain were conscious of the cataclysm. The monk-solitary of Farne, a former Durham Benedictine, was appalled by the awful waste of towns and other settlements and of the population as a whole.[77] Of course, there were notable exceptions to the experience: the nuns of Swaffham Bulbeck, near Bury, were numerous and well enough resourced to begin a building programme during the first outbreak.[78] The impact of the recurrence of plague was apparently less marked, although individual losses were still suffered: Henry Hunstanton, abbot-elect of Bury St Edmunds, died during the 'second plague' of 1361–2; Wilton Abbey succumbed again in 1528.[79]

There are fewer contemporary accounts of the effects of the outbreaks upon Continental convents. It is plausible to apply Boccaccio's general account of plague deaths at Florence in 1348 to the Benedictine Badia in particular although the number of dead at the abbey is not recorded.[80] The experience of Francesco Petrarca's brother Gerardo, who was the only one of his thirty-five brethren at the Carthusian community of Montrieu (Marseilles) to survive, may not have been exceptional.[81] An account of the arrival of the pestilence at Padua in 1405, perhaps the worst of the fifteenth-century outbreaks, gives an impression of general devastation in both secular and religious households.[82] A measure of the losses suffered by the religious houses, not only in Italy but also parts of the Empire, and central and southern France, may be provided by the critically low numbers

---

[75] *GASA*, ii. 370.

[76] *MRH*, p. 61; Gottfried, *Bury St Edmund's and the Urban Crisis*, p. 51.

[77] 'Civitates quondam populose in solidtudinem fere redacte sunt, extinctis habitatoribus in eis, et in pluribus locis Anglie non relinquitur unus pro mille et duo propter decem milia': W. A. Pantin, 'The Monk-Solitary of Farne: A Fourteenth-Century English Mystic', *EHR* 59 (1944), 162–86.

[78] *VCH Cambridgeshire*, ii. 226–9.

[79] *Heads of Religious Houses*, ed. Knowles et al., ii. 27; *VCH Wiltshire*, iii. 231–42.

[80] D. Herlihy, *The Black Death and the Transformation of the West*, ed. S. K. Cohn (Boston, MA, 1997), pp. 24, 40–1; S. K. Cohn, *The Black Death Transformed: Disease and Culture in Early Renaissance Europe* (London, 2001), pp. 58–60.

[81] B. F. Leavy, *To Blight with Plague: Studies in a Literary Theme* (New York, 1992), p. 188. See also Cohn, *Black Death Transformed*, pp. 30, 35, 102–8.

[82] Cohn, *Black Death Transformed*, p. 109.

recorded later in the fifteenth century. Levels of mortality rose above 40 per cent in Languedoc.[83]

There can be no doubt the pestilence interrupted monastic life in Britain and Europe for many months at least, between in 1348 and 1351, and also during subsequent outbreaks. Liturgical duties were badly disrupted. Urgent petitions presented to the Papal Curia by the greater English abbeys and priories after 1350 for dispensation from the canons concerning profession and ordination bear witness to a chronic shortage of monks capable of fulfilling the daily demands of the *horarium*.[84] Abbot William [de] Bernham of Bury was dispensed from canonical restrictions to ordain ten monks below the age of twenty-four.[85] The shortage of both priests and senior obedientiaries must also have affected the internal dynamics of the monastic community, interrupting capitular discipline, confession and the process of education and formation. It seems the subsistence of the monks was also threatened, although perhaps cloister-monks suffered more than their superiors, given the unequal division of stores: at Rochester 'the monks were obliged to grind their own bread. The prior, however, had plenty of good things.'[86] The income of the monasteries also came under intense strain, at least in the immediate aftermath. Temporal income fell sharply following the pandemic of 1347–51. Religious houses in southern England saw returns fall by between one-third and one-half. Estates were left without tenants and, at least in the quarter century after 1350, monastic landlords struggled to replace them. The domestic management of the monastery also came under strain since labour in all forms was scarce and wages soared. The Rochester Priory chronicler recorded that labourers now demanded 'triple wages'.[87] At Bury St Edmunds it has been suggested the town centre was blighted, and both within and beyond the precincts offices stood empty and their associated infrastructure fell into dereliction.[88] It would be wrong to attribute these difficulties to the Black Death alone. In England patterns of tenure, property management and labour service were shifting even before the Black Death, and it may be that its main effect was to set into sharp relief economic and social transformations that were already in train.[89] Certainly, some monastic commentators considered the

[83] R. S. Gottfried, *The Black Death: Natural and Human Disaster in Medieval Europe* (London and New York, 1983), pp. 50–1.

[84] For example, *CPP*, 171–2 (1349), 202 (1350); *CPL*, iii. *1342–62*, 331, 337 (1349).

[85] *CPL*, iii. *1342–62*, 383.

[86] *The Black Death*, ed. R. Horrox (Manchester, 1994), p. 73.

[87] Ibid., p. 70.

[88] Gottfried, *Bury St Edmunds and the Urban Crisis*, pp. 34–45 at 45 (urban blight), 46–72 at 71: [depopulation] 'hurt the burgesses far less than it did the monks of the abbey'.

[89] For these transformations, see J. Bolton, 'The World Turned Upside Down', in *The Black Death in England*, ed. W. Ormrod and P. G. Lindley (Stamford, 1996), pp. 17–78; C. Platt, *King Death: The Black Death and its Aftermath in Late-Medieval England* (London, 1996), pp. 177–92. For a nuanced if not sceptical approach to the claim that the Black Death and subsequent outbreaks acted to accelerate changes already apparent, see S. H. Rigby, *English Society in the Later Middle Ages: Class, Status, Gender* (Basingstoke, 1996), pp. 80–1, 91–2.

pestilence only compounded their existing problems. John of Reading regarded the death from the plague of Abbot Bircheston of Westminster as damaging only because it exposed the abbey unexpectedly to the debts he had accrued.[90]

The extent to which these problems endured after the pestilence had passed remains difficult to gauge across Benedictine Europe as a whole. Clearly there were houses that never recovered either the size or the vitality they had known before the Black Death. Although the paucity of case studies leaves any conclusion provisional, it would appear that Italy and the imperial territories suffered far more than other regions. By contrast, in England, there are signs of a rapid recovery. It seems the greater abbeys – Bury, Glastonbury, St Albans, Westminster – were restored to their pre-1349 numbers before the end of the fourteenth century in spite of the subsequent outbreaks.[91] These houses held on to the dispensations secured *in extremis* and exploited them to stimulate growth in the decades that followed. By the beginning of the fifteenth century it had become customary for Bury, St Albans and Westminster to admit as many as half a dozen novices at any one time and to progress them from minor orders to the priesthood as soon as practically possible.[92] At St Albans Abbot Thomas de la Mare also made efforts to restore the ragged *horarium* after the pressures of the plague years. As early as 1351, in a series of constitutions issued for the abbey and its dependent cells, he called upon his brethren to resume due observance of the Office of the Dead which of late had been so badly neglected.[93] These great abbeys also appear to have recovered their income to a great extent in the half-century after the first appearance of the plague. Responding pragmatically to the prevailing economic climate, a portion of their estates were brought back into demesne, while others were further subdivided, rent-farmed, or sold. These houses also increased their investment in commercial enterprises, such as urban tenements, shops and even inns.[94] The growing involvement of the great Benedictine monasteries in industrial ventures – open-face coal-mining, tin, etc. – might also be seen as a response to economic pressures of the period.[95]

Throughout Europe the years of pestilence also profoundly affected the emotional, psychological and spiritual dynamics of the monastic community. While historians have been rightly reluctant to characterise the prevailing attitudes of the post-1349 generations as a culture of morbidity, the signs of renewed religious intensity in this period, of an ascetic revival

[90] *Chronica Johannis de Reading et Anonymi Cantuariensis, 1346–1367*, ed. J. Tait (Manchester, 1914), pp. 106–10 at 106.
[91] *MRH*, pp. 61, 66.
[92] Harvey, 'A Novice's Life at Westminster', pp. 51–73.
[93] *GASA*, ii. 418–44; Clark, *Monastic Renaissance*, p. 12.
[94] Smith, *Canterbury Cathedral Priory*, p. 200.
[95] See above, p. 143.

even, are pronounced.[96] In England the number of the Benedictines seeking transfer to a reformed order – Carthusians, Cistercians and Brigittines – rose steadily between 1360 and 1425. Several St Albans monks sought the reformed life early in the reign of Abbot Thomas de la Mare, among them his own brothers.[97] De la Mare himself was said to have cultivated a strictly aesthetic regime which appears to have involved severe forms of mortification. One of De la Mare's subordinate priors, William of Belvoir, was also known for his conspicuous asceticism and resigned his office to enter eremitic retirement within the precincts of his monastery.[98] These same impulses might also explain the increased incidence of monks seeking dispensation to make a personal pilgrimage.[99] They may also have stimulated the interest in contemplative texts that is so marked in monastic books of the later fourteenth and early fifteenth centuries.[100]

It would be wrong, of course, to suggest there now settled over the order – or, indeed, any other religious – some form of existential malaise. The Benedictines that survived the Black Death were among the most energetic that the order had seen for several generations. Their number included a handful of influential prelates – Adam Easton, Simon Langham – and several prolific scholars and writers, not the least of whom were Henry Kirkstead (Bury St Edmunds) and Thomas Walsingham (St Albans). Moreover, it was the generation born against the background of the pestilence – Luigi Barbo, for example, of Santa Giustina di Padua – that inaugurated the reform movements of the fifteenth century.

Warfare

The conditions of life for the Benedictines were also affected by armed conflicts both widespread and protracted in the period after 1215. The first monasteries had suffered frequently from incursions and occasionally from conquering forces but rarely on the scale, or with the far-reaching economic, political and social consequences, of later medieval warfare. Europe did not erupt into war after 1215, nor were the conflicts it witnessed wholly unconnected with the troubles of earlier centuries. The emergence of national monarchies, and systems of governance to support them, however, combined with the continuing instability of empire and papacy,

---

[96] For discussions of post-Back Death morbidity, see Platt, *King Death*, pp. 177–92; Rigby, *English Society in the Later Middle Ages*, pp. 321–2.

[97] *GASA*, ii. 373.

[98] BL, Add. MS 4936, fo. 129r; Clark, *Monastic Renaissance*, p. 25.

[99] For example, Cambridge University Library, MS Ee 4. 20, fos. 66v–67r, 82r; *CPL*, VI. 404–15, pp. 5–21 (Richard Scherman, monk of Peterborough); a Battle monk, *VCH Sussex*, ii. 52–6 at 56.

[100] For example, *AL*, nos. 1493 ('Speculum laicorum'), 1495 ('Dieta salutis'), 1506, 1576 ('Lumen laicorum'), 1511 ('Doctrina bone vite'), pp. 370–2; *EBL*, B43. 14, B68. 80, 340, B100. 13, 35, pp. 222, 359, 387, 599–601; *Dover*, BM103aa, v, 130a, pp. 72, 87; *Peterborough*, B21. 347g, pp. 176, 247–8.

created a climate more explosive (in the old Europe at least) than at any time since the First Crusade. The resurgence of heresy and the sharpening of other perceived threats to Christian unity – Islam, Judaism, paganism – also offered an impetus for further, multi-lateral, offensive campaigns. No conflict did more to destabilise Europe in this period than the struggle for sovereignty between England and France (1337–1453); it drew in, and unsettled, neighbouring polities (Burgundy, Flanders, Scotland) and extended the European battleground from the Mediterranean to the North Sea. This was a fight for ascendancy in northern Europe; to the south and east the vapid political authority of empire and papacy encouraged a proliferation of urban, magnate and – at least over the Neapolitan succession – dynastic conflicts. Internal strife exposed even the heartland of the old Europe to external threats. The campaigns of the Ottoman Mehmet the Conquerer (d. 1481) extended further west than any of his predecessors and proved near-fatal to the infrastructure of the Christian frontier. The resurgence of English, French, Iberian and imperial monarchies at the turn of the fifteenth century served only to stimulate a search for new hegemonies. The widespread suppression of monastic religion after 1517 reflected not only the rise of new religious orthodoxies, but also the priorities of a society still organised for war.

For much of the period, the Benedictines found themselves in the path of armed forces and suffered damage and, in some cases, total destruction. It was the opening of the Plantagenet offensive under Edward I that generated perhaps the order's greatest war story: in August 1295 a French raiding-party sacked Dover Priory and murdered one Thomas de la Hale, the only member of the monastic community not to flee; Hale was subsequently promoted as a popular saint. The abbot of Colchester attempted to profit, illicitly purchasing the custody of a Crécy prisoner in 1346.[101] It was in the second and subsequent phases of the Anglo-French conflict, following the failure of the peace of Brétigny (1360), that the monasteries were most affected. In England the resumption of war saw persistent piracy in the channel and sporadic assaults on the property of coastal monasteries. In 1370 Prior Haimo [of] Offington of Lewes won widespread admiration for his spirited resistance to, and subsequent capture by, the French sailors.[102] At the same time the Scots' repeated raids ravaged the land, and at times, the buildings, of the border monasteries. The prior of Tynemouth (Northumbria) complained to his superiors at St Albans that his church had been rendered almost ruinous both before and after the invasion of

---

[101] C. R. Haines, *Dover Priory: A History of the Priory of St Mary the Virgin and St Martin of the New Work* (Cambridge, 1930), pp. 161, 469–78. *VCH Essex*, ii. 93–102 at 96.

[102] The incident was reported with pride by contemporary monastic chroniclers: *St Albans Chronicle*, ed. Taylor and Childs, pp. 132–3, 162–3. For the consequences of coastal attack on Abbotsbury (Dorset), see *VCH Dorset*, ii. 48–53 at 51–2.

1385.[103] The rumbling of Welsh rebellion also disturbed the Black Monks of Worcester and, half a century after its suppression, the tiny Tewkesbury outpost of Goldcliff.[104] The mainland campaigns of this period, and in particular the Lancastrian invasion of 1417, brought the conflict to the precincts of the monasteries of Normandy, Gascony and the Touraine. In Normandy, Fécamp was seized, and held, by English captains and the buildings of Jumièges were badly damaged. Mont Saint-Michel, crowned by its Benedictine abbey, was besieged in the winter of 1423, although the English forces never took the town.[105] The Anglo-French war weakened monasteries as much by attrition as by violent assault. This was not the experience of their counterparts in central and eastern Europe. The magnate (*Vögte*) violence in the Austro-Swiss counties of the empire saw the destruction of the abbeys of Beinwil (Basel) and Muri (Canton of Aargau).[106] The bitter battles of Hussite Bohemia brought the burning of Sázava and explusion of the Polish community from Krzeszów; the royal abbey of Broumov was besieged but never taken.[107] The advance of the Ottomans across the Danube led to the systematic destruction of Hungarian monasteries; the royal house of Pannonhalma was heavily fortified but finally succumbed to the Turks in 1590.[108] Their rising hegemony in the eastern Mediterranean removed the Black Monks from Nicosia (Cyprus) in 1426. In the second quarter of the sixteenth century conflict continued to be as great a threat as Reformation theology: the reformist monks of Liessies (Flanders) abandoned their abbey for the priory of Ath after the French invasion of 1537.[109]

Only a minority of Benedictine monasteries was damaged or destroyed but many more suffered from the political, social and economic pressures of war. The monasteries of Aquitaine-Guyenne, Normandy, the Pas-de-Calais and Champagne saw their revenues tumble through successive waves of English *chevauchées*: in 1384 the abbot and convent of Rheims reported on the matter of rent(s) 'on ne paie pas la moitié, tant pour causes des guerres, comme des mortalities'.[110] The decimation of their incomes and the disruption of their manorial administration left them vulnerable

[103] Walsingham, *Historia Anglicana*, ed. Riley, i. 144, 152. See also W. Bower, *Scotichronicon: in Latin and English*, ed. D. E. R. Watt et al., 9 vols. (Edinburgh, 1993–8), vii. 446–7.

[104] *Chapters*, ed. Pantin, iii. 205, 209: 'horribilium insurrecionem Wallicorum'; *VCH Gloucestershire*, ii. 61–6; *MRH*, p. 67.

[105] *L'abbaye bénédictine de Fécamp*, i. 144–9 at 145–7; J. Huynes, *Histoire générale de l'abbaye du Mont St Michel au péril de la mer*, 2 vols. (Rouen, 1873), ii. 101–9 at 105–9; *Gallia monastica*, i. 16–17.

[106] R. C. Hend, 'Shared Lordship, Authority and Administration: The Exercise of Dominion in the Genevan *Herrschaften*, 1417–1600', *Central European History* 30 (1997), 489–512 at 505, n. 59.

[107] F. G. Heymann, *John Žižka and the Hussite Revolution* (Princeton, 1955), p. 303.

[108] R. J. W. Evans, *The Making of the Habsburg Monarchy, 1550–1700: an Interpretation* (Oxford, 1979), p. 252.

[109] Schmitz, *Histoire*, iii. 225–9 at 225; G. de Blois, *A Benedictine of the Sixteenth Century: Louis de Blois*, trans. Lady Lovat (London, 1878), pp. 93–5 at 95.

[110] *Gallia monastica*, i. 26.

to encroachment following the recovery of royal authority under Charles VII. Even the region's greater abbeys, such as Rheims and Saint-Trond, were subject to *commendam* grants during the reign of Louis XI (1461–83).[111]

An entire sector of Benedictine England was disrupted and, finally, dispersed as a result of the Anglo-French war. The 'alien' priories, convents founded and supervised by parent communities in France, faced mounting pressures from the outbreak of war; some had suffered earlier during the Saint-Sardos conflict of 1324. Communications with their mother-houses were strained at the height of the English campaigns and by the last quarter of the fourteenth century the few remaining French brethren had already drained away. Before the peace of 1394 the greater French abbeys had abandoned their properties: the abbey of Bec sold Steventon Priory as early as 1363.[112] The peace encouraged a rapprochement and several abbeys (Caen, Conches) resumed the supervision of their English colonies.[113] The human and material resources of these houses had been irrevocably undermined, however, and the new campaigns of Henry V and his regents broke the remaining bonds with the French abbeys. In 1414 no fewer than forty-two priories were suppressed; further followed them in 1415, 1420, 1442 and 1447. In a number of cases their endowments were redeployed for collegiate foundations.[114] The constant levies of taxation in England and France should not be underestimated as a new pressure upon even the more venerable, and best endowed Benedictine houses.[115] The impact of continuous conflict on the community of monks itself should not be underestimated. An embattled mentality is evoked in many contemporary chronicles.[116] The profusion of personal weapons in the monastic enclosure may be indicative not only of the social context of late medieval Benedictines but also of their consciousness – at Lewes, Mont Saint-Michel or Broumov – of the threats beyond the precinct wall. Perhaps it was not only at St Albans where the brethren were eager to take up arms themselves – here to join Bishop Despenser's doomed crusade.[117]

---

[111] Ibid., i. 26–7.

[112] *MRH*, p. 89; *VCH Berkshire*, pp. 112–13 at 113.

[113] *MRH*, pp. 85 (Frampton, Hykeham: Caen), 87 (Monkland: Conches), 88, 91 (Panfield with Well Hall: Caen), 93 (Wooton Wawen: Conches); *Heads of Religious Houses*, ed. Knowles *et al.*, iii. 177.

[114] For example, the priories of Stogursey (Somerset) and Wooton Wawen (Warwickshire, having previously been returned to its Norman proprietor) presented respectively to Eton College and King's College, Cambridge: *MRH*, pp. 90, 93.

[115] For example, M. Mate, 'The Impact of War on the Economy of Canterbury Cathedral Priory, 1294–1340', *Speculum* 57 (1982), 761–78.

[116] For example, the suspicion of the St Albans chronicler, Thomas Walsingham, towards John of Gaunt, duke of Lancaster who threatened to 'disturb the whole commonalty' ('ad totius communitatis incommodum'): *St Albans Chronicle*, ed. Taylor and Childs, pp. 72–3.

[117] Walsingham, *Historia Anglicana*, ed. Riley, ii. 416. For the 'crusade', see also *St Albans Chronicle*, ed. Taylor and Childs, pp. 672–82, 684–8, 690–704.

Urbanisation

The monasteries were affected not only by sudden crises but also by fundamental structural changes which, while they may have come into focus in the fourteenth or fifteenth centuries, were the fruit of many generations. The building of urban Europe began before the thirteenth century, but the century after 1250 saw the establishment of further towns of small and middle size and the steady expansion of existing cities, markets and ports. The infrastructure of the greatest cities grew rapidly and with it the raft of commercial and political privileges exercised by their governing elite. The demographic drift which underpinned these developments forced fissures in the feudal bonds between labourer and lord and even before the Black Death a number of new status groups were readily apparent. The transformation of the social and economic environment challenged the established magnate elite. It would be premature to trace the fall of the traditional aristocracy from as early as the fourteenth century, but there is no doubt that in this period, and in the decades before the Reformation, the men who had been the principal patrons of monasticism, and much else besides, were now compelled to seek out new sources of power.

The expansion of the urban environment brought a new challenge to the status of the Benedictines. By contrast with their mendicant counterparts, many of their monasteries pre-dated the urban community that surrounded them and could claim seigniorial authority from time out of mind. Their control of labour and trade had been contested before the fourteenth century, but the conditions prevailing between the Great Famine (1315–17) and the Black Death, and for decades after, brought these bonds to breaking point. In 1327, at a time also of intense political upheaval, the subjects of the Black Monks of Bury and St Albans rose against their superiors. They rose again in 1381, when the commons of Essex and Kent converged on London and challenged the Crown: the men of the monastic boroughs were aroused less by the collapse of royal authority than by the general crisis of lordship it temporarily provoked.[118] Now the challenge to lordship was not confined to the Home Counties: the Benedictines of Chester were threatened by their Wirral tenants who made brief recourse to arms.[119] The urban monasteries of mainland Europe experienced sporadic challenges to their temporal authority, most notably perhaps in the commune protests of the Italian peninsula; although the scenes of violent revolts (1358, 1378, 1382), in Flanders and France the monasteries were largely unscathed.[120] The greater abbeys and priories recovered their authority as economic and social stability returned in the years after 1450, but their supervision of their

[118] Dobson, *The Peasants' Revolt of 1381*, pp. 269–77.
[119] *VCH Cheshire*, iii. 132–46 at 1410.
[120] S. K. Cohn, *Popular Protest in Late Medieval Europe: Italy, France, and Flanders* (Manchester, 2004), pp. 110–22, 303–5.

subjects was transformed. Labour services were widely commuted and wage labour became the norm.[121] Craft and commercial restrictions were lifted: before 1500 the abbot and convent permitted the Bury weavers to foregather as a guild.[122] The governance of the secular community was not ceded to the commonalty but they were now recognised as a corporate body.

The reinvigoration of the urban economy brought changes to the material condition of many Benedictine monasteries. The fall in benefaction and the local constraints on the alienation of estates, such as the Statute of Mortmain (1279) in England and Wales, led them, far more frequently than before, into the purchase of property. In the half century after the Black Death, some houses amassed a substantial portfolio, much of it city tenements and commercial premises. As the development of the urban infrastructure resumed, in the second half of the fifteenth century and after, monastic landlords played a leading role in the reconfiguration of the cityscape.[123] The dissolution of the monasteries in England may have left a political and spiritual vacuum in many urban centres, but the release of much new-build property into the marketplace must have appeared to the local populace a positive boon.

This increasing interaction with urban society also left its imprint on internal life. As landlord and proprietor, the monastic superior was drawn into participation in civic affairs, political, social, and, perhaps especially, devotional. Their civic experiences reshaped their own observances. The proliferation of monastic confraternities in the post-Black Death period is directly attributable to the influence of urban life.

Europe in the Later Middle Ages: Culture and Belief

The decades either side of the Black Death also unsettled beliefs, values and patterns of thought in many parts of Europe. Indeed, it is frequently to this period that historians trace the first fractures that led to the collapse of the cultural framework – concepts, institutions, modes of discourse – of the Latin Middle Ages. The intellectual integrity of the institutional church – which Aquinas had aimed to encapsulate in his *Summae* – was challenged, from as early as the mid-thirteenth century, by radical masters in the same schools that had formed him, while its unity had been shattered by the friars to whom he was professed. At the same time the clamour of extra-clerical voices on matters of doctrine and knowledge of the divine undermined not only magisterial authority but also the spiritual and pastoral purpose

---

[121] See above, p. 160.
[122] Gottfried, *Bury St Edmunds and the Urban Crisis*, pp. 104–7. See also *Memorials of St Edmund's Abbey*, ed. Arnold, iii. 358–68.
[123] For example, Dobson, *Durham Priory*, p. 29; G. Rosser, *Medieval Westminster, 1200–1540* (Oxford, 1989), p. 45.

of the priesthood itself. The vigour of vernacular literatures tended to translate this dissent into a threatening counter-culture. Meanwhile, an artistic and scholarly elite of middle Italy recovered the traces of a classical *cultus* against which their own time could be considered only an age of darkness. The religious orders in general, and the oldest monastic order in particular, are often represented as the principal casualties of this state of cultural flux. Their identity as custodians of church, doctrine and orthodox observance appeared now to leave them at the margins of a society captivated by alternative authorities and their own autonomy. Yet it would be wrong to suggest the foundations of monastic culture were somehow fatally undermined. There were communities of Benedictines that engaged with, and even absorbed, these new approaches in theology, language and literature. Recent research has recast the Black Monks as pioneers of classicism and (proto-)humanism in late medieval England.

Asceticism and Mysticism

The enduring appeal of the *RB* in the Middle Ages lay in its combination of genuine asceticism – chastise the body, relieve the poor, forsake the world ('corpus castigare, pauperes recreare, saeculi actibus se facere alienum': *RB*, iv. 11, 13, 20) – with a regime of general moderation. The counterpoint between these two themes did much to shape the Benedictine experience as it evolved from Monte Cassino to Cluny, but the great spiritual renewal of the Gregorian period, and the spread of the reformed monastic orders, exposed their obvious contradictions. Reports of a 'crisis of cenobiticism' between *c.* 1050 and *c.* 1150 may have been exaggerated, but there were many Black Monks of this period moved to echo John of Fécamp's plea, 'Free the soul of your servant from these struggles and squabbles' ('Libera animam servi tui ab his iurgiis et contentionibus').[124] The spiritual currents of the later Middle Ages – mendicant *paupertas Christi*, millenarian prophecy, the revelatory theology of the unschooled and the *devotio moderna* – renewed these tensions and tended to unsettle observant life on both sides of the precinct wall. In this climate the oldest monastic order confronted a challenge not only to its corporate power, but also to its pastoral authority, perhaps to the spiritual value of the monastic vocation itself.

Certainly these later medieval trends made a powerful impression upon the intellectual life of the Benedictines. The vigour of internal debates over the original *ascèse* of the *RB* may have subsided after 1200, but the mystical and spiritual literature of the reformed religious, and some radical works of prophecy and revelation, still attracted readers. The English Black Monks were early enthusiasts for Hildegard of Bingen and perhaps played a role

---

[124] Van Engen, 'Crisis of Cenobiticism Reconsidered', p. 271n.

in the initial transmission of Elizabeth of Schönau's *Liber viarum Dei*.[125] Two Bury manuscripts of the second half of the thirteenth century both contain Joachimite prophecies.[126] A fourteenth-century compilation connected with Ramsey Abbey suggests Joachimite *revelatio* retained a certain currency after 1349.[127] The English Benedictines also engaged with aspects of the Franciscan controversy, and especially the anti-fraternal response of William of Saint-Amour. They were eager champions of Archbishop Richard Fitzralph of Armagh, whose *De pauperie Salvatoris* renewed corporate tensions in 1357, and his pastoral perspective perhaps eclipsed William's apocalypticism.[128] The English abbeys also absorbed the influence of other insular trends: the anti-scholastic theology of Richard Rolle of Hampole and the Carthusian Walter Hilton attracted a number of early Benedictine readers: Abbot Thomas Spofford of St Mary's, York, appears to have encouraged the reading of Rolle among his brethren, and his own monastic chaplain, Christopher Braystanes, was both a reader and a convert to the Carthusian habit.[129] The interest in these texts must also account for the early reception of the *Revelationes* of Birgitta of Sweden: it was an English Benedictine, Cardinal Adam Easton, who led English clergy in the promotion of her cult, composing a *Defensorium Beatae Birgittae*.[130] The prominence of these genres in English houses generated a handful of original Benedictine contributions to the growing corpus of contemplative literature. The anonymous monk of Farne Island (*fl.* 1349), affiliated to Durham Priory, produced a short compendium of meditations – on angels, the Virgin Mary, and the Durham patron, St Cuthbert – against the background of the Black Death.[131] Another Durham monk, John Uthred of Boldon (d. 1390), composed a *meditatio devota* on Christ's passion which circulated, and was perhaps deliberately published throughout, the English congregation.[132]

[125] K. Kerby-Fulton, *Books under Suspicion: Censorship and the Tolerance of Revelatory Writing in Late Medieval England* (Notre Dame, IN, 2006), pp. 101–8.

[126] Ibid., pp. 101, 103, 108.

[127] Cambridge, Corpus Christi College, MS 321. See also Kerby-Fulton, *Books under Suspicion*, p. 97.

[128] K. L. Walsh, *A Fourteenth-Century Scholar and Primate: Richard Fitzralph in Oxford, Avignon and Armagh* (Oxford, 1981), pp. 446, 455.

[129] M. Deanesly, 'The *Incendium Amoris* of Richard Rolle and St Bonaventura', *EHR* 29 (1914), 98–101 at 99–100.

[130] The best evidence is from female convents: a book in English called 'Bridget' was acquired at Thetford, and a compilation made probably for Carrow was influenced by the text: M. C. Erler, *Women, Reading and Piety in Late Medieval England* (Cambridge, 2002), pp. 42&n., 76. It is worth noting a copy among books donated to the Cistercian women of Swine perhaps before 1400: Bell, *What Nuns Read*, pp. 168–9 at 169. A copy was among the books of Monk Bretton priory before the Dissolution: *EBL*, B55. 22, p. 271. See also F. Johnson, 'The English Cult of Birgitta of Sweden', *Analecta Bollandiana* 103 (1985), 75–92. For Easton, see R. B. Dobson, 'Adam Easton, *c.* 1330–97', *ODNB*, 8417; B. Morris, *St Birgitta of Sweden* (Woodbridge, 1999), p. 154; J. A. Schmidtke, '"Saving" by Faint Praise: St Birgitta of Sweden, Adam Easton and Medieval Antifeminism', *American Benedictine Review* 33 (1982), 149–61.

[131] Pantin, 'Monk-Solitary of Farne', 162–86.

[132] H. Farmer, 'The *Meditacio devota* of Uthred of Boldon', *Analecta monastica*, 5th series, 43 (1958), 187–206; Sharpe, *Latin Writers*, pp. 699–702 at 701.

The engagement of Continental convents with these post-1215 trends is not nearly so well documented. There are glimpses of an early awareness of Joachimite prophecies in a handful of French and German houses. The Black Monks of both northern and southern regions also responded to the revelations of Catherine of Siena and Birgitta of Sweden. In a Tuscan convent Catherine was so much a part of the devotional landscape as to be commemorated in a commissioned altarpiece by Beccafumi.[133] Birgitta's *Revelationes* appear to have been as well known to European Benedictines as to their English counterparts.[134] The monks of northern Europe were also attracted to the ascetic programme of the brethren of the *devotio moderna*. Their pioneering community at Windesheim and its subsequent congregation provided the model for the Benedictine reforms begun at Melk (1418) and Bursfeld (1430).[135] The texts of the *devotio moderna* were taken up by the reformed monasteries in England but it would appear had scarcely any impact upon the Benedictines at least until the advent of print; a solitary, mid-fifteenth-century manuscript of the *Imitatio Christi* may be connected with St Albans Abbey, but there is no trace of this or other Windesheim works in Benedictine book lists.[136]

There is no doubt these spiritual and theological trends also left their imprint upon the observant life of the Black Monks, both by their own design, and as determined by congregational, episcopal and papal supervisors. The renewed profile of ascetic and contemplative programmes persuaded a number of individual Benedictines to seek greater rigour, if necessary, even beyond their commitment to the *RB*. There are several recorded cases of religious adopting an eremitic existence while remaining within their community, and the contemporary response suggests their actions were not wholly uncommon. In the middle years of the fourteenth century a hermitage on Farne Island was reoccupied by at least one representative of Durham Cathedral Priory.[137] Abbot Thomas de la Mare of St Albans (d. 1396) adopted a punishing regime of personal mortification alongside his public, and political, responsibilities as a prelate.[138] Abbot Thomas Spofford of St Mary's Abbey, York, resigned his office and retired

---

[133] B. P. Gordley, 'A Dominican Saint for the Benedictines: Beccafumi's "Stigmatization of St. Catherine"', *Zeitschrift für Kunstgeschichte* 55 (1992), 394–412.

[134] *EBL*, B55. 22, p. 271 (Monk Bretton); Erler, *Women, Reading and Piety*, pp. 41–2; *Prophets Abroad: The Reception of Continental Holy Women in Late Medieval England*, ed. R. Voaden (York, 1996), especially pp. 71–114, 161–76.

[135] W. Scheepsma, *Medieval Religious Women in the Low Countries: the 'Modern Devotion', the Canonesses of Windesheim and their Writings* (Woodbridge, 2004); R. Fuller, *The Brotherhood of the Common Life and its Influence* (Albany, NY, 1995), pp. 76–86.

[136] R. Lovatt, 'The "Imitation of Christ" in Late Medieval England', *TRHS* 5th Series 18 (1968), 97–121. The misattribution to a thirteenth-century Benedictine 'Abbot Gerson' was current among fifteenth-century readers: A. Gwyn, 'New Light on the Imitation of Christ', *Studies* 29 (1940), 84–94 at 85. The possible St Albans copy is Oxford, Bodleian Library, MS Laud Misc. 215.

[137] Pantin, 'Monk-Solitary of Farne', 162–86.

[138] *GASA*, iii. 403, 404–5.

to a cell, although, as an advocate of the New Learning, this might be seen as a deliberate appropriation of the humanist *topos* of *otium* versus *negotium*.[139] This was not a pattern exclusive to England: Abbot Gutolf von Heiligenkreuz of Marienburg resigned his office to return to the cloister as an eremite.[140] The Benedictine convent at Sarlat built a colony of dry-stone, beehive cells, *cabanes*, deep in the Dordogne forest at Breuil to which they might retreat at regular intervals.[141] At the beginning of the fifteenth century, a number of English Benedictines abandoned the order for the Carthusians, and the Brigittine community of Syon. A resumption of *ad literam* observance, if not also a re-creation of the 'pristine' condition of early monasticism, also informed the injunctions of congregational and episcopal visitors in England over the course of the pre-Reformation centuries. It is difficult not to hear in their requirements for the exposition of the *RB* in the vernacular, the daily delivery of a biblical lecture, and the resumption of the craftwork of book production an echo of the values of the *devotio moderna*.[142] It should be emphasised, of course, that the populous and sophisticated precincts of the Benedictines were not wholly separated from the practice of eremites, even in the later period. England's most celebrated anchoress, Julian, lived in the churchyard of the parochial chapel of St Julian under the patronage of the nuns of Carrow (Norfolk).[143]

Among the convents of central and eastern Europe the spirit of reform was palpable. The community of Windesheim drew under its wing two Benedictine houses of Lower Saxony, Hildesheim and Lüneburg, both of which were subsequently affiliated to the Bursfeld congregation.[144] The effect of their exchanges on the Benedictine *opus Dei* may have been significant since Windesheim despised the polyphonic complexity of monastic music, preferring (according to their annalist, Johann Busch) 'Bearded men of ripe age ... moving with noble gravity ... booming forth the psalms of David with no childish or womanly treble but with a manly vigour.'[145] The Windesheim revival of the *ars scribendi* also resounded in these and other German houses: specimen writing books survive from Augsburg, Kremsmünster and Melk.[146]

Perhaps more significant from a community perspective was the extent to which these trends appear to have affected the involvement of some Benedictines in the spiritual life of their lay subjects. Their own interest in

---

[139] Emden, *BRUO*, iii. 1744.

[140] G. B. Fowler, 'Learning in Austria about 1300: Notes and Suggestions', *Church History* 20-1 (1951), 56–71 at 66.

[141] See illustration 7.

[142] *Chapters*, ed. Pantin, i. 74-28 at 75, 95, 111; ii. 50-1 at 51; ii. 127-8; *Visitations*, ed. Thompson, i. 102 (Peterborough, 1432), 106 (Ramsey, 1432).

[143] Oliva, *Convent and Community*, pp. 155–6.

[144] Coulton, *Five Centuries of Religion*, iv. 157.

[145] Coulton, 'The Last Generations of Medieval Monachism', 442.

[146] Steinberg, 'Instructions in Writing'.

the expanding corpus of contemplative literature appears to have provided a new foundation for a productive relationship with the lay *devotus*. The exchange of devotional texts between Benedictines and their lay associates was not uncommon after 1350; personal testamentary bequests suggest some monks also assumed the role of spiritual advisor.[147] Their exposure to popular theology in all its variety appears to have encouraged the monks to seek a more prominent pastoral profile. It was not only the diocesan, and mendicant representatives, who counselled the would-be vowess Margery Kempe at Norwich in the early fifteenth century, but also Prior William Worsted of the Benedictine Cathedral Priory.[148] Prior Edmund Bocking of Canterbury Cathedral Priory counselled Elizabeth Barton when she claimed to have experienced visions of the Virgin Mary between 1530 and 1534, and also appears to have promoted the provocative, and political, message of her visions.[149]

Anticlericalism

The wide spectrum of popular theology, Latin and vernacular, that emerged in this period, and to which the Black Monks were exposed, shared a common undertone of anticlericalism. Of course, the criticism of the clergy, from light comedy to outright condemnation, was a literary trope well established before 1215, and the monastic order had been targeted as frequently as any of their regular and secular colleagues.[150] The range and register of the later medieval discourse, however, set it apart from earlier models and has been regarded by some historians as expressive of a deep-seated rejection of traditional clerical status. Certainly, the assaults on the monastic life now appeared sharper and more searching. Comic representations of the monk as glutton, drunkard or bawd were not entirely discarded but were now, generally speaking, subordinate to the discussion of more fundamental matters such as monastic observance, the nature, origin and value of monastic vows, and the necessity for temporal endowment.[151] In the wake of the Fourth Lateran Council the quality of Benedictine observance was widely debated, not only in popular broadsides but also in the legal and pastoral manuals prepared for the parish clergy.[152] The debates

[147] For example, New York Public Library, Spence 19 (Marrick): Scott, *Later Gothic Manuscripts*, ii. 217–19 (cat. 74); Beeleigh Abbey, Miss C. Foyle, Paris, Bibliothèque nationale, Fr. 1038 (Barking): Bell, *What Nuns Read*, pp. 107–8, 115–16. See also the book donations of Lady Ann Scrope of Harling to nunneries in Norwich diocese: Oliva, *Convent and Community*, p. 70.
[148] N. P. Tanner, 'The Cathedral and the City', in *Norwich Cathedral*, ed. I. Atherton *et al.*, pp. 255–80 at 275.
[149] For a summary of Prior Bocking's involvement in the case, see Bernard, *King's Reformation*, pp. 88, 92–3, 96–8.
[150] For background, see A. G. Rigg, 'Satire', in *Medieval Latin*, ed. Mantello and Rigg, pp. 562–8.
[151] Kaartinen, *Religious Life and English Culture*, pp. 13–22, 49–62.
[152] For example, the *Summa praedicantium* of John Bromyard, who did not confine his criticism of contemporary practice to the older monastic order, and the *Summa summarum* of William of Pagula

generated by Wyclif, Hus and their disciples transferred attention to the endowment of the monastic and other regular orders. The researches of the first generation of Christian humanists in the mid-fifteenth century, and after, turned the debate again to the validity, and exclusivity, of religious vows.[153]

The books and book lists of the later medieval Benedictines, albeit an unrepresentative sample of their original holdings, suggest a high degree of engagement with this disturbing, emerging discourse. Whether by official or unofficial channels, it would seem a wide selection of this material passed into English precincts in the centuries either side of 1350. One of the very earliest witnesses to *Piers Plowman* is a manuscript associated with Ramsey Abbey, perhaps compiled by its prominent graduate monk, John Wellys (*fl.* 1370).[154] Fifteenth-century compilers of miscellanies at Glastonbury and St Albans Abbey were able to secure copies of such anti-monastic works as Richard Trivetlam's *De laude universitatis Oxoniae*.[155] John Wheathampstead of St Albans, or his amanuensis, also held a fragment of John Swetstock's Lollard manifesto.[156] The humanist critiques attracted the attention of Benedictines in England and Continental Europe; in the precincts of northern Italy and the empire *De voto religionis* was vigorously debated, albeit the most vocal contributors came from the reformed convents of Carthusians.[157]

The principal effect of this rising tide of anticlericalism was to project the Black Monks into public – and, increasingly, political – controversy, perhaps to a greater extent, in certain congregations, than ever experienced before. The English Benedictines added their voices to the anti-fraternal chorus at the height of the Fitzralph affair and from this platform began to articulate their own apologia for the monastic order itself.[158] Even before the advent of Wyclif made such apologias an essential weapon in their armoury, the monks of Bury St Edmunds had begun to compile monastic apologetics,

---

[Paull], which reiterated the principle that the monastic order should not undertake pastoral care. For Bromyard, see G. R. Owst, *Literature and Pulpit in Medieval England*, 2nd edn (Oxford, 1961), pp. 247–66 at 262–4; K. Walls, *John Bromyard on Church and State: The Summa Praedicantium and Early Fourteenth-Century England: A Dominican's Books and Guide for Preachers* (Market Weighton, 2007). For Pagula, see L. E. Boyle, *Proceedings of the Second Congress of Canon Law* (Vatican City, 1965), pp. 415–56. See also Coulton, *Five Centuries of Religion*, iii. 580.

[153] C. Trinkaus, 'Humanist Treatises on the Status of the Religious: Petrarch, Salutati, Valla', *Studies in the Renaissance* 11 (1964), 7–45.

[154] Now Oxford, Bodleian Library, MS Bodley 851, fos. 124r–208r. For Wellys, see Emden, *BRUO*, iii. 2008.

[155] *Glastonbury miscellany*, ed. Rigg, pp. 75–6 [Cambridge, Trinity College, MS O.9.38]. For Trevytlam, see Emden, *BRUO*, ii. 1904; Sharpe, *Latin Writers*, p. 516.

[156] *Registrum abbatiae Johannis Whethamstede*, ed. Riley, i. 457–8.

[157] An anthology compiled at St Peter and St Paul, Erfurt, contained traditional monastic and contemporary authorities on the different nature of the monastic and secular clerical vocation: BL, Add. MS 15105.

[158] Walsh, *A Fourteenth-Century Scholar and Primate*, pp. 446, 455; E. Doyle, 'A Bibliographical List by William Woodford OFM', *Franciscan Studies* 35 (1976 for 1975), 93–100.

histories and hagiographies which circulated among affiliate houses and may have originated with a now lost *speculum cenobitarum*.[159] Later renderings incorporated an explicit challenge to the heterodox and 'other detractors of this present time'.[160] The English monks also advanced their defence of the order from the pulpit. The growing number of graduate monks brought with it a rise in Benedictine preaching. Sermons surviving from the period 1370–1425 show a preoccupation with the shortcomings of the secular clergy, the spread of irreligion and heresy, and the enduring spiritual power of the country's great monastic shrines (Canterbury, Durham, St Albans, Walsingham).[161]

It could be argued that the flowering of anticlerical literature in this period also served, paradoxically, to reinforce the status of certain monastic values, some of them characteristically Benedictine. The textual assault on the religious orders, whether in Latin or in the vernacular, was by no means indiscriminate. The exclusivity of their vows may have been challenged, but not the value of their observant lives. It was not without admiration that Clergie, in Passus X of *Piers Plowman*, envisaged a cloister, 'a place of harmonious co-operation, given over to study and to learning'.[162]

Vernacular

The great expansion of extra-clerical literature in the later Middle Ages was powered by the (re-)emergence of viable vernaculars throughout Europe. The dissemination of these vernaculars in a variety of documentary, literary and scholarly genres represented a challenge to the old monopoly of the clerical establishment, especially when, at the end of the fourteenth century, they appeared to become the vehicle of the heterodox.[163] In the century after the Black Death secular society steadily substituted Latin with the written vernacular in a wide variety of official and personal documents.[164] Clerical communities evinced greater caution, but before 1400 parish clergy, preachers and teachers of grammar in elementary schools experimented

---

[159] For the work at Bury see Pantin, 'Some Medieval English Treatises', 194–6, 198. See also Oxford, Bodleian Library, MS Bodley 240, pp. 7656–8526. The apologetics reached as far as the abbey of Tournus (Burgundy).

[160] Pantin, 'Some Medieval English Treatises', 214.

[161] S. Wenzel, *Latin Sermon Collections from Later Medieval England: Orthodox Preaching in the Age of Wyclif* (Cambridge, 2005), pp. 278–87; Clark, *Monastic Renaissance*, pp. 239–67.

[162] *Piers Plowman: A New Translation of the B-Text*, ed. A. V. C. Schmidt (Oxford, 1992), p. 104.

[163] For the intersection between vernacular literary and popular and heterodox religion, see S. McSheffrey, 'Heresy, Orthodoxy and English Vernacular Religion, 1480–1525', *PP* 186 (2005), 47–80; G. Hasenohr, 'Religious Reading among the Laity in France in the Fifteenth Century', in *Heresy and Literacy, 1000–1530*, ed. P. Biller and A. Hudson (Cambridge, 1996), pp. 205–21; F. Šmahel, 'Literacy and Heresy in Hussite Bohemia', in *Heresy and Literacy*, ed. Biller and Hudson, pp. 237–54.

[164] For this trend, see *Pragmatic Literacy: East and West, 1250–1330*, ed. R. H. Britnell (Woodbridge, 1997); E. Steiner, *Documentary Culture and the Making of Medieval English Literature* (Cambridge, 2003), pp. 1–16.

with macaronics, parallel texts and even complete translations.[165] The supervisors of women religious (bishops, monastic prelates) seized on vernacular translations as a valuable means of advancing observance in communities where Latin literacy had never become universal.[166] The reformed religious orders also readily adopted the written vernacular not only to disseminate their devotional manuals outside strictly clerical circles but also to distinguish their voices from those of the old order.

For their part the Black Monks remained equivocal over the use of the vernacular. Superiors did not endorse the use of translations of the *RB* or other canonical authorities; nor did capitular or episcopal visitors propose them. It appears the studies of novice and junior monks were assisted by at least bilingual glossaries and grammars.[167] In England novice masters made use of the manuals of secular schoolmasters such as Thomas Sampson (whose manuals were in French, not English), and later John Leyland; the popular *Medulla grammaticae*, which featured a full glossary of English words, also appears in a number of surviving novice 'readers'.[168]

Beyond the monastic *schola*, there was scarcely a trace of the vernacular in the observant life of the community. Reports of conversation inside the monastic enclosure are as rare in this as in earlier centuries, but a brief exchange recorded in the St Albans Abbey register shows obedientiaries and other seniors squabbling in the Latin of the *RB*.[169] The reading of professed monks remained predominantly Latinate.[170] In English book lists there are glimpses of romances in French (especially) and English, but barely a single example of the burgeoning devotional literature.[171] In the wake of the Peasants' Revolt and Wyclifism, there was widespread suspicion towards

[165] For this trend, see C. R. Bland, *The Teaching of Grammar in Late Medieval England: An Edition, with Commentary, of Oxford, Lincoln MS Lat 130*, Medieval Texts and Studies 6 (East Lansing, 1991); R. Copeland, 'Vernacular Translation and Instruction in Grammar in Fifteenth-Century England', in *Papers in the History of Linguistics: Proceedings of the Third International Conference on the History of the Language Sciences*, ed. H. Aarsleff, L. G. Kelly and H. J. Niederehe (Amsterdam, 1987), pp. 143–54; J. Fellman, 'The Earliest Renaissance Vernacular Grammar', *Orbis* 26:2 (1977), 409–10.

[166] Notably, Bishop Richard Fox of Winchester, who presented his own English translation of the *RB* to the women religious of his diocese in 1517; see Collett, *Female Monastic Life in Early Tudor England*. See also Power, *Medieval English Nunneries*, pp. 246–7.

[167] For examples of these texts, see *EBL*, B30. 6–10, pp. 139–40, especially the anthology, B30.10 (Evesham); Dover, BM1. 439, pp. 168–9; *Peterborough*, BP21. 149, 333b, pp. 110–11, 172. The popular Latin-English glossary *Medulla grammaticae* also appears to have found monastic readers. See also Worcester Cathedral Library, MS F 61, a fourteenth-century compendium of grammar texts, where the verb *amo–amare* is declined in English on fo. 283r.

[168] A. Bellenger, 'A Medieval Novice's Formation: Reflections on a Fifteenth-Century Manuscript at Downside Abbey', in *Medieval Monastic Education and Formation*, ed. G. Ferzoco and C. Muessig (London, 2000), pp. 35–55. See also Worcester Cathedral Library, F 123, fos. 99v–100r; Thomson, *Descriptive Catalogue*, pp. 84–5 at 85.

[169] *Registrum abbatiae Johannis Whethamstede*, ed. Riley, i. 110.

[170] See the selection of books recorded in rare borrowers' lists from Thorney and St Albans: *EBL*, B87, B100 (pp. 555–63, 598–604).

[171] For example at Evesham, Glastonbury and Ramsey: *EBL*, B30. 69a, 72–3, B39. 202, B68. 491, pp. 145, 192, 402; *Peterborough*, BP21.203b, 331b, 338a-b, pp. 130–1, 171–4.

written English, but the Benedictines' preference for Latin was perhaps more pedagogic than it was political, a product of their growing engagement with the universities and their academic syllabus. If their studies in the Schools strengthened their attachment to Latin culture it only intensified in the fifteenth century as the scholarly values of Italian humanism pervaded the cloister. It may be an accurate reflection of the cultural essence of the Benedictine community of this period that much of the extant ephemera – doggerel verses, obituaries, personal letters – is written in an allusive and florid, pseudo-classical Latin.[172] Here the divergence of male and female cultural values was marked: in Benedictine nunneries of the post-Black Death period vernacular reading was predominant; there was an increasing interdependence of their book culture and that of the noble or upper gentry household from which they had come.[173]

The internal idiom of the male monastery was juxtaposed with the development of a vernacular discourse in their dealings with the secular world. Over the course of the fifteenth century it became increasingly common for conventual correspondence, grants of confraternity and many other public documents to be written in the local language.[174] It would appear that when preaching to mixed congregations, the monks were also prepared to use the vernacular, although the macaronic reportage of contemporary sermons cannot be treated as an accurate guide to the actual mode of delivery.[175]

Civility

The spread of vernacular languages in this period and the literature that sustained them were symptoms of a fundamental shift in the cultural and social identity of Europe's secular elite. Between the Black Death and the Reformation it is generally understood that the nobility and the knightly class turned from their traditional martial and highly mobile existence towards a more settled, even pastoral state in which they cultivated alternative aesthetic, cultural and social values expressed in new patterns

---

[172] For example, A. G. Rigg, *A Glastonbury Miscellany of the Fifteenth Century: A Descriptive Index of Trinity College, Cambridge, MS O.9.38* (London, 1968), pp. 40–100, describing the poetry and prose in an anthology from Glastonbury Abbey; Weiss, *Humanism in England*, p. 118&n; A. L. Brown, 'The Latin Letters in MS All Souls 182', *EHR* 87 (1972), 565–73 at 565.

[173] For the book culture of the nuns, see Bell, *What Nuns Read*, pp. 17–20 at 18, 20, 59–60, 103–217 (books presented by provenance). See also Erler, *Women, Reading and Piety*, pp. 22–47; Oliva, *Convent and Community*, pp. 65–70.

[174] Of course, the customary names for comestibles had also introduced transliteration, if not a degree of macaronics, into obedientiary rolls, but in the century before the suppression it was not uncommon for the administrative documents of English monks to be written in the vernacular: Harvey, *Obedientiaries of Westminster*, p. 95 (Warden of the Lady Chapel).

[175] For vernacular sermons, see S. Wenzel, *Macaronic Sermons: Bilingualism and Preaching in Late-Medieval England* (Ann Arbor, MI, 1994); Wenzel, *Latin Sermon Collections*, pp. 89–90. See also P. J. Horner, *A Macaronic Sermon Collection from Late Medieval England: Oxford, MS Bodley 649* (Toronto, 2006).

of behaviour, recreation and building. This civil culture also attracted the gentry and mercantile communities whose wealth and public voice now encroached on the status of the old elite. The men and women of the religious orders were not only observers of these shifts and tensions but also active participants. Some, of course, were born into these milieus and carried at least a vestige of their values into the cloister, but even those of lower status were bound by the obligations of conventual administration and intercession into a constant interaction with the social elite.

Many patterns of elite behaviour and values penetrated Benedictine monasteries in the pre-Reformation period. Like the *arriviste* gentry and mercantile families from which a number of them were recruited, the monks of this period aspired to the recreations of the old nobility – hawking, hunting and even perhaps competing 'at the [archery] butts'. Visitation injunctions from fifteenth- and sixteenth-century England show the owning of dogs and diverse weaponry was not uncommon; likewise the dress of equestrian display.[176] Perhaps more benign forms of behaviour, such as dining in private – in the oriel of the refectory, for example – an evening collation, or reading in bed were also borrowed from the secular household.[177] The decision of Abbot Henry V of Tegernsee to establish a bathing-place at Wilbad Kreuth in 1511 might also be taken as a sign of the assimilation of essentially secular recreations.[178] It is tempting to see the tendentious table talk of which pre-Reformation English Benedictines were frequently suspected as another custom of civil society transplanted into the monastic enclosure.[179] Notwithstanding the obvious restrictions of the habit prescribed under the *RB*, these pre-Reformation Benedictines also inclined to the dress code of their middle-class kinsfolk. Episcopal visitors in England complained of the unnecessary, and notably unmonastic, luxury of the hoods, stoles, linen-shirts and fur-lined boots that they found at the greater abbeys and priories.[180] As Barbara Harvey recovered from the compotus rolls of Westminster Abbey, this taste for gentle comforts extended to the common table where, especially in the century before the Dissolution, were seen game and sweetmeats that would not have disgraced the dais of any knightly dining-hall.[181] It is a morbid index of the integration of the monastic and secular society in this period that remains from monastic cemeteries

---

[176] *Visitations*, ed. Thompson, ii. 280 (Peterborough, 1437), 296–7 (Peterborough, 1446–7); *Visitations*, ed. Jessopp, pp. 21, 279–80; *VCH Yorkshire*, iii. 101–5 (St Mary's York, 1535).

[177] *Visitations*, ed. Thompson, ii. 284–5, 294–5 (Peterborough, 1437, 1446–7), 303–4 (Ramsey, 1439). See also Erler, 'Private Reading', at 134.

[178] *Handbuch der deutschen Kunstdenkmäler*, iv. *München und Oberbayern*, ed. E. Gotz and G. Dehio (Munich, 1990), 1285.

[179] For example, *LP*, xiv/2, 454.

[180] *Visitations*, ed. Thompson, ii. 142–3, 154–5, 168; *VCH Durham*, ii. 103–5; Harvey, *Monastic Dress*, pp. 16–19. See also Hodges, *Chaucer and Clothing*, pp. 112–33 at 115–18.

[181] Harvey, *Living and Dying*, pp. 34–71 at 39, 52; J. Greatrex, 'Rabbits and Eels at High Table', in *Monasteries and Society in Medieval Britain*, ed. Thompson, pp. 312–28.

have revealed a predisposition to diffuse idiopathic skeletal hyperitosis (DISH), the bone disease that is the hallmark of high living.[182]

Their absorption of secular values was also reflected in the aesthetics of the monastic enclosure. Communal spaces were filled with the painted panels and tapestries fashionable in the secular household.[183] For their private chambers Benedictine prelates of the fifteenth and sixteenth centuries chose the grand chimney pieces pioneered in secular palaces: the abbot of Muchelney (Somerset) was regarded by Cromwell's commissioners as a model of a monastic superior but the comforts of his solar were almost indistinguishable from those of any fashionable secular lord.[184] These pre-Reformation superiors also superimposed their monastic status with expressions of personal and family identity. The personal rebus – often involving symbols that made a punning allusion to the family name – was widely adopted by abbots and priors; some also cultivated the use of a personal blazon of arms.[185] A fifteenth-century portrait (oil on board, *c.* 1480, French origin, now at the Metropolitan Museum of Art) of a haughty Black Monk in a detached attitude of prayer perhaps offers an impression of how far some Benedictines had appropriated the self-image of secular gentility.[186]

Church and State

The later medieval centuries not only brought changes to the economic, social and cultural fabric of Europe but also a fundamental restructuring of the institutions of Church and State. The Fourth Lateran Council marked the culmination of a century, or more, of papal, episcopal and monastic reform, but it also represented the inception of a new phase of ecclesiastical and seigniorial reorganisation that continued to the Black Death and beyond. The post-1215 papacy struggled to retain the authority realised under Innocent III, but although it reached its nadir under Boniface VIII (1294–1303), the ensuing Avignon exile (1305–77) ushered in a period (under Clement V (1305–14) and Benedict XII (1334–42)) of progressive reform. The Great Schism (1378–1417) stifled this spirit but it returned during the series of General Councils (Pisa, 1409; Constance, 1414–17; Basel, 1430–8),

---

[182] C. Daniell, *Death and Burial in Medieval England, 1066–1550* (London, 1997), p. 139. See also J. Rogers and T. Waldron, 'DISH and the Monastic Life', *International Journal of Osteoarchaeology* 1 (2001), 357–65; G. Stroud and R. L. Kemp, *Cemeteries of St Andrew Fishergate: The Medieval Cemeteries*, 12/2 (York, 1993).

[183] T. Tolley, 'Visual Culture', in *Gentry Culture in Late Medieval England*, ed. R. Radulescu and A. Truelove (Manchester, 2005), pp. 167–82. See also Luxford, *Art and Architecture*.

[184] *LP*, v, 10, 88; Luxford, *Art and Architecture*, p. 18.

[185] For example, the rebus of Prioress Isabel Wygun of Carrow (1503–35) which adorns the parlour fireplace of her lodgings, among other locations: *Greater Medieval Houses of England and Wales, 1300–1500*, ed. A. Emery (Cambridge, 2000), p. 73.

[186] H. B. Wehle, 'A Fifteenth-Century French Portrait', *The Metropolitan Museum of Art Bulletin* 33:2 (1938), 44–6.

if not to the papacy then at least to a number of its generals.[187] Secular rulers saw their authority extended in this period, not least as the strength of the institutional church appeared to falter. Their adoption of a framework of permanent institutions – exchequers, judiciaries, parliaments – diminished their old dependence on the infrastructure and personnel of the church: the *Eigenklöster* may have retained a symbolic importance but it was no longer an instrument of government.[188] For the Benedictines, as for many of their monastic and mendicant counterparts, the developments of this period within and between Church and State led to permanent changes in their own institutional and internal life. Increasingly, their independence was constrained as spiritual and temporal powers sought to legislate for the clergy in general and the religious orders in particular. Perhaps above all, they were drawn into cycles of reform driven by the competing priorities of congregational, papal and seigniorial authorities. After eight centuries governed almost exclusively by the *RB* and its later (re-)formulations, the Benedictines were constrained by a complex, and at times conflicting, weave of structures. The experience of the brethren of this period, with its different levels of visitation, legislative exposition, etc., would have been barely recognisable to their high medieval forebears.

Papacy and Councils

The Fourth Lateran Council represented a turning point in the papacy's relationship with the Benedictines as it began a process of intervention in their organisation and observance that continued almost to the brink of the Reformation. Monastic reform was not the primary concern of the council but nonetheless it promulgated a programme of change.[189] Canon 12 called for the adoption of a capitular structure among the monastic order in every province. Triennial meetings of the chapter were to supersede all other governing authorities and each chapter was to co-ordinate its own (also triennial) cycle of visitations, their regularity and rigour to be guaranteed, where necessary, by the diocesan; to compound any perceived assault on the autonomy of the order, the council advised the Benedictines to seek the counsel of the White Monks: 'Let two neighbouring abbots of the

---

[187] For reform in the age of the Schism and Councils see C. M. D. Crowder, *Unity, Heresy and Reform: The Conciliar Response to the Great Schism* (London, 1977), pp. 1–39, 182–9; Swanson, *Universities, Academics and the Great Schism*, pp. 181, 187, 189; C. M. Bellitto, *Nicolas de Clamanges: Spirituality, Personal Reform and Pastoral Renewal on the Eve of the Reformations* (Washington, DC, 2005), pp. 127–34.

[188] For the development of secular government in this period, see G. L. Harriss, 'Political Society and the Growth of Government in Late Medieval England', *PP* 138 (1993), 28–57; D. Potter, 'The King and his Government under the Valois, 1328–1498', in *France in the Later Middle Ages, 1200–1500*, ed. D. Potter, The Short Oxford History of France (Oxford, 2002), pp. 226–9; H. S. Offler, 'Aspects of Government in the Late Medieval Empire', in H. S. Offler, *Church and Crown in the Fourteenth Century: Studies in European History and Political Thought*, ed. A. I. Doyle (Aldershot, 2000), pp. 217–47.

[189] For the Fourth Lateran Council, see Morris, *Papal Monarchy*, pp. 433–8, 447–51; Bolton, *Innocent III*.

Cistercian order be invited to give them counsel and opportune assistance, since among them the celebration of such chapters is of long standing.' A number of other canons affected the order: Canon 11 called upon all cathedral churches, regular and secular, to appoint a master of theology; Canons 59–61 sought to restrict the receipt of spiritual and temporal properties by regular or secular clerks; Canon 64 forbade the payment of fees at the admission of a novice. By contrast, two canons also touched on the priority of the order to which the Benedictine hierarchy aspired: Canon 57 ascribed to them the right to bury during an Interdict, no small concession in England, where the sentence had been lifted barely eighteen months before; Canon 13 also asserted that any new religious order should adopt only a rule – such as the *RB* – already well established. The effect of the canons was uneven. The English Black Monks adhered to them almost *ad literam*. Chapters of the northern (York) and southern (Canterbury) provinces were in place within three years, and the first triennial meetings are recorded in 1218.[190] The English chapters also initiated a cycle of visitations, although accounts before the end of the thirteenth century are sparse. The cycle of chapters and visitations continued in England until 1532.[191] The monastic cathedral chapters made provision for masters, although perhaps not until the turn of the century.[192] In Continental provinces the capitular requirements appear to have been evaded: in France and Italy the regional power of the pre-existing networks such as Cluny and Montecassino was perhaps too great to make them meaningful. The German Benedictines were conscious enough of the capitular requirements to convene chapters in 1417 and 1451, but there is little evidence of regular conventions before the earlier date. In Spain a general chapter of monks met at Tarragona in November 1229 but there is no evidence of either an earlier gathering or any after this date; there were annual chapter meetings at the abbeys of Santa Maria de Benevivere, Palencia and San Victorián, Huesca, but these were not the triennial chapters conceived in 1215 but an administrative mechanism to supervise regional networks of dependent priories.[193]

Innocent's successors continued the papal supervision of the order. In 1235 Gregory IX (1227–41) issued a decree directed at monastic superiors, requiring their presence in the refectory at meal times; a subsequent revision in 1237 softened this obligation but spoke in general terms of their reintegration into claustral life. In 1239, the same year he sponsored the abortive Thibautian crusade, Gregory issued a complete set of statues for the

[190] *Chapters*, ed. Pantin, i. 3.
[191] Ibid., iii. 262.
[192] B. Dobson, 'The Monks of Canterbury in the Later Middle Ages', in *A History of Canterbury Cathedral*, ed. P. Collinson, N. Ramsey and M. Sparks (Oxford, 1995), pp. 69–153 at 109&n. See also *Canterbury College, Oxford*, ed. Pantin, iv. 69–70.
[193] P. Linehan, *The Spanish Church and the Papacy in the Thirteenth Century* (Cambridge, 1971), p. 39.

Black Monks.[194] In the same spirit as the Lateran canons, but more systematic in their scrutiny of community life, these statutes set stringent conditions for conventual administration, diet, and discipline derived from the strict standards of the *RB*. Gregory's programme for reform was underpinned by a series of legatine visitations. In England the first commission was conducted by the Cardinal Legate Otto in 1234; he returned in 1237 and remained for four years in an effort to enforce the papal statutes.[195] It seems English superiors were receptive to the reforms, perhaps since they did not represent an undue departure from their current practice. In Normandy they aroused resistance: Abbot Robert d'Ételan of Jumièges secured a papal dispensation from them in 1253 on the grounds they were contrary to the substance of the *RB*.[196] Innocent IV (1243–54) reissued the Gregorian code in 1245 and further legatine commissions followed in a number of provinces. A second legation, commissioned by Clement IV (1265–8), arrived in England in 1268, under the authority of Cardinal Ottobuono Fieschi. In April Ottobuono issued canons for the community of clergy in England, seventeen of which were addressed to the regulars and returned to the matters of conventual and individual property raised by Gregory, and the perennial problem of diet.[197] Their provisions were widely circulated and they appear to have been more familiar to the monks of later medieval England than any previous codes, not least the canons of 1215. Few if any of the themes tackled by Ottobuono were wholly new, but the clarity and rigour of his prescriptions, and their range, guaranteed their longevity as a point of reference. The canons were incorporated in collections of monastic canons compiled and circulated in England over the next two centuries; they, together with the *Benedictina* (the canons *Summi magistri* of 1336), became required reading for late medieval novices.[198] Episcopal visitors in England also routinely referred to them in framing their own injunctions.[199] The examination of the monks of Selby Abbey undertaken by Archbishop William Wickwane in 1279 appears to have been founded on both the legatine canons and the Gregorian code of 1239.[200] Legations also passed through Spain during the pontificate of Gregory but here the monks proved more obstructive (or less co-operative) than their English counterparts; a legatine visitation charged

[194] For the canons of 1235 and 1237, see Paris, *Chronica majora*, ed. Luard, vi. 235–47; Morris, *Papal Monarchy*, p. 545; *RO*, i. 270; Cheney, *Episcopal Visitations*, p. 72. See also J. Sayers, 'Peter's Throne and Augustine's Chair: Rome and Canterbury from Baldwin (1184–90) to Robert Winchelsey (1297–1313)', *JEH* 51:2 (2000), 249–66.

[195] D. M. Williamson, 'Some Aspects of the Legation of Cardinal Otto in England, 1237–4', *EHR* 64 (1949), 145–73.

[196] Cheney, *Episcopal Visitations*, p. 155.

[197] *Councils and Synods*, ii.2, 783; *RO*, i. 80. R. Graham, 'Cardinal Ottoboni and the Monastery of Stratford Langthorne', *EHR* 33 (1918), 213–25.

[198] For example, *EBL*, B43 41c, B120. 595b, 599, pp. 226, 743; *Peterborough*, BP21. 175d, p. 120.

[199] For example, the visitation injunctions of 1323 at Burton upon Trent: *VCH Staffordshire*, iii. 199–213.

[200] *VCH Yorkshire*, iii. 95–100.

to the abbots of Samos and Celanova appears to have been approached only as an opportunity to settle local scores.[201]

Neither the papal codes, nor successive legatine commissions, stifled clerical, or indeed, extra-clerical, interest in the matter of monastic reform. In spite of their own explosive bouts of self-examination, the mendicants of the later thirteenth century continued to pressure the Curia, and senior prelates, to confront the 'problem' of monastic observance. In 1274 on the eve of the Council of Lyons, Humbert de Romans (d. 1277), Minister General of the Dominicans, urged Gregory X (1271–6) to undertake a dissolution of 'those utterly decayed abbeys for which there is no hope of reform', with their endowments channelled into the support of a new crusade.[202] The distinguished Bishop Guillaume Durand of Mende (d. 1296) also urged prelates: 'the monastic order is now almost fallen'.[203] At the Council of Vienne in 1311, a delegation of English mendicants complained publicly 'quod monachi sunt indiscreti in confessionibus', an allegation that appeared to capture the mood of the meeting.[204]

The clamour over monastic reform in the councils and other clerical arena encouraged the independent initiatives of provincial prelates. In 1269 Filippo Augustariccio of Amalfi consolidated the members of one male and three female monasteries into a reformed convent at Atrani.[205] In 1301 Bishop Bernard von Prambach of Passau began a systematic visitation of the canon houses and monasteries 'unter der Enns' to which he appointed both an Augustinian and a Benedictine as commissioners.[206] In the same year in England Archbishop Robert Winchelsea (1294–1313) mounted a metropolitan visitation which subjected the monasteries to systematic scrutiny for the first time since Ottobuono's legation.[207] There were suspicions of further papal intervention from Pope John XXII (1316–34) in 1317.[208] Certainly, action on monastic observance appears to have remained a priority at Avignon in the first and second quarters of the fourteenth century.

The election of another monastic pontiff, the Cistercian Jacques Fournier (Benedict XII), in 1334 initiated perhaps the most important intervention in monastic affairs since 1215. In a succession of canons and decrees Benedict sought to legislate systematically for the monastic order as a whole, i.e. Benedictines, Cistercians and Canons Regular. He prefigured this programme of reform in 1335 with the decree *Pastor bonus*, which addressed

[201] Linehan, *The Spanish Church and the Papacy*, p. 39.

[202] Pixton, *German Episcopacy*, p. 467.

[203] Coulton, *Five Centuries of Religion*, iv. 71.

[204] *Chapters*, ed. Pantin, i. 173–4 at 174.

[205] R. Brentano, *Two Churches: England and Italy in the Thirteenth Century* (Berkeley, 1988), pp. 285–7.

[206] Fowler, 'Learning in Austria', 63.

[207] Graham, 'Metropolitan Visitation'.

[208] New constitutions issued in that year included prescriptions on the minimum age (17) for entry into clerical office. Pope John addressed Archbishop Winchelsea 'de voltentia commissa in legatos suos ulciscenda': *Concilia magnae*, ed. Wilkins, ii. 465, 469.

the specific issue of apostasy.[209] In 1336 he issued canons for the reform of the Benedictine order, *Summi magistri*; comparable codes addressed to the White Monks and the Black Canons also ensued.[210] *Summi magistri* was not an original document. Benedict returned to the matters of administration, diet and discipline first addressed in the Gregorian statutes of 1239 and to the capitular structure created in 1215; he also considered the arrangements for university study, although here too his provisions only codified what was already common practice. Its significance lay in the pragmatic – some contemporaries preferred to say lenient – approach adopted to some of the most controversial matters of conventual discipline, such as the eating of meat, which was now to be permitted outside the refectory on four days out of seven. In their codes the semantically sensitive schoolmen Innocent and Gregory had intended to recover the sense of the *RB ad literam*; Benedict the monk recognised that its literal observance was as irrevocable as the society in which it was written.[211]

Summi magistri was promulgated in England in 1337, and the general chapter of Benedictines which it brought into being convened the following year.[212] There were voices which condemned the code as 'oppressive' (*gravissima*), which tends to confirm the suggestion that the earlier, stricter Gregorian code had been all but forgotten. At any rate, the English chapter encouraged a loose interpretation of those prescriptions – on the rendering of accounts, on property, both conventual and private – which challenged current practice. Only the seventh chapter, 'On study', was followed almost without variation.[213] Nonetheless, *Summi magistri*, or the *Benedictina* as it and its sister codes came to be known in some quarters, were invested with a symbolic importance in English monasteries, matched only, after the *RB* itself, by the early English *consuetudines* (*Regularis Concordia, Decreta Lanfranci*). The text was read regularly and expounded; it was widely reproduced and in the course of the fourteenth and fifteenth centuries became a staple of the anthologies compiled for the training of novices.[214] For these later generations of Benedictines, it was not the specific prescriptions of *Summi magistri* that resonated but the status of the code as a whole, marking an official watershed between the pure observance of the remote past and pragmatic monasticism of their own day: a shibboleth for embattled Benedictines of the later Middle Ages. One fifteenth-century celebration of monastic pontiffs (a text which may have originated in

[209] G. Mollat, *The Popes at Avignon, 1305–78*, trans. J. Love (London, 1963), p. 30; *RO*, ii. 3.
[210] *Concilia magnae*, ed. Wilkins, ii. 585–613 at 588–613.
[211] *RO*, ii. 4; Mollat, *Popes at Avignon*, p. 31.
[212] *Chapters*, ed. Pantin, ii. 5–12 (June, 1338).
[213] *Concilia*, ed. Wilkins, ii. 588–613 at 596.
[214] *EBL*, B30. 44, B43.83x, B120. 601, pp. 143, 231, 744; *AL*, nos. 1827–31, p. 405 (St Augustine's, Canterbury).

Benedictine England) commended Benedict as one 'multas constituciones circa ordinem monachorum reperandum edidit salubriter et devoto'.[215]

Benedictine XII also provided papal recognition for the Olivetan reform (1344), which, with affiliate monasteries at Florence, Naples and San Gimignano, served to renew Benedictinism in middle Italy.[216] Urban V sought to reform Montecassino in 1370, presenting the Camaldolese Benedictine, Andrew of Faenza, as superior (although reserving the title of abbot for himself). He demanded subventions throughout Benedictine Europe to support the work of reconstruction and sought to recruit brethren to enter the reinvigorated community. The recovery was short lived, however, and before the mid-fifteenth century the order's premier abbey was again in the possession of secular commendators.[217] The Franciscan Sixtus IV (1471–84) promulgated constitutions for the reform of the order of Fontevraud in 1479; a mission from the mother-house to its three English dependencies had been mooted the year before, but there is no evidence of the effect of either the regional or corporate reform.[218] Martin V (1417–31), first pontiff of the restored papacy, championed (1420) the convent of Cervara (Genoa) as a centre of reform; although it was also favoured by Eugenius IV (1431–47), its force had faded by the mid-fifteenth century.[219]

While they were frequently the focus of papal reform initiatives, it should be noted that at times the fortunes of the monasteries were subordinated to other papal priorities. Throughout the later Middle Ages, monasteries were subject to papal grants *in commendam*, under which terms the house passed into the hands of a secular, or occasionally a lay, beneficiary, who became titular abbot. Generally the *commendam* abbot exercised authority over the temporal and spiritual possessions of the monastery but did not govern it directly. Therefore such grants invariably undermined the material condition of the monastery and led to indiscipline, depopulation and even desertion. *Commendam* was widespread in those regions where papal interventions were most vigorous. In England, where the Crown sought to curtail papal provisions, *commendam* grants of monasteries were almost

---

[215] BL, MS Harley 2268, fo. 283r.

[216] M.-P. Dickson, 'La congrégation bénédictine de Monte Olivet au premier siècle de sa foundation et sa place dans l'histoire de l'ordre', in *Saggi e ricerche nel VII centenario della nascita del b. Bernardo Tolomei (1272–1972)*, Studia Olivetana 1 (Siena, 1972), pp. 25–47; P. Lugnano, 'L'istituzione di Monte Oliveto nella seconda metà del Trecento', in ibid., pp. 49–84; See also D. F. Stramara, 'Une nouvelle facette de la spiritualité olivétane primitive: l'adoration de la Saint Trinité', *Studia Monastia* 39:2 (1997) 365–75; G. Picasso, 'La spiritualità dell'antico monachesmo alle origini di Monte Oliveto', in *Charisma und religiose Gemeinschaften im Mittelalter*, ed. G. Andenna, M. Breitensen and G. Melville, Vita regularis: Ordnungen unde Deutungen religiosen Lebens im Mittelalter 26 (Münster, 2005), pp. 443–52.

[217] D. Hay, 'The Quality of Italian Religious Life', in *The Church in Italy in the Fifteenth Century* (London, 1972), pp. 72–90 at 75.

[218] L. Coudanne, 'De la règle reformée de Fontevraud (1479) aux statuts d'Étienne Poncher (1505)', *Revue Mabillon* 59 (1979), 393–408.

[219] Schmitz, *Histoire*, iii. 168–9.

unknown until Thomas Wolsey (d. 1530) secured St Albans in 1521; the Estates of Brabant also actively resisted.[220] During the Avignon exile the abbeys of France could scarcely evade *commendam*. Cardinal Talleyrand of Périgord amassed as many as nine (dependent) priories and one abbey in only two decades (1331–48).[221] Undoubtedly it was the monasteries of Italy that were the most vulnerable.[222] Some of the most distinguished, and earliest, of Italy's Benedictine houses were surrendered to a *commendator*. Farfa became a cardinalate commendatory before the close of the fourteenth century.[223] *Commendam* diminished many, while some were left wholly desolate: when Carone Abbey (Bari) was granted *in commendam* in 1477 a contemporary recalled 'they filched all that was valuable in the way of pictures or manuscripts: the monastery building and churches went to ruin; the offices and vestments could not be kept up for want of vestments and books; the monks starved and were forced to from place to place begging for sustenance'.[224] Yet, occasionally, a period *in commendam* proved to be a prelude to reform. Luigi Barbo's tenure of Santa Giustina di Padua was *in commendam* with his Augustinian Abbey of San Giorgio, Alga, but his connection with the Benedictine convent was a fruitful one that culminated in a process of reform.[225] The commendatory abbot of San Prospero, Reggio-Emilia, presented his monastery to the reformist congregation of Santa Giustina di Padua.[226]

The General Councils of the fifteenth century encouraged a resurgence of the reform impulse. The early councils were attended by public pleas from secular prelates and masters of the schools for delegates to address, and arrest, the decline of monasticism. The Dominican theologian Johan Nider regarded a 'reformation' of religious orders as a possibility 'but Almighty God knoweth with how much difficulty'.[227] Only months after Pisa (1409), Jean Gerson (d. 1429), chancellor of Paris, urged Emperor Sigismund to initiate a process of reform specifically 'so that monks might live in observance of the rule'.[228] After Constance convened in November 1414, Gerson's

[220] *Heads of Religious Houses*, ed. Knowles *et al.*, iii. 64; Coulton, *Five Centuries of Religion*, iii. 435–5; iv. 664.

[221] *Gallia monastica*, i. 27; Pfaff, *The Liturgy in Medieval England*, p. 268&n. See also N. P. Zacour, *Talleyrand, the Cardinal of Perigord, 1301–1364* (Phildelphia, 1960).

[222] Stump, *Reforms of the Council of Constance*, pp. 66–7; Hay, *The Church in Italy in the Fifteenth Century*, pp. 18–19, 74–5. See also the abbey and priories held *in commendam* by the Cardinal Giovanni Gaetano Orsini in B. R. Beattie, *Angelus pacis: The Legation of Cardinal Giovanni Gaetao Orsini, 1326–1334* (Leiden, 2007), pp. 217–18; G. M. Varanini, 'From Seigneurial Foundation to Commendam: the monastery of San Pietro di Vilanova at San Bonifacio, near Verona from the Twelfth to the Fifteenth Century', *Bulletin of the John Rylands University Library of Manchester* 73:1 (1991), 47–63.

[223] Boynton, *Shaping a Monastic Identity*, p. 14&n.

[224] Coulton, *Five Centuries of Religion*, iv. 65.

[225] Collett, *Italian Benedictine Scholars*, p. 2.

[226] Coulton, *Five Centuries of Religion*, iii. 433.

[227] Ibid., iv. 592.

[228] Ibid., iv. 46.

Paris colleague Pierre d'Ailly (d. *c.* 1420), Cardinal Bishop of Cambrai, and a number of other seculars, sought to direct delegates towards a systematic restoration of monasticism.[229] Another, open letter to Sigismund in February 1415 outlined the condition of contemporary monasteries, 'which have now departed from God's commandments ... daily betraying Christ, like Judas and the Jews ... monks in naught but their habit and their tonsure'.[230] Cardinal d'Ailly reprised this theme in a personal address to the council in November 1416 in which he proposed measures to tackle specific abuses of superiors, the integrity of the monastic enclosure, and the observance of the liturgical hours.[231] Other delegates also drew unfavourable comparisons between the monasteries and the mendicant friars: Jean de Vincelles contrasted the *commendam* monastery with 'the decency of the friaries', notwithstanding his Cluniac status; another, perhaps mendicant delegate complained of the general decay of the monastic order.[232]

The consideration of pastoral issues at Constance was repeatedly interrupted by more immediate political tensions. The decrees that did emerge on the matter of the monasteries were mild – novices must be taught grammar and chant; abbots should reside in the enclosure; apostates were to be properly disciplined – and fell far short of the root-and-branch reform envisaged by d'Ailly and his colleagues. Nonetheless, it seems the council debates did serve to stimulate a reform initiative among delegates from the German monasteries. A general chapter of German Benedictines was convened at Peterhausen, close to Constance, in February 1417 to address the 'utterly and miserably desolate' (Trittenheim) condition of the order.[233] The chapter was presided over by Benedictine delegates from Constance itself, one of whom was the English superior Thomas Spofford of St Mary's, York.[234] After due deliberation, the chapter issued injunctions for monasteries in the province of Mainz and the adjoining dioceses of Bamberg and Constance. The injunctions were neither original nor radical but they were more thorough than the conciliar decrees.[235] The canons *Summi magistri* of 1336 (i.e. the *Benedictina*) were reiterated and a revised customary was offered to delegates. With no tradition of capitular governance in the region, the authority of the Peterhausen code was nebulous. At the close of the fifteenth century Johann Trittenheim recalled how Abbot Friedrich of Hirsau had returned from Peterhausen to implement the injunctions

[229] Ibid., iv. 48.
[230] Ibid., iv. 50.
[231] Ibid., iv. 48. See also Stump, *Reforms of the Council of Constance*, p. 168.
[232] *Acta Concilii Constanciensis*, ed. H. von Finke, 4 vols. (Münster, 1896–1928), ii. 430, 500–4. See also Coulton, *Five Centuries of Religion*, iv. 51–2.
[233] Coulton, *Five Centuries of Religion*, iv. 165; Brann, *Abbot Trithemius*, p. 11; Stump, *Reforms of the Council of Constance*, pp. 154–9 at 155–6.
[234] Schmitz, *Histoire*, iii. 177; Stump, *Reforms of the Council*, pp. 155, 161, 168.
[235] *Magnum oecumenicum Constantiense concilium*, ed. H. Von der Hardt, 7 vols. (Leipzig, 1697), i.26. 1095–1110, esp. 1000–1.

'and all the brethren with one accord resisted him'.[236] It may be possible to connect with Constance the impulse for change evinced by Abbot Robert de Chaudesoles (1416–23) in 1417: 'Cet ordre qui a été si grand ... est maintenant presque anéanti dans la célébration du culte divin.'[237]

The reform agenda of d'Ailly and his disciples resurfaced at the Council of Basel (1431–49) but in its protracted discussions drew less concerted support from its delegates.[238] The presence of several vocal, and well-connected, monastic reformers, at least in the early sessions, did facilitate further efforts at regional reform. Under the aegis of the council, a general visitation of monasteries in Saxony, Thuringia, Franconia and Westphalia was undertaken by Johann Dederoth of Nordheim (Göttingen), himself a veteran of Constance.[239] Dederoth took the abbacy of Clus, a house notorious for its abuses, and then (in 1433) of Bursfeld, from where he co-ordinated a network of reformed convents, discussed in detail below. At the same time Nicholas of Cusa, another delegate, advanced monastic reform in his own jurisdictions. He first promoted reform of the secular and regular clergy at the diets of Mainz, Frankfurt and Nuremberg (1441–2, 1444), he presided at a provincial chapter of Benedictines at Würzburg (1451), and undertook a general visitation of monasteries in the dioceses of Erfurt, Hildesheim, Magdeberg, Minden and Thuringia (1451–2).[240]

In a sermon Nicholas declared 'the religious orders with few exceptions, have now sunk into empty superficiality, as we see in many places where only the outer form of church order is left, without the spirit of the founders'.[241] In a mandate to the archbishop of Salzburg, Nicholas warned monasteries they would be deprived of their privileges if they did not reform themselves within a year; to the truly reformed he offered a papal plenary indulgence. He passed from Germany into the Netherlands, where he sought assistance from the duke of Burgundy; he also made use of the chapter of Windesheim. Trittenheim concluded 'all took the oath but few accepted the observance within the year; thus, therefore, many became perjured'.[242] Later Trittenehim wrote, 'Where now is that reform which Cardinal Nicholas of Cusa as Papal legate began with incredible zeal?'[243]

---

[236] Coulton, *Five Centuries of Religion*, iv. 57.

[237] Schmitz, *Histoire*, iii. 207.

[238] For Basel, see Tanner, *Decrees*, i. 453–591; G. Alberigo, 'The Conciliar Church', in *The Church, the Councils and Reform*, ed. G. Christianson, T. M. Izbicki and C. M. Bellitto (Washington DC, 2008), pp. 271–90; M. Watanabe, 'Pope Eugenius IV, the Conciliar Movement, and the Primacy of Reform', in ibid., pp. 177–93; A. N. E. D. Schofield, 'Some Aspects of English Representation at the Council of Basle', *Councils and Assemblies*, ed. G. J. Cumming and D. Baker, Studies in Church History 7 (1971), pp. 219–27; J. W. Stieber, *Pope Eugenius IV, the Council of Basel and the Secular and Ecclesiastical Authorities in the Empire* (Leiden, 1978).

[239] Stieber, *Pope Eugenius IV, the Council of Basel*, pp. 96–8.

[240] P. E. Tillinghast, 'Nicholas of Cusa vs Sigmund of Habsburg: an Attempt at Post-Conciliar Reform', *Church History* 36 (1967), 371–90.

[241] Coulton, *Five Centuries of Religion*, iv. 197.

[242] Ibid., iv. 206.

[243] Ibid., iv. 206.

The Germans were dominant among the monastic delegates at Basel but its progress was followed in England and France. The new injunctions issued by the English chapter (1444) and the general chapter of Cluny (1458) might be connected to the climate of reform engendered by the council.[244]

Congregations

For the Benedictines, the legacy of the General Councils was a genuine commitment to reform which did much to renew monasticism in the old imperial territories. As the councils dispersed, this commitment was channelled into the creation of a number of new congregations. The origins of the first, and perhaps the foremost, of these congregations, of Santa Giustina di Padua, pre-date the Council of Constance.[245] Ironically, the first cause of the Paduan reform was the politics of the schismatic popes: in attempt to secure Venetian support after his absence from Pisa in 1409, Gregory XII appointed Luigi Barbo to restore the once-great abbey of Santa Giustina. Barbo embraced the *RB* and began a systematic reform. His success led a number of neighbouring monasteries to seek affiliation. Santa Giustina was soon recast as the centre-point of a circle of reformed houses. By 1439 there were sixteen convents following Barbo's Paduan customs; by 1462 there were twenty-nine. The nascent congregation won the support of Eugenius IV (1431–47) who gave papal recognition to its capitular organisation and congregational status in 1432; he also granted it exemption from episcopal visitation and to the president of its chapter general privileged rights of absolution. The pope also placed St Paul's, Rome, and the Badia, Florence, under its jurisdiction, and expelled the Humiliati from the convent of SS Peter and Paul in Milan so that it might also become a Paduan convent; in 1460 the modest, regional congregation of Cervara (Genoa) was also affiliated to Santa Giustina.[246]

Like so many earlier efforts at Benedictine reform, Barbo aimed to restore the *ad literam* observance of the *RB*. The originality of the Paduan programme lay in the importance attached to the congregation structure. Santa Giustina and its affiliates were administered and governed as a congregation, with absolute authority vested in the chapter general and its president, itself an annual appointment. Superiors were appointed by the chapter and subject to its annual scrutiny: to this extent Barbo abandoned the traditional autonomy of the abbot as envisaged in the *RB*.[247]

[244] *Chapters*, ed. Pantin, ii. 183–220 at 187–220.
[245] For Santa Giustina, see Schmitz, *Histoire*, iii. 157–74 at 157–64; Collett, *Italian Benedictine Scholars*, pp. 2–5.
[246] Schmitz, *Histoire*, iii. 157–64 at 161–3, 168–9 at 169; Collett, *Italian Benedictine Scholars*, pp. 2–3; N. Rubinstein, 'Lay Patronage and Observant Reform in Fifteenth-Century Florence', in *Christianity and the Renaissance: Image and Religious Imagination in the Quattrocento*, ed. T. Verdon and J. Henderson (Syracuse, NY, 1990), pp. 63–82 at 64–6.
[247] Collett, *Italian Benedictine Scholars*, p. 4.

Whatever monastery they entered, every monk made his profession to the congregation and their deployment to one house or another within the network was determined by the chapter general. Brethren of potential or proven scholarly ability were dispersed – a *mutationes fratrum* – to ensure the even distribution of ability across talent in the affiliate houses.[248]

Santa Giustina and its affiliates served as both symbol and source of monastic reform throughout the fifteenth century. The Paduan code was adopted beyond Italy, at Augsburg, at the ancient abbey of SS Ulrich and Afra and thence to Saint-Gall; in France it inspired and informed the reform code of Chezal-Benoît and its satellites in the diocese of Bourges (Clermont), Normandy (Jumièges) and Brittany (Landévennec).[249] The significance of Santa Giustina as a guardian of Benedictinism was acknowledged in 1505 when the founder's own Montecassino joined and the congregation was recast as the Cassinese congregation.[250] In turn the Cassinese congregation secured the Sicilian Benedictines (in 1506) and later the abbey of Lérins and its subordinates in Provence; earlier (1485) it had also subsumed the Vallombrosan congregation.[251] Before the Reformation there were forty-five affiliate abbeys and 145 smaller houses and as many 2,500 monks under the banner of Cassinese-Paduan Benedictinism.[252]

The congregation that cohered around the Austrian abbey of Melk was more directly connected to the debates at Constance. The monks of Melk had mounted their own mission to Subiaco (Rome) in 1364 to revive observance at one of Benedict's own foundations.[253] A colony of Austrian brethren remained there in the early fifteenth century, and at the direction of their brethren in attendance at the council, they now returned to Melk in 1418 to supervise its own restoration. Prior Nicholas von Matzen took the abbacy, and the customary was replaced with that of Subiaco, recast as the *Consuetudines Mellicenses*.[254] The leader of the delegation, Peter von Rosenheim, who had himself attended Constance, established the position of *cursor biblicus*, to provide a programme of scriptural instruction for the brethren.[255]

The Melk reformers were perhaps less purist in their approach to the *RB* than their Paduan counterparts. With an unusually high number of university men and more than a hint of humanist inspiration, they placed particular emphasis on learning – never at the heart of the *RB* – as an

---

[248] Ibid., p. 8.

[249] Schmitz, *Histoire*, iii. 167, 209–10; Collett, *Italian Benedictine Scholars*, pp. 3–4.

[250] Collett, *Italian Benedictine Scholars*, p. 5. See also M. W. Anderson, 'Gregorio Cortèse and Roman Catholic Reform, *Sixteenth-Century Essays and Studies* 1 (1970), 75–106 at 79.

[251] Anderson, 'Gregorio Cortese and Roman Catholic Reform', 75–106.

[252] Collett, *Italian Benedictine Scholars*, p. 98&n.

[253] D. D. Martin, *Fifteenth-Century Carthusian Reform: The World of Nicholas Kempf* (Leiden, 1992), pp. 61–7.

[254] Schmitz, *Histoire*, iii. 183; for *Consuetudines Mellicense*, see Steinberg, 'Instructions in Writing', 210.

[255] Schmitz, *Histoire*, iii. 184; Posset, *Renaissance Monks*, p. 20.

instrument of reform. In addition to a programme of scriptural teaching, the Melk customs promoted book production as both a practical and symbolic support for monastic observance.[256] Here it is possible to detect the influence of the *devotio moderna* and the practices of the Windesheim congregation. Over the course of the century Melk became known both its scholars and scribes. Leonhard Wagner, author of the *Proba centum scripturarum una manu exaratarum* was commemorated by Hans Holbein the Elder as 'de guot schreiber'.[257]

The scholarly, indeed humanist, spirit of the Melk customs attracted early support from secular masters. Chancellor Gerson himself sojourned at Melk in 1418 while at work on his *De consolatione theologia*.[258] The *Consuetudines* were adopted by a number of Austrian and Bavarian houses: Peter von Rosenheim carried the customs to Tegernsee, from where they were transmitted to Oldenburg, Mariazell, Ratisbon, Salzburg and the Scots abbey of Kremsmünster, near Vienna.[259] The Melk monasteries struggled to formalise their union. It was not until 1470 that seventeen superiors confirmed their observance of its customs at Erfurt and thereafter the ties that bound Padua and Bursfeld still eluded them. Abbot Benedikt of Tegernsee feared their shortcomings threatened the very survival of monastic religion in Austria: 'everywhere ... monasteries are ravaged, plundered, and laid waste; nor is there anyone to save us or to sympathise in pity or mercy'.[260] Yet a succession of reformist superiors served to stimulate both monastic and pastoral reform in their own regions. Monks of the Melk customary also contributed to the Cusan reform movement. Abbot Martin von Sening (d. 1460×1470) of the Vienna Schottenkloster assisted the archbishop in his regional campaign of 1451, in which as many as fifty-two monasteries (by no means all of which had already been touched by the congregational reform) were subject to visitation.[261] Abbot Bernard of Waging (d. 1472) at Tegernsee worked alongside Bishop Johann Eich of Eichstatt to promote reform in their diocese.[262]

The Council of Basel was the key stimulus for a second monastic congregation in this same region. The restoration of Clus led Duke Otto I of Brunswick to transfer Johann Dederoth to the abbey of Bursfeld where, according to a contemporary chronicler, 'The buildings were in ruins, [the] possessions dissipated, only one monk was left, compelled to live on

---

[256] Steinberg, 'Instructions in Writing'.

[257] Posset, *Renaissance Monks*, p. 142.

[258] Martin, '*Via Moderna*, Humanism and Hermeneutics', 188.

[259] Schmitz, *Histoire*, iii. 184; Martin, *Fifteenth-Century Carthusian Reform*, pp. 61–2.

[260] Coulton, *Five Centuries of Religion*, iv. 210.

[261] Ibid., ii. 602. See also D. Sullivan, 'Nicholas of Cusa as Reformer: the Papal Legation to the Germanies, 1451–2', *Mediaeval Studies* 36 (1974), 382–428.

[262] D. D. Martin, 'Popular and Monastic Pastoral Issues in the Later Middle Ages', *Church History* 56 (1987), 320–32 at 327; Martin, *Fifteenth-Century Carthusian Reform*, pp. 209–10.

the meagre produce of a single cow.[263] Dederoth returned the house to the disciplined observance of the *RB*. He retired to Reinhausen (Göttingen), where he died in 1439, but his successor Johann Hagen extended the reform to three further houses – Cismar in Schleswig-Holstein, St Jacob, near Mainz, and Huysburg near Magdeburg, from where it soon spread further afield. Trier, the subject of an independent reform, was also incorporated into the network.[264] The Basel council recognised Bursfeld in 1446; papal recognition followed in 1451, together with the exemption privileges granted to Padua twenty years before. It is worth noting its identity, indeed self-image, was that of a confederation, a *union* of confrères and not a formal congregation.[265] Ettenheimmünster, Würzburg and Hirsau were admitted to the congregation in 1457, and in the next quarter century a further fifty monasteries followed, in Alsace, Bavaria and the Low Countries.[266] William III, Landgrave of Hesse, even called upon the Bursfelders to colonise new foundations, for which he would provide endowment. By 1517 there were almost 100 monasteries under the Bursfeld banner.[267]

As at Padua, the primary objective of the Bursfeld reformers was the recovery of the pure essence of Benedictinism. There was a notable antiquarianism in their approach to the *RB* and their interpretation of patterns of observance. It was typical of Johann Hagen that he sought permission from the Basel delegates in 1445 to follow the original form of the Benedictine breviary, without the accretions and adaptations of later centuries.[268] Visiting from Melk in 1457, Martin von Senging witnessed the *opus manuum* as it was conceived in the *RB*: 'all through summer and autumn they have manual labour with earth ... and the gathering of fruits from the trees and so forth, sometimes daily two hours at a time'.[269] Their interest in earlier expressions of Benedictinism also led the Bursfelders to overlook corporate niceties and acknowledge the achievement of the Cistercians: the title page of the edition of the *RB* printed from the Mainz Benedictines in 1528/9 incorporated a typical Cistercian motif of the *amplexus Bernardi* (i.e. the embrace of Bernard by Christ crucified).[270]

A congregational movement arose in Iberia whose progress paralleled that of Bursfeld and Padua. Its focal point was the community of St Benedict, Valladolid (founded by Juan I in 1390), and its affiliates included the ancient abbey of San Martín, Compostela, as well as houses at Montserrat,

---

[263] Coulton, *Five Centuries of Religion*, iv. 167. See also Schmitz, *Histoire*, iii. 189.

[264] Schmitz, *Histoire*, iii. 189–91 at 190–1.

[265] Stieber, *Pope Eugenius IV, the Council of Basel*, p. 96.

[266] Schmitz, *Histoire*, iii. 190–4 at 191, 194n. See also *Hirsau St Peter und Paul*, ed. Schreiner.

[267] Coulton, *Five Centuries of Religion*, iv. 168–71; Schmitz, *Histoire*, iii. 192–4 at 194&n.

[268] Coulton, *Five Centuries of Religion*, iv. 171.

[269] Ibid., iv. 171.

[270] Posset, *Renaissance Monks*, pp. 70–1.

6 Benedictine congregations and unions, *c.* 1517

Salamanca, Silos and Sahagún, the largest monastic community in Spain.[271] The congregation was formally established in 1450 and received papal recognition in 1489.[272] Its organisation was modelled on Padua (and its earlier Cistercian prototypes); superiors were subject to annual elections, and the congregational general chapter asserted visitorial authority over all its constituent communities.[273]

---

[271] J. N. Hillgarth, *The Spanish Kingdoms, 1250–1516*, 2 vols. (Oxford, 1976), ii. 103–4. See also E. Zaragoza Pascual, *Los Generales de la Congregación de San Benito de Valladolid*, 6 vols (Silos, 1973–87), i, passim.

[272] Schmitz, *Histoire*, iii. 230–41 at 233–40; Hillgarth, *Spanish Kingdoms*, ii. 103–4 at 104; E. A. Lehfeldt, *Religious Women in Golden Age Spain: The Permeable Cloister*, Women and Gender in the Early Modern World (Aldershot, 2005), pp. 117–18 at 117.

[273] Schmitz, *Histoire*, iii. 234; Hillgarth, *Spanish Kingdoms*, ii. 104.

While the network of affiliate houses continued to grow, the congregations remained divided over the direction, and the efficacy, of their reform. As early as 1465, the Paduan general chapter was compelled to remind its brethren not to allow the *studia litterarum* (in Greek and Latin) to obscure the scriptures.[274] Offering the first historical perspective on the progress of the Bursfeld reform, Johann Busch maintained 'it is very marvellous that such ancient monasteries of Black Monks could be brought to so perfect reform'.[275] By contrast, among the younger generation of Bursfelders, Abbot Trittenheim warned that zeal of the pioneers was already fading: 'The greater part of our walls have fallen; for in many of them religion hath perished, devotion is grown cold, charity hath expired ... a minority along shine with reformation, while the rest, the many still remain in desolation. ... Lo how many reforms have flourished in our order yet men's hardened minds still shrink from that Benedictine rule which they profess.'[276] His verdict was shared by Johannes Legatius of St Godehard, Hildesheim, who wrote, *c.* 1500, 'They strayed from the path of righteousness and corrupted the way of the Holy Rule, becoming disobedient, unchaste and proprietary.'[277] There is no doubt that the congregational movement itself served as a stimulus for reform initiatives in other regions. Before the close of the Council of Basel, Renier de St Marguerite of the abbey of Saint-Jacques, Liège, led a revival of Benedictine observance at Gembloux, Hasnon and Stavelot.[278] Valladolid, perhaps the premier Benedictine house of the Iberian peninsula, also directed a restoration of discipline in Castilian convents. The reformed monasteries were placed under the jurisdiction of Valladolid in the manner of Padua. Valladolid was formally recognised as a congregation in 1489; with the support of the Catholic Monarchs its customs were applied further afield and by 1504 there were no fewer than forty-five houses under its affiliation.[279]

The regional congregations of the Gregorian age were also roused by the impulse for reform. Eschewing academia for a Cluniac profession, the Paris master Jean Raulin promoted reform at the general chapter and in his *Collatio de perfecta religionis plantatione* of 1499: as the century turned, an observant reform advanced in central and south-west France.[280] Also at the turn of the fifteenth century the regional convent of Chezal-Benoît

---

[274] Collett, *Italian Benedictine Scholars*, p. 29.
[275] Coulton, *Five Centuries of Religion*, iv. 169.
[276] Ibid., iv. 178.
[277] Ibid., iv. 185.
[278] P. Annaert, 'La situation du clergé régulier dans les Pays Bas bourguignons au début du XVe siècle', in *La miracle du Saint Sang: Bois-Seigneur-Isaac, 1405–2005, actes du colloque organisé au prieuré des Prémonstrés de Bois-Seigneur-Isaac*, ed. J.-M. Cauchies and M.-A. Collet-Lombard (Munster, 2009), pp. 19–36 at 28–9.
[279] Schmitz, *Histoire*, iii. 230–41; Lehfeldt, *Religious Women in Golden Age Spain*, pp. 115–17.
[280] Schmitz, *Histoire*, iii. 208–9.

reinvigorated the Black Monks at Bourges, Clermont, Le Mans, Lyons and Paris itself.[281]

Crown and Nobility

The expansion of monastic Europe in the early and high Middle Ages occurred alongside, and at times in tandem with, the advance of royal authority. To the under mighty rulers of this period, monasteries were virtually an instrument of government, their material and spiritual resources providing essential reinforcement for a personal monarchy. As permanent institutions – an exchequer, judiciary, representative assembly – evolved after 1200, monarchs no longer had need of such supports and now regarded religious houses, much as they did the magnate nobility, as potential obstacles to be neutralised or even removed. Monastic commentators after 1215 were conscious of the fracture of their old affinity with the Crown and frequently complained of the coercion and fear they suffered.[282] The material condition of many Benedictine monasteries was much diminished in this period and a small number were destroyed. But it is mistaken to see in these encounters the seeds of the systematic assault on monastic religion initiated in the sixteenth century. The monarchs of the later Middle Ages may have possessed a concept of kingship and may even have engaged with contemporary debates over the nature of dominion, but their approach to the monasteries remained more pragmatic than philosophical. Their infrastructure, money and personnel still offered much that was useful to them, and armed with the tools of institutional government, these resources appeared more accessible than ever before.

Perhaps the primary objective of monarchs in this period was to contain the power of competing lordships, both lay and ecclesiastical. The means to achieve containment were extended in the course of the thirteenth and fourteenth centuries to encompass not only the customary interference in rights of succession but also new fiscal obligations and legal constraints on the acquisition and transmission of offices, titles and other forms of property. The lords of the institutional church were affected as much by these measures as any lay magnate; for Benedictine monasteries, which had known only exemption and privilege since their tenth-century recovery, the change was profound indeed. The English Benedictines in fact saw comparatively little interference in the appointment of superiors, but this was not the experience of their Celtic counterparts, or of Continental convents. Secular governments in France, Iberia and the imperial territories

[281] Ibid., iii. 209–11 at 210; Le Gall, 'Les moines et la ville', p. 255. See also U. Berlière, 'La congrégation bénédictine de Chezal-Benoît', *Rév. Bén.* 17 (1900), 29–50, 113–27, 252–74, 37–61.
[282] For example, *St Albans Chronicle*, ed. Taylor and Childs, pp. 780–1 at 781: 'one of these knights ... wanted to make a thousand marks annually from [our] temporalities'. See also n. 115 above.

were complicit in *commendam* grants, sometimes promoting the candidacy of their own placemen.[283] The resistance of monarchs to papal provisions also appears to have resulted in less, not more freedom in monastic appointments and elections. From the end of the thirteenth century the Black Monks were also subject to an expanding regime of internal taxation. A parliamentary levy of a tenth on the income of regular and secular clergy in England was established under Edward I (1272–1307) and had become almost a customary grant by the beginning of the fifteenth century.[284] The monks' independence was compromised further by the Crown's demand that some of their number serve as collectors of the subsidy for the diocese.[285]

Edward I of England also placed restrictions on the continuing endowment of religious communities. The Statute of Mortmain (1279) required that, without licence, 'No person, religious or other, whatsoever presume to buy or sell any lands or tenements, or under colour of gift or lease, or of any other term or title whatever to receive them from any one … whereby such lands and tenements may come into mortmain [i.e. into permanent possession].[286] Thus any grant of property made to a monastery of any colour required a licence from the Crown, which, as the tone of the statute implied, would not be issued as a matter of course. Whether the statute itself served as a deterrent, or the costs of such donations had already risen above and beyond the means of many prospective benefactors, there is no doubt the endowment of the monasteries in England declined sharply in the century after 1279.[287] Case studies have suggested that some houses came to negotiate the terms of the statute successfully, or nullified them by turning to the purchase of (particularly) urban properties.[288]

A century after Mortmain the English crown extended its supervision of monastic endowments by its summary alienation of properties held by priories under the jurisdiction of, and in many cases founded by, French monasteries. A number of these alien priories were seized in 1395; further suppressions followed in 1414–15, and again between 1442 and 1447.[289] These seizures constituted the largest redistribution of estates since the Conquest, and in manner, if not also in motive, they anticipated the suppressions of the sixteenth century, since the properties were in many cases redeployed for new (secular) collegiate foundations. The notion of disendowment itself was never very far from public debates in this period both in

---

[283] For example, Riche, *L'ordre de Cluny*, pp. 279–80, 428–30; X. Hermand, 'La réforme de l'abbaye de Saint-Trond et les réseaux monastiques au début du XVIe siècle: Autour d'un recueil de textes réformateurs: Bruxelles, Bibliothèque royale, 20929–20930', *Rev. Bén.* 112 (2002), 356–78.

[284] M. Prestwich, *War, Politics and Finance under Edward I* (London, 1972), p. 186.

[285] *GASA*, iii. 282–5.

[286] *Councils and Synods*, ii.2, 864–5.

[287] Raban, *Mortmain Legislation and the English Church*. See also Jones, 'The Crown, Three Benedictine Houses, and the Statute of Mortmain'; Brand, 'The Mortmain Licensing System'.

[288] Smith, *Canterbury Cathedral Priory* pp. 192–7; Rosser, *Medieval Westminster*, pp. 61–2.

[289] As many as forty houses were suppressed in 1414–15: *MRH*, pp. 83–93.

England and Continental Europe. As early as 1310 Pierre Dubois, a member of the Estates General and an accomplished legal authority, proposed such as course to Philip IV of France as a means of funding the crusade.[290] The matter was apparently raised in Ricardian England at the parliament of 1385, and another schedule surfaced a generation later, in 1410.[291]

In some regions of Continental Europe monastic estates suffered a similar attrition, although more often at the hands of magnates whose regional authority was greater than the governing regime. The Black Monks of South Germany and the Swiss Confederation saw properties of commercial or strategic value subject to violent seizure. Here however it was possible for the monks to exploit regional rivalries and to submit to one *vogte* to secure protection from another. The abbot and convent of Rheinau concluded a treaty with the counts of Sulz (1455) to counter the threat of the Klettgau.[292]

In Bohemia in the first half of the fifteenth century the endowments of the monasteries were not merely restricted but subject to a systematic process of secularisation, fuelled by a powerful confessional impulse. By 1425, the estates of the major Bohemian monasteries had all been confiscated. The major beneficiaries were the magnates: Ulrich of Rožmberk formed a formidable patrimony from the portions of Milevsko, Zlatá Koruna, Zvíkov and Sedlčany; the might of the Hussite magnates of the north and east – Kolda of Žampach, Ptacek of Pirkštejn and George of Poděbrady – were vested in monastic estates. The restoration of Sigismund in 1436 saw the return of some, but by no means all, of these confiscations to the revived communities.[293]

It would be wrong to represent the monasteries' relations with monarchy as a sudden fall from exemption to exploitation. The desire to curb their territorial presence was coterminous with the routine defence of their rights against over-mighty magnates, urban communes, and occasional popular uprisings. While the English crown evinced little enthusiasm in principle for the temporal and spiritual power of such Benedictine abbeys as Bury St Edmunds and St Albans, their place in the political and social order was preferable to the revolutionary programme of the rebels in 1327 and 1381. In mainland Europe, monarchs were also moved to protect the essential rights and properties of their principal monasteries. The Swiss abbey of Einsiedeln

[290] For Pierre Dubois, see Pierre Dubois, *The Recovery of the Holy Land*, trans. W. Brandt (New York, 1936); Coulton, *Five Centuries of Religion*, iv. 430.

[291] Walsingham, *Historia Anglicana*, ed. Riley, ii. 139–40; *The St Albans Chronicle*, ed. V. H. Galbraith (Oxford, 1937), p. 56. See also M. Aston, *Faith and Fire: Popular and Unpopular Religion, 1350–1600* (London, 1993), pp. 95–31, 109; F. Somerset, *Clerical Discourse and Lay Audience in Late Medieval England* (Cambridge, 1998), p. 8.

[292] P. Blickle, *Communal Reformation: The Quest for Salvation in Sixteenth-Century Germany*, trans. T. Dunlap (Atlantic Highlands, NJ, 1992), p. 139.

[293] R. R. Betts, 'Social and Constitutional Development in Bohemia in the Hussite Period', *PP* 7 (1955), 37–54 at 43. It is notable that Sigismund, ostensibly the orthodoxy opponent of Hussite anticlericalism himself granted seized monastic estates to George of Podebrady.

was granted the singular rights of self-contained principality by Rudolf I in 1274. The Florentine authorities offered certain of the city's monasteries exemption from the gabelle.[294] Nor did their covetousness towards the monasteries prevent new acts of royal patronage. In England the later Plantagenets and Lancastrians upheld their status as benefactors of the Benedictines of Canterbury (Christ Church), Bury St Edmunds, Durham, St Albans, Westminster and Worcester.[295]

In the greater European polities – notably England and France – the Benedictines retained at least a vestige of their early involvement in the practice of government. In fourteenth-century England the Black Monks re-emerged as favoured counsellors of the Crown. Successive abbots of St Albans, Hugh Eversden, Thomas de la Mare and William Heyworth, were welcomed into the inner circle of, respectively, Edward II, Edward III and Henry V.[296] Here it is worth noting that the Tudor monarchy itself still reserved a place for premier Benedictines. The abbots of St Albans, Westminster and Winchcombe were all regular recipients of seasonal gifts (Christmas, New Year), and also in attendance at occasions of dynastic significance, such as the birth of Prince Arthur and Henry VIII's marriage to Catherine of Aragon.[297]

The monasteries were also affected indirectly by a parallel set of measures to restrict the exercise of papal authority within the realm. The Statutes of Provisors and Praemunire promulgated in England by Edward III (1351–2) sought to insulate both regular and secular clergy from papal impositions although among the Benedictines such interference was relatively rare after 1215.[298] The Pragmatic Sanction of Bourges secured by Charles VII of France in 1438 similarly preserved the right of the regulars freely to elect their superiors.[299] In practice these instruments signalled an increase in royal interventions not only in appointments but also their temporal and spiritual administration. The Pragmatic Sanction was repealed in 1516 but under the Concordat of Bologna François I renewed his supervision of monastic appointments and restricted the right of appeal to the Curia.[300] Yet there is nothing to suggest these statutory protections diminished the profile of the papacy in monastic precincts. The Benedictines of late medieval Europe

[294] W. J. Connell, *Society and Individual in Renaissance Florence* (Berkeley, 2002), p. 209.

[295] Dobson, *Durham Priory*, pp. 187–202; Dobson, 'Monks of Canterbury in the Later Middle Ages', pp. 65–153; Clark, *Monastic Renaissance*, pp. 35–7; P. Binski, *Westminster Abbey and the Plantagenets: Kingship and the Representation of Power, 1200–1400* (New Haven, 1995).

[296] Clark, *Monastic Renaissance*, pp. 17–18.

[297] *LP*, i/1, 308, 1549.

[298] *RO*, ii. 207. See also W. T. Waugh, 'The Great Statute of Praemunire', *EHR* 37 (1922), 173–205; C. Davies, 'The Statute of Provisors of 1351', *History* 38 (1953). 116–33.

[299] P. Santoni, 'Les nominations royales aux bénéfices ecclésiastiques sous le régime de la pragmatique sanction', in *Crises et réformes dans l'Église de la Réforme grégorienne a la préréforme: Actes du 115e congrès national des sociétés savantes, Avignon, 1990, section d'histoire médiévale et de philologie* (Paris, 1991), pp. 357–70; P. S. Lewis, *Later Medieval France: The Polity* (London, 1968), p. 319.

[300] R. J. Knecht, *François I* (Cambridge, 1984), pp. 51–65.

showed an equal, or even greater, willingness to pursue grievances against episcopal, seigniorial and royal authorities in the Curia.[301]

The impulse to intervene was not confined to the material or seigniorial properties of the monasteries. The secular powers were now inclined also to claim some authority in matters of reform. There was a perception widespread among clerical and lay elites that the spread of heresy and irreligion threatened the social order, and the present weakness of the institutional church provided monarchs with a new opportunity to reassert the priority of the temporal over the spiritual sword. Yet it these royal reform initiatives should not be regarded as narrowly political acts. Several monarchs of this period were themselves students of monastic custom, or drew counsel from men (clerks and magnates) inspired by contemporary currents of reform.

The English Black Monks faced a succession of royal reforms after the Black Death: Henry VIII's 1535 visitation of religious houses should be understood as part of a tradition of interventions that may be traced back over 200 years. Edward III had presided over a visitation of premier Benedictine houses between *c.* 1362–6, apparently acting in response to petitions which had highlighted cases of corruption and indiscipline.[302] In 1421 Henry V summoned representatives of the Black Monks to a council at Westminster to propose a reform of observant life.[303] The Crown continued to exercise a disciplinary authority later in the fifteenth century: in 1437 Chester Abbey was placed in royal custody (the Stafford earls acting as agents) 'for reason its misrule'.[304] In 1489 Henry VII appointed John Morton, Cardinal Archbishop of Canterbury, to conduct a visitation of the exempt Benedictine monasteries, beginning at the abbey of St Albans. Morton's collection of *comperta* which recorded the corruption of the monastic community anticipated the conduct of the Henrician visitation forty years on.[305] Perhaps only the first of these visitations, which was placed in the hands of the president of the Benedictine chapter, proved wholly successful. The canons of the Westminster council were rejected at first by the congregation and in revised form did not differ significantly from their own capitular statutes. Cardinal Morton's *comperta* and *monitio* subjected exempt houses – notably St Albans Abbey and St Andrew's Priory, Northampton – to a period of public humiliation, but both prevented further intervention by renewing their exempt status in the Papal Curia. The efforts of the English crown to subject the greater abbeys and priories served only to encourage them to reinforce their papal privileges and exemptions. Between 1350 and 1400 no fewer than four Benedictine

[301] For example, the cause of Norwich Priory (1366): *Chapters*, ed. Pantin, iii. 61–3.
[302] Ibid., iii. 34–5, 36–52, 62–3. For witness to these visitations, see also *GASA*, ii. 405–7 at 405–6.
[303] *Chapters*, ed. Pantin, ii. 98–134 at 98–101.
[304] *VCH Cheshire*, iii. 132–48.
[305] D. Knowles, 'The Case of St Albans Abbey in 1490', *JEH* 3:2 (1952), 144–58.

houses secured exempt status; cases in pursuit of such status continued into the fifteenth century.[306] The discourse of reform formulated in 1421 and renewed in 1489 was again revived by Thomas Wolsey in 1520.[307]

Like Henry V, conqueror of Normandy, in 1421, on the eve of his Italian campaign Charles VIII of France (d. 1498) initiated a reform of the monasteries in his realm. The Council of Tours (1493) issued injunctions for the restoration of religious observance and commissioned Cardinal Archbishop Georges d'Amboise (d. 1510) to implement them.[308]

In other parts of Europe, it was the provincial nobility or merchant class that now seized the initiative in matters of reform. At Florence (1434–6, 1439–43) and Venice (1519), it was the commune that conducted a systematic reform of the cities' convents, albeit with the acknowledged support of the incumbent pope.[309] The duke of Transylvania initiated the reform of Sponheim in 1469, inviting brethren from Bursfeld to assume authority over the abbey.[310] It was the efforts of Dukes Albrecht III (1438–60) and IV (1467–1508), father and son, that established the Bursfeld reform in Bavaria; William, Landgrave of Thuringia espoused the cause of monastic reform in Saxony.[311]

The Sixteenth-Century Renaissance

There is no doubt the Benedictine communities that entered the sixteenth century differed significantly from their forebears in constitutional, cultural and material terms. Modern historians have generally regarded the monks of this generation as already detached from the medieval monastic tradition and caught, however unconsciously, in an inexorable drift towards their own extinction. Even apologist monastic authorities have preferred to look beyond their brethren of the pre-Reformation period to the revivalist programme of the post-Tridentine congregations.[312] Consequently, the first three decades of the sixteenth century remain among the most neglected in monastic history. However, a number of new discoveries and case studies have served not only to bring the era into

[306] Evesham, Glastonbury, Malmesbury, St Albans: *RO*, i. 277–8.
[307] *Chapters*, ed. Pantin, iii. 117–24.
[308] Coulton, *Five Centuries of Religion*, iv. 701.
[309] Penco, *Storia del monachesimo*, p. 313.
[310] Brann, *Abbot Trithemius*, pp. 10–11; D. I. Howie, 'Benedictine Monks, Manuscript Copying and the Renaissance: Johannes Trithemius' *De laude scriptorum*', *Rev. Bén.* 76 (1976), 129–54 at 132–5.
[311] G. Strauss, 'The Religious Policies of Dukes Willhelm and Ludwig of Bavaria, in the First Decade of the Protestant Era', *Church History* 28 (1959), 350–73 at 357; C. Scott-Dixon, 'The Princely Reformation in Germany', in *The Reformation World*, ed. A. Pettegree (London, 2000), pp. 146–68 at 152.
[312] D. Lunn, *The English Benedictines, 1540–1688: From Reformation to Revolution* (London, 1980). See also B. Green, *The English Benedictine Congregation: A Short History* (London, 1980); *Monks of England: The Benedictines in England from Augustine to the Present Day*, ed. D. Rees (London, 1997).

sharper focus but also to challenge some, if not all, of these conventional assumptions.[313]

In many parts of Europe, and perhaps especially in the north and west (notably England), the Benedictine population rose significantly at the turn of the fifteenth and sixteenth centuries. The total number of professed religious in England had risen by a factor of almost 50 per cent from approximately 6,000–8,000 in 1400 to 10,000–12,000 at the beginning of the new century.[314] Many of the greater Benedictine abbeys and priories had grown in numbers and had also seen a greater frequency of admissions; just as significant was the stability of the numbers in the smaller houses, many which maintained their post-plague levels until the visitation of 1535.[315] The rising population was not only an English phenomenon. Saint-Germain-des-Prés rose from twenty-four to fifty between 1480 and 1520, a doubling which was matched by all the monasteries in the diocese of Paris.[316] The continuing restrictions on new professions in the Paduan congregation certainly suggest no diminution in new vocations after 1500.[317]

Notwithstanding the economic pressures of the preceding century, it would appear many Benedictine monasteries now experienced a degree of prosperity not seen in many parts of monastic Europe since before the Black Death. One measure of their material well-being is offered by the programmes of new building which many now initiated. Many of the best-known churches of Benedictine England were rebuilt or extended between 1485 and 1540.[318] It was a reflection of their confidence that works on the church and cloister at Chester continued even under the eye of the Cromwellian commissioners in the autumn of 1539.[319] It was an indication both of their wealth and their continuing cultural engagement that their buildings incorporated the motifs of contemporary renaissance design. It is notable these styles penetrated northern and eastern Europe: the Polish Black Monks at Mogilno and Tyniec (Kraków) both transformed their buildings in the High Renaissance style.[320]

The observant life of the sixteenth-century Benedictines is poorly

[313] For England most significant is the recovery of the remarkable pre-Reformation decoration of the chapter house of Coventry Cathedral Priory: R. W. Dunning, 'Revival at Glastonbury, 1530–9', in *Renaissance and Renewal in Christian History: Papers Read at the Fifteenth Summer Meeting and the Sixteenth Winter Meeting of the Ecclesiastical History Society*, ed. D. Baker, Studies in Church History 14 (1977), 213–32.
[314] Rigby, *English Society in the Later Middle Ages*, p. 215.
[315] For example, Chester, Malvern, Pershore and Winchcombe: *MRH*, pp. 62, 67, 73, 81.
[316] Le Gall, 'Les moines et la ville', pp. 255–70 at 256.
[317] Collett, *Italian Benedictine Scholars*, p. 73.
[318] For example, Milton Abbey: Traskey, *Milton Abbey*, pp. 150–6.
[319] S. W. Ward, 'Dissolution or Reformation: A Case Study from Chester's Urban Landscape', in *The Archaeology of Reformation, c. 1480–1580*, ed. D. Gaimster and R. Gilchrist (Leeds, 2003), pp. 267–79.
[320] For these houses, see M. Derwich, 'Les foundations et implantations des monastères bénédictins en Pologne jusqu'au début du XVIe siècle', in *Moines et monastères dans les sociétés de rite grec et latin*, ed. Lemaître *et al.*, pp. 49–69.

documented but there are signs of spiritual renewal. It was not without substance that Leo X claimed, at the inception of the eleventh session of the Fifth Lateran Council in December 1516, that 'The religious have done much in the field of the Lord for the defence and advance of the Christian religion.'[321] There was a resurgence of the earlier reform impulse both in the old imperial territories and the Low Countries. Under Bernard Waging, Tegernsee, notionally an affiliate of the Melk congregation, became a seminary for a form of Benedictine observance far stricter (and less bookish) than that of the Melk reformer Peter von Rosenheim.[322] Abbot Ludovicus II of Einsiedeln reformed the ancient Swiss abbey between 1526 and his death in 1544.[323] Abbot Ulrich Schoppenzaun (d. 1484) of Kremsmünster, and his successor, Johann Schreiner (d. 1524), revived *ad literam* observance in the house that had once been at the heart of the conciliar reform.[324] In Flanders, after a process of reform Afflighem and Stavelot sought affiliation to the Bursfeld congregation. The abbey at Gembloux also assumed membership of Bursfeld (1505) following its restoration by the Cistercian Arnould de Solbrecq.[325] Abbot François-Louis Blosius (de Blois) of Liessies (d. 1566) initiated a reform of the ancient Flemish abbey which attracted papal recognition in 1545, and for Blosius himself the offer of the metropolitan see of Cambrai. Blosius codified the principles of his reform in his *Speculum monachorum* (1538), perhaps the final pre-Reformation discourse on monastic reform.[326] The union of Montecassino and Padua also stimulated a subsequent phase of reform. In 1516 Giovanni Andrea Cortese, former papal auditor and ally of Leo X, led a delegation of reformers to the ancient abbey of Lérins. The essence of the Cassinese was to revive observance through the recovery of monastic studies. At Lérins, Cortese established a humanist academy; he held the abbacy from 1524 to 1529, when he carried the reform to San Pietro di Perugia, and from there to Subiaco and San Giorgio Maggiore at Venice.[327]

A congregation of the Gregorian age, the Camaldolese were also renewed, if not wholly reinforced, in this climate of reform. In 1513 the brethren compacted a union with the region congregation of San Michele di Murano; yet a faction under Paolo Giustiniani (1476–1528), seeking to recover the original observance of the eleventh century, was also recognised

[321] Tanner, *Decrees*, 593–655. See also N. Minnich, *The Fifth Lateran Council (1512–17): Studies on its Membership, Diplomacy and Proposals for Reform* (London, 1993).
[322] Martin, *Fifteenth-Century Carthusian Reform*, pp. 209–23 at 209–10. For Tegernsee, see also Posset, *Renaissance Monks*, p. 20.
[323] B. Gordon, *The Swiss Reformation*, New Frontiers in History (Manchester, 2002), p. 49.
[324] Steinberg, 'Instructions in Writing', 212.
[325] Schmitz, *Histoire*, iii. 194, 223–4.
[326] Ibid., iii. 225–7 at 226; Blois, *Louis de Blois*, pp. 97&n, 102–3. See also L. Vos, *Louis de Blois, abbé de Liessies (1506–1566), recherches bibliographiques sur son œuvre* (Turnhout, 1992).
[327] For Cortèse, see Anderson, 'Gregorio Cortèse and Roman Catholic Reform'.

as a discrete congregation in 1523. The constituencies were not reconciled until 1540.[328]

There are also signs of a late blossoming of Benedictine learning. In England it has been estimated the number of brethren at university rose in the forty years before the Dissolution.[329] In the greater abbeys and priories, teaching and private study appear to have been at least as vigorous as they had been a century before. The academic exercises encouraged at Winchcombe by Richard Kidderminster may have continued to the end of his abbacy (1525).[330] At St Augustine's Canterbury, Glastonbury and Reading, and perhaps a number of other houses, there were exchanges, both personal and epistolographical, with secular humanists.[331] Desiderius Erasmus of Rotterdam was widely read and responded to (notably by Abbot Richard Kidderminster of Winchcombe) if not uncritically admired.[332] The monks of this period had embraced the emergent culture of print: at Durham Priory, Thomas Swalwell had purchased a personal library of some forty or fifty printed books.[333] At Abingdon, St Albans, St Augustine's, Canterbury and Tavistock the brethren provided conventual patronage to commercial printers and, at least in two cases, presented their own compositions for publication.[334]

The re-emergence of the learned monk was equally marked in mainland monasteries. A generation of humanists now gravitated towards the greater abbeys of France. From Abbot Briçonnet's Saint-Germain there radiated a movement for the recovery and renewal of the early authorities of the monastic tradition and the return of patristic and scriptural syllabus to the cloister; this cadre of editors and exegetes, such as Josse Clichtove and Guy Jouenneaux, also composed a sequence of tracts to rouse their brethren to the project of reform.[335] Mondsee, a monastery of the Melk reform on the margins of Bavaria, attracted the accomplished schoolman Jerome (d. 1475).[336] Nearby Salzburg, which played a pivotal role in the transmission

---

[328] S. D. Bowd, *Reform before the Reformation: Vicenzo Querini and the Renaissance in Italy*, Studies in Medieval & Renaissance Thought 87 (Leiden, 2002), pp. 113–16.

[329] P. Cunich, 'Benedictine Monks at the University of Oxford and the Dissolution of the Monasteries', in *Benedictines in Oxford*, ed. H. Wansbrough and A. Marret-Crosby (London, 1997), pp. 155–84 at 155&n.

[330] Pantin, 'Abbot Kidderminster and Monastic Studies'.

[331] J. G. Clark, 'Humanism and Reform in Pre-Reformation English Monasteries', *TRHS* 6th Series 19 (2009), 57–93.

[332] *RO*, iii. 154.

[333] A. J. Piper, 'Dr Thomas Swalwell: Monk of Durham, Archivist and Bibliophile (d. 1539)', in *Books and Collectors, 1200–1700: Essays Presented to Andrew Watson*, ed. J. P. Carley and C. G. C. Tite, British Library Studies in the History of the Book (London, 1996), pp. 71–100.

[334] Clark, 'Print and Pre-Reformation Religion', 77–92.

[335] Jouenneaux's *Reformationis monasticae vindiciae seu defensio* was published at Paris in 1503, Clichtove's *De laude monasticae religionis* in 1515: Le Gall, 'Les moines et la ville', pp. 256, 264–6; G. Bedouelle and B. Rousell, *Les temps des réformes et la Bible*, Bible de tous les temps 5 (Paris, 1989), pp. 22–6 at 24–5; Posset, *Renaissance Monks*, p. 17.

[336] D. D. Martin, 'The *Via Moderna*, Humanism, and the Hermeneutics of Late Medieval Monastic Life', *Journal of the History of Ideas* 51:2 (1990), 179–97 at 184.

of the *Consuetudines Mellicenses*, became a centre for biblical studies where the works of both traditional and contemporary exegetes – Augustine, Bernard of Clairvaux, Johann Nider, Thomas von Kempen – were translated into the regional vernacular.[337] At Mainz, the hub of the Bursfeld affinity, historical writing flourished: Hermannus Piscator published his *Chronicon urbis et ecclesiae Maguntinensis* in the same year as Luther's triptych of pamphlets; at the fount of the Bursfeld reform, Clus, there also emerged the chronicle of Heinrich Bodo, begun in 1523.[338] The *studia humanitatis* also succeeded at Laach, a Bursfeld house since 1474, earning it the sobriquet of 'the nursery of the Bursfeld reform'.[339] The Bursfeld Benedictines embraced printing a generation before their English counterparts. Mainz and its affiliate monasteries were among the first buyers of the forty-two-line Bible and the Mainz Psalter; perhaps one of them also provided the manuscript exemplar for these pioneering editions.[340] Its union with Santa Giustina di Padua stimulated a resurgence of scholarship at Montecassino. The Cassinese monk Onorato Fascitelli di Isernia collaborated with Paolo Manutius (son of Aldo) on editions of the *opera* of Cicero, Lactantius, Ovid and Petrarch; Leonardo Sforza sojourned there in 1520 and, struck by the learning of the brethren, composed his verses *De laudibus Montis Casini*.[341] Padua itself appears to have benefited from the Cassinese connection. Following the union the abbey acquired the library of the Florentine humanist Palla di Noferi Strozzi.[342]

The cultural profile of this pre-Reformation generation brought some of them wider public attention. In England Abbot Kidderminster (d. 1528) attracted particular interest not only as an elder statesman among the prelacy but as a willing and persuasive mouthpiece of traditional orthodoxy.[343] In the Bursfeld congregation, Abbot Johann Trittenheim of Sponheim (d. 1516) attracted a degree of celebrity for his widely printed historical and pastoral works, although his self-image as a spokesman for the Benedictines was challenged by his own brethren.[344] At Paris the Black Monks were prominent, perhaps predominant in the academic press, being responsible for 19 per cent of the scholarly output between 1500 and 1536.[345]

[337] Posset, *Renaissance Monks*, p. 20.
[338] Ibid., p. 20.
[339] H. E. J. Cowdrey, Review of *Germania Sacra*, EHR 111 (1996), 447–8 at 447.
[340] Davies, *Gutenberg Bible*, pp. 42–53; Kapr, *Johann Gutenberg*, pp. 61–4, 182–3; N. E. Van Deusen, *The Place of the Psalms in the Intellectual Culture of the Middle Ages* (New York, 1999), p. 177; S. Fussel, *Gutenberg and the Impact of Printing* (Aldershot, 2005), p. 55.
[341] Collett, *Italian Benedictine Scholars*, p. 113.
[342] Ibid., p. 32.
[343] RO, iii. 92–4.
[344] Finally, in 1506 he resigned Sponheim and assumed the abbacy of Würzburg, saying 'Sponheim, Sponheim, you who from the beginning of your reformation have always abhorred good and useful men': Brann, *Abbot Trithemius*, p. 55.
[345] Le Gall, 'Les moines et la ville', p. 264.

੨*

It should be recognised, of course, that the spirit of renewal was concentrated on (if never wholly confined to) a small number of long-favoured houses at the heart of the Bursfeld, Cassinese and English congregations. In fact for the first time since the tenth century, some of the order's most venerable foundations – Lérins, Montecassino, Tegernsee (and in England, Durham, Glastonbury, Winchester) – were in the vanguard of the monastic mission. The condition of Benedictine life outside these distinguished, and well-documented, monasteries remains only impressionistic. There can be little doubt, however, that the consequence of a century or more of diminishing benefactions was a permanent change in the character of houses of moderate or modest size. They could no longer accept the number of professions they had once known; some adapted to a monastic community that was half its pre-1349 proportions. This change in scale also curbed the scope of their activities, not only in terms of spiritual or social outreach – almonry schools established only a century before were abandoned – but also their ability to meet the seasonal requirements of the liturgy. A surviving cellarer's roll from *c.* 1530 and its careful calculation of annual expenditure on candles and other sundries for the side-altars of the church is sharply evocative of community constrained even in the fulfilment of the observance for which it was founded.[346] The internal dynamics of the monastery were also increasingly distorted (and permanently so) at least by the standard of the *RB*. The community of the monks retained its symbolic significance verbally and visually, and still in key liturgical rituals, but it bore little relation to the daily experience of the brethren.[347] Apart from the offices, the daily occupations of the monks were no longer shared: the meal was taken outside the refectory; senior officers occupied private chambers from where they conducted conventual and personal affairs; dormitories were subdivided to afford almost complete privacy to their occupants.[348] A private life facilitated, and perhaps encouraged, different patterns of personal conduct. Breaches of the Benedictine code – drunkenness, incontinence – were widely reported by pre-Reformation visitors although whether their frequency was greater than in earlier times is wholly unclear.[349] There can be little doubt, however, that this greater independence introduced a new level of dissension and division into many of these monasteries. Even the observant houses of this period it seems possessed little of a common

---

[346] Evans, 'Battle Abbey at the Dissolution: Expenses'.
[347] Contrast, for example, the representation of Islip's Westminster and the well-documented private luxuries of its monks: Harvey, *Living and Dying*, pp. 34–71.
[348] *LP*, xiv/2, 454; *Rites of Durham*, ed. Raine, pp. 72–3; Erler, 'Private Reading', 141–2.
[349] *Visitations*, ed. Jessopp, p. 74 (Norwich, 1514).

identity. Liessies was badly divided under Abbot Blosius.[350] This tendency to fragment into factions, or individuals, was as corrosive for the future of the Benedictines as any rising tide of moral corruption.

---

[350] His reform brought 'uneasiness' and a plea 'to let them go on as they had done': Blois, *Louis de Blois*, pp. 74–87 at 83. See also Schmitz, *Histoire*, iii. 225–9.

CHAPTER SIX

Reformations

The dissolution of the monasteries has always been overshadowed by the political and popular dramas of the European Reformation. Indeed, the perceived ease of the suppressions – which began in Saxony and Hesse in the 1520s and ended (for the sixteenth century at least) in the States of Holland in 1584 – has encouraged the view that the experience of the religious orders represented only a brief epilogue to a story that ended long before 1517, one that could be connected only coincidentally with the sixteenth-century spirit of reform. Successive waves of revisionism have reinforced this view, recasting Europe's Reformation on the one hand as a highly regional and popular process of community reorganisation, and on the other as a wholly political enterprise. There can be little doubt that after a century and more of religious change in Europe, the balance between church and state had shifted, and even in Catholic polities much of the energy in religious life was now generated outside the institutional church; but it would be a mistake to leave either the regular (or, indeed, the secular) clergy at the margins of this Reformation. From the turn of the fifteenth century the convents of the reinvigorated orders of monks and friars, among them the Benedictine congregations of Bursfeld and Padua, proved to be seed-beds of reform. The values of both Erasmus (an erstwhile Augustinian canon) and Martin Luther (an Augustinian friar) were formed at least in part through their exchanges with monastic divines. The early fervour of the populace was fuelled – on both sides of the confessional battle lines – by the spiritual and seigniorial power of the monasteries. The first stirrings of Counter-Reformation strategy can also be traced to both British and Continental monasteries of Benedictines. Later, after much of the infrastructure of traditional religion had been dismantled, the monasteries continued to draw the interest of (particularly) Continental reformers in search of a plausible prototype for the Protestant seminary.

The prevailing perceptions of the Dissolution have stifled its study for many years. In his exposition of the English experience, David Knowles sensed the need to explain why an account of the 'Tudor Age' of the monasteries was necessary at all.[1] The diverse and protracted processes of dissolution have barely registered in discussions of reformation in mainland

[1] *RO*, iii. ix–x.

Europe; only the swift suppressions of Vasan Sweden have been the sub-ject of systematic study.[2] However, new discoveries, both of documentary and material sources, have offered the possibility of fresh insights. The number of suppression papers known to survive from England and Wales has recently grown.[3] The post-1540 careers of ex-religious of some regions (e.g. the province of York) have now been chronicled in depth.[4] Excavations have even afforded us a glimpse of patterns of demolition in a major English city (i.e. Coventry).[5] The Reformation records of key German convents have been collated, and contemporary accounts of the suppressions in Eastern Europe and Scandinavia have emerged from the manuscript shadows for the first time.[6]

These records bring into focus a reformation of the monasteries that challenges a number of our received assumptions. As an order, the Benedictines did not surrender either easily, or rapidly, to a pre-ordained end. The century after 1517 was certainly amongst the most troubled in their pre-modern history. Their presence in the northern and western peripheries of Europe was extinguished; their place in the public and private religion of their old European heartland was also much diminished. Yet even towards the close of the Council of Trent (1564), a trace of the old Benedictine observance was to be found in many of their early centres, even in Tudor England. It was only in the last quarter of the sixteenth century, when the first phase of Catholic recovery began in earnest, that their ties to medieval tradition truly were severed.

The Benedictines and Reform

The Benedictines were not mere bystanders at the beginnings of Europe's Reformation. The early catalysts – the dissemination of Luther's theses at Wittenberg, the *cause célèbre* of the unfortunate Richard Hunne – were located in contexts outside the old clerical establishment, but as these (and other) controversies passed via print and pulpit to a wider public, the Black

---

[2] For example, M. Berntson, *Klostren och Reformationen: Upplösningen av Kloster och Konvent I Sverige, 1523–96* (Gothenburg, 2003).

[3] See the English Monastic Archives project at www.ucl.ac.uk.

[4] For example, C. Cross and N. Vickers, *Monks, Friars and Nuns in Sixteenth-Century Yorkshire*, Yorkshire Record Society, Record Series 150 (Leeds, 1995); J. G. Clark, 'Reformation and Reaction at St Albans Abbey, 1530–1558', *EHR* 114 (2000), 297–328.

[5] R. K. Morris, 'The Lost Cathedral Priory Church of St Mary, Coventry', *Coventry's First Cathedral, 1043–1993: The Cathedral and Priory of St Mary: Papers from the 1993 Symposium*, ed. G. Demidowicz (Stamford, 1994), pp. 17–66.

[6] For example, C. Ocker, *Church Robbers and Reformers in Germany, 1525–1547: Confiscation and Religious Purpose in the Holy Roman Empire*, Studies in Medieval and Renaissance Traditions 114 (Leiden, 2006).

Monks did become closely engaged.[7] In many ways, the monks were well prepared for the doctrinal and ecclesiological debates that ensued after 1517. The councils of the fifteenth century had inculcated an interest in the governance of the church, and the general matter of reform, that had never entirely subsided, at least in the greater abbeys. Their presence in the universities – growing again at the turn of the sixteenth century – placed them at the centre-point of contemporary theology; their numbers may have been greater at the older universities but still they encountered the novel exegesis of Erasmus and Jacques Lefèvre d'Étaples.[8] The brethren of the greater Italian monasteries could not fail to be conscious of currents in theology, since, for structural reasons, much university teaching in the subject was delivered in their own precincts.[9] Only a fraction of Europe's Benedictines were graduates, but at the same time almost every community of any size could claim an active role in the ministry of diocese and parish. Here they confronted resurgent Lollards (in England) and other expressions of anti-clericalism and occasionally even early disciples of Masters Martin, Philip and Ulrich.[10] The monks may not have anticipated all of the political and social consequences of these movements, but they were aware of their advent and early development and not wholly unsympathetic to them.

Reformist literature was well established in the greater Benedictine abbeys and priories for some time before 1517. Jean Gerson, the great reformer of the conciliar period, was widely popular; the Celestine Benedictines contributed to the transmission of his works.[11] The manuals of the modern devotion – Thomas's *Imitatio*, Ludolphus's *De vita Christi* – attracted a monastic readership even before they were printed for the first time.[12] The new exegesis, born of humanist commentators at both old and

---

[7] For the first response to Luther, see A. McGrath, *Reformation Thought: An Introduction* (Oxford, 1999), pp. 86–100. For the Hunne case, see R. M. Wunderli, 'Pre-Reformation London Summoners and the murder of Richard Hunne', *JEH* 33 (1982), 209–24; S. M. Jack, 'The Conflict of Common Law and Canon Law in Early Sixteenth-Century England: Richard Hunne Revisited', *Parergon*, n.s. 3 (1985), 131–45; S. Brigden, *London and the Reformation* (Oxford, 1991), pp. 98–103; Haigh, *English Reformations*, pp. 77–80, 83–4, 86–7.

[8] For example, the awareness of contemporary authorities attested in the letters of Robert Joseph, monk of Evesham: *Letter Book of Robert Joseph*, ed. Aveling and Pantin, Letters 18, 24, 35, 83, pp. 26, 31–2, 43–5, 124 (citing Baptista Mantuanus, Erasmus, Jacques Lefèvre d'Étaples, Josse von Clichtove).

[9] P. F. Grendler, *The Universities of the Italian Renaissance* (Baltimore, 2002), pp. 42–3, 71, 129.

[10] For resurgent (or at least residual) Lollardy in early sixteenth-century England, see J. A. F. Thomson, *The Later Lollards, 1414–1520* (Oxford, 1965); M. Aston, 'Lollardy and the Reformation: Survival or Revival?', *History* 49:166 (1964), 149–70; R. Lutton, *Lollardy and Orthodox Religion in Pre-Reformation England: Reconstructing Piety* (Woodbridge, 2006).

[11] B. P. McGuire, *Jean Gerson and the Last Medieval Reformation* (University Park, PA, 2005), p. 26.

[12] For the reception of Kempen's meditation, see Lovatt, 'The "Imitation of Christ" in Late Medieval England'. For Ludolf of Saxony, see D. D. Martin, 'Behind the Scene: The Carthusian Presence in Late Medieval Spirituality', in *Nicholas of Cusa and his Age: Intellect and Spirituality: Essays Dedicated to the Memory of F. Edward Cranz, Thomas P. McTighe and Charles Trinkaus*, ed. T. M. Izbicki and C. M. Bellitto, Studies in the History of Christian Thought 105 (Leiden, 2002), pp. 29–62; Constable, *Three Studies*, pp. 234, 239. See also M. C. Erler, 'Devotional Literature', in *The Cambridge History of the Book in Britain*, iii. *1400–1557*, ed. L. Hellinga and J. B. Trapp (Cambridge, 1999).

new universities, was represented in personal book collections, if not always in conventual libraries. Robert Joseph, sometime novice master of Evesham Abbey, was already familiar with the work of Jacques Lefèvre d'Étaples and Erasmus (the *Enarrationes in psalmos*) when he began his correspondence in *c.* 1521.[13] The Benedictines were early enthusiasts for Erasmus: 'the glory of our age' ('decus nostrae aetatis'), as Joseph described him.[14] The Rotterdamer favoured a number of monks with his personal letters. During his two short sojourns in England he identified the Benedictine superiors Richard Bere (d. 1525) of Glastonbury and Richard Kidderminster (d. 1528) of Winchcombe as scholars of like mind.[15] He presented a personal letter to Abbot Paul Volz of Hugshofen Abbey (1480–1544) as the preface to his *Enchiridion* (1518). The letter rebuked Volz and his brethren for valuing *verbum Benedicti* above *verbum Dei*: 'I do not blame [them] for cherishing their rules but I blame those of them who think their rule more efficacious than the gospel', although the Benedictine devotion to Erasmus was apparently undimmed.[16] Given their general interest in print culture, it must be assumed that at least a trace of the expanding corpus of polemic, satire and contemporary political discourse was to be found in monastic book collections of this period. There is scarcely a single surviving example of certain provenance but reading communities that proved so receptive to *Piers Plowman* and *Dives et Pauper* could surely not fail to respond to the comic critiques of such authors as Sebastian Brant and John Skelton.[17] There was a significant difference in tenor and tone, of course, between these polemics and the pamphlets of the truly radical reformers. Yet the writings of Luther, Thomas Müntzer, John Frith, and George Joye also passed into the precincts, just as the work of Hus and Wyclif had done a century before.[18] John Skelsyn, a monk of Ely, purchased an unspecified volume of Luther's writings perhaps as early as 1519, presumably in Cambridge where he was a student.[19] Robert Joseph's brethren were familiar enough with the Wittenberg reformer for one of their number to be nicknamed 'Lutherus'.[20] Given the later 'conversions' to Lutheranism documented in a number of

---

[13] *Letter Book of Robert Joseph*, ed. Aveling and Pantin, pp. 19, 21, 26–7, 262.

[14] Ibid., letter 97, p. 147. See also letter 24, pp. 31–2.

[15] *RO*, iii. 153.

[16] *RO*, iii. 150. The epistolary preface is numbered 858 among the collected letters of Erasmus: *Correspondence of Erasmus*, ed. Mynors *et al.*, vi. 72–91.

[17] Brant (1457/8–1521) published *Das Narrenschiff* (Ship of Fools) in 1494; Skelton (*c.* 1460–1529), composed *Colyn Cloute*, a bitter satire of the contemporary church, in *c.* 1519. Although he was condemned by Cardinal Thomas Wolsey he attracted the patronage and protection of the Benedictine Abbot John Islip of Westminster: B. F. Harvey and H. Summerson, 'John Islip (1464–1532)', *ODNB*, 14492.

[18] Certainly this was the case at Reading, arising from the book acquisitions of Prior John Shirbourn; subsequently, in 1532, scarcely a year before his execution, John Frith visited: Martin, 'Leadership and Priorities in Reading during the Reformation', 114. See also below, p. 320.

[19] Greatrex, *BRECP*, pp. 438–9.

[20] *Letter Book of Robert Joseph*, ed. Aveling and Pantin, p. 106 (Letter 74).

Dutch, German and Italian monasteries, here his works, whether through the conventual library, or personal book collections, must also have gained a wide currency. An order in 1549 to search the cells or chambers of Scots monks for heretical texts might suggest the works of Luther and others had already penetrated the northernmost monasteries.[21] In a handful of cases the monks' exposure to the radical ideas extended to direct interaction with the reformers themselves. The Wittenberg theologian Johann von Staupitz (c. 1460–1524) entered the Benedictine abbey of St Peter, Salzburg, in 1522 after a series of scholarly exchanges with Luther. Staupitz advised his colleague in the aftermath of the Indulgences controversy; their association drew suspicions of heresy toward Staupitz himself, and in 1520 he was compelled to make his own public profession of faith.[22] In England in 1528 John Sherborne, prior of Reading, attracted the suspicion of the ecclesiastical and then the secular authorities through his association with the acknowledged Lutheran Thomas Garrett, from whom he had acquired as many as sixty (unspecified) books. He was committed to the Tower of London and was also compelled to abjure his heresy.[23] Sherborne may not have been the only monk of Reading to have made contact with the early English Lutherans. John Frith appears to have passed through the town at the beginning of the 1530s and was known to be an associate of the abbey schoolmaster, Leonard Coxe, himself a favoured subject of Abbot Hugh Faringdon.[24] The pastoral and social profile of the monks also appears to have made them conscious of the confessional climate in the local lay community. At Evesham, Robert Joseph regaled a correspondent with news of the will of one William Tracy of Toddington, notorious in the region for its evangelical expressions ('certe in Tracaeo evangelica effectum sortiuntur verba').[25]

The surviving accounts, generated for the most part by episcopal visitors and royal, seigniorial or civic commissioners at the point of suppression, allow us only to glimpse the effects of this discourse of reform on the climate of the monastic community. The reports of the royal commissioners in England give the general impression that reform, broadly defined, dominated now the daily dialogue of the brethren. We cannot know the whole truth of the reports of 'treasonable words' passed repeatedly to Thomas Cromwell between 1534 and 1539, but it is perhaps a measure of the general mood in the monastery that they invariably emerged from the wide-ranging discussion of political or public affairs at times of communal activity, such

---

[21] W. Stanford Reid, 'The Scottish Counter-Reformation before 1560', *Church History* 14 (1945), 104–25 at 114.

[22] H. A. Oberman, *Luther: Man between God and the Devil*, trans. E. Walliser-Schwarzbart (New Haven, 2006), pp. 180–3.

[23] *LP*, iv, 4004, 4017. Sherborne did not easily submit to his superior, however, refusing re-entry to the convent or a proffered benefice: *LP*, vi, 942.

[24] S. F. Ryle, 'Leonard Cox (*b. c.* 1495, *d.* in or after 1549)', *ODNB*, 6525.

[25] *Letter Book of Robert Joseph*, ed. Aveling and Pantin, p. 102 (Letter, 71).

as the midday mealtime or the evening collation.[26] Their exposure to the reformers did give shape and voice to a conservative element in the community. Yet it also appears to have given rise to what might be termed a 'reformed conscience' among certain monks. These seem to have been the sensibilities expressed by Richard Beerley, monk of Pershore, in a letter to Thomas Cromwell in 1536, in which he confessed: 'It is grudging in [my] conscience that the religion they [his brethren] keep is no rule of St Benet nor commandment of God nor of any saint, but light and foolish ceremonies ... [in which they] let the precepts of God go.'[27] The gulf, as Beerley perceives it, between the observance of his brethren and the precepts of both God and the *RB*, echoes Erasmus, not only in the *Enchiridion*, but in his savage swipes in the *Adagiae* and *Colloquiae*.[28] This moderate reformism – or Erasmianism – may have been more common in Benedictine communities of the 1520s and 30s than the dearth of documentary evidence can corroborate. It is in these terms that Staupitz at Salzburg might more accurately be characterised. These were also the scholarly underpinnings of the reformist regime of Blosius at Liessies and Cortese at Lérins.[29] And it was this common impulse for what would later be called 'Catholic' reform that projected Richard Kidderminster into the circle of progressive English prelates such as Richard Fox (bishop of Winchester, d. 1528) and John Longland (bishop of Lincoln; d. 1547).[30]

In a handful of houses the radical reformation did take hold, although it was far fewer than among the mendicant orders. Abbot Michael Eggenstorfer of All Saints, Schaffhausen, had sent his brethren to study at Wittenberg in the *annus momenti* of 1520.[31] Abbot Kraft Myle of Hersfeld embraced Lutheranism at the time of the Peasants' War, and when the prophet of Wittenberg himself entered the city in 1525, Myle accompanied him in public procession.[32] The Swiss monastery of Saint-Gall was said to have been roused with a spirit of reform under Abbot Franz von Gaisberg (d. 1529).[33] Abbot Odet de Châtillon of Vézelay (Burgundy) transformed

---

[26] For example, the depositions used in the arraignment of the abbot of Colchester, which reported political discourse over 'a dish of "baces" and a pottle of wine: *LP*, xiv/2, 458. See also the reports concerning William Ashwell of St Albans: *LP*, xi, 354.

[27] BL, Cotton MS Cleopatra E IV, fo. 161r. (*LP*, xi, 1449).

[28] Ibid.

[29] Vos, *Louis de Blois*; Schmitz, *Histoire*, iv. 225; Collett, *Italian Benedictine Scholars*, pp. 79–80.

[30] *RO*, iii. 91.

[31] Gordon, *Swiss Reformation*, p. 112.

[32] For Abbot Meyle, see D. B. Miller, 'The Dissolution of the Religious Houses of Hesse during the Reformation' (PhD diss., Yale, 1971), p. 144; *The German Peasants' War: A History in Documents*, ed. T. Scott and R. W. Scribner (1991), p. 38.

[33] For Abbot Gaisberg: Schmitz, *Histoire*, iii. 283. Gaisberg had exercised seigniorial authority as any medieval superior (Blickle, *Communal Reformation*, p. 36), but finally he departed the convent, committing, it would seem, to his monastic identity and his brethren: K.-H. Ludwig, 'Miners, Pastors and the Peasant War in Upper Austria, 1524–26', in *Religion and Rural Revolt: Papers Presented to the Fourth Interdisciplinary Workshop on Peasant Studies, University of British Columbia, 1982*, ed. J. M. Bak and G. Benecke (Manchester, 1984), pp. 154–73 at 163.

his community into a secular chapter in 1538 and professed himself to be a follower of Jean Calvin.[34] A small number of Benedictine converts abandoned unsympathetic communities to assist the enterprise of reform elsewhere: Gottschalk Kruse of St Giles, Braunschweig (1499–1540), apostasised to preach reform in northern Germany;[35] Ambrose Blaurer (Bauer) (1492–1564) forswore the Benedictine abbey of Alpirsbach in 1522 to promote reform at Constance;[36] Michael Sattler (d. 1527) of St Peter in the Black Forest abandoned his monastery for Anabaptism and was executed for his radicalism;[37] the Italian Benedictines Benedetto da Mantova (of Venice, c. 1490–1555) and Giorgio Rioli (of San Nicolo, Catania) espoused heterodox views which the authorities (inaccurately) interpreted as Lutheran; Benedetto was the first author of the *Beneficio di Cristo*, a devotion, of, at the very least, dubious orthodoxy, that sold 40,000 copies at Venice alone before it was prescribed in the Papal Index of 1549.[38]

The Benedictines' exposure to radical ideas led them perhaps more frequently into an involvement in Counter-Reformation activities. As early as 1521 Abbot Richard Kidderminster of Winchcombe was appointed to a commission charged by the English crown to examine Leo X's bull *Exsurge Domini*. No trace of his refutation has been recovered, although it is likely it became the basis for King Henry's own study of Luther.[39] The commissioners were returned to the communities to compose their own defence of orthodoxy and Kidderminster was said to have written ably on indulgences, although no text survives. The English Black Monks do not appear to have preached publicly on the dangers of Luther as they had done on Wyclif, although again scarcely a single monastic sermon survives from this period: Abbot Kidderminster was praised by Bishop Longland for his sermons.[40] The Black Monks also contributed to the Counter-Reformation of mid-century Scotland. Abbot James Hamilton of Paisley has been credited with the (albeit brief) reconciliation of the Regent Arran with Cardinal David Beaton in 1542.[41] In the dying moments of Catholic Scotland, Quintin Kennedy (c. 1520–64), abbot of Crossraguel, composed the *Compendius Tractive*, a confutation of Protestantism which conveyed a view of Catholicism closer to fifteenth-

[34] For Vézelay, see A. Turgot, *Histoire de la ville et abbaye de Vézelay* (repr., Autun, 1997), p. 184.

[35] U. Bubenheimer, *Thomas Müntzer: Herkunft und Bildung*, Studies in Medieval and Reformation Thought 46 (Leiden, 1989), p. 114&n.

[36] Schmitz, *Histoire*, iii. 284–5; Posset, *Renaissance* Monks, p. 22. Blaurer was celebrated in Theodore Beza's *Icones* (1580).

[37] C. A. Snyder, 'The Case of Michael Sattler', *Church History* 50 (1981), 276–87; C. A. Snyder, *The Life and Thought of Michael Sattler* (Scottdale, PA, 1984).

[38] M. A. Overell, *Italian Reformers and English Reformations, c. 1535–c. 1585* (Aldershot, 2008), pp. 29–31 at 29. See also R. Prelowski, 'Beneficio di Christo', in *Reform Thought in Sixteenth-Century Italy, 1465–1600*, ed. E. G. Gleason (Chicago, 1981), pp. 103–61.

[39] Emden, *BRUO*, ii. 1047; *RO*, iii. 91–5 at 93.

[40] Ibid., 63.

[41] J. Wormald, *Mary Queen of Scots: A Study in Failure* (London, 1988), p. 54.

century Conciliarism than it was to the Tridentine creed. He also agreed to a public disputation with Protestant John Wilcock, although the event was abandoned.[42]

Reformation, Secularisation and Suppression

From the outset the Benedictines – and their monastic and mendicant colleagues – can have had little doubt of the threat even moderate reformism, or Erasmianism, posed to their order. The reformers often represented the religious as indifferent to, or disengaged from, the drift of popular opinion and public policy. In England the Cromwellian commissioners claimed to have found monastic superiors – and sometimes entire communities – in a state of torpor. In the account of the royal commissioner Richard Layton, Abbot Richard Whiting of Glastonbury (elected 1525) appears almost pathologically passive at the time of his arrest in December 1539.[43] Modern historians have often treated this testimony at face value: A. G. Dickens represented the Dissolution in England as the sudden descent of royal and seigniorial authority upon 'a jolly dinner-party under the greenwood tree'.[44] In fact the prospects of an enforced programme of reform, and even of permanent suppression, were recognised by the regulars not only after 1517 but also arguably for decades before. The governors of the English Benedictine congregation had been conscious of the inclination of the Crown to intervene in monastic affairs for at least a century. Henry V's Council of Westminster (1421) had proved not to be a passing interest in monastic reform; a similar convention was envisaged (but not realised) by his son and in 1489–90 Henry VII had resumed the royal assault on monastic exemptions and privileges.[45] The Lancastrians and the first of the Tudors had also shown themselves inclined towards suppression as a tool of reform; they had also failed to stifle the discussion of disendowment in parliament, a discourse closely monitored by the Black Monks. The resistance of Richard Kidderminster to the rising star of Erasmus in the early years of Henry VIII may have been motivated by his awareness that the celebrated humanist could lend clerical credibility to a court long since eager for a confrontation with the monasteries. Indeed, there are signs of a partisan spirit formed among the monastic leadership and certain conservative

---

[42] J. E. A. Dawson, *Scotland Re-formed, 1488–1587*, New Edinburgh History of Scotland 6 (Edinburgh, 2007), p. 188.

[43] *LP*, xiv/2, 206; *RO*, iii. 379–82 at 380.

[44] A. G. Dickens, *Late Monasticism and the Reformation* (London, 1994), p. 23.

[45] For Henry VII's conduct towards the religious orders in general and the exempt houses of the Benedictines in particular, see C. Harper-Bill, 'Archbishop John Morton and the Province of Canterbury, 1486–1500', *JEH* 29 (1978), 6–11. For the Council of Westminster, see *Chapters*, ed. Pantin, ii. 98–101.

courtiers.[46] The climate was not dissimilar in Continental Europe. The Black Monks of France, Italy and Scotland had known to their great cost the capacity of Crown, nobility and secular church to sequestrate their incomes since at least the beginning of the fourteenth century. Suppression was less common than in Lancastrian England but Continental monks had witnessed the fall of a whole order of regulars – the Knights Templar – an event which appears to have caused remarkably few ripples, or shudders, in England and Wales. Not only was the machinery for the reform and suppression of the religious orders well established in Europe before the advent of Luther, it had also become widely accepted as part and parcel of their interface with the secular church, and with seigniorial and royal authorities. The monastic suppressions that spread across the Continent from 1522 to 1618 (and beyond) were remarkable not, by and large, for the means by which they were undertaken, but for the pace and the permanence with which they were carried through.

The 'Dissolution of the Monasteries' was not a unitary process. The suppression of Benedictine houses, as much as those of other orders, followed a different course, and brought into focus different impulses, in different regions of Europe; it was also pursued at a different pace. Germany was the crucible of the radical Reformation, but it provided neither the model nor the momentum for the assault on religious houses. The Lutheran suppressions began not in Saxony, but in its southern neighbour, Hesse, and in 1526, almost a decade after the advent of Luther.[47] The surge of support for Luther in Saxony between 1517 and 1525 did not initiate the mass suppression or surrender of monasteries or mendicant houses and even the voluntary dispersal of communities was sporadic, and in some cases short-lived.[48] In fact the first phase of dissolution driven by a reforming zeal occurred among the Swiss cantons, at Zurich: in June 1523 the Council of Zurich permitted (and passively promoted) voluntary surrenders; a council resolution the following December made the surrenders coercive.[49] In the same year (1524), the Tudor regime in England embarked on the selective suppression of monasteries under a rationale of Catholic (i.e. not Lutheran) reform: of the twenty-eight foundations dissolved, seven were Benedictine.[50] At the same time, Albrecht of Hohenzollern seized and secularised ecclesiastical property (regular and secular) in Ducal Prussia (Poland). The German dissolution

---

[46] For example, the exchanges between Christopher Urswick, dean of York minster, and veteran of Henry VII's court, and Prior Thomas Goldstone of Christ Church, Canterbury: P. I. Kaufmann, 'Polydore Vergil and the Strange Disappearance of Christopher Urswick', *Sixteenth-Century Journal* 17:1 (1986), 69–85.

[47] For Hesse, see Miller, 'Dissolution of the Religious Houses of Hesse'.

[48] P. Blickle, *The Revolution of 1525: The German Peasants' War from a New Perspective*, trans. T. A. Brady and H. C. E. Midelfort (Baltimore, 1981); H. J. Cohn, 'Anticlericalism in the German Peasants' War, 1525', *PP* 83 (1979), 3–31.

[49] Gordon, *Swiss Reformation*, pp. 57–60.

[50] *RO*, iii. 157–64; *MRH*, pp. 60, 62, 66, 75, 77, 80, 96, 100; M. Heale, *The Dependent Priories of Medieval English Monasteries* (Woodbridge, 2005), p. 238.

gathered pace at the end of the decade: Saxony followed Hesse in 1527, and Frisia followed in 1528.[51] The formation of the Schmalkaldic League (1531) intensified the pressure for dissolution in the remaining states of Germany: Württemberg began suppressions in 1535, but Bavaria and Brandenburg remained intact until the middle years of the century.[52] The suppressions also spread through the Swiss cantons. Berne's dissolution accounted for the Benedictine abbeys of Erlach and Trub in 1528 and 1529 respectively.[53] Geneva expelled its bishop in 1530 but its regular communities were not broken up until 1535.[54] The cantons that did not officially favour reform also saw religious houses abandoned: both Einsiedeln (Schwyz) and Fischingen (Thurgau) succumbed to the radicals in 1526.[55] The 1523 election of King Gustav Vasa advanced a reformation in Sweden and the regular religious were among the early targets.[56] The clergy and people of Denmark and Norway were also receptive to the reformers, but the suppression of monasteries and mendicant convents did not begin before 1537.[57] At this time the Tudor regime resumed, and extended, its assault on monasteries of England, Wales and its dominion in Ireland, at a point when the monastic orders of north-western Europe were already dispersed. The English suppressions were complete by early 1540, but much of monastic northern Europe survived, including the scattered settlements of the Celtic British Isles.[58] The Scots monasteries were subject to visitation and subsequent injunctions in 1552 but were not formally suppressed until after 1560.[59] Their Irish counterparts never faced formal sanctions but faded slowly over the second half of the century after the loss of their English and Scots affiliations.[60] The monks and mendicants of the Low Countries

[51] While Luther's protector, Elector John of Saxony, pursued a programme of reform, ducal Saxony resisted until the death of Duke George in 1539. The succession of Count Enno precipitated religious change in Frisia: A. Pettegree, *Emden and the Dutch Revolt: Reformation and the Development of Reformed Protestantism* (Oxford, 1992), pp. 29–31. See also E. Cameron, *The European Reformation* (Oxford, 1991), pp. 267–72; Schmitz, *Histoire*, iii. 272.

[52] Schmitz, *Histoire*, iii. 272–3, 279, 281; Strauss, 'Religious Policies of Dukes Willhelm and Ludwig', 357.

[53] Schmitz, *Histoire*, iii. 282–3; Gordon, *Swiss Reformation*, pp. 86–119 at 101–8.

[54] W. G. Naphy, *Calvin and the Consolidation of the Genevan Reformation* (Manchester, 1994), pp. 20–1.

[55] Schmitz, *Histoire*, iii. 283–4.

[56] E. I. Kouri, 'The Early Reformation in Sweden and Finland, c. 1520–1560', in *The Scandinavian Reformation*, ed. O. P. Grell (Cambridge, 1995), pp. 42–69. See also O. P. Grell, 'The Catholic Church and its Leadership', ibid., pp. 70–114 at 104–7.

[57] M. S. Lausten, 'The Early Reformation in Denmark and Norway, 1520–1559', in *The Scandinavian Reformation: From Evangelical Movement to Institutionalisation of Reform*, ed. O. P. Grell (Cambridge, 1995), pp. 12–41 at 35–7.

[58] For the chronology of the suppressions in England, see *RO*, iii. 304–19, 330–49. For Scotland, see M. Dilworth, *Scottish Monasteries in the Late Middle Ages* (Edinburgh, 1995), pp. 75–88. For the successive suppression 'campaigns' in Ireland, see B. Bradshaw, *The Dissolution of the Religious Orders in Ireland under Henry VIII* (Cambridge, 1974), pp. 39–46, 66–77, 110–22.

[59] Dilworth, *Scottish Monasteries*, pp. 75–88 at 75. See also Stanford Reid, 'Scottish Counter Reformation before 1560', 104–25.

[60] Only 55 per cent of Ireland's 140 monasteries were suppressed; although many dispersed, it was a protracted process and there was some survivalism: Bradshaw, *Dissolution of Religious Orders in Ireland*, pp. 125–30, 206.

were threatened only after the close of the Council of Trent (1564); popular uprisings in 1566–7 undermined regular communities in Flanders and Holland but they survived on depleted numbers and diminished resources until a systematic led by William of Orange in 1584.[61]

In many parts of Europe the process against the monasteries was undertaken using the mechanisms long established for the management of ecclesiastical foundations. This fact may account for the failure of monasteries to form effective resistance. Not only did the conventional machinery of reform conceal the possible outcomes of state intervention but also, perhaps more importantly, it restricted their scope, their freedom of manœuvre. It was customary to admit the visitor and to accept his injunctions for the correction of the community, even if the remedy recommended was suppression.[62] In Hesse, Saxony, Württemberg, England, Scotland and Wales the religious houses were in the first instance subject to visitation; in Ireland a visitation was prevented only by the eruption of the Silken Thomas rebellion.[63] The involvement of secular authorities in such a visitation did not represent a significant departure from customary practice: since the Council of Constance, the German dukes had initiated several cycles of reform in their own domains, and the English crown had also attempted the reform of leading Benedictine abbeys.[64] Even Gustav Vasa (1496–1560) was initially inclined to act within the accepted norms: his reform of the Swedish church was heralded by a conventional challenge to papal provisions.[65] Of course, the secular authorities now arrogated to themselves powers – spiritual dominion, supremacy – which had no precedent in medieval practice but at least at first these were exercised within the established framework of diocese, province and parliament. The visitations and subsequent suppressions in the German states were advanced not by princely proclamation but by the proceedings of the state Diet.[66] In England the royal supremacy, the visitations, injunctions and suppressions were enforced with the assistance of episcopal authority and parliamentary statutes, the latter promulgated with the apparent approval of representative abbots in the House of Lords.[67] In fact the

[61] J. D. Tracy, *The Founding of the Dutch Republic: War, Finance and Politics in Holland, 1572–88* (Oxford, 2008), p. 71.

[62] For the practice of visitation, see J. H. Tillotson, 'Visitation and Reform of the Yorkshire Nunneries in the Fourteenth Century', *Northern History* 30 (1994), 1–21. See above, pp. 122–3.

[63] Miller, 'Dissolution of the Religious Houses of Hesse', pp. 223–6 at p. 223; Strauss, 'Religious Policies of Dukes Wilhelm and Ludwig', 357; Bradshaw, *Dissolution of Religious Orders in Ireland*, pp. 17–21.

[64] See above, pp. 204–9.

[65] E. I. Kouri, 'The Early Reformation in Sweden and Finland, c. 1520–1560', in *Scandinavian Reformation*, ed. Grell, pp. 42–69.

[66] Landgrave Philip of Hesse appointed a commission which prepared an ordinance for reform, *Reformatio ecclesiarum Hessiae*, which addressed monastic foundations among other matters, but thereafter he proceeded by means of royal memoranda: Miller, 'Dissolution of the Religious Houses of Hesse', pp. 203, 206, 214, 218.

[67] *RO*, ii. 291–303.

novel authority of national governments was frequently tempered by the intervention of regional jurisdictions: in Germany evangelical city councils acted in anticipation of the approval of their prince;[68] for the States of Holland and the Swiss cantons, the suppression of monastic religion was wholly a matter for civic government.[69]

For the majority of European monks, dissolution was born of a familiar disciplinary process, but for a minority, notably on the Continental mainland, it was the consequence of violent conflict. Such violence was very rare in the British Isles. It was only after their initial suppression and subsequent reoccupation in 1536 that the northern English monasteries witnessed skirmishes with the King's militia.[70] The fiercest struggles were seen at houses of Cistercians and Regular Canons; the Benedictines appear largely unaffected.[71] Some 5,000–6,000 radicals may have mustered at Edinburgh in 1543 to confront monks, mendicants and other symbols of Catholicism, but their mood was not widely shared, and they were swiftly dispersed.[72] There was one monastic casualty here, but only after the Scots Reformation was underway. The abbot of Kelso was murdered by the Edinburgh mob in March 1566 on the night that Mary Stuart's minion David Riccio also met his death.[73]

The most sustained violence was witnessed in Lutheran Germany in 1524–6, as Saxony and its neighbours suffered a sudden spate of popular uprisings. From his vantage point at Basel, Erasmus observed the violence as *Pfaffenkrieg*, a peasants' war, with, in his view, the religious orders as the common enemy: 'the wickedness of [the monasteries] provoked them to it', he wrote, 'since they could not be controlled by the law'.[74] Modern research has provided a more nuanced reading of the confessional, social and political impulses of the peasants of neighboring regions but there is no doubt that assaults on monastic and mendicant communities were widespread. In Würzburg diocese as many as thirty-one monasteries were destroyed; in Thuringia, nineteen were also laid waste, ten of which were houses of Black Monks.[75] Pilgrim shrines were particular targets: the abbey of Einsiedeln, renowned for its Black Madonna, was attacked at the beginning of the 'war'

[68] C. Scott-Dixon, *The Reformation in Germany* (Oxford, 2002), pp. 98–114.
[69] Gordon, *Swiss Reformation*, p. 326.
[70] *RO*, iii. 325–33. The (few) armed confrontations did not occur at Benedictine foundations. Both in Linolnshire and Yorkshire it was among Cistercian convents that there were conspicuous signs of support for the rebels, for example at Jervaulx: R. W. Hoyle, *The Pilgrimage of Grace and the Politics of the 1530s* (Oxford, 2001), pp. 386–7.
[71] The Cistercian houses of the East Riding of Yorkshire, Jervaulx and Rievaulx, witnessed scenes of violent opposition: *RO*, iii. 320–35; Hoyle, *Pilgrimage of Grace*, pp. 386–7.
[72] Stanford Reid, 'The Scottish Counter-Reformation before 1560', 108; A. Ryrie, *The Origins of the Scottish Reformation* (Manchester, 2006), pp. 53–72 at 67.
[73] W. Stanford Reid, 'The Coming of the Reformation to Edinburgh', *Church History* 42 (1973), 27–44 at 36.
[74] *The German Peasants' War of 1525: New Viewpoints*, ed. B. Scribner and G. Benecke (London, 1979), pp. 45–6 at 45.
[75] O. Chadwick, *The Early Reformation on the Continent* (Oxford, 2001), p. 163.

in 1524.[76] The peasants also 'punished' houses that had actively opposed the reformers: Fulda, whose abbot had held Thomas Müntzer captive, was targeted in 1525.[77] Some attacks aimed at the annihilation of the monastic institution, not only to destroy the church and conventual buildings and disperse the community, but also to dismantle the wider infrastructure and sources of income in the manner of a medieval *chevauchée*. In a state of war it was the monastery's status as an entrepôt as much as its spiritual significance that made it a popular target. According to the chronicler of Metz, the mob passing through the Vosges mountains 'did not leave those monks and great abbots anything that was not essential for their sustenance, saying that their goods were the goods of the poor, and that such persons should have only what they needed to feed and clothe themselves'.[78] Some were iconoclastic in intent, notably the Saxon peasants' assault on Anhausen and Bildhausen. Others only harried the community to the point that their habitual observances became impossible. The spectacle of *Pfaffenkrieg* intensified the popular pressure on the regulars in neighbouring states. Bavaria, where there was no early impulse for suppression, saw sporadic outbreaks of violence. Amorbach was sacked in 1525, although the monastic community subsequently reassembled and survived.[79] From 1524, monasteries in the Swiss confederation suffered a series of attacks: Ittingen was set upon by incensed famers in July 1524; Ottobeuren and Rüti were also ravaged by rebel bands in March 1525; Beinwil was wholly destroyed in 1527; Rheinau was dispersed in 1529 and in the same year the abbey of Saint-Gall was coercively confiscated by the townspeople.[80]

Direct action against the religious returned during the Dutch revolt (1566–84). Iconoclastic riots erupted in southern Flanders in August 1566 and the ancient Benedictine abbey of Egmond was threatened.[81] The army of William of Orange (1533–84) renewed the assault from 1578, and over the next six years almost every monastery in the region was plundered and many communities were permanently dispersed. In the confessional flux of the Low Countries, some of the brethren allied themselves with the radicals. In Friesland and Groningen, as so-called hedge-preachers stirred the crowds gathered at the city gates, there were professed religious that acted as *agents provocateurs*.[82]

---

[76] B. Gordon, 'Switzerland', in *The Early Reformation in Europe*, ed. A. Pettegree (Cambridge, 1992), pp. 70–93 at 74.

[77] Miller, 'Dissolution of the Religious Houses of Hesse', p. 150.

[78] Cohn, 'Anticlericalism and the German Peasants' War', 11.

[79] Schmitz, *Histoire*, iii. 277–8.

[80] Ibid., iii./1 282–3; Gordon, *Swiss Reformation*, p. 77; G. R. Potter, *Zwingli* (Cambridge, 1984), pp. 144–9; H. J. Cohn, 'Changing Places: Peasants and Clergy, 1525', in *Anticlericalism in Late Medieval and Early Modern Europe*, ed. P. A. Dykema and H. A. Oberman (Leiden, 1993), pp. 545–69 at 546.

[81] A. C. Duke, *Reformation and Revolt in the Netherlands* (London, 1989), pp. 133, 146–7.

[82] Ibid., 78–9, 121, 129.

There may have been common mechanisms and motives evident in the assault on the monasteries in northern Europe, but rarely did they result in the same outcome. The complete surrender or suppression of communities that occurred in England and Wales between 1536 and early 1540 was not typical of the Continent as a whole. In Hesse and Sweden the interventions of the secular authorities lead directly (and swiftly) to the seizure of houses, the sequestration of their estates and the dispersal of their members.[83] However, incremental appropriation and secularisation was witnessed in Scotland, the Swiss cantons, and even in Luther's Saxony.[84] In Geneva the religious were stripped of their material assets, their seigniorial authority, and the centrepiece of their observance, the Mass, but they remained *in situ* for another five years.[85] The Scots abbeys were transferred to lay administrators – called commendators, from *commendam* – but the brethren were not forcibly dispersed but drifted away *ad hoc*.[86] At Wittenberg itself, although the corporate identity of the houses was stifled and their estates seized, initially the brethren continued to occupy the conventual buildings. The mass was still celebrated in Wittenberg cloisters even four years after the advent of Luther.[87] Where and when it did occur, the appropriation of endowments did not itself follow a common course. The Swiss cantons recycled monastic resources in a range of charitable and education foundations.[88] The resources of some of Saxony's religious houses were channelled in this way, while others were allowed to remain and were evangelised (see below). Elsewhere, significant houses were transformed into collegiate foundations.[89] It should be noted that a series of secularisations also occurred in the reformed south-west of France: between 1532 and 1540 such significant monastic churches as Montauban and Castres (Languedoc) became chapters of secular canons.[90] English reformers had favoured such an expedient although in the event only a handful of such churches were created.[91] The transfer (by grant or purchase) of monastic endowments to

[83] Schmitz, *Histoire*, iii. 1. 289; Miller, 'Dissolution of the Religious Houses of Hesse', pp. 227–36; R. Cahill, 'The Sequestration of the Hessian Monasteries', in *Reformations Old and New: Essays on the Social and Economic Impact of Religious Change, c. 1470–1630*, ed. B. A. Kümin (Aldershot, 1996), p. 76.

[84] For Scotland, see Dilworth, *Scottish Monasteries*, pp. 75–88. For Switzerland, see K. von Greyerz, 'Switzerland', in *Reformation in National Context*, ed. R. W. Scribner, R. Porter and M. Teich (Cambridge, 1994), pp. 30–46 at 36–7; Gordon, *Swiss Reformation* p. 104.

[85] Cameron, *European Reformation*, pp. 223–6; Gordon, *Swiss Reformation*, pp. 150–3; C. M. N. Eire, *War against Idols: The Reformation of Worship from Erasmus to Calvin* (Cambridge, 1989), p. 127.

[86] Dilworth, *Scottish Monasteries*, pp. 75–88; Ryrie, *Origins of the Scottish Reformation*, p. 14.

[87] For Wittenberg, see C. Lindberg, 'Wait for No-one: the Implementation of Reform in Wittenberg', in *The European Reformation* (Oxford, 2009), pp. 87–109.

[88] Gordon, *Swiss Reformation*, p. 65. Berne had intended school foundations but failed.

[89] For example, Schmitz, *Histoire*, iii. 220–1.

[90] Schmitz, *Histoire*, iii. 220.

[91] For the aspirations of reformist English clergy, see F. Heal, *Reformation in Britain and Ireland* (Oxford, 2003), pp. 196–7. For cathedrals: S. E. Lehmberg, *The Reformation of Cathedrals: Cathedrals in English Society, 1485–1603* (Princeton, 1988). Of course, some radicals rejected secular chapters just as they did regular convents: C. Cross, 'Dens of Loitering Lubbers: Protestant Protest against Cathedral Foundations, 1540–1640', in *Schism, Heresy and Religious Protest*, ed. D. Baker, Studies in Church History 10 (1972), pp. 231–2.

lay beneficiaries which was widespread in England was not paralleled in mainland Europe.

By contrast, in a number of regions, once secured under secular jurisdiction, there was a conscious effort to recast the monasteries as evangelical communities. The Saxon abbey of Oldenstadt survived under Lutheran supervision until 1541.[92] Gengenbach (Württemberg) also adopted evangelical customs under the direction of Abbot Friedrich von Keppenbach, an early disciple of Calvin.[93] Elizabeth of Brandenburg, regent during the minority of her son Erich II, 1543–6, sought to recast the monasteries in her custody as evangelical seminaries; the brethren were to receive four sermons weekly and to hear passages from the Confession of Augsburg and Melanchthon's *Loci communes* from the refectory lector.[94] The monastic community at Bursfeld accepted such terms and survived until the Catholic resurgence in the region allowed the return of Benedictine customs.[95] Brandenburg's convents cast off the cloak of evangelism under the Catholic Erich II, but the prescriptions were reintroduced at the end of the century during the overlordship of Henri Jules de Brunswick-Wolfenbüttel (d. 1613).[96] The monasteries of Württemberg were subject to a degree of evangelism after the resurgence of ducal authority in 1552. Their 'superstitious rites' were suppressed, which meant the abandonment of the mass and the full scope of the Benedictine offices; they were also required to keep a school, reflecting the notion widespread among Continental reformers that monastic foundation might best serve the reformed church as seminaries.[97] Some, already susceptible to the influence of the reformers, initiated the transformation for themselves, Abbot Jacques Russinger of Pfäfers, a follower of Zwingli, converted his community in 1530.[98] In Scotland uniquely there had been an attempt to refashion the monasteries as reformed communities before the kingdom's Calvinist Reformation. In 1549 each house was required to appoint a special lecturer, to be supported by a benefice, to provide scriptural instruction.[99]

The assault on monastic religion is often presented as a measure of the might of princely government in the sixteenth century. The early, speedy and systematic suppressions effected in England and Wales, Hesse and Sweden must to a certain extent stand as testament to the skilful manipulation of legal machinery, personnel and resources by their respective regimes. At the same time it is important to acknowledge the willingness of religious in

[92] Chadwick, *Early Reformation on the Continent*, p. 168.
[93] Ibid., p. 160.
[94] Schmitz, *Histoire*, iii. 272–3.
[95] Ibid.
[96] Ibid., 273.
[97] Ibid., 279–80 at 280.
[98] Ibid., 283.
[99] Dilworth, *Scottish Monasteries*, p. 66.

many regions to surrender peaceably to royal, seigniorial or civic authorities. Whatever the individual motivations involved, it is unlikely such a comprehensive redeployment of people and resources could have been achieved without the complicity – both passive and active – of the monastic communities themselves.[100]

It would be wrong, however, to suggest the period passed without any resistance from the monastic communities and their supporters. The pace of the royal commissioners, and the growing capacity of the Tudor regime to command the provinces (and mobilise a militia), diminished in England and Wales the prospect of a nationwide challenge to the reformers. Before the royal visitation of 1535 a handful of regulars had expressed their hostility to the Henrician supremacy. The Carthusians of London, together with individual brethren from their provincial houses, remained resolute and, between 1535 and 1538, no fewer than eighteen were executed.[101] Of the Benedictines, only the prior of Christ Church, Canterbury, Edmund Bocking, provoked an early confrontation with the Crown. His patronage of Elizabeth Barton, whose 'prophecies' conveyed popular anger at the break with Rome and the king's divorce, provided a vehicle for his own opposition to the drift of royal policy; but it also led him to the scaffold.[102] The enforcement of the first act of dissolution by the royal commissioners in Lincolnshire and the ridings of Yorkshire in the summer and early autumn of 1536 contributed to the only concerted rebellion against the reformers in England.[103] The men of Lincolnshire attempted an armed challenge from 30 September, but it was quickly quelled; a parallel but much more widespread revolt erupted in the Northern Province towards the end of October.[104] Robert Aske, a figurehead for the Yorkshire insurgents, articulated their alarm at the 'spreading of heretics [i.e. Lutherans], the suppression of houses of religion and other matters touching the commonwealth'.[105] Recent studies have suggested the Pilgrimage of Grace, as it came to be known, was motivated as much by Aske's 'other matters', such the enforcement of First Fruits and other fiscal novelties, as it was by the assault on monastic

---

[100] The disposition of religious during the European reformations is largely unstudied. For general reflections, see *RO*, iii. 367–82. See also P. Cunich, 'The Ex-Religious in Post-Dissolution Society: Symptoms of Post-Traumatic Stress Disorder?', in *The Religious Orders in Pre-Reformation England*, ed. J. G. Clark (Woodbridge, 2002), pp. 227–38.

[101] For the Carthusian opposition, see *RO*, iii. 222–40.

[102] For Bocking, see Bernard, *King's Reformation*, pp. 88–92–3, 96–8. See also *RO*, iii. 182, 184–90.

[103] For the monastic dimension to the Pilgrimage of Grace, see *RO*, iii. 322–30; Hoyle, *Pilgrimage of Grace*, pp. 48–9: 'evidence for Aske's monastophilia being a general northern preference is decidedly lacking. The monasteries may well have been a familiar and valued part of the fabric of early sixteenth-century society but the risings of 1536 were not primarily about their defence.'

[104] Here there were skirmishes in the precincts or the environs of a number of houses but none of them was Benedictine.

[105] 'The Manner of Taking Robert Aske': *LP*, xii, 1 (6); M. Bateson, 'The Pilgrimage of Grace', *EHR* 5 (1890), 331–43 at 335.

religion.[106] Yet the houses of the dales and the moors momentarily became a battleground. The most spirited resistance came from the Regular Canons and Cistercians, however, who (at Jervaulx) skirmished with King's militia from their own gatehouse.[107] As they had done during the enforcement of the supremacy, generally the Benedictines remained at one remove. There were isolated instances of armed resistance in midland and south-western England – at Norton Priory, Cheshire, and the priory of St Nicholas, Exeter – although again it was the houses of other orders that appear most unstable.[108] The periphery of the Tudor realm proved to be more explosive. The rebellion of Thomas Fitzgerald, 10th earl of Kildare was intended as political challenge to the English rule, but it also interrupted the progress of the visitors of religious houses between June 1534 and March the following year. 'Silken Thomas' seized on the public alarm over religious reform, rallying his supporters at the gates of Dublin's Cistercian abbey of St Mary.[109]

During this period, however, the Black Monks did engage in a degree of passive resistance to the interventions of the commissioners and the aims of the Crown. The abbot and convent of St Albans allowed a pro-papal preacher to remain active in their liberty by providing him to the parochial chapel (of St Andrew) within their precincts.[110] In 1536 it was reported that John Stoneywell, abbot of Benedictine Pershore, had failed to remove references to the pope and to Rome from the monastery's service books; two years later it was alleged he still openly asserted the papal supremacy.[111] Even after the process of suppression had begun, some continued to confound the authorities. The properties of the monastery, both temporal and spiritual, were granted to favoured benefactors – and on occasion, kinsfolk – on leases so lengthy as to place them beyond the reach of the Crown for a generation.[112] In a number of notorious cases, even the livestock of the monastery's demesne were sold so as to avoid their surrender to the royal commissioners.[113] Such an alienation – known as 'concealment' – had been explicitly prohibited under the first Act of Dissolution (1536)

---

[106] Hoyle, *Pilgrimage of Grace*, pp. 48–9.

[107] *RO*, iii. 325, 331.

[108] For contemporary reports of these protests, see *LP*, x, 296. See also P. Greene, *Norton Priory: The Archaeology of a Medieval Religious House* (Cambridge, 2004), pp. 151–2; P. Greene, 'The Impact of the Dissolution of the Monasteries in Cheshire: The Case of Norton', in *Medieval Archaeology, Art and Architecture at Chester*, ed. A. Thacker (Leeds, 2000), pp. 152–66 at pp. 155–6; Youings, *Dissolution of the Monasteries*, pp. 53–4, 164–5.

[109] Bradshaw, *Dissolution of Religious Orders in Ireland*, pp. 42, 49–61. See also L. McCorristine, *The Revolt of Silken Thomas: A Challenge to Henry VIII* (Dublin, 1987).

[110] See *LP*, viii/406–7. The preacher was Thomas Kyng: Clark, 'Reformation and Reaction', 297–328 at 301–2.

[111] *LP*, xi/2, 449; xiii/1, 822.

[112] For example, Sir Richard Lister's report on the nuns of Romsey in 1538: *LP*, xiii/2, 352.

[113] *LP*, xiv/1, 324; xiv/2, 49 (15) (Reading Abbey); G. H. Cook, *Letters to Cromwell and others on the Suppression of the Monasteries* (London, 1965), p. 141.

and thus constituted a deliberate act of treason.[114] The commissioners were conscious of concealment but were commonly too late – and perhaps too disconnected from provincial society – to prevent it. The Crown's litigation to retrieve concealed monastic properties continued into the reign of James I.[115]

The closing months of the Dissolution in England brought a final confrontation between the reformers and the remaining communities of Benedictines. Between September and December 1539 the superiors of three of the foremost abbeys of the English congregation – Colchester, Glastonbury and Reading – were arraigned, convicted and executed.[116] The nature of their treason was shadowy. They had consistently obstructed to the work of the commissioners and now resisted the final surrender of their houses. For its part, the government had grown weary of the struggle over the 'great and solemn' monasteries and were perhaps already aware that the material gains of the suppression did not far outweigh its costs. The abbots approached their death not as an act of resistance but of sacrifice, one which the government, whether consciously or not, amplified in the execution at Glastonbury: Abbot Whiting was paraded through the town and then taken to the Tor, beyond where he was executed with men convicted of common thievery placed on either side.[117]

The suppression in Continental Europe was more protracted and generally more peaceable. Some German convents confronted the insurgents directly during the disturbances of the Peasants' War (1524–6). The monks of Neresheim Abbey (Württemberg) held firm throughout the uprising under the direction of their remarkable superior, Johannes Vinsternau (d. 1529).[118] Many more reoccupied their houses and resumed their observance as best they could as soon as the plunderers had passed.[119] In the early stages of the reform, monastic communities also exploited the rivalry of regional jurisdictions to insulate themselves against the injunctions of the Diet, diocesan or prince. The Benedictines of Überwasser refused to surrender their abbey in 1536, asserting their ancient exemption from episcopal authority.[120] Elsewhere episcopal authority was itself mobilised as a means of preservation. Even in Hesse, the progress of Landgrave Philip's reform was hindered within the jurisdiction of the archbishop of Mainz.[121] The Black Monks of Lippe survived (until 1571) through the protection of their

[114] *The Tudor Constitution: Documents and Commentary*, ed. G. R. Elton, 2nd edn (Cambridge, 1982), no. 186, pp. 383–7.
[115] C. J. Kitching, 'The Quest for Concealed Lands in the Reign of Elizabeth I: The Alexander Prize Essay', *TRHS* 5th Series 24 (1974), 63–78.
[116] *RO*, iii. 367–82.
[117] *LP*, xi, 382; xii/1, 907 (2); xiv/2, 531.
[118] Schmitz, *Histoire*, iii. 286.
[119] Ibid. 285–6.
[120] R. P.-C. Hsia, *Society and Religion in Münster, 1535–1618* (New Haven, 1984), p. 34.
[121] Miller, 'Dissolution of the Religious Houses of Hesse', p. 236.

patron, the bishop of Paderborn.[122] In Brabant both bishops and nobles came together to assist the monasteries in their resistance to princely authority, when the annexation of abbeys to create a series of new sees was conceived in 1561.[123] In regions where the regulars had been reformed but not removed there was growing passive resistance by mid-century. Even after the mass had been suppressed and the material assets of these houses sequestrated, a number of their brethren remained. Whether they were unable to follow another form of life, or unwilling to surrender, they presented a substantial obstacle to the state authorities.

Survival and Revival

Historians within and outside the Benedictine order have always been sharply divided in their reading of the sixteenth-century suppressions. Monastic authorities, viewing the problems of the period on a European scale, have preferred to treat the reformations of Germany, Scandinavia and the British Isles as regional episodes that did not threaten the continuity of observance across the Continent as a whole (although there was an early, internal dispute over the apparent discontinuity of the English congregation).[124] Secular Catholic historians have similarly sought to highlight the continuities – at times in their accounts remarkable, even heroic – not only in the ministry of regular and secular clergy but also in the resilient spirituality of the laity.[125] Yet from a Protestant perspective the assault on the religious orders has always represented, unequivocally, the final extinction of the medieval monastic tradition in Europe.[126] The pace and pattern of monastic suppression was so variable that it is difficult to identify any moment in the sixteenth century that might stand as an absolute turning point in their fortunes. Such were the exigencies of the Reformation in Germany that some regions saw successive revivals of monastic religion in the century after Luther; indeed, on the eve of the Thirty Years War monasticism was stronger in some areas than it had been at any time since 1517.[127] Recent research has uncovered evidence of regional monastic survival even in Elizabethan England.[128]

Of course, the loss of a large proportion of Benedictine Europe in this period cannot be overlooked. By the spring of 1540 every one of

---

[122] Chadwick, *Early Reformation on the Continent*, p. 172.

[123] Duke, *Reformation and Revolt in the Netherlands*, p. 169.

[124] *RO*, iii. 444–54 at 449–51.

[125] For example, Duffy, *Stripping of the Altars*; E. Duffy, *Voices of Morebath: Reformation and Rebellion in an English Village* (New Haven, 2003).

[126] For example, G. G. Coulton's pejorative subtitle for the final volume of his *Five Centuries of Religion*, published posthumously in 1950, 'The Last Days of Medieval Monachism'.

[127] Schmitz, *Histoire*, iii. 284–8, iv. 117–26.

[128] M. C. Cross, 'A Medieval Yorkshire Library', *Northern History* 25 (1989), 281–90.

England's 120 Benedictine houses had been suppressed and almost all of their inhabitants had abandoned their vows and adopted the life of the secular clerk.[129] The loss of monasteries in Germany was on a far greater scale: between 1522 and 1541 perhaps as many as 500 houses had been abandoned, surrendered or suppressed; as many as another hundred had been transformed (albeit not permanently in every case) into communities of reformed observance.[130] The fortunes of the ex-religious are not nearly so well documented here as they have been for England and Wales, but the profound disturbance of the Peasants' War, and, for some regions, the imperial counter-attack mid-century may have caused a higher degree of destitution among the monastic cohorts. Elsewhere, in Denmark, Norway, Bohemia, Ducal Prussia and regions of Hungary – ravaged by Ottoman invasion, not Reformation – the communities of Benedictines, like those of other religious, had been entirely extinguished.[131] Once again the fortunes of their former inhabitants remain obscure. Certainly in the case of both Scandinavia and Hungary it was centuries before the monks could return.[132]

The Benedictine houses that had escaped suppression were also badly diminished. The states of southern Germany that saw no early reform suffered shrinkage. Bursfeld, once the beacon of reform, survived the reform of Elizabeth of Brandenburg only as a much-reduced community: a visitor in 1585 recorded only five brethren.[133] By the middle years of the century, the communities at Admont, Lambach and even Melk, the crucible of fifteenth-century reform, had fallen to six brethren or fewer.[134] In the Catholic cantons of Switzerland there was also a steady decline. The Benedictine convent of Beinwil, once considered a prize by the region's land-hungry nobility, retained only the smallest colony of monks until it came under the benign supervision of the revived abbey of Einsiedeln in 1587.[135]

Yet the monastic tradition was not wholly expunged from northern and western Europe. Even in the most fervently reformist regions of Germany, there were houses that held firm against the authorities or, after the early assaults had receded, returned to resume some semblance of the observant life. Luther himself was responsible for the retention of the Benedictine community at Oldenstadt, which remained unchallenged by the authorities

---

[129] For a list of houses and dates of suppression, see *MRH*, pp. 58–82, 95–101. For the conversion of monks to seculars, see D. Chambers, *Faculty Office Registers, 1534–49: A Calendar of the First Two Registers of the Archbishop of Canterbury's Faculty Office* (Oxford, 1966).

[130] Schmitz, *Histoire*, iv. 272, 276–78; Chadwick, *Early Reformation on the Continent*, pp. 168–70.

[131] See also R. Portner, *The Counter-Reformation in Central Europe: Styria, 1580–1630* (Oxford, 2001), pp. 62–3, where houses declined but were not destroyed.

[132] *Scandinavian Reformation*, ed. Grell, p. 87.

[133] Schmitz, *Histoire*, iii. 274.

[134] Ibid., iii. 282.

[135] Ibid.

until 1541.[136] The Lutheran toleration of monastic observance was not matched in all reformed territories. There is evidence that monastic observance survived in Holland after the Orange Reformation, but only in clandestine ceremonies.[137] There are glimpses of at least a tacit commitment to the monastic tradition in England of the 1540s and 1550s. The wills of former monks that died as much as a decade after the Dissolution bear witness to the maintenance of their old fraternal ties.[138] The wills of two monks of St Albans Abbey who died in 1540 and 1545 respectively refer to one another and request burial side by side in the parochial chapel adjoining their abbey church, the only place of worship still in use within the monastic precincts.[139] In a number of cases these ties were buttressed by cohabitation: several former monks of the Cluniac priory of Monk Bretton shared a household from the suppression until their deaths in the 1560s and 70s.[140] Whether such coexistence amounted to an approximation of the life-in-common is not captured in the sources, but it may be significant that Monk Bretton brethren retained some of the books and other paraphernalia of their former community.[141] A handful of the ex-Benedictine nuns of Shaftesbury may have held together in the years immediately following the dissolution of their great abbey in 1539.[142] Moreover, monastic identity endured after the energy, or opportunity, for a life-in-common had passed: Mary Dennys, former prioress of Kington St Michael (Wiltshire), lived on, unmarried, maintaining her own household, for more than fifty years after the suppression of her house.[143]

Moreover, in the middle years of the century these northern regions also experienced a reversal of religious policy that saw the selective restoration of the monastic order. Entering his majority in 1546, Erich II of Brandenburg (1528–84) reversed the reform of religious houses initiated during the regency of his mother, Elizabeth. His efforts ensured the recovery of monastic observance in the region of Hanover and Lower Saxony.[144] The recovery of imperial authority in Württemberg in 1547 enabled the revival of observant life at Hirsau and other celebrated Benedictine convents at least

[136] Luther wrote to Abbot Heino Gottschalk of Oldestadt that a monk whose life accords with the precepts of the Gospel may 'with great benefit remain in the monastery': *The Pastoral Luther: Essays on Luther's Practical Theology* (Grand Rapids, MI, 2009), ed. T. J. Wengert, p. 350; Chadwick, *Early Reformation on the Continent*, p. 168.
[137] Pettegree, *Emden and the Dutch Revolt*, p. 32.
[138] Cross and Vickers, *Monks, Friars and Nuns in Sixteenth-Century Yorkshire*, p. 428.
[139] Clark, 'Reformation and Reaction', 297–328.
[140] Cross, 'A Medieval Yorkshire Library'.
[141] *EBL*, B55, 266–87, discussion at 266–8. See also Cross, 'A Medieval Yorkshire Library'; C. Cross, 'Monastic Learning and Libraries in Sixteenth-Century Yorkshire', in *Humanism and Reform: The Church in Europe, England and Scotland, 1400–1643: Essays in Honour of James K. Cameron*, ed. J. Kirk, Studies in Church History, Subsidia 8 (Oxford, 1991), pp. 255–70.
[142] J. Chandler, *A Higher Reality: The History of Shaftesbury's Royal Nunnery* (East Knoyle, 2003), p. 98.
[143] *VCH, Wiltshire*, ii. 259–61 at 261. See illustration 8.
[144] Schmitz, *Histoire*, iii. 272–3.

until the resurgence of ducal authority – under Christoph of Württemberg (1515–68) – gave a further stimulus to reform.[145] The emergence of the Catholic cantons of the Swiss *Eidgenossenschaft* enabled the revival of several Benedictine houses. Einsiedeln was placed in the hands of Louis Barer of Saint-Gall as early as 1526; Rheinau was restored in 1532 and Fischingen ten years later.[146]

The accession of Mary Tudor in England and Wales in July 1553, assured only by a noble *coup d'état*, also signalled a change in the confessional climate that had prevailed for almost twenty years.[147] Provincial England appears to have anticipated a general programme of monastic restoration, and in a number of the old abbey towns testators prepared the ground with bequests 'lest the abbay be sett up again'.[148] The manner of Mary's accession made the reappropriation of monastic properties politically impossible, however, and her government sanctioned only a handful of restorations, favouring the reformed orders, of Brigittines and Observant Friars. Only one Benedictine abbey, Westminster, was reoccupied, and only after protracted negotiations with the secular chapter that had been its custodians for almost two decades. The Black Monks finally returned to Westminster on 21 November 1557, 21 November, a date which both early modern and modern Benedictines have hallowed as a *dies memorabilis*. There were twenty-eight of them, none of them originally professed to Westminster but representative of the order's principal English houses, *inter alia* Evesham, Glastonbury and St Albans. Their superior was John Feckenham (*c.* 1510–84), formerly a monk of Evesham. Feckenham had passed barely a decade in the Benedictine habit before the suppression of his house and for much of this period he had been a student at Oxford (from which position he appears among the correspondents of the fellow Evesham monk, Robert Joseph). Like many of his brethren, Feckenham had taken a 'capacity' and secured a secular benefice, but in the wake of Henry's death (April 1547) he emerged as a Catholic polemicist preaching his 'odious opinions' (as a contemporary report gives it) publicly at Paul's Cross. For much of Edward's reign Feckenham was in detention but he was also used by the reformist government as the opponent in contrived disputations with a series of conformist diocesans. Undoubtedly it was Feckenham's currency and public profile as a Catholic propagandist, and not his status as a Benedictine, that led to his appointment at Westminster Abbey. His

---

[145] Ibid., iii. 279–80; Scott-Dixon, *Reformation in Germany*, p. 137.

[146] Schmitz, *Histoire*, iii. 283.

[147] 'The Marian Church establishment belonged to a different era ... and its objectives were not so much reactionary as evangelical and reformist': L. Wooding, *Rethinking Catholicism in Reformation England* (Oxford, 2000), p. 115. For the manner of Mary's accession, see D. M. Loades, *Mary Tudor: A Life* (Oxford, 1989; repr. 1992), pp. 171–88.

[148] For example, Clark, 'Reformation and Reaction', 297–328; Litzenberger, 'The Coming of Protestantism to Elizabeth Tewkesbury'.

presence underlined the aim of the Marian restorations, not primarily to initiate a new monastic (or mendicant) mission but to assist in a more imperative enterprise, the recovery of popular Catholic piety throughout the realm. These priorities were reflected in the renewed monastic church: the shrine of St Edward the Confessor was restored, and the abbey's celebrated rights of sanctuary were resumed, but, so far as the scanty documentary record allows, it would appear that Benedictine observance was not fully realised. According to the seventeenth-century researches of Augustine Baker (1575–1641), on the testimony of Siegbert Buckley, the last living survivor, the devotional climate was 'more akin to a college (i.e. a chapter of secular clergy) than a monastery'.

Further Benedictine communities were contemplated between 1555 and 1558, at least by the former monks and their benefactors, if not by the government itself. Richard Bourman, abbot of St Albans at its surrender, petitioned for, and secured, the use of his abbey church in 1557; among the local elite it appears to have been public knowledge that he intended to reoccupy the site with a community of monks. Several men of property pledged support for the projected monastery in a will drafted between the summer of 1557 and the autumn of 1558. Hopes for a restoration were also expressed by testators at Bury St Edmunds, Glastonbury, Montacute and Tewkesbury, and perhaps elsewhere, although there is no indication their aspirations were translated into actions. Feckenham's Westminster functioned uninterrupted for only a year before Mary's death in November 1558. The brethren observed the feast of the Lord's Nativity before being forcibly dispersed in January 1559. Outside the abbey Feckenham attempted to resume his role as Catholic apologist but the deep insecurity of the Elizabethan regime led to his early, and permanent, imprisonment.[149]

Epilogue: Re-formation

If it is possible to identify a moment in time to mark the conclusion of the Benedictines' medieval history, it should properly be the November day in 1557 that Feckenham and his twenty-eight fellows were found in Westminster. These men were not Benedictines, not, that is, in the mould of their thousands of medieval predecessors, or even those two decades before that had surrendered or succumbed to suppression. They had passed almost twenty years in the role of the parochial clergy, presiding over the

---

[149] For restorations desired and realised, see *RO*, iii. 421–43 at 423–38; NA, Prob. 11/26; 11/27 (Bury); Clark, 'Reformation and Reaction'. For Tewkesbury see Litzenberger, 'The Coming of Protestantism to Elizabethan Tewkesbury'. For the restored Westminster see *RO*, iii; G. Bodenwein, 'John Feckenham: The Last Abbot of Westminster', *American Benedictine Review* 17 (1996), 85–91; P. Tudor-Craig, 'John Feckenham and Tudor Religious Controversies', in *The Cloister and the World: Essays in Honour of Barbara Harvey*, ed. J. Blair and B. Golding (Oxford, 1996), pp. 302–33; *Westminster Abbey Reformed*, ed. C. S. Knighton and R. Mortimer (Aldershot, 2003).

patterns of vernacular worship prescribed in the King's Book. Not only had they held benefices – sometimes in plurality – but they had been sustained both by pensions quite unlike the *peculium* of the medieval monk and by temporal possessions and property of some substance. In the wake of the Dissolution they had become the provincial gentlemen-of-substance that their critics had assumed them to be before the Reformation. These men were also separated from the medieval monastic tradition not only by their own change in circumstances, but also by the wider transformation of traditional religion that had occurred since the spring of 1540. These men, and many of their Continental counterparts that sought to resume the cenobitic life in the old imperial territories and the Swiss cantons, now identified themselves as *Catholic*. Not only did they accept the permanence of the schism in the Christian community but they also acknowledged the ways in such a profound discontinuity altered their own profession of faith and forms of worship; many of them also now recognised the necessity for continued Catholic reform.

The Catholic reforms – or Counter-Reformation – of the second half of the sixteenth century reinforced the separation of Europe's surviving Benedictines from their medieval past. The Council of Trent (1545–64) turned to the monastic orders only towards the end of its protracted proceedings but the decrees 'concerning monks and nuns' promulgated in session twenty-five detached them further from their medieval past. The exempt status which had become a shibboleth for many Benedictines in the later Middle Ages was to be stripped away and after centuries of conflict the diocesan was to be assigned direct supervision of the monasteries in their jurisdiction. The decrees also reduced the number of 'endowed' or private masses that might be undertaken – always a conspicuous feature of pre-Reformation observance – and also required monastic liturgical calendars to conform more closely with those of the diocesan see. In the wake of Trent, provincial churches continued the work of reorganisation. At the direction of Pius V, the Benedictines of Portugal were translated into a Portuguese congregation in 1566.[150] The Tarragonese congregation of Benedictines was compelled to accept canons of reform in 1582 after their resistance to Philip II's proposed combination of the two Spanish congregations under Valladolid.[151] The measures taken at Trent and in the Catholic provinces reflected a new determination not only to integrate the Benedictines into the ecclesiastical mainstream but also, in the light of the success of the new orders, to make them more properly an arm of the Church militant, an objective articulated in Clement VII's 1592 bull *Sacer et religiosus monachorum status*.[152] In Catholic Germany under the direction of

---

[150] Schmitz, *Histoire*, iv. 169.
[151] Ibid., 164–5.
[152] Ibid., 165.

their diocesan, the reinvigorated monasteries were made centres not only of Catholic devotion but also of Catholic teaching and preaching. In Italy and Spain the Benedictine Congregations contributed to the continuing battle against the Lutheran heresy. For the first time in almost a millennium, the Black Monks were also charged with the work of conversion, on the emerging pagan frontier of New Spain. Benedictine missionaries arrived at Brazil in 1581; in 1598 priories dependent upon Montserrat were founded at Lima and Mexico City.[153]

The reduced ranks of the English Benedictines remained detached from these enterprises to the end of the sixteenth century. In exile they were dispersed and to a large extent itinerant. Some entered convents of the Cassinese congregation; at least two made their way to Spain while a larger number found refuge in Flanders. But the pressure of numbers and corporate (and possibly national) differences prevented any permanent settlement. Their fragmentation, coupled perhaps with mounting tensions in the Flemish monasteries, fuelled a false, but pervasive, view throughout the Continent that the English Black Monks had always been dependent, subject to Cluny from foundation to dissolution. The contention attracted credence, and the imprimatur of the Counter-Reformation elite, when repeated in Robert Parsons's *Memoriall of the Reformation in England* (1596).[154] By this date, however, a new generation of English converts had begun to emerge and enter voluntary exile in pursuit of their monastic vocation. Gregory Sayer, the first English Benedictine of the post-Reformation period, was professed at Montecassino in 1588.[155] The number of expatriate professions grew steadily at the turn of the sixteenth century and in 1602 – some thousand years after the arrival of Augustine of Canterbury – a Benedictine mission returned to England. According to a legend, one of the missionaries, Augustine Bradshaw, encountered in Worcestershire an elderly gentleman named Littleton who claimed to have been a monk of Evesham more than sixty years before; if he was the William Littleton that signed the deed of surrender at Evesham in January 1540, he would have been ninety-seven years old.[156]

❧

The Benedictines' own historians have been tempted to interpret Bradshaw's strange meeting as a symbol of the living link between their medieval forebears and the monks of the post-Reformation world. Yet what, if anything, William Littleton gave Bradshaw, a Tridentine Catholic trained in the Cassinese observance of Cortèse, was only a glimpse of a monastic

---

[153] Ibid., 169.
[154] Lunn, *English Benedictines*, p. 23.
[155] Ibid., p. 16.
[156] Ibid., p. 27.

past that for him and for the majority of his brethren, whether Englishmen or Continental Europeans, was already remote. The Benedictines' experience of Reformation was neither as sudden and unforeseen cataclysm, nor as a decisive and irrevocable discontinuity, but it would be entirely wrong to suggest the order was not profoundly changed by the ebb and flow of reform that passed throughout the Continent in the century after 1517.

Select Bibliography

Manuscript Sources

Chantilly, Musée Condé

MS XIX B1   Benedictine history of Jean de Stavelot

London, British Library

Add. 74236   'Sherborne Missal' (15th C.)
Cotton Julius D VIII   The 'Charge' of the Cellaress of Barking Abbey (15th C.)

Oxford, Bodleian Library

Auct. F. 4. 32   Dunstan's 'Classbook'
Bodley 240   Hagiography and History of the Monastic Order (14th C.)
Bodley 649   Sermon Collection, probably Benedictine (15th C.)
Bodley 692   Notebook of a Benedictine student at Oxford (15th C.)
Hatton 48   Rule of St Benedict (8th C)

Printed Sources

HISTORIES OF THE BENEDICTINES

Pre-Reformation

Pantin, W. A., 'Some Medieval English Treatises on the Origins of Monastic Life', in *Medieval Studies presented to Rose Graham*, ed. V. Ruffer and A. J. Taylor (Oxford, 1950), pp. 189–215

Post-Reformation

Newman, John Henry, 'The Mission of Saint Benedict', in his *Historical Sketches*, 3 vols. (London, 1888), ii. 363–430

Reyner, Clement, *Apostolatus Benedictinorum in Anglia, sive disceptatio historia de antiquitate ordinis congregationique monachorum nigrorum S Benedicti in regno Angliae*, 3 pts (Douai, 1626)

Modern Classics

Butler, E. C., *Benedictine Monachism: Studies in the Benedictine Life and Rule* (London, 1919)

Coulton, G. G., *Five Centuries of Religion*, IV. *The Last Days of Medieval Monachism* (Cambridge, 1950)

Décarreaux, J., *Monks and Civilisation from the Barbarian Invasions to the Reign of Charlemagne*, trans. C. Haldane (London, 1965)

Knowles, D., *The Monastic Order in England* (Cambridge, 1940)

—— *The Religious Orders in England*, 3 vols. (Cambridge, 1948–59)

Schmitz, P., *Histoire de l'Ordre de Saint-Benoît*, 7 vols. (Paris, 1942–56)

PRE-BENEDICTINE MONASTICISM

Sources

Alcuin, *Vita Willibrordi*, ed. W. Levison, MGH, Scriptores rerum Merovingicarum 7 (Hanover, 1920), pp. 81–141

Bede, *Historia gentis Anglorum ecclesiasticus*, ed. R. A. B. Mynors and B. Colgrave (Oxford, 1969)

Jonas, *The Life of St Columban by the Monk Jonas*, ed. D. Carleton Munro (repr., Llanerch, 1993)

The Life of Bishop Wilfrid, by Eddius Stephanus, ed. and trans. B. Colgrave (Cambridge, 1927)

McNamara, J. A., and J. E. Halborg, *The Ordeal of Community: The Rule of Donatus of Besançon and the Rule of a Certain Father to the Virgins* (Toronto, 1993)

La règle du maître, ed. and trans. A. de Vogüé, 3 vols., Sources chrétiennes 105–7, Serie des texts monastiques d'occident 14–16 (Paris, 1964–5)

The Rule of the Master: Regula magistri, Cistercian Studies Series 6 (1977)

Studies

Bazell, D. M., 'Strife among the Table-Fellows: Conflicting Attitudes of Early and Medieval Christians toward the Eating of Meat', *Journal of the American Academy of Religion* 65:1 (1997), 73–99

Blair, J., *The Church in Anglo-Saxon Society* (Oxford, 2005)

Columbanus and Merovingian Monasticism, ed. H. B. Clarke and M. Brennan, British Archaeological Reports, International Series 113 (Oxford, 1981)

Dunn, M., *The Emergence of Monasticism: From the Desert Fathers to the Early Middle Ages*, 2nd edn (Oxford, 2005)

Fouracre, P., and R. A. Gerberding, *Late Merovingian France: History and Hagiography, 640–720*, Manchester Medieval Source Series 1 (Manchester, 1996)

Klingshirn, W., *Caesarius of Arles: The Making of a Christian Community in Late Antique Gaul*, Cambridge Studies in Medieval Life and Thought 22 (Cambridge, 1994)

Richter, M., *Bobbio in the Early Middle Ages: the Abiding Legacy of Columbanus* (Dublin, 2008)

St Cuthbert, his Cult and his Community to AD 1200, ed. G. Bonner, D. Rollason and C. Stancliffe (Woodbridge, 1998)

Wood, I., 'The Mission of Augustine of Canterbury to the English', *Speculum* 69:1 (1994), 1–17

—— *The Missionary Life: Saints and the Evangelisation of Europe, 400–1050* (Harlow, 2001)

The World of Gregory of Tours, ed. K. Mitchell and I. Wood (Leiden, 2002)

Wormald, P., 'Bede and Benedict Biscop', in *Famulus Christi: Essays in Commemoration of the Thirteenth-Centenary of the Birth of the Venerable Bede*, ed. G. Bonner (London, 1976), pp. 141–69

ST BENEDICT AND HIS RULE

Sources

Gregory, *Dialogues*, ed. A. de Vögué, 3 vols., Sources chrétiennes 251, 260, 265 (Paris, 1978)

La règle du saint Benoît, trans. A. de Vogüé and ed. J. Neufville, Sources chrétiennes 181, Série des textes monastiques d'Occident 49 (Paris, 1972)

Studies

Bloch, H., *Monte Cassino in the Middle Ages*, Edizioni di Storia e Letteratura, 3 vols. (Rome and Cambridge, MA, 1986)

Dunn, M., 'Mastering Benedict: Monastic Rules and their Authors in the Early Medieval West', *EHR* 105 (1990), 567–94

Meyvaert, P., 'Problems Concerning the "Autograph" Manuscript of Saint Benedict's Rule', *Rev. Bén.* 69 (1959), 3–21

——'Towards a History of the Textual Transmission of the *Regula sancti Benedicti*', *Scriptorium* 17 (1963), 83–110

Vogüé, A. de, *Community and Abbot in the Rule of St Benedict*, Cistercian Studies Series 5:1 (Kalamazoo, 1979)

——*Le Maître, Eugippe et Saint Benoît: Recueil d'articles* (Hildesheim, 1984)

——'The Master and St Benedict', *EHR* 107 (1992), 95–103

EARLY BENEDICTINES

Sources

The Anglo-Saxon Missionaries in Germany, being the lives of SS Wilibrord, Boniface, Sturm, Leoba and Lebium, together with the Hodoeporicon of St Willibald and a selection from the correspondence of St Boniface, ed. C. H. Talbot (London and New York, 1954)

McNamara, J. A., and J. E. Halborg, *The Ordeal of Community: The Rule of Donatus of Besançon and the Rule of a Certain Father to the Virgins* (Toronto, 1993)

Paulus Diaconus, *Historia Langobardorum*, ed. L. Bethmann and G. Waitz, MGH Scriptores rerum Langobardicarum (Hanover, 1878)

Schroll, A. M., *Benedictine Monasticism, as Reflected in the Commentaries of Hildemar and Warnefrid*, Studies in History, Economics and Public Law, v. 478 (New York, 1941)

Studies

Bernhardt, J., *Itinerant Kingship and Royal Monasteries in Early Medieval Germany* (Cambridge and New York, 1993)

Bloch, H., 'Monte Cassino, Byzantium and the West in the Earlier Middle Ages', *Dumbarton Oaks Papers* 3 (1946), 163–224

Costambeys, M., *Power and Patronage in early Medieval Italy: Local Society, Italian Politics and the Abbey of Farfa, c. 700–900*, Cambridge Studies in Medieval Life and Thought 4th Series 70 (Cambridge, 2007)

Hen, Y., *Culture and Religion in Merovingian Gaul, AD 481–751*, Culture, Beliefs and Traditions 1 (Leiden, 1995)

Wallace-Hadrill, J. M., *The Frankish Church* (Oxford, 1981)

THE CAROLINGIAN REFORM

Sources

Ardo, *Life of St Benedict of Aniane*, in *Soldiers of Christ: Saints and Saints' Lives from Late Antiquity and the Early Middle Ages*, ed. T. Head and T. F. X. Noble (London, 1995)

Benedict of Aniane, *Benedicti Ananiensis Concordia regularum*, ed. P. Bonnerue, CCCM 168 (1999)

—— *Regula sancti Benedicti abbatis Anianensis siue collectio capitularis*, ed. J. Semmler, in *Initia consuetinis Benedictinae consuetudinem saeculi octavi et noni*, ed. K. Hallinger, CCM 1 (Siegburg, 1963), pp. 501–36

Studies

Bouchard, C. B., 'Merovingian, Carolingian and Cluniac Monasticism: Reform and Renewal in Burgundy', *JEH* 41 (1990), 365–88

Claussen, M. A., *The Reform of the Frankish Church: Chrodegang of Metz and the Regula canonicorum in the eighth century* (Cambridge, MA, 2004)

Jong, M. de, 'Charlemagne's Church', in *Charlemagne: Empire and Society*, ed. J. Story (Manchester, 2005), pp. 103–35

McKitterick, R., *The Frankish Church and the Carolingian Reforms, 789–895*, Royal Historical Society, Studies in History (London, 1977)

—— 'Le rôle culturel des monastères dans les royaumes carolingiens du VIIIe au Xe siècle', *Rev. Bén.* 103 (1993), 117–30

Nightingale, J., *Monasteries and Patrons of the Gorze Reform: Lotharingia, c. 850–1000*, Oxford Historical Monographs (Oxford, 1997)

Sears, E., 'Louis the Pious as *Miles Christi*', in *Charlemagne's Heir: New Perspectives on the Reign of Louis the Pious*, ed. P. Godman and R. Collins (Oxford, 1990)

Wemple, S. F., *Women in Frankish Society: Marriage and the Cloister, 500–900* (Philadelphia, 1985)

ANGLO-SAXON ENGLAND

Sources

Aldhelm, *The Prose Works of Aldhelm*, ed. M. Lapidge and M. Herren (Cambridge, 1979)

Ælfric, *Ælfric's Letter to the Monks of Eynsham*, ed. C. A. Jones (Cambridge, 1995)

Byrhtferth of Ramsey, *The Lives of St Oswald and St Ecgwine*, ed. M. Lapidge, Oxford Medieval Texts (Oxford, 2009)

Dunstan, *Memorials of St Dunstan, Archbishop of Canterbury*, ed. W. Stubbs, RS 63 (London, 1874)

John of Worcester, *The Chronicle of John of Worcester, 450–1141*, ed. R. R. Darlington and P. McGurk, 3 vols. (Oxford, 1995–8)

Wulfstan of Winchester, *The Life of St Æthelwold*, ed. M. Lapidge and M. Winterbottom, Oxford Medieval Texts (Oxford, 1991)

Studies

Ælfric's Letter to the Monks of Eynsham, ed. C. A. Jones, Cambridge Studies in Anglo-Saxon England 24 (Cambridge, 1998)

Gretsch, M., *The Intellectual Foundations of the English Benedictine Reform*, Cambridge Studies in Anglo-Saxon England 25 (Cambridge, 1991)

St Cuthbert, his Cult and his Community to AD 1200, ed. G. Bonner, D. Rollason, and C. Stancliffe (Woodbridge, 1989)

Wood, I., 'The Mission of Augustine of Canterbury to the English', *Speculum* 69:1 (1994), 1–17

Yorke, B., ed., *Bishop Æthelwold: His Career and Influence* (Woodbridge, 1988)

THE GREGORIAN AGE

Sources

The Book of the Foundation of Walden Monastery, ed. D. Greenway and L. Watkiss, Oxford Medieval Texts (Oxford, 1999)

Chronicle of Hugh of Flavigny: Reform and the Investiture Contest in the Late Eleventh Century, ed. P. Healy, Church, Faith and Culture in the Medieval West (Aldershot, 2006)

The Chronicle of Jocelin of Brakelond, ed. H. E. Butler, Nelson's Medieval Classics (London, 1949)

Eadmer, *The Life of St Anselm, Archbishop of Canterbury*, ed. R. W. Southern (London, 1962)

Libellus de diversis ordinibus et professionibus qui sunt in aecclesia, ed. G. Constable and B. Smith, Oxford Medieval Texts (Oxford, 1972)

Memoirs of Abbot Guibert de Nogent: Self and Society in Medieval France, ed. J. F. Benton (Toronto, 1989)

St. Odo of Cluny, being the Life of St. Odo of Cluny by John of Salerno and the Life of St. Gerald of Aurillac by St. Odo, The Makers of Christendom, trans. and ed. Gerard Sitwell (London, 1958)

Studies

Bethell, D. L., 'English Black Monks and Episcopal Elections in the 1120s', *EHR* 8 (1969), 673–98

Burton, J. E., *The Monastic Order in Yorkshire, 1069–125* (Cambridge, 1999)

Cantor, N. F., 'The Crisis of Western Monasticism, 1050–1130', *American Historical Review* 66 (1960–1), 47–67

Chibnall, M., *The World of Orderic Vitalis* (Oxford, 1984)

Constable, G., *Cluny from the Tenth to the Twelfth Centuries: Further Studies* (Aldershot, 2000)

Cowdrey, H. E. J., *The Cluniacs and the Gregorian Reform* (Oxford, 1970)

—— *The Age of Abbot Desiderius: Montecassino, the Papacy and the Normans in the Eleventh and Early Twelfth Century* (Oxford, 1983)

Jestice, P. G., *Wayward Monks and the Religious Revolution of the Eleventh Century*, Brill's Studies in Intellectual History 76 (Leiden, 1997)

Kerr, B., *Religious Life for Women, c. 1100–c. 1350*, Oxford Historical Monographs (Oxford, 1999)

Smith, M. F., R. Fleming and P. Halpin, 'Court Piety in Late Anglo Saxon England', *Catholic Historical Review* 81(2001), 569–602

Thompson, S., *Women Religious: The Founding of English Nunneries after the Norman Conquest* (Oxford, 1991)

Van Engen, J., 'The Crisis of Cenobitism Reconsidered: Benedictine Monasticism, 1050–1150', *Speculum* 61:1 (1986), 269–304

REGIONS AND COMMUNITIES

Cowley, F. G., *The Monastic Order in South Wales, 1066–1349*, Studies in Welsh History 1 (Cardiff, 1977)

The Irish Benedictines: A History, ed. M. Browne and C. Ó'Clabaigh (Dublin, 2005)

Johnson, P. D., *Equal in Monastic Profession: Religious Women in Medieval France* (Chicago, 1991)

Nyberg, T., *Monasticism in North-Western Europe, 800–1200* (Aldershot, 2000)

Potts, C., *Monastic Revival and Religious Identity in Early Normandy*, Studies in the History of Medieval Religion 11 (Woodbridge, 1995)

OBSERVANCE

Sources

The Customary of the Benedictine Abbey of Eynsham in Oxfordshire, ed. A. Gransden, Corpus consuetudinum monasticarum 2 (Siegburg, 1963)

Customary of the Benedictine Monasteries of Saint Augustine, Canterbury, and Saint Peter, Westminster, ed. E. M. Thompson, HBS 23, 28, 2 vols. (London, 1902–4)

Rites of Durham: A Description of all the Ancient Monuments, Rites and Customes with the Monastical Church of Durham before the Suppression, ed. J. Raine, Surtees Society 15 (1842)

Three Treatises from Bec on the Nature of Monastic Life, ed. G. Constable and B. S. Smith (Toronto, 2008),

Studies

Bowers, R., 'An Early Tudor Monastic Enterprise: Choral Polyphony for the Liturgical Service', in *The Culture of Medieval English Monasticism*, ed. J. G. Clark (Woodbridge, 2007), pp. 21–54

Boynton, S., *Shaping a Monastic Identity: Liturgy and History at the Imperial Abbey of Farfa, 1000–1125* (Ithaca, 2006)

Bruce, S. G., *Silence and Sign Language in Medieval Monasticism: The Cluniac Tradition, c. 900–1200* (Cambridge, 2007)

Cheney, C. R., *Episcopal Visitation of Monasteries in the Thirteenth Century*, 2nd edn (Philadelphia and Manchester, 1982)

The Divine Office in the Latin Middle Ages: Methodology and Source Studies, Regional Developments, Hagiography: Written in Honor of Professor Ruth Steiner, ed. M. E. Fassler and R. A. Baltzer (Oxford, 2000)

From Dead of Night to End of Day: The Medieval Customs of Cluny/Du cœur de la nuit à la fin du jour: Les coutumes clunisiennes en Moyen Âge, ed. S. Boynton and I. Cochelin, Disciplina monastica 3 (Turnhout, 2005)

Harper, S., *Medieval English Benedictine Liturgy: Studies in the Formation, Structure and Content of the Monastic Votive Office, c. 950–1540* (New York, 1993)

Harvey, B. F., *Monastic Dress in the Middle Ages: Precept and Practice*, William Urry Memorial Trust (Canterbury, 1988)

Kelly, T. F., *The Beneventan Chant*, Cambridge Studies in Music (Cambridge, 1989)

Robertson, A. W., *The Service Books of the Royal Abbey of Saint-Denis: Images of Ritual and Music in the Middle Ages*, Oxford Monographs on Music (Oxford, 1991)

CULTURE

Sources

Bell, D. N., *What Nuns Read: Books and Libraries in Medieval English Nunneries*, Cistercian Studies Series 188 (1995)

Dover Priory, ed. W. P. Stoneman, CBMLC (1999)

English Benedictine Libraries: The Shorter Catalogues, ed. R. Sharpe, J. P. Carley, K. Friis-Jensen and A. G. Watson, CBMLC (1996)

Friis-Jensen, K., and J. Willoughby, *Peterborough Abbey*, CBMLC (2002)

James, M. R., *Ancient Libraries of Canterbury and Dover* (Cambridge, 1903)

Suger, *Abbot Suger on the Abbey Church of St Denis and its Arts Treasures*, ed. and trans. E. Panofsky, 2nd edn (Princeton, 1979)

Studies

Alexander, J. J. G., *Norman Illumination at Mont St Michel, 966–1100* (Oxford, 1970)

Beach, A. I., *Women as Scribes: Book Production and Monastic Reform in Twelfth-Century Bavaria*, Cambridge Studies in Palaeography and Codicology (Cambridge, 2004)

Binski, P., *Westminster Abbey and the Plantagenets: Kingship and the Representation of Power, 1200–1400* (New Haven, 1995)

Bischoff, B., 'Benedictine Monasteries and the Survival of Classical Literature', in *Manuscript and Libraries in the Age of Charlemagne* (Cambridge, 1994), 134–60

Brann, N. L., *The Abbot Trithemius (1462–1516): The Renaissance of Monastic Humanism*, Studies in the History of Christian Thought 24 (Leiden, 1981)

Carolingian Culture: Emulation and Innovation, ed. R. McKitterick (Cambridge, 1994)

Clark, J. G., *A Monastic Renaissance at St Albans: Thomas Walsingham and his Circle, 1350–1440* (Oxford, 2004)

Collett, B., *Italian Benedictine Scholars and the Reformation: The Congregation of Santa Giustina of Padua* (Oxford, 1985)

Cyrus, C. J., *The Scribes for Women's Convents in Late Medieval Germany* (Toronto, 2009)

The Eadwine Psalter: Text, Image and Monastic Culture at Canterbury in the Twelfth Century, ed. M. T. Gibson, T. A. Heslop R. W. Pfaff, Publications of the Modern Humanities Research Association 14 (Philadelphia, 1992)

Ganz, D., *Corbie in the Carolingian Renaissance*, Beihefte der Francia 20 (Sigmaringen, 1990)

Grotans, A. A., *Reading in Medieval St Gall*, Cambridge Studies in Palaeography and Codicology 13 (Cambridge, 2006)

Lapidge, M., *The Anglo-Saxon Library* (Oxford, 2006)

Leclercq, J., *The Love of Learning and the Desire for God: A Study of Monastic Culture*, trans. C. Misrahi (New York, 1961)

Luxford, J. M., *The Art and Architecture of English Benedictine Monasteries, 1300–1540: A Patronage History* (Woodbridge, 2006)

McGuire, B. P., *Friendship and Community: the Monastic Experience, 350–1250*, Cistercian Studies Series 95 (Kalamazoo, MI, 1988)

North, J. D., *Richard of Wallingford and the Invention of Time* (London, 2005)

Piper, A. J., 'The Libraries of the Monks of Durham', in *Medieval Scribes, Manuscripts and Libraries: Essays presented to N. R. Ker*, ed. M. B. Parkes and A. G. Watson (London, 1978), pp. 213–49

—— 'The Durham Monks and the Study of Scripture', in *The Culture of Medieval English Monasticism*, ed. J. G. Clark (Woodbridge, 2007), pp. 86–103

Posset, F., *Renaissance Monks: Monastic Humanism in Six Biographical Sketches*, Studies in Medieval and Renaissance Tradition 108 (Leiden, 2005)

Southern, R. W., *Saint Anselm: A Portrait in a Landscape* (Cambridge, 1991)

Steinberg, S. H., 'Instructions in Writing by Members of the Congregation of Melk', *Speculum* 16:2 (1941), 210–15

Thomson, R. M., *William of Malmesbury*, rev. edn (Woodbridge, 2003)

—— 'Worcester Monks and Education, c. 1300', in *The Culture of Medieval English Monasticism*, ed. J. G. Clark (Woodbridge, 2007), pp. 104–10

Van Engen, J. H., *Rupert of Deutz* (Berkeley, 1983)

Vaughan, R., *Matthew Paris* (Cambridge, 1958)

Weiss, R., *Humanism in England during the Fifteenth Century*, 2nd edn (Oxford, 1957)

SOCIETY

Sources

The Account Rolls of the Obedientiaries of Peterborough, ed. J. Greatrex, Northamptonshire Record Society 33 (1984)

The Chronicle of Battle Abbey, ed. E. Searle, Oxford Medieval Texts (Oxford, 1980)

Documents Illustrating the Rule of Abbot Walter de Wenlok, 1283–1307, ed. B. F. Harvey, Camden Society, 4th Series 2 (1965)

Historia ecclesiae Abbendonensis: The History of the Church of Abingdon, ed. Hudson, Oxford Medieval Texts (Oxford, 2002–7)

Liber Eliensis, ed. E. O. Blake, Camden Society, 3rd Series 92 (1962)

Monastery and Society in the Late Middle Ages: Selected Account rolls from Selby Abbey, Yorkshire, 1398–1537, ed. J. H. Tillotson (Woodbridge, 1988)

Morton, William, *The Book of William Morton, Almoner of Peterborough Monastery, 1448–67*, ed. W. T. Mellows, intr. C. N. L. Brooke, Northamptonshire Record Society 16 (1954)

Studies

Bowers, R., 'The Almonry Schools of the English Monasteries, *c.* 1265–1540', in *Monasteries and Society in Medieval Britain: Proceedings of the 1994 Harlaxton Symposium*, ed. B. J. Thompson, Harlaxton Medieval Studies 6 (Stamford, 1999), pp. 177–222

Costambeys, M., *Power and Patronage in Early Medieval Italy, Local Society, Italian Politics and the Abbey of Farfa, c. 700–900*, Cambridge Studies in Medieval Life and Thought 70 (Cambridge, 2004)

Gilchrist, R., *Gender and Material Culture: The Archaeology of Religious Women* (London and New York, 1994)

Gottfried, R. S., *Bury St Edmunds and Urban Crisis, 1290–1539* (Princeton, 1982)

Gransden, A., *A History of the Abbey of Bury St Edmunds, 1182–1256: Samson of Tottington to Edmund of Walpole*, Studies in the History of Medieval Religion 31 (Woodbridge, 2007)

Harvey, B. F., *Living and Dying in England: The Monastic Experience, c. 1100–1540* (Oxford, 1993)

—— *The Obedientiaries of Westminster Abbey and their Financial Records, c. 1275–1540*, Westminster Abbey Record Series 3 (Woodbridge, 2002)

—— *Westminster Abbey and its Estates in the Middle Ages* (Oxford, 1977)

Harvey, M., *Lay Religious Life in Late Medieval Durham*, Regions and Regionalism in History 6 (Woodbridge, 2006)

Heale, M., 'Monastic Parochial Churches in Late Medieval England', in *The Parish in Late Medieval England*, ed. C. Burgess and E. Duffy, Harlaxton Medieval Studies 14 (Donnington, 2006), pp. 54–77

Kerr, J., *Monastic Hospitality: The Benedictines in England, c. 1050–1250* (Woodbridge, 2007)

King, E., *Peterborough Abbey, 1086–1310: A Study in the Land Market* (Cambridge, 1973)

Levett, A. E., *Studies in Manorial History*, ed. H. Cam and L. Sutherland (Oxford, 1938)

Oexle, O. G., 'Les moines d'Occident et la vie politique et sociale dans le Haut Moyen Âge', *Rev. Bén.* 103 (1993), 255–72

Potter, J., 'The Benefactors of Bec and the Politics of Priories', *Anglo-Norman Studies* 21 (1998), 175–92

Raban, S., *Mortmain Legislation and the English Church, 1279–1500* (Cambridge, 1982)

Rushton, N. S., and W. Sigle-Rushton, 'Monastic Poor Relief in Sixteenth-Century England', *Journal of Interdisciplinary History* 32:2 (2001), 193–216

Savine, A., 'English Monasteries on the Eve of the Dissolution' in *Oxford Studies in Social and Legal History*, ed. P. Vinogradoff, vol. 1 (Oxford, 1909), pp. 1–303

Slater, T. R., 'Benedictine Town Planning in England: Evidence from St Albans', in *The Church in the Medieval Town*, ed. T. R. Slater and G. Rosser (Aldershot, 1998), pp. 155–76

Smith, R. A. L., 'The Central Financial System of Christ Church, Canterbury, 1186–1512', *EHR* 55 (1940), 353–69

—— 'The *Regimen Scaccarii* in English Monasteries: The Alexander Prize Essay', *TRHS*, 4th Series 24 (1942), 73–94

Threlfall-Holmes, M., *Monks and Markets: Durham Cathedral Prior, 1460–1520* (Oxford, 2005)

Verhulst, A. E., *Carolingian Economy*, Cambridge Medieval Textbooks (Cambridge, 2002)

Wood, S., *The Proprietary Church in the Medieval West* (Oxford, 2006)

LATER MIDDLE AGES
Sources

Christ Church Canterbury, I. *The Chronicle of John Stone*; II. *Lists of the Deans, Priors and Monks of Christ Church, Canterbury*, ed. W. G. Searle, Cambridge Antiquarian Society Publications, Octavo Series, 34 (1902)

Female Monastic Life in Early Tudor England: with an Edition of Richard Fox's Translation of the Benedictine Rule for Women, 1517, ed. B. Collett, Early Modern Englishwomen, 1500–1750 (Aldershot, 2002)

Lydgate, John, *Testament*, in *The Minor Poems of John Lydgate*, ed. H. N. MacCracken, EETS, Extra Series 107 (1911), pp. 329–62

A Macaronic Sermon Collection from Late Medieval England: Oxford, MS Bodley 649, ed. P. J. Horner (Toronto, 2006)

Memorials of St Edmunds Abbey at Bury, ed. T. Arnold, 3 vols., Rolls Series 96 (1896)

Morton, William, *The Book of William Morton, Almoner of Peterborough Monastery, 1448–67*, ed. W. T. Mellows, intr. C. N. L. Brooke, Northamptonshire Record Society 16 (1954)

Thorne, William, *William Thorne's Chronicle of St Augustine's Canterbury, now rendered into English*, trans. A. H. Davis (Oxford, 1934)

Visitations of Religious Houses in the Diocese of Lincoln, ed. A. H. Thompson, Lincoln Record Society 7, 14, 21, 27, 4 vols. (Lincoln, 1914–47)

Studies

Derwich, M., *Réforme et la vie quotidienne dans les abbayes bénédictines en Pologne au XVe siècle* (Wrocław, 1995)

Dilworth, M., *Scottish Monasteries in the Late Middle Ages* (Edinburgh, 1995)

Dobson, R. B., *Durham Priory, 1400–1450*, Cambridge Studies in Medieval Life and Thought 3rd Series 6 (Cambridge, 1973)

Haines, R. M., 'Some Visitation Injunctions for Worcester Cathedral Priory Appended to the Register of Bishop Simon de Montacute', *Rev. Bén.* 106 (1996), 332–55

Harvey, B. F., 'A Novice's Life at Westminster in the Century before the Dissolution', in *The Religious Orders in Pre-Reformation England*, ed. J. G. Clark (Woodbridge, 2002), pp. 51–73

Kaartinen, M., *Religious Life and English Culture in the Reformation* (Basingstoke, 2002)

Logan, D., *Runaway Religious in Medieval England, c. 1240–1540*, Cambridge Studies in Medieval Life and Thought 4th Series 32 (Cambridge, 1996)

McGuire, B. P., *Jean Gerson and the Last Medieval Reformation* (University Park, PA, 2005)

Martin, D. D., *Fifteenth-Century Carthusian Reform: The World of Nicholas Kempf*, Studies in the History of Christian Thought 99 (Leiden, 1992)

Mate, M. E., 'The Impact of War on the Economy of Canterbury Cathedral Priory', *Speculum* 57 (1982), 761–78

Oliva, M., *The Convent and the Community in Late Medieval England: Female Monasteries in the Diocese of Norwich, 1350–1540* (Woodbridge, 1998)

Pantin, W. A., 'The Monk-Solitary of Farne: A Fourteenth-Century English Mystic', *EHR* 59 (1944), 162–86

Posset, F., *Renaissance Monks: Monastic Humanism in Six Biographical Sketches*, Studies in Medieval and Reformation Traditions 108 (Leiden, 2005)

Power, E., *Medieval English Nunneries, c. 1275–1535*, Cambridge Studies in Medieval Life and Thought (Cambridge, 1922)

Raban, S., *Mortmain Legislation and the English Church, 1279–1500* (Cambridge, 1982)

Riche, D., *L'ordre de Cluny à la fin du moyen âge: le vieux pays clunisien, XIIe–XVe siècles* (Saint-Étienne, 2000)

Stieber, J. W., *Pope Eugenius IV, the Council of Basel and the Secular and Ecclesiastical Authorities in the Empire*, Studies in the History of Christian Thought 13 (Leiden, 1978),

Strocchia, S. T., *Nuns and Nunneries in Renaissance Florence* (Baltimore, MD, 2009)

Stump, P. H., *The Reforms of the Council of Constance, 1414–1418*, Studies in the History of Christian Thought 53 (Leiden, 1994)

Tillotson, J. H., 'Visitation and Reform of the Yorkshire Nunneries in the Fourteenth Century', *Northern History* 30 (1994), 1–21

REFORMATIONS

Sources

Cross, C., and N. Vickers, *Monks, Friars and Nuns in Sixteenth-Century Yorkshire*, Yorkshire Record Society, Record Series, 150 (Leeds, 1995)

The Letter Book of Robert Joseph, Monk-Scholar of Evesham and Gloucester College, 1530–33, ed. H. Aveling and W. A. Pantin, Oxford Historical Society, New Series, 19 (1967)

Three Chapters of Letters relating to the Suppression of the Monasteries, ed. T. Wright, Camden Society (1843)

Studies

Anderson, M. W., 'Gregorio Cortese and Roman Catholic Reform', *Sixteenth-Century Essays and Studies* 1 (1970), 75–106

Bernard, G. W., *The King's Reformation: Henry VIII and the Remaking of the English Church* (New Haven, 2005)

Blois, G. de, *A Benedictine of the Sixteenth Century: Louis de Blois*, trans. Lady Lovat (London, 1878)

Bowker, M., *The Henrician Reformation: The Diocese of Lincoln under John Longland, 1521–47* (Cambridge, 1981)

Bradshaw, B., *The Dissolution of the Religious Orders in Ireland under Henry VIII* (Cambridge, 1974)

Clark, J. G., 'Reformation and Reaction at St Albans Abbey, 1530–1558', *EHR*, 114 (2000), 297–328

Dunning, R. W., 'Revival at Glastonbury, 1530–9', in *Renaissance and Renewal in Christian History: Papers read at the Fifteenth Summer Meeting and the Sixteenth Winter Meeting of the Ecclesiastical History Society*, ed. D. Baker, Studies in Church History 14 (1977), 213–32

Evans, A., 'Battle Abbey at the Dissolution: Expenses', *Huntington Library Quarterly* 6 (1942), 53–101

Le Gall, J.-M., 'Les moines et la ville: l'exemple de Paris au début du XVIe siècle', in *Moines et monastères dans les sociétés de rite grec et latin*, ed. J.-L. Lemaître, M. Dmitriev and P. Gonneau, École pratique des hautes études, IVe section, Sciences historique et philologique, Hautes études médiévales et modernes 76 (Geneva, 1996), 255–70

Morris, R. K., 'The Lost Cathedral Priory Church of St Mary, Coventry', *Coventry's First Cathedral, 1043–1993: The Cathedral and Priory of St Mary: Papers from the 1993 Symposium*, ed. G. Demidowicz (Stamford, 1994), pp. 17–66

Index

354

Bavaria, 48, 193, 301, 312, 325, 328

Beaton, David, 322

Beaume (Hautes-Alpes), abbey, 40

Bec Abbey (Normandy), 73, 84, 198, 214, 217, 220, 246, 275

Beccafumi, Domenico di Pace, altarpiece, 280

Becket, Thomas, St (1118–70), archbishop of Canterbury, 167

Bede, the Venerable (673–735), 21, 27, 32, 110, 133, 135, 196, 201, 202–3, 208–9, 226

  Homily on John, 96

Beerley, Richard, 321

Beinwil (Aargau), 274, 328, 335

Benedetto da Mantova, 322

Benedict of Aniane, St (747–821), 24, 30, 34, 36, 38, 40, 46, 60, 61, 76, 77, 92, 94, 99, 112, 116–17, 141, 172, 186–7, 193, 195

  Concordia regularum, 30, 35, 37, 46, 61, 75

Benedict of Nursia, St (c. 480–c. 547), 1, 5, 7, 8, 10, 12–13, 16–18, 22, 25–9, 31, 33–4, 37, 62–4, 70, 74, 91–3, 95, 101–3, 105, 106, 108, 110–13, 116–19, 122, 130–2, 134, 139, 149, 153, 157, 163, 165, 169, 171–2, 182, 187, 189, 190–1, 193–4, 212–13, 237–8, 247, 265, 267–8, 301

  birth, 132

  family, 157

  feast of, 265

  death, 12, 16

  relics, 176

  Regula Benedicti, 1, 5, 13, 22–5, 27–30, 34, 35, 37, 41, 42, 44, 46–7, 50, 52–4, 56, 58, 60–4, 66, 70–2, 74–5, 77, 80–3, 87–93, 95, 97, 101–6, 108, 110, 111–26, 128, 130–2, 139, 149, 150, 153, 157, 162–3, 165, 167, 169–72, 177, 179, 182, 185–97, 203, 209, 213, 218, 225, 237–8, 257, 259, 262, 267, 281, 285, 287, 289, 291, 293, 298, 301, 314

  early dissemination, 23–6

  textus interpolatus, 23, 24, 26

  textus purus, 25

  textus receptus, 24

  translation into Old English, 44

  translation into Swabian German, 192

Benedict XII, pope (1334–42), 7, 109, 111, 123, 288, 292

Benedict Biscop, abbot of Monkwearmouth and Jarrow, 26, 27, 29, 70, 213

Benedictina. See Summi magistri

Benedictine order, 1–3, 6–8, 12, 14, 17, 37, 50, 59, 61, 82, 92, 108, 113, 130–1, 150, 176, 180, 183, 190, 196, 204, 210, 225, 235–7, 243, 245, 250, 255–6, 261, 263, 265–7, 281, 292–4, 296, 303, 314, 317, 334, 337, 341

  beginnings, 30–9

  ascendancy, 56–8

canons of (1247), 201; (1277), 72, 76, 78, 92, 94, 117, 193, 201n, 238, 242; (1343), 76, 92, 94, 117, 165, 238; (1444), 92

English chapters, 2, 7, 72, 78, 92, 94, 109, 117, 121, 123, 165, 176, 178, 183, 193, 201–2, 238, 242, 261, 264–5, 290, 298, 308

  in Germany, 296

  women of, 87

Benedictines, general

  precursors, 17–22

  academic studies, 230–7

  almonry schools, 186

  book-craft, 111–12, 238–47

  Classical literature, 212–24

  decorative arts, 248–9

  daily chapter, 117

  diet, 118–20

  dress, 121

  education, 83–91

  election of a superior, 114–15

  historical writing, 224–30

  lay brethren, 71–2

  manual labour, 105–12

  music, 102–5

  noviciate, 74–83

  oblation, 64–6

  Opus Dei, 91–102

  ordination, 87–9

  portraits of, 288

  profession, 89–91

  regulation of time by, 125–6

  seigniorial obligations, 158–9

  seigniorial responsibilities, 159–61

  social culture, 128

  social origins, 66–9

  and secular values, 286–8

  and vernacular, 284–6

Benedictine women

  book craft, 87

  craft skills, 249

  education, 83–4

  foundations for, 51, *69*

  literacy, 83

  oblates among, 65

  social origins, 67–8

Benedikt, abbot of Tegernsee, 300

Benediktbeuren (Bavaria), abbey, 50, *302*

Beneventan chant, 103

Benevento, 191

Bere, Richard, abbot of Glastonbury, 319

Berkshire, parishes of, 145

Bermondsey Abbey (Greater London), 184, 261

Bernard, abbot of Montecassino, 58, 78, 200, 267

William of Volpiano, 42, 51, 173
Willibald, St (d. *c.* 787), 12, 33
Willibrord, St (*c.* 658–739), 32, 34, 133
  Life of, 64
Wilton (Wiltshire), 46, *49*, 63, *69*, 147–8, 269
Wiltshire, 336
Winchcombe (Gloucestershire), 45, *49*, 54,
  203, 236, 246, 307, 312, 322
Winchelsea, Robert of, 292
Winchester (Hampshire), 39, 44, 45, 46, *49*,
  54, *55*, 66, 72, 82, 84, 91, 173, 197, 205,
  209, 219, 226–7, 239, 246, 314, 321
  diocese, 83
  Old Minster, 109, 173
  Psalter, 243
  St Swithun's Cathedral Priory, 142, 261,
    314
  style, 245
Windesheim (Holland), monastery, 280, 281,
  297, 300
Windsor, 188
Winfrith (St Boniface), 33
Wirral, the (Merseyside), 276
Wittenberg, 203, 317, 319–21, 329
Wolsey, Thomas, cardinal, archbishop of York
  (1514–30), 115, 295, 309
women religious
  books of, 242, 279n, 286
  children in custody of, 170, 186
  Cluniac observance for, 51
  culture of, 129
  devotional interests of, 279n
  enclosure of, 121
  estates of, 143
  foundations of, *69*
  hospitals under supervision of, 185
  interaction with males, 170
  late medieval foundations for, 259
  location of, 134, 136
  needlework of, 249
  obedientiaries, 153

post-Reformation, 336
priests of, 166
relations with monasteries of men, 260
scribes among, 242
social origins of, 67–8
vernacular literacy of, 83, 192, 286
See also Benedictines
Woodford, William, 202, 230
Worcester
  early monastery, 24, *25*, 45, *55*
  cathedral priory, 100, 176, 184, 197, 198,
    207, 227, 229, 231, 234, 246, 274, 307
Worcester, William, 221, 230
Wulfald, abbot of Fleury, 116
Wulfsige, disciple of Dunstan, 45
Wulfstan of Winchester, 81, 82, 84, 107, 109,
  118, 122, 176, 226
Württemberg, region of, 326, 333, 336
Wurzburg (Franconia), 220, 260, 301
  diocese, 327
  provincial chapter, 297
Wyclif, John, 202, 229, 231, 235–6, 236, 266,
  283
Wyclifites, 285

York, St Mary's abbey, 185, 260, 279, 280, 296
  hospital of St Nicholas, 185
  province of, 265, 290, 317, 331
Yorkshire, 155, 331
Youghal, 260

Zachary, pope (741–52), 17, 34
Zalavár (Bohemia), 53
Želiv (Bohemia), 259
Zlatá Koruna (Bohemia), abbey, 306
Zobor (Slovakia), abbey, 53
Zurich, 324
  Council of, 324
Zvíkov (Bohemia), 306
Zwingli, Ulrich, 318
  follower of, 330

Lightning Source UK Ltd.
Milton Keynes UK
UKOW06f1250280617

304218UK00002B/5/P

9 781843 839736